Kanji & Kana
Revised Edition

漢字 かな

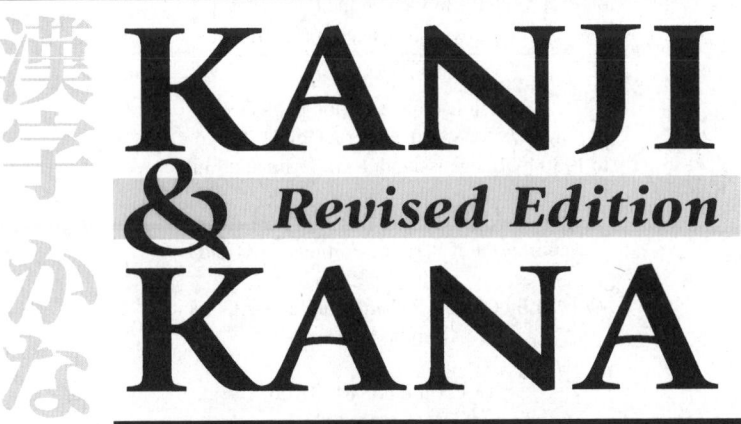

KANJI & KANA

Revised Edition

A Handbook of
the Japanese Writing System

by Wolfgang Hadamitzky & Mark Spahn

CHARLES E. TUTTLE COMPANY
Rutland · Vermont : Tokyo · Japan

Visit Tuttle Web on the Internet at:
http://www.tuttle.co.jp/~tuttle/

German language edition published
in 1979 by Verlag Enderle GmbH, Tokyo
in 1980 by Langenscheidt KG, Berlin and Munich

Published by Charles E. Tuttle Publishing,
an imprint of Periplus Editions (HK) Ltd.

LCC Card No. 81-50106
ISBN 0-8048-2077-5

First edition, 1981
First revised edition, 1997
Second printing, 1998

Printed in Singapore

Distributed by:

USA **Charles E. Tuttle Company, Inc.**
Airport Industrial Park
RR1 Box 231-5
North Clarendon, VT 05759
Tel: (802) 773-8930
Fax: (802) 773-6993

Japan **Tuttle Shokai Ltd.**
1-21-13 Seki
Tama-ku, Kawasaki-shi
Kanagawa-ken 214, Japan
Tel: (81) (44) 833-0225
Fax: (81) (44) 822-0413

Southeast Asia
Berkeley Books Pte Ltd.
5 Little Road #08-01
Singapore 536983
Tel: (65) 280 3320
Fax: (65) 280 6290

Tokyo Editorial Office:
2-6, Suido 1-chome,
Bunkyo-ku, Tokyo 112, Japan

Boston Editorial Office:
153 Milk Street, 5th Floor
Boston, MA 02109, USA

Singapore Editorial Office:
5 Little Road #08-01
Singapore 536983

TABLE OF CONTENTS

Preface 6

Introduction 9

Romanization 11

The Kana 16

    Origin 16

    Order 20

    Writing 24

    Orthography 27

    Usage 31

Punctuation 35

The Kanji 42

    Brief Historical Outline 42

    Form and Construction 43

Readings 54

Writing the Strokes in the Correct
    Direction and Sequence 56

How to Use a Kanji Dictionary 63

Explanation of the *Jōyō Kanji*
    List 68

The *Jōyō Kanji* List 73

Explanation of the *Jinmei-yō*
    Kanji List 352

The *Jinmei-yō Kanji* List 353

Kanji Indexes:

    By Radicals 374

    By Stroke Count 384

    By Readings 392

LIST OF TABLES

1. The 79 Radicals (without variants) (inside front cover)

2. The 79 Radicals (with variants) (front end paper)

3. Transliteration 14

4. Hiragana Derivations 18

5. Katakana Derivations 19

6. Example of Dictionary Order 22

7. The *Iroha* 23

8. Writing Hiragana 25

9. Writing Katakana 26

10. Important Katakana Combinations .. 30

11. The Most Important of the 214 Traditional Radicals 47

12. The 214 Traditional Radicals and Their Meanings 48

13. The 80 Graphemes (without variants) 52

14. The 80 Graphemes (with variants) 53

15. The Syllabaries: Hiragana, Katakana (back end paper)

16. Checklist for Determining the Radical of a Character (according to Spahn & Hadamitzky) (inside back cover)

Preface

Fifteen years after it first was published, this handbook and dictionary of the Japanese writing system has been reissued in a fully revised and expanded version. In addition to reworking and updating the main text, a section has been added covering the 284 kanji officially recognized for use in given names (the *Jinmei-yō Kanji*). Perhaps the most striking new feature is a separate English-Japanese/Japanese-English dictionary that lists, in alphabetical order by their reading, all the individual kanji and multiple-kanji compounds and names that appear in this handbook.

This two-volume basic text, along with the accompanying writing-practice manuals, is designed for those who wish to acquire in the shortest possible time a practical working knowledge of the written language, either active or passive. It contains all kanji recommended for general use and found in various certification tests, and its indexes and tables allow the user to look up any of its approximately 2,300 characters and 15,000 compounds and proper names.

In addition, the introductory chapters will be of use to linguists, travelers, devotees of Japanese calligraphy, art, and culture, and others who desire only to familiarize themselves with the basics or certain aspects of the writing system.

This work, which presents all Japanese characters and words in transliteration, is also suitable for self-study.

This handbook consists of a discussion of transliteration; an extensive presentation of the hiragana and katakana syllabaries (known collectively as kana); punctuation; and the origin, form, reading, writing, and dictionary arrangement of kanji. The bulk of this volume consists of a list of the 1,945 *Jōyō Kanji* recommended by the Japanese government in 1981 for general use. The order of presentation is based on pedagogical principles, proceeding from the simplest and most often used characters to those which are more complex and occur less frequently. Within this general framework, characters that are graphically similar are presented together in order to call attention to their similarities and differences in form, reading, and meaning.

Each character is presented along with its stroke order, its components (radical and graphemes), references to where it may be found in more-comprehensive kanji dictionaries, its readings, its meanings, and a brief list of its most important compounds, consisting exclusively of characters that have appeared previously, along with the cross-reference number of each.

Associated with the 1,945 *Jōyō Kanji* are over 4,000 readings, some 2,000 of which represent independent words. Approximately 9,000 compounds are given to show how the char-

acters are used in combination. In all, the *Jōyō Kanji* part of this work contains a basic vocabulary of about 11,000 words.

The *Jōyō Kanji* part is followed by a list of 284 more kanji (the *Jinmei-yō Kanji*) officially permitted (along with the *Jōyō Kanji* themselves) for use in given names.

The 1,945 *Jōyō Kanji* and the 284 name kanji are included in three indexes at the back of this book as well as in the Japanese-English/English-Japanese dictionary, and the dictionary also includes all the compounds and names listed in this volume.

The authors hope that this revised and expanded work will serve its users well by making possible direct access to written sources and providing a solid basis for a more than superficial treatment of the language and culture of Japan. For it is primarily the barriers of the spoken and written language that hinder the foreigner in his understanding of a country that deserves our interest for more reasons than its economic and political importance alone.

The authors wish to thank Teisuke Higuchi, who wrote the characters in the main section; Mariko Atsumi, who wrote the characters in the name section and in the accompanying writing-practice materials; Yōko Hintz, who helped prepare the name section; Rainer Weihs and Seiko Harada, who created the database and typeset the text, including the preparation of special characters; and Karl Ludwig Warnecke, Dr. Wolfgang Lemm, Claus-Ulrich Liepke-Nakamura, Wolfgang Kaufmann, Susanne Scheermann, Professor James W. Heisig, Wolfgang Mayer-Lauingen, Helmut Busch, Hiroshi Kitamura, and all other users who have written with constructive suggestions for improvements to the first edition.

Berlin, March 1996   Wolfgang Hadamitzky

West Seneca, New York, March 1996   Mark Spahn

Introduction

Japanese is written in a mixture (called *kanji-kana majiri*) of three types of symbols, each with its own function:

Kanji

These pictographic-ideographic characters, adopted from the Chinese language, are used for conceptual words (mainly substantives, verbs, and adjectives) and indigenous names.

Kana

These phonetic symbols were developed in Japan. Each symbol represents the sound of one syllable. *Kana* are divided into two groups (syllabaries):

1. *Hiragana* are used to write the inflectional endings of the conceptual words written in kanji, as well as all types of native words not written in kanji.
2. *Katakana* are used chiefly for words of foreign origin.

Besides these, one often finds in Japanese texts roman letters and arabic numerals; for example, the name of the semigovernmental radio and television broadcasting corporation, *Nippon Hōsō Kyōkai*, is abbreviated *NHK* (the letters are pronounced as in English), and in horizontal writing, the use of arabic numerals rather than the corresponding kanji is usual.

There has never existed an independent, purely Japanese system of writing. Around the seventh century the attempt was first made to use Chinese characters to note down Japanese speech. In the ninth century the Japanese simplified the complex Chinese ideographs into what are now the kana. Each of the two kana syllabaries allows one to represent any syllable occurring in the Japanese language, so that it is quite possible to write excusively in *kana* (and in fact telegrams used to be written in katakana alone). In practice, however, this would hamper communication due to the large number of words pronounced alike but different in meaning (homophones), which are distinguished from one another by the use of different kanji. The same problem of ambiguity holds for romanized Japanese, which otherwise presents no problems.

Japanese today is written either in vertical columns proceeding from right to left or in horizontal lines which are read from left to right. The traditional vertical style is seen mostly in literary works. The horizontal European style, recommended by the Ministry of Education, is found more in technical literature and works dealing with the natural sciences. Newspapers use both styles: most articles are written vertically, headlines and advertisements appear in both styles, and radio and television program listings are given horizontally.

Letters and other handwritten Japanese may be written vertically or horizontally. The type of manuscript paper (*genkō yōshi*) commonly used in Japan contains either 200 or 400

squares per page, usually arranged in vertical columns. Each written symbol, including the punctuation marks, takes up a full space. For writing practice it is recommended that the beginner use either *genkō yōshi* or the practice manuals which accompany this text.

Whether handwritten or printed, the individual characters are written separately one after another; the characters of a single word are not strung together, nor are any blank spaces left between words. There is no distinction analogous to that between capital and lowercase letters. Hence the conventions governing the use of kanji and kana for various types of words aid the reader in determining where one word ends and the next begins.

As with roman letters, there are a few differences between the printed and handwritten forms, and these differences sometimes make character recognition difficult for the beginner. In order to familiarize the student with these differences, each of the 1,945 kanji presented in the main section of this book and in the practice manuals appears three ways: in brush form, in pen form, and in printed form. Within the printed form there are various typefaces, but the differences between them are usually insignificant.

In handwriting (with brush or pen) three styles are distinguished:

1. The standard style (*kaisho*), which is taught as the norm in elementary school and which is practically identical to the printed form. All the handwritten characters in this volume are given in the standard style.
2. The semicursive style (*gyōsho*), a simplification of the standard style which allows one to write more flowingly and rapidly.
3. The cursive style or "grass hand" (*sōsho*), which is a kind of calligraphic shorthand resulting from extreme simplification according to esthetic standards.

| Kaisho | Gyōsho | Sōsho |

In addition, several frequently used characters are sometimes written in greatly simplified forms which are not officially recognized; for example, the character 門 is sometimes simplified to 门, 曜 to 旺, and 第 to 才. And let it be noted in passing that there is also a Japanese shorthand intended for purely practical rather than artistic purposes. Since the early 1980s computers have made it almost as easy to type Japanese as it is to type an alphabet-based language like English. In Japanese word processing, one uses a keyboard to spell out words phonetically in either roman letters or kana. Consulting a built-in dictionary, the word processing software converts this phonetic input, phrase by phrase, into what it surmises is its proper kanji-kana spelling, displaying it on the computer's monitor screen, along with a list

of alternative spellings to choose from when a phonetic phrase could be spelled in several different ways. Among other features, Japanese word processing programs compete in how cleverly they can facilitate input by guessing the correct spelling of a phonetic phrase, perhaps by remembering what spelling choices the user has made previously.

Japanese word processing, as well as the typesetting of Japanese text, is a matter of software, which can be written to run on any computer, even one made in the U.S. or Europe. Indeed, the typesetting for this revised edition of *Kanji & Kana* was done on a "western" computer.

Now that Japanese is most often written, even by non-Japanese writers, on a computer, the ability to recognize the correct kanji (from alternative spellings displayed on a computer screen) has perhaps become more useful than the ability to write kanji by hand. Each individual will have to decide whether writing kanji by hand is a didactically wise use of time for learning new kanji.

Romanization

The transliteration of Japanese words and texts into roman letters presents no problems; the Japanese language can easily be transliterated by using only 22 roman letters and 2 simple diacritical marks.

Why then have the Japanese not adopted such an alphabet to replace a system of writing which even they find difficult? The answer lies in the large number of homophones, especially in the written language: even in context it is frequently impossible to uniquely determine the sense of a word without knowing the characters it is written with. Other rational as well as more emotional considerations, including a certain inertia, make it very unlikely that the Japanese writing system will undergo a thorough overhaul anytime soon.

In 1952 the Japanese government issued recommendations for the transliteration of Japanese into roman letters. Table 3 on pages 14 and 15 summarizes the two recommended systems of romanization, the *kunrei-shiki rōmaji* system and the Hepburn system, which differ only slightly and are both in use today. Where the two systems differ, the table gives both romanizations, in the form: Hepburn/*kunrei-shiki rōmaji*. Parentheses enclose romanizations that apply only when the kana are used as grammatical particles.

The *kunrei-shiki rōmaji* system
This system is patterned after the Fifty-Sounds Table (*gojū-on zu*), the five-by-ten grid in which each *kana* syllabary is conventionally arranged (although the layout contains several blank spaces, and diacritical marks are not shown). In the *kunrei-shiki* the initial consonant

11

sound of all five syllables in each row is represented uniformly with the same roman letter, despite any phonetic variation associated with different final vowel sounds. The government introduced the *kunrei-shiki* for official use in 1937, in a form which differs only slightly from that used today.

The *Hebon-shiki rōmaji* or Hepburn system
This system is similar to the *kunrei-shiki*, except that the consonant sounds in the same row are not represented uniformly with the same letter. The *Hebon-shiki* was developed by a commission of Japanese and foreign sholars in 1885 and was widely disseminated a year later through use in a Japanese-English dictionary compiled by the American missionary and philologist James Curtis Hepburn (in Japanese: *Hebon*). In the Hepburn system the consonant sounds are spelled as in English, and the vowel sounds as in Italian.

Although the *kunrei-shiki* has a more systematic one-to-one relationship with actual Japanese orthography, the much more widely known *Hebon-shiki* is better suited to texts intended for foreigners. "Fuji", the name of Japan's sacred mountain, is written *Huzi* in the *kunrei-shiki* and *Fuji* in the Hepburn system. As illustrated by this example, the Hepburn system allows an English speaker to approximate the original Japanese pronunciation without the need to remember any unfamiliar pronunciation rules, and is therefore less likely to lead the student into mispronunciations. For these reasons the Hepburn system has been adopted for all transliterations in this book.

The following additional transliteration rules are from official recommendations. The examples as well as the remarks in parentheses have been added. (For an explanation of the corresponding kana orthography, see Orthography, page 27.)

1. The end-of-syllable sound ん is always written *n* (even when it appears before the labials *b*, *p*, or *m* and is phonetically assimilated to *m*: *konban*, *kanpai*, *kanmuri*).
2. When the end-of-syllable sound *n* is followed by vowel or *y*, an apostrophe ['] is inserted to indicate that *n* should not be slurred together with the following syllable: *man'ichi*, *kon'yaku*.
3. Assimilated, or "stretched," sounds (*soku-on*) are represented (as in Italian) by double consonants: *mikka*, *massugu*, *hatten*, *kippu*; *sh* becomes *ssh*, *ch* becomes *tch*, and *ts* becomes *tts*: *ressha*, *botchan*, *mittsu*.
4. Long (double) vowels are marked with a circumflex [^] (this does not correspond to the kana orthography), and if a long vowel is capitalized it may be doubled instead. (In practice the simpler macron [‾] has become prevalent: *mā*, *yūjin*, *dōzo*. The long *i* is indicated by double *i*: *oniisan*. The long *e* is indicated in words of Chinese origin by writing *ei*: *meishi*; and in words of Japanese origin by a macron: *onēsan*. In foreign words and

names written in katakana, the long *i* and *e* are written with a macron if they are represented by a lengthening stroke [ー]: ビール *bīru*, メートル *mētoru*, ベートーベン *Bētōben*; but the long *e* vowel is written *ei* if it is represented by successive katakana instead of a lengthening stroke: スペイン *Supein*, エイト *eito*.)

5. For the representation of certain sounds there are no binding rules. (Short, suddenly broken-off vowels at the ends of words or syllables—glottal stops, or *soku-on*—are denoted in this book by adding an apostrophe: *a', are', ji'*.)

6. Proper names and the first word of every sentence are capitalized. The capitalization of substantives is optional: *Ogenki desu ka? Nippon, Tōkyō, Tanaka,* Genji Monogatari, *jūdō* or *Jūdō*.

A close examination of Table 3 and these six rules shows that the transliteration system is based partly on the Japanese syllabary and partly on phonetic considerations.

The only real problem in romanizing Japanese text, in which there are no spaces between words, is in deciding where one word ends and the next begins. There are no universal rules for this, but, as a basic principle, components which are perceived to be independent units are written separately: *Hon o sagashite iru n desu.* Hyphenation is used for various suffixes and other word units that one does not want to run together but does not want to write separately: *Tōkyō-to, Minato-ku, Endō-san.* For readability, long compounds are broken up into smaller units: *Nihon Shoki, kaigai ryokō, minshu shugi.*

Table 3. Transliteration

	The Fifty-Sounds Table (within darker lines) and supplementary tables, with				
	あ ア a	い イ i	う ウ u	え エ e	お オ o
k	か カ ka	き キ ki	く ク ku	け ケ ke	こ コ ko
s	さ サ sa	し シ shi/si	す ス su	せ セ se	そ ソ so
t	た タ ta	ち チ chi/ti	つ ツ tsu/tu	て テ te	と ト to
n	な ナ na	に ニ ni	ぬ ヌ nu	ね ネ ne	の ノ no
h	は ハ ha (wa)	ひ ヒ hi	ふ フ fu/hu	へ ヘ he (e)	ほ ホ ho
m	ま マ ma	み ミ mi	む ム mu	め メ me	も モ mo
y	や ヤ ya	—	ゆ ユ yu	—	よ ヨ yo
r	ら ラ ra	り リ ri	る ル ru	れ レ re	ろ ロ ro
w	わ ワ wa	ゐ* ヰ* i	—	ゑ* ヱ* e	を ヲ o
	* Obsolete				ん ン n
g	が ガ ga	ぎ ギ gi	ぐ グ gu	げ ゲ ge	ご ゴ go
z	ざ ザ za	じ ジ ji/zi	ず ズ zu	ぜ ゼ ze	ぞ ゾ zo
d	だ ダ da	ぢ ヂ ji/zi	づ ヅ zu	で デ de	ど ド do
b	ば バ ba	び ビ bi	ぶ ブ bu	べ ベ be	ぼ ボ bo
p	ぱ パ pa	ぴ ピ pi	ぷ プ pu	ぺ ペ pe	ぽ ポ po
	a	i	u	e	o

—	—	—
きゃ キャ kya	きゅ キュ kyu	きょ キョ kyo
しゃ シャ sha/sya	しゅ シュ shu/syu	しょ ショ sho/syo
ちゃ チャ cha/tya	ちゅ チュ chu/tyu	ちょ チョ cho/tyo
にゃ ニャ nya	にゅ ニュ nyu	にょ ニョ nyo
ひゃ ヒャ hya	ひゅ ヒュ hyu	ひょ ヒョ hyo
みゃ ミャ mya	みゅ ミュ myu	みょ ミョ myo
—	—	—
りゃ リャ rya	りゅ リュ ryu	りょ リョ ryo
—	—	—

ぎゃ ギャ gya	ぎゅ ギュ gyu	ぎょ ギョ gyo
じゃ ジャ ja/zya	じゅ ジュ ju/zyu	じょ ジョ jo/zyo
—	—	—
びゃ ビャ bya	びゅ ビュ byu	びょ ビョ byo
ぴゃ ピャ pya	ぴゅ ピュ pyu	ぴょ ピョ pyo

The Kana

Origin

The characters in Chinese texts brought into Japan via Korea, beginning in the fourth century, gradually came to be adopted by the Japanese for the writing of their own language, for which there was no native system of writing. The Chinese characters were used phonetically to represent similar-sounding Japanese syllables; the meanings of the characters were ignored. In this way one could represent phonetically any Japanese word. But since each Chinese character corresponded to only one syllable, in order to write a single multisyllabic Japanese word one had to employ several kanji, which frequently consist of a large number of strokes. To simplify this bothersome process, instead of the full angular style (*kaisho*) of the kanji a cursive, simplified, derivative style (*sōsho*) was used. In addition, the flowing and expressive lines of the *sōsho* style were felt to be better suited to literary notation. Toward the end of the Nara period (710–794) and during the Heian period (794–1185) these symbols underwent a further simplification, in which esthetic considerations played a part, resulting in a stock of phonetic symbols which was extensive enough to encompass the entire sound system of the Japanese language. This was the decisive step in the formation of a purely phonetic system of representing syllables. These simple syllable-symbols, today known as hiragana, were formerly referred to as *onna-de*, "ladies' hand," since they were first used, in letters and literary writing, by women of the Heian period, who were ignorant of the exclusively male domain of Chinese learning and literature and the use of Chinese characters. But the hiragana gradually came to prevail as a standard syllabary.

The katakana symbols were developed only a little later than the hiragana. While listening to lectures on the classics of Buddhism, students wrote in their texts notations on the pronunciations of meanings of unfamiliar characters, and sometimes wrote commentaries between the lines of certain passages. This practice required some sort of phonetic shorthand, and this need led to the development of a new script based on Chinese characters. Like hiragana, each katakana was developed from a Chinese character corresponding to a particular syllable and was thenceforth used purely phonetically to represent that syllable. But unlike hiragana, which are cursive simplifications of entire kanji, the more angular katakana were made by taking a single component of a kanji in *kaisho* style. In a few cases (チ, ハ, ミ) the katakana is only a slight alteration of a simple kanji. Since katakana were closely associated with science and learning, this angular syllabary was for a long time used only by men. (Tables 4 and 5 on pages 18 and 19 show the kanji from which each kana was derived.)

The selection of the hiragana and katakana in use today was laid down in the year 1900 in a decree for elementary schools. Two obsolete hiragana (ゐ *wi*, ゑ *we*) and the corresponding katakana (ヰ *wi*, ヱ *we*) were dropped as part of orthographic reforms made shortly after World War II. As a result, today there are 46 officially recognized symbols in each syllabary.

First lines from the famous *Gakumon no susume* by *Fukuzawa Yukichi* (1835–1901), the prominent educator and propagator of Western knowledge during the Meiji period.

RIGHT HAND SIDE: 1873 edition, written with a mixture of katakana and old kanji.

BELOW: same text in modern orthography.

学問のすすめ　　　　　福沢諭吉・小幡篤次郎　同著

天は人の上に人を造らず、人の下に人を造らず
と云えり。されば天より人を生ずるには、万人
は万人皆同じ位にして、生れながら貴賤上下の
差別なく、万物の霊たる身と心との働きを以
て、天地の間にあるよろずの物を……

學問ノスヽメ

福澤　諭吉

小幡篤次郎

同著

○天ハ人ノ上ニ人ヲ造ラズ人ノ下ニ人ヲ造ラズト云
ヘリサレバ天ヨリ人ヲ生ズルニハ萬人ハ萬人皆同シ
位ニシテ生レナガラ貴賤上下ノ差別ナク萬物ノ靈タ
ル身ト心トノ働ヲ以テ天地ノ間ニアルヨロヅノ物ヲ

First lines from the *Genji Monogatari*, the supreme classic of Japanese literature, written by the court lady *Murasaki Shikibu* (ca. 973–ca. 1014).

RIGHT HAND SIDE: manuscript written with kana and a few kanji in calligraphic *sōsho* style, 16th century edition.

BELOW: same text in modern orthography.

　いづれの御時にか、女御更衣あまた｜侍ひ給
ひけるなかに、いとやむごとな｜ききはにはあ
らぬが、すぐれて時｜めき給ふ、ありけり。
　はじめよりわれは｜と思ひあがり給へる御
方々、めざましき｜ものにおとしめそねみ給
ふ。同じほど、それ｜……

17

Table 4. Hiragana Derivations

あ 安	い 以	う 宇	え 衣	お 於
か 加	き 幾	く 久	け 計	こ 己
さ 左	し 之	す 寸	せ 世	そ 曽
た 太	ち 知	つ 川	て 天	と 止
な 奈	に 仁	ぬ 奴	ね 祢	の 乃
は 波	ひ 比	ふ 不	へ 部	ほ 保
ま 末	み 美	む 武	め 女	も 毛
や 也		ゆ 由		よ 与
ら 良	り 利	る 留	れ 礼	ろ 呂
わ 和				を 遠
ん 无				

Table 5. Katakana Derivations

ア 阿	イ 伊	ウ 宇	エ 江	オ 於
カ 加	キ 幾	ク 久	ケ 介	コ 己
サ 散	シ 之	ス 須	セ 世	ソ 曽
タ 多	チ 千	ツ 川	テ 天	ト 止
ナ 奈	ニ 仁	ヌ 奴	ネ 祢	ノ 乃
ハ 八	ヒ 比	フ 不	ヘ 部	ホ 保
マ 末	ミ 三	ム 牟	メ 女	モ 毛
ヤ 也		ユ 由		ヨ 與
ラ 良	リ 利	ル 流	レ 礼	ロ 呂
ワ 和				ヲ 乎
ン 尓				

Order

The order of arrangement of the sounds of Japanese, shown in Table 3 on pages 14 and 15, has a history of one thousand years of development. Around the year 1000, people began to arrange systematically, according to their sounds, the kana which had been in use since the beginning of the Heian period. The result is the *Gojū-on Zu*, the "Fifty-Sounds Table," which forms an "alphabet" for the Japanese language. The table is read from left to right across each row, starting with the top row; its order is therefore *a, i, u, e, o; ka, ki, ku, ke, ko....* The five characters of each row (*gyō*) are arranged according to the final (vowel) sound of the syllables (*a i u e o*), and the ten characters of each column (*dan*) are arranged according to the initial (consonant) sound of the syllables (Ø *k s t n h m y r w*; this is sometimes memorized as *a ka sa ta na, ha ma ya ra wa* in the sing-song musical rhythm of do-re-mi-fa-so, so-fa-mi-re-do). This systematic ordering makes it easy to memorize the Japanese *Aiueo* syllable alphabet.

The *Gojū-on Zu* can be written in either hiragana or katakana. Although the symbols composing the two systems are different, the systems represent the same sounds and arrange them in the same order.

Linguistic changes over the centuries caused some sounds to fall into disuse. Thus, the number of kana in the Fifty-Sounds Table in use today has decreased to 45 (46 if ん/ン *n* is counted). At the same time, new sounds become part of the language, requiring new symbols or diacritical marks, or an extended usage of the old symbols.

Strictly speaking, the end-of-syllable *n* is not part of the *Gojū-on Zu*, since this sound did not occur in the Japanese kanguage until after the kana syllabaries had been constructed. Today, however, *n* is included at the end of the *Gojū-on Zu*. Similarly, the designation of the "muddied," that is, voiced, sounds *g, z, d*, and *b* (*daku-on*) by a *daku-ten* or *nigori-ten* [˝], and the representation of the "half-muddied" sound *p* (*handaku-on*) by a *handaku-ten* or *maru* [°] did not come until later. The same is true of the "twisted" sounds (*yō-on*: consonant + *y* + *a, u,* or *o*) and the assimilated sounds (soku-on: unvoiced long [double] consonant, or glottal stop), which did not appear until about the middle of the Heian period. There are no special diacritical marks for *yō-on* or *soku-on*; instead, as shown in the examples below, they are written with two kana, the second of which is written smaller. As seen in the example of きゃっか *kyakka*, the one-syllable combination of *yō-on* + *soku-on* (きゃっ *kya'*) is written with three kana, the final two of which are written small.

Soku-on	*Soku-on*	*Yō-on*	*Soku-on* and *Yō-on*
あっ アッ	あっか アッカ	きゃ キャ	あっきゃ アッキャ
a'	*akka*	*kya*	*akkya*

かっ カッ　　　　かっか カッカ　　　　　　　きゃっか キャッカ
ka'　　　　　　*kakka*　　　　　　　　　　　*kyakka*

Japanese dictionaries, encyclopedias, and other reference works whose entries must appear in a definite order are "alphabetized", in the order (called *a-i-u-e-o jun* or *gojū-on jun*) of the *Gojū-on Zu*.

In determining dictionary order, no distinction is made between whether a *kana* is written with a diacritical mark or not, whether a kana is written large or small, or whether it is hiragana or katakana, except when one of these distinctions must be used to differentiate between two otherwise identical words. This corresponds to the roman-letter alphabetization convention which dictates that a capital letter is treated like its lowercase counterpart, except where capitalization is the only feature that distinguishes the spelling of two waords (like "china" and "China"). In these cases the rule is that the lowercase word comes first. In Japanese dictionary order the situation is more complex. The "same" *kana* may have as many as six versions; for example, は, ハ, ば, バ, ぱ, and パ are considered the same for purposes of dictionary order except in otherwise identical words.

Different reference books use different rules to govern this aspect of dictionary order. These are usually explained in detail in an introductory section of the reference book and should be consulted by the user. Below is a typical set of such rules:

1. A shorter word precedes a longer word beginning with the same *kana* (as "china" comes before "chinaware" in English-language dictionaries): あぶら before あぶらかす. (Virtually all reference books follow this convention.)
2. A character with no diacritical mark precedes its counterpart with a *daku-ten* or *handaku-ten*, and a character with a *daku-ten* precedes its counterpart with a *handaku-ten*: はり, then ばり, then ぱり. (Another virtually universal rule.)
3. A *kana* written large precedes its counterpart written small (this applies mostly to *soku-on* with a small つ and *yō-on* with a small や, ゅ, or ょ): かつて before かって, and いしや before いしゃ.
4. A *hiragana* precedes its *katakana* counterpart: これら before コレラ.

In cases of confict between these rules, Rule 1 takes precedence over Rule 2, Rule 2 over Rule 3, and Eule 3 over Rule 4. A few examples will help to make this clear. Because Rule 1 takes precedence over Rule 2: ばりき before はりきって.

Rule 1 over Rule 3: ちょ	before ちよがみ
Rule 1 over Rule 4: カッパ	before かっぱつ
Rule 2 over Rule 3: はっき	before はつぎ
Rule 2 over Rule 4: キス	before きず
Rule 3 over Rule 4: アツシ	before あっし

21

Table 6. Example of Dictionary Order

あ	あいかぎ	あいぎん
ア	あいき	あいく
ああ	あいぎ	………
アー	あいきどう	あち
アート	あいきゃく	あつ
ああら	アイキュー	あっ
あい	あいきょう	あつい
あいか	あいぎょう	あつか
あいが	あいきわ	あっか
あいがえし	あいきん	あつかい

In Japanese dictionary order, there is also the issue of how to handle the mark ‾ (called *chō-on kigō* or simply *bō*), which is used in foreignderived words written in katakana to show the lengthening of the preceding vowel sound. Some dictionaries simply ignore it, as a hyphen would be ignored in English-language alphabetization. Others take it to represent the katakana for the preceding vowel sound, so that for example ウーリー "wooly" is ordered as if it were written ウウリイ. This latter convention is the one we adopt here.

22

Table 7. The *Iroha*

い i	ろ ro	は ha	に ni	ほ ho	へ he	と to
chi ち	り ri	ぬ nu	る ru	を wo		
わ wa	か ka	よ yo	た ta	れ re	そ so	
つ tsu	ね ne	な na	ら ra	む mu		
う u	ゐ wi	の no	お o	く ku	や ya	ま ma
け ke	ふ fu	こ ko	え e	て te		
あ a	さ sa	き ki	ゆ yu	め me	み mi	し shi
ゑ we	ひ hi	も mo	せ se	す su		

Table 6 (page 22) presents further examples of the order in which words written in kana are arranged in dictionaries and the like. In order to use Japanese reference works with assurance, mastery of this ordering is essential. First read down the left-hand column, then down the middle column, then down the right-hand column.

In addition to the *Gojū-on Zu*, the hiragana may be ordered according to the *Iroha* arrangement, which is presented in Table 7. While both systems developed during the Heian period, the *Iroha* is falling into disuse in this century. The *Iroha* arranges all the hiragana in the form of a Buddhist poem, and is today used mostly for labeling things in sequence, such as subheadings or items in a list.

Note: This table includes the two obsolete hiragana ゐ *wi* and ゑ *we* (see page 14), as well as the obsolete reading *wo* for を.

23

Writing

The best first step toward mastery of the Japanese writing system is to begin with the kana, for these reasons:

1. They are limited in number (46 per syllabary).
2. They are simple in form (one to four strokes each).
3. There is a one-to-one correspondence between sound and symbol (with a few exceptions; see page 29, Rule 10).
4. Each syllabary encompasses all the sounds of the Japanese language, so that any text can be written down in kana.

It is debatable which syllabary ought to be learned first. With katakana the beginner can write many familiar words, derived from English for the most part. But the hiragana occur far more frequently.

The following two principles govern the sequence and direction of writing the strokes of kana (as well as kanji):

1. From top to bottom
2. From left to right

In the writing tables, the small numbers at the beginning of each stroke indicate the direction in which it is written, the sequence of the strokes, and the number of strokes which compose the kana.

Japanese is normally written not on lines, but rather in a printed (or at least imaginary) grid of squares or rectangles. In practicing writing, foreigners would be well advised to use, right from the beginning, either the printed manuscript paper which Japanese use, or the practice manuals which accompany this textbook. Tracing over the gray-tone characters in the practice manuals is the quickest way to get a feel for the proper proportions of each character.

Table 8. Writing Hiragana

あ	い	う	え	お
か	き	く	け	こ
さ	し	す	せ	そ
た	ち	つ	て	と
な	に	ぬ	ね	の
は	ひ	ふ	へ	ほ
ま	み	む	め	も
や		ゆ		よ
ら	り	る	れ	ろ
わ				を
ん				

Table 9. Writing Katakana

ア	イ	ウ	エ	オ
カ	キ	ク	ケ	コ
サ	シ	ス	セ	ソ
タ	チ	ツ	テ	ト
ナ	ニ	ヌ	ネ	ノ
ハ	ヒ	フ	ヘ	ホ
マ	ミ	ム	メ	モ
ヤ		ユ		ヨ
ラ	リ	ル	レ	ロ
ワ				ヲ
ン				

26

Orthography

Modern kana orthography (*gendai kanazukai*) reflects pronunciation closely. This section explains, with examples, the most important orthographic rules.

1. In hiragana, the long vowels (*chō-on*) *ā*, *ii*, and *ū* are represented by adding あ, い, or う to a hiragana containing the same vowel sound:

ああ	*ā*	Ah! Oh!
おかあさん	*okāsan*	mother
いいえ	*iie*	no
おにいさん	*oniisan*	elder brother
ゆうがた	*yūgata*	evening
すうがく	*sūgaku*	mathematics

2. In hiragana, the vowel *ē*, which occurs in words of Japanese origin, is written by adding え to a hiragana containing the *e* vowel sound:

ねえ	*nē*	indeed, right?
おねえさん	*onēsan*	elder sister

The identically pronounced long vowel *ei*, which occurs in words of Chinese origin, is written by adding い to a hiragana containing the *e* vowel sound:

ていねい	*teinei*	polite
きれい	*kirei*	pretty

3. In hiragana *ō* is normally represented by adding う to a hiragana containing the *o* sound:

どうぞ	*dōzo*	please
おはよう	*ohayō*	Good morning.

In some cases, however, お is used instead of う:

おおい	(多い)	*ōi*	numerous
おおきい	(大きい)	*ōkii*	big
オオカミ		*ōkami*	wolf
おおやけ	(公)	*ōyake*	public, official
こおり	(氷)	*kōri*	ice
とお	(十)	*tō*	ten
とおい	(遠い)	*tōi*	far
とおる	(通る)	*tōru*	go along/through, pass
ほのお	(炎)	*honō*	flame
もよおす	(催す)	*moyōsu*	sponsor

27

The student need not concern himself too long with these historically based exceptions, since these words are usually written with kanji in such a way (shown in the parentheses) that the problem does not arise.

4. In the transliteration of foreign words into katakana, long vowels are represented with a lengthening stroke:

コーヒー	_kōhī_	coffee
ビール	_bīru_	beer
ボール	_bōru_	ball
ダンサー	_dansā_	dancer
エスカレーター	_esukarētā_	escalator

Exceptions:

| エイト | _eito_ | eight |
| スペイン | _Supein_ | Spain |

5. The voiced sounds (_daku-on_) g, z, and b are denoted by placing a pair of short diagonal strokes (_daku-ten_) on the upper right corner of the kana for the corresponding unvoiced sound. The p sound (_handaku-on_) is denoted by adding a small circle (_handaku-ten_) on the upper right corner of the corresponding kana from the _ha_ row of the _Gojū-on Zu_ (given on page 14) :

| が ガ | ざ ザ | だ ダ | ば バ | ぱ パ |
| _ga_ | _za_ | _da_ | _ba_ | _pa_ |

6. The "twisted" sounds (_yō-on_) are denoted by two kana, which coalesce phonetically into a single syllable. The first one is selected from the _i_ column and the second from the _ya_ row of the _Gojū-on Zu_. The second kana, which is written smaller, is positioned toward the lower part of its space when the text is written horizontally, and toward the right side of its space when the text is written vertically:

| _kya_ | きゃ | キャ | きゃ | キャ |
| _gya_ | ぎゃ | ギャ | ぎゃ | ギャ |

7. Assimilated sounds (_soku-on_), i.e., those sounds which are represented in romanization by double consonants, are denoted by a small っ/ッ before the consonant sound:

れっしゃ	_ressha_	train
じっぷん	_jippun_	10 minutes
ロケット	_roketto_	rocket
ちょっと	_chotto_	a little

8. Short, broken-off vowels at the ends of words or syllables (final glottal stops, or soku-on) are also denoted by a small つ/ッ:

あっ	*a'*	Oh!
きゃっ	*kya'*	Eek!
ジッ	*ji'*	(a Chinese reading used in compounds)

9. The sounds *ji* and *zu* are usually written じ/ジ and ず/ズ:

まじめ	*majime*	serious, sober
まずい	*mazui*	bad-tasting
ラジオ	*rajio*	radio
ジャズ	*jazu*	jazz

But ぢ and づ are used

a. when the preceding syllable (of the same word) consists of the same character without the *daku-ten*:

つづり	*tsuzuri*	syllable, spelling
つづく	*tsuzuku*	continue
ちぢむ	*chijimu*	shrink

b. when the syllables ち and つ are voiced in compound words:

かなづかい	(かな＋つかい)	*kanazukai*	*kana* orthography
きづかれ	(き＋つかれ)	*kizukare*	mental fatigue
はなぢ	(はな＋ち)	*hanaji*	nosebleed

10. The syllables *e*, *o*, and *wa* are written え/エ, お/オ, and わ/ワ when part of a word:

いいえ	*iie*	no
なお	*nao*	further, still
わたし	*watashi*	I, me
エネルギー	*enerugī*	energy
オペラ	*opera*	opera
ワシントン	*Washinton*	Washington

But the same three sounds are written へ/ヘ, を/ヲ, and は/ハ when they represent postpositional "auxiliary words" or particles (*joshi*):

こんにちは	*konnichi wa*	Hello!
テヘランへ	*Teheran e*	to Teheran

わたしははがきをポストへいれた。 *Watashi wa hagaki o posuto e ireta.*
I put the postcard in the mailbox.

11. The word 言う "say" is pronounced ゆう *yū* but written いう *iu.*

Table 10. Important Katakana Combinations
(according to western alphabetical order)

	a	e	i	o	u
c		che チェ			
d			di ディ		
f	fa ファ	fe フェ	fi フィ	fo フォ	
g	gwa グァ				
h		hye ヒェ			
j		je ジェ			
k	kwa クァ	kwe クェ	kwi クィ	kwo クォ	
s		she シェ			
t			ti ティ		
ts	tsa ツァ	tse ツェ		tso ツォ	
v	va ヴァ	ve ヴェ	vi ヴィ	vo ヴォ	vu ヴ
w		we ウェ	wi ウィ	wo ウォ	

As shown in this table, a foreign sound that does not normally occur in Japanese is sometimes represented by a normal-size katakana followed by a smaller-size katakana vowel character. In practice, however, foreign words are often "nipponized" so that, for example, the Spanish *viva* is represented not by ヴィヴァ but simply by ビバ.

Usage

As mentioned previously, modern texts usually consist of a mixture of kanji and hiragana, with a sprinkling of katakana (*kanji-kana majiri*). Each of these scripts serves definite functions. The following rules outline what the kana syllabaries are used for.

Usages of hiragana

1. All types of native words other than substantives, verbs, and adjective:

よく	*yoku*	well, often
たぶん	*tabun*	probably
この	*kono*	this, these
あそこ	*asoko*	there
だから	*dakara*	so, therefore
まだ	*mada*	still, not yet
だけ	*dake*	only
へ	*e*	to

2. Substantives, verbs, and adjectives in certain cases (as when the formerly used kanji have become obsolete):

いす	*isu*	chair
(お)はし	*(o)hashi*	chopsticks
する	*suru*	do, make
できる	*dekiru*	can, be able
きれい	*kirei*	pretty
うれしい	*ureshii*	happy

3. Inflectional endings of all words written with kanji:

行く	*i-ku*	go
行かない	*i-kanai*	not go
白い	*shiro-i*	white
祭り	*matsu-ri*	festival

Hiragana used for writing word endings (*gobi*) are called *okurigana*. But it must be noted that in many cases not only the inflectional ending but also part of the stem (*gokan*) is written in kana (in particular, this incudes adjectives ending in *-shii*, and *ichi-dan* or "vowel" verbs, which end in *-eru* or *-iru*):

新しい	*atara-shii*	new
大きい	*ō-kii*	big

31

| 食べる | *ta-beru* | eat |
| 幸せ | *shiawa-se* | happiness |

Usages of katakana

1. Foreign-derived words:

ビル	*biru*	building
ビール	*bīru*	beer
パン	*pan*	bread
テーブル	*tēburu*	table
タバコ	*tabako*	tobacco, cigarette

But one also sees:

| たばこ | *tabako* | tobacco, cigarette |

2. Foreign words and foreign proper names (with the exception of Chinese and Korean proper names, which are written in kanji):

アメリカ	*Amerika*	America
ドイツ	*Doitsu*	Germany
パリ	*Pari (Fr. pron.)*	Paris
シェークスピア	*Shēkusupia*	Shakespeare

In transcribing foreign words and proper names, the basic rule is that the katakana should follow as closely as possible the pronunciation of the original word, the ever-growing vocabulary of foreign-derived words being overwhelmingly of English origin. Despite a general trend toward unification of the transcription rules, one occasionally encounters foreign words and names which are rendered into katakana in more than one way:

ベット	*betto*	bed
ベッド	*beddo*	bed
ジェネレーション	*jenerēshon*	generation
ゼネレーション	*zenerēshon*	generation
ダーウィン	*Dāwin*	Darwin
ダーウイン	*Dāuin*	Darwin

For many foreign sounds there is nothing in the traditional Japanese sound and writing system that corresponds. Diacritical marks and many new combinations of katakana

(some written small to show phonetic coalescence into one syllable) are used to represent such sounds (see also Table 10 on page 30):

テイー	tī	tea
クォータリー	quōtarī	a quarterly
フィリピン	Firipin	the Philippines
ダーウィン	Dāwin	Darwin
ヴィーン*	Vīn	Vienna
ジュネーヴ*	Junēvu	Genève
デュッセルドルフ*	Dyusserudorufu	Düsseldorf

*The ministry of Education presently recommends that these be written ウイーン *Uīn*, ジュネーブ *Junēbu*, and ジュッセルドルフ *Jusserudorufu*.

In many cases Japanese prefer to give foreign words a more Japanese-sounding pronunciation:

バイオリン	baiorin	violin
ビタミン	bitamin	vitamin
チーム	chīmu	team
ラジオ	rajio	radio
ベートーベン	Bētōben	Beethoven

The consonant *l*, which does not occur in the Japanese language, is transcribed with a katakana from the *ra* row of the *Gojū-on* table:

| ホール | hōru | hall; hole (in golf) |
| ラブレター | raburetā | love letter |

Katakana are also used for the following:

3. Names of plants and animals (especially in scientific contexts):

ネズミ	nezumi	mouse, rat
マグロ	maguro	tuna
サクラ	sakura	cherry tree

But kanji and hiragana are also used:

犬	inu	dog
桜	sakura	cherry tree
みかん	mikan	mandarin orange

4. Some female given names:

エミ	*Emi*
マリ	*Mari*

5. Onomatopoeic words such as animal cries and other sounds; children's words; exclamations:

ワンワン	*wan wan*	bowwow
ニャーニャー	*nyā nyā*	meow
ガタガタ	*gata gata*	(rattling sound)
トントン	*ton ton*	(knocking sound)
ピューピュー	*pyū pyū*	(sound of the wind)
アレ / アレッ	*are / are'*	Huh!?
オヤ / オヤッ	*oya / oya'*	Oh!

6. Colloquialisms and slang:

インチキ	*inchiki*	fake, phony
デカ	*deka*	detective

7. Words and proper names which are to be emphasized:

もうダメだ	*mō dame da*	It's too late.
ナゾの自殺	*nazo no jisatsu*	mysterious suicide
トヨタ	*Toyota*	Toyota (auto company)
ヨコハマ	*Yokohama*	Yokohama (port city)

The limited usage of words written in *katakana* makes them stand out and often lends them a certain weight. This highvisibility, which is often made use of in advertising, has somewhat the same effect that italics have in Western languages.

Usages of both hiragana and katakana

1. To show the pronunciation of kanji:

一つ (ひと)	*hitotsu*	片 (カタ)
平仮名 (ひらがな)	*hiragana*	仮 (カ)
漢字 (カンジ)	*kanji*	名 (ナ) *katakana*

34

These small kana, written either above or below the kanji in horizontal writing and to the right of the kanji in vertical writing, are calls *furigana* or *rubi*.

2. In transliterating individual kanji, katakana are used for Chinese-derived (*on*) readings, and hiragana for Japanese (*kun*) readings:

人   ジン, ニン, ひと   *JIN, NIN (on), hito (kun)*   person

The repetition symbols (*kurikaeshi fugō*)

If, within a single word, the same kana symbols occur one after the other, the second one can be replaced by the repetition symbol ヽ :

| あヽ | *ā* | Ah! Oh! |
| かヽし | *kakashi* | scarecrow |

The repetition symbol may also be used in combination with the *daku-ten*:

ほゞ	*hobo*	almost, nearly
たゞし	*tadashi*	but, however
すゞり	*suzuri*	inkstone

The repetition symbol for two syllables is used only in vertical writing:

| いろ〳〵 | *iroiro* | various | わざ〳〵 | *wazawaza* | on purpose |

Punctuation

There are no compulsory and uniform rules for the usage and nomenclature of the various punctuation marks (*kugiri fugō* or *kutōten*), and this chapter is but an attempt to present in a systematic way a uniform terminology and practical explication of Japanese punctuation as it is used today.

In general, a punctuation mark is given the same amount of space as any other character; that is, on *genkō yōshi* an entire square is used even for a punctuation mark. However, a pair of successive punctuation marks like 「 「 or 。) are written in a single space, the *tensen* is written three dots per space, and some punctuation marks (see examples under 4, 5, 10, and 11 below) extend over several spaces.

Some punctuation marks take different orientations or forms when used in vertical and horizontal writing:

﹁﹂ → 「」   ﹃﹄ → 『』   〝〟 → " "
︵︶ → （ ）   ︵︵︶ → （ ）   ～ → ～
ひる、 → ひる   よる → よる

1. *Maru* or *kuten* [。]

Indicates the conclusion of a sentence or utterance (a)–(c), like the period in English. When the presence of the question particle *ka* or an interrogative word makes it clear that the sentence is a question, a *maru* is used in preference to a question mark (d), (cf. 12).

(a) 日本は島国です。

(b) 「どうぞ、こちらへ。」

(c) 「おおい、田中君。」

(d) 「どちらへ。」

2. *Ten* or *tōten* [、]

Used like the comma in English to indicate a pause and clarify the structure of the sentence (a)–(e); to separate successive numbers (f); and to divide numbers of four or more digits into three-digit groups (g). To show how the presence or absence of a *ten* can change the meaning of a sentence, (e) has been written with a *ten* ("A man wearing large glasses").

(a) はい、そうです。

(b) ただ、例外として、……

(c) 「行きますか」と、彼にきいた。

(d) 見ましたか、今朝の新聞を。

(e) 大きな、めがねをかけた男。

(f) 二、三日

(g) 二、三二〇円

3. *Nakaguro* or *nakaten* [・]

Used to separate words of the same type (a), (b); to link words together into one unit, when opposed to *ten* which separates (c), (d); to separate the year, month, and day when citing dates (e); to indicate the decimal point (f); and to separate the component words of foreign phrases and names written in katakana (g).

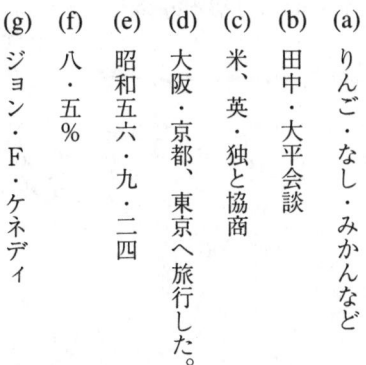

(a) りんご・なし・みかんなど

(b) 田中・大平会談

(c) 米・英・独と協商

(d) 大阪・京都、東京へ旅行した。

(e) 昭和五六・九・二四

(f) 八・五％

(g) ジョン・F・ケネディ

4. *Nakasen* [│]

Has the same functions as the dash in English. It is used to indicate that a sentence or thought has been broken off while still incomplete (a) or to set off explanatory information inserted into a sentence (b); when used for lengths of time or distance it has the meaning of "from … to …" or "between … and …" (c)–(e); and in Japanese addresses it separates the numbers for the *-chōme, -ban,* and *-gō* (f).

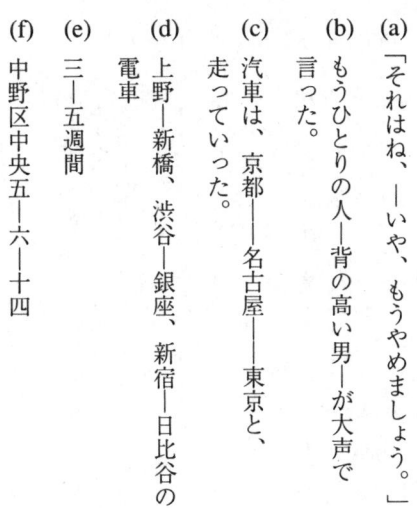

(a) 「それはね、―いや、もうやめましょう。」

(b) もうひとりの人―背の高い男―が大声で言った。

(c) 汽車は、京都―名古屋―東京と、走っていった。

(d) 上野―新橋、渋谷―銀座、新宿―日比谷の電車

(e) 三―五週間

(f) 中野区中央五―六―十四

5. *Tensen* [⋮]

Consists of a string of centered dots (usually six), three to a space. It corresponds to the English ellipsis […] and denotes a pause in speech indicating that a sentence or thought has been left uncompleted (a), (cf. 4a), the trailing off of the voice at the end of an utterance (b), or silence (c). Long strings of successive three-dot *tensen* groups are sometimes used in tables of contents and the like to form lines connecting chapter titles and page number (d).

(a) 「それからね……いやいや、もうなんにも申し上げますまい。」

(b) 「それもそうだけど……」

(c) 「………」
「ごめんネ、由美ちゃん。」

(d) 第一章　序説……………一頁

6. *Kagikakko* [「」]

Correspond to the quotation marks of English (a), (b).

Futaekagi [『』]

Used for quotations within quotations (c), (d).

(a) 国歌「君が代」

(b) 漢字の読み方は「音」と「訓」との二つがある。

(c) 「母も『よろしく』と申しておりました。」

(d) 彼は「人生に大切なのは『努力』ということだ」と言った。

38

7. *In'yōfu* [„ "]

Today often used instead of *kagikakko*, especially with short phrases in the sence of "so-called."

これは有名な „月光の曲" です。

8. *Kakko* or *marukakko* [⌒]

Used like parentheses in English (a), (b).

Futaegakko [◌]

Like brackets in English, used for parentheses within parentheses (c).

Yokogakko [( )]

Enclose the umbers or letters that mark off various sections, articles, paragraphs, etc., of a text (d).

(d)	(c)	(b)	(a)
（一）	和英辞典	（第二回	（田中）
（イ）	（修訂	（完）	
（a）	《新装》	（終）	
	版昭和五十六年刊）	（続く）	

39

9. *Namigata* [〳]

Used to idicate a range "from … to …" (a)–(c), (cf. 4c–4e). It is usually read aloud as kana, "from".

(c) 東京～大阪　(b) 四月～六月　(a) 一～三時間

10. *Wakiten* [⋮]

Used to "italicize" words and phrases (a); also applied to words which for some reason are written in kana instead of the usual kanji (b), and sometimes used to distinguish slang, dialect, of other types of unconventional words (c).

(a) まず、句点は文の終わりに、つけるというのが……

(b) ひるという言葉は、

(c) ぴんからきりまで、である。

11. *Wakisen* [│]

Directs the reader's attention to certain phrases (a), words, or parts of words (b) like a kind of "vertical underlining" (cf. 10a).

(a) 名辞は、単一の名詞から成ることもあり、あるいは、長い名詞句から成ることもある。人はパンのみにて生くるものにあらず。

(b) 次の傍線を引いた語について説明せよ。そう考えられる。

40

12. *Gimonfu* [?]

Used in place of the *maru* when it would otherwise be unclear whether the sentence is a question or a statement (a), (b), (cf. 1d).

(b) 「きのう見に行った?」

(a) 「ええ? なんですって?」

13. *Kantanfu* [!]

Like the exclamation point in English, indicates emotional intensity and should be used sparingly.

「ちがう、ちがう、ちがうぞ!」

14. *Piriodo*, "period" [.]

Used in horizontal writing as a delimiter between the year, month, and day in dates (see example), and sometimes also instead of the *maru*.

平成 8.4.30

15. *Konma*, "comma" [,]

Used in horizontal writing instead of the *ten*.

はい, そうです。

The Kanji
Brief Historical Outline

The oldest known Chinese characters date back to the sixteenth century B.C., but their number and advanced form indicate that they had already gone through a development of several hundred years. Like the Egyptian hieroglyphics, the earliest characters started with simple illustrations, which during the course of time became increasingly abstract and took on forms better adapted to the writing tools of the time. These characters, along with many other elements of Chinese culture, came to Japan by way of the Korean peninsula in the fourth century A.D. Since the Japanese had no writing of their own, the Chinese characters soon came to be used for the Japanese language as well.

At first these monosyllabic Chinese characters were used purely phonetically, with no reference to their meanings, to represent similar Japanese sounds:

久尔 *ku-ni* country

This method enabled one to write down any word, but a single multisyllabic Japanese word required several Chinese characters, each consisting of many strokes.

A second method soon developed: the characters were used ideographically, with no reference to their Chinese pronunciations, to represent Japanese words of the same or related meaning:

国 *kuni* country

Both methods are used in the *Man'yōshū*, the oldest (eighth-century) Japanese collection of poetry. Here, words denoting concepts are written with the corresponding Chinese characters, which are then given the Japanese pronunciation. All other words, as well as proper names and inflectional endings, are represented phonetically by kanji which are read with a Japanese approximation to their Chinese pronunciations.

The characters used for this latter, phonetic function are called *Man'yōgana*. The kana syllabaries developed from these characters after great simplification.

For centuries kanji, hiragana, and katakana were used independently of one another, and the number of symbols in use and their readings kept growing. Toward the end of the 1800s, after the Meiji Restoration, the government as part of its modernization program undertook to simplify the writing system for the first time.

The latest major writing reform came shortly after World War II:

1. In 1946 the number of kanji permitted for use in official publications was limited to 1,850 *Tōyō Kanji* (1,945 *Jōyō Kanji* in the cabinet order of 1981); of these, 900 (presently 1006) were selected as *Kyōiku Kanji* to be learned in the first six years of schooling.

2. The *on* and *kun* readings of the 1,850 kanji were limited in number to about 3,500 (over 4,000 in the *Jōyō Kanji* of 1981).
3. Many kanji were simplified or replaced by others easier to write.
4. Uniform rules were prescribed for how to write the kanji (sequence and umber of strokes).

The press strives to follow these and other government recommendations concerning how Japanese is to be written. A knowledge of the set of characters treated in this book will therefore be sufficient for reading Japanese newspapers without time-consumung reference to character dictionaries.

Since 1951 the government has from time to time published an ever-growing supplementary list of kanji which, in addition to the *Jōyō Kanji*, are permitted for use in given names. This list of *Jinmei-yō Kanji* currently (as of 1991) numbers 284 kanji.

A Japanese of average education is familiar with about 3,000 characters. Today roughly 6,000–7,000 characters are used in written Japanese, including technical and literary writing. The most comprehensive modern Japanese character dictionary, the *Kō Kan-Wa Jiten* by Morohashi et al., includes more than 20,000 kanji, while Chinese dictionaries which attempt to record every character that has ever been in use have entries for some 40,000.

Form and Construction

Most characters are built up from a limited number of basic elements according to principles which are easily grasped. How these elements are put together is related to the meaning, and often the pronunciation, of a kanji, and therefore familiarity with the most important elements and their use will make it much easier to understand and memorize the 1,945 *Jōyō Kanji* and 284 name kanji as well as all those not incuded here. Chinese characters can be divided, according to their origins and structures, into three categories: pictographs, ideographs, and complex characters.

Pictographs

The first characters developed from simple illustrations of objects and phenomena of daily life. Even in the abstract form used today, the object depicted can often still be recognized:

山	*yama*	mountain (three towering peaks)
木	*ki*	tree (trunk with branches)
田	*ta*	field, paddy (square plot of land with furrows)

There are only a few pictographs which are used today as independent characters. But they serve as building blocks for almost all the other characters in use.

Ideographs

For abstract concepts, characters were invented which indicate meaning in only a few strokes:

一	*ICHI*	one		上	*ue*	above
二	*NI*	two		下	*shita*	below
				中	*naka*	middle

Complex characters

To increase the stock of word signs, the characters already available were put together in new combinations. At first two or three pictographs with the same or similar meanings were combined into a single new character (logogram):

林	*hayashi*	woods	(木 tree + 木 tree)
森	*mori*	forest	(木 tree + 木 tree + 木 tree)
明	*akarui*	light	(日 sun + 月 moon)

In other cases, the Chinese took the reading of one part of a newly created complex character as the reading of the entire character (phonologogram):

理	*RI*	reason

The sound-indicating part is in this case the character 里, whose reading is *ri*. Over 90 percent of all kanji are combinations constructed according to this principle, which is therefore often helpful for guessing at the *on* reading of a newly encountered character. Usually the component indicationg the pronunciation is on the right, while that on the left indicates the meaning. Most phonologograms can be classed into six groups, corresponding to the positions of the sound- and meaning-indicating components (P = pronunciation, M = meaning):

M on left, P on right:	銅	*DŌ*	copper	(金 metall + 同 *DŌ*)
P on left, M on right:	歌	*KA*	sing	(欠 yawn + 可 *KA*)
M on top, P on bottom:	花	*KA*	flower	(艹 grass + 化 *KA*)
P on top, M on bottom:	盛	*SEI*	fill	(皿 dish + 成 *SEI*)
M outside, P inside:	園	*EN*	garden	(囗 enclosure + 袁 *EN*)
P outside, M inside:	問	*MON*	ask	(口 mouth + 門 *MON*)

The 17 structures:

Just as there is a limited number of elements (graphemes) from which kanji are built up, there is likewise a limited number of structures that kanji assume. There are basically 16 kanji structures that occur with any frequency. All other structures are denoted in this book by a square containing three dots. These structures, listed approximately in decreasing order of their frequency, are:

In the lists of *Jōyō Kanji* and name kanji in this book, the structure of each kanji is given, as well as its radical and graphemes.

This additional information is meant to show that kanji are not just a bunch of disordered strokes but are made up of a limited number of meaning- and pronunciation-indicating elements that are organized with a certain regularity. Knowing the most important radicals and graphemes and how they are put together helps in becoming familiar with a newly encountered kanji.

Table 11 (page 47) provides an overview of the most important of the 214 traditional radicals, their position within a character (denoted by crosshatching), and their Japanese term. Listed beside each radical are two example kanji that contain the radical.

Knowledge of radicals not only helps in understanding and memorizing a kanji; it is also essential for using a conventional character dictionary. In addition, knowing what each radical is called is very useful in identifying kanji verbally (such as in describing the spelling of someone's name over the telephone).

Table 12 (pages 48–51) lists all 214 traditional radicals along with their meanings.

In some cases the meaning and name of a radical is more a matter of tradition and convention than firm scientific knowledge. There is no sure way to derive the meaning of a kanji from its radical and the meanings of its other components, and this is especially true of those kanji which were simplified after World War II. Often these interpretations are nothing more than a *pons asinorum* the kanji learner must overcome.

Table 1 (inside front cover) presents an overview of the 79 Radicals in the Index by Radicals in this book, in *The Kanji Dictionary* (1996), and in *The Learner's Kanji Dictionary* (1997) of Spahn & Hadamitzky. With one exception, these radicals are a subset of the 214 traditional radicals. Practice has verified the plausible proposition that a smaller number of radicals makes it easier and quicker to look up a kanji.

Table 2 (front end paper) presents the 79 radicals with their variants.

Table 13 (page 52) lists 80 graphemes (graphical elements) especially selected for looking up kanji in computer programs. These graphemes were first used in the programs *MacSUNRISE Script* (1990) and *MacSUNRISE Kanji Dictionary* (1993) and since then have been adopted by other programs. In number and form, these graphemes mostly coincide with the 79 radicals in Tables 1 and 2. But while in the traditional radical system and the 79-radical system derived from it there is exactly one radical per kanji, all the graphemes contained in a kanji can be put to use in specifying kanji and compounds.

Table 14 (page 53) shows the 80 standard forms of the graphemes along with their variants. Each variant grapheme is associated with one of the standard graphemes on the basis of similarity, common traits, and, in individual cases, same meanings.

Table 11. The Most Important of the 214 Traditional Radicals

(ordered according to their position within a character)

hen 偏				koromohen ネ	初 裸		takekanmuri 竹	筆 答
亻 ninben	体 住		言 gonben	語 話		耂 oikanmuri	者 老
冫 nisui	次 冷		貝 kaihen	財 貯		雨 amekanmuri	雲 電
口 kuchihen	味 呼		車 kurumahen	転 輪		**ashi** 脚	
土 tsuchihen	地 場		金 kanehen	鉄 針		儿 hitoashi	先 免
女 onnahen	好 始		馬 umahen	駅 験		心 kokoro	想 悪
弓 yumihen	引 強		**tsukuri** 旁			灬 rekka/renga	無 照
彳 gyōninben	役 御		刂 rittō	別 制		皿 sara	盗 盟
阝 kozatohen	防 院		力 chikara	助 効		貝 kogai	貨 負
忄 risshinben	性 情		卩 fushizukuri	印 却		**kamae** 構	
扌 tehen	持 招		彡 sanzukuri	形 彫		冂 dōgamae	円 同
方 katahen	放 旅		阝 ōzato	都 郡		匚 hakogamae	区 医
日 hihen	明 曜		攵 nobun	故 政		囗 kunigamae	国 四
木 kihen	林 村		斤 onozukuri	新 断		戈 hokogamae	戦 成
氵 sanzui	海 池		欠 akubi	歌 欧		行 gyōgamae	街 術
火 hihen	畑 灯		殳 rumata	段 殺		門 mongamae	間 問
牛 ushihen	物 特		隹 furutori	難 雑		**tare** 垂	
犭 kemonohen	独 犯		頁 ōgai	類 顔		厂 gandare	原 厚
王 ōhen	理 現		**kanmuri** 冠			尸 shikabane	局 居
目 mehen	眼 眠		亠 nabebuta	交 京		广 madare	広 庁
矢 yahen	知 短		八 hachigashira	分 公		疒 yamaidare	病 痛
石 ishihen	砂 破		冖 wakanmuri	写 冠		**nyō** 繞	
衤 shimesuhen	社 礼		宀 ukanmuri	家 安		廴 ennyō	建 延
禾 nogihen	和 私		艹 kusakanmuri	花 茶		辶 shinnyō	進 返
米 komehen	粉 精		癶 hatsugashira	発 登		走 sōnyō	起 超
糸 itohen	続 約		宀 anakanmuri	空 窓			
月 nikuzuki	胴 服		罒 amigashira	買 罪			
舟 funehen	般 航						

47

Table 12. The 214 Traditional Radicals and Their Meanings
(arranged by stroke count)

	– 1 –		26	卩	stamp, seal
1	一	one; (horizontal stroke)	27	厂	cliff
2	丨	(vertical stroke)	28	厶	private
3	丶	(dot stroke)	29	又	again; hand
4	丿	(diagonal stroke)			
5	乙	No. 2		**– 3 –**	
6	亅	(vertical stroke with hook)	30	口	mouth
			31	囗	border
	– 2 –		32	土	earth
7	二	two	33	士	man; scholar
8	亠	lid, top; up	34	夂	follow
9	人, 亻	man, human being	35	夊	go slowly
10	儿	legs	36	夕	evening
11	入	enter	37	大	large
12	八	eight	38	女	woman
13	冂	enclose	39	子	child, son
14	冖	cover	40	宀	roof
15	冫	ice	41	寸	inch
16	几	table	42	小	small
17	凵	container	43	尤	lame
18	刀, 刂	knife, sword	44	尸	corpse
19	力	power	45	屮	sprout
20	勹	wrap	46	山	mountain
21	匕	spoon	47	川	river
22	匚	box	48	工	work
23	匸	conceal	49	己	self
24	十	ten	50	巾	cloth
25	卜	oracle	51	干	dry; shield
			52	幺	young; slight

53	广	slanting roof
54	夂	move
55	廾	folded hands
56	弋	javelin
57	弓	bow (in archery)
58	彐, 彑	pig's head
59	彡	hair-style; light rays
60	彳	step, stride

– 4 –

61	心, 忄, 㣺	heart
62	戈	spear
63	戶, 戸	weapon; door
64	手, 扌	hand
65	支	branch
66	攴, 攵	strike, hit
67	文	literature
68	斗	(unit of volume)
69	斤	ax
70	方	direction
71	无	not
72	日	sun; day
73	曰	say
74	月	moon; month
75	木	tree, wood
76	欠	lack
77	止	stop
78	歹	decompose
79	殳	lance shaft
80	母	mother; not
81	比	compare
82	毛	hair
83	氏	family, clan

84	气	breath, air
85	水, 氵	water
86	火, 灬	fire
87	爪	claw, nail
88	父	father
89	爻	mix
90	爿, 丬	split wood (left half)
91	片	split wood (right half)
92	牙	fang, canine tooth
93	牛	cow
94	犬, 犭	dog

– 5 –

95	玄	darkness
96	玉, 王	jewel
97	瓜	melon
98	瓦	tile
99	甘	sweet
100	生	be born, live
101	用	use
102	田	rice paddy
103	疋, 乛	roll of cloth
104	疒	sickness
105	癶	outspread legs
106	白	white
107	皮	skin, hide
108	皿	bowl, dish
109	目	eye
110	矛	halberd
111	矢	arrow
112	石	stone
113	示, 礻	show, announce
114	禸	footprint

115	禾	grain
116	穴	hole
117	立	stand

– 6 –

118	竹, ⺮	bamboo
119	米	rice
120	糸, 糹	thread
121	缶	earthen jar
122	网, 罒	net
123	羊	sheep
124	羽, 羽	feather
125	老	old
126	而	and also
127	耒	plow
128	耳	ear
129	聿	writing brush
130	肉, 月	flesh, meat
131	臣	retainer, minister
132	自	self
133	至	arrive, reach
134	臼	mortar
135	舌	tongue
136	舛	contrary, err
137	舟	ship, boat
138	艮, 艮	boundary
139	色	color
140	艸, 艹	grass, plant
141	虍	tiger
142	虫	worm, insect
143	血	blood
144	行	go
145	衣, 衤	clothing

146	西	cover; west

– 7 –

147	見	see
148	角	horn; corner
149	言	speak, say
150	谷	valley
151	豆	bean
152	豕	pig
153	豸	badger; reptile
154	貝	shell, mussel; money
155	赤	red
156	走	run
157	足	foot, leg
158	身	body
159	車	vehicle, wheel
160	辛	bitter
161	辰	(fifth zodiac sign); 7–9 A.M.
162	辵, 辶	advance, move ahead
163	邑, 阝	community
164	酉	wine jug; bird
165	釆	separate
166	里	(2.44 miles); village

– 8 –

167	金	metal, gold
168	長	long
169	門	gate, door
170	阜, 阝	hill
171	隶	capture
172	隹	small bird
173	雨	rain

174	靑, 青	green, blue		197	鹵	salt
175	非	wrong; non-		198	鹿	deer
				199	麥	wheat
	– 9 –			200	麻	hemp
176	面	face; surface				
177	革	leather			**– 12 –**	
178	韋	leather		201	黃	yellow
179	韭	leek		202	黍	millet
180	音	sound, noise		203	黑, 黒	black
181	頁	head; page		204	黹	embroider
182	風	wind				
183	飛	fly			**– 13 –**	
184	食	food, eat		205	黽	frog
185	首	head		206	鼎	3-legged kettle
186	香	scent		207	鼓	drum
				208	鼠	rat, mouse
	– 10 –					
187	馬	horse			**– 14 –**	
188	骨	bone		209	鼻	nose
189	高	high		210	齊, 斉	alike
190	髟	long hair				
191	鬥	fighting			**– 15 –**	
192	鬯	herbs		211	齒, 歯	tooth
193	鬲	tripod				
194	鬼	demon			**– 16 –**	
				212	龍, 竜	dragon
	– 11 –					
					– 17 –	
195	魚	fish		213	龜, 亀	turtle
196	鳥	bird		214	龠	flute

Table 13. The 80 Graphemes (without variants)

1	一 1	丨 2							
2	亻 3	二 4	冫 5	孑 6	阝 7	力 8	又 9	匕 10	亠 11	十 12
	卜 13	厂 14	𠂉 15	儿 16	厶 17	厂 18	辶 19	冂 20
3	氵 21	土 22	扌 23	口 24	女 25	巾 26	犭 27	弓 28	彳 29	夕 30
	彡 31	艹 32	宀 33	大 34	小 35	山 36	寸 37	工 38	ヨ 39	尸 40
4	木 41	月 42	日 43	火 44	礻 45	王 46	牛 47	方 48	攵 49	斤 50
	心 51	戈 52								
5	石 53	立 54	目 55	禾 56	衤 57	罒 58	皿 59	疒 60		
6	糸 61	米 62	舟 63	虫 64	耳 65	竹 66				
7	言 67	貝 68	車 69	𧾷 70	酉 71					
8-11	金 72	食 73	隹 74	雨 75	門 76	頁 77	馬 78	魚 79	鳥 80	

52

Table 14. The 80 Graphemes (with variants)

一 **1**	ㄱ	ㄱ	ㄱ	ㄱ	ㄱ	ㄟ	乙	之	ㅣ **2**	ㄴ	ㄴ	ㄴ	ㄴ
ㄴ	丿	㇀	㇀	㇏	㇀	㇀	丶	亻 **3**	人	入	ㄥ	ㄥ	二 **4**
二	氵	冫	孑	阝 **7**	卩 **8**	巳	力	刀	乃	又 **9**	ㄷ	又	ㄴ **10**
㇀	亠 **11**	上	工 **12**	十	十	ㄗ	七	九	ナ	ナ	ㄕ	卄
与	乂	乂	乂	乂	七	卜 **13**	卜	匕	ㅑ	丆	丁 **14**
丁	匸	万	宀 **15**	ㄅ	ㄅ	ㄅ	ㄅ	儿 **16**	ㄦ	八	八	八	㇀
川	㇚	㇙	刂	‖	厶 **17**	厶	ㄅ	ㅗ	厂 **18**	厂	厂	ㄈ	厂
广	广	广	辶 **19**	辶	廴	冂 **20**	几	冂	冂	冂	冂	ㄦ	冖
凵	匚	ㄷ	氵 **21**	水	永	氺	氺	土 **22**	土	士	扌 **23**	手	手
口 **24**	口	口	囗	女 **25**	母	毌	巾 **26**	犭 **27**	勿	昜	豸	㇀	犬
尤	弓 **28**	己	己 **29**	彳	夕 **30**	夂	夕	彡 **31**	艹 **32**	廾	廾	廾	廾
宀 **33**	大 **34**	六	小 **35**	丷	丷	屵 **36**	寸 **37**	工 **38**	彐 **39**	ㅌ	ㅌ	ㅌ
彐	ㅌ	ㄱ	习	尸 **40**	卩	卩	户	户	户	巴	木 **41**	木	朩
月 **42**	冃	日	月	日 **43**	火 **44**	灬	父	灬	灬	灬	衤 **45**	示	王 **46**
王	壬	丰	牛 **47**	方 **48**	夊 **49**	夂	夂	夂	欠	斤 **50**	斤	心 **51**	小
忄	戈 **52**	弋	石 **53**	立	立 **54**	日 **55**	罒	禾 **56**	衤 **57**	衣	辰	氐	飞
夊 **58**	田	皿 **59**	疒 **60**	糸 **61**	米 **62**	舟 **63**	虫 **64**	耳 **65**	耳	竹 **66**	竹	言 **67**	貝 **68**
見 **69**	車 **70**	跍	足 **71**	酉 **72**	金 **73**	食	食	會	侖	良	良	艮	艮
目	隹 **74**	隹	雨 **75**	雫	雨	門 **76**	頁 **77**	馬 **78**	魚 **79**	鳥 **80**			

Readings

When Chinese texts were introduced into Japan, the Japanese adopted not only the Chinese characters but their Chinese readings as well. In being adapted to the Japanese phonetic system, the Chinese pronunciations were modified. For example, the distinctions between the four tones of Chinese were ignored. (This is one reason for the large number of homophones in Japanese.) Later, Chinese characters were used to represent Japanese words of identical or similar meaning and were given Japanese readings. This explains why most kanji have both Chinese-derived (*on*) and native Japanese (*kun*) readings. Moreover, a single kanji may have two or more *on* or *kun* readings, each indicating a different meaning or nuance (in contrast to Chinese, in which each character has only one reading).

In prescribing the basic kanji, the Ministry of Education limited not only the number of characters recognized for geneal use but also the number of officially authorized readings. Of the 1,945 *Jōyō Kanji* dealt with in this book, 1,200 have both Chinese and Japanese readings, a little more than 700 have only Chinese readings, and 43 have only Japanese readings. The kanji which have only a *kun* reading consist almost entirely of characters which were created by Japanese in imitation of the Chinese pattern (*kokuji*). The character 働 meaning "work" is the only *kokuji* to which a pseudo-*on*-reading is attached; its *on* reading is *dō* and its *kun* reading is *hatara(ku)*.

By convention, when it is necessary to distinguish *on* and *kun* readings, an *on* reading is spelled with katakana or uppercase roman letters, and a *kun* reading is spelled with hiragana or lowercase roman letters.

Whether a word is to be read with an *on* or with a *kun* reading can be determined in most cases by means of the following criteria:

1. One-character words are read with their *kun* readings:

人	*hito*	person
口	*kuchi*	mouth
日	*hi*	sun; day

Most of the relatively few single-character words which are pronounced with *on* readings have no *kun* readings, so the problem of choosing between two different readings seldom arises.

2. Words incorporating *okurigana* are pronounced with *kun* readings:

一つ	*hitotsu*	one
明かり	*akari*	light
大きい	*ōkii*	big

| 出す | *dasu* | take out |
| 入り口 | *iriguchi* | entrance |

3. Kanji sequences without *okurigana* are usually read with *on* readings:

| 見物 | *KENBUTSU* | sight-seeing |
| 人口 | *JINKŌ* | population |

4. Personal names are usually read with *kun* readings:

| 田中 | *Tanaka* | 山田 *Yamada* |

The characters composing a given compound word are generally read either all *on* or all *kun*.

Some character combinations have two, and in rare cases three, different readings, which may be associated with similar or with different meanings:

明日	*myōnichi, asu*	tomorrow
一日	*ichinichi, ichijitsu*	1 day
	tsuitachi	1st of the month

Sometimes kanji are used either (a) exclusively to convey the meaning of a word, disregarding the usual readings of the kanji; or (b) exclusively as phonetic symbols, disregarding the meanings of the individual kanji. Both types of kanji are called *ateji*:

| (a) | 大人 | *otona* | adult |
| | お母さん | *okāsan* | mother |

The readings *asu* and *tsuitachi* for the compounds 明日 and 一日 given above belong to this group.

| (b) | 出来る | *dekiru* | can, be able |

A number of kanji are used in compounds to refer to countries. Most are *ateji* of the second type, derived from an obsolete phonetic kanji spelling of the name of the country. The following list gives the most frequently encounterd kanji which denote countries; those marked with an asterisk [*] are not among the 1,945 basic kanji.

日	*Nichi, Nit-*	Japan	米	*Bei*	America, U.S.A.
中	*Chū*	China	英	*Ei*	Britain, England
韓*	*Kan*	South Korea	独	*Doku*	Germany
越	*Etsu*	Vietnam	仏	*Futsu*	France
印	*In*	India	伊*	*I*	Italy
比	*Hi*	the Philippines	露	*Ro*	Russia
豪, 濠*	*Gō*	Australia	西	*Sei*	Spain

Writing the Strokes in the Correct Direction and Sequence

At least in the beginning, reading practice should be supplemented by writing practice. Only by repeatedly writing the individual characters and their compounds can one gain confidence in reading. In addition, stroke counting, which is indispensable in using character dictionaries, can be mastered only trough writing. Writing the most complex kanji will present no difficulties once one knows to apply the writing rules to the limited number of elements which make up any kanji. The main problem is active writing: that is, reproducing from memory a character that has already been learned.

The small numbers given at the beginning of each stroke in the kanji illustrations in the following examples, and in the List of the *Jōyō Kanji*, indicate the direction in which each stroke is to be written and the order in which the strokes are to be written, as well as the total number of strokes in the kanji.

Stroke direction

1. Horizontal strokes are written from left to right:

2. Vertical or slanting strokes are written from top to bottom:

An exception is the combination of a short slanting down-stroke followed by a short slanting up-stroke, as in the radicals 氵 *sanzui*, 冫 *nisui*, and 疒 *yamaidare* and in 求 *kyū*, *moto(meru)* and other related kanji:

3. A stroke may change direction several times:

Stroke order

1. From top to bottom:

2. From left to right:

川 竹

3. Middle part before short flanking side-strokes:

小 当 水 氺

Exceptions:

忄 火

4. Horizontal stroke before intersecting vertical stroke:

十 土 七

Exceptions:

田 王 隹

and elements and characters built from these.

5. When slanting strokes intersect, the one running from upper right to lower left is written first:

文 父 攵

6. A piercing vertical stroke is written last:

中 申 車 半 聿 平 手

When the vertical middle stroke protrudes neither above nor below, the writing sequence is: upper part, middle stroke, lower part:

里 重 星

57

7. A piercing horizontal stroke is written last:

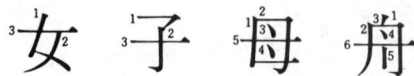

8. First the vertical stroke, then the short horizontal stroke which adjoins it on the right:

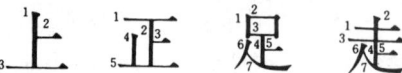

9. The enclosure is written first:

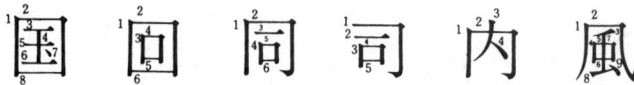

Exceptions:

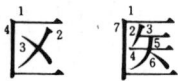

10. *Shinnyō, shinnyū* ⻌ is written last:

11. The kanji repetition symbol is written:

This symbol denotes the repetition of the immediately preceding kanji in the same word, but not when kanji are repeated merely by coincidence:

山々	*yamayama*	mountain
人々	*hitobito*	people

But:

民主主義	*minshu shugi*	democracy

In order to avoid confusing the beginner, not all details of the strokeorder rules set forth by the Ministry of Education have been given here.

For all *Jōyō Kanji* listed in this book the beginning of each stroke and the stroke order are shown by small numbers attached to the big main entry characters in the Kanji List. The main entry characters also serve as a model for the length of each stroke and its direction (vertical or slanted, straight or curved). The typeface of the main entry characters is very close to the standard handwritten form of the kanji.

Note that even within handwritten characters some strokes may differ in length and direction, depending on personal habits or whether a kanji is written with pen or brush.

A number of strokes in printed characters differ considerably in length and direction from their handwritten counterparts. (In the same way that a printed "a" may look quite different from a handwritten "*a*" in the Roman alphabet.)

But even printed characters may look quite different, depending on the typeface used.

Note that in some cases a handwritten stroke may look like two strokes in its printed version or is actually written with two strokes in calligraphy. When counting strokes, be aware that in this handbook we consider the following components to consist of the following number of strokes: 了 (1), 子 (2), 阝 (2), 辶 (2), 比 (4), 𠂆 (4), 臣 (7)

The following list gives examples for the most frequently occurring differences in direction and length of strokes. The first two kanji in a row are the forms that are considered "standard" in written and printed form, while the following ones are variants usually tolerated as "still correct". The number preceding the kanji is the entry number for that kanji in the two Kanji Lists of this handbook; the number at the end of each line is the number of the stroke that differs between the standard and variant form of the kanji.

Length of strokes

① 雨 雨 雨 雨   30 (likewise 雲 636, etc.)   雨 雨

① 天 天 夭 夭   141   夭 夭

① 戸 戸 尸 戸   152 (likewise 所 153, 戻 1238, etc.)   戸 戸

② 商 商 商 商   412   商 商

⑧ 無 無 無 無   93   無 無

Length of first stroke may likewise vary in these and related kanji:
百 14, 面 273, 夏 461, 再 782, 丙 984, 吏 1007, 更 1008

59

Direction of strokes

①	言 言 言 言	66 (likewise 語 67, etc.)		言 言	
①	安 安 安 安	105 (likewise 字 110, etc.)		安 安	
①	立 立 立 立	121 (likewise 六 8, 方 70, 文 111, 高 190, 広 694, 玄 1225, etc.)		立 立	
①	主 主 主 主	155 (likewise 注 357, etc.)		主 主	
①	社 社 社 社	308 (likewise 礼 620, etc.)		社 社	
①	良 良 良 良	321 (likewise 食 322, etc.)		良 良	
⑥	第 第 第 第	404 (likewise 等 569, etc.)		第 第	
④–⑥	終 終 終 終	458 (likewise 紙 180, etc.)		終 終	
③	化 化 化 化	254 (likewise 北 73, 死 75, 能 386, 考 541, 老 543, 比 798, etc.)		化 化	
③	集 集 集 集	436 (likewise 進 437, etc.)		集 集	
⑤	令 令 令 令	831 (likewise 冷 832, etc.)		令 令	
③	含 含 含 含	1249		含 含	

Up-sweeping hook at end of strokes

②	木 木 木 木	22 (likewise 本 25, 村 191, 架 755, etc.)		木 木	
④	米 米 米 米	224 (likewise 来 69, 料 319, etc.)		米 米	
⑩	第 第 第 第	404 (likewise 弟)		第 第	
④	糸 糸 糸 糸	242 (likewise 終 458, 系 908, etc.)		糸 糸	
③	特 特 特 特	282 (likewise 株 741, etc.)		特 特	

Curving of strokes

④	六 六 六 六	8 (likewise 分 38, 外 83, 公 126, 船 376)		六	六
⑤	央 央 央 央	351 (likewise 美 401, 奥 476, 検 531, 漢 556, etc.)		央	央
⑩	家 家 家 家	165 (likewise 録 537, 求 724, 像 740, 隊 795, etc.)		家	家
④	返 返 返 返	442 (likewise 経 548, etc.)		返	返
⑤	青 青 青 青	208 (likewise 通 150, 育 246, 有 265, 背 1265, 骨 1266, etc.)		青	青
①	子 子 子 子	103 (likewise 了 941, 承 942, etc.)		子	子
④	手 手 手 手	57		手	手
⑤	空 空 空 空	140 (likewise 商 412, 深 536, 陸 647, etc.)		空	空
④	令 令 令 令	831 (likewise 冷 832, etc.)		令	令
②	心 心 心 心	97 (likewise 必 520, etc.)		心	心
②	人 人 人 人	1 (likewise 火 20, 欠 383, 入 52, 込 776, etc.)		人	人
④	込 込 込 込	776 (likewise 進 437, etc.)		込	込

Touching strokes

⑫ – ⑬	楽 楽 楽 楽	358 (likewise 果 487, 条 564, 栄 723, etc.)		楽	楽
① – ②	又 又 又 又	1594 (likewise 文 111)		又	又
③ – ④	月 月 月 月	17 (likewise 日 5, 田 35, 目 55, 耳 56, 当 77, 理 143, 門 161, 進 437, 酒 517, 恵 1219, etc.)		月	月
① – ②	立 立 立 立	121 (likewise 玄 1225, etc.)		立	立
③ – ④	不 不 不 不	94 (likewise 否 1248, etc.)		不	不

Crossing strokes

②-③ 女 女 女 女   102 (likewise 好 104, 安 105, etc.)   せ 女

Number of strokes

② 比 比 比 比   798 (likewise 皆 587, etc.)   比 比

④ 衣 衣 衣 衣   677 (likewise 依 678, 表 272, 裏 273, etc.)   衣 衣

③ 公 公 公 公   126 (likewise 育 246, 流 247, etc.)   公 公

③ 茶 茶 茶 茶   251 (likewise 花 255, 薬 359, etc.)   茶 茶

② 之 之 之 之   2004   之 之

Position of strokes

③ 北 北 北 北   73 (likewise 背 1265)   北 北

How to Use a Kanji Dictionary

Many people have sought in vain to arrange Chinese characters in some logical way that would make it easy to look up a character whose readings are unknown.

In 1716 a character dictionary known as the *Kōki Jiten* was published in China. In this work 214 character components called "radicals" were used to classify some 47,000 Chinese characters into an equal number of groups. Since in general a character contains a number of radicals, a decision had to be made concerning which of its constituent radicals each character would be classified under. Unfortunately, this was not decided according to any consistent graphical principle, but rather the radical which indicates the meaning of the character was selected. This classical radical system, despite all its shortcomings, is still used as the basis for almost all character dictionaries. The 214 radicals are arranged in order of stroke count, as are the characters within each group.

This traditional system of arrangement is so complex that even for Japanese it is easier to use an index to locate a character than it is to search for the character directly. The character dictionaries used by Japanese (*Kan-Wa jiten*) often include three indexes: an index by radicals (*bushu sakuin*), a troke-count index (*sōkaku sakuin*), and an index by readings (*on-kun sakuin*). This book also includes three such indexes, which makes it possible to quickly look up any of the 1,945 kanji in the main part and the 284 kanji in the name part, and thus use this book as a concise kanji dictionary encompassing these *Jōyō Kanji* and name kanji. The second volume, the dictionary, contains all the individual kanji and all the compounds in this book, arranged alphabetically by reading in the first part and by meaning in the second part. All together, this provides five possible ways to look up a character or compound.

How to use the indexes:

To the right of a kanji entry in the indexes is the running number of the kanji in the main part of the book, in which the *Jōyō Kanji* are numbered from 1 to 1,945 and the name kanji are numbered from 2,001 to 2,284.

1. Index by Readings (page 394)

The alphabetically arranged index by readings is used when one knows one of the readings of the desired kanji. Since many kanji have the same *on* reading (among the *Jōyō Kanji* alone there are 45 characters that have the reading *KAN*), one should whenever possible look for the kanji under its *kun* reading.

Since often a reading will belong to many kanji, the kanji listed under a given reading are first subdivided into groups sharing the same component (generally the pronunciation-determining component), then subdivided by increasing stroke count.

At the end of each group are kanji which could be sought in this group because of the component they share with it, but which have a different reading. These kanji appear in parentheses, with their actual reading given to the right.

The end of each group is denoted by a horizontal line. Following a group of kanji that share both the same component and the same reading are more kanji, arranged in order of increasing stroke count, that share the component but have a different reading.

This arrangement allows the user to quickly find the running number of the kanji of known reading that he is looking for by zeroing in on the group having the kanji's distinctive grapheme or, if not found there, the remaining kanji of the same reading. If a kanji is sought under an erroneous reading, a cross-reference directs the user to the right reading. Other advantages of this arrangement are that it calls attention to the systematic way in which kanji are put together, it shows etymological connections, it points out the commonalities and differences between certain kanji, it provides groupings of kanji containing similar graphical components for repetition and self-testing, and it aids in expanding one's kanji vocabulary by learning new kanji in a group in which most of the kanji have already been learned.

2. Index by Radicals (page 376)

If none of the readings of a kanji are known, it is usually looked up via the radical index.

Modern character dictionaries often list a kanji under a different radical than the radical under which it was traditionally listed. This is a result of the attempt to make the lookup system simpler and more logical, and a consequence of the fact that many kanji were simplified in the years after the Second World War thereby no longer contained their traditional radical.

Andrew N. Nelson, in his *Modern Reader's Japanese-English Character Dictionary*, which first came out in 1962, attempted to arrange the characters according to easy-to-follow, logical rules while still maintaining the classical radicals. The idea was to allow the reader, after having familiarized himself with the system, to look up characters directly, without resorting to a register of radicals.

Spahn and Hadamitzky (S&H), in their *Kanji Dictionary*, which first came out in 1989 under the title *Japanese Character Dictionary*, carried this a step further by reducing the cumbersomely numerous 214 radicals to a set of 79 and arranging radicals with the same number of strokes into a systematic sequence.

The present book includes a radical index according to the S&H rules. To gain familiarity with this radical system, the user should examine Tables 1 (inside front cover), 2 (front end paper), and the Rules for determining the radical of a kanji (page 65).

Traditional radical systems list radicals having the same stroke count with no other apparent ordering principle, thus making the search more time-consuming than it needs to be to find one of 214 radicals. In S&H, radicals having the same stroke count are listed according to their usual position within a character (in the order of left side, right side, top, bottom, enclosure), and are sub-ordered according to their relative frequency of occurrence.

A kanji will typically contain several graphical components (graphemes) that are listed in a character dictionary's table of radicals, so the problem is to devise rules for determining which of these graphemes is its radical, that is, the radical under which is it will be found in the dictionary.

In the classical system, the meaning-bearing part of the character is taken to be its radical. But since one usually wants looks up a character precisely to find its meaning, one is faced with the problem of knowing or guessing its meaning before one can find it in the dictionary. This presents, in extreme form, the same difficulty an ordinary dictionary poses: you need to know how to spell a word in order to find it to check its spelling. The problem is accentuated with those kanji that where simplified in the orthographic reforms following the Second World War so as to lose their meaning-bearing part (for example, 醫 → 医. The classical radical system still survives because, apart from ordinary conservativism, in most cases it is safe to assume that the meaning-bearing part of a kanji (its radical) is found on its left or top.

Spahn & Hadamitzky (1989) elected to determine the radical of a character not from the character's meaning but from its structure and the position of the "candidate radicals" within it. For example, if both the left part and right part of a kanji are listed in the radical table, the left part is chosen as the radical. Here are the priority rules for S&H according to which the radical is determined by the first description that applies to the kanji.

Rules for Determining the Radical of a Kanji (according to Spahn & Hadamitzky):

Position of the radical   *Examples*

0. ▨ all of kanji = radical   人　水　手　木　日　門

1. ▧ left   休　湖　押　村　明　際

2. ▨ right   外　彫　教　期　旧　部

3. ▨ up   今　谷　花　査　早　思

4. ▨ down   想　泰　撃　架　書　無

5. ▨ ▨ ▨ ▨ ▨ ▨ around   進　式　原　区　間　国

6. ? anywhere

    a) 1 only one   止　右　契　友　缶　面

    b) > greater stroke count   向　靴　鞘　殺　者　題

    c) ← leftmost extending   喪　叛　鼻

    d) ↑ highest extending   段　栽　舗

7. 0 nowhere (pseudo-radical 0a)   一　七　五　中　来　東

Having determined the radical of a kanji, the kanji can be found listed under that radical in the Index by Radicals (page 376). In this index, the radicals are listed in increasing order of stroke-count, and under each radical the kanji are listed in increasing order of residual stroke-count (the number of strokes in the kanji, not counting the strokes in its radical).

3. Index by Stroke Count (page 386)

If no reading of a character is known and it seems too troublesome to determine its radical, the character can be found in the Index by Stroke Count, which lists all the characters in this book in increasing order of stroke-count, sub-ordered by radical. Counting strokes requires some knowledge of how kanji are written; for example, someone who knew nothing about how 田 is written might see it as three vertical and three horizontal strokes, for a stroke-count of 6, even though its actual stroke-count is 5. Strokes of some radicals are counted differently in different kanji dictionaries. In the Index by Stroke Count, the following radicals are taken to have the following number of strokes: 子 2, 阝 2, 辶 2, 比 4, 臣 7.

How to look up a multiple-character compound (*jukugo*)

Both purely Japanese and Japanese-English character dictionaries list not only individual kanji but also compound words (*jukugo*) consisting of two or more kanji, along with their readings and meanings. In most dictionaries, however, a compound must be sought under its first character. The *Japanese Character Dictionary* (retitled *The Kanji Dictionary* in its later edition) and *The Learner's Kanji Dictionary* by Spahn & Hadamitzky were the first to list each *jukugo* under each of its constituent kanji, allowing the user to find a compound via a reading or radical of its second, third, or fourth kanji, even when the compound's first kanji is unknown. In the dictionary volume of *Kanji & Kana*, compounds can be looked up either by their reading or by their meaning in English, thereby constituting a two-way dictionary of the words appearing in this book.

Here are some recommendations on how to study the 1,945 units of the *Jōyō Kanji* list:

1. On the first reading, accentuate with a colored marker those readings and words which you already know. For the compounds, mark the kanji, not the *rōmaji*; try to get away as soon as possible from relying on the romanization, which after all is not even Japanese. The known readings and words will be used later in forming new words and meanings.

2. Write the kanji, first by itself, then as part of the compounds in which it occurs, until you can reproduce it readily from memory. In practicing writing, foreigners would be well advised to use, right from the beginning, either the printed manuscript paper which Japanese use, or the practice manuals that accompany this textbook.

3. Keep firmly in mind the association between the writing, readings, meanings, and compounds of each character. Learn this information together as a single unit so that you do not wind up knowing, for example, the meaning of a kanji but not its readings. With many kanji you may find it possible to make up your own mnemonics. For example, the kanji 親 *oya*, "parent" is composed of the kanji 立 *ta(tsu)*, "stand"; 木 *ki*, "tree"; and 見 *mi(ru)*, "see, watch," so one can remenber this character by picturing an image of parents standing in a tree watching over their children at play.

4. On each repetition of a unit, learn at least one new reading or character combination and mark it (perhaps in a different color).

5. Test yourself on the writing, readings, and meanings of the characters you have learned. You can use a bookmark to cover up the part which is to be reproduced. Or make a self-testing card, with a notch or window positioned to expose only the desired part of the entry.

6. Using the computer program *SUNRISE Script*, you can listen to studio-recorded pronunciation by a native speaker for every reading of every kanji.

Explanation of the *Jōyō Kanji* List

A sample entry from the *Jōyō Kanji* list appears below, with annotations explaining the arrangement and typography.

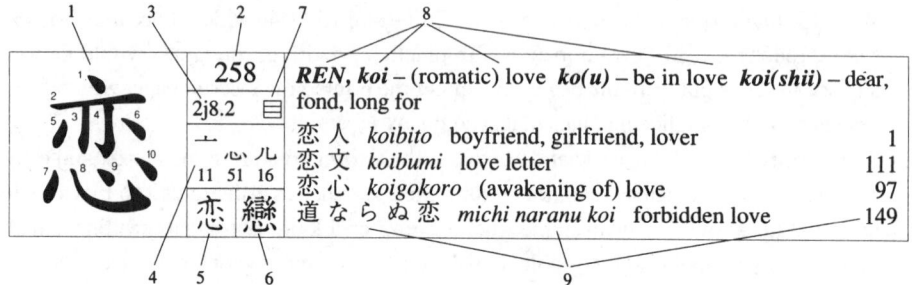

1. The kanji in brush form, with numbers showing stroke order positioned at the beginning of each stroke.

2. Number of the kanji in this book (in this case, 258)

3. Name of the radical (2j) of the kanji and descriptor (2j8.2) giving the kanji's location in Spahn & Hadamitzky's *The Kanji Dictionary* (1996) and *The Learner's Kanji Dictionary* (1997).

4. Up to three graphemes, according to the computer programs *SUNRISE Kanji Dictionary* and *SUNRISE Script*, with the number of the grapheme written beneath each grapheme (see the table of graphemes on pp. 52 and 53). The first grapheme is always the kanji's radical. When the kanji's radical is only a part of a grapheme in the kanji (as 目 is a part of 見 in 観), the first grapheme appears in parentheses (see K&K number 604).

5. The kanji in pen form. There are minor differences in style, stroke order, and even stroke count between the brush, pen, and printed forms of a number of kanji.

6. Variant of the kanji (usually an obsolete form)

7. Structure of the kanji according to the computer programs *SUNRISE Kanji Dictionary* and *SUNRISE Script* (for a list of the structures, see p. 45)

8. Readings and meanings of the kanji, with *on* readings in capital letters, *kun* readings in lowercase italics, and *okurigana* in parentheses. Readings which are infrequent or used only in special cases are given in brackets. All officially recognized readings of the kanji are listed, plus as many of the most important meanings as space allows. As in the official *Jōyō Kanji* list, the first reading given is the one by which the kanji is alphabetized (in *aiueo* order); this is usually the kanji's most frequent *on* reading. *On* readings are

68

listed before *kun* readings, and within these divisions the more frequently used readings are given first.

9. Compounds, with romanization, meanings, and cross-reference numbers to the main entries for the other characters in the compound. Officially sanctioned *ateji* are listed among the compounds. Note that the readings of a kanji sometimes undergo slight modification when it is combined with other kanji to form a compound; examples here are the voicings *hito* → *-bito, fumi* → *-bumi*, and *kokoro* → *-gokoro*. As with the individual kanji, because of space limitations, only the most important meanings of the compounds are listed.

A few other conventions have been used to save space or enhance clarity. The abbreviations "tr." and "intr." indicate where necessary whether a Japanese verb is transitive (that is, can be used with the particle を *o*) or intransitive. Similar English meanings are separated by a comma, but meanings which differ more sharply are marked off by a semicolon: "gem, jewel; ball."

Besides *okurigana*, parentheses enclose explanatory information and examples of usage. Parentheses also contain optional additions: "(sum) total" is short for "total, sum total"; and *nyūmon(sho)* for *nyūmon* or *nyūmonsho*. When additions appear on both the Japanese and English sides of an entry, there is correspondence between them: "*(rōdō) undō* (labor) movement" is a condensed way of writing "*undō* movement" and "*rōdō undō* labor movement." A parenthesized English preposition in the definition of a Japanese word corresponds to a Japanese particle (usually the particle に *ni*); compare "*saga(su)* look for" with "*masu(ru)* be superior (to)."

The slash [/] is used to save space by indicating alternative choices; thus, "comic book/ strip" is short for "comic book, comic strip"; *jizen/go* for *jizen* and *jigo*; and *su(mu/mau)* for *su(mu), su(mau)*. When needed, a hyphen is used in conjunction with the slash to make its scope clear: *kigen-zen/go* is short for *kigenzen* and *kigengo*. When slashes appear on both the Japanese and English sides of an entry, they indicate one-to-one correspondence between the respective alternatives: "*hok/nan-kyoku* north/south pole" indicates that *hokkyoku* means "north pole" and *nankyoku* means "south pole."

The articles "a," "an," and "the" are used only when needed to clarify the meaning or connotation of an English definition, for example to indicate a noun which could otherwise be mistaken for a verb: "a jump," "a shout." Many Japanese words can also be used either as nouns or, by attaching a form of *suru*, as verbs. Wherever possible, this happy coincidence has been exploited by giving an English "noun-verb" as the equivalent of a Japanese noun-verb: "*henji* reply." Where this is not possible, usually only the more common form is given.

The *Jōyō Kanji* List

人	1	***JIN, NIN, hito*** – human being, man, person
	2a0.1 ☐	アメリカ人 *Amerikajin* an American
	イ	100人 *hyakunin* 100 people
	3	5,6人 *go-rokunin* 5 or 6 people
	人	あの人 *ano hito* that person, he, she
		人々 = 人びと *hitobito* people

一	2	***ICHI, ITSU, hito(tsu), hito-*** – one
	0a1.1 ☐	一ページ *ichi pēji* 1 page; page 1
	一	りんご一つ *ringo hitotsu* 1 apple
	1	一つ一つ *hitotsu-hitotsu* one by one, individually
		一人 *hitori* 1 person; alone 1
	一	一人一人 *hitori-hitori* one by one, one after another 1

二	3	***NI, futa(tsu), futa-*** – two
	0a2.1 ☐	二人 *futari, ninin* 2 people 1
	二	一人二人 *hitori futari* 1 or 2 people 2, 1
	4	二人ずつ *futarizutsu* two by two, every two people 1
		二人とも *futaritomo* both people, both (of them) 1
	二	二けた *futaketa* 2 digits; 2-digit, double-digit

三	4	***SAN, mit(tsu), mi(tsu), mi-*** – three
	0a3.1 ☐	三人 *sannin* 3 people 1
	二 一	二,三人 *ni-sannin* 2 or 3 people 3, 1
	4 1	三キロ *san kiro* 3 kg; 3 km
		三つぞろい *mitsuzoroi* 3-piece suit
	三	二つ三つ *futatsu mittsu* 2 or 3 3

日	5	***NICHI, JITSU, hi, -ka*** – day; sun; (short for) Japan
	4c0.1 ☐	一日 *ichinichi, ichijitsu* 1 day 2
	日	*tsuitachi* 1st of the month
	43	二日 *futsuka* 2 days; 2nd of the month 3
		三日 *mikka* 3 days; 3rd of the month 4
	日	二,三日 *ni-sannichi* 2 or 3 days 3, 4

四	6	***SHI, yot(tsu), yo(tsu), yo-, yon*** – four
	3s2.2 ▣	四人 *yonin* 4 people 1
	口 儿	四日 *yokka* 4 days; 4th of the month 5
	24 16	三,四日 *san-yokka* 3 or 4 days 4, 5
		三,四人 *san-yonin* 3 or 4 people 4, 1
	四	四つんばい *yotsunbai* (on) all fours

五	7	***GO, itsu(tsu), itsu-*** – five
	0a4.27 ⋯	五人 *gonin* 5 people 1
	一 一	五日 *itsuka* 5 days; 5th of the month 5
	14 1	四,五日 *shi-gonichi* 4 or 5 days 6, 5
		四,五人 *shi-gonin* 4 or 5 people 6, 1
	五	三々五々 *san-san go-go* in small groups, by twos and threes 4

六	**8** 2j2.2 ⊟ 亠 儿 11 16 六	***ROKU, mut(tsu), mu(tsu), mu-, [mui-]*** – six		
		六 人　*rokunin*　6 people	1
		五, 六 人　*go-rokunin*　5 or 6 people	7, 1
		六 日　*muika*　6 days; 6th of the month	5
		五, 六 日　*go-rokunichi*　5 or 6 days	7, 5
		六つぐらい　*muttsu gurai*　about 6	
七	**9** 0a2.13 ▢ 十 12 七	***SHICHI, nana(tsu), nana, [nano-]*** – seven		
		七 人　*shichinin*　7 people	1
		七 日　*nanoka*　7 days; 7th of the month	5
		七 メ ー ト ル　*nana mētoru, shichi mētoru*　7 meters	
		七 五 三　*Shichi-go-san*　festival day for 3-, 5-, and 7-year- olds (Nov. 15) 7, 4	
八	**10** 2o0.1 ▢ 丷 16 八 八	***HACHI, yat(tsu), ya(tsu), ya-, [yō-]*** – eight		
		八 人　*hachinin*　8 people	1
		八 日　*yōka*　8 days; 8th of the month	5
		八 ミ リ　*hachi miri*　8 mm	
		八 グ ラ ム　*hachi guramu*　8 grams	
		お 八 つ　*oyatsu*　afternoon snack	
九	**11** 0a2.15 ▢ 十 12 九	***KYŪ, KU, kokono(tsu), kokono-*** – nine		
		九 人　*kyūnin, kunin*　9 people	1
		九 日　*kokonoka*　9 days; 9th of the month	5
		九 ド ル　*kyū doru*　9 dollars	
		九 マ ル ク　*kyū maruku*　9 German mark	
		九 九　*kuku*　multiplication table	
十	**12** 2k0.1 ▢ 十 12 十	***JŪ, JI', tō, to-*** – ten		
		十 人　*jūnin*　10 people	1
		十 日　*tōka*　10 days; 10th of the month	5
		二 十 日　*hatsuka*　20 days; 20th of the month	3, 5
		十 四 日　*jūyokka*　14 days; 14th of the month	6, 5
		十 八 日　*jūhachinichi*　18 days; 18th of the month	10, 5
円	**13** 2r2.1 ▢ 冂 亠 20 11 円 圓	***EN*** – circle; yen　***maru(i)*** – round		
		一 円　*ichi en*　1 yen	2
		二 円　*ni en*　2 yen	3
		三 円　*san en*　3 yen	4
		四 円　*yo en*　4 yen	6
		十 円　*jū en, tō en*　10 yen	12
百	**14** 4c2.3 ⊟ 日 一 43 14 百	***HYAKU*** – hundred		
		百 人　*hyakunin*　100 people	1
		八 百 円　*happyaku en*　800 yen	10, 13
		九 百　*kyūhyaku*　900	11
		三 百 六 十 五 日　*sanbyaku rokujūgonichi*　365 days 4, 8, 12, 7, 5	

千	**15** 2k1.2 […] 十 丨 12 2 千	**SEN, chi** – thousand

一 千　*issen*　1,000　　2
三 千　*sanzen*　3,000　　4
八 千　*hassen*　8,000　　10
千 円　*sen en*　1,000 yen　　13
千 人　*sennin*　1,000 people　　1

万	**16** 0a3.8 […] 一 一 14 1 万 萬	**MAN** – ten thousand　**BAN** – many, all

一 万 円　*ichiman en*　10,000 yen　　2, 13
百 万　*hyakuman*　1 million　　14
一 千 万 円　*issenman en*　10 million yen　　2, 15, 13
二, 三 万 円　*ni-sanman en*　20,000 – 30,000 yen　　3, 4, 13
万 一　*man' ichi*　by any chance, should happen to　　2

月	**17** 4b0.1 □ 月 42 月	**GETSU, tsuki** – moon; month　**GATSU** – month

一 月　*ichigatsu*　January　　2
　　　hitotsuki　1 month
一 か 月　*ikkagetsu*　1 month　　2
一 月 八 日 = 1 月 8 日　*ichigatsu yōka*　January 8　　2, 10, 5
月 ロ ケ ッ ト　*tsuki-roketto*　moon rocket

明	**18** 4c4.1 □ 日 月 43 42 明	**MEI** – light　**MYŌ** – light; next　**a(kari)** – light, clearnes **aka(rui)** – bright　**aki(raka)** – clear　**a(keru), aka(rumu),** **aka(ramu)** – become light　**a(ku)** – be open　**a(kasu)** – pass (the night); divulge　**a(kuru)** – next, following

明 日　*myōnichi, asu*　tomorrow　　5
明 く る 日　*akuru hi*　the next/following day　　5

曜	**19** 4c14.1 ⊞ 日 隹 ヨ 43 74 39 曜	**YŌ** – day of the week

日 曜 (日)　*nichiyō(bi)*　Sunday　　5
月 曜 (日)　*getsuyō(bi)*　Monday　　17, 5
曜 日　*yōbi*　day of the week　　5

火	**20** 4d0.1 □ 火 44 火	**KA, hi, [ho]** – fire

火 曜 (日)　*kayō(bi)*　Tuesday　　19, 5
9 月 4 日 (火)　*kugatsu yokka (ka)*　(Tue.) Sept. 4th　　17, 5

水	**21** 3a0.1 □ 氵 21 水	**SUI, mizu** – water

水 曜 (日)　*suiyō(bi)*　Wednesday　　19, 5
水 が め　*mizugame*　water jug/jar
水 か さ　*mizukasa*　volume of water (of a river)

	22	**BOKU, MOKU, ki, [ko]** – tree; wood	
木	4a0.1 □	木曜(日) *mokuyō(bi)* Thursday	19, 5
	朮 41	木こり *kikori* woodcutter, lumberjack, logger	
		木々 *kigi* every tree; many trees	
	木	千木 *chigi* ornamental crossbeams on a Shintō shrine	15
		三木 *Miki* (surname)	4

	23	**KIN, KON** – gold; metal; money **kane** – money **[kana]** – metal	
金	8a0.1 □	金曜(日) *kin'yō(bi)* Friday	19, 5
	釒 72	月・水・金 *ges-sui-kin* Monday, Wednesday, Friday	17, 21
		金メダル *kinmedaru* gold medal	
	金	金ぱく *kinpaku* gold leaf/foil	
		金もうけ *kanemōke* making money	

	24	**DO, TO, tsuchi** – earth, soil, ground	
土	3b0.1 □	土曜(日) *doyō(bi)* Saturday	19, 5
	土 22	土木 *doboku* civil engineering	22
		土人 *dojin* native, aborigine	1
	土	土のう *donō* sandbag	

	25	**HON** – book; origin; main; this; (counter for long, thin objects) **moto** – origin	
本	0a5.25 ...	日本(人) *Nihon(jin), Nippon(jin)* (a) Japan(ese)	5, 1
	朮 一 41 1	本日 *honjitsu* today	5
		本人 *honnin* the said person, the person himself	1
	本 本	ビール六本 *bīru roppon* 6 bottles of beer	8

	26	**DAI, TAI, ō(kii), ō-** – big, large **ō(i ni)** – very much, greatly	
大	0a3.18 □	大金 *taikin* large amount of money	23
	大 34	大きさ *ōkisa* size	
		大水 *ōmizu* flooding, overflow	21
	大	大みそか *Ōmisoka* New Year's Eve	
		大人 *otona* adult	1

	27	**SHŌ, chii(sai), ko-, o-** – little, small	
小	3n0.1 □	小人 *kobito* dwarf, midget	1
	⺌ 35	*shōjin* insignificant person; small-minded man	
		shōnin child	
	小	大小 *daishō* large and small; size	26
		小金 *kogane* small sum of money; small fortune	23

	28	**CHŪ** – middle, inside; throughout; (short for) China **naka** – middle, inside	
中	0a4.40 ...	日本中 *Nihonjū, Nipponjū* all over Japan	5, 25
	口 丨 24 2	一日中 *ichinichijū* all day long	2, 5
		日中 *nitchū* during the daytime	5
	中	*Nit-Chū* Japanese-Chinese, Sino-Japanese	

風	29	**FŪ, [FU]** – wind; appearance, style ***kaze, [kaza]*** – wind
	2s7.1 □	日本風 *Nihon-fū* Japanese-style 5, 25
	几 虫 |	風土 *fūdo* natural features, climate 24
	20 64 2	中風 *chūbū, chūfū* paralysis, palsy 28
	風	そよ風 *soyokaze* gentle breeze

雨	30	**U, ame, [ama]** – rain
	8d0.1 □	風雨 *fūu* wind and rain 29
	⻗	大雨 *ōame* heavy rain, downpour 26
	75	小雨 *kosame* light rain, fine rain 27
		雨水 *amamizu* rainwater 21
	雨	にわか雨 *niwakaame* sudden shower

下	31	**KA, GE, shita, moto** – lower, base ***shimo*** – lower part
	2m1.2 ···	***sa(geru), o(rosu), kuda(su)*** – lower, hand down (a verdict)
	⼘ 一 |	***sa(garu)*** – hang down, fall ***o(riru)*** – get out of, get off (a vehicle)
	(13) 14 2	***kuda(ru)*** – go/come down ***kuda(saru)*** – give
	下	下水 *gesui* sewer system, drainage 21
		風下 *kazashimo* leeward side 29

上	32	**JŌ, [SHŌ], ue** – upper ***kami, [uwa-]*** – upper part ***a(geru)*** – raise
	2m1.1 ⊟	***a(garu), nobo(ru)*** – rise ***nobo(seru), nobo(su)*** – bring up (a topic)
	⼘ 一	水上 *suijō* on the water 21
	13 1	上下 *jōge* high and low, rise and fall; [volume] 1.2 31
	上	上り下り *nobori-kudari* ascent and descent, ups and
		downs 31

川	33	**SEN, kawa** – river
	0a3.2 ⊞	川上 *kawakami* upstream 32
	几 |	川下 *kawashimo* downstream 31
	16 2	小川 *ogawa* stream, brook, creek 27
		ミシシッピー川 *Mishishippī-gawa* Mississippi River
	川 巛	中川 *Nakagawa* (surname) 28

山	34	**SAN, yama** – mountain
	3o0.1 □	山水 *sansui* landscape, natural scenery 21
	凵	火山 *kazan* volcano 20
	36	下山 *gezan* descent from a mountain 31
		小山 *koyama* hill 27
	山	山々 *yamayama* mountains

田	35	**DEN, ta** – rice field, paddy
	5f0.1 □	水田 *suiden* rice paddy 21
	田	田中 *Tanaka* (surname) 28
	58	本田 *Honda* (surname) 25
		山田 *Yamada* (surname) 34
	田	下田 *Shimoda* (city on Izu Peninsula) 31

	36	**hata, hatake** – cultivated field	
畑	4d5.1 ⊞	田畑 *tahata* fields	35
	火 田	みかん畑 *mikan-batake* mandarin orange/tangerine orchard	
	44 58		
	畑		

	37	**TŌ, katana** – sword, knife	
刀	2f0.1 □	日本刀 *Nihon-tō* Japanese sword	5, 25
	刂 力	大刀 *daitō* long sword	26
	16 8	小刀 *shōtō* short sword	27
		kogatana knife, pocketknife	
	刀 釖	山刀 *yamagatana* woodsman's hatchet	34

	38	**BUN** – portion **BU** – portion, 1 percent **FUN** – minute (of	
分	2o2.1 ⊟	time/arc) **wa(keru), wa(katsu)** – divide, share, distinguish	
	ハ 力	**wa(kareru)** – be separated **wa(karu)** – understand	
	16 8	十分 *jūbun* enough, sufficient, adequate (cf. No. 828)	12
		jippun 10 minutes	
	分 分	十分の一 *jūbun no ichi* one tenth, 10 percent	12, 2

	39	**SETSU, [SAI], ki(ru)** – cut **ki(reru)** – cut well; break off; run	
切	2f2.2 ⊞	out of	
	刂 十 力	大切 *taisetsu* important; precious	26
	(16) 12 8	一切れ *hitokire* slice, piece	2
		切り上げ *kiriage* conclusion; rounding up; revaluation	32
	切	切り下げ *kirisage* reduction; devaluation	31

	40	**KOKU, kuni** – country	
国	3s5.1 ▣	大国 *taikoku* large/great country, major power	26
	口 王 丨	万国 *bankoku* all countries, world	16
	24 46 2	六か国 *rokkakoku* 6 countries	8
		四国 *Shikoku* (one of the 4 main islands of Japan)	6
	国 國	中国 *Chūgoku* China; (region in western Honshū)	28

	41	**JI, tera** – temple	
寺	3b3.5 ⊟	国分寺 *Kokubunji* (common temple name)	40, 38
	土 寸	山寺 *yamadera* mountain temple	34
	22 37		
	寺		

	42	**JI, toki** – time; hour	
時	4c6.2 ⊞	四時二十分＝4時20分 *yoji nijippun*	6, 3, 12, 38
	日 土 寸	一時 *ichiji* for a time; 1 o'clock ⌐4:20	2
	43 22 37	*hitotoki, ittoki* a while, moment	
		時々 *tokidoki* sometimes	
	時	日時 *nichiji* time, date, day and hour	5

間	**43** 8e4.3 □ 門日 76 43 間	**KAN, KEN, aida** – interval (between) **ma** – interval (between); a room
		時 間 *jikan* time; hour 42 中 間 *chūkan* middle, intermediate 28 人 間 *ningen* human being 1 間 も な く *mamonaku* presently, in a little while, soon

生	**44** 0a5.29 日 牛 一 47 1 生	**SEI, SHŌ** – life *i(kiru/keru)* – be alive *i(kasu)* – revive, bring to life; let live *u(mu)* – bear (a child) *u(mareru)* – be born *ha(yasu/eru), o(u)* – grow *nama* – raw, draft (beer) *ki-* – pure
		人 生 *jinsei* life, human life 1 一 生 *isshō* one's whole life 2 生 ビ ー ル *namabīru* draft beer

年	**45** 0a6.16 □ ノ 牛 午 15 12 11 年	**NEN, toshi** – year
		生 年 月 日 *seinengappi* date of birth 44, 17, 5 三 年 生 *sannensei* third-year student, junior 4, 44 五 年 間 *gonenkan* for 5 years 7, 43 年 金 *nenkin* pension, annuity 23 1 9 9 6年 *senkyūhyaku kyūjūrokunen* 1996

以	**46** 0a5.1 □ 亻 丨 3 2 以	**I** – (prefix)
		以 上 *ijō* or more; more than; above-mentioned 32 三 時 間 以 上 *san jikan ijō* at least 3 hours 4, 42, 43, 32 以 下 *ika* or less; less than; as follows 31 三 つ 以 下 *mittsu ika* 3 or fewer 4, 31

前	**47** 2o7.3 日 ソ 月 一 16 42 1 前	**ZEN, mae** – before, in front of, earlier
		以 前 *izen* ago, previously, formerly 46 前 も っ て *maemotte* beforehand, in advance 人 前 (で) *hitomae (de)* before others, in public 1 分 け 前 *wakemae* one's share 38 二 人 前 *nininmae, futarimae* enough for 2 people 3, 1

後	**48** 3i6.5 田 彳 夂 ム 29 49 17 後	**GO, nochi** – after, later **KŌ, ushi(ro)** – behind **ato** – afterward, subsequent, back, retro- **oku(reru)** – be late, lag behind
		以 後 *igo* hereafter; since then 46 前 後 *zengo* approximately; front and rear 47 明 後 日 *myōgonichi, asatte* day after tomorrow 18, 5 そ の 後 *sono go* thereafter, later

午	**49** 2k2.2 □ ノ 午 12 15 午	**GO** – noon
		午 前 *gozen* morning; a.m. 47 午 後 *gogo* afternoon; p.m. 48 午 前 中 *gozenchū* all morning, before noon 47, 28 午 後 四 時 *gogo yoji* 4:00 p.m. ⌈afternoon 48, 6, 42 午 前 も 午 後 も *gozen mo gogo mo* both morning and 47, 48

先	**50**	**SEN, saki** – earlier; ahead; priority; future; destination; the tip	
	3b3.7 🗒	先 日 *senjitsu* recently, the other day	5
	土 儿 丨	先 月 *sengetsu* last month	17
	22 16 2	先 々 月 *sensengetsu* month before last	17
	先	先 生 *sensei* teacher	44

今	**51**	**KON, KIN, ima** – now	
	2a2.10 🗒	今 日 *konnichi, kyō* today	5
	亻 一	今 月 *kongetsu* this month	17
	3 1	今 年 *kotoshi* this year	45
	今	今 後 *kongo* after this, from now on	48
		今 ご ろ *imagoro* about this time (of day)	

入	**52**	**NYŪ, hai(ru), i(ru)** – go/come/get in, enter **i(reru)** – put/let in	
	0a2.3 ☐	入 国 *nyūkoku* entry (into a country)	40
	亻	金 入 れ *kaneire* cashbox; purse, wallet	23
	3	日 の 入 り *hi no iri* sunset	5
	入	入 り 日 *irihi* setting sun	5

出	**53**	**SHUTSU, [SUI], da(su)** – take out; send **de(ru)** – go/come out	
	0a5.22 ⋯	出 火 *shukka* outbreak of fire	20
	凵 冂	出 入 り *deiri* coming and going (of people)	52
	36 20	人 出 *hitode* turnout, crowds	1
	出	日 の 出 *hi no de* sunrise	5

口	**54**	**KŌ, KU, kuchi** – mouth	
	3d0.1 ☐	人 口 *jinkō* population, number of inhabitants	1
	口	入 (り) 口 *iriguchi* entrance	52
	24	出 口 *deguchi* exit	53
	口	川 口 *kawaguchi* mouth of a river	33
		口 出 し *kuchidashi* meddling, butting in	53

目	**55**	**MOKU, [BOKU], me, [ma]** – eye, (suffix for ordinals)	
	5c0.1 ☐	一 目 *ichimoku, hitome* a glance	2
	目	人 目 *hitome* notice, public attention	1
	55	目 上 *meue* one's superior/senior	32
	目	目 下 *1. meshita, 2. mokka* 1. one's subordinate/junior 2.	31
		三 日 目 *mikkame* at the 3rd day ⌐at present	4, 5

耳	**56**	**JI, mimi** – ear	
	6e0.1 ☐	耳 目 *jimoku* eye and ear; attention, notice	55
	耳	中 耳 *chūji* the middle ear	28
	65	耳 た ぶ *mimitabu* earlobe	
	耳		

手	**57** 3c0.1 □ 扌 23 手	**SHU, te, [ta]** – hand

切手 *kitte* (postage) stamp   39
小切手 *kogitte* (bank) check   27, 39
手本 *tehon* model, example, pattern   25
上手 *jōzu* skilled, good, good at   32
下手 *heta* unskilled, poor, poor at   31

足	**58** 7d0.1 □ 跫 70 足	**SOKU, ashi** – foot, leg *ta(ru), ta(riru)* – be enough, sufficient *ta(su)* – add up, add (to)

一足 *issoku* 1 pair (of shoes/socks)   2
     hitoashi a step
手足 *teashi* hands and feet, limbs   57
足下に *ashimoto ni* at one's feet; (watch your) step   31

身	**59** 0a7.5 ⊟ 月 丨 42 2 身	**SHIN, mi** – body

身上 *shinjō* strong point, merit; personal background   32
     shinshō one's fortune, property
出身 … *shusshin* (be) from …   53
前身 *zenshin* one's past life; predecessor   47
身分 *mibun* one's social standing; identity   38

休	**60** 2a4.2 ⊞ 亻 木 3 41 休	**KYŪ, yasu(mu)** – rest *yasu(meru)* – give it a rest *yasu(maru)* – be rested

休日 *kyūjitsu* holiday, day off   5
一休み *hitoyasumi* short rest   2
休み中 *yasumichū* Closed (shop sign)   28
休火山 *kyūkazan* nonactive volcano   20, 34

体	**61** 2a5.6 ⊞ 亻 木 一 3 41 1 体 體	**TAI, TEI, karada** – body

身体 *shintai* body   59
人体 *jintai* the human body   1
五体 *gotai* the whole body   7
大体 *daitai* gist; on the whole, generally   26
風体 *fūtai, fūtei* (outward) appearance   29

自	**62** 5c1.1 ⊟ 目 丨 55 2 自	**JI, SHI, mizuka(ra)** – self

自分 *jibun* oneself, one's own   38
自身 *jishin* oneself, itself   59
自体 *jitai* one's own body; itself   61
自国 *jikoku* one's own country   40
自らの手で *mizukara no te de* with one's own hands   57

見	**63** 5c2.1 □ 目 貝 (55) 68 見	**KEN, mi(ru)** – see *mi(eru)* – be visible *mi(seru)* – show

一見 *ikken* (quick) glance   2
先見 *senken* foresight   50
見本 *mihon* sample (of merchandise)   25
見出し *midashi* heading, headline   53
見分ける *miwakeru* tell apart, recognize   38

聞	64 8e6.1 ⬚ 門 耳 76 65 聞	**BUN, MON, ki(ku)** – hear; heed; ask **ki(koeru)** – be audible	
		見 聞 *kenbun* information, observation, experience	63
		風 聞 *fūbun* hearsay, rumor	29
		聞 き 手 *kikite* listener	57
		聞 き 入 れ る *kikiireru* accede to, comply with	52

取	65 6e2.2 ⬚ 耳 又 65 9 取	**SHU, to(ru)** – take	
		取 り 出 す *toridasu* take out; pick out	53
		足 取 り *ashidori* way of walking, gait	58
		聞 き 取 る *kikitoru* catch, follow (what someone says)	64
		日 取 り *hidori* appointed day	5
		取 り 上 げ る *toriageru* take up; adopt; take away	32

言	66 7a0.1 ⬚ 言 67 言	**GEN, GON, -koto** – word **i(u)** – say	
		一 言 *ichigon, hitokoto* a word, brief comment	2
		一 言 二 言 *hitokoto futakoto* a word or two	2, 3
		言 明 *genmei* declaration, definite statement	18
		小 言 *kogoto* a scolding; complaints, griping	27
		言 い 分 *iibun* one's say; objection	38

語	67 7a7.6 ⬚ 言 ロ 一 67 24 14 語	**GO** – word **kata(ru)** – talk, relate **kata(rau)** – converse	
		日 本 語 *Nihongo* Japanese language	5, 25
		国 語 *kokugo* national/Japanese language	40
		言 語 *gengo* speech, language	66
		一 語 一 語 *ichigo-ichigo* word for word, verbatim	2
		語 り 手 *katarite* narrator, storyteller	57

行	68 3i3.1 ⬚ 彳 二 丨 29 4 2 行	**KŌ, [AN], i(ku), yu(ku)** – go **GYŌ** – line (of text) **okona(u)** – do, perform, carry out	
		一 行 *ikkō* party, retinue *ichigyō* a line (of text)	2
		行 間 *gyōkan* space between lines (of text)	43
		行 き 先 *ikisaki, yukisaki* destination	50

来	69 0a7.6 ⬚ 米 一 62 1 来 耒	**RAI, ku(ru), kita(ru)** – come **kita(su)** – bring about	
		来 年 *rainen* next year	45
		来 月 *raigetsu* next month	17
		来 日 *rainichi* come to Japan	5
		本 来 *honrai* originally, primarily	25
		以 来 *irai* (ever) since	46

方	70 4h0.1 ⬚ 方 48 方	**HŌ** – direction, side **kata** – person; method; side; c/o	
		一 方 *ippō* one side; on the other hand; only	2
		四 方 *shihō* north, south, east, west; all directions	6
		八 方 *happō* all directions, all sides	10
		方 言 *hōgen* dialect	66
		目 方 *mekata* weight	55

	71	**TŌ, higashi** – east	
東	0a8.9 ⸬	東 方 *tōhō* the eastward, east	70
	木 日	中 東 *Chūtō* Middle East	28
	41 43	東 大 *Tōdai* Tōkyō University (abbr. for *Tōkyō Daigaku*)	26
	東	東 ア ジ ア *Higashi-Ajia* East Asia	
		東 ヨ ー ロ ッ パ *Higashi-Yōroppa* East Europe	

	72	**SEI, SAI, nishi** – west; (SEI = short for) Spain	
西	0a6.20 ⸬	西 方 *seihō* the westward, west	70
	口 ̄		東 西 *tōzai* east and west	71
	24 14 2	西 風 *seifū, nishikaze* westerly wind	29
		西 日 *nishibi* the afternoon sun	5
	西	西 ヨ ー ロ ッ パ *Nishi-Yōroppa* Western Europe	

	73	**HOKU, kita** – north	
北	0a5.5 ⊔	北 方 *hoppō* the northward, north	70
	⼌ ̄ ｜	北 風 *hokufū, kitakaze* wind from the north	29
	13 1 2	東 北 *Tōhoku* (region in northern Honshū)	71
		北 東 *hokutō* northeast	71
	北	北 北 東 *hokuhokutō* north-northeast	71

	74	**NAN, [NA], minami** – south	
南	2k7.1 ⊟	西 南 *seinan* southwest	72
	十 月 几	東 南 ア ジ ア *Tōnan-Ajia* Southeast Asia	71
	12 42 16	南 北 *nanboku* south and north, north-south	73
		南 ア ル プ ス *Minami-Arupusu* Southern (Japan) Alps	
	南	南 口 *minamiguchi* southern entrance/exit	54

	75	**SA, hidari** – left	
左	0a5.20 ⧈	左 方 *sahō* left side	70
	エ ナ	左 手 *hidarite* left hand; (on) the left	57
	38 12	左 足 *hidariashi* left foot/leg	58
		左 目 *hidarime* left eye	55
	左	左 上 *hidariue* upper left	32

	76	**U, YŪ, migi** – right	
右	3d2.15 ⧈	右 方 *uhō* right side	70
	口 ナ	左 右 *sayū* left and right; control	75
	24 12	右 手 *migite* right hand; (on) the right	57
		右 か ら 左 へ *migi kara hidari e* from right to left; quickly	75
	右	右 と 言 え ば 左 *migi to ieba hidari* (always) argumenting	66, 75

	77	**TŌ, a(teru), a(taru)** – hit, be on target	
当	3n3.3 ⊟	本 当 *hontō* truth; really	25
	⺌ ∃	当 時 *tōji* at present; at that time	42
	35 39	当 分 *tōbun* for now, for a while	38
		手 当 て *teate* allowance, compensation; medical treatment	57
	当 當	一 人 当 た り *hitoriatari* per person, per capita	2, 1

	78	**SEKI, [SHAKU], ishi** – stone **[KOKU]** – (unit of volume, about 180 liters)
石	5a0.1 □	
	石 53	石けん *sekken* soap
		木石 *bokuseki* trees and stones; inanimate objects — 22
	石	小石 *koishi* small stone, pebble — 27
		石切り *ishikiri* stonecutting, quarrying — 39

	79	**BUTSU, MOTSU, mono** – object, thing
物	4g4.2 □	人物 *jinbutsu* person, personage — 1
	牛 犭 47 27	生物 *seibutsu* living beings, life — 44
		見物 *kenbutsu* sightseeing — 63
	物	物語 *monogatari* tale, story — 67
		本物 *honmono* genuine, the real thing — 25

	80	**JI, [ZU], koto** – thing, affair
事	0a8.15 □	人事 *jinji* human/personnel affairs — 1
	口 ヨ 十 24 39 12	火事 *kaji* a fire — 20
		事前, 事後 *jizen, jigo* before the fact, after the fact — 47, 48
	事 事	大事 *daiji* great thing, important — 26
		出来事 *dekigoto* event, occurrence — 53, 69

	81	**SEKI, yū** – evening
夕	0a3.14 □	一夕 *isseki* one evening — 2
	夕 30	夕方 *yūgata* evening — 70
		夕日 *yūhi* evening/setting sun — 5
	夕	夕月 *yūzuki* evening moon — 17
		七夕 *tanabata* Star Festival (July 7) — 9

	82	**MEI, MYŌ, na** – name; reputation
名	3d3.12 □	人名 *jinmei* name of a person — 1
	口 夕 24 30	名人 *meijin* master, expert, virtuoso — 1
		名物 *meibutsu* noted product (of a locality) — 79
	名	大名 *daimyō* (Japanese) feudal lord — 26
		名前 *namae* a name — 47

	83	**GAI, GE, soto** – outside **hoka** – other **hazu(reru/su)** – slip off; miss
外	2m3.1 □	外(国)人 *gai(koku)jin* foreigner — 40, 1
	┠ 夕 十 (13) 30 12	外来語 *gairaigo* word of foreign origin, loanword — 69, 67
		外出 *gaishutsu* go out — 53
	外	以外 *igai* besides, except (for) — 46

	84	**NAI, [DAI], uchi** – inside
内	0a4.23 □	国内 *kokunai* domestic, internal — 40
	亻 冂 3 20	体内 *tainai* inside the body — 61
		内外 *naigai* inner and outer; domestic and foreign — 83
	内	年内に *nennai ni* before the year is out — 45
		一年以内に *ichinen inai ni* within a year — 2, 45, 46

	85	**SHI** – death **shi(nu)** – die	
死	0a6.6 ⊟ 夕 ト 一 30 13 1 死	死体 *shitai* dead body, corpse 死人 *shinin* dead person, the dead 死後 *shigo* after death 水死 *suishi* drowning 死語 *shigo* dead language	61 1 48 21 67

	86	**BU** – part, section; copy of a publication	
部	2d8.15 ⊟ 阝 立 口 7 54 24 部	一部 *ichibu* a part; a copy (of a publication) 部分 *bubun* a part 大部分 *daibubun* greater part, most 本部 *honbu* headquarters 北部 *hokubu* the north (of a country)	2 38 26, 38 25 73

	87	**BAI** – double, times, -fold	
倍	2a8.14 ⊞ イ 立 口 3 54 24 倍	一倍 *ichibai* as much again 二倍 *nibai* double, twice as much 三倍 *sanbai* 3 times as much, threefold 三倍以上 *sanbai ijō* at least 3 times as much 倍にする *bai ni suru* double	2 3 4 4, 46, 32

	88	**HAN, naka(ba)** – half	
半	0a5.24 ⠿ 小 二 35 4 半	半分 *hanbun* half 半年 *hantoshi* half a year, 6 months 三時半 *sanjihan* 3:30 前半 *zenhan, zenpan* first half 大半 *taihan* greater part, majority	38 45 4, 42 47 26

	89	**ZEN, matta(ku)** – all, whole, entirely	
全	2a4.16 ⊟ イ 王 3 46 全	全部 *zenbu* all 全国 *zenkoku* the whole country 全体 *zentai* the whole, (in) all 全身 *zenshin* the entire body 万全 *banzen* perfect, absolutely sure	86 40 61 59 16

	90	**KAI, [E]** – times, repetitions **mawa(su)** – send around, rotate **mawa(ru)** – go around, revolve	
回	3s3.1 ⊡ 口 24 回 囘	十回 *jikkai* 10 times 今/前回 *kon/zenkai* this/last time 言い回し *iimawashi* expression, turn of phrase 上回る *uwamawaru* be more than, exceed	12 51, 47 66 32

	91	**SHŪ, mawa(ri)** – lap; circumference; surroundings	
周	2r6.1 ⠿ 冂 月 口 20 42 24 周	一周 *isshū* 1 lap, 1 revolution 半周 *hanshū* semicircle, halfway around 円周 *enshū* circumference (of a circle) 百周年 *hyakushūnen* 100th anniversary	2 88 13 14, 45

92

週

2q8.7 ⌐⌐

辶 月 日
19 42 24

週

SHŪ – week

二 週 間	*nishūkan*	2 weeks	3, 43
先 週	*senshū*	last week	50
今 週	*konshū*	this week	51
来 週	*raishū*	next week	69
週 日	*shūjitsu*	weekday	5

93

無

4d8.8 目

火 艹 ⌐
44 32 15

無

MU, BU, na(i) – not be; (prefix) un-, without, -less

無 名	*mumei*	anonymus; unknown	82
無 口	*mukuchi*	taciturn, laconic	54
無 言	*mugon*	silent, mute	66
無 休	*mukyū*	no holidays, always open (shop)	60
無 事	*buji*	safe and sound	80

94

不

0a4.2 ⌐⌐

一 丨
14 2

不

FU, BU – (prefix) not, un-

不 足	*fusoku*	insufficiency, shortage	58
不 十 分	*fujūbun*	not enough, inadequate	12, 38
行 方 不 明	*yukue fumei*	whereabouts unknown,	68, 70, 18
不 当	*futō*	improper, unjust ⌐missing	77
不 死 身	*fujimi*	invulnerable	85, 59

95

長

0a8.2 日

衤 ⌐ 二
57 13 4

長

CHŌ – long; chief, head **naga(i)** – long

部 長	*buchō*	department head, director	86
身 長	*shinchō*	person's height	59
長 時 間	*chōjikan*	long time, many hours	42, 43
長 年	*naganen*	many years, long years	45
長 い 間	*nagai aida*	for a long time	43

96

発

0a9.5 日

火 艹 一
44 32 1

発 發

HATSU, HOTSU – emit; start from; depart

発 明	*hatsumei*	invention	18
発 見	*hakken*	discovery	63
発 行	*hakkō*	publish, issue	68
出 発	*shuppatsu*	departure, start out	53
発 足	*hossoku, hassoku*	start, inauguration	58

97

心

4k0.1 ⌐

心
51

心

SHIN, kokoro – heart, mind; core

中 心	*chūshin*	center, midpoint	28
心 身	*shinshin*	body and mind/spirit	59
本 心	*honshin*	one's real mind; real intention	25
内 心	*naishin*	one's inmost heart, true intent	84
一 心 に	*isshin ni*	with singlehearted devotion, fervently	2

98

性

4k5.4 田

心 牛 一
51 47 1

性

SEI – sex; nature (of) **SHŌ** – temperament

中 性	*chūsei*	neuter gender	28
性 行	*seikō*	character and conduct	68
発 が ん 性	*hatsugansei*	carcinogenic, cancer-causing	96
性 分	*shōbun*	nature, temperament	38
本 性	*honshō, honsei*	true nature/character	25

思	99 5f4.4 田 58 51 思	**SHI, omo(u)** – think, believe	
		思い出 *omoide* memories	53
		思い出す *omoidasu* remember	53
		思い切って *omoikitte* resolutely, daringly	39
		思いやり *omoiyari* compassion, considerateness	
		思い上がった *omoiagatta* conceited, cocky	32

力	100 2g0.1 力 8 力	**RYOKU, RIKI, chikara** – force, power	
		体力 *tairyoku* physical strength	61
		水力 *suiryoku* water power, hydraulic power	21
		風力 *fūryoku* force of the wind	29
		全力 *zenryoku* all one's power, utmost efforts	89
		無力 *muryoku* powerless, helpless	93

男	101 5f2.2 田 力 58 8 男	**DAN, NAN, otoko** – man, human male	
		男性 *dansei* man; masculine gender	98
		長男 *chōnan* eldest son	95
		男の人 *otoko no hito* man	1
		山男 *yamaotoko* mountain dweller; mountaineer	34
		大男 *ōotoko* giant, tall man	26

女	102 3e0.1 女 25 女	**JO, NYO, [NYŌ], onna** – woman *me* – feminine	
		女性 *josei* woman; feminine gender	98
		長女 *chōjo* eldest daughter	95
		男女 *danjo* men and women	101
		女中 *jochū* maid	28
		女の人 *onna no hito* woman	1

子	103 2c0.1 子 6 子	**SHI, SU, ko** – child	
		男子 *danshi* boy, man	101
		男の子 *otokonoko* boy	101
		女子 *joshi* girl, woman	102
		女の子 *onnanoko* girl	102
		分子 *bunshi* molecule; numerator of a fraction	38

好	104 3e2.1 女 子 25 6 好	**KŌ, kono(mu), su(ku)** – like	
		好物 *kōbutsu* favorite food	79
		好人物 *kōjinbutsu* good-natured person	1, 79
		物好き *monozuki* idle curiosity	79
		大好き *daisuki* like very much	26
		好き好き *sukizuki* matter of individual preference	

安	105 3m3.1 宀 女 33 25 安	**AN** – peace, peacefulness *yasu(i)* – cheap	
		安心 *anshin* feel relieved/reassured	97
		安全 *anzen* safety	89
		不安 *fuan* unease, anxiety, fear	94
		目安 *meyasu* standard, yardstick	55
		安物 *yasumono* cheap goods	79

案	**106** 3m7.6 目 宀 木 女 33 41 25 案	**AN** – plan, proposal	
		案 内　*annai*　guidance, information	84
		案 外　*angai*　contrary to expectations	83
		名 案　*meian*　good idea	82
		思 案　*shian*　consideration, reflection	99
		案 出　*anshutsu*　contrieve, devise	53

用	**107** 2r3.1 ⋯ 冂 月 丨 20 42 2 用	**YŌ** – business; usage　***mochi(iru)*** – use	
		用 事　*yōji*　business affair; errand	80
		用 語　*yōgo*　(technical) term, vocabulary	67
		無 用　*muyō*　useless; unnecessary	93
		男 子 用　*danshiyō*　for men, men's	101, 103
		用 水　*yōsui*　city/tap water	21

電	**108** 8d5.2 日 雨 日 丨 75 43 2 電	**DEN** – electricity	
		電 力　*denryoku*　electrical power/energy	100
		電 子　*denshi*　electron	103
		発 電　*hatsuden*　generation of electricity	96
		外 電　*gaiden*　telegram from abroad	83

学	**109** 3n4.2 目 ⺍ 冖 子 35 20 6 学 學	**GAKU** – science, study　***mana(bu)*** – learn	
		大 学　*daigaku*　university, college	26
		学 部　*gakubu*　academic department; faculty	86
		入 学　*nyūgaku*　entry/admission into a school	52
		学 生　*gakusei*　student	44
		語 学　*gogaku*　linguistics	67

字	**110** 3m2.1 目 宀 子 33 6 字	**JI** – character, letter　***aza*** – village section	
		国 字　*kokuji*　national/Japanese script	40
		当 て 字　*ateji*　kanji used phonetically/for meaning	77
		ロ ー マ 字　*rōmaji*　roman letters	
		字 体　*jitai*　form of a character, type font	61
		十 字　*jūji*　a cross	12

文	**111** 2j2.4 目 亠 丶 11 12 文 文	**BUN, MON** – literature, text, sentence　***fumi*** – letter, note	
		文 字　*moji, monji*　letter, character	110
		文 学　*bungaku*　literature	109
		本 文　*honbun, honmon*　text, wording	25
		文 語　*bungo*　the written language	67
		文 明　*bunmei*　civilization	18

母	**112** 0a5.36 ⋯ 母 丨 25 2 母	**BO, haha** – mother	
		母 子　*boshi*　mother and child	103
		生 母　*seibo*　one's biological mother	44
		母 国 語　*bokokugo*　one's mother tongue	40, 67
		母 方　*hahakata*　maternal, on the mother's side	70
		お 母 さ ん　*okāsan*　mother	

父	**113**	**FU, chichi** – father
	2o2.3 ☐	父母 *fubo, chichihaha* father and mother ... 112
	ソ 十	父子 *fushi* father and child/son ... 103
	16 12	父方 *chichikata* paternal, on the father's side ... 70
	父	父上 *chichiue* father ... 32
		お父さん *otōsan* father

交	**114**	**KŌ** – intersection; coming and going *ma(jiru/zaru)* – (intr.) mix
	2j4.3 ☐	*maji(eru), ma(zeru)* – (tr.) mix *maji(waru), ka(u)* – associate
	亠 儿 十	(with) *ka(wasu)* – exchange (greetings)
	11 16 12	国交 *kokkō* diplomatic relations ... 40
	交	外交 *gaikō* foreign policy, diplomacy ... 83
		性交 *seikō* sexual intercourse ... 98

校	**115**	**KŌ** – school; (printing) proof
	4a6.24 ☐	学校 *gakkō* school ... 109
	木 亠 儿	小学校 *shōgakkō* elementary school ... 27, 109
	41 11 16	中学校 *chūgakkō* junior high school ... 28, 109
	校	母校 *bokō* alma mater ... 112
		校長 *kōchō* principal, headmaster ... 95

毎	**116**	**MAI** – every, each
	0a6.25 ☐	毎年 *mainen, maitoshi* every year, yearly, annual ... 45
	母 ⼓ 丨	毎月 *maigetsu, maitsuki* every month, monthly ... 17
	25 15 2	毎週 *maishū* every week, weekly ... 92
	毎	毎日 *mainichi* every day, daily ... 5
		毎時 *maiji* every hour, hourly, per hour ... 42

海	**117**	**KAI, umi** – sea, ocean
	3a6.20 ☐	大海 *taikai* an ocean ... 26
	氵 母 ⼓	海上 *kaijō* ocean, seagoing, marine ... 32
	21 25 15	海外 *kaigai* overseas, abroad ... 83
	海 海	内海 *uchiumi, naikai* inland sea ... 84
		日本海 *Nihonkai* Sea of Japan ... 5, 25

地	**118**	**CHI, JI** – earth, land
	3b3.1 ☐	土地 *tochi* land, soil ... 24
	土 十 丨	地下 *chika* underground, subterranean ... 31
	22 12 2	地方 *chihō* region, area ... 70
	地	地名 *chimei* place name ... 82
		生地 *kiji* material, cloth ... 44

池	**119**	**CHI, ike** – pond
	3a3.4 ☐	用水池 *yōsuichi* water reservoir ... 107, 21
	氵 十 丨	電池 *denchi* battery ... 108
	21 12 2	池田 *Ikeda* (surname) ... 35
	池	

	120	*TA* – other, another
他	2a3.4	他人　*tanin*　another person; stranger ... 1
	イ 十 丨	他国　*takoku*　another/foreign country ... 40
	3 12 2	他方　*tahō*　the other side/party/direction ... 70
	他	自他　*jita*　oneself and others ... 62
		その他　*sonota*　and so forth

	121	*RITSU, [RYŪ], ta(tsu)* – stand (up)　*ta(teru)* – set up, raise
立	5b0.1	国立　*kokuritsu*　national, state-supported ... 40
	立	自立　*jiritsu*　independent, self-supporting ... 62
	54	中立　*chūritsu*　neutral, neutrality ... 28
		目立つ　*medatsu*　be conspicuous, stick out ... 55
	立	立ち上がる　*tachiagaru*　stand up ... 32

	122	*I, kurai* – rank, position
位	2a5.1	地位　*chii*　position, rank ... 118
	イ 立	学位　*gakui*　academic degree ... 109
	3 54	上位　*jōi*　higher rank ... 32
		本位　*hon'i*　monetary standard; basis, principle ... 25
	位	位取り　*kuraidori*　position (before/after decimal point) ... 65

	123	*HŌ, HA', HO'* – law
法	3a5.20	国法　*kokuhō*　laws of the country ... 40
	氵 土 厶	立法　*rippō*　enactment of legislation ... 121
	21 22 17	法案　*hōan*　bill, legislative proposal ... 106
		文法　*bunpō*　grammar ... 111
	法	方法　*hōhō*　method ... 70

	124	*WA, [O]* – peace, harmony; (short for) Japanese　*yawa(rageru), yawa(ragu), nago(mu)* – soften, calm down　*nago(yaka)* – mild, gentle, congenial
和	5d3.1	
	禾 口	和風　*wafū*　Japanese style ... 29
	56 24	不和　*fuwa*　disharmony, discord, enmity ... 94
	和	大和　*Yamato*　(old) Japan ... 26

	125	*SHI, watakushi* – I; private
私	5d2.2	私事　*shiji*　personal affairs ... 80
	禾 厶	私物　*shibutsu*　private properity ... 79
	56 17	私用　*shiyō*　private use ... 107
		私立　*shiritsu*　private, privately supported ... 121
	私	私自身　*watakushi jishin*　personally, as for me ... 62, 59

	126	*KŌ, ōyake* – public, official
公	2o2.2	公安　*kōan*　public peace/security ... 105
	ヽ 厶	公法　*kōhō*　public law ... 123
	16 17	公立　*kōritsu*　public ... 121
		公海　*kōkai*　international waters ... 117
	公 公	公言　*kōgen*　public declaration, avowal ... 66

127	**RIN, hayashi** – woods, forest
4a4.1 ⊞	山 林 *sanrin* mountains and forests; mountain forest 34
木 41	(山) 林 学 *(san)ringaku* forestry 34, 109
林	林 立 *rinritsu* stand close together in large numbers 121
	小 林 *Kobayashi* (surname) 27

128	**SHIN, mori** – woods, forest
4a8.39 ⊞	森 林 *shinrin* woods, forest 127
木 41	大 森 *Ōmori* (area of Tōkyō) 26
森	

129	**CHIKU, take** – bamboo
6f0.1 ☐	竹 林 *chikurin, takebayashi* bamboo grove/thicket 127
⺮ 66	竹 刀 *shinai* bamboo sword (for *kendō*) 37
	さ お 竹 *saodake* bamboo pole
竹	竹 の つ え *take no tsue* bamboo cane
	竹 や ぶ *takeyabu* bamboo thicket

130	**HITSU, fude** – writing brush
6f6.1 ⊟	万 年 筆 *mannenhitsu* fountain pen 16, 45
⺮ 彐 ⼗	自 筆 *jihitsu* one's own handwriting; autograph 62
66 39 12	筆 名 *hitsumei* pen name, pseudonym 82
	文 筆 *bunpitsu* literary work, writing 111
筆	筆 先 *fudesaki* tip of the writing brush 50

131	**SHO, ka(ku)** – write
4c6.6 ⊟	書 物 *shomotsu* book 79
日 土 彐	文 書 *bunsho, monjo* (in) writing, document 111
43 22 39	書 名 *shomei* book title 82
	前 書 き *maegaki* foreword, preface 47
書	書 き 取 り *kakitori* dictation 65

132	**I** – will, heart, mind, thought; meaning, sense
5b8.2 ⊟	意 見 *iken* opinion 63
立 日 心	用 意 *yōi* preparations, readiness 107
54 43 51	好 意 *kōi* goodwill, good wishes, kindness 104
	意 外 *igai* unexpected, surprising 83
意	不 意 *fui* sudden, unexpected 94

133	**SHA, kuruma** – vehicle; wheel
7c0.1 ☐	電 車 *densha* electric train 108
車 69	人 力 車 *jinrikisha* rickshaw 1, 100
	発 車 *hassha* departure 96
車	下 車 *gesha* get off (a train) 31
	水 車 *suisha* waterwheel 21

気	134 0a6.8 □ ⌐ 十 一 15 12 1 気 氣	**KI, KE** – spirit, soul, mood	
		人 気 *ninki* popularity	1
		気 分 *kibun* feeling, mood	38
		本 気 *honki* seriousness, (in) earnest	25
		気 体 *kitai* a gas	61
		電 気 *denki* electricity	108

汽	135 3a4.16 ⊞ ⺡ ⌐ 一 21 15 1 汽 滊	**KI** – steam	
		汽 車 *kisha* train drawn by steam locomotive	133

原	136 2p8.1 ⊟ 厂 日 小 18 43 35 原	**GEN** – original, fundamental **hara** – plain, field, wilderness	
		原 案 *gen'an* the original plan/proposal	106
		原 書 *gensho* (in) the original (text)	131
		原 文 *genbun* the text, the original	111
		原 生 林 *genseirin* primeval/virgin forest	44, 127
		原 子 *genshi* atom	103

元	137 0a4.5 ⊟ 二 儿 4 16 元	**GEN** – yuan, yüan, (Chinese monetary unit) **GAN, moto** – origin, foundation	
		元 日 *ganjitsu* New Year's Day	5
		元 金 *gankin* principal (vs. interest)	23
		元 気 *genki* healthy, peppy	134
		地 元 *jimoto* local	118

光	138 3n3.2 ⊟ ⺌ 一 丨 35 14 2 光	**KŌ, hikari** – light **hika(ru)** – shine	
		日 光 *nikkō* sunlight, sunshine	5
		月 光 *gekkō* moonlight	17
		光 年 *kōnen* light-year	45
		発 光 *hakkō* luminosity, emit light	96
		電 光 *denkō* electric light, lightning	108

工	139 0a3.6 □ 工 38 工 互	**KŌ, KU** – artisan; manufacturing, construction	
		工 事 (中) *kōji(chū)* (under) construction	80, 28
		大 工 *daiku* carpenter	26
		女 工 *jokō* woman factory-worker	102
		工 学 *kōgaku* engineering	109
		人 工 *jinkō* man-made, artificial	1

空	140 3m5.12 ⊟ 宀 工 儿 33 38 16 空	**KŪ, sora** – sky **a(keru/ku)** – make/be unoccupied **kara** – empty	
		空 気 *kūki* air	134
		(時 間 と) 空 間 *(jikan to) kūkan* (time and) space	42, 43
		空 車 *kūsha* empty car, For Hire (taxi)	133
		空 手 *karate* empty-handed; karate	57
		大 空 *ōzora* sky, firmament	26

天	141 0a4.21 日 大 一 34 1 天	**TEN, ame, [ama]** – heaven
		天 気　*tenki*　weather　　　　　　　　　　　　134 天 文 学　*tenmongaku*　astronomy　　　　111, 109 天 国　*tengoku*　paradise　　　　　　　　　40 天 性　*tensei*　nature, natural constitution　98 天 の 川　*amanogawa*　Milky Way　　　　33

里	142 0a7.9 ... 日 土 43 22 里	**RI** – (old unit of length, about 2.9 km)　*sato* – village; one's parents' home
		千 里　*senri*　1,000 *ri*; a great distance　　　15 海 里　*kairi*　nautical mile　　　　　　　　117 里 子　*satogo*　foster child　　　　　　　　103 里 心　*satogokoro*　homesickness　　　　　97

理	143 4f7.1 ⊞ 王 日 土 46 43 22 理	**RI** – reason, logic, principle
		地 理 (学)　*chiri(gaku)*　geography　　　118, 109 心 理 学　*shinrigaku*　psychology　　　　97, 109 理 学 部　*rigakubu*　department of science　109, 86 無 理　*muri*　unreasonable; impossible; (by) force　93 理 事　*riji*　director　　　　　　　　　　80

少	144 3n1.1 ... ʼʼ 丨 35 2 少	**SHŌ, suko(shi)** – a little　**suku(nai)** – little, few, slight
		少 年　*shōnen*　boy　　　　　　　　　　　45 少 年 法　*shōnenhō*　the Juvenile Law　　45, 123 少 女　*shōjo*　girl　　　　　　　　　　　102 少 々　*shōshō*　a little 少 し ず つ　*sukoshizutsu*　little by little, a little at a time

省	145 5c4.7 ... 日 小 丨 55 35 2 省	**SEI, kaeri(miru)** – reflect upon, give heed to　**SHŌ** – (government) ministry　**habu(ku)** – omit; cut down on
		自 省　*jisei*　reflection, introspection　　　62 内 省　*naisei*　introspection　　　　　　　84 人 事 不 省　*jinjifusei*　unconsciousness, fainting　1, 80, 94 文 部 省　*Monbushō*　Ministry of Education　111, 86

相	146 4a5.3 ⊞ 木 日 41 55 相	**SŌ** – aspect, phase　**SHŌ** – (government) minister　**ai-** – together, fellow, each other
		相 当　*sōtō*　suitable, appropriate　　　　77 文 相　*bunshō*　minister of education　　　111 外 相　*gaishō*　foreign minister　　　　　83 相 手　*aite*　the other party, partner, opponent　57

想	147 4k9.18 ⊞ 心 日 木 51 55 41 想	**SŌ, [SO]** – idea, thought
		思 想　*shisō*　idea, thought　　　　　　　99 回 想　*kaisō*　retrospection, reminiscense　90 理 想　*risō*　an ideal　　　　　　　　　143 空 想　*kūsō*　fantasy, daydream　　　　　140 め い 想　*meisō*　meditation

148

SHU, kubi – neck, head

2o7.2 目

16 55 14

首

首相	shushō	prime minister	146
元首	genshu	sovereign, ruler	137
首位	shui	leading position, top spot	122
部首	bushu	radical of a kanji	86
手首	tekubi	wrist	57

149

DŌ, [TŌ], michi – street, way, path

2q9.14 辶

19 55 16

道

国道	kokudō	national highway	40
水道	suidō	water conduits, running water	21
北海道	Hokkaidō	(northernmost of the 4 main	73, 117
書道	shodō	calligraphy	⌐islands of Japan) 131
回り道	mawarimichi	a detour	90

150

TSŪ, [TSU], tō(ru) – go through, pass   **tō(su)** – let through
kayo(u) – commute

2q7.18 辶

19 42 1

通

交通	kōtsū	traffic, transportation	114
文通	buntsū	correspondence, exchange of letters	111
通学	tsūgaku	attend school	109
見通し	mitōshi	prospects, outlook	63

151

RO, -ji – street, way

7d6.5 田

70 49 24

路

道路	dōro	street, road	149
十字路	jūjiro	intersection, crossroads	12, 110
水路	suiro	waterway, aqueduct	21
海路	kairo	sea route	117
通路	tsūro	passageway, walkway, aisle	150

152

KO, to – door

4m0.1 □

戸

40

戸 戸

戸外で	kogai de	outdoors, in the open air	83
下戸	geko	nondrinker, teetotaler	31
戸口	toguchi	doorway	54
木戸	kido	gate, entrance; castle gate	22
雨戸	amado	storm door, shutter	30

153

SHO, tokoro – place

4m4.3 □

戸 斤

40 50

所 所

案内所	annaijo	inquiry office, information desk	106, 84
名所	meisho	noted place, sights (to see)	82
所長	shochō	director, head, manager	95
長所	chōsho	strong point, merit, advantage	95
原子力発電所	genshiryoku hatsudensho	nuclear power plant	

154

JŌ, ba – place

3b9.6 田

土 日 勿

22 43 27

場 塲

工場	kōjō, kōba	factory, plant	139
出場	shutsujō	stage appearance; participation	53
場所	basho	place, location	153
立ち場	tachiba	standpoint, point of view	121
相場	sōba	market price	146

主 155 4f1.1 王 丨 46 2 主 主	**SHU, [SU], nushi** – lord, master, main **omo** – main, principal	
	主人 *shujin* husband, head of household	1
	主人公 *shujinkō* hero, main character	1, 126
	自主 *jishu* independence, autonomy	62
	主語 *shugo* subject (in grammar)	67
	地主 *jinushi* landowner, landlord	118

住 156 2a5.19 亻王 丨 3 46 2 住 住	**JŪ, su(mu), su(mau)** – live, dwell, reside	
	住所 *jūsho* an address	153
	住人 *jūnin* inhabitant, resident	1
	安住 *anjū* peaceful living	105
	住まい *sumai* residence, where one lives, address	
	住み心地 *sumigokochi* comfortableness, livability	97, 118

信 157 2a7.1 亻言 3 67 信	**SHIN** – faith, trust, belief	
	信用 *shin'yō* trust	107
	不信 *fushin* bad faith, insincerity; distrust	94
	自信 *jishin* (self-)confidence	62
	所信 *shoshin* one's conviction, opinion	153
	通信 *tsūshin* communication, correspondence, dispatch	150

会 158 2a4.19 亻二 ム 3 4 17 会 會	**KAI** – meeting; association **E, a(u)** – meet	
	国会 *kokkai* parliament, diet, congress	40
	大会 *taikai* mass meeting; sports meet, tournament	26
	学会 *gakkai* learned/academic society	109
	会見 *kaiken* interview, news conference	63
	出会う *deau* happen to meet, run into	53

合 159 2a4.18 亻口 一 3 24 1 合	**GŌ, GA', [KA'], a(u)** – fit **a(waseru), a(wasu)** – put together	
	合意 *gōi* mutual consent, agreement	132
	場合 *baai, bawai* (in this) case	154
	(お)見合い *(o)miai* marriage interview	63
	間に合う *maniau* be in time (for); will do, suffice	43
	見合わせる *miawaseru* look at each other; postpone	63

答 160 6f6.12 竹 口 亻 66 24 3 答	**TŌ, kota(e)** – an answer **kota(eru)** – answer	
	回答 *kaitō* an answer, reply	90
	口答 *kōtō* oral answer	54
	筆答 *hittō* written answer	130
	名答 *meitō* correct answer	82
	答案 *tōan* examination paper	106

門 161 8e0.1 門 76 門 门	**MON, kado** – gate	
	入門(書) *nyūmon(sho)* introduction, primer	52, 131
	部門 *bumon* group, category, branch	86
	名門 *meimon* distinguished/illustrious family	82
	門下生 *monkasei* (someone's) pupil	31, 44
	門口 *kadoguchi* front door, entrance	54

	162	*MON, to(i), [ton]* – question, problem *to(u)* – matter, care about
問	8e3.1	問 答 *mondō* questions and answers, dialogue 160
	門 口	学 問 *gakumon* learning, science 109
	76 24	問 い 合 わ せ る *toiawaseru* inquire, ask 159
	問 向	問 い た だ す *toitadasu* inquire, question

	163	*IN* – member
員	3d7.10	会 員 *kaiin* member (of a society) 158
	口 貝	海 員 *kaiin* seaman, sailor 117
	24 68	工 員 *kōin* factory worker 139
	員	人 員 *jin'in* staff, personnel 1
		全 員 *zen'in* all members, entire staff 89

	164	*SHA, mono* – person
者	4c4.13	学 者 *gakusha* scholar 109
	日 土 丨	日 本 学 者 *Nihongakusha* Japanologist 5, 25, 109
	43 22 2	筆 者 *hissha* writer, author 130
	者 者	信 者 *shinja* believer, the faithful 157
		後 者 *kōsha* the latter 48

	165	*KA, KE, ie, ya* – house; family
家	3m7.1	家 事 *kaji* family affairs; household chores 80
	宀 犭 乀	家 内 *kanai* (one's own) wife 84
	33 27 10	家 来 *kerai* retainer, vassal 69
	家	国 家 *kokka* state, nation 40
		家 主 *yanushi* landlord, house owner 155

	166	*SHITSU* – a room *muro* – greenhouse; cellar
室	3m6.4	和 室 *washitsu* Japanese-style room 124
	宀 土 厶	私 室 *shishitsu* private room 125
	33 22 17	室 内 *shitsunai* in a room, indoor 84
	室	分 室 *bunshitsu* isolated room; annex 38
		室 長 *shitsuchō* senior roommate; section chief 95

	167	*OKU, ya* – roof; house; shop, dealer
屋	3r6.3	家 屋 *kaoku* house, building 165
	尸 土 厶	屋 上 *okujō* roof, rooftop 32
	40 22 17	部 屋 *heya* a room 86
	屋	小 屋 *koya* cottage, hut, shack 27
		八 百 屋 *yaoya* vegetable shop, greengrocer 10, 14

	168	*TEN, mise* – shop, store
店	3q5.4	書 店 *shoten* bookstore 131
	广 口 卜	本 店 *honten* head office, main shop 25
	18 24 13	店 員 *ten'in* store employee, clerk 163
	店	店 先 *misesaki* storefront 50
		出 店 *demise* branch store 53

169

点 點

2m7.2 目
⼢ 火 口
13 44 24
点

TEN – point

出発点	shuppatsuten starting point	53, 96
原点	genten starting point; origin (of coordinate)	136
合点	gaten, gatten understanding; consent	159
点字	tenji Braille	110
点火	tenka ignite	20

170

局

3r4.4 囗
尸 口 一
40 24 1
局

KYOKU – bureau, office

当局	tōkyoku the authorities, responsible officials	77
局長	kyokuchō director of a bureau; postmaster	95
局員	kyokuin staff member of a bureau	163
局外者	kyokugaisha outsider, onlooker	83, 164
時局	jikyoku the situation	42

171

居

3r5.3 囗
尸 口 十
40 24 12
居

KYO, i(ru) – be (present), exist

住居	jūkyo dwelling, residence	156
居住地	kyojūchi place of residence	156, 118
居間	ima living room	43
長居	nagai stay (too) long	95
居合わせる	iawaseru (happen to) be present	159

172

古

2k3.1 目
十 口
12 24
古

KO, furu(i) – old **furu(su)** – wear out

古風	kofū old customs; antiquated	29
古語	kogo archaic word; old adage	67
古文	kobun classical literature, ancient classics	111
古今東西	kokon-tōzai all ages and countries	51, 71, 72
古本	furuhon secondhand/used book	25

173

故

4i5.2 田
攵 口 十
49 24 12
故

KO – deceased **yue** – reason, cause; circumstances

故人	kojin the deceased	1
故事	koji historical event	80
事故	jiko accident	80
故国	kokoku one's homeland, native country	40
故意	koi intention, purpose	132

174

新

5b8.3 田
立 木 斤
54 41 50
新

SHIN, atara(shii), ara(ta), nii- – new

新聞	shinbun newspaper	64
古新聞	furushinbun old newspapers	172, 64
新年	shinnen the New Year	45
新人	shinjin newcomer, new face	1
一新	isshin renovation, reform	2

175

親

5b11.1 田
立 貝 木
54 68 41
親

SHIN – intimacy; parent **oya** – parent **shita(shii)** – intimate, close (friend) **shita(shimu)** – get to know better

親切	shinsetsu kind, friendly	39
親日	shin-Nichi pro-Japanese	5
母親	hahaoya mother	112
親子	oyako parent and child	103

質	**176** 7b8.7 貝 斤 68 50 質 质	**SHITSU** – quality, nature **SHICHI, [CHI]** – hostage; pawn 質問　*shitsumon*　a question　162 性質　*seishitsu*　nature, property　98 物質　*busshitsu*　matter, material, substance　79 本質　*honshitsu*　essence, substance　25 人質　*hitojichi*　hostage　1
民	**177** 0a5.23 尸 ナ 40 12 民	**MIN, tami** – people, nation 国民　*kokumin*　people, nation, citizen　40 人民　*jinmin*　the people, citizens　1 (原)住民　*(gen)jūmin*　(aboriginal) native of a place　136, 156 民間　*minkan*　private (not public)　43 民意　*min'i*　will of the people　132
宅	**178** 3m3.4 宀 ナ 丨 33 12 2 宅	**TAKU** – house, home, residence 住宅　*jūtaku*　house, residence　156 自宅　*jitaku*　one's own home, private residence　62 私宅　*shitaku*　one's private residence　125 宅地　*takuchi*　land for housing, residential site　118 家宅　*kataku*　house, the premises　165
宿	**179** 3m8.3 宀 日 亻 33 43 3 宿	**SHUKU, yado** – lodging, inn **yado(ru)** – take shelter; be pregnant **yado(su)** – give shelter, conceive (a child) 下宿　*geshuku*　room and board; boardinghouse　31 合宿　*gasshuku*　lodging together　159 宿屋　*yadoya*　inn　167 民宿　*minshuku*　private house providing tourist lodging　177
紙	**180** 6a4.4 糸 厂 ナ 61 18 12 紙 帋	**SHI, kami** – paper 和紙　*washi*　Japanese paper　124 日本紙　*Nihonshi*　Japanese paper　5, 25 新聞紙　*shinbunshi*　newspaper; newsprint　174, 64 質問用紙　*shitsumon yōshi*　questionnaire　176, 162, 107 手紙　*tegami*　letter　57
市	**181** 2j3.1 亠 巾 11 26 市	**SHI** – city, town; market **ichi** – market 市長　*shichō*　mayor　95 市会　*shikai*　municipal assembly, city council　158 市立　*shiritsu*　municipal　121 市民　*shimin*　citizen, townspeople　177 市場　*ichiba, shijō*　marketplace, market　154
町	**182** 5f2.1 田 一 58 14 町 甼	**CHŌ, machi** – town, quarter 町民　*chōmin*　townsman, townsfolk　177 町人　*chōnin*　merchant; townsfolk　1 町内　*chōnai*　neighborhood　84 下町　*shitamachi*　(low-lying) downtown area　31 室町　*Muromachi*　(historical period, 1392–1573)　166

	183	**KU** – municipal administrative district, ward	
区	2t2.1 回	地 区 *chiku* district, area, zone	118
	匚 十	区 間 *kukan* section, interval	43
	20 12	区 切 る *kugiru* partition; punctuate	39
		区 分 *kubun* division, partition; classification	38
	区 區	北 区 *Kita-ku* Kita Ward (Tōkyō)	73

	184	**CHŌ** – even number; (counter for blocks of houses/blocks of tofu/	
丁	0a2:4 □	guns/dishes of prepared food) **TEI** – D, No. 4 (in a series); adult;	
	一	T shape	
	14	一 丁 目 *itchōme* city block no. 1 (in addresses)	2, 55
		丁 年 *teinen* (age of) majority, adulthood	45
	丁	丁 字 路 *teijiro* T-shaped street intersection	110, 151

	185	**BAN** – keeping watch; number; order	
番	5f7.4 目	一 番 *ichiban* the first; number one, most	2
	囲 米 丨	二 番 目 *nibanme* the second, No. 2	3, 55
	58 62 2	番 地 *banchi* lot/house number	118
		局 番 *kyokuban* exchange (part of a phone number)	170
	番	交 番 *kōban* police box	114

	186	**GAI, [KAI], machi** – street	
街	3i9.2 □	街 路 *gairo* street	151
	彳 土 二	街 道 *kaidō* street, highway	149
	29 22 4	市 街 *shigai* the streets (of a city); town	181
		名 店 街 *meitengai* arcade of well-known stores	82, 168
	街	地 下 街 *chikagai* underground shopping mall	118, 31

	187	**JUTSU** – art, technique, means, conjury	
術	3i8.2 □	手 術 *shujutsu* (surgical) operation	57
	彳 木 二	手 術 室 *shujutsushitsu* operating room	57, 166
	29 41 4	学 術 *gakujutsu* science, learning	109
		(学) 術 (用) 語 *(gaku)jutsu (yō)go* technical term,	
	術 術	terminology	109, 107, 67

	188	**TO, TSU, miyako** – capital (city)	
都	2d8.13 □	(大) 都 市 *(dai)toshi* (major/large) city	26, 181
	阝 日 土	都 会 *tokai* city	158
	7 43 22	首 都 *shuto* capital (city)	148
		都 内 *tonai* in (the city of) Tōkyō	84
	都 都	都 合 *tsugō* circumstances, reasons	159

	189	**KYŌ, KEI** – the capital	
京	2j6.3 目	東 京 (都) *Tōkyō(-to)* (City of) Tōkyō	71, 188
	亠 口 小	京 都 (市) *Kyōto(-shi)* (City of) Kyōto	188, 181
	11 24 35	上 京 *jōkyō* go/come to Tōkyō	32
		北 京 *Pekin* Peking, Beijing	73
	京 京	南 京 *Nankin* Nanking	74

高	**190** 2j8.6 ⽬ 一 ⼝ 冂 11 24 20 高 髙	**KŌ, taka(i)** – high; expensive **taka** – amount, quantity **taka(maru)** – rise **taka(meru)** – raise
		高原 *kōgen* plateau, heights, tableland 136
		上高地 *Kamikōchi* (scenic valley in Japanese Alps) 32, 118
		高校 *kōkō* senior high school (cf. No. 569) 115
		名高い *nadakai* renowned, famous 82

村	**191** 4a3.11 ⼝ 木 寸 41 37 村 邨	**SON, mura** – village
		市町村 *shichōson* cities, towns, and villages 181, 182
		村会 *sonkai* village assembly 158
		村長 *sonchō* village mayor 95
		村民 *sonmin* villager 177
		村人 *murabito* villager 1

付	**192** 2a3.6 ⼝ 亻 寸 3 37 付	**FU, tsu(ku)** – be attached, belong (to) **tsu(keru)** – attach, apply (cf. No. 1843)
		交付 *kōfu* deliver, hand over 114
		日付け *hizuke* date (of a letter) 5
		気付く *kizuku* (take) notice 134
		付き物 *tsukimono* what (something) entails, adjunct 79

郡	**193** 2d7.12 ⼝ 阝 ⺕ ⼝ 7 39 24 郡	**GUN** – county, district
		郡部 *gunbu* rural district 86
		新田郡 *Nitta-gun* Nitta District (in Gunma Prefecture) 174, 35

県	**194** 3n6.3 ⽬ ⺍ ⽬ ⼁ 35 55 2 県 縣	**KEN** – prefecture, province
		郡県 *gunken* districts/counties and prefectures 193
		県立 *kenritsu* prefectural, provincial 121
		県道 *kendō* prefectural highway 149
		県会 *kenkai* prefectural assembly 158
		山口県 *Yamaguchi-ken* Yamaguchi Prefecture 34, 54

州	**195** 2f4.1 ⊞ 刂 16 州	**SHŪ** – state, province **su** – sandbank, shoals
		本州 *Honshū* (largest of the 4 main islands of Japan) 25
		九州 *Kyūshū* (one of the 4 main islands of Japan) 11
		カリフォルニア州 *Kariforunia-shū* (State of) California
		五大州 *godaishū* the 5 continents (Asia, Africa, Europe, 7, 26
		中州 *nakasu* sandbank in a river ⌊America, and Australia) 28

共	**196** 3k3.3 ⽬ ⼗ 儿 一 32 16 1 共	**KYŌ, tomo** – together, both, all
		共学 *kyōgaku* coeducation 109
		共通 *kyōtsū* in common, shared 150
		共用 *kyōyō* common, shared 107
		公共 *kōkyō* the public, community 126
		共和国 *kyōwakoku* republic 124, 40

供	**197** 2a6.13 ⊞ 亻 艹 儿 3 32 16 供	**KYŌ, [KU], tomo** – retinue, attendant; serve ***sona(eru)*** – offer
		供 出 *kyōshutsu* delivery 53 自 供 *jikyō* confession, admission 62 供 物 *kumotsu* votive offering 79 子 供 *kodomo* child 103 (お) 供 *(o)tomo* accompany (someone)

同	**198** 2r4.2 ◫ 冂 卩 一 20 24 1 同 全	**DŌ, ona(ji)** – same
		同 時 に *dōji ni* at the same time, simultaneously 42 共 同 *kyōdō* joint, communal, cooperative 196 合 同 *gōdō* combination, merger, joint 159 同 意 *dōi* agreement, consent 132 同 居 *dōkyo* live in the same house, live together 171

向	**199** 3d3.10 ⊟ 卩 冂 丨 24 20 2 向	**KŌ, mu(kau)** – face (toward); proceed (to) ***mu(keru)*** – (tr.) turn ***mu(ku)*** – (intr.) turn ***mu(kō)*** – opposite side
		方 向 *hōkō* direction 70 向 上 *kōjō* elevation, betterment 32 意 向 *ikō* intention, inclination 132 外 人 向 け *gaijinmuke* for foreigners 83, 1

両	**200** 0a6.11 ⊟ 山 冂 一 36 20 1 両 兩	**RYŌ** – both; (obsolete Japanese coin)
		両 親 *ryōshin* parents 175 両 方 *ryōhō* both 70 両 手 *ryōte* both hands 57 両 立 *ryōritsu* coexist, be compatible (with) 121 車 両 *sharyō* car, vehicle 133

満	**201** 3a9.25 ⊞ 氵 艹 山 21 32 36 満 滿	**MAN, mi(chiru)** – become full ***mi(tasu)*** – fill; fulfill
		満 足 *manzoku* satisfaction 58 不 満 *fuman* dissatisfaction, discontent 94 満 員 *man'in* full to capacity 163 満 点 *manten* perfect score 169 円 満 *enman* harmonious, peaceful, perfect 13

平	**202** 2k3.4 ⸛ 小 二 35 4 平 平	**HEI, BYŌ, tai(ra), hira** – flat, level
		平 行 *heikō* parallel 68 平 和 *heiwa* peace 124 不 平 *fuhei* discontent, complaint 94 平 家 *Heike* (historical clan name) 165 平 家, 平屋 *hiraya* 1-story house 165, 167

実	**203** 3m5.4 ⊟ 宀 大 二 33 34 4 実	**JITSU** – truth, actuality ***mi*** – fruit, nut ***mino(ru)*** – bear fruit
		事 実 *jijitsu* fact 80 口 実 *kōjitsu* pretext, excuse 54 実 行 *jikkō* put into practice, carry out, realize 68 実 力 *jitsuryoku* actual ability, competence 100 実 用 *jitsuyō* practical use 107

	204	SHOKU, SHIKI, iro – color; erotic passion	
色	2n4.1 ☐	原色 genshoku primary color	136
	宀 尸 丨	好色 kōshoku sensuality, lust, eroticism	104
	15 40 2	色紙 shikishi (type of calligraphy paper)	180
	色	irogami colored paper	
		金色 kin'iro, kinshoku, konjiki gold color	23

	205	HAKU, BYAKU, shiro(i), shiro, [shira] – white	
白	4c1.3 ☐	白紙 hakushi white/blank paper	180
	日 丨	白書 hakusho a white paper (on), report	131
	43 2	白人 hakujin a white, Caucasian	1
	白	自白 jihaku confession, admission	62
		空白 kūhaku a blank; vacuum	140

	206	KOKU, kuro(i), kuro – black	
黒	4d7.2 ☐	黒人 kokujin a black, Negro	1
	火 日 土	黒白 kuroshiro, kokubyaku black and/or white; right and	205
	44 43 22	黒字 kuroji (in the) black, black figures ⌐wrong	110
	黒 黒	黒子 kuroko black-clad Kabuki stagehand	103

	207	SEKI, [SHAKU], aka(i), aka – red aka(ramu) – become red, blush aka(rameru) – make red, blush	
赤	3b4.10 ☐	赤十字 Sekijūji Red Cross	12, 110
	土 儿	赤道 sekidō equator	149
	22 16	赤字 akaji deficit, red figures, (in the) red	110
	赤	赤ちゃん akachan baby	

	208	SEI, [SHŌ], ao(i), ao – blue, green; unripe	
青	4b4.10 ☐	青年 seinen young man/people	45
	月 土 一	青少年 seishōnen young people, youth	144, 45
	42 22 1	青空 aozora blue sky	140
	青 青	青空市場 aozora ichiba open-air market	140, 181, 154
		青物 aomono green vegetables	79

	209	JŌ, [SEI], nasa(ke) – emotion, sympathy; circumstances	
情	4k8.9 ⊞	人情 ninjō human feelings, humanity	1
	心 月 土	同情 dōjō sympathy	198
	51 42 22	無情 mujō heartlessness, callousness	93
	情 情	事情 jijō circumstances, situation	80
		実情 jitsujō actual situation, the facts	203

	210	TEKI – (attributive suffix) mato – target	
的	4c4.12 ⊞	目的 mokuteki purpose, aim, goal	55
	日 勹 丨	一時的 ichijiteki temporary	2, 42
	43 15 2	民主的 minshuteki democratic	177, 155
	的 的	理想的 risōteki ideal	143, 147
		自発的 jihatsuteki voluntary, spontaneous	62, 96

	211	**YAKU** – approximately; promise	
約	6a3.7 ⬚	公 約 *kōyaku* public commitment	126
	糸 宀 ｜	口 約 *kōyaku* verbal promise	54
	61 15 2	約 三 キ ロ *yaku sankiro* approximately 3 km/kg	4
		約 半 分 *yaku hanbun* approximately half	88, 38
	約	先 約 (が あ る) *sen'yaku (ga aru)* (have a) previous en-⌐gagement	50

	212	**KYŪ, yumi** – bow (for archery/violin)	
弓	3h0.1 ☐	弓 術 *kyūjutsu* (Japanese) archery	187
	弓	弓 道 *kyūdō* (Japanese) archery	149
	28		
	弓		

	213	**SHI, ya** – arrow	
矢	0a5.19 ⊟	弓 矢 *yumiya* bow and arrow	212
	大 宀		
	34 15		
	矢		

	214	**CHI, shi(ru)** – know	
知	3d5.14 ⊞	通 知 *tsūchi* a notification, communication	150
	口 大 宀	周 知 *shūchi* common knowledge, generally known	91
	24 34 15	知 事 *chiji* governor (of a prefecture)	80
		知 人 *chijin* an acquaintance	1
	知	知 り 合 い *shiriai* an acquaintance	159

	215	**TAN, mijika(i)** – short	
短	3d9.27 ⊞	長 短 *chōtan* (relative) length; good and bad points	95
	口 大 宀	短 刀 *tantō* short sword, dagger	37
	24 34 15	短 気 *tanki* short temper, touchiness, hastiness	134
		短 所 *tansho* defect, shortcoming	153
	短	短 大 *tandai* junior college (cf. No. 449)	26

	216	**IN, hi(ku)** – pull; attract **hi(keru)** – be ended; make cheaper	
引	3h1.1 ☐	引 力 *inryoku* attraction, gravitation	100
	弓 ｜	引 用 *in'yō* quotation, citation	107
	28 2	引 き 出 し *hikidashi* drawer	53
		取 り 引 き *torihiki* transaction, trade	65
	引	引 き 上 げ *hikiage* raise, increase	32

	217	**KYŌ, GŌ, tsuyo(i)** – strong **tsuyo(maru)** – become strong(er) **tsuyo(meru)** – make strong(er), strengthen **shi(iru)** – force	
強	3h8.3 ⊞	強 力 *kyōryoku* strength, power	100
	弓 虫 ム	強 国 *kyōkoku* strong country, great power	40
	28 64 17	強 情 *gōjō* stubbornness, obstinacy	209
	強	強 引 に *gōin ni* by force	216

	218	
弱	3h7.2 ⊟	**JAKU, yowa(i)** – weak(er) **yowa(ru), yowa(maru)** – become weak(er) **yowa(meru)** – make weak(er), weaken
	弓 冫 28 5	強弱 *kyōjaku* strengths and weaknesses, strenth 217
	弱 弱	弱点 *jakuten* a weakness, weak point 169
		弱体 *jakutai* weak 61
		弱気 *yowaki* faintheartedness; bearishness (of market) 134

	219	
独	3g6.1 ⊟	**DOKU** – alone; (short for) Germany **hitori** – alone
	犭 虫 27 64	独立 *dokuritsu* independence 121
	独 獨	独身 *dokushin* unmarried, single 59
		独学 *dokugaku* self-study 109
		日独 *Nichi-Doku* Japan and Germany, Japanese-German 5
		和独 *Wa-Doku* Japanese-German (dictionary) 124

	220	
医	2t5.2 ▣	**I** – medicine, healing
	匸 大 匚 20 34 15	医学 *igaku* medicine 109
	医 醫	医学部 *igakubu* medical department/school 109, 86
		医学用語 *igaku yōgo* medical term 109, 107, 67
		医者 *isha* physician, doctor 164
		女医 *joi* woman physician, lady doctor 102

	221	
族	4h7.3 ⊞	**ZOKU** – family, tribe
	方 大 匚 48 34 15	家族 *kazoku* family 165
	族	親族 *shinzoku* relative, kin 175
		一族 *ichizoku* one's whole family, kin 2
		部族 *buzoku* tribe 86
		民族 *minzoku* race, people, nation 177

	222	
旅	4h6.4 ⊞	**RYO, tabi** – trip, travel
	方 匚 亻 48 15 3	旅行 *ryokō* trip, travel 68
	旅	旅行者 *ryokōsha* traveler, tourist 68, 164
		旅人 *tabibito* traveler, wayfarer 1
		旅先 *tabisaki* destination 50
		旅立つ *tabidatsu* start on a journey 121

	223	
肉	2a4.20 ⋯	**NIKU** – meat, flesh
	亻 冂 3 20	肉屋 *nikuya* butcher (shop) 167
	肉	肉体 *nikutai* the body, the flesh 61
		肉親 *nikushin* blood relationship/relative 175
		肉付きのよい *nikuzuki no yoi* well-fleshed, plump 192
		肉筆 *nikuhitsu* one's own handwriting; autograph 130

	224	
米	6b0.1 □	**BEI** – rice; (short for) America **MAI, kome** – rice
	米 62	白米 *hakumai* polished rice 205
	米	新米 *shinmai* new rice; novice 174
		外米 *gaimai* imported rice 83
		日米 *Nichi-Bei* Japan and America, Japanese-U.S. 5
		南米 *Nanbei* South America 74

	225	**SŪ, [SU], kazu** – number **kazo(eru)** – count	
	4i9.1	数字 *sūji* digit, numeral, figures	110
	攵米女	数学 *sūgaku* mathematics	109
	49 62 25	人数 *ninzū* number of people	1
		無数 *musū* countless, innumerable	93
	数 數	手数 *tesū* trouble, bother	57

	226	**RUI** – kind, type, genus	
	9a9.1	親類 *shinrui* relative, kin	175
	頁米 大	人類 *jinrui* mankind	1
	77 62 34	書類 *shorui* papers, documents	131
		分類 *bunrui* classification	38
	類 類	類語 *ruigo* synonym	67

	227	**JŪ, CHŌ, omo(i)** – heavy **kasa(naru)** – lie on top of one another	
	0a9.18	**kasa(neru)** – pile on top of one another **-e** – -fold, -ply	
	車 一 丨	体重 *taijū* body weight	61
	69 1 2	重力 *jūryoku* gravity, gravitation	100
		重大 *jūdai* weighty, grave, important	26
	重	二重 *nijū, futae* double, twofold	3

	228	**SHU** – kind, type; seed **tane** – seed; species; cause	
	5d9.1	種類 *shurui* kind, type, sort	226
	禾車 一	一種 *isshu* kind, sort	2
	56 69 1	人種 *jinshu* a human race	1
		種子 *shushi* seed, pit	103
	種	不安の種 *fuan no tane* cause of unease	94, 105

	229	**TA, ō(i)** – much, many, numerous	
	0a6.5	多少 *tashō* much or little, many or few; some	144
	夕	多数 *tasū* large number (of); majority	225
	30	大多数 *daitasū* the overwhelming majority	26, 225
		多元的 *tagenteki* pluralistic	137, 210
	多 多	数多く *kazuōku* many, great number (of)	225

	230	**HIN** – refinement; article **shina** – goods; quality	
	3d6.15	上品 *jōhin* refined, elegant, graceful	32
	口	下品 *gehin* unrefined, gross, vulgar	31
	24	品質 *hinshitsu* quality	176
		部品 *buhin* (spare/machine) parts	86
	品 品	品物 *shinamono* merchandise	79

	231	**DŌ, ugo(ku)** – (intr.) move **ugo(kasu)** – (tr.) move	
	2g9.1	自動車 *jidōsha* automobile, car	62, 133
	力車 丨	動物 *dōbutsu* animal	79
	8 69 2	動力 *dōryoku* moving force, (electric) power	100
		行動 *kōdō* action	68
	動	動員 *dōin* mobilize	163

働	232 2a11.1 ⊞ 亻 車 力 3 69 8 働 仂	**DŌ, hatara(ku)** – work

実 働 時 間　*jitsudō jikan*　actual working hours　203, 42, 43
働 き　*hataraki*　work; functioning; ability
働 き 口　*hatarakiguchi*　job, position　54
働 き 者　*hatarakimono*　hard worker　164
働 き 手　*hatarakite*　worker, breadwinner; capable man　57

労	233 3n4.3 目 ⺍ 冂 力 35 20 8 労 勞	**RŌ** – labor, toil

労 働　*rōdō*　work, labor　232
労 働 者　*rōdōsha*　worker, laborer　232, 164
労 働 時 間　*rōdō jikan*　working hours　232, 42, 43
労 力　*rōryoku*　trouble, effort; labor　100
心 労　*shinrō*　worry, concern　97

協	234 2k6.1 田 十 力 12 8 協	**KYŌ** – cooperation

協 力　*kyōryoku*　cooperation　100
協 力 者　*kyōryokusha*　collaborator, coworker　100, 164
協 同　*kyōdō*　cooperation, collaboration, partnership　198
協 会　*kyōkai*　society, association　「Society　158
日 米 協 会　*Nichi-Bei Kyōkai*　the America-Japan　5, 224, 158

務	235 4i7.6 田 夂 一 力 49 14 8 務	**MU, tsuto(meru)** – work, serve

事 務 所　*jimusho*　office　80, 153
公 務 員　*kōmuin*　government employee　126, 163
国 務　*kokumu*　affairs of state　40
外 務 省　*Gaimushō*　Ministry of Foreign Affairs　83, 145
法 務 省　*Hōmushō*　Ministry of Justice　123, 145

野	236 0a11.5 田 甲 土 一 43 22 14 野 埜	**YA, no** – field, plain

野 生　*yasei*　wild (animal/plant)　44
平 野　*heiya*　a plain　202
　　　　Hirano　(surname)
分 野　*bun'ya*　field (of endeavor)　38
野 原　*nohara*　field, plain　136

活	237 3a6.16 田 氵 口 ⺌ 21 24 12 活	**KATSU** – life, activity

生 活　*seikatsu*　life　44
活 発　*kappatsu*　active, lively　96
活 動　*katsudō*　activity　231
活 用　*katsuyō*　practical use; conjugate, inflect　107
活 字　*katsuji*　printing/movable type　110

話	238 7a6.8 田 言 口 ⺌ 67 24 12 話	**WA, hanashi** – conversation, story **hana(su)** – speak

会 話　*kaiwa*　conversation　158
電 話　*denwa*　telephone　108
立 ち 話　*tachibanashi*　chat while standing　121
話 し 手　*hanashite*　speaker　57
話 し 合 う　*hanashiau*　talk over, discuss　159

売	**239** 3p4.3 目 士 冂 儿 22 20 16 売 賣	**BAI, u(ru)** – sell **u(reru)** – be sold	
		売店 *baiten* stand, newsstand, kiosk	168
		売り子 *uriko* store salesclerk	103
		売り手 *urite* seller	57
		売り切れ *urikire* sold out	39
		小売り *kouri* retailing, retail	27

貝	**240** 7b0.1 口 貝 68 貝	**kai** – shellfish (cf. No. 453)	
		貝類 *kairui* shellfish (plural)	226
		ほら貝 *horagai* trumpet shell, conch	
		貝ボタン *kaibotan* shell button	

買	**241** 5g7.2 目 罒貝 55 68 買	**BAI, ka(u)** – buy	
		売買 *baibai* buying and selling, trade, dealing	239
		買い物 *kaimono* shopping, purchase	79
		買い手 *kaite* buyer	57
		買い主 *kainushi* buyer	155
		買い入れる *kaiireru* purchase, stock up on	52

糸	**242** 6a0.1 口 糸 61 糸 絲	**SHI, ito** – thread	
		一糸まとわぬ *isshi matowanu* stark naked	2
		糸口 *itoguchi* end of a thread; beginning; clue	54
		糸車 *itoguruma* spinning wheel	133
		糸目 *itome* a fine thread	55
		生糸 *kiito* raw silk	44

続	**243** 6a7.5 田 糸 土 冂 61 22 20 続 續	**ZOKU, tsuzu(ku)** – (intr.) continue **tsuzu(keru)** – (tr.) continue	
		続出 *zokushutsu* appear one after another	53
		続行 *zokkō* continuation	68
		相続 *sōzoku* succession; inheritance	146
		手続き *tetsuzuki* procedures, formalities	57
		引き続いて *hikitsuzuite* continuously, uninterruptedly	216

読	**244** 7a7.9 田 言 土 冂 67 22 20 読 讀	**DOKU, TOKU, [TŌ], yo(mu)** – read	
		読者 *dokusha* reader	164
		読書 *dokusho* reading	131
		読本 *tokuhon* reader, book of readings	25
		読み物 *yomimono* reading matter	79
		読み方 *yomikata* reading, pronunciation (of a word)	70

教	**245** 4i6.1 田 攵 土 子 49 22 6 教 敎	**KYŌ, oshi(eru)** – teach **oso(waru)** – be taught, learn	
		教室 *kyōshitsu* classroom	166
		教員 *kyōin* teacher, instructor; teaching staff	163
		教会 *kyōkai* church	158
		回教 *kaikyō* Islam, Muhammadanism	90
		教え方 *oshiekata* teaching method	70

育	**246**	***IKU, soda(tsu)*** – grow up ***soda(teru)*** – raise	
	2j6.4 目	教育 *kyōiku* education	245
	亠 月 厶	体育 *taiiku* physical education	61
	11 42 17	発育 *hatsuiku* growth, development	96
		生育 *seiiku* growth, development	44
	育 毓	育ての親 *sodate no oya* foster/adoptive parent	175

流	**247**	***RYŪ*** – a current; style, school (of thought)	
	3a7.10 田	***[RU], naga(reru)*** – flow ***naga(su)*** – pour	
	氵 亠 厶	流通 *ryūtsū* circulation, distribution, ventilation	150
	21 11 17	海流 *kairyū* ocean current	117
		流行 *ryūkō* fashion, fad, popularity	68
	流	一流 *ichiryū* first class	2

早	**248**	***SŌ, [SA'], haya(i)*** – early; fast ***haya(maru)*** – be hasty	
	4c2.1 日	***haya(meru)*** – hasten	
	日 十	早々 *sōsō* early, immediately	
	43 12	早目に *hayame ni* a little early (leaving leeway)	55
		早耳 *hayamimi* quick-eared, in the know	56
	早	手早い *tebayai* quick, nimble, agile	57

草	**249**	***SŌ, kusa*** – grass, plants	
	3k6.13 目	草原 *sōgen* grassy plain, grasslands	136
	艹 日 十	草木 *sōmoku, kusaki* plants and trees, vegetation	22
	32 43 12	草本 *sōhon* herb	25
		草書 *sōsho* (cursive script form of kanji)	131
	草	草案 *sōan* (rough) draft	106

芝	**250**	***shiba*** – lawn	
	3k2.1 目	芝生 *shibafu* lawn	44
	艹 一 丨	芝草 *shibakusa* lawn	249
	32 1 2	人工芝 *jinkō shiba* artificial turf	1, 139
		芝居 *shibai* stage play, theater	171
	芝	芝居小屋 *shibai-goya* playhouse, theater	171, 27, 167

茶	**251**	***CHA, SA*** – tea	
	3k6.19 目	茶色 *chairo* brown	204
	艹 木 亻	茶畑 *chabatake* tea plantation	36
	32 41 3	茶室 *chashitsu* tea-ceremony room	166
		茶の間 *cha no ma* living room	43
	茶	茶道 *chadō, sadō* tea ceremony	149

世	**252**	***SEI, SE, yo*** – world, era	
	0a5.37 ⋯	二世 *nisei* second generation	3
	艹 一 丨	中世 *chūsei* Middle Ages	28
	32 1 2	世間 *seken* the world, public, people	43
		出世 *shusse* success in life, getting ahead	53
	世 丗	世話 *sewa* taking care of, looking after	238

葉	**253** 3k9.21 艹 木 一 32 41 1 葉	**YŌ, ha** – leaf, foliage

YŌ, ha – leaf, foliage

葉書	*hagaki* postcard	131
青葉	*aoba* green foliage	208
言葉	*kotoba* word; language	66
木の葉	*ko no ha* tree leaves, foliage	22
千葉	*Chiba* (prefecture east of Tōkyō)	15

254 2a2.6 亻 ㅏ 3 13 化

KA, KE, ba(keru) – turn oneself (into) **ba(kasu)** – bewitch

文化	*bunka* culture	111
化学	*kagaku* chemistry	109
強化	*kyōka* strengthening	217
合理化	*gōrika* rationalization, streamlining	159, 143
化け物	*bakemono* spook, ghost, monster	79

255 3k4.7 艹 亻 32 3 13 花 花

KA, hana – flower, blossom

草花	*kusabana* flower, flowering plant	249
生け花	*ikebana* flower arranging	44
花屋	*hanaya* flower shop, florist	167
花見	*hanami* viewing cherry blossoms	63
花火	*hanabi* fireworks	20

256 2a3.3 亻 戈 3 52 代

DAI – generation; age; price **TAI, ka(waru)** – represent **ka(eru)** – replace **yo** – generation **shiro** – price; substitution

時代	*jidai* era, period	42
古代	*kodai* ancient times, antiquity	172
世代	*sedai* generation	252
代理	*dairi* representation; agent	143

257 2j7.3 亠 夂 儿 11 49 16 変 變

HEN, ka(waru) – (intr.) change **ka(eru)** – (tr.) change

変化	*henka* change, alteration	254
変動	*hendō* change, fluctuation	231
変種	*henshu* variety, strain	228
変人	*henjin* an eccentric	1
不変	*fuhen* immutability, constancy	94

258 2j8.2 亠 心 儿 11 51 16 恋 戀

REN, koi – (romantic) love **ko(u)** – be in love **koi(shii)** – dear, fond, long for

恋人	*koibito* boyfriend, girlfriend, lover	1
恋文	*koibumi* love letter	111
恋心	*koigokoro* (awakening of) love	97
道ならぬ恋	*michi naranu koi* forbidden love	149

259 4i10.1 夂 心 小 49 51 35 愛

AI – love

恋愛	*ren'ai* love	258
愛情	*aijō* love	209
愛国心	*aikokushin* patriotic sentiment, patriotism	40, 97
愛読	*aidoku* like to read	244
愛想	*aisō* amiability, sociability	147

260 2h6.2 目 又 小 冂 9 35 20 受	**JU, u(keru)** – receive **u(karu)** – pass (an exam)	
	受 理 *juri* acceptance	143
	受 動 *judō* passive	231
	受 け 身 *ukemi* passivity; passive (in grammar)	59
	受 け 取 る *uketoru* receive, accept, take	65
	受 (け) 付 (け) *uketsuke* receptionist, reception desk	192

261 4n2.1 口 戈 宀 52 15 成	**SEI, [JŌ], na(ru)** – become; consist (of) **na(su)** – do; form	
	成 長 *seichō* growth	95
	成 年 *seinen* (age of) majority, adulthood	45
	成 立 *seiritsu* establishment, founding	121
	平 成 *Heisei* (Japanese era, 1989–)	202
	成 り 行 き *nariyuki* course (of events), development	68

262 4k9.21 目 心 戈 口 51 52 24 感 憾	**KAN** – feeling, sensation	
	五 感 *gokan* the 5 senses	7
	感 心 *kanshin* admire	97
	感 想 *kansō* one's thoughts, impressions	147
	感 情 *kanjō* feelings, emotion	209
	感 受 性 *kanjusei* sensibility, sensitivity	260, 98

263 4c8.10 目 日 耳 又 43 65 9 最	**SAI, motto(mo)** – highest, most	
	最 後 *saigo* end; last	48
	最 新 *saishin* newest, latest	174
	最 大 *saidai* maximum, greatest, largest	26
	最 高 *saikō* maximum, highest, best	190
	最 上 *saijō* best, highest	32

264 2h2.3 口 又 十 9 12 友	**YŪ, tomo** – friend	
	友 人 *yūjin* friend	1
	学 友 *gakuyū* fellow student, classmate; alumnus	109
	親 友 *shin'yū* close friend	175
	友 好 *yūkō* friendship	104
	友 情 *yūjō* friendliness, friendship	209

265 4b2.3 口 月 十 42 12 有	**YŪ, U, a(ru)** – be, exist, have	
	国 有 *kokuyū* state-owned	40
	私 有 *shiyū* privately owned	125
	所 有 *shoyū* possession, ownership	153
	有 名 *yūmei* famous	82
	有 力 *yūryoku* influential, powerful	100

266 3d2.10 目 口 一 24 14 号 號	**GŌ** – number; pseudonym	
	番 号 *bangō* (identification) number	185
	三 号 室 *sangōshitsu* Room No. 3	4, 166
	年 号 *nengō* name/year of a reign era	45
	信 号 *shingō* signal	157
	号 外 *gōgai* an extra (edition of a newspaper)	83

別	**267** 2f5.3　⊟ 刂口　宀 16　24　15 別	**BETSU** – different, separate; another, special **waka(reru)** – diverge, part, bid farewell

区 別　*kubetsu*　difference, distinction　183
分 別　*funbetsu*　discretion, good judgment　38
別 人　*betsujin*　different person　1
別 居　*bekkyo*　(legal) separation; live separately　171

在	**268** 3b3.8　⊡ 土　十　丨 22　12　2 在	**ZAI** – outskirts, country; be located　**a(ru)** – be, exist

所 在 地　*shozaichi*　(prefectural) capital, (county) seat;　153, 118
在 日　*zainichi*　(stationed) in Japan　⌐location　5
在 外　*zaigai*　overseas, abroad　83
不 在　*fuzai*　absence　94

存	**269** 2c3.1　⊡ 子　十　丨 6　12　2 存	**SON, ZON** – exist; know, believe

存 在　*sonzai*　existence　268
生 存　*seizon*　existence, life　44
存 続　*sonzoku*　continuance, duration　243
共 存　*kyōson, kyōzon*　coexistence　196
存 分 に　*zonbun ni*　as much as one likes, freely　38

麦	**270** 4i4.2　⊟ 夂　土　一 49　22　1 麦　麥	**BAKU, mugi** – wheat, barley, rye, oats

小 麦　*komugi*　wheat　27
大 麦　*ōmugi*　barley　26
麦 畑　*mugibatake*　wheat field　36
麦 わら　*mugiwara*　(wheat) straw
麦 茶　*mugicha*　wheat tea, barley water　251

素	**271** 6a4.12　⊟ 糸　土　一 61　22　1 素	**SO** – element; beginning　**SU** – naked, uncovered, simple

素 質　*soshitsu*　nature, makeup　176
質 素　*shisso*　simple, plain　176
元 素　*genso*　chemical element　137
水 素　*suiso*　hydrogen　21
素 人　*shirōto*　amateur, layman　1

表	**272** 0a8.6　⚃ 衤　二 57　4 表	**HYŌ** – table, chart; surface; expression　**omote** – surface, obverse **arawa(reru)** – be expressed　**arawa(su)** – express, manifest

時 間 表　*jikanhyō*　timetable, schedule　42, 43
代 表 的　*daihyōteki*　representative, typical　256, 210
表 情　*hyōjō*　facial expression　209
発 表　*happyō*　announcement, publication　96

裏	**273** 2j11.2　⊟ 一　衤　日 11　57　43 裏　裡	**RI, ura** – reverse side, back, rear

表 裏　*hyōri*　inside and outside; double-dealing　272
裏 口　*uraguchi*　back door, rear entrance　54
裏 道　*uramichi*　back street; secret path　149
裏 付 け　*urazuke*　backing, support; corroboration　192
裏 切 る　*uragiru*　betray, double-cross　39

面	**274** 3s6.1 ⊟ 口 一 儿 24 14 16 面	**MEN** – face, mask, surface, aspect **omote, omo, tsura** – face
		方面 *hōmen* direction, side 70
		表面 *hyōmen* surface, exterior 272
		面会 *menkai* interview, meeting 158
		面目 *menmoku, menboku* face, honor, dignity 55

正	**275** 2m3.3 ⋯ ㅏ 工 一 (13) 38 1 正	**SEI, SHŌ, tada(shii)** – correct, just **tada(su)** – correct **masa (ni)** – just, exactly; certainly
		校正 *kōsei* proofreading 115
		不正 *fusei* injustice 94
		正面 *shōmen* front, front side 274
		正月 *shōgatsu* January; New Year 17

頭	**276** 9a7.6 ⊞ 頁 口 儿 77 24 16 頭	**TŌ, [TO], ZU, atama, kashira** – head, leader, top
		後頭 (部) *kōtō(bu)* back of the head 48, 86
		出頭 *shuttō* appearance, attendance, presence (at official 53
		先頭 *sentō* (in the) front, lead ⌐proceeding) 50
		口頭 *kōtō* oral, verbal 54
		頭上 *zujō* overhead 32

顔	**277** 9a9.3 ⊞ 頁 立 彡 77 54 31 顔 顔	**GAN, kao** – face
		顔面 *ganmen* face 274
		顔色 *kaoiro* complexion; a look 204
		素顔 *sugao* face without makeup 271
		新顔 *shingao* stranger; newcomer 174
		知らん顔 *shirankao* pretend not to notice, ignore 214

産	**278** 5b6.4 ⊟ 立 牛 一 54 47 1 産 產	**SAN** – childbirth; production; property **u(mu)** – give birth/rise to **u(mareru)** – be born **ubu** – birth; infant
		出産 *shussan* childbirth, delivery 53
		生産 *seisan* production 44
		産物 *sanbutsu* product 79
		不動産 *fudōsan* immovable property, real estate 94, 231

業	**279** 0a13.3 ⊟ ʼʼ 王 一 16 46 1 業	**GYŌ** – occupation, business, undertaking **GŌ** – karma **waza** – act, deed, work, art
		工業 *kōgyō* industry 139
		産業 *sangyō* industry 278
		事業 *jigyō* undertaking, enterprise 80
		実業家 *jitsugyōka* businessman, industrialist 203, 165

犬	**280** 3g0.1 ☐ 犭 27 犬	**KEN, inu** – dog
		番犬 *banken* watchdog 185
		愛犬 *aiken* pet/favorite dog 259
		野犬 *yaken* stray dog 236
		小犬 *koinu* puppy 27
		犬小屋 *inugoya* doghouse 27, 167

281	**GYŪ, ushi** – cow, bull, cattle
4g0.1 □	牛肉 *gyūniku* beef — 223
牛	野牛 *yagyū* buffalo, bison — 236
47	水牛 *suigyū* water buffalo — 21
牛	小牛, 子牛 *koushi* calf — 27, 103
	牛小屋 *ushigoya* cowshed, barn — 27, 167

282	**TOKU** – special
4g6.1 田	特別 *tokubetsu* special — 267
牛 土 寸	特色 *tokushoku* distinguishing characteristic — 204
47 22 37	特有 *tokuyū* characteristic, peculiar (to) — 265
特	独特 *dokutoku* peculiar, original, unique — 219
	特長 *tokuchō* strong point, forte — 95

283	**BA, uma, [ma]** – horse
10a0.1 □	馬車 *basha* horse-drawn carriage — 133
馬	馬力 *bariki* horsepower — 100
78	馬術 *bajutsu* horseback riding, dressage — 187
馬	竹馬 *takeuma, chikuba* stilts — 129
	馬小屋 *umagoya* a stable — 27, 167

284	**EKI** – (train) station
10a4.4 田	東京駅 *Tōkyō-eki* Tōkyō Station — 71, 189
馬 尸		当駅 *tōeki* this station — 77
78 40 2	駅前 *ekimae* (in) front of/opposite the station — 47
駅 驛	駅長 *ekichō* stationmaster — 95
	駅員 *ekiin* station employee — 163

285	**CHŌ, tori** – bird
11b0.1 □	白鳥 *hakuchō* swan — 205
鳥	野鳥 *yachō* wild bird — 236
80	花鳥 *kachō* flowers and birds — 255
鳥	一石二鳥 *isseki-nichō* killing 2 birds with 1 stone — 2, 78, 3
	鳥居 *torii* torii, Shintō shrine archway — 171

286	**TŌ, shima** – island
3o7.9 日	半島 *hantō* peninsula — 88
屵 尸 一	島民 *tōmin* islander — 177
36 40 1	無人島 *mujintō* uninhabited island — 93, 1
島 嶋	島国 *shimaguni* island country — 40
	島々 *shimajima* (many) islands

287	**MŌ, ke** – hair, fur, feather, down
0a4.33 ⋯	原毛 *genmō* raw wool — 136
十 |	毛筆 *mōhitsu* brush (for writing/painting) — 130
12 2	不毛 *fumō* barren, sterile — 94
毛	毛糸 *keito* wool yarn, knitting wool — 242
	まゆ毛 *mayuge* eyebrow

羊	**288** 2o4.1 ⊟ ⌄王 16 46 羊	**YŌ, hitsuji** – sheep 羊毛 *yōmō* wool — 287 羊肉 *yōniku* mutton — 223 小羊, 子羊 *kohitsuji* lamb — 27, 103
洋	**289** 3a6.19 ⊞ 氵王儿 21 46 16 洋	**YŌ** – ocean; foreign, Western 大洋 *taiyō* ocean — 26 東洋 *tōyō* the East, Orient — 71 西洋 *seiyō* the West, Occident — 72 大西洋 *Taiseiyō* Atlantic Ocean — 26, 72 洋書 *yōsho* foreign/Western book — 131
魚	**290** 11a0.1 ☐ 魚 79 魚	**GYO, sakana, uo** – fish 魚類 *gyorui* a variety of fish — 226 金魚 *kingyo* goldfish — 23 魚肉 *gyoniku* fish (meat) — 223 魚市場 *uoichiba* fish market — 181, 154 魚屋 *sakanaya* fish shop/dealer — 167
義	**291** 2o11.3 ⊟ ⌄王戈 16 46 52 義	**GI** – justice, honor; meaning; in-law; artificial 民主主義 *minshu shugi* democracy — 177, 155 義務 *gimu* obligation, duty — 235 義理 *giri* duty, debt of gratitude — 143 同義語 *dōgigo* synonym — 198, 67 類義語 *ruigigo* word of similar meaning, synonym — 226, 67
議	**292** 7a13.4 ⊞ 言王戈 67 46 52 議	**GI** – deliberation; proposal 会議 *kaigi* conference, meeting — 158 協議 *kyōgi* council, conference — 234 議会 *gikai* parliament, diet, congress — 158 議員 *giin* M.P., dietman, congressman — 163 不思議 *fushigi* marvel, wonder, mystery — 94, 99
論	**293** 7a8.13 ⊞ 言 ⺮ 亻 67 32 3 論	**RON** – discussion, argument; thesis, dissertation 論理 *ronri* logic — 143 理論 *riron* theory — 143 世論 *yoron, seron* public opinion — 252 論議 *rongi* discussion, argument — 292 論文 *ronbun* thesis, essay — 111
王	**294** 4f0.1 ☐ 王 46 王	**Ō** – king 王国 *ōkoku* kingdom — 40 国王 *kokuō* king — 40 女王 *joō* queen — 102 王子 *ōji* prince — 103 法王 *hōō* pope — 123

	295	**GYOKU, tama** – gem, jewel; sphere, ball	
玉	4f0.2 ⬚	玉石 *gyokuseki* wheat and chaff, good and bad	78
	王 丨	玉子 *tamago* egg (cf. No. 1058)	103
	46 2	水玉 *mizutama* drop of water	21
		目玉 *medama* eyeball	55
	玉	十円玉 *jūendama* 10-yen piece/coin	12, 13

	296	**HŌ, takara** – treasure	
宝	3m5.2 ⬚	宝石 *hōseki* precious stone, gem	78
	宀 王 丨	宝玉 *hōgyoku* precious stone, gem	295
	33 46 2	国宝 *kokuhō* national treasure	40
		家宝 *kahō* family heirloom	165
	宝 寶	宝物 *hōmotsu, takaramono* treasure, prized possession	79

	297	**KŌ, Ō** – emperor	
皇	4f5.9 ⬚	天皇 *tennō* emperor	141
	王 日 丨	皇女 *kōjo* imperial princess	102
	46 43 2	皇居 *kōkyo* imperial palace	171
		皇室 *kōshitsu* imperial household	166
	皇	皇位 *kōi* imperial throne	122

	298	**GEN** – present **arawa(reru)** – appear **arawa(su)** – show	
現	4f7.3 ⬚	現代 *gendai* contemporary, modern	256
	王 貝 丨	現在 *genzai* current, present; present tense	268
	46 68	現金 *genkin* cash	23
		表現 *hyōgen* an expression	272
	現	実現 *jitsugen* realize, attain; come true	203

	299	**SEN** – line	
線	6a9.7 ⬚	光線 *kōsen* light, light ray	138
	糸 日 氵	内線 *naisen* (telephone) extension	84
	61 43 21	無線 *musen* wireless, radio	93
		二番線 *nibansen* Track No. 2	3, 185
	線	地平線 *chiheisen* horizon	118, 202

	300	**TAN** – single, simple	
単	3n6.2 ⬚	単語 *tango* word	67
	丷 日 十	単位 *tan'i* unit, denomination	122
	35 43 12	単一 *tan'itsu* single, simple, individual	2
		単数 *tansū* singular (in grammar)	225
	単 單	単独 *tandoku* independent, single-handed	219

	301	**SEN, tataka(u)** – wage war, fight **ikusa** – war, battle	
戦	4n9.2 ⬚	内戦 *naisen* civil war	84
	戈 日 小	交戦 *kōsen* war, warfare	114
	52 43 35	合戦 *kassen* battle; contest	159
		休戦 *kyūsen* truce, cease-fire	60
	戦 戰	戦後 *sengo* postwar	48

Kanji	Entry	Reading & Meaning	Examples	Ref
争	**302** 2n4.2 ケ ヨ 亅 15 39 2 争 争	**SŌ, araso(u)** – dispute, argue, contend for	戦争　*sensō*　war 争議　*sōgi*　dispute, strife 論争　*ronsō*　argument, controversy 争点　*sōten*　point of contention, issue 言い争う　*iiarasou*　quarrel, argue	301 292 293 169 66
急	**303** 2n7.2 ケ 心 ヨ 15 51 39 急 急	**KYŪ** – urgent, sudden　*iso(gu)* – be in a hurry	急行　*kyūkō*　an express (train) 特急　*tokkyū*　a special express (train) 急変　*kyūhen*　sudden change 急用　*kyūyō*　urgent business 急性　*kyūsei*　acute	68 282 257 107 98
悪	**304** 4k7.17 心 エ 口 51 38 24 悪 惡	**AKU, O, waru(i)** – bad, evil	悪化　*akka*　change for the worse 悪性　*akusei*　malignant, vicious 悪事　*akuji*　evil deed 最悪　*saiaku*　the worst, at worst 悪口　*akkō, warukuchi*　abusive language, speaking ill of	254 98 80 263 54
末	**305** 0a5.26 木 一 41 1 末	**MATSU, BATSU, sue** – end	週末　*shūmatsu*　weekend 月末　*getsumatsu*　end of the month 年末　*nenmatsu*　year's end 末代　*matsudai*　all ages to come, eternity 末っ子　*suekko*　youngest child	92 17 45 256 103
未	**306** 0a5.27 木 一 41 1 未	**MI** – not yet	未来　*mirai*　future 未知　*michi*　unknown 前代未聞　*zendai-mimon*　unprecedented 未満　*miman*　less than, under 未明　*mimei*　early dawn, before daybreak	69 214 47, 256, 64 201 18
味	**307** 3d5.3 口 木 一 24 41 1 味	**MI, aji** – taste　*aji(wau)* – taste; relish, appreciate	意味　*imi*　meaning, significance, sense 正味　*shōmi*　net (amount/weight/price) 不気味　*bukimi*　uncanny, eerie, ominous 地味　*jimi*　plain, subdued, undemonstrative 三味線　*shamisen*　samisen (3-stringed instrument)	132 275 94, 134 118 4, 299
社	**308** 4e3.1 ネ 土 45 22 社 社	**SHA** – Shintō shrine; company, firm　*yashiro* – Shintō shrine	社会　*shakai*　society, social 会社　*kaisha*　company, firm 本社　*honsha*　our company; head office 社長　*shachō*　company president 社員　*shain*　employee, staff member	158 158 25 95 163

309 申

0a5.39
日 丨
43 2
申

SHIN, mō(su) – say; be named

答申	tōshin	report, findings	160
上申	jōshin	report (to a superior)	32
内申	naishin	unofficial/confidential report	84
申し入れ	mōshiire	offer, proposal, notice	52
申し合わせ	mōshiawase	an understanding	159

310 神

4e5.1
ネ 日 丨
45 43 2
神 神

SHIN, JIN, kami, [kan], [kō] – god, God

神道	shintō	Shintoism	149
神社	jinja	Shintō shrine	308
神話	shinwa	myth, mythology	238
神父	shinpu	(Catholic) priest, Father	113
神風	kamikaze	divine wind; kamikaze	29

311 失

0a5.28
大 ノ
34 15
失

SHITSU, ushina(u) – lose

失業	shitsugyō	unemployment	279
失意	shitsui	disappointment, despair	132
失神	shisshin	faint, lose consciousness	310
失恋	shitsuren	unrequited love	258
見失う	miushinau	lose sight of	63

312 鉄

8a5.6
金 大 ノ
72 34 15
鉄 鐵

TETSU – iron

鉄道	tetsudō	railroad	149
地下鉄	chikatetsu	subway	118, 31
私鉄	shitetsu	private railway	125
鉄かぶと	tetsukabuto	steel helmet	

313 銀

8a6.3
金 食
72 73
銀

GIN – silver

銀行	ginkō	bank	68
日銀	Nichigin	the Bank of Japan	5
銀色	gin'iro	silver color	204
水銀	suigin	mercury	21
銀メダル	ginmedaru	silver medal	

314 根

4a6.5
木 食
41 73
根

KON – root; perseverance **ne** – root, base, origin

大根	daikon	daikon, Japanese radish	26
根本的	konponteki	fundamental; radical	25, 210
根気	konki	patience, perseverance	134
屋根	yane	roof	167
根強い	nezuyoi	deep-rooted, firmly established	217

315 夫

0a4.31
大 一
34 1
夫

FU, [FŪ], otto – husband

夫人	fujin	wife, Mrs.	1
人夫	ninpu	laborer	1
水夫	suifu	sailor, seaman	21
工夫	kōfu	laborer	139
	kufū	contrivance, scheme, means	

婦	316 3e8.6 ⊞ 女 ⿻ 巾 25 39 26 婦 婦	**FU** – woman, wife	
		夫婦 *fūfu* husband and wife, married couple	315
		主婦 *shufu* housewife	155
		婦人 *fujin* lady, woman	1
		婦女(子) *fujo(shi)* woman	102, 103
		婦長 *fuchō* head nurse	95

帰	317 2f8.8 ⊞ 刂 ⿻ 巾 16 39 26 帰 歸	**KI**, *kae(ru)* – return *kae(su)* – let return, dismiss	
		帰国 *kikoku* return to one's country	40
		帰宅 *kitaku* return/come/get home	178
		帰路 *kiro* the way home	151
		帰化 *kika* become naturalized	254
		日帰り *higaeri* go and return in a day	5

支	318 2k2.1 ⊟ 十 又 12 9 支	**SHI** – branch; support *sasa(eru)* – support	
		支出 *shishutsu* expenditure, disbursement	53
		支社 *shisha* branch (office)	308
		支店 *shiten* branch office/store	168
		支部 *shibu* branch, local chapter	86
		支流 *shiryū* tributary (of a river)	247

料	319 6b4.4 ⊞ 米 十 丨 62 12 2 料	**RYŌ** – materials; fee	
		料理 *ryōri* cooking, cuisine; dish, food	143
		原料 *genryō* raw materials	136
		料金 *ryōkin* fee, charge, fare	23
		手数料 *tesūryō* fee; commission	57, 225
		有/無料 *yū/muryō* pay, toll, charging a fee/free	265, 93

科	320 5d4.3 ⊞ 禾 十 丨 56 12 2 科	**KA** – academic course, department, faculty	
		科学 *kagaku* science	109
		理科 *rika* natural sciences (department)	143
		外科 *geka* surgery	83
		産婦人科医 *sanfujinkai* gynecologist	278, 316, 1, 220
		教科書 *kyōkasho* textbook, schoolbook	245, 131

良	321 0a7.3 ☐ 食 73 良 良	**RYŌ**, *yo(i)* – good	
		良好 *ryōkō* good, favorable, satisfactory	104
		良質 *ryōshitsu* good quality	176
		最良 *sairyō* best	263
		不良 *furyō* bad, unsatisfactory; delinquency	94
		良心 *ryōshin* conscience	97

食	322 8b0.1 ☐ 食 73 食	**SHOKU, [JIKI]** – food; eating *ta(beru), ku(u), ku(rau)* – eat	
		食事 *shokuji* meal, dinner	80
		食料品 *shokuryōhin* food, foodstuffs	319, 230
		和/洋食 *wa/yōshoku* Japanese/Western food	124, 289
		夕食 *yūshoku* evening meal, supper	81
		食べ物 *tabemono* food	79

323

飲

8b4.1

食 攵
73 49

飲 飲

IN, no(mu) – drink

飲食	*inshoku*	food and drink, eating and drinking	322
飲料	*inryō*	drink, beverage	319
飲料水	*inryōsui*	drinking water	319, 21
飲み水	*nomimizu*	drinking water	21
飲み物	*nomimono*	(something to) drink, beverage	79

324

反

2p2.2

厂 又
18 9

反

HAN, [HON] – anti- **[TAN]** – (unit of land/cloth measurement)
so(ru/rasu) – (intr./tr.) warp, bend back

反発	*hanpatsu*	repulsion, repellence; opposition	96
反日	*han-Nichi*	anti-Japanese	5
反面	*hanmen*	the other side	274
反省	*hansei*	reflection, introspection; reconsideration	145

325

飯

8b4.5

食 厂 又
73 18 9

飯

HAN, meshi – cooked rice; meal, food

ご飯	*gohan*	cooked rice; meal, food	
赤飯	*sekihan*	(festive) rice boiled with red beans	207
夕飯	*yūhan, yūmeshi*	evening meal, supper, dinner	81
飯ごう	*hangō*	mess kit, eating utensils	
飯場	*hanba*	construction camp/bunkhouse	154

326

官

3m5.6

宀 尸 口
33 40 20

官

KAN – government, authorities

半官半民	*hankan-hanmin*	semigovernmental	88, 177
国務長官	*kokumu chōkan*	secretary of state	40, 235, 95
外交官	*gaikōkan*	diplomat	83, 114
高官	*kōkan*	high government official/office	190
神官	*shinkan*	Shintō priest	310

327

館

8b8.3

食 宀 尸
73 33 40

館 舘

KAN – (large) building, hall

旅館	*ryokan*	Japanese-style inn	222
水族館	*suizokukan*	(public) aquarium	22, 221
会館	*kaikan*	(assembly) hall	158
本館	*honkan*	main building	25
別館	*bekkan*	annex, extension	267

328

管

6f8.12

竹 宀 尸
66 33 40

管

KAN – pipe; wind instrument; control **kuda** – pipe, tube

管内	*kannai*	(area of) jurisdiction	84
管理	*kanri*	administration, supervision	143
水道管	*suidōkan*	water pipe/conduit	21, 149
気管	*kikan*	wind pipe, trachea	134
鉄管	*tekkan*	iron tube/pipe	312

329

利

5d2.1

禾 刂
56 16

利

RI – advantage; (loan) interest **ki(ku)** – take effect, work

有利	*yūri*	profitable, advantageous	265
利子	*rishi*	interest (on a loan)	103
利用	*riyō*	make use of	107
利口	*rikō*	smart, clever, bright	54
左利き	*hidarikiki*	left-hander	75

便	**330** 2a7.5	**BEN** – convenience; excrement **BIN** – opportunity; mail **tayo(ri)** – news, tidings
	亻日 一 3 43 14	便利 *benri* convenient, handy 329 不便 *fuben* inconvenient 94 便所 *benjo* toilet 153
	便便	別便 *betsubin* separate mail 267

使	**331** 2a6.2	**SHI** – use; messenger **tsuka(u)** – use
	亻口 艹 3 24 12	大使 *taishi* ambassador 26 公使 *kōshi* minister, envoy 126 天使 *tenshi* angel 141 使用法 *shiyōhō* how to use, directions for use 107, 123
	使使	使い方 *tsukaikata* how to use, way to handle 70

史	**332** 0a5.38	**SHI** – history, chronicles
	口 艹 24 12	日本史 *Nihon shi* Japanese history 5, 25 中世史 *chūsei shi* medieval history 28, 252 文学史 *bungaku shi* history of literature 111, 109 史実 *shijitsu* historical fact 203
	史史	女史 *joshi* (honorific) Madame, Miss, Mrs. 102

仕	**333** 2a3.2	**SHI, [JI], tsuka(eru)** – serve
	亻土 3 22	仕事 *shigoto* work, job 80 仕立て屋 *shitateya* tailor; dressmaker 121, 167 仕方 *shikata* way, method, means 70 仕手 *shite* protagonist, leading role (in Noh) 57
	仕	仕上げる *shiageru* finish up, complete 32

任	**334** 2a4.9	**NIN** – duty, responsibility; office **maka(seru/su)** – entrust (to)
	亻王 3 46	主任 *shunin* person in charge, manager, head 155 信任 *shinnin* confidence, trust 157 後任 *kōnin* successsor 48 任務 *ninmu* duty, office, mission 235
	任	任意 *nin'i* optional, voluntary 132

権	**335** 4a11.18	**KEN, [GON]** – authority, power; right
	木 隹 亠 41 74 15	権利 *kenri* a right 329 人権 *jinken* human rights 1 特権 *tokken* special right, privilege 282 主権 *shuken* sovereignty 155
	権權	三権分立 *sanken bunritsu* seperation of powers 4, 38, 121

極	**336** 4a8.11	**KYOKU** – end, pole **GOKU** – very, extremely **kiwa(mi)** – height, end **kiwa(meru)** – carry to its end **kiwa(maru)** – reach its end
	木 口 一 41 24 14	極東 *kyokutō* the Far East 71 北/南極 *hok/nankyoku* north/south pole 73, 74 見極める *mikiwameru* see through, discern 63
	極	極上 *gokujō* finest, top quality 71

句	**337** 3d2.13 □ 口 ᅮ 24 15 句	**KU** – phrase, sentence, verse	
		語句 *goku* words and phrases	67
		成句 *seiku* set phrase, idiom	261
		文句 *monku* words, expression; objection	111
		句読点 *kutōten* punctuation mark	244, 169
		引用句 *in'yōku* quotation	216, 107
旬	**338** 4c2.5 □ 日 ᅮ 43 15 旬	**JUN** – 10-day period	
		上旬 *jōjun* first 10 days of a month (1st to 10th)	32
		中旬 *chūjun* second 10 days of a month (11th to 20th)	28
		下旬 *gejun* last third of a month (21th to end)	31
図	**339** 3s4.3 □ 口 艹 丨 24 12 2 図 圖	**ZU** – drawing, diagram, plan **TO, haka(ru)** – plan	
		地図 *chizu* map	118
		図表 *zuhyō* chart, table, graph	272
		合図 *aizu* signal, sign, gesture	159
		意図 *ito* intention	132
		図書館 *toshokan* library	131, 327
計	**340** 7a2.1 □ 言 十 67 12 計	**KEI** – measuring; plan; total **haka(ru)** – measure, compute **haka(rau)** – arrange, dispose of, see about	
		時計 *tokei* clock, watch	42
		会計 *kaikei* accounting; paying a bill	158
		合計 *gōkei* total	159
		家計 *kakei* household finances	165
針	**341** 8a2.3 □ 金 十 72 12 針	**SHIN, hari** – needle	
		方針 *hōshin* course, line, policy	70
		針路 *shinro* course (of a ship)	151
		長針, 分針 *chōshin, funshin* minute hand	95, 38
		短針 *tanshin* hour hand	215
		針金 *harigane* wire	23
調	**342** 7a8.16 □ 言 月 口 67 42 24 調 調	**CHŌ, shira(beru)** – investigate, check **totono(eru)** – prepare, arrange, put in order **totono(u)** – be prepared, arranged	
		協調 *kyōchō* cooperation, harmony	234
		好調 *kōchō* good, favorable	104
		調子 *chōshi* tone; mood; condition	103
		取り調べ *torishirabe* investigation, questioning	65
画	**343** 0a8.7 … 日 一 冂 43 14 20 画 畫	**GA** – picture **KAKU** – stroke (in writing kanji)	
		画家 *gaka* painter ⌐painting	165
		日本/洋画 *Nihon/yōga* Japanese/Western-style	5, 25, 289
		画用紙 *gayōshi* drawing paper	107, 180
		画面 *gamen* (TV/computer/movie) screen	274
		計画 *keikaku* plan, project	340

344

演 3a11.13
氵日宀
21 43 33
演

EN – performance, play, presentation

上演	*jōen* performance, dramatic presentation	32
公演	*kōen* public performance	126
独演	*dokuen* solo performance	219
出演	*shutsuen* appearance, performance	53
演出	*enshutsu* production, staging (of a play)	53

345

絵 6a6.8
糸亻二
61 3 4
絵 繪

KAI, E – picture

絵画	*kaiga* pictures, paintings, drawings	343
絵葉書	*ehagaki* picture postcard	253, 131
絵本	*ehon* picture book	25
口絵	*kuchie* frontispiece	54
大和絵	*Yamato-e* ancient Japanese-style painting	26, 124

346

給 6a6.7
糸口亻
61 24 3
給

KYŪ – supply

給料	*kyūryō* pay, wages, salary	319
月給	*gekkyū* monthly salary	17
支給	*shikyū* supply, provisioning, allowance	318
供給	*kyōkyū* supply	197
給水	*kyūsui* water supply	21

347

音 5b4.3
立日
54 43
音

ON, IN, oto, ne – sound

発音	*hatsuon* pronunciation	96
表音文字	*hyōon moji* phonetic symbol	272, 111, 110
母音	*boin* vowel	112
本音	*honne* one's true intention	25
足音	*ashioto* sound of footsteps	58

348

暗 4c9.2
日立
43 54
暗

AN, kura(i) – dark, dim

暗黒	*ankoku* darkness	206
暗室	*anshitsu* darkroom	166
暗号	*angō* (secret) code, cipher	266
明暗	*meian* light and darkness, shading	18
暗がり	*kuragari* darkness	

349

韻 7b12.2
貝立日
68 54 43
韻 韵

IN – rhyme

音韻学	*on'ingaku* phonology	347, 109
韻文	*inbun* verse, poetry	111
韻語	*ingo* rhyming words	67
頭韻	*tōin* alliteration	276

350

損 3c10.12
扌貝口
23 68 24
損

SON – loss, damage **soko(nau), soko(neru)** – harm, injure
-soko(nau) – fail to, err in

損失	*sonshitsu* loss	311
大損	*ōzon* great loss	26
見損なう	*misokonau* miss (seeing); misjudge	63
読み損なう	*yomisokonau* misread	244

351

0a5.33 […]

大 冂
34 20

央

Ō – center, middle

中央	chūō	center	28
中央口	chūōguchi	main/middle exit	28, 54
中央部	chūōbu	central part, middle	28, 86
中央線	Chūō-sen	the Chūō (train) Line	28, 299
中央区	Chūō-ku	Chūō Ward (Tōkyō)	28, 183

352

4c5.1 □

日 大 冂
43 34 20

映 暎

EI, utsu(su) – reflect, project **utsu(ru)** – be reflected, projected
ha(eru) – shine, be brilliant

映画	eiga	movie	343
反映	han'ei	reflection	324
上映	jōei	showing, screening (of a movie)	32
夕映え	yūbae	the glow of sunset	81

353

3k5.5 日

艹 大 冂
32 34 20

英

EI – brilliant, talented, gifted; (short for) England

英気	eiki	energetic spirit, enthusiasm	134
石英	sekiei	quartz	78
英語	Eigo	the English language	67
和英	Wa-Ei	Japanese-English	124
英会話	Ei-kaiwa	English conversation	158, 238

354

9a9.7 […]

頁日 一
77 43 14

題

DAI – topic, theme; title

問題	mondai	problem, question	162
議題	gidai	topic for discussion, agenda	292
話題	wadai	topic	238
表題	hyōdai	title, caption	272
宿題	shukudai	homework	179

355

3m5.8 日

宀 一 亻
33 14 3

定

TEI, JŌ, sada(meru) – determine, decide **sada(maru)** – be
determined, decided **sada(ka)** – certain, definite

安定	antei	stability, equilibrium	105
協定	kyōtei	agreement, pact	234
定食	teishoku	meal of fixed menu, complete meal	322
未定	mitei	undecided, unsettled, not yet fixed	306

356

3a4.6 □

氵 大 一
21 34 1

決 決

KETSU, ki(meru) – decide **ki(maru)** – be decided

決定	kettei	decision, determination	355
決心	kesshin	determination, resolution	97
決意	ketsui	determination, resolution	132
議決	giketsu	decision (of a committee)	292
未決	miketsu	pending	306

357

3a5.16 田

氵 王 丨
21 46 2

注 注

CHŪ – note, comment **soso(gu)** – pour, flow

注意	chūi	attention, caution, warning	132
注目	chūmoku	attention, notice	55
注文	chūmon	order, commission	111
発注	hatchū	order, commission	96
注入	chūnyū	injection; pour into, infuse	52

358	**GAKU** – music **RAKU** – pleasure **tano(shimu)** – enjoy **tano(shii)** – fun, enjoyable, pleasant	
4a9.29 目	音楽 *ongaku* music	347
木 日 冫	文楽 *bunraku* Japanese puppet theater	111
41 43 5	楽天家 *rakutenka* optimist	141, 165
楽 樂	安楽死 *anrakushi* euthanasia	105, 85

359	**YAKU, kusuri** – medicine	
3k13.15目	薬学 *yakugaku* pharmacy	109
艹 木 日	薬品 *yakuhin* medicine, drugs	230
32 41 43	薬味 *yakumi* spices	307
	薬局 *yakkyoku* pharmacy	170
藥 藥	薬屋 *kusuriya* drugstore, pharmacy	167

360	**SAKU, SA, tsuku(ru)** – make	
2a5.10 囗	作家 *sakka* writer	165
亻 宀 卜	作品 *sakuhin* (literary) work, work (of art), opus	230
3 15 13	作戦 *sakusen* military operation, tactics	301
	作り話 *tsukuribanashi* made-up story, fabrication	238
作	手作り *tezukuri* handmade	57

361	**SAKU** – past; yesterday	
4c5.3 囗	昨年 *sakunen* last year	45
日 宀 卜	昨日 *sakujitsu, kinō* yesterday	5
43 15 13	一昨日 *issakujitsu, ototoi* day before yesterday	2, 5
	一昨年 *issakunen, ototoshi* year before last	2, 45
昨	昨今 *sakkon* these days, recent	51

362	**DAN** – step; stairs; rank; column	
2s7.2 田	一段 *ichidan* step; single-stage	2
几 又 厂	石段 *ishidan* stone stairway	78
20 9 18	段々畑 *dandanbatake* terraced fields	36
	手段 *shudan* means, measure	57
段	段取り *dandori* program, plan, arrangements	65

363	**YU, YŪ, [YUI], yoshi** – reason, cause; significance	
0a5.35 …	由来 *yurai* origin, derivation	69
日 丨	理由 *riyū* reason, grounds	143
43 2	自由 *jiyū* freedom	62
	不自由 *fujiyū* discomfort; want, privation	94, 62
由	事由 *jiyū* reason, cause	80

364	**YU, abura** – oil	
3a5.6 囗	石油 *sekiyu* oil, petroleum	78
氵 日 丨	原油 *gen'yu* crude oil	136
21 43 2	油田 *yuden* oil field	35
	給油所 *kyūyusho, kyūyujo* filling/gas station	346, 153
油	油絵 *aburae* oil painting	345

対	**365** 2j5.5 ⊞ 亠 寸 11 37 12 対 對	**TAI** – against **TSUI** – pair	
		反対 *hantai* opposite; opposition	324
		対立 *tairitsu* confrontation	121
		対決 *taiketsu* showdown	356
		対面 *taimen* interview, meeting	274
		対話 *taiwa* conversation, dialogue	238
曲	**366** 0a6.27 ⋯ 日 儿 43 16 曲	**KYOKU** – curve; melody, musical composition **ma(geru)** – bend, distort **ma(garu)** – (intr.) bend, turn	
		作曲 *sakkyoku* musical composition	360
		名曲 *meikyoku* famous/well-known melody	82
		曲線 *kyokusen* a curve	299
		曲がり道 *magarimichi* winding street	149
典	**367** 2o6.5 ⊟ ソ 艹 冂 16 32 20 典	**TEN** – law code; ceremony	
		古典 *koten* classical literature, the classics	172
		百科事典 *hyakka jiten* encyclopedia	14, 320, 80
		法典 *hōten* code of laws	123
		出典 *shutten* literary source, authority	53
		特典 *tokuten* special favor, privilege	282
興	**368** 2o14.2 ⊟ ソ 冂 厂 16 24 18 興	**KŌ, KYŌ** – interest; entertainment; liveliness; prosperity **oko(ru)** – flourish, prosper **oko(su)** – revive, retrieve	
		興行 *kōgyō* entertainment, industry; performance	68
		興業 *kōgyō* industrial enterprise	279
		興味 *kyōmi* interest	307
		興信所 *kōshinjo* private inquiry/detective agency	157, 153
農	**369** 2p11.1 ⊟ 厂 衤 日 18 57 43 農	**NŌ** – agriculture	
		農業 *nōgyō* agriculture	279
		農村 *nōson* farm village	191
		農民 *nōmin* farmer, peasant	177
		農家 *nōka* farmhouse, farm household; farmer	165
		農産物 *nōsanbutsu* agricultural product	278, 79
己	**370** 0a3.12 ▢ 弓 28 己	**KO, KI, onore** – self	
		自己 *jiko* self-	62
		自己中心 *jiko chūshin* egocentric	62, 28, 97
		利己 *riko* selfishness, egoism	329
		利己的 *rikoteki* selfish, self-centered	329, 210
		知己 *chiki* acquaintance	214
記	**371** 7a3.5 ▢▢ 言 弓 67 28 記	**KI, shiru(su)** – write/note down	
		記者 *kisha* newspaperman, journalist	164
		記事 *kiji* article, report	80
		日記 *nikki* diary	5
		暗記 *anki* memorize	348
		記号 *kigō* mark, symbol	266

紀	**372** 6a3.5 ☐ 糸 弓 61 28 紀	**KI** – narrative, history

紀元　*kigen*　era (of year reckoning)　137
紀元前／後　*kigenzen/go*　B.C./A.C.　137, 47, 48
世紀　*seiki*　century　252
紀行 (文)　*kikō(bun)*　account of a journey　68, 111
風紀　*fūki*　discipline, public morals　29

起	**373** 3b7.11 ⋯ 土 弓 ⊢ 22 28 13 起	**KI** – awakening, rise, beginning　*o(kiru)* – get/wake/be up *o(koru)* – occur　*o(kosu)* – give rise to; wake (someone) up

起原　*kigen*　origin, beginning　136
起点　*kiten*　starting point　169
早起き　*hayaoki*　get up early　248
起き上がる　*okiagaru*　get up, pick oneself up　32

得	**374** 3i8.4 ⊞ 彳 日 寸 29 43 37 得	**TOKU** – profit, advantage　*e(ru), u(ru)* – gain, acquire

損得　*sontoku*　profit and loss　350
所得　*shotoku*　income　153
得点　*tokuten*　one's score, points made　169
得意　*tokui*　prosperity; pride; one's strong point　132
心得る　*kokoroeru*　know, understand　97

役	**375** 3i4.2 ⊞ 彳 冂 又 29 20 9 役	**YAKU** – service, use; office, post　**EKI** – battle; service

役所　*yakusho*　government office/bureau　153
役人　*yakunin*　public official　1
役員　*yakuin*　(company) officer, director　163
役者　*yakusha*　player, actor　164
使役　*shieki*　employment, service　331

船	**376** 6c5.4 ⊞ 舟 口 儿 63 24 16 船 船	**SEN, fune, [funa]** – ship

船長　*senchō*　captain　95
船員　*sen'in*　crewman, seaman, sailor　163
船室　*senshitsu*　cabin　166
汽船　*kisen*　steamship, steamer　135
船旅　*funatabi*　sea voyage　222

度	**377** 3q6.1 ☐ 广 廿 又 18 32 9 度	**DO, [TAKU], [TO]** – degree, measure, limit; times　*tabi* – times

一度　*ichido*　once; 1 degree (of temperature)　2
今度　*kondo*　this time; soon; next time　51
年度　*nendo*　business/fiscal year　45
高度成長　*kōdo seichō*　high growth　190, 261, 95
支度, 仕度　*shitaku*　preparations　318, 333

渡	**378** 3a9.35 ☐ 氵 廿 厂 21 32 18 渡	**TO, wata(ru)** – cross　*wata(su)* – hand over

渡来　*torai*　introduction (into); visit　69
渡し船　*watashibune*　ferryboat　376
渡り鳥　*wataridori*　migratory bird　285
見渡す　*miwatasu*　look out over　63
手渡す　*tewatasu*　hand deliver, hand over　57

	379	*SEKI* – seat, place	
席	3q7.4	出 席 *shusseki* attendance	53
	广 艹 巾	満 席 *manseki* full, fully occupied	201
	18 32 26	議 席 *giseki* seat (in parliament)	292
		主 席 *shuseki* top seat, head, chief	155
	席	席 上 *sekijō* (at) the meeting; (on) the occasion	32

	380	*BYŌ, [HEI], ya(mu)* – fall ill, suffer from **yamai** – illness	
病	5i5.3	病 気 *byōki* sickness, disease	134
	疒 一 冂	重 病 *jūbyō* serious illness	227
	60 14 20	急 病 *kyūbyō* sudden illness	303
		性 病 *seibyō* venereal disease	98
	病	病 人 *byōnin* sick person	1

	381	*OKU* – remember, think	
憶	4k13.5	記 憶 *kioku* memory, recollection	371
	忄 立 日	憶 病 *okubyō* cowardice, timidity	380
	51 54 43		
	憶 憶		

	382	*OKU* – 100 million	
億	2a13.6	一 億 *ichioku* 100 million	2
	亻 立 日	億 万 長 者 *okuman chōja* multimillionaire	16, 95, 164
	3 54 43	数 億 年 *sūokunen* hundreds of millions of years	225, 45
	億 億		

	383	*KETSU, ka(ku)* – lack *ka(keru)* – be lacking	
欠	4j0.1	欠 点 *ketten* defect, flaw	169
	欠	出 欠 *shukketsu* attendance (and/or absence)	53
	49	欠 席 *kesseki* absence, nonattendance	379
		欠 員 *ketsuin* vacant position, opening	163
	欠 缺	欠 損 *kesson* deficit, loss	350

	384	*JI, SHI, tsugi* – next *tsu(gu)* – come/rank next	
次	2b4.1	次 官 *jikan* vice-minister	326
	冫 欠	次 男 *jinan* second-oldest son	101
	5 49	二 次 *niji* second, secondary	3
		目 次 *mokuji* table of contents	55
	次	相 次 ぐ *aitsugu* follow/happen one after another	146

	385	*SHOKU* – employment, job, occupation, office	
職	6e12.1	職 業 *shokugyō* occupation, profession	279
	耳 日 戈	職 場 *shokuba* place of work, jobsite	154
	65 43 52	職 員 *shokuin* personnel, staff, staff member	163
		現 職 *genshoku* one's present post	298
	職 耺	無 職 *mushoku* unemployed	93

能	**386** 4b6.15 田 月 厶 ⼘ 42 17 13 能	**NŌ** – ability, function; Noh play

能 力 *nōryoku* capacity, talent — 100
本 能 *honnō* instinct — 25
能 筆 *nōhitsu* calligraphy, skilled penmanship — 130
能 楽 *nōgaku* Noh play — 358
能 面 *nōmen* Noh mask — 274

態	**387** 4k10.14 目 心 月 厶 51 42 17 態	**TAI** – condition, appearance

態 度 *taido* attitude — 377
生 態 *seitai* mode of life, ecology — 44
変 態 *hentai* metamorphosis; abnormality — 257
事 態 *jitai* situation, state of affairs — 80
実 態 *jittai* actual conditions/situation — 203

可	**388** 3d2.12 日 口 一 24 14 可	**KA** – good; possible; approval

可 能 (性) *kanō(sei)* possibility — 386, 98
不 可 能 *fukanō* impossible — 94, 386
不 可 欠 *fukaketsu* indispensable, essential — 94, 383
不 可 分 *fukabun* indivisible — 94, 38
可 決 *kaketsu* approval (of a proposed law) — 356

河	**389** 3a5.30 田 氵 口 一 21 24 14 河	**KA, kawa** – river

河 川 *kasen* rivers — 33
河 口 *kakō, kawaguchi* mouth of a river — 54
大 河 *taiga, ōkawa* large river — 26
銀 河 *ginga* the Milky Way — 313
河 原 *kawara* dry riverbed — 136

何	**390** 2a5.21 田 亻 口 一 3 24 14 何	**KA, nani, [nan]** – what, which, how many

何 事 *nanigoto* what, whatever — 80
何 曜 日 *nan'yōbi* what day of the week — 19, 5
何 日 *nannichi* how many days; what day of the month — 5
何 時 *nanji* what time — 42
何 時 間 *nanjikan* how many hours — 42, 43

荷	**391** 3k7.10 田 艹 口 亻 32 24 3 荷	**KA, ni** – load, cargo, baggage

在 荷 *zaika* stock, inventory — 268
入 荷 *nyūka* fresh supply/arrival of goods — 52
出 荷 *shukka* shipment, shipping — 53
(手)荷 物 *(te)nimotsu* (hand) baggage, luggage — 57, 79
重 荷 *omoni* heavy burden — 227

歌	**392** 4j10.2 田 欠 口 一 49 24 14 歌 詞	**KA, uta** – poem, song *uta(u)* – sing

歌 手 *kashu* singer — 57
国 歌 *kokka* national anthem — 40
和 歌 *waka* 31-syllable Japanese poem — 124
短 歌 *tanka* (synonym for *waka*) — 215
流 行 歌 *ryūkōka* popular song — 247, 68

予	393 0a4.12 ☐ 亠 一 丨 14 1 2 予 豫	**YO** – previously, in advance

予 約 *yoyaku* subscription, reservation, booking — 211
予 定 *yotei* plan; expectation — 355
予 想 *yosō* expectation, supposition — 147
予 知 *yochi* foresee, predict — 214
予 言 *yogen* prophecy, prediction — 66

預	394 9a4.5 ☐ 頁 亠 一 77 14 1 預	**YO, azu(keru)** – entrust for safekeeping **azu(karu)** – receive for safekeeping

預 金 *yokin* deposit, bank account — 23
預 か り 所 *azukarisho/jo* depository, warehouse — 153
手荷物一時預かり(所) *tenimotsu ichiji azukari(sho/jo)* (place for) temporary handbaggage storage — 57, 391, 79, 2, 42, 153

形	395 3j4.1 ☐ 彡 卅 一 31 32 1 形	**KEI, GYŌ, katachi, kata** – form, shape

円 形 *enkei* round/circular shape — 13
正 方 形 *seihōkei* square — 275, 70
無 形 *mukei* formless, immaterial, intangible — 93
人 形 *ningyō* doll, puppet — 1
手 形 *tegata* (bank) bill, note, draft — 57

開	396 8e4.6 ☐ 門 卅 一 76 32 1 開	**KAI** – opening, development **a(ku)** – (intr.) open **a(keru)** – (tr.) open **hira(keru)** – become developed **hira(ku)** – (itr./tr.) open

公 開 *kōkai* open to the public — 126
開 会 *kaikai* opening of a meeting — 158
未 開 *mikai* uncivilized, backward, savage — 306
開 発 *kaihatsu* development — 96

閉	397 8e3.3 ☐ 門 十 丨 76 12 2 閉 閉	**HEI, shi(meru), to(jiru), to(zasu)** – close, shut **shi(maru)** – become closed

開 閉 *kaihei* opening and closing — 396
閉 会 *heikai* closing, adjournment — 158
閉 店 *heiten* store closing — 168
閉 口 *heikō* be dumbfounded — 54

関	398 8e6.7 ☐ 門 大 儿 76 34 16 関 關	**KAN, seki** – barrier

関 門 *kanmon* gateway, barrier — 161
関 心 *kanshin* interest — 97
関 東 *Kantō* (region including Tōkyō) — 71
関 西 *Kansai* (region including Ōsaka and Kyōto) — 72
関 所 *sekisho* barrier station, checkpoint — 153

税	399 5d7.4 ☐ 禾 口 儿 56 24 16 税	**ZEI** – tax

税 金 *zeikin* tax — 23
所 得 税 *shotokuzei* income tax — 153, 374
関 税 *kanzei* customs, duty, tariff — 398
税 関 *zeikan* customs, customshouse — 398
無 税 *muzei* tax-free, duty-free — 93

説	**400**	***SETSU*** – opinion, theory ***ZEI, to(ku)*** – explain; persuade	
	7a7.12	説明 *setsumei* explanation	18
	言 口 儿	社説 *shasetsu* an editorial	308
	67 24 16	小説 *shōsetsu* novel, story	27
		演説 *enzetsu* a speech	344
	説	説教 *sekkyō* sermon	245

美	**401**	***BI, utsuku(shii)*** – beautiful	
	2o7.4	美術館 *bijutsukan* art museum/gallery	187, 327
	ソ 王 大	美学 *bigaku* esthetics	109
	16 46 34	美人 *bijin* beautiful woman	1
		美化 *bika* beautification	254
	美	美点 *biten* beauty, merit, good point	169

養	**402**	***YŌ, yashina(u)*** – rear; adopt; support; recuperate	
	2o13.1	養育 *yōiku* upbringing, nurture	246
	ソ 食 王	養成 *yōsei* training, cultivation	261
	16 73 46	教養 *kyōyō* culture, education	245
		養子 *yōshi* adopted child	103
	養	休養 *kyūyō* rest, recreation; recuperation	60

様	**403**	***YŌ*** – way, manner; similarity; condition ***sama*** – condition; Mr.,	
	4a10.25	様子 *yōsu* situation, aspect, appearance ⌐Mrs., Miss	103
	木 王 儿	同様 *dōyō* same	198
	41 46 16	多様 *tayō* diversity, variety	229
		神様 *kamisama* God	310
	様 様	田中明様 *Tanaka Akira sama* Mr. Akira Tanaka	35, 28, 18

第	**404**	***DAI*** – (prefix for ordinals); degree	
	6f5.5	第一 *dai-ichi* No. 1; first, best, main	2
	竹 弓 丨	第三者 *daisansha* third person/party	4, 164
	66 28 2	次第 *shidai* sequence; circumstances; as soon as	384
		毎月第二土曜日 *maitsuki dai-ni doyōbi* second	
	第 才	Saturday of every month	116, 17, 3, 24, 19, 5

弟	**405**	***TEI, [DAI], [DE], otōto*** – younger brother	
	2o5.1	義弟 *gitei* younger brother-in-law	291
	ソ 弓 丨	子弟 *shitei* sons, children	103
	16 28 2	弟子 *deshi* pupil, apprentice, disciple	103
		門弟 *montei* pupil, follower	161
	弟	弟分 *otōtobun* like a younger brother	38

兄	**406**	***KEI, [KYŌ], ani*** – elder brother	
	3d2.9	兄弟 *kyōdai* brothers, brothers and sisters	405
	口 儿	父兄 *fukei* parents and brothers; guardians	113
	24 16	義兄 *gikei* elder brother-in-law	291
		実兄 *jikkei* one's brother by blood	203
	兄	兄さん *niisan* elder brother	

姉	**407** 3e5.8 ⊞ 女 巾 一 25 26 11 姉	**SHI, ane** – elder sister 義姉 *gishi* elder sister-in-law　　291 姉さん *nēsan* elder sister; young lady
妹	**408** 3e5.4 ⊡ 女 朩 一 25 41 1 妹	**MAI, imōto** – younger sister 姉妹 *shimai* sisters　　407 姉妹都市 *shimai toshi* sister cities　　407, 188, 181 弟妹 *teimai* younger brothers and sisters　　405 義妹 *gimai* younger sister-in-law　　291
師	**409** 3f7.2 ⊞ 巾 尸 冂 26 40 20 師	**SHI** – teacher; army 教師 *kyōshi* teacher, instructor　　245 医師 *ishi* physician　　220 法師 *hōshi* Buddhist priest　　123 山師 *yamashi* speculator; adventurer; charlatan　　34 師弟 *shitei* master and pupil　　405
童	**410** 5b7.3 ⊟ 立 日 土 54 43 22 童	**DŌ, warabe** – child 学童 *gakudō* schoolchild　　109 童話 *dōwa* nursery story, fairy tale　　238 童顔 *dōgan* childlike/boyish face　　277 童心 *dōshin* child's mind/feelings　　97 神童 *shindō* child prodigy　　310
量	**411** 4c8.9 ⊟ 日 土 一 43 22 1 量	**RYŌ** – quantity　**haka(ru)** – (tr.) measure, weigh 大/小量 *tai/shōryō* large/small quantity　　26, 27 雨量 *uryō* (amount of) rainfall　　30 大量生産 *tairyō seisan* mass production　　26, 44, 278 分量 *bunryō* quantity, amount; dosage　　38 重量 *jūryō* weight　　227
商	**412** 2j9.7 ⊟ 亠 口 儿 11 24 16 商	**SHŌ, akina(u)** – deal (in), trade 商人 *shōnin* merchant, dealer　　1 商品 *shōhin* goods, merchandise　　230 商業 *shōgyō* commerce, business　　279 商売 *shōbai* trade, business; one's trade　　239 商工 *shōkō* commerce and industry　　139
過	**413** 2q9.18 ⊡ 辶 口 冂 19 24 20 過	**KA, su(giru)** – pass, exceed; too much　**su(gosu)** – spend (time) **ayama(tsu)** – err　**ayama(chi)** – error 過度 *kado* excessive, too much　　377 通過 *tsūka* passage, transit　　150 過半数 *kahansū* majority, more than half　　88, 225 食べ過ぎる *tabesugiru* eat too much, overeat　　322

131

去	**414** 3b2.2 田 ± ム 22 17 去	**KYO, KO, sa(ru)** – leave, move away; pass, elapse	
		去年 *kyonen* last year	45
		死去 *shikyo* death	85
		去来 *kyorai* coming and going	69
		過去 *kako* past	413
		立ち去る *tachisaru* leave, go away	121

適	**415** 2q11.3 匚 辶 口 宀 19 24 11 適	**TEKI** – fit, be suitable	
		適当 *tekitō* suitable, appropriate	77
		適度 *tekido* to a proper degree, moderate	377
		適切 *tekisetsu* pertinent, appropriate	39
		適用 *tekiyō* application (of a rule)	107
		適合 *tekigō* conformity, compatibility	159

敵	**416** 4i11.2 田 攵 口 宀 49 24 11 敵	**TEKI, kataki** – enemy, opponent, competitor	
		宿敵 *shukuteki* old/hereditary enemy	179
		強敵 *kyōteki* powerful foe, formidable rival	217
		敵意 *tekii* enmity, hostility	132
		敵対 *tekitai* hostility, antagonism	365
		不敵 *futeki* fearless, daring	94

程	**417** 5d7.2 田 禾 王 口 56 46 24 程	**TEI, hodo** – degree, extent	
		程度 *teido* degree, extent, grade	377
		過程 *katei* a process	413
		工程 *kōtei* progress of the work; manufacturing process	139
		日程 *nittei* schedule for the day	5
		音程 *ontei* musical interval, step	347

組	**418** 6a5.7 田 糸 月 一 61 42 1 組	**SO, kumi** – group, crew, class, gang **ku(mu)** – put together	
		組成 *sosei* composition, makeup	261
		番組 *bangumi* (TV) program	185
		労働組合 *rōdō kumiai* labor union	233, 232, 159
		組み立て *kumitate* construction; assembling	121
		組み合わせる *kumiawaseru* combine, fit together	159

要	**419** 3e6.11 田 女 口 宀 25 24 14 要 要	**YŌ** – main point, necessity **i(ru)** – need, be necessary	
		重要 *jūyō* important	227
		主要 *shuyō* principal, major	155
		要点 *yōten* main point, gist	169
		要素 *yōso* element, factor	271
		要約 *yōyaku* summary	211

具	**420** 5c3.1 田 目 儿 一 55 16 1 具 具	**GU** – tool	
		具体的 *gutaiteki* concrete, specific	61, 210
		道具 *dōgu* tool, implement	149
		家具 *kagu* furniture	165
		金具 *kanagu* metal fitting	23
		不具 *fugu* deformity, crippled	94

421

KA, atai – price, value

2a6.3 □

イ 口 一
3 24 14

価 價

物価	bukka	prices (of commodities)	79
米価	beika	price of rice	224
単価	tanka	unit price	300
定価	teika	fixed/list price	355
現金正価	genkin seika	cash price	298, 23, 275

422

SHIN – truth, genuineness, reality   ma – true, pure, exactly

2k8.1 目

十 目 儿
12 55 16

真 眞

真実	shinjitsu	the truth, a fact	203
真理	shinri	truth	143
真相	shinsō	the truth, the facts	146
真空	shinkū	vacuum	140
真っ暗	makkura	pitch-dark	348

423

CHOKU, JIKI – honest, frank, direct   nao(su) – fix, correct
nao(ru) – be fixed, corrected   tada(chi ni) – immediately

2k6.2 目

十 目 丨
12 55 2

直

直線	chokusen	straight line	299
直前/後	chokuzen/go	immediately before/after	47, 48
正直	shōjiki	honest, upright	275
書き直す	kakinaosu	write over again, rewrite	131

424

SHOKU, u(eru) – plant   u(waru) – be planted

4a8.32 田

木 相 十
41 55 12

植

植物	shokubutsu	a plant	79
動植物	dōshokubutsu	animals and plants	231, 79
植民地	shokuminchi	colony	177, 118
植木	ueki	garden/potted plant	22
田植え	taue	rice planting	35

425

CHI, ne, atai – value, price

2a8.30 □

イ 目 十
3 55 12

値

価値	kachi	value	421
値うち	neuchi	value; public estimation	
値段	nedan	price	362
値上げ	neage	price increase	32
値切る	negiru	haggle over the price, bargain	39

426

CHI, o(ku) – put, set; leave behind, leave as is

5g8.8 目

罒 十 丨
55 12 2

置

位置	ichi	position, location	122
置き物	okimono	ornament; figurehead	79
物置き	monooki	storeroom, shed	79
前置き	maeoki	introductory remarks, preface	47
一日置き	ichinichioki	every other day	2, 5

427

SEI – system; regulations

2f6.1 □

刂 牛 冂
16 47 20

制

制度	seido	system	377
税制	zeisei	system of taxation	399
新制	shinsei	new order, reorganization	174
強制	kyōsei	compulsion, force	217
管制	kansei	control	328

製	**428** 5e8.9 衤 牛 冂 57 47 20 製	**SEI** – produce, manufacture, make	
		製作 *seisaku* a work, production	360
		製品 *seihin* product	230
		製鉄 *seitetsu* iron manufacturing	312
		木製 *mokusei* wooden, made of wood	22
		日本製 *nihonsei* Japanese-made, Made in Japan	5, 25

走	**429** 3b4.9 土 ⼧ 亻 22 13 3 走 赱	**SŌ, hashi(ru)** – run	
		走路 *sōro* (race) track, course	151
		走行時間 *sōkō jikan* travel time	68, 42, 43
		走り回る *hashirimawaru* run around	90
		走り書き *hashirigaki* flowing/hasty handwriting	131
		口走る *kuchibashiru* babble, blurt out	54

徒	**430** 3i7.1 彳 土 ⼧ 29 22 13 徒	**TO** – on foot; companions; vain, useless	
		生徒 *seito* pupil, student	44
		教徒 *kyōto* believer, adherent	245
		使徒 *shito* apostle	331
		徒手 *toshu* empty-handed; penniless	57
		徒労 *torō* vain effort	233

歩	**431** 3n5.3 ⺌ ⼧ ⼇ 35 13 11 歩 歩	**HO, BU, [FU], aru(ku), ayu(mu)** – walk	
		歩道 *hodō* footpath, sidewalk	149
		歩行者 *hokōsha* pedestrian	68, 164
		一歩 *ippo* a step	2
		歩調 *hochō* pace, step	342
		歩合 *buai* rate, percentage; commission	159

渉	**432** 3a8.20 氵 小 ⼧ 21 35 13 渉 涉	**SHŌ** – cross over; have to do with	
		交渉 *kōshō* negotiations	114

転	**433** 7c4.3 車 二 厶 69 4 17 転 轉	**TEN, koro(bu), koro(garu), koro(geru)** – roll over, fall down **koro(gasu)** – roll, knock down	
		自転車 *jitensha* bicycle	62, 133
		回転 *kaiten* rotation, revolution	90
		空転 *kūten* idling (of an engine)	140
		転任 *tennin* transfer of assignments/personnel	334

伝	**434** 2a4.14 亻 二 厶 3 4 17 伝 傳	**DEN, tsuta(eru)** – transmit, impart **tsuta(waru)** – be transmitted, imparted **tsuta(u)** – go along	
		伝記 *denki* biography	371
		伝説 *densetsu* legend, folklore	400
		伝道 *dendō* evangelism, missionary work	149
		手伝い *tetsudai* help, helper	57

芸	**435** 3k4.12 目 卄 二 ム 32 4 17 芸 藝	**GEI** – art, craft

芸者	*geisha* geisha	164
芸術	*geijutsu* art	187
文芸	*bungei* literary art, literature	111
演芸	*engei* performance, entertainment	344
民芸	*mingei* folkcraft	177

集	**436** 8c4.2 日 隹 木 74 41 集	**SHŪ, atsu(maru/meru)** – (intr./tr.) gather **tsudo(u)** – (intr.) gather

集金	*shūkin* bill collecting	23
集中	*shūchū* concentrating	28
全集	*zenshū* the complete works	89
特集	*tokushū* special edition	282
万葉集	*Man'yōshū* (Japan's oldest anthology of ⌐poems)	16, 253

進	**437** 2q8.1 □ 辶 隹 19 74 進	**SHIN, susu(mu)** – advance, progress **susu(meru)** – advance, ⌐promote

進歩	*shinpo* progress, improvement	431
進行	*shinkō* progress, onward movement	68
進学	*shingaku* entrance to a higher school	109
前進	*zenshin* advance, forward movement	47
先進国	*senshinkoku* developed/advanced country	50, 40

軍	**438** 2i7.1 目 冖 車 20 69 軍	**GUN** – army, troops; war

軍人	*gunjin* soldier, military man	1
軍事	*gunji* military affairs, military	80
海軍	*kaigun* navy	117
敵軍	*tekigun* enemy army/troops	416
軍国主義	*gunkoku shugi* militarism	40, 155, 291

運	**439** 2q9.10 □ 辶 車 冂 19 69 20 運	**UN** – fate, luck **hako(bu)** – carry, transport

運転手	*untenshu* driver, chauffeur	433, 57
(労働)運動	*(rōdō) undō* (labor) movement	233, 232, 231
運動不足	*undōbusoku* lack of exercise	231, 94, 58
運河	*unga* canal	389
不運	*fuun* misfortune	94

連	**440** 2q7.2 □ 辶 車 19 69 連	**REN** – group; accompaniment **tsu(reru)** – take (someone) **tsura(naru)** – stand in a row **tsura(neru)** – link, put in a row

連続	*renzoku* series, continuity	243
連合	*rengō* combination, league, coalition	159
国連	*Kokuren* UN, United Nations	40
家族連れ	*kazokuzure* with the family	165, 221

送	**441** 2q6.9 □ 辶 ハ 儿 19 34 16 送	**SŌ, oku(ru)** – send

運送	*unsō* transport, shipment	439
回送	*kaisō* forwarding	90
送金	*sōkin* remittance	23
送別会	*sōbetsukai* going-away/farewell party	267, 158
見送る	*miokuru* see (someone) off; escort	63

	442	**HEN, kae(su)** – (tr.) return **kae(ru)** – (itr.) return
返	2q4.5 □	返事 *henji* reply ⌈postcard 80
	辶 厂 又	返信用葉書 *henshin'yō hagaki* reply 157, 107, 253, 131
	19 18 9	見返す *mikaesu* look back; triumph over (an old enemy) 63
		読み返す *yomikaesu* reread 244
	返	送り返す *okurikaesu* send back 441

	443	**HAN, saka** – slope, hill
坂	3b4.7 □	急な坂 *kyū na saka* steep slope/hill 303
	土 厂 又	坂道 *sakamichi* road on a slope 149
	22 18 9	上り坂 *noborizaka* ascend 32
		下り坂 *kudarizaka* descent; decline 31
	坂	赤坂 *Akasaka* (area of Tōkyō) 207

	444	**GYAKU** – reverse, inverse, opposite; treason **saka** – reverse,
逆	2q6.8 □	inverse **saka(rau)** – be contrary (to)
	辶 儿 一	逆転 *gyakuten* reversal 433
	19 16 14	逆説 *gyakusetsu* paradox 400
		反逆 *hangyaku* treason 324
	逆	逆立つ *sakadatsu* stand on end 121

	445	**KIN, chika(i)** – near, close
近	2q4.3 □	近所 *kinjo* vicinity, neighborhood 153
	辶 斤	付近 *fukin* vicinity, environs 192
	19 50	最近 *saikin* recent; most recent, latest 263
		近代 *kindai* modern times, modern 256
	近	近道 *chikamichi* shortcut, shorter way 149

	446	**EN, [ON], tō(i)** – far, distant
遠	2q10.4 □	遠方 *enpō* great distance, (in) the distance 70
	辶 衤 土	遠近法 *enkinhō* (law of) perspective 445, 123
	19 57 22	遠足 *ensoku* excursion, outing 58
		遠心力 *enshinryoku* centrifugal force 97, 100
	遠	遠回し *tōmawashi* indirect, roundabout 90

	447	**EN, sono** – garden
園	3s10.1 回	公園 *kōen* (public) park 126
	口 衤 土	動物園 *dōbutsuen* zoo 231, 79
	24 57 22	植物園 *shokubutsuen* botanical garden 424, 79
		学園 *gakuen* educational institution, academy 109
	園 薗	楽園 *rakuen* paradise 358

	448	**TATSU** – reach, arrive at
達	2q9.8 □	上達 *jōtatsu* progress; proficiency 32
	辶 立 土	発達 *hattatsu* development 96
	19 54 12	達成 *tassei* achieve, attain 261
		達人 *tatsujin* expert, master 1
	達 達	友達 *tomodachi* friend 264

449 4b8.11 田 月 卄 二 42 32 4 期 萛	**KI, [GO]** – time, period, term	
	期 間　*kikan*　period of time, term	43
	定 期　*teiki*　fixed period	355
	過 渡 期　*katoki*　transition period	413, 378
	学 期　*gakki*　semester, trimester, school term	109
	短 期 大 学　*tanki daigaku*　junior college	215, 26, 109

450 3b8.12 目 土 卄 二 22 32 4 基	**KI, moto, motoi** – basis, foundation, origin	
	基 本　*kihon*　basics, fundamentals; standard	25
	基 金　*kikin*　fund, endowment	23
	基 地　*kichi*　(military) base	118
	基 石　*kiseki*　foundation stone, cornerstone	78
	基 調　*kichō*　keynote	342

451 3c6.8 田 扌 土 寸 23 22 37 持	**JI, mo(tsu)** – have, possess; hold, maintain	
	支 持　*shiji*　support	318
	持 続　*jizoku*　continuance, maintenance	243
	持 ち 主　*mochinushi*　owner, possessor	155
	金 持 ち　*kanemochi*　rich person	23
	気 持 ち　*kimochi*　mood, feeling	134

452 3i6.4 田 彳 土 寸 29 22 37 待	**TAI, ma(tsu)** – wait for	
	期 待　*kitai*　expectation, anticipation	449
	特 待　*tokutai*　special treatment, distinction	282
	待 ち 合 い 室　*machiaishitsu*　waiting room	159, 166
	待 ち 合 わ せ る　*machiawaseru*　wait for (as previously	159
	待 ち ぼ う け　*machibōke*　getting stood up 　⌐arranged)	

453 2a2.9 ⋯ 亻 儿 3 16 介	**KAI** – shellfish (cf. No. 240); be in between, mediate	
	介 入　*kainyū*　intervention	52
	介 在　*kaizai*　lie/stand/come between	268
	魚 介　*gyokai*　fish and shellfish, marine products	290
	一 介 の　*ikkai no*　mere, only	2

454 5f4.7 目 田 亻 儿 58 3 16 界 畍	**KAI** – world	
	世 界　*sekai*　world	252
	世 界 史　*sekai shi*　world history	252, 332
	学 界　*gakkai*　academic world	109
	外 界　*gaikai*　external world, outside	83
	下 界　*gekai*　this world, the earth below	31

455 3c5.22 田 扌 口 力 23 24 8 招	**SHŌ, mane(ku)** – beckon to, invite, cause	
	招 待　*shōtai*　invitation	452
	手 招 き　*temaneki*　beckoning	57

	456	**SHŌ** – introduction
紹	6a5.10 ⊞ 糸 口 力 61 24 8 紹	紹介 *shōkai* introduction, presentation .... 453 自己紹介 *jiko shōkai* introduce oneself ... 62, 370, 453

	457	**KAN** – coldest season; coldness **samu(i)** – cold
寒	3m9.3 目 宀 艹 二 33 32 4 寒 寒	寒気 *kanki* the cold .... 134 寒中 *kanchū* the cold season .... 28 極寒 *gokkan* severe cold .... 336 寒村 *kanson* poor/lonely village .... 191 寒空 *samuzora* wintry sky, cold weather 140

	458	**SHŪ, o(waru)** – come to an end **o(eru)** – bring to an end
終	6a5.9 ⊞ 糸 夂 丨 61 49 2 終	最終 *saishū* last .... 263 終戦 *shūsen* end of the war .... 301 終点 *shūten* end of the line, last stop, terminus . 169 終身 *shūshin* for life, lifelong .... 59 終日 *shūjitsu* all day long 5

	459	**TŌ, fuyu** – winter
冬	4i2.1 目 夂 丨 49 2 冬	立冬 *rittō* first day of winter .... 121 真冬 *mafuyu* midwinter, dead of winter .... 422 冬向き *fuyumuki* for winter .... 199 冬物 *fuyumono* winter clothing .... 79 冬空 *fuyuzora* winter sky 140

	460	**SHUN, haru** – spring
春	4c5.13 ▭ 日 大 二 43 34 4 春	春分 (の日) *shunbun (no hi)* vernal equinox .... 38, 5 立春 *risshun* beginning of spring .... 121 青春 *seishun* springtime of life, youth ...... 208 売春 *baishun* prostitution .... 239 春画 *shunga* obscene picture, pornography 343

	461	**KA, [GE], natsu** – summer
夏	4i7.5 目 夂 日 一 49 55 14 夏	夏期 *kaki* the summer period .... 449 立夏 *rikka* beginning of summer .... 121 真夏 *manatsu* midsummer, height of summer .... 422 夏物 *natsumono* summer clothing .... 79 夏休み *natsuyasumi* summer vacation 60

	462	**SHŪ, aki** – fall, autumn
秋	5d4.1 ▯ 禾 火 56 44 秋 穐	春夏秋冬 *shunkashūtō* all the year round . 460, 461, 459 春秋 *shunjū* spring and autumn; years, age ... 460 秋分 (の日) *shūbun (no hi)* autumnal equinox .. 38, 5 秋気 *shūki* the autumn air .... 134 秋風 *akikaze* autumn breeze 29

即	**463** 2e5.1 ▯ 卩 食 7 73 即 即	**SOKU** – immediately; conform (to); namely, i.e.	
		即時 *sokuji* instantly, immediately, on the spot	42
		即日 *sokujitsu* on the same day	5
		即金 *sokkin* cash; payment in cash	23
		即席 *sokuseki* extemporaneous, impromptu	379
		即興 *sokkyō* improvised, ad-lib	368

節	**464** 6f7.3 ▦ ⺮ 食 卩 66 73 7 節 節	**SETSU, [SECHI]** – season; occasion; section, paragraph; verse **fushi** – joint, knuckle; melody; point	
		時節 *jisetsu* time of the year; the times	42
		調節 *chōsetsu* adjustment, regulation	342
		使節 *shisetsu* envoy, mission	331
		節約 *setsuyaku* economizing, thrift	211

季	**465** 5d2.3 ▤ 禾 子 56 6 季	**KI** – season	
		季節 *kisetsu* season, time of the year	464
		四季 *shiki* the 4 seasons	6
		季節風 *kisetsufū* seasonal wind, monsoon	464, 29
		季節外れ *kisetsuhazure* out of season	464, 83
		季語 *kigo* word indicating the season (in haiku)	67

委	**466** 5d3.2 ▤ 禾 女 56 25 委	**I** – entrust	
		委任 *inin* trust, mandate, authorization	334
		委員 *iin* committee member	163
		委員会 *iinkai* committee	163, 158

湖	**467** 3a9.8 ▥ 氵月口 21 42 24 湖	**KO, mizuumi** – lake	
		湖水 *kosui* lake	21
		火口湖 *kakōko* crater lake	20, 54
		湖面 *komen* surface of a lake	274
		山中湖 *Yamanaka-ko* (lake near Mt. Fuji)	34, 28
		十和田湖 *Towada-ko* (lake in Tōhoku)	12, 124, 35

潮	**468** 3a12.1 ▥ 氵日月 21 43 42 潮	**CHŌ, shio** – tide; salt water; opportunity	
		満潮 *manchō* high tide	201
		潮流 *chōryū* tidal current; trend of the times	247
		風潮 *fūchō* tide; tendency, trend	29
		潮時 *shiodoki* favorable tide; opportunity	42
		黒潮 *Kuroshio* Japan Current	206

朝	**469** 4b8.12 ▤ 月日 十 42 43 12 朝 朝	**CHŌ** – morning; dynasty **asa** – morning	
		朝食 *chōshoku* breakfast	322
		平安朝 *Heianchō* Heian period (794 – 1185)	202, 105
		朝日 *asahi* morning/rising sun	5
		毎朝 *maiasa* every morning	116
		今朝 *kesa, konchō* this morning	51

昼	470	***CHŪ, hiru*** – daytime, noon	
	4c5.15 ☐	昼食 *chūshoku* lunch	322
	日 尸 一	白昼に *hakuchū ni* in broad daylight	205
	43 40 1	昼飯 *hirumeshi* lunch	325
		昼間 *hiruma* daytime	43
	昼 畫	昼休み *hiruyasumi* lunch break, noon recess	60

夜	471	***YA, yoru, yo*** – night	
	2j6.1 ☐	昼夜 *chūya* day and night	470
	亠 夕 イ	今夜 *kon'ya* tonight	51
	11 30 3	夜行 *yakō* traveling by night; night train	68
		夜学 *yagaku* evening class	109
	夜	夜明け *yoake* dawn, daybreak	18

液	472	***EKI*** – liquid, fluid	
	3a8.29 ☐	液体 *ekitai* liquid, fluid	61
	氵 夕 亠	液化 *ekika* liquefaction	254
	21 30 11	だ液 *daeki* saliva	
	液		

角	473	***KAKU*** – angle, corner ***kado*** – corner, angle ***tsuno*** – horn, antlers	
	2n5.1 ☐	角度 *kakudo* degrees of an angle, angle	377
	𠂉 月 丨	三角(形) *sankaku(kei)* triangle	4, 395
	15 42 2	直角 *chokkaku* right angle	423
	角	街角 *machikado* street corner	186

解	474	***KAI, GE, to(ku)*** – untie; solve ***to(keru)*** – come loose; be solved	
	4g9.1 ☐	理解 *rikai* understanding ⌊***to(kasu)*** – comb	143
	牛 月 𠂉	解説 *kaisetsu* explanation, commentary	400
	47 42 15	解決 *kaiketsu* solution, settlement	356
		和解 *wakai* compromise	124
	解 解	解任 *kainin* dismissal, release	334

菊	475	***KIKU*** – chrysanthemum	
	3k8.30 ☐	白菊 *shiragiku* white chrysanthemum	205
	艹 米 勹	菊の花 *kiku no hana* chrysanthemum	255
	32 62 15	菊作り *kikuzukuri* chrysanthemum growing	360
		菊人形 *kikuningyō* chrysanthemum doll	1, 395
	菊	菊地 *Kikuchi* (surname)	118

奥	476	***Ō, oku*** – interior	
	6b6.9 ☐	奥義 *ōgi, okugi* secrets, hidden mysteries	291
	米 六 冂	奥行き *okuyuki* depth (vs. height and width)	68
	62 34 20	山奥 *yamaoku* deep in the mountains	34
		奥付け *okuzuke* colophon	192
	奥 奥	奥さん *okusan* wife; ma'am	

477 止 — 2m2.2 · 止 · 13 11

SHI, to(maru) – come to a stop **to(meru)** – bring to a stop

終止	*shūshi*	termination	458
休止	*kyūshi*	pause, suspension	60
通行止め	*tsūkōdome*	Road Closed, No Thoroughfare	150, 68
口止め料	*kuchidomeryō*	hush money	54, 319
足止め	*ashidome*	keep indoors, confinement	58

478 歯 — 6b6.11 · 歯 歯 · 62 13 11

SHI, ha – tooth

門/犬歯	*mon/kenshi*	incisor/canine	161, 280
義歯	*gishi*	false teeth, dentures	291
歯科医	*shikai*	dentist	320, 220
歯医者	*haisha*	dentist	220, 164
歯車	*haguruma*	toothed wheel, gear	133

479 歳 — 4n9.5 · 歳 · 52 35 13

SAI – year, years old **[SEI]** – year

満四歳	*man'yonsai*	4 (full) years old	201, 6
二十歳	*hatachi*	20 years old	3, 12
万歳	*banzai*	Hurrah! Long live … !	16
歳月	*saigetsu*	time, years	17
歳入歳出	*sainyū-saishutsu*	yearly revenue and expenditure	52, 53

480 歴 — 2p12.4 · 歴 歴 · 18 41 13

REKI – continuation, passing of time

歴史	*rekishi*	history	332
学歴	*gakureki*	school career, academic background	109
前歴	*zenreki*	one's personal history, background	47
歴任	*rekinin*	successive holding of various posts	334

481 企 — 2a4.17 · 企 · 3 13 11

KI, kuwada(teru) – plan, undertake, attempt

企業	*kigyō*	enterprise, undertaking	279
企画	*kikaku*	planning, plan	343
企図	*kito*	plan, project, scheme	339
中小企業	*chūshō kigyō*	small- and medium-size enterprises	28, 27, 279

482 禁 — 4e8.3 · 禁 · 45 41

KIN – prohibition

禁止	*kinshi*	prohibition	477
解禁	*kaikin*	lifting of a ban	474
禁制	*kinsei*	prohibition, ban	427
禁物	*kinmotsu*	forbidden things, taboo	79
発禁	*hakkin*	prohibition of sale	96

483 政 — 4i5.1 · 政 · 49 38 1

SEI, [SHŌ], matsurigoto – government, rule

政局	*seikyoku*	political situation	170
行政	*gyōsei*	administration	68
内政	*naisei*	domestic politics, internal affairs	84
市政	*shisei*	municipal government	181
家政	*kasei*	management of a household, housekeeping	165

証	**484** 7a5.5 ☐ 言 エ 一 67 38 1 証 證	**SHŌ** – proof, evidence, certificate

証明 *shōmei* proof, testimony, corroboration — 18
証人 *shōnin* witness — 1
証言 *shōgen* testimony — 66
反証 *hanshō* counterproof, counterevidence — 324
内証 *naishō, naishō* secret — 84

結	**485** 6a6.5 ☐ 糸 土 口 61 22 24 結	**KETSU, musu(bu)** – tie, bind; conclude (a contract); bear (fruit) **yu(waeru)** – tie **yu(u)** – do up (one's hair)

結論 *ketsuron* conclusion — 293
結成 *kessei* formation, organization — 261
結合 *ketsugō* union, combination — 159
終結 *shūketsu* conclusion, termination — 458

接	**486** 3c8.10 ☐ 扌 立 女 23 54 25 接	**SETSU** – touch, contact **tsu(gu)** – join together

直接 *chokusetsu* direct — 423
間接 *kansetsu* indirect — 43
面接 *mensetsu* interview — 274
接続 *setsuzoku* connecting, joining — 243
接待 *settai* reception, welcome; serving, offering — 452

果	**487** 0a8.8 … 日 木 43 41 果	**KA** – fruit; result **ha(tasu)** – carry out, complete **ha(teru)** – come to an end **ha(te)** – end, limit; result

結果 *kekka* result — 485
成果 *seika* result — 261
果実 *kajitsu* fruit — 203
果物 *kudamono* fruit — 79

課	**488** 7a8.2 ☐ 言 日 木 67 43 41 課	**KA** – lesson; section

第一課 *dai-ikka* Lesson 1 — 404, 2
課目 *kamoku* subject (in school) — 55
課程 *katei* course, curriculum — 417
課長 *kachō* section chief — 95
人事課 *jinjika* personnel section — 1, 80

保	**489** 2a7.11 ☐ 亻 木 口 3 41 24 保	**HO, tamo(tsu)** – keep, preserve, maintain

保証 *hoshō* guarantee, warranty — 484
保証人 *hoshōnin* guarantor, sponsor — 484, 1
保存 *hozon* preservation — 269
保育所 *hoikusho, hoikujo* daycare nursery — 246, 153
保養所 *hoyōsho, hoyōjo* sanatorium, rest home — 402, 153

守	**490** 3m3.2 ☐ 宀 寸 33 37 守	**SHU, [SU], mamo(ru)** – protect; obey, abide by **mori** – babysitter;

保守的 *hoshuteki* conservative ⌐(lighthouse) keeper — 489, 210
子守 *komori* baby-sitting; baby-sitter, nursemaid — 103
子守歌 *komoriuta* lullaby — 103, 392
見守る *mimamoru* keep watch over; stare at — 63
お守り *omamori* charm, amulet

団	**491**	**DAN, [TON]** – group
	3s3.3 回	団体 (旅行) *dantai (ryokō)* group (tour) 61, 222, 68
	口 寸	集団 *shūdan* group, mass 436
	24 37	団地 *danchi* public housing development/complex 118
		団結 *danketsu* unity, solidarity 485
	団 團	師団 *shidan* (army) division 409

台	**492**	**DAI, TAI** – stand, pedestal, platform, plateau
	3d2.11 日	台所 *daidokoro* kitchen 153
	口 厶	天文台 *tenmondai* observatory 141, 111
	24 17	高台 *takadai* high ground, a height 190
		台本 *daihon* script, screenplay, libretto 25
	台 臺	台風 *taifū* typhoon 29

治	**493**	**JI, CHI** – peace; government; healing *osa(meru)* – govern; suppress *osa(maru)* – be at peace, quelled *nao(ru/su)* – (intr./tr.) heal
	3a5.28 田	政治 *seiji* politics 483
	氵 口 厶	自治 *jichi* self-government, autonomy 62
	21 24 17	明治時代 *Meiji jidai* Meiji era (1868–1912) 18, 42, 256
	治	

始	**494**	**SHI, haji(maru)** – (intr.) start, begin **haji(meru)** – (tr.) start, begin
	3e5.9 田	始末 *shimatsu* circumstances; management, disposal 305
	女 口 厶	始終 *shijū* from first to last, all the while 458
	25 24 17	始発 *shihatsu* the first (train) departure 96
		開始 *kaishi* beginning, opening 396
	始	原始的 *genshiteki* primitive, original 136, 210

党	**495**	**TŌ** – party, faction
	3n7.2 目	政党 *seitō* political party 483
	⿱ 口 儿	野党 *yatō* party out of power, opposition 236
	35 24 16	党員/首 *tōin/shu* party member/leader 163, 148
		徒党 *totō* confederates, clique, conspiracy 430
	党 黨	社会党 *Shakaitō* Socialist Party 308, 158

堂	**496**	**DŌ** – temple, hall
	3n8.4 目	食堂 *shokudō* dinig hall, restaurant 322
	⿱ 口 土	能楽堂 *nōgakudō* Noh theater 386, 358
	35 24 22	公会堂 *kōkaidō* public hall, community center 126, 158
		本堂 *hondō* main temple 25
	堂	国会議事堂 *kokkai gijidō* Diet Building 40, 158, 292, 80

常	**497**	**JŌ, tsune** – normal, usual, continual **toko-** – ever-, always
	3n8.3 目	日常生活 *nichijō seikatsu* everyday life 5, 44, 237
	⿱ 口 巾	正常 *seijō* normal 275
	35 24 26	通常 *tsūjō* ordinary, usual ⌐(director) 150
		常務 *jōmu* regular business, routine duties, executive 235
	常	常任委員 *jōnin iin* member of a standing committee 334, 466, 163

非	**498** 0a8.1 … 二 儿 一 4 16 1 非	**HI** – mistake; (prefix) non-, un-

非常口 *hijōguchi* emergency exit — 497, 54
非常事態 *hijō jitai* state of emergency — 497, 80, 387
非公開 *hikōkai* not open to the public, private — 126, 396
非人間的 *hiningenteki* inhuman, impersonal — 1, 43, 210
非合法 *higōhō* illegal — 159, 123

掌	**499** 3n9.4 ⽬ ツ 口 扌 35 24 23 掌	**SHŌ** – palm of the hand; administer

合掌 *gasshō* clasp one's hands (in prayer) — 159
掌中 *shōchū* pocket (edition), in the hand — 28
掌中の玉 *shōchū no tama* apple of one's eye, one's jewel — 28, 295
車掌 *shashō* (train) conductor — 133

賞	**500** 3n12.1 ⽬ ツ 貝 口 35 68 24 賞	**SHŌ** – prize; praise

文学賞 *bungaku-shō* prize for literature — 111, 109
ノーベル賞 *Nōberu-shō* Nobel Prize
賞品 *shōhin* a prize — 230
賞金 *shōkin* cash prize, prize money — 23
受賞者 *jushōsha* prizewinner — 260, 164

束	**501** 0a7.8 … 木 口 41 24 束	**SOKU, taba** – bundle, sheaf

一束 *issoku, hitotaba* a bundle — 2
約束 *yakusoku* promise, appointment — 211
結束 *kessoku* unity, union, bond — 485
花束 *hanataba* bouquet — 255
束ねる *tabaneru* tie in a bundle; control

速	**502** 2q7.4 ⼞ 辶 木 口 19 41 24 速	**SOKU, haya(i), sumi(yaka)** – fast, quick, prompt **haya(meru)** – quicken, accelerate

速力, 速度 *sokuryoku, sokudo* speed, velocity — 100, 377
高速道路 *kōsoku dōro* expressway, freeway — 190, 149, 151
速達 *sokutatsu* special/express delivery — 448
速記 *sokki* shorthand, stenography — 371

整	**503** 4i12.3 ⽥ 攵 木 口 49 41 24 整	**SEI, totono(eru)** – put in order; prepare **totono(u)** – be put in order, prepared

整理 *seiri* arrangement, adjustment — 143
調整 *chōsei* adjustment, modulation — 342
整形外科 *seikei geka* plastic surgery — 395, 83, 320
整数 *seisū* integer — 225

府	**504** 3q5.2 ⼞ 广 寸 亻 18 37 3 府	**FU** – storehouse; government office; capital city

政府 *seifu* government — 483
無政府 *museifu* anarchy — 93, 483
首府 *shufu* the capital — 148
京都府 *Kyōto-fu* Kyōto Prefecture — 189, 188
都道府県 *to-dō-fu-ken* the Japanese prefectures — 188, 149, 194

符	**505** 6f5.12 ☐ ⺮ 寸 亻 66 37 3 符	**FU** – sign, mark; amulet

切 符 *kippu* ticket — 39
切 符 売 り 場 *kippu uriba* ticket office/window — 39, 239, 154
音 符 *onpu* diacritical mark; musical note — 347
符 号 *fugō* mark, symbol — 266
符 合 *fugō* coincidence, agreement, correspondence — 159

券	**506** 2f6.10 ☐ �v 火 二 16 44 4 券 券	**KEN** – ticket, certificate

入 場 券 *nyūjōken* admission ticket — 52, 154
旅 券 *ryoken* passport — 222
回 数 券 *kaisūken* coupon ticket — 90, 225
定 期 券 *teikiken* commutation ticket, (train) pass — 355, 449
(有 価) 証 券 *(yūka) shōken* securities — 265, 421, 484

巻	**507** 0a9.11 ☐ v 火 弓 16 44 28 巻 巻	**KAN, maki** – roll, reel; volume **ma(ku)** – roll, wind

上/中/下 巻 *jō/chū/gekan* first/middle/last volume — 32, 28, 31
第 一 巻 *dai-ikkan* Volume 1 — 404, 2
絵 巻 (物) *emaki(mono)* picture scroll — 345, 79
葉 巻 *hamaki* cigar — 253
取 り 巻 く *torimaku* surround, encircle — 65

圏	**508** 3s9.1 回 口 火 弓 24 44 28 圏 圏	**KEN** – circle, range, sphere

共 産 圏 *kyōsanken* the Communist bloc/countries — 196, 278
極 地 圏 *kyokuchiken* polar region — 336, 118
北/南 極 圏 *hok/nankyokuken* Arctic/Antarctic Circle — 73, 336, 74
首 都 圏 *shutoken* the capital region — 148, 188
圏 内/外 *kennai/gai* within/outside the range (of) — 84, 83

勝	**509** 4b8.4 ☐ 月 火 二 42 44 4 勝 勝	**SHŌ, ka(tsu)** – win **masa(ru)** – be superior (to)

勝 利 *shōri* victory — 329
勝 (利) 者 *shō(ri)sha* victor, winner — 329, 164
決 勝 *kesshō* decision (of a competition) — 356
連 勝 *renshō* series of victories, winning streak — 440
勝 ち 通 す *kachitōsu* win successive victories — 150

負	**510** 2n7.1 ☐ ⺈ 貝 15 68 負	**FU, ma(keru)** – be defeated, lose; give a discount **ma(kasu)** – beat, defeat **o(u)** – carry, bear; owe

勝 負 *shōbu* victory or defeat; game, match — 509
自 負 *jifu* conceit, self-importance — 62
負 け ん 気 *makenki* unyielding/competitive spirit — 134
負 け 犬 *makeinu* loser — 280

敗	**511** 7b4.1 ☐ 貝 攵 68 49 敗	**HAI, yabu(reru)** – be defeated, beaten, frustrated

敗 北 *haiboku* defeat — 73
勝 敗 *shōhai* victory or defeat, outcome — 509
失 敗 *shippai* failure, blunder — 311
敗 戦 *haisen* lost battle, defeat — 301
敗 者 *haisha* the defeated, loser — 164

	512 4h4.1 ▯ 方 攵 48 49 放	**HŌ, hana(tsu)** – set free, release; fire (a gun); emit **hana(su)** – set free, release **hana(reru)** – get free of
放		解 放 *kaihō* liberation, emancipation	474
		放 送 *hōsō* (radio/TV) broadcasting	441
		放 火 *hōka* arson	20
		放 置 *hōchi* let alone, leave as is, leave to chance	426

	513 2d4.1 ▯ 阝 方 7 48 防	**BŌ, fuse(gu)** – defend/protect from, prevent
防		防 止 *bōshi* prevention, keeping in check	477
		予 防 *yobō* prevention, precaution	393
		国 防 *kokubō* national defense	40
		防 火 *bōka* fire prevention/fighting	20
		防 水 *bōsui* waterproof, watertight	21

	514 4i3.1 ▯ 攵 弓 49 28 改	**KAI, arata(meru)** – alter, renew, reform **arata(maru)** – be altered, renewed, corrected
改		改 正 *kaisei* improvement; revision	275
		改 良 *kairyō* improvement, reform	321
		改 新 *kaishin* renovation, reformation	174
		改 名 *kaimei* changing one's name	82

	515 7e3.2 ▯ 酉 弓 71 28 配	**HAI, kuba(ru)** – distribute, pass out
配		心 配 *shinpai* worry, concern	97
		支 配 *shihai* management, administration, rule	318
		配 達 *haitatsu* deliver	448
		配 置 *haichi* arrangement, placement	426
		気 配 *kehai* sign, indication	134

	516 7e7.2 ⊞ 酉 攵 厶 71 49 17 酸	**SAN, su(i)** – acid, sour
酸		酸 味 *sanmi* acidity, sourness	307
		酸 性 *sansei* acidity	98
		酸 化 *sanka* oxidation	254
		酸 素 *sanso* oxygen	271
		青 酸 *seisan* prussic acid, hydrogen cyanide	208

	517 3a7.1 ▯ 氵 酉 21 71 酒	**SHU, sake, [saka]** – sakè, rice wine, liquor
酒		日 本 酒 *Nihon-shu* sakè, Japanese rice wine	5, 25
		ぶ ど う 酒 *budōshu* (grape) wine	
		禁 酒 *kinshu* abstinence from drink; temperance	482
		酒 屋 *sakaya* wine dealer, liquor store	167
		酒 場 *sakaba* bar, saloon, tavern	154

	518 3m7.4 目 宀 土 口 33 22 24 害	**GAI** – injury, harm, damage
害		公 害 *kōgai* pollution	126
		水 害 *suigai* flood damage, flooding	21
		損 害 *songai* injury, loss	350
		利 害 *rigai* advantages and disadvantages, interests	329

割	**519** 2f10.1 リ宀士 16 33 22 割	**KATSU, wa(ru)** – divide, separate, split **wa(reru)** – break, crack/ split apart **wari** – proportion; profit; 10 percent **sa(ku)** – cut up; separate; spare (time) 分割 *bunkatsu* division, partitioning　　　　　　　38 割合 *wariai* rate, proportion, percentage　　　　159 割引き *waribiki* discount　　　　　　　　　　　216
必	**520** 0a5.16 心 丿 51 2 必	**HITSU, kanara(zu)** – surely, (be) sure (to), without fail 必要 *hitsuyō* necessary, requisite　　　　　　　419 必死 *hisshi* certain death; desperation　　　　　85 必読 *hitsudoku* required reading　　　　　　　244 必勝 *hisshō* sure victory　　　　　　　　　　509 必ずしも … ない *kanarazu shimo … nai* not necessarily
憲	**521** 3m13.2 宀目 心 33 55 51 憲 憲	**KEN** – law 憲法 *kenpō* constitution　　　　　　　　　　123 改憲 *kaiken* constitutional revision　　　　　514 憲政 *kensei* constitutional government　　　　483 立憲 *rikken* constitutional　　　　　　　　121 官憲 *kanken* the (government) authorities　　326
毒	**522** 0a8.14 土 母 一 22 25 1 毒 毒	**DOKU** – poison 毒薬 *dokuyaku* poison　　　　　　　　　　　359 有毒 *yūdoku* poisonous　　　　　　　　　　265 中毒 *chūdoku* poisoning　　　　　　　　　　28 毒草 *dokusō* poisonous plant　　　　　　　249 気の毒 *kinodoku* pitiable, regrettable, unfortunate　134
乗	**523** 0a9.19 禾 卅 一 41 32 1 乗 乘	**JŌ, no(ru)** – get in/on, ride, take (a train); be fooled **no(seru)** – let ride, take aboard; deceive, trick, take in 乗用車 *jōyōsha* passenger car　　　　　　107, 133 乗車券 *jōshaken* (passenger) ticket　　　133, 506 乗組員 *norikumiin* (ship's) crew　　　　418, 163 乗っ取る *nottoru* take over, commandeer, hijack　65
郵	**524** 2d8.12 阝 卅 土 7 32 22 郵	**YŪ** – mail 郵便局 *yūbinkyoku* post office　　　ᴦpostman 330, 170 郵便配達(人) *yūbin haitatsu(nin)* mailman,　330, 515, 448, 1 郵便料金 *yūbin ryōkin* postage　　　　330, 319, 23 郵税 *yūzei* postage　　　　　　　　　　　399 郵送料 *yūsōryō* postage　　　　　　　　441, 319
式	**525** 4n3.2 弋 工 52 38 式	**SHIKI** – ceremony, rite; style, form; method; formula 正式 *seishiki* prescribed form, formal　　　　275 公式 *kōshiki* formula (in mathematics); formal, official　126 様式 *yōshiki* mode, style　　　　　　　　　403 方式 *hōshiki* formula, mode; method, system　　70 新式 *shinshiki* new type　　　　　　　　　174

	526	**SHI, kokoro(miru), tame(su)** – give it a try, try out, attempt
	7a6.18 ⬚	試 合 *shiai* game, match — 159
	言 戈 工	試 作 *shisaku* trial manufacture/cultivation — 360
	67 52 38	試 食 *shishoku* sample, taste — 322
		試 運 転 *shiunten* trial run — 439, 433
	試	試 金 石 *shikinseki* touchstone; test — 23, 78

	527	**KI, utsuwa** – container, apparatus; capacity, ability
	3d12.13…	楽 器 *gakki* musical instrument — 358
	口 大	器 楽 *kigaku* instrumental music — 358
	24 34	器 具 *kigu* utensil, appliance, tool, apparatus — 420
		食 器 *shokki* eating utensils — 322
	器 器	(不)/(無) 器 用 *(bu)kiyō* (not) dexterous — 94, 107, 93

	528	**KI** – opportunity; machine **hata** – loom
	4a12.1 ⬚	機 関 *kikan* engine; machinery, organ, medium — 398
	木 戈 厶	制 動 機 *seidōki* a brake — 427, 231
	41 52 17	起 重 機 *kijūki* crane — 373, 227
		機 能 *kinō* a function — 386
	機	機 会 *kikai* opportunity, occasion, chance — 158

	529	**KAI** – fetters; machine
	4a7.22 ⬚	器 械 *kikai* instrument, apparatus, appliance — 527
	木 戈 艹	機 械 *kikai* machine, machinery — 528
	41 52 32	機 械 化 *kikaika* mechanization — 528, 254
		機 械 文 明 *kikai bunmei* technological civilization
	械	— 528, 111, 18

	530	**HI, to(bu)** – fly **to(basu)** – let fly; skip over, omit
	0a9.4 …	飛 行 *hikō* flight, aviation — 68
	ｾ 十 一	飛 行 機 *hikōki* airplane — 68, 528
	10 12 1	飛 行 場 *hikōjō* airport — 68, 154
		飛 び 石 *tobiishi* stepping-stones — 78
	飛	飛 び 火 *tobihi* flying sparks, leaping flames — 20

	531	**KEN** – investigation, inspection
	4a8.28 ⬚	検 事 *kenji* public procurator/prosecutor — 80
	木 口 亻	検 定 *kentei* official approval, inspection — 355
	41 24 3	検 証 *kenshō* verification, inspection — 484
		検 死 *kenshi* coroner's inquest, autopsy — 85
	検 検	点 検 *tenken* inspection, examination — 169

	532	**KEN** – effect; testing *[GEN]* – beneficial effect
	10a8.4 ⊞	実 験 *jikken* experiment — 203
	馬 口 亻	試 験 *shiken* examination, test — 526
	78 24 3	入 学 試 験 *nyūgaku shiken* entrance exam — 52, 109, 526
		体 験 *taiken* experience — 61
	験 験	受 験 *juken* take a test/exam — 260

	533	**KEN, kewa(shii)** – steep, inaccessible; stern, harsh	
險	2d8.8 ⊞	保 険　*hoken*　insurance	489
	阝口亻	険 悪　*ken'aku*　dangerous, threatening	304
	7 24 3	険 路　*kenro*　steep path	151
		険 し い 道　*kewashii michi*　steep/treacherous road	149
	険 險	険 し い 顔 つ き　*kewashii kaotsuki*　stern/fierce look	277

	534	**KI, abu(nai), aya(ui)** – dangerous	
危	2n4.3 ⊟	危 険　*kiken*　danger	533
	⺈厂阝	危 機　*kiki*　crisis, critical moment	528
	15 18 7	危 急　*kikyū*　emergency, crisis	303
		危 害　*kigai*　injury, harm	518
	危	危 ぐ　*kigu*　fear, misgivings, apprehension	

	535	**TAN, sagu(ru)** – search/grope for　**saga(su)** – look for	
探	3c8.16 ⊞	探 検/険　*tanken*　exploration, expedition	53†, 533
	扌朩冂	探 知　*tanchi*　detection	214
	23 41 20	探 り 出 す　*saguridasu*　spy/sniff out (a secret)	53
	探	探 し 回 る　*sagashimawaru*　look/search around for	90

	536	**SHIN, fuka(i)** – deep　**fuka(meru)** – make deeper, intensify	
深	3a8.21	**fuka(maru)** – become deeper, more intense	
	氵朩冂	深 度　*shindo*　depth, deepness	377
	21 41 20	深 夜　*shin'ya*　dead of night, late at night	471
		情 け 深 い　*nasakebukai*　compassionate, merciful	209
	深	興 味 深 い　*kyōmibukai*　very interesting	368, 307

	537	**RYOKU, [ROKU], midori** – green	
緑	6a8.15 ⊞	緑 地　*ryokuchi*　green tract of land	118
	糸彐氵	新 緑　*shinryoku*　fresh verdure/greenery	174
	61 39 21	葉 緑 素　*yōryokuso*　chlorophyll	253, 271
		緑 青　*rokushō*　verdigris, green/copper rust	208
	緑 綠	緑 色　*midoriiro*　green, green-colored	204

	538	**ROKU** – record	
録	8a8.16 ⊞	記 録　*kiroku*　record	371
	釒彐氵	録 音　*rokuon*　(sound) recording	347
	72 39 21	録 画　*rokuga*　videotape recording	343
		目 録　*mokuroku*　catalog, inventory, list	55
	録 錄	付 録　*furoku*　supplement, appendix, addendum	192

	539	**YO, ata(eru)** – give, grant	
与	0a3.23 ⋯	与 党　*yotō*　party in power, government	495
	十一	関 与　*kan'yo*　participation	398
	12 1	給 与　*kyūyo*　allowance, wage	346
		供 与　*kyōyo*　give, grant, furnish	197
	与 與	賞 与　*shōyo*　bonus	500

	540 2i3.1 □ ⼍ ⼗ 一 20 12 1 写 寫	**SHA, utsu(su)** – copy down; copy, duplicate; depict; photograph **utsu(ru)** – be taken, turn out (photo)	
		写真 *shashin* photograph	422
		映写機 *eishaki* projector	352, 528
		写生 *shasei* sketch, painting from nature	44
		写実的 *shajitsuteki* realistic, graphic	203, 210

	541 2k4.4 □ ⼗ ⼟ 一 (12) 22 1 考 攷	**KŌ, kanga(eru)** – think, consider	
		思考 *shikō* thinking, thought	99
		考案 *kōan* conception, idea, design	106
		考証 *kōshō* historical research	484
		考古学 *kōkogaku* archaeology	172, 109
		考え方 *kangaekata* way of thinking, viewpoint	70

	542 2k4.3 □ ⼗ ⼟ ⼦ (12) 22 6 孝	**KŌ** – filial piety	
		(親)孝行 *(oya)kōkō* filial piety, obedience to parents	175, 68
		孝養 *kōyō* discharge of filial duties	402
		(親)不孝 *(oya)fukō* undutifulness to one's parents	175, 94

	543 2k4.5 □ ⼗ ⼟ ⼘ (12) 22 13 老	**RŌ, o(iru), fu(keru)** – grow old	
		老人 *rōjin* old man/woman/people	1
		長老 *chōrō* elder, senior member	95
		元老 *genrō* genro; elder statesman	137
		老夫婦 *rōfūfu* old married couple	315, 316
		老子 *Rōshi* Laozi, Lao-tzu	103

	544 3k5.12 □ ⼌ ⼝ ⼗ 32 24 12 若	**JAKU, [NYAKU], waka(i)** – young **mo(shikuwa)** – or	
		老若 *rōnyaku, rōjaku* young and old, youth and age	543
		若者 *wakamono* young man/people	164
		若手 *wakate* young man, a younger member	57
		若人 *wakōdo* young man, a youth	1
		若死に *wakajini* die young	85

	545 3k5.24 ▤ ⼌ ⼝ ⼗ 32 24 12 苦	**KU, kuru(shimu)** – suffer **kuru(shimeru)** – torment **kuru(shii)** – painful **niga(i)** – bitter **niga(ru)** – scowl	
		苦労 *kurō* trouble, hardship, adversity	233
		苦心 *kushin* pains, efforts	97
		病苦 *byōku* the pain of illness	380
		重苦しい *omokurushii* oppressed, gloomy, ponderous	227

	546 7c9.5 ⊞ 車 月 ⼂ 69 42 3 輸 輸	**YU** – send, transport	
		輸入 *yunyū* import	52
		輸出 *yushutsu* export	53
		輸送 *yusō* transport	441
		運輸 *un'yu* transport, conveyance	439
		空輸 *kūyu* air transport, shipment by air	140

	547	**KEI, karu(i), karo(yaka)** – light	
軽	7c5.3 ⊞	軽工業 *keikōgyō* light industry	139, 279
	車 士 又	軽食 *keishoku* light meal	322
	69 22 9	軽音楽 *keiongaku* light music	347, 358
		手軽 *tegaru* easy, light, simple, cheap	57
	軽 輕	気軽 *kigaru* lighthearted, cheerful, feel free (to)	134

	548	**KEI** – longitude; sutra; passage of time **KYŌ** – sutra	
経	6a5.11 ⊞	**he(ru)** – pass, elapse	
	糸 士 又	経験 *keiken* experience	532
	6I 22 9	経歴 *keireki* one's life history, career	480
		経理 *keiri* accounting	143
	経 經	神経 *shinkei* a nerve	310

	549	**SAI, su(mu)** – come to an end; be paid; suffice	
済	3a8.30 ⊞	**su(masu)** – finish, settle; pay; make do, manage	
	氵 亠 艹	経済 *keizai* economy, economics	548
	21 11 12	返済 *hensai* payment, repayment	442
		決済 *kessai* settlement of accounts	356
	済 濟	使用済み *shiyōzumi* used up	331, 107

	550	**ZAI** – medicine, dose	
剤	2f8.6 ⊞	薬剤 *yakuzai* medicine, drug	359
	⼁⼁ 亠 艹	薬剤師 *yakuzaishi* pharmacist, druggist	359, 409
	16 11 12	調剤 *chōzai* compounding/preparation of medicines	342
		下剤 *gezai* laxative	31
	剤 劑	解毒剤 *gedokuzai* antidote	474, 522

	551	**SAI** – talent, genius	
才	0a3.27 ⋯	天才 *tensai* a genius	141
	亠 丨	才子 *saishi* talented person	103
	12 2	才能 *sainō* talent, ability	386
		多才 *tasai* many-talented	229
	才	十八才 *jūhassai* 18 years old	12, 10

	552	**ZAI** – wood; material; talent	
材	4a3.7 ⊡	材料 *zairyō* materials, ingredients	319
	木 亠 丨	取材 *shuzai* collection of material, news gathering	65
	41 12 2	教材 *kyōzai* teaching materials	245
		題材 *daizai* subject matter, theme	354
	材 杖	材木 *zaimoku* wood, lumber	22

	553	**ZAI, [SAI]** – money, wealth, property	
財	7b3.1 ⊡	財産 *zaisan* estate, assets, property	278
	貝 亠 丨	財政 *zaisei* finances, financial affairs	483
	68 12 2	財務 *zaimu* financial affairs	235
		財界 *zaikai* financial world, business circles	454
	財 賊	文化財 *bunkazai* cultural asset	111, 254

因	554 3s3.2 回 口 大 24 34 因	**IN** – cause **yo(ru)** – depend (on); be limited (to)
		原因 *gen'in* cause 136 主因 *shuin* primary/main cause 155 死因 *shiin* cause of death 85 要因 *yōin* important factor, chief cause 419 因果 *inga* cause and effect 487

恩	555 4k6.23 日 心 口 大 51 24 34 恩	**ON** – kindness, goodness; favor; gratitude
		恩給 *onkyū* pension 346 恩賞 *onshō* a reward 500 恩人 *onjin* benefactor; patron 1 恩返し *ongaeshi* repayment of a favor 442 恩知らず *onshirazu* ingratitude; ingrate 214

漢	556 3a10.17 日 氵 艹 口 21 32 24 漢 漢	**KAN** – Han (Chinese dynasty); China; man, fellow
		漢字 *kanji* Chinese character 110 漢文 *kanbun* Chinese writing; Chinese classics 111 漢時代 *Kan jidai* Han dynasty/period 42, 256 好/悪漢 *kō/akkan* nice fellow/scoundrel, villain 104, 304 門外漢 *mongaikan* outsider, layman 161, 83

難	557 8c10.2 日 隹 艹 口 74 32 24 難 難	**NAN, muzuka(shii), kata(i)** – difficult
		難題 *nandai* difficult problem/question 354 難病 *nanbyō* incurable disease 380 難民 *nanmin* refugees 177 海難 *kainan* disaster at sea, shipwreck 117 非難 *hinan* adverse criticism 498

困	558 3s4.1 回 口 木 24 41 困	**KON, koma(ru)** – be distressed
		困難 *konnan* difficulty, trouble 557 困苦 *konku* hardships, adversity 545 困り切る *komarikiru* be in a bad fix, at a loss 39 困り果てる *komarihateru* be greatly troubled, nonplussed 487

勤	559 2g10.1 日 力 艹 口 8 32 24 勤 勤	**KIN, [GON], tsuto(meru)** – be employed **tsuto(maru)** – be fit for
		勤労 *kinrō* work, labor 233 勤務 *kinmu* service, being on duty/at work 235 通勤 *tsūkin* going to work, commuting 150 転勤 *tenkin* be transferred (to another job) 433 勤め先 *tsutomesaki* place of work, employer 50

抵	560 3c5.18 口 扌 厂 十 23 18 12 抵	**TEI** – resist
		抵当 *teitō* mortgage, hypothec 77 大抵 *taitei* generally, for the most part, usually 26

561 2a5.15 □ 亻 厂 十 3 18 12 低 低	***TEI, hiku(i)*** – low ***hiku(meru)*** – make lower ***hiku(maru)*** – become lower	263
	最 低 *saitei* lowest, minimum	
	低 地 *teichi* low ground, lowlands	118
	低 所 得 *teishotoku* low income	153, 374
	低 成 長 *teiseichō* low growth	261, 95
	低 能 *teinō* weak intellect, mental deficiency	386
562 3q5.3 □ 广 十 一 18 12 1 底	***TEI, soko*** – bottom	
	根 底 *kontei* base, foundation	314
	海 底 *kaitei* bottom of the sea, ocean floor	117
	河 底 *katei* bottom of a river, riverbed	389
	底 力 *sokojikara* latent energy/power	100
	底 値 *sokone* rock-bottom price	425
563 2d5.10 □ 阝 厂 十 7 18 12 邸	***TEI*** – mansion, residence	
	公 邸 *kōtei* official residence	126
	官 邸 *kantei* official residence	326
	私 邸 *shitei* one's private residence	125
	邸 宅 *teitaku* residence, mansion	178
	邸 内 *teinai* the grounds, the pemises	84
564 4i4.1 □ 夂 木 49 41 条 條	***JŌ*** – article, clause; line, stripe	
	条 約 *jōyaku* treaty	211
	条 文 *jōbun* the text, provisions	111
	第 一 条 *dai-ichijō* Article 1 (in a law/contract/treaty)	404, 2
	条 理 *jōri* logic, reason	143
	信 条 *shinjō* a belief, article of faith	157
565 2f7.6 □ 刂 土 大 (16) 22 34 契	***KEI, chigi(ru)*** – pledge, vow, promise	
	契 約 *keiyaku* contract	211
	契 機 *keiki* opportunity, chance	528
566 0a4.25 □ 厂 十 18 12 氏	***SHI*** – family, surname; Mr. ***uji*** – family, lineage	
	氏 名 *shimei* (full) name	82
	坂 本 氏 *Sakamoto-shi* Mr. Sakamoto	443, 25
	同 氏 *dōshi* the said person, he	198
	両 氏 *ryōshi* both (gentlemen)	200
	氏 神 *ujigami* tutelary deity, genius loci	310
567 3e8.4 □ 女 日 厂 25 43 18 婚	***KON*** – marriage	
	結 婚 *kekkon* marriage	485
	結 婚 式 *kekkonshiki* marriage ceremony, wedding	485, 525
	婚 約 *kon'yaku* engagement	211
	未 婚 *mikon* unmarried	306
	新 婚 旅 行 *shinkon ryokō* honeymoon	174, 222, 68

級	**568** 6a3.2 □ 糸 力 丨 61 8 2 級 級	**KYŪ** – rank, class 進級 *shinkyū* (school/military) promotion — 437 高級 *kōkyū* high rank; high class, de luxe — 190 上級 *jōkyū* upper grade, senior — 32 学級 *gakkyū* class in school — 109 同級生 *dōkyūsei* classmate — 198, 44
等	**569** 6f6.9 目 竹 土 寸 66 22 37 等	**TŌ** – class, grade; equality; etc. *hito(shii)* – equal 等級 *tōkyū* class, grade, rank — 568 一等 *ittō* first class — 2 平等 *byōdō* equality — 202 同等 *dōtō* equality, same rank — 198 高等学校 *kōtō gakkō* senior high school — 190, 109, 115
詩	**570** 7a6.5 ⊞ 言 土 寸 67 22 37 詩	**SHI** – poetry, poem 詩人 *shijin* poet — 1 詩歌 *shiika, shika* poetry — 392 詩情 *shijō* poetic sentiment — 209 詩集 *shishū* collection of poems — 436 漢詩 *kanshi* Chinese poem/poetry — 556
侍	**571** 2a6.11 ⊞ 亻 土 寸 3 22 37 侍	**JI, samurai** – samurai 侍者 *jisha* attendant, valet, page — 164 侍女 *jijo* lady-in-waiting, lady's attendant — 102 侍医 *jii* court physician — 220 侍気質 *samurai katagi* the samurai spirit — 134, 176 七人の侍 *Shichinin no Samurai* (The Seven Samurai) — 9, 1
士	**572** 3p0.1 □ 士 22 士	**SHI** – samurai; man; scholar 人間同士 *ningen dōshi* fellow human being — 1, 43, 198 力士 *rikishi* sumo wrestler — 100 代議士 *daigishi* dietman, congressman, M.P. — 256, 292 学士 *gakushi* university graduate — 109 税理士 *zeirishi* (licensed) tax accountant — 399, 143
志	**573** 3p4.1 目 士 心 22 51 志	**SHI, kokorozashi** – will, intention, aim *kokoroza(su)* – intend, aim at, have in view 意志 *ishi* will — 132 志向 *shikō* intention, inclination — 199 同志 *dōshi* like-minded (person) — 198 有志 *yūshi* voluntary; those interested — 265
誌	**574** 7a7.8 ⊞ 言 心 士 67 51 22 誌	**SHI** – write down, chronicle; magazine 誌上 *shijō* in a magazine — 32 誌面 *shimen* page of a magazine — 274 日誌 *nisshi* diary — 5 書誌学 *shoshigaku* bibliography — 131, 109 地誌 *chishi* a topography, geographical description — 118

575 雑

ZATSU, ZŌ – miscellany, a mix

8c6.2 田
隹木 十
74 41 12
雑 雜

雑 誌	*zasshi* magazine	574
雑 音	*zatsuon* noise, static	347
雑 感	*zakkan* miscellaneous thoughts/impressions	262
雑 草	*zassō* weeds	249
雑 木 林	*zōkibayashi* thicket of assorted trees	22, 127

576 殺

SATSU, [SAI], [SETSU], koro(su) – kill

4a6.35 田
木 十 几
41 12 20
殺 殺

自 殺	*jisatsu* suicide	62
暗 殺	*ansatsu* assassination	348
毒 殺	*dokusatsu* killing by poison	522
殺 人	*satsujin* a murder	1
人 殺 し	*hitogoroshi* murder, murderer	1

577 設

SETSU, mō(keru) – establish, set up, prepare

7a4.7 田
言 冂 又
67 20 9
設

設 立	*setsuritsu* establishment, founding	121
設 定	*settei* establishment, creation	355
新 設	*shinsetsu* newly established/organized	174
私 設	*shisetsu* private	125
設 置	*setchi* establishment, founding, institution	426

578 命

MEI – command; fate; life **MYŌ, inochi** – life

2a6.26 田
亻 口 卩
3 24 7
命

生 命 (保 険)	*seimei (hoken)* life (insurance)	44, 489, 533
運 命	*unmei* fate	439
使 命	*shimei* mission, errand	331
短 命	*tanmei* a short life	215
任 命	*ninmei* appointment, nomination	334

579 念

NEN – thought, idea; desire; concern, attention

2a6.24 目
亻 心 一
3 51 1
念

記 念 日	*kinenbi* memorial day, anniversary	371, 5
記 念 切 手	*kinen kitte* commemorative stamp	371, 39, 57
理 念	*rinen* idea, doctrine, ideology	143
信 念	*shinnen* belief, faith, conviction	157
念 入 り	*nen'iri* careful, scrupulous, thorough	52

580 源

GEN, minamoto – source, origin

3a10.25 口
氵 日 小
21 43 35
源

起 源	*kigen* origin	373
根 源	*kongen* origin	314
財 源	*zaigen* source of revenue	553
源 平	*Gen-Pei* Genji and Heike clans	202
源 氏 物 語	*Genji Monogatari* (The Tale of Genji)	566, 79, 67

581 願

GAN, nega(u) – petition, request, desire

9a10.2 口
頁 日 小
77 43 35
願

大 願	*taigan* great ambition, earnest wish	26
念 願	*nengan* one's heart's desire	579
出 願	*shutsugan* application	53
願 書	*gansho* written request, application	131
志 願	*shigan* application, volunteering, desire	573

	582	**FUTSU, hara(u)** – pay; sweep away	
払	3c2.2 □	払 底 *futtei* shortage, scarcity	562
	扌 ム	支 払 い *shiharai* payment	318
	23 17	前 払 い *maebarai* payment in advance	47
		現 金 払 い *genkinbarai* cash payment	298, 23
	払 拂	分 割 払 い *bunkatsubarai* payment in installments	38, 519

	583	**BUTSU, hotoke** – Buddha *[FUTSU]* – (short for) France	
仏	2a2.5 □	仏 教 *bukkyō* Buddhism	245
	亻 ム	大 仏 *daibutsu* great statue of Buddha	26
	3 17	石 仏 *sekibutsu* stone image of Buddha	78
		念 仏 *nenbutsu* Buddhist prayer	579
	仏 佛	日 仏 *Nichi-Futsu* Japanese-French	5

	584	**KAN, hi(ru)** – get dry **ho(su)** – dry; drink up	
干	2k1.1 ⚏	(潮 の) 干 満 *(shio no) kanman* tide, ebb and flow	468, 201
	十 丁 一	干 潮 *kanchō* ebb/low tide	468
	(12) 14 1	干 渉 *kanshō* interfere, meddle	432
		若 干 *jakkan* some, a number of	544
	干	物 干 し *monohoshi* frame for drying clothes	79

	585	**KAN** – publish	
刊	2f3.1 □	週 刊 (誌) *shūkan(shi)* weekly magazine	92, 574
	リ 丁 一	日 刊 紙 *nikkanshi* daily newspaper	5, 180
	16 14 1	夕 刊 *yūkan* evening newspaper/edition	81
		新 刊 *shinkan* new publication	174
	刊	未 刊 行 *mikankō* unpublished	306, 68

	586	**GAN, kishi** – bank, shore, coast	
岸	3o5.11 ⊟	西 岸 *seigan* west bank/coast	72
	屮 厂 一	対 岸 *taigan* opposite shore	365
	36 18 14	海 岸 *kaigan* seashore, coast	117
		河 岸 *kawagishi, kagan* riverbank	389
	岸	川 岸 *kawagishi* riverbank	33

	587	**KAI, mina** – all	
皆	4c5.14 ⊞	皆 済 *kaisai* payment in full	549
	日 ⼘ |	皆 勤 *kaikin* perfect attendance (at work/school)	559
	43 13 2	皆 無 *kaimu* nothing/none at all	93
		皆 目 *kaimoku* utterly; (not) at all	55
	皆	皆 さ ん *minasan* everybody; Ladies and Gentlemen!	

	588	**KAI** – stair, story, level	
階	2d9.6 ⊞	三 階 *sangai, sankai* third floor	4
	阝 日 ⼘	階 段 *kaidan* stairs, stairway	362
	7 43 13	段 階 *dankai* stage, phase	362
		階 級 *kaikyū* social class	568
	階	音 階 *onkai* musical scale	347

陛	**589** 2d7.6 田 阝 土 卜 7 22 13 陛	***HEI*** – steps (of the throne)

天 皇 陛 下	*tennō heika* H.M. the Emperor 141, 297, 31
国 王 陛 下	*kokuō heika* H.M. the King 40, 294, 31
女 王 陛 下	*joō heika* H.M. the Queen 102, 294, 31
両 陛 下	*ryōheika* Their Majesties the Emperor and Empress 200, 31

羽	**590** 2b4.5 囗 冫 彐 2b 39 羽 羽	***U, ha, hane*** – feather; wing

羽 毛	*umō* feather, plumage 287
白 羽	*shiraha* white feather 205
羽 音	*haoto* flapping of wings 347
一 羽	*ichiwa* 1 bird 2
羽 田	*Haneda* (airport in Tōkyō) 35

習	**591** 4c7.11 田 日 彐 丨 43 39 2 習 習	***SHŪ, nara(u)*** – learn

学 習	*gakushū* learning, study 109
独 習	*dokushū* self-study 219
予 習	*yoshū* preparation of lessons 393
常 習	*jōshū* custom; habit 497
習 字	*shūji* penmanship, calligraphy 110

翌	**592** 5b6.6 田 立 彐 54 39 翌 翌	***YOKU*** – the next, following

翌 朝	*yokuasa, yokuchō* the next morning 469
翌 日	*yokujitsu* the next/following day 5
翌 々 日	*yokuyokujitsu* 2 days later/thereafter 5
翌 年	*yokunen* the following year 45
翌 週	*yokushū* the following week, the week after that 92

談	**593** 7a8.7 田 言 火 67 44 談	***DAN*** – conversation

会 談	*kaidan* a conversation, conference 158
対 談	*taidan* face-to-face talk, conversation 365
談 話	*danwa* conversation 238
相 談	*sōdan* consultation 146
下 相 談	*shitasōdan* preliminary negotiations 31, 146

訳	**594** 7a4.8 囗 言 尸 丨 67 40 2 訳 譯	***YAKU*** – translation ***wake*** – reason; meaning; circumstances

通 訳	*tsūyaku* interpreting, interpreter 150
英 訳	*eiyaku* a translation into English 353
全 訳	*zen'yaku* a complete translation 89
訳 者	*yakusha* translator 164
言 い 訳	*iiwake* apology; excuse 66

釈	**595** 6b5.5 囗 米 尸 丨 62 40 2 釈 釋	***SHAKU*** – explanation

解 釈	*kaishaku* interpretation, construal 474
釈 明	*shakumei* explanation, vindication 18
釈 放	*shakuhō* release, discharge 512
保 釈	*hoshaku* (prison) bail 489
注 釈	*chūshaku* comments, annotation 357

翻	**596** 6b12.3 田 米 田 ヨ 62 58 39 翻 飜	**HON, hirugae(su)** – (tr.) turn over; change (one's opinion); wave (a flag) **hirugae(ru)** – (intr.) turn over; wave 翻 訳 *hon'yaku* translation, translate　　　　　594 翻 案 *hon'an* an adaptation　　　　　　　　106 翻 意 *hon'i* change one's mind　　　　　　　132 翻 ろ う *honrō* trifle with, make sport of
橋	**597** 4a12.8 田 木 大 口 41 34 24 橋	**KYŌ, hashi** – bridge 歩 道 橋 *hodōkyō* pedestrian bridge　　　431, 149 鉄 橋 *tekkyō* iron bridge; railway bridge　　　312 石 橋 *ishibashi* stone bridge　　　　　　　　78 つ り 橋 *tsuribashi* suspension bridge 日 本 橋 *Nihonbashi* (area of Tōkyō)　　　5, 25
柱	**598** 4a5.12 田 木 王 丨 41 46 2 柱	**CHŪ, hashira** – pillar, column, pole 支 柱 *shichū* prop, support, strut　　　　　318 電 柱 *denchū* utility/electric pole　　　　　108 水 銀 柱 *suiginchū* column of mercury　　21, 313 円 柱 *enchū* column, cylinder　　　　　　　13 大 黒 柱 *daikokubashira* central pillar, mainstay　26, 206
駐	**599** 10a5.2 田 馬 王 丨 78 46 2 駐	**CHŪ** – stop; reside 駐 車 場 *chūshajō* parking lot　　　　　133, 154 駐 在 *chūzai* stay, residence　　　　　　　268 駐 日 *chūnichi* resident/stationed in Japan　　5 進 駐 *shinchū* stationing, occupation　　　437 常 駐 *jōchū* permanently stationed　　　　497
専	**600** 0a9.16 日 日 寸 十 43 37 12 専 專	**SEN, moppa(ra)** – entirely, exclusively 専 門 家 *senmonka* specialist, expert　　161, 165 専 任 *sennin* exclusive duty, full-time　　334 専 制 *sensei* absolutism, despotism　　　427 専 売 *senbai* monopoly　　　　⌜(parking lot) 239 専 用 (駐 車 場) *sen'yō (chūshajō)* private　107, 599, 133, 154
博	**601** 2k10.1 田 十 日 寸 12 43 37 博 博	**HAKU, [BAKU]** – extensive, broad; many 博 物 館 *hakubutsukan* museum　　　　79, 327 博 学 *hakugaku* broad knowledge, erudition　109 博 士 *hakase, hakushi* doctor　　　　　　572 博 愛 *hakuai* philantrophy　　　　　　　259 万 博 *banpaku* international exhibition　　16
授	**602** 3c8.15 田 扌 小 冖 23 35 20 授	**JU, sazu(keru)** – grant; teach **sazu(karu)** – be granted, taught 授 業 *jugyō* teaching, instruction　　　　279 教 授 *kyōju* instruction; professor　　　245 授 受 *juju* giving and receiving, transfer　260 授 与 *juyo* conferment, presentation　　　539 授 賞 *jushō* awarding a prize　　　　　　500

603

確

5a10.3

石 隹 冂
53 74 20

確

KAKU, tashi(ka) – certain **tashi(kameru)** – make sure of, verify

確立	kakuritsu	establishment, settlement	121
確定	kakutei	decision, settlement	355
確実	kakujitsu	certain, reliable	203
確信	kakushin	firm belief, conviction	157
正確	seikaku	accurate, precise, correct	275

604

観

5c13.7

目 隹見
(55) 74 68

観 觀

KAN – appearance, view

観光	kankō	sight-seeing, tourism	138
外観	gaikan	(external) appearance	83
主観的	shukanteki	subjective	155, 210
楽観的	rakkanteki	optimistic	358, 210
観念	kannen	idea; sense (of duty/justice)	579

605

覚

3n9.3

⺍ 貝 冂
35 68 20

覚 覺

KAKU, obo(eru) – remember, bear in mind; learn; feel **sa(meru/masu)** – (intr./tr.) awake, wake up

感覚	kankaku	sense, sensation, feeling	262
直覚	chokkaku	intuition, insight	423
見覚え	mioboe	recognition, knowing by sight	63
目覚まし (時計)	mezamashi(dokei)	alarm clock	55, 42, 340

606

視

4e7.1

ネ 貝
45 68

視 視

SHI – seeing, regarding as

視力	shiryoku	visual acuity, eyesight	100
近視	kinshi	nearsightedness, shortsightedness	445
重視	jūshi	attach importance to, stress	227
無視	mushi	ignore, disregard	93
視界	shikai	field of vision	454

607

規

5c6.9

目 貝 大
(55) 68 34

規

KI – standard, measure

規定	kitei	stipulations, provisions, regulations	355
定規	jōgi	ruler, square; standard, norm	355
正規	seiki	regular, formal, regulation	275
新規	shinki	new	174
法規	hōki	laws and regulations, legislation	123

608

則

7b2.1

貝 刂
68 16

則

SOKU – rule, law

規則	kisoku	rule, regulation	607
原則	gensoku	general rule, principle	136
法則	hōsoku	a law	123
変則	hensoku	irregularity, anomaly	257
会則	kaisoku	rules of an association	158

609

側

2a9.4

亻 貝 刂
3 68 16

側

SOKU, kawa – side

側面	sokumen	side, flank	274
側近者	sokkinsha	one's close associates	445, 164
左側	hidarigawa	left side	75
反対側	hantaigawa	opposite side	324, 365
日本側	Nihongawa, Nippongawa	the Japanese side	5, 25

	610	**SOKU, haka(ru)** – measure	
測	3a9.4 □□	測量 *sokuryō* measurment, surveying	411
	氵貝 儿	測定 *sokutei* measuring	355
	21 68 16	観測 *kansoku* observation	604
		目測 *mokusoku* measurement by eye, estimation	55
	測	予測 *yosoku* estimate, forecast	393

	611	**RETSU** – row	
列	2f4.4 ⊞	列車 *ressha* train	133
	刂 夕 一	列島 *rettō* chain of islands, archipelago	286
	16 30 1	列国 *rekkoku* world powers, nations	40
		行列 *gyōretsu* queue; procession; matrix	68
	列	後列 *kōretsu* back row	48

	612	**REI** – example; custom, precedent ***tato(eru)*** – compare	
例	2a6.7 □□	例外 *reigai* exception	83
	亻夕 儿	特例 *tokurei* special case, exception	282
	3 30 16	先例 *senrei* previous example, precedent	50
		例年 *reinen* normal year; every year	45
	例	条例 *jōrei* regulations, ordinance	564

	613	**KAN** – completion	
完	3m4.6 目	完結 *kanketsu* completion	485
	宀 二 儿	完全 *kanzen* complete, perfect	89
	33 4 16	完成 *kansei* completion, accomplishment	261
		未完成 *mikansei* incomplete, unfinished	306, 261
	完	完敗 *kanpai* complete defeat	511

	614	**IN** – institution	
院	2d7.9 ⊞	病院 *byōin* hospital	380
	阝宀二	入院 *nyūin* admission to a hospital	52
	7 33 4	大学院 *daigakuin* graduate school	26, 109
		養老院 *yōrōin* old folks' home	402, 543
	院	両院 *ryōin* both houses (of the Diet/Congress/Parliament)	200

	615	**JI, SHI, shime(su)** – show	
示	4e0.1 □	公示 *kōji* public announcement	126
	礻	明示 *meiji* clear statement	18
	45	教示 *kyōji* instruction, teaching	245
		暗示 *anji* hint, suggestion	348
	示	示談 *jidan* out-of-court settlement	593

	616	**SHŪ, SŌ** – religion, sect	
宗	3m5.1 目	宗教 *shūkyō* religion	245
	宀 礻	宗門 *shūmon* sect	161
	33 45	宗徒 *shūto* adherent, believer	430
		改宗 *kaishū* conversion, become a convert	514
	宗	宗家 *sōke* the head family	165

	617	**SAI, matsu(ru)** – deify, worship **matsu(ri)** – festival	
祭	4e6.3	祭日 *saijitsu* holiday; festival day	5
	ネ 夕 又	百年祭 *hyakunensai* centennial	14, 45
	45 30 9	文化祭 *bunkasai* cultural festival	111, 254
	祭	秋祭り *akimatsuri* autumn festival	462
		後の祭り *ato no matsuri* Too late!	48

	618	**SAI** – time, occasion **kiwa** – side, brink, edge	
際	2d11.1	国際 *kokusai* international	40
	阝 ネ 夕	交際 *kōsai* association, company, acquaintance	114
	7 45 30	実際 *jissai* truth, reality, actual practice	203
	際	水際 *mizugiwa* water's edge, shore	21
		際立つ *kiwadatsu* be conspicuous, stand out	121

	619	**SATSU** – surmise, judge, understand, sympathize	
察	3m11.6	観察 *kansatsu* observation	604
	宀 ネ 夕	検察 *kensatsu* criminal investigation, prosecution	531
	33 45 30	視察 *shisatsu* inspection, observation	606
	察	考察 *kōsatsu* consideration, examination	541
		明察 *meisatsu* discernment, keen insight	18

	620	**REI, RAI** – courtesy; salutation; gratitude, remuneration	
礼	4e1.1	祭礼 *sairei* religious festival	617
	ネ 丨	礼式 *reishiki* etiquette	525
	45 2	失礼 *shitsurei* rudeness	311
	礼 禮	非礼 *hirei* impoliteness	498
		無礼 *burei* rudeness, impertinence, affront	93

	621	**KI, ino(ru)** – pray	
祈	4e4.3	祈念 *kinen* a prayer	579
	ネ 斤	祈願 *kigan* a prayer	581
	45 50	祈とう(書) *kitō(sho)* prayer (book)	131
	祈 祈	祈り *inori* a prayer	
		主の祈り *shu no inori* the Lord's Prayer	155

	622	**SO** – ancestor	
祖	4e5.4	祖先 *sosen* ancestor, forefather	50
	ネ 月 一	祖母/父 *sobo/fu* grandmother, grandfather	112, 113
	45 42 1	祖国 *sokoku* one's homeland/fatherland	40
	祖 祖	元祖 *ganso* originator, founder, inventor	137
		宗祖 *shūso* founder of a sect	616

	623	**JO, tasu(keru)** – help, rescue **tasu(karu)** – be helped, rescued **suke** – assistance	
助	2g5.1	助力 *joryoku* help, assistance	100
	力 月 丨	助言 *jogen* advice	66
	8 42 2	助手 *joshu* helper, assistant	57
	助	助け合う *tasukeau* help each other	159

161

	624	SA – investigate	
査	4a5.32 目	調査 chōsa investigation, inquiry, observation	342
	木 月 一	検査 kensa inspection, examination	531
	41 42 1	査問 samon inquiry, hearing	162
	査	査察 sasatsu inspection, observation	619
		査定 satei assessment	355

	625	SEN – announce	
宣	3m6.2 目	宣言 sengen declaration, manifesto ┌independence	66
	宀 日 一	独立宣言 dokuritsu sengen declaration of	219, 121, 66
	33 43 1	宣伝 senden propaganda; advertising, publicity	434
	宣	宣戦 sensen declaration of war	301
		宣教師 senkyōshi a missionary	245, 409

	626	JŌ – condition, circumstances; form; letter	
状	2b5.1 ▥	状態 jōtai circumstances, situation	387
	冫 犭 丨	現状 genjō present situation	298
	5 27 2	白状 hakujō confession	205
	状 狀	礼状 reijō letter of thanks	620
		招待状 shōtaijō written invitation	455, 452

	627	SHŌ – commander, general; soon	
将	2b8.3 ⊞	将来 shōrai future	69
	冫 小 寸	将軍 shōgun shogun, general	438
	5 35 37	大将 taishō general, leader	26
	将 將	主将 shushō (team) captain	155
		将校 shōkō officer	115

	628	TEI – present, submit sa(geru) – carry (in the hand)	
提	3c9.4 ⊞	提案 teian proposition, proposal	106
	扌 日 一	提供 teikyō offer	197
	23 43 14	提議 teigi proposal, suggestion	292
	提	提出 teishutsu presentation, filing	53
		前提 zentei premise	47

	629	TAI, TA, futo(i) – fat, thick futo(ru) – get fat/thick	
太	0a4.18 …	太平洋 Taiheiyō Pacific Ocean	202, 289
	大 丨	皇太子 kōtaishi crown prince	297, 103
	34 2	太古 taiko ancient times, antiquity	172
	太	太字 futoji thick character, boldface	110
		太刀 tachi (long) sword	37

	630	YŌ – positive; male; sun	
陽	2d9.5 ⊞	太陽 taiyō sun	629
	阝 日 犭	陽光 yōkō sunshine, sunlight	138
	7 43 27	陽気 yōki season, weather; cheerfulness, gaiety	134
	陽	陽性 yōsei positive	98
		陽子 yōshi proton	103

	631	**YŌ, a(geru)** – raise; fry **a(garu)** – rise
揚	3c9.5 ⊞	高揚 *kōyō* uplift, surge 190
	扌 日 勿	揚水車 *yōsuisha* scoop wheel 21, 133
	23 43 27	意気揚々 *ikiyōyō* triumphantly, exultantly 132, 134
	揚	荷揚げ *niage* unloading, discharge, landing 391
		引き揚げ *hikiage* withdrawal, evacuation 216

	632	**TŌ, yu** – hot water
湯	3a9.23 ⊞	湯治 *tōji* hot-spring cure 493
	氵 日 勿	湯元 *yumoto* source of a hot spring 137
	21 43 27	湯ぶね *yubune* bathtub
	湯	茶の湯 *cha no yu* tea ceremony 251
		湯上がり *yuagari* just after a bath 32

	633	**SHŌ, kizu** – wound, injury **ita(mu)** – hurt **ita(meru)** – injure
傷	2a11.10 ⊞	負傷 *fushō* wound, injury 510
	亻 日 勿	傷害 *shōgai* injury, damage 518
	3 43 27	重/軽傷 *jū/keishō* severe/minor injuries 227, 547
	傷	死傷者 *shishōsha* the killed and injured, casualties 85, 164
		中傷 *chūshō* slander 28

	634	**ON, atata(kai), atata(ka)** – warm **atata(meru)** – (tr.) warm up **atata(maru)** – (intr.) warm up
温	3a9.21 ⊞	温度 *ondo* temperature 377
	氵 皿 日	気/水/体温 *ki/sui/tai-on* air/water/body temperature 134, 21, 61
	21 59 43	温室 *onshitsu* hothouse, greenhouse 166
	温 温	温和 *onwa* mild, gentle 124

	635	**DAN, atata(kai), atata(ka)** – warm **atata(meru)** – (tr.) warm up **atata(maru)** – (intr.) warm up
暖	4c9.4 ⊞	寒暖計 *kandankei* thermometer 457, 340
	日 小 二	温暖 *ondan* warm 634
	43 35 4	暖流 *danryū* warm ocean current 247
	暖 暖	暖冬 *dantō* warm/mild winter 459

	636	**UN, kumo** – cloud
雲	8d4.1 ⊟	風雲 *fūun* wind and clouds; situation 29
	雨 二 ム	暗雲 *an'un* dark clouds 348
	75 4 17	雨雲 *amagumo* rain cloud 30
	雲	入道雲 *nyūdōgumo* cumulonimbus, thunderhead 52, 149
		出雲大社 *Izumo Taisha* Izumo Shrine 53, 26, 308

	637	**DON, kumo(ru)** – cloud up, get cloudy
曇	4c12.1 ⊟	曇天 *donten* cloudy/overcast sky 141
	日 雨 二	曇りがち *kumorigachi* broken clouds, mostly cloudy
	43 75 4	曇りガラス *kumori garasu* ground/frosted/mat glass
	曇	花曇り *hanagumori* cloudy weather in cherry-blossom season 255

	638	**SHO, atsu(i)** – hot (weather)	
暑	4c8.5	寒暑 *kansho* cold and heat	457
	日 土 丨	暑気 *shoki* the heat	134
	43 22 2	暑中 *shochū* middle of summer	28
	暑	大暑 *taisho* Japanese Midsummer Day (about July 24)	26
		暑苦しい *atsukurushii* oppressively hot, sultry	545

	639	**KŌ, atsu(i)** – thick; kind, cordial	
厚	2p6.1	厚意 *kōi* kind intentions, kindness	132
	厂 日 子	厚顔 *kōgan* impudence, effrontery	277
	18 43 6	厚生省 *Kōseishō* Ministry of Health and Welfare	44, 145
	厚	厚相 *kōshō* minister of health and welfare	146
		厚紙 *atsugami* thick paper, cardboard	180

	640	**EN** – feast, banquet	
宴	3m7.3	宴会 *enkai* dinner party, banquet	158
	宀 日 女	宴席 *enseki* (one's seat in) a banquet hall	379
	33 43 25	酒宴 *shuen* feast, drinking bout	517
	宴	きょう宴 *kyōen* banquet, feast, dinner	

	641	**KYAKU, KAKU** – guest, customer	
客	3m6.3	客間, 客室 *kyaku-ma, kyaku-shitsu* guest room	43, 166
	宀 夂 口	客船 *kyakusen* passenger ship	376
	33 49 24	乗客 *jōkyaku* passenger	523
	客	旅客 *ryokaku* passenger, traveler	222
		客観的 *kyakkanteki* objective	604, 210

	642	**KAKU, onoono** – each, every, various	
各	4i3.3	各地 *kakuchi* every area; various places	118
	夂 口	各国 *kakkoku* all/various countries	40
	49 24	各種 *kakushu* every kind, various types	228
	各	各人 *kakujin* each person, everyone	1
		各自 *kakuji* each person, everyone	62

	643	**KAKU, [KŌ]** – status, rank; standard, rule; case	
格	4a6.17	人格 *jinkaku* personality, character	1
	木 夂 口	性格 *seikaku* character, personality	98
	41 49 24	価格 *kakaku* price; value	421
	格	合格 *gōkaku* pass (an exam)	159
		格子 *kōshi* lattice, bars, grating, grille	103

	644	**GAN, maru(i)** – round **maru(meru)** – make round, form into a ball **-maru** – (suffix for names of ships)	
丸	0a3.28	丸薬 *gan'yaku* pill	359
	十 丿 丨	丸太小屋 *marutagoya* log cabin	629, 27, 167
	12 2	日本丸 *Nihon-maru* the ship Nihon	5, 25
	丸	日の丸 *Hi no Maru* (Japanese) Rising-Sun Flag	5

	645	***NETSU*** – heat, fever ***atsu(i)*** – hot (object)	
熱	4d11.4 日	熱病 *netsubyō* fever	380
	火 土 儿	高熱 *kōnetsu* high fever	190
	44 22 16	熱湯 *nettō* boiling water	632
		情熱 *jōnetsu* passion	209
	熱	熱心 *nesshin* enthusiasm, zeal	97

	646	***SEI, ikio(i)*** – force, energy, vigor; trend	
勢	2g11.6 日	勢力 *seiryoku* influence, force	100
	力 土 儿	国勢 *kokusei* state/condition of a country	40
	8 22 16	情勢 *jōsei* the situation	209
	勢	大勢 *taisei* general situation/trend	26
		ōzei many people, large crowd	

	647	***RIKU*** – land	
陸	2d8.4 田	大陸 *tairiku* continent, mainland	26
	阝土 儿	陸上 *rikujō* land, ground	32
	7 22 16	上陸 *jōriku* landing, going ashore	32
		陸路 *rikuro* land route	151
	陸	陸軍 *rikugun* army	438

	648	***SEN*** – money; 1/100 yen ***zeni*** – money	
銭	8a6.1 田	金銭 *kinsen* money	23
	金 戈 二	口銭 *kōsen* commission, percentage	54
	72 52 4	悪銭 *akusen* ill-gotten money	304
		銭湯 *sentō* public bath	632
	銭 錢	小銭 *kozeni* small change	27

	649	***SEN, asa(i)*** – shallow	
浅	3a6.4 田	浅海 *senkai* shallow sea	117
	氵戈 二	浅見 *senken* superficial view	63
	21 52 4	浅学 *sengaku* superficial knowledge	109
		浅黒い *asaguroi* dark-colored, swarthy	206
	浅 淺	遠浅 *tōasa* shoaling beach	446

	650	***ZAN, noko(ru)*** – remain behind ***noko(su)*** – leave behind	
残	0a10.11 田	残念 *zannen* regret, disappointment; too bad	579
	戈 夕 二	残業 *zangyō* overtime	279
	52 30 4	残高 *zandaka* balance, remainder	190
		残り物 *nokorimono* leftovers	79
	残 殘	生き残る *ikinokoru* survive	44

	651	***ZEN, NEN*** – as, like	
然	4d8.10 田	全然 *zenzen* (not) at all; completely	89
	火 夕 犭	当然 *tōzen* naturally, (as a matter) of course	77
	44 30 27	必然 *hitsuzen* inevitability, necessity	520
		自然 *shizen* nature	62
	然	天然 *tennen* natural	141

燃	**652** 4d12.2 火 夕 犭 44 30 27 燃	**NEN, mo(eru)** – (intr.) burn **mo(yasu), mo(su)** – (tr.) burn 燃料 *nenryō* fuel — 319 不燃性 *funensei* nonflammable, fireproof — 94, 98 可燃性 *kanensei* flammable, combustible 「engine — 388, 98 内燃機関 *nainen kikan* internal-combustion — 84, 528, 398 燃え上がる *moeagaru* blaze up, burst into flames — 32
谷	**653** 2o5.3 ソ 火 口 (16) 44 24 谷	**KOKU, tani** – valley 谷間 *tanima* valley — 43 谷底 *tanisoko* bottom of a ravine/gorge — 562 谷川 *tanigawa* mountain stream — 33 長谷川 *Hasegawa* (surname) — 95, 33 四ツ谷 *Yotsuya* (area of Tōkyō) — 6
容	**654** 3m7.8 宀 火 口 33 44 24 容	**YŌ** – form, appearance; content 美容院 *biyōin* beauty parlor, hairdresser's — 401, 614 形容 *keiyō* form; metaphor — 395 内容 *naiyō* content — 84 容器 *yōki* container — 527 容量 *yōryō* capacity, volume — 411
責	**655** 7b4.4 貝 土 一 68 22 1 責	**SEKI, se(meru)** – condemn, censure; torture 責任 *sekinin* responsibility — 334 重責 *jūseki* heavy responsibility — 227 責務 *sekimu* duty, obligation — 235 自責 *jiseki* self-reproach, pangs of conscience — 62 引責 *inseki* assume responsibility — 216
積	**656** 5d11.5 禾 貝 土 56 68 22 積	**SEKI, tsu(mu)** – heap up, load **tsu(moru)** – be piled up, accumulate **tsu(mori)** – intention; estimate 面積 *menseki* (surface) area — 274 積極的 *sekkyokuteki* positive, active — 336, 210 見積(書) *mitsumori(sho)* (written) estimate — 63, 131 積み重ねる *tsumikasaneru* stack up one on another — 227
着	**657** 2o10.1 ソ 目 王 16 55 46 着	**CHAKU, [JAKU]** – arrival; clothing **ki(ru), tsu(keru)** – put on, wear **ki(seru)** – dress (someone) **tsu(ku)** – arrive 着陸 *chakuriku* (airplane) landing — 647 決着 *ketchaku* conclusion, settlement, decision — 356 着物 *kimono* kimono; clothing — 79 下着 *shitagi* underwear — 31
差	**658** 2o8.4 ソ 王 エ 16 46 38 差	**SA** – difference **sa(su)** – hold (an umbrella); wear (a sword); offer (a cup of sakè) 時差 *jisa* time difference/lag — 42 差別 *sabetsu* discrimination — 267 交差点 *kōsaten* intersection — 114, 169 差し支え *sashitsukae* impediment; objection — 318

	659	**SEI, [SHŌ]** – spirit; energy, vitality	
精	6b8.1 ⊞	精力 *seiryoku* energy, vigor, vitality	100
	米 月 土	精神 *seishin* mind, spirit	310
	62 42 22	精液 *seieki* semen, sperm	472
		精進 *shōjin* diligence, devotion; purification	437
	精 精	不/無 精 *bushō* sloth, laziness, indolence	94, 93

	660	**SEI, [SHŌ], kiyo(i)** – pure, clean, clear **kiyo(meru)** – purify, cleanse **kiyo(maru)** – be purified, cleansed	
清	3a8.18 ⊞	清酒 *seishu* refined sakè	517
	氵 月 土	清書 *seisho* fair/clean copy	131
	21 ·42 22	清水 *seisui, shimizu* pure/clean water	21
	清 清	清水寺 *Kiyomizu-dera* (temple in Kyōto)	21, 41

	661	**SEI, SHIN, ko(u)** – ask for **u(keru)** – receive	
請	7a8.8 ⊞	請願 *seigan* petition, application	581
	言 月 土	要請 *yōsei* demand, requirement, request	419
	67 42 22	申請 *shinsei* application, petition	309
		強請 *kyōsei* importunate demand; extortion	217
	請 請	下請け *shitauke* subcontract	31

	662	**SEI, ha(reru)** – (intr.) clear up **ha(rasu)** – (tr.) clear up	
晴	4c8.2 ⊞	晴天 *seiten* clear sky, fine weather	141
	日 月 土	晴曇 *seidon* changeable, fair to cloudy	637
	43 42 22	秋晴れ *akibare* clear autumn weather	462
		見晴らし *miharashi* view, vista	63
	晴 晴	気晴らし *kibarashi* pastime, diversion	134

	663	**SEI, [JŌ], shizu, shizu(ka)** – quiet, peaceful, still **shizu(meru)** – make peaceful **shizu(maru)** – become peaceful	
静	4b10.9 ⊞	静物 *seibutsu* still life	79
	月 土 ヨ	静止 *seishi* stillness, rest, stationary	477
	42 22 39	安静 *ansei* rest, quiet, repose	105
	静 靜	平静 *heisei* calm, serenity	202

	664	**JŌ** – pure	
浄	3a6.18 ⊞	清浄 *seijō* purity, cleanliness	660
	氵 ヨ 宀	浄化 *jōka* purification	254
	21 39 15	不浄 *fujō* dirtiness, impurity	94
	浄 淨	浄土宗 *Jōdoshū* the Jōdo sect (of Buddhism)	24, 616

	665	**HA, yabu(ru)** – tear, break **yabu(reru)** – get torn/broken	
破	5a5.1 ⊡	破産 *hasan* bankruptcy	278
	石 厂 又	破局 *hakyoku* catastrophe, ruin	170
	53 18 9	破約 *hayaku* breach of contract/promise	211
		破れ目 *yabureme* a tear, split	55
	破	見破る *miyaburu* see through	63

	666	**HA, nami** – wave	
波	3a5.9 ⊞	波止場 *hatoba* wharf, pier	477, 154
氵 厂 又		電波 *denpa* electric/radio wave	108
21 18 9		短波 *tanpa* shortwave	215
波		波長 *hachō* wavelength	95
		波乗り *naminori* surfing	523

	667	**RITSU, [RICHI]** – law, regulation	
律	3i6.1 ⊞	法律 *hōritsu* law	123
彳 ヨ 十		規律 *kiritsu* order, discipline, regulations	607
29 39 12		不文律 *fubunritsu* unwritten law	94, 111
律		韻律 *inritsu* rhythm, meter	349
		自律神経 *jiritsu shinkei* autonomic nerve	62, 310, 548

	668	**SHIN, tsu** – harbor; ferry	
津	3a6.1 ⊞	津波 *tsunami* tsunami, "tidal" wave	666
氵 ヨ 十		興味津々 *kyōmi-shinshin* very interesting	368, 307
21 39 12		津軽半島 *Tsugaru Hantō* Tsugaru Peninsula	547, 88, 286
津			

	669	**KŌ, minato** – harbor, port	
港	3a9.13 ⊞	空港 *kūkō* airport	140
氵 ㅛ 弓		商/軍港 *shō/gunkō* trading/naval port	412, 438
21 32 28		内港 *naikō* inner harbor	84
港 港		港内 *kōnai* in the harbor	84
		港町 *minatomachi* port city	182

	670	**WAN** – bay	
湾	3a9.15 ⊞	東京湾 *Tōkyō-wan* Tōkyō Bay	71, 189
氵 弓 亠		湾曲 *wankyoku* curvature, bend	366
21 28 11		港湾 *kōwan* harbor ⌈borer, longshoreman	669
湾 灣		港湾労働者 *kōwan rōdōsha* port la-	669, 233, 232, 164
		台湾 *Taiwan* Taiwan, Formosa	492

	671	**SAI, tsuma** – wife	
妻	3e5.10 ⊟	夫妻 *fusai* husband and wife, Mr. and Mrs.	315
女 ヨ 十		妻子 *saishi* wife and child/children, family	103
25 39 12		後妻 *gosai* second wife	48
妻		良妻 *ryōsai* good wife	321
		老妻 *rōsai* one's aged wife	543

	672	**BŌ, [MŌ]** – die **na(i)** – dead, deceased	
亡	2j1.1 ⊟	死亡者 *shibōsha* the dead	85, 164
亠 乚		亡父 *bōfu* one's late father	113
11 2		亡夫 *bōfu* one's late husband	315
亡 亡		未亡人 *mibōjin* widow	306, 1
		亡命 *bōmei* fleeing one's country, going into exile	578

望	**673** 4f7.6 ⊟ 王 夕 亠 46 30 11 望	**BŌ, MŌ, nozo(mu)** – desire, wish, hope for

志望 *shibō* wish, aspiration — 573
宿望 *shukubō* long-cherished desire — 179
要望 *yōbō* demand, wish — 419
失望 *shitsubō* despair, disappointment — 311
大望 *taimō* great desire, ambition — 26

聖	**674** 4f9.9 ⊟ 王 耳 口 46 65 24 聖 聖	**SEI** – holy

聖人 *seijin* sage, holy man — 1
神聖 *shinsei* sacredness, sanctity — 310
聖書 *Seisho* the Bible — 131
聖堂 *seidō* Confucian temple; church — 496
聖母 *Seibo* the Holy Mother, the Blessed Mary — 112

布	**675** 3f2.1 ⫟ 巾 十 26 12 布	**FU** – spread; cloth **nuno** – a cloth

財布 *saifu* purse, wallet — 553
毛布 *mōfu* a blanket — 287
分布 *bunpu* distribution, range — 38
配布 *haifu* distribution, distributing widely — 515
公布 *kōfu* official announcement, promulgation — 126

希	**676** 3f4.1 ⊟ 巾 十 26 12 希	**KI** – hope, desire; rarity, scarcity

希望 *kibō* wish, hope — 673
希少 *kishō* scarce, rare — 144
希少価値 *kishō kachi* scarcity value — 144, 421, 425
メーカー希望価格 *mēkā kibō kakaku* manufacturer's suggested price, list price — 673, 421, 643

衣	**677** 5e0.1 □ 衤 57 衣	**I, koromo** – garment, clothes

衣類 *irui* clothing — 226
黒衣 *kokui* black clothes — 206
法衣 *hōi* priestly robes, vestment — 123
衣食住 *ishokujū* food, clothing, and shelter — 322, 156
羽衣 *hagoromo* robe of feathers — 590

依	**678** 2a6.1 ⊞ 亻 衤 3 57 依	**I, [E]** – depend on, be due to; request

依存 (度) *izon(do)* (extent of) dependence — 269, 377
依然として *izen toshite* as ever, as before — 651
帰依 *kie* faith, devotion; conversion — 317

初	**679** 5e2.1 ⊞ 衤 力 57 8 初	**SHO, haji(me)** – beginning **haji(mete)** – for the first time **hatsu-, ui-** – first **-so(meru)** – begin to

最初 *saisho* beginning, first — 263
初歩 *shoho* rudiments, ABCs — 431
初演 *shoen* first performance, premiere — 344
初恋 *hatsukoi* one's first love — 258

680

織

6a12.6 □

糸 戈日
61 52 43

織

SHOKU, SHIKI, o(ru) – weave

織機	shokki	loom	528
組織	soshiki	organization, structure; tissue	418
織物	orimono	cloth, fabric, textiles	79
毛織 (物)	keori(mono)	woolen fabric	287, 79
羽織	haori	haori, Japanese half-coat	590

681

識

7a12.6 □

言 戈日
67 52 43

識

SHIKI – know; discriminate

意識	ishiki	consciousness	132
知識	chishiki	knowledge	214
常識	jōshiki	common sense/knowledge	497
学識	gakushiki	learning	109
識別	shikibetsu	discrimination, recognition	267

682

編

6a9.13 □

糸 戸 艹
61 40 32

編

HEN, a(mu) – knit, crochet; compile, edit

編集	henshū	editing	436
短編小説	tanpen shōsetsu	short novel, story	215, 27, 400
編成	hensei	organizing, formation	261
編み物	amimono	knitting; knitted goods	79
手編み	teami	knitting by hand	57

683

服

4b4.6 □

月 阝 又
42 7 9

服

FUKU – clothes, dress; dose

衣服	ifuku	clothing	677
洋/和服	yō/Wafuku	Western/Japanese clothing	289, 124
心服	shinpuku	admiration and devotion	97
着服	chakufuku	embezzlement, misappropriation	657
服役	fukueki	penal servitude; military service	375

684

幸

3b5.9 日

土 立 艹
(22) 54 12

幸

KŌ, saiwa(i), shiawa(se), sachi – happiness, good fortune

| 幸運 | kōun | good fortune, luck | 439 |
| 不幸 | fukō | unhappiness, misfortune | 94 |

685

報

3b9.16 日

土 立 艹
(22) 54 12

報

HŌ – news, report; remuneration **muku(iru)** – reward, requite

天気予報	tenki yohō	weather forecast	141, 134, 393
報道機関	hōdō kikan	news media, the press	149, 528, 398
情報	jōhō	information	209
報知	hōchi	information, news, intelligence	214
電報	denpō	telegram	108

686

執

3b8.15 日

土 立 艹
(22) 54 12

執

SHITSU, SHŪ, to(ru) – take, grasp; carry out, execute

執行	shikkō	execution, performance	68
執権	shikken	regent	335
執心	shūshin	devotion, attachment, infatuation	97
執着	shūjaku, shūchaku	attachment to; tenacity	657
執念	shūnen	tenacity of purpose; vindictiveness	579

	687	**JUKU, u(reru)** – ripen, come to maturity	
熟	4d10.5 田	円 熟 *enjuku* maturity, mellowness	13
	火 口 一	成 熟 *seijuku* ripeness, maturity	261
	44 24 11	未 熟 *mijuku* unripe, immature, green	306
		半 熟 *hanjuku* half-cooked, soft-boiled (egg)	88
	熟	熟 語 *jukugo* compound word; phrase	67

	688	**JI** – word; resignation **ya(meru)** – quit, resign	
辞	5b8.4 田	辞書, 辞典 *jisho, jiten* dictionary	131, 367
	立 口 十	(お) 世 辞 *(o)seji* compliment, flattery	252
	54 24 12	式 辞 *shikiji* address, oration	525
		辞 職 *jishoku* resignation	385
	辞 辭	辞 表 *jihyō* (letter of) resignation	272

	689	**RAN** – riot, rebellion; disorder **mida(reru)** – get in disorder/ confusion **mida(su)** – put in disorder/confusion	
乱	3d4.21 田	反 乱 *hanran* rebellion, insurgency, insurrection	324
	口 十 |	内 乱 *nairan* internal strife, civil war	84
	24 12 2	乱 雑 *ranzatsu* disorder, confusion	575
	乱 亂	乱 筆 *ranpitsu* hasty writing, scrawl	130

	690	**KOKU, tsu(geru)** – tell, announce, inform	
告	3d4.18 日	報 告 *hōkoku* report	685
	口 土 |	通 告 *tsūkoku* notice, notification	150
	24 22 2	申 告 *shinkoku* report, declaration, (tax) return	309
		告 発 *kokuhatsu* prosecution, indictment, accusation	96
	告	告 白 *kokuhaku* confession, avowal, profession	205

	691	**ZŌ, tsuku(ru)** – produce, build	
造	2q7.11 凵	製 造 *seizō* manufacture, production	428
	辶 口 土	造 船 *zōsen* shipbuilding	376
	19 24 22	木 造 *mokuzō* made of wood, wooden	22
		人 造 *jinzō* man-made, artificial	1
	造	手 造 り *tezukuri* handmade	57

	692	**SEN, ara(u)** – wash	
洗	3a6.12 田	洗 剤 *senzai* detergent	550
	氵 土 儿	洗 面 器 *senmenki* wash basin	274, 527
	21 22 16	面 所 *senmenjo* washroom, lavatory	274, 153
		(お) 手 洗 い *(o)tearai* washroom, lavatory	57
	洗	洗 い 立 て る *araitateru* inquire into, rake up, ferret out	121

	693	**O, kitana(i), kega(rawashii)** – dirty **yogo(reru)**, **kega(reru)** – become dirty **yogo(su), kega(su)** – make dirty	
汚	3a3.5 田	汚 職 *oshoku* corruption, bribery	385
	氵 一 一	汚 物 *obutsu* dirt, filth; sewage	79
	21 14 1	汚 点 *oten* blot, blotch, blemish, tarnish	169
	汚	汚 名 *omei* stigma, stain on one's name, dishonor	82

171

	694	**KŌ, hiro(i)** – broad, wide **hiro(geru)** – extend, enlarge
広	3q2.1	**hiro(garu)** – spread, expand **hiro(meru)** – broaden, propagate
	广 厶	**hiro(maru)** – spread, be propagated
	18 17	広告 *kōkoku* advertisement — 690
	広 廣	広大 *kōdai* vast, extensive, huge — 26
		広場 *hiroba* plaza, public square — 154

	695	**SAI** – narrow, small, fine **hoso(i)** – thin, narrow, slender
細	6a5.1	**hoso(ru)** – get thinner **koma(kai), koma(ka)** – small, detailed
	糸 田	委細 *isai* details, particulars — 466
	61 58	細工 *saiku* work, workmanship; artifice, trick — 139
	細	細説 *saisetsu* detailed explanation — 400
		細長い *hosonagai* long and thin, lean and lanky — 95

	696	**SHŌ, matsu** – pine
松	4a4.16	松原 *matsubara* pine grove — 136
	木 儿 厶	松林 *matsubayashi* pine woods — 127
	41 16 17	松葉 *matsuba* pine needle — 253
	松 杦	門松 *kadomatsu* pine decoration for New Year's — 161
		松島 *Matsushima* (scenic coastal area near Sendai) — 286

	697	**SŌ** – general, overall
総	6a8.20	総会 *sōkai* general meeting, plenary session — 158
	糸 心 儿	総合 *sōgō* synthesis, comprehensive — 159
	61 51 16	総計 *sōkei* (sum) total — 340
	総 總	総理 *sōri* prime minister (cf. No. 835) ⌐product — 143
		国民総生産 *kokumin sōseisan* gross national — 40, 177, 44, 278

	698	**SŌ, mado** – window
窓	3m8.7	同窓生 *dōsōsei* schoolmate, alumnus — 198, 44
	宀 心 儿	車窓 *shasō* car window — 133
	33 51 16	窓口 *madoguchi* (ticket) window — 54
	窓 窗	二重窓 *nijūmado* double window — 3, 227
		窓際の席 *madogiwa no seki* seat next to the window — 618, 379

	699	**GYO, RYŌ** – fishing
漁	3a11.1	漁業 *gyogyō* fishery, fishing industry — 279
	氵 魚	漁船 *gyosen* fishing boat/vessel — 376
	21 79	漁場 *gyojō* fishing ground/banks — 154
	漁	漁村 *gyoson* fishing village — 191
		漁師 *ryōshi* fisherman — 409

	700	**GEI, kujira** – whale
鯨	11a8.9	鯨肉 *geiniku* whale meat — 223
	魚 口 小	鯨油 *geiyu* whale oil — 364
	79 24 35	鯨飲 *geiin* drink like a fish, guzzle — 323
	鯨	白鯨 *Hakugei* (Moby Dick, or The White Whale –
		Melville) 205

Kanji	No.	Entry
鮮	**701** 11a6.7 田 魚 王 儿 79 46 16 鮮	**SEN, aza(yaka)** – fresh, vivid, clear, brilliant

新 鮮　*shinsen*　fresh　174
鮮 明　*senmei*　clear, distinct　18
鮮 度　*sendo*　(degree of) freshness　377
鮮 魚　*sengyo*　fresh fish　290
朝 鮮　*Chōsen*　Korea　469

Kanji	No.	Entry
遅	**702** 2q9.17 囗 辶 王 尸 19 46 40 遅 遅	**CHI, oso(i)** – late, tardy; slow　**oku(reru)** – be late (for); be slow (clock)　**oku(rasu)** – defer; put back (a clock)

遅 着　*chichaku*　late arrival　657
遅 配　*chihai*　late arrival; delay in apportioning/delivery　515
遅 速　*chisoku*　speed　502
乗 り 遅 れ る　*noriokureru*　be too late to catch, miss (a bus/train)　523

Kanji	No.	Entry
導	**703** 5c9.3 日 目 寸 辶 55 37 19 導	**DŌ, michibi(ku)** – lead, guide

主 導　*shudō*　leadership, guidance　155
先 導　*sendō*　guidance, leadership　50
導 入　*dōnyū*　introduction　52
導 火 線　*dōkasen*　fuse; cause, occasion　20, 299
半 導 体　*handōtai*　semiconductor　88, 61

Kanji	No.	Entry
尊	**704** 2o10.3 目 丷 酉 寸 16 71 37 尊 尊	**SON, tatto(bu), tōto(bu)** – value, esteem, respect **tatto(i), tōto(i)** – valuable, precious, noble, august

尊 重　*sonchō*　value, respect, pay high regard to　227
自 尊 (心)　*jison(shin)*　self-respect, pride　62, 97
尊 大　*sondai*　haughtiness, arrogance　26
本 尊　*honzon*　Buddha; idol; he himself, she herself　25

Kanji	No.	Entry
敬	**705** 4i8.4 田 夂 艹 口 49 32 24 敬	**KEI, uyama(u)** – respect, revere

尊 敬　*sonkei*　respect, deference　704
敬 意　*keii*　respect, homage　132
敬 老　*keirō*　respect for the aged　543
敬 遠　*keien*　keep at a respectful distance　446
敬 語　*keigo*　an honorific, term of respect　67

Kanji	No.	Entry
警	**706** 7a12.7 田 言 夂 艹 67 49 32 警	**KEI** – admonish, warn

警 察　*keisatsu*　police　619
警 官　*keikan*　policeman　326
警 視　*keishi*　police superintendent　606
警 告　*keikoku*　warning, admonition　690
警 報　*keihō*　warning (signal), alarm　685

Kanji	No.	Entry
卸	**707** 2e7.1 囗 卩 丿 十 7 15 12 卸	**oro(su)** – sell wholesale　**oroshi** – wholesaling

卸 商　*oroshishō*　wholesaler　412
卸 値　*oroshine*　wholesale price　425
卸 し 売 り 物 価　*oroshiuri bukka*　wholesale prices　239, 79, 421

	708	**GYO, GO, on-** – (honorific prefix)	
御	3i9.1 ⊞	制御 *seigyo* control, governing, suppression	427
	彳 阝 宀	御飯 *gohan* boiled rice; meal	325
	29 7 15	御用の方 *goyō no kata* customer, inquirer	107, 70
		御所 *gosho* imperial palace	153
御		御中 *onchū* Dear sirs:, Gentlemen:, Messrs.	28

	709	**KA, kuwa(eru)** – add, append **kuwa(waru)** – join, take part (in)	
加	2g3.1 ⊞	加入 *kanyū* joining	52
	力 口	加工 *kakō* processing	139
	8 24	加法 *kahō* addition (in mathematics)	123
		倍加 *baika* doubling ⌐tax	87
加		付加価値税 *fukakachi-zei* value-added 192, 421, 425, 399	

	710	**SAN** – three (in documents); go, come, visit **mai(ru)** – go, come,	
参	3j5.1 ⽇	visit, visit a temple/shrine	
	彡 大 厶	参加 *sanka* participation	709
	31 34 17	参列 *sanretsu* attendance, presence	611
		参考書 *sankōsho* reference book/work	541, 131
参 参		参議院 *Sangiin* (Japanese) House of Councilors	292, 614

	711	**BEN** – speech, dialect; discrimination; petal; valve	
弁	0a5.30 ⽇	弁当 *bentō* box/sack lunch	77
	艹 厶	駅弁 *ekiben* box lunch sold at a train station	284
	32 17	答弁 *tōben* reply, answer	160
		弁解 *benkai* explanation, justification, excuse	474
弁 辯		関西弁 *Kansai-ben* Kansai dialect/accent	398, 72

	712	**ZŌ, ma(su), fu(eru)** – increase, rise **fu(yasu)** – increase, raise	
増	3b11.3 ⊞	増加 *zōka* increase, rise, growth	709
	土 甲 日	増産 *zōsan* increase in production	278
	22 58 43	増税 *zōzei* tax increase	399
		増進 *zōshin* increase, furtherance, improvement	437
増 增			

	713	**FU, [FŪ], tomi** – wealth **to(mu)** – be/become rich	
富	3m9.5 ⽇	国富 *kokufu* national wealth	40
	宀 甲 日	富強 *fukyō* wealth and power	217
	33 58 24	富力 *furyoku* wealth, resources	100
		富者 *fusha, fūsha* rich person, the wealthy	164
富 冨		富士山 *Fuji-san* Mount Fuji	572, 34

	714	**FUKU** – assistant, accompany, supplement	
副	2f9.2 ⊞	副社長 *fukushachō* company vice-president	308, 95
	刂 甲 口	副業 *fukugyō* side business, sideline	279
	16 58 24	副産物 *fukusanbutsu* by-product	278, 79
		副作用 *fukusayō* side effects	360, 107
副		副題 *fukudai* subtitle, subheading	354

	715	**GEN, he(ru)** – decrease, diminish **he(rasu)** – decrease, shorten	
減	3a9.37 ⯐ 氵 戈 口 21 52 24 減	増減 *zōgen* increase and/or decrease 加減 *kagen* addition and subtraction; state of health 減少 *genshō* decrease, reduction 半減 *hangen* reduction by half 減法 *genpō* subtraction (in mathematics)	712 709 144 88 123
益	716 2o8.5 目 ⸌ 皿 一 16 59 1 益	**EKI, [YAKU]** – profit, use, advantage 利益 *rieki* profit, advantage 公益 *kōeki* the public good 有益 *yūeki* useful, beneficial, profitable 無益 *mueki* useless, in vain 益鳥 *ekichō* beneficial bird	 329 126 265 93 285
盟	717 5h8.1 日 皿 日 月 59 43 42 盟	**MEI** – oath; alliance 連盟 *renmei* league, federation 同盟 *dōmei* alliance, confederation 加盟 *kamei* joining, affiliation 盟主 *meishu* the leader, leading power 盟約 *meiyaku* pledge, pact; alliance	 440 198 709 155 211
誠	718 7a6.3 ⯐ 言 戈 一 67 52 15 誠	**SEI, makoto** – truth, reality; sincerity, fidelity 誠実 *seijitsu* sincere, faithful, truthful 誠意 *seii* sincerity, good faith 誠心誠意 *seishin-seii* sincerely, wholeheartedly 誠に *makoto ni* truly, indeed; sincerely; very	 203 132 97, 132
盛	719 5h6.1 目 皿 戈 ⸌ 59 52 15 盛	**SEI, [JŌ], saka(n)** – prosperous, energetic **saka(ru)** – flourish, prosper **mo(ru)** – serve (food); heap up 盛大 *seidai* thriving, grand, magnificent 全盛 *zensei* height of prosperity, zenith, heyday 最盛期 *saiseiki* golden age, zenith 花盛り *hanazakari* in full bloom, at its best	 26 89 263, 449 255
城	720 3b6.1 ⯐ 土 戈 ⸌ 22 52 15 城	**JŌ, shiro** – castle 城下町 *jōkamachi* castle town 城主 *jōshu* feudal lord of a castle 開城 *kaijō* surrender of a fortress, capitulation 城門 *jōmon* castle gate 古城 *kojō* old castle	 31, 182 155 396 161 172
宮	721 3m7.5 目 宀 口 丨 33 24 2 宮	**KYŪ, GŪ, [KU], miya** – shrine; palace; prince 宮城 *kyūjō* imperial palace 神宮 *jingū* Shintō shrine 宮参り *miyamairi* visit to a shrine 宮城県 *Miyagi-ken* Miyagi Prefecture 子宮 *shikyū* uterus, womb	 720 310 710 720, 194 103

722

EI, itona(mu) – perform (a ceremony); conduct (business)

3n9.2 目
ｿ 口 冂
35 24 20

営

経営	*keiei*	management, administration	548
運営	*un'ei*	operation, management, running	439
公営	*kōei*	public management, municipally run	126
営業	*eigyō*	(running a) business	279
営利	*eiri*	profit, profit-making	329

723

EI, ha(e) – glory, honor, splendor **ha(eru)** – shine, be brilliant
saka(eru) – thrive, prosper

3n6.1
ｿ 木 冂
35 41 20

栄 榮

栄養	*eiyō*	nutrition	402
光栄	*kōei*	honor, glory	138
栄光	*eikō*	glory	138
見栄え	*mibae*	outward appearance	63

724

KYŪ, moto(meru) – want; request, demand, seek

2b5.5 ⬚
冫 氵 一
(5) 21 1

求

請求	*seikyū*	a claim, demand	661
要求	*yōkyū*	demand	419
求職	*kyūshoku*	seeking employment, job hunting	385
求人	*kyūjin*	job offer, Help Wanted	1
探求	*tankyū*	research, investigation	535

725

KYŪ, suku(u) – rescue, aid

4i7.1 ⬚
攵 氵 一
49 21 1

救

救急	*kyūkyū*	first aid	303
救助	*kyūjo*	rescue, relief	623
救済	*kyūsai*	relief, aid, redemption, salvation	549
救命ボート	*kyūmei bōto*	lifeboat	578
救世軍	*Kyūseigun*	Salvation Army	252, 438

726

KYŪ, tama – ball, sphere

4f7.2 ⬚
王 氵 一
46 21 1

球

野球	*yakyū*	baseball	236
球場	*kyūjō*	baseball stadium, ball park	154
電球	*denkyū*	light bulb	108
(軽)気球	*(kei)kikyū*	(hot-air/helium) balloon	547, 134
地球	*chikyū*	the earth, globe	118

727

GI – rule; ceremony; affair, matter

2a13.4 ⊞
亻 王 戈
3 46 52

儀

礼儀	*reigi*	politeness, courtesy, propriety	620
礼儀正しい	*reigi tadashii*	courteous, decorous	620, 275
儀式	*gishiki*	ceremony, formality, ritual	525
儀典長	*gitenchō*	chief of protocol	367, 95
地球儀	*chikyūgi*	a globe	118, 726

728

GI – sacrifice

4g13.1 ⊞
牛 王 戈
47 46 52

犠 犧

牲	**729** 4g5.1 ⊞ 牛 一 47 1 牲	**SEI** – sacrifice

犠 牲 *gisei* sacrifice   728
犠 牲 者 *giseisha* victim   728, 164

星	**730** 4c5.7 ⊟ 日 牛 一 43 47 1 星	**SEI, [SHŌ], hoshi** – star

火 星 *kasei* Mars   20
明 星 *myōjō* morning star, Venus   18
すい星 *suisei* comet
流れ星 *nagareboshi* shooting star, meteor   247
星 空 *hoshizora* starry sky   140

牧	**731** 4g4.1 ⊞ 牛 攵 47 49 牧	**BOKU, maki** – pasture

牧 場 *bokujō, makiba* pasture, meadow   154
牧 草 地 *bokusōchi* pasture, grassland, meadowland   249, 118
放 牧 *hōboku* pasturage, grazing   512
牧 羊 者 *bokuyōsha* sheep raiser, shepherd   288, 164
牧 師 *bokushi* pastor, minister   409

件	**732** 2a4.4 ⊞ 亻 牛 3 47 件	**KEN** – matter, affair, case

事 件 *jiken* incident, affair, case   80
条 件 *jōken* condition, terms, stipulation   564
要 件 *yōken* important matter; condition, requisite   419
用 件 *yōken* (item of) business   107
案 件 *anken* matter, case, item   106

免	**733** 2n6.1 ⊟ ⺈ 口 儿 15 24 16 免 免	**MEN, manuka(reru)** – escape, avoid, be exempt from

御 免 *gomen* pardon; declining, refusal   708
免 責 *menseki* exemption from responsibility   655
免 税 *menzei* tax exemption   399
免 状 *menjō* diploma; license   626
免 職 *menshoku* dismissal from one's job/office   385

逸	**734** 2q8.6 ⊡ 辶 口 ⺈ 19 24 15 逸 逸	**ITSU** – idleness; diverge, deviate from

逸 話 *itsuwa* anecdote   238
逸 品 *ippin* superb article, masterpiece   230
放 逸 *hōitsu* self-indulgence, licentiousness   512

勉	**735** 2n8.1 ⊡ ⺈ 口 儿 15 24 16 勉 勉	**BEN** – effort, hard work

勉 強 *benkyō* studying; diligence; sell cheap   217
勉 強 家 *benkyōka* diligent student; hard worker   217, 165
勉 学 *bengaku* study, pursuit of one's studies   109
勤 勉 *kinben* industriousness, diligence, hard work   559

晩 736	**BAN** – evening, night	
4c8.3 田	今晩 konban this evening, tonight	51
日 口 厂	毎晩 maiban every evening	116
43 24 15	一晩 hitoban a night, all night	2
	朝晩 asaban mornings and evenings, day and night	469
晩 晩	晩年 bannen latter part of one's life	45

許 737	**KYO, yuru(su)** – permit, allow	
7a4.3 口	免許 menkyo permission, license	733
言 广 十	許可 kyoka permission, approval, authorization	388
67 15 12	許容 kyoyō permission, tolerance	654
	特許 tokkyo special permission; patent	282
許	特許法 tokkyo-hō patent law	282, 123

認 738	**NIN, mito(meru)** – perceive; recognize; approve of	
7a7.10 田	認可 ninka approval	388
言 心 力	認定 nintei approval, acknowledgment	355
67 51 8	確認 kakunin confirmation, certification	603
	公認 kōnin official recognition/sanction	126
認	認識 ninshiki cognition, recognition, perception	681

象 739	**SHŌ** – image, shape **ZŌ** – elephant	
2n10.1 目	具象的 gushōteki concrete, embodied	420, 210
宀 口 豸	現象 genshō phenomenon	298
15 24 27	対象 taishō object, subject, target	365
	気象学 kishōgaku meteorology	134, 109
象	象げ zōge ivory	

像 740	**ZŌ** – statue, image	
2a12.8 田	仏像 butsuzō statue/image of Buddha	583
亻 口 豸	自画像 jigazō self-portrait	62, 343
3 24 27	受像機 juzōki television set	260, 528
	現像 genzō (photographic) development	298
像	想像 sōzō imagination	147

株 741	**kabu** – share, stock; stump	
4a6.3 口	株式会社 kabushiki-gaisha Co., Ltd.	525, 158, 308
木 广	株券 kabuken share, stock certificate	506
41 15	株主 kabunushi stockholder ⌐shareholders	155
	株主総会 kabunushi sōkai general meeting of	155, 697, 158
株	切り株 kirikabu (tree) stump, (grain) stubble	39

絶 742	**ZETSU, ta(eru)** – die out, end **ta(tsu)** – cut off, interrupt;	
6a6.11 田	eradicate **ta(yasu)** – kill off, let die out	
糸 尸 广	絶対 zettai absolute	365
61 40 15	絶大 zetsudai greatest, immense	26
	絶望 zetsubō despair	673
絶	根絶 konzetsu root out, eradicate, stamp out	314

743	**REN, ne(ru)** – knead; train; polish up	
6a8.2 ⬚	練習 *renshū* practice, exercise	591
糸 木 日	教練 *kyōren* (military) drill	245
61 41 43	試練 *shiren* trial, test, ordeal	526
	熟練 *jukuren* practiced skill, expertness, mastery	687
練 練	洗練 *senren* polish, refine	692

744	**TAI, ka(eru)** – replace **ka(waru)** – be replaced	
4c8.12 ⬚	代替 *daitai, daigae* substitution	256
日 大 一	両替 *ryōgae* exchanging/changing money	200
43 34 1	着替える *kigaeru, kikaeru* change clothes	657
	切り替え *kirikae* renewal, changeover	39
替	取り替え *torikae* exchange, swap, replacement	65

745	**SAN** – praise; agreement	
7b8.6 ⬚	賛成 *sansei* agreement, approbation	261
貝 大 一	賛助 *sanjo* support, backing	623
68 34 1	協賛 *kyōsan* approval, consent, support	234
	賞賛 *shōsan* praise, admiration	500
賛 贊	賛美 *sanbi* praise, glorification	401

746	**SEI, [SHŌ], koe, [kowa-]** – voice	
3p4.4 ⬚	声明 *seimei* declaration, statement, proclamation	18
声 尸 丨	名声 *meisei* fame, reputation	82
22 40 2	音声学 *onseigaku* phonetics	347, 109
	声変わり *koegawari* change/cracking of voice	257
声 聲	声色 *kowairo* imitated/assumed voice	204

747	**SAN** – calculate	
6f8.7 ⬚	計算 *keisan* calculation, computation	340
竹 目 廾	公算 *kōsan* probability, likelihood	126
66 55 32	予算 *yosan* an estimate; budget	393
	精算 *seisan* exact calculation; (fare) adjustment	659
算	暗算 *anzan* mental arithmetic/calculation	348

748	**TAI, ka(su)** – rent out	
7b5.9 ⬚	貸与 *taiyo* lend, loan	539
貝 戈 亻	貸し家 *kashiya* house for rent, rented house	165
68 52 3	貸しボート *kashibōto* boat for rent, rented boat	
	貸し出す *kashidasu* lend/hire out	53
貸	貸し切り *kashikiri* reservations, booking	39

749	**HI, tsui(yasu)** – spend **tsui(eru)** – be wasted	
7b5.4 ⬚	経費 *keihi* expenses, cost	548
貝 弓 儿	費用 *hiyō* expense, cost	107
68 28 16	生活費 *seikatsuhi* living expenses, cost of living	44, 237
	光熱費 *kōnetsuhi* heating and lighting expenses	138, 645
費	旅費 *ryohi* traveling expenses	222

資 750

7b6.7 ⊟

貝 攵 冫
68 49 5

資

SHI – resources, capital, funds

資源	*shigen*	resources	580
資本	*shihon*	capital	25
資金	*shikin*	funds	23
物資	*busshi*	goods, (raw) materials	79
資格	*shikaku*	qualification, competence	643

賃 751

7b6.6 ⊟

貝 王 亻
68 46 3

賃

CHIN – rent; wages; fare, fee

賃金	*chingin*	wages, pay	23
賃上げ	*chin'age*	raise in wages	32
運賃	*unchin*	passenger fare; shipping charges	439
電車賃	*denshachin*	train fare	108, 133
家賃	*yachin*	rent	165

貨 752

7b4.5 ⊟

貝 亻 ⺊
68 3 13

貨

KA – freight; goods, property

貨物	*kamotsu*	freight	79
百貨店	*hyakkaten*	department store	14, 168
通貨	*tsūka*	currency	150
外貨	*gaika*	foreign goods/currency	83
銀貨	*ginka*	silver coin	313

貧 753

2o9.5 ⊟

貝 儿 力
68 16 8

貧 貧

HIN, BIN, mazu(shii) – poor

貧富	*hinpu*	poverty and wealth, the rich and poor	713
貧困	*hinkon*	poverty, need	558
貧弱	*hinjaku*	poor, meager, scanty	218
貧相	*hinsō*	poor-looking, seedy	146
清貧	*seihin*	honest poverty	660

乏 754

0a3.11 ⊟

一 丨
1 2

乏

BŌ, tobo(shii) – scanty, meager, scarce

貧乏	*binbō*	poor	753
欠乏	*ketsubō*	shortage, deficiency	383

架 755

4a5.36 ⊟

木 口 力
41 24 8

架

KA, ka(keru) – hang, build (bridge) **ka(karu)** – hang, be built

架設	*kasetsu*	construction, laying	577
架橋	*kakyō*	bridge building	597
書架	*shoka*	bookshelf	131
十字架像	*jūjikazō*	crucifix	12, 110, 740
架空	*kakū*	overhead, aerial; fanciful	140

賀 756

7b5.10 ⊟

貝 口 力
68 24 8

賀

GA – congratulations, felicitations

賀状	*gajō*	greeting card	626
年賀	*nenga*	New Year's greetings	45
年賀状	*nengajō*	New Year's card	45, 626
賀正	*gashō*	New Year's greetings	275
志賀高原	*Shiga Kōgen*	Shiga Highlands	573, 190, 136

	757	**SHŪ**, *osa(meru)* – obtain, collect *osa(maru)* – be obtained, end
収	2h2.2	収支 *shūshi* income and expenditures 318
	又 丨	収入 *shūnyū* income, earnings, receipts 52
	9 2	買収 *baishū* purchase; buying off, bribery 241
		収益 *shūeki* earnings, proceeds, profit 716
	収 収	収容 *shūyō* admission, accommodation 654

	758	**NŌ**, [**TŌ**], [**NA**], [**NA'**], [**NAN**], *osa(meru)* – pay; supply; accept,
納	6a4.5	store *osa(maru)* – be paid (in), supplied
	糸 亻 冂	納税 *nōzei* payment of taxes 399
	61 3 20	出納 *suitō* receipts and disbursements 53
		納得 *nattoku* consent, understanding 374
	納	納屋 *naya* (storage) shed 167

	759	**EKI** – devination **I**, *yasa(shii)* – easy
易	4c4.9	易者 *ekisha* fortune-teller 164
	日 彡	不易 *fueki* immutability, unchangeableness 94
	43 27	交易 *kōeki* trade, commerce, barter 114
		容易 *yōi* easy, simple 654
	易	難易 (度) *nan'i(do)* (degree of) difficulty 557, 377

	760	**BŌ** – exchange, trade
貿	7b5.8	貿易 *bōeki* foreign trade, trade 759
	貝 厂 力	自由貿易 *jiyū bōeki* free trade 62, 363, 759
	68 18 8	貿易会社 *bōeki-gaisha* trading firm/company 759, 158, 308
		貿易収支 *bōeki shūshi* balance of trade 759, 757, 318
	貿	日米貿易 *Nichi-Bei bōeki* Japan-U.S. trade 5, 224, 759

	761	**RYŪ**, [**RU**], *to(meru)* – fasten down; hold, keep (in)
留	5f5.4	*to(maru)* – stay, settle
	甼 厂 力	留学 *ryūgaku* study abroad 109
	58 18 8	留守 *rusu* absence from home 490
		書留 *kakitome* registered mail 131
	留 畱	局留 (め) *kyokudome* general delivery 170

	762	**CHO** – storage
貯	7b5.1	貯金 *chokin* savings, deposit 23
	貝 宀 丁	貯水池 *chosuichi* reservoir 21, 119
	68 33 14	
	貯	

	763	**CHŌ** – government office, agency
庁	3q2.2	官庁 *kanchō* government office, agency 326
	广 丁	警視庁 *Keishichō* Metropolitan Police Department 706, 606
	18 14	気象庁 *Kishōchō* Meteorological Agency 134, 739
	庁 廳	県庁 *kenchō* prefectural office 194

	764 3k5.28 目 艹 日 一 32 43 1 昔	**SEKI, [SHAKU], mukashi** – antiquity, long ago
昔		今昔 *konjaku* past and present — 51
		大昔 *ōmukashi* remote antiquity, time immemorial — 26
		昔々 *mukashi-mukashi* Once upon a time ...
		昔話 *mukashi-banashi* old tale, legend — 238
		昔 の 事 *mukashi no koto* thing of the past — 80

	765 4k8.11 目 忄 日 艹 51 43 32 惜	**SEKI, o(shii)** – regrettable; precious; wasteful **o(shimu)** – regret; value; begrudge, be sparing of
惜		惜敗 *sekihai* narrow defeat (after a hard-fought contest) — 511
		愛惜 *aiseki* be loath to part — 259
		口惜しい *kuchioshii* regrettable, vexing — 54
		負け惜しみ *makeoshimi* unwillingness to admit defeat — 510

	766 2a8.22 田 亻 日 艹 3 43 32 借	**SHAKU, ka(riru)** – borrow, rent
借		借金 *shakkin* debt — 23
		借財 *shakuzai* debt — 553
		貸借 *taishaku* debits and credits — 748
		転借 *tenshaku* subleasing — 433
		賃借, 賃借り *chinshaku, chingari* lease — 751

	767 4i8.1 田 攵 月 艹 49 42 32 散	**SAN, chi(rakasu)** – scatter, disarrange **chi(rakaru)** – lie scattered, be in disorder **chi(rasu)** – (tr.) scatter **chi(ru)** – (intr.) scatter
散		解散 *kaisan* breakup, dissolution, disbanding — 474
		散会 *sankai* adjournment — 158
		散文 *sanbun* prose — 111
		散歩 *sanpo* walk, stroll — 431

	768 2a10.4 田 亻 月 艹 3 42 32 備	**BI, sona(eru)** – furnish, provide (for) **sona(waru)** – possess
備		設備 *setsubi* equipment, facilities — 577
		整備 *seibi* maintenance, servicing — 503
		軍備 *gunbi* military preparations, armaments — 438
		予備費 *yobihi* reserves, reserve funds — 393, 749
		備考 *bikō* explanatory notes, remarks — 541

	769 9a3.2 川 頁 儿 丨 77 16 2 順	**JUN** – order, sequence
順		順番 *junban* order, one's turn — 185
		順位 *jun'i* ranking, standing — 122
		語順 *gojun* word order — 67
		五十音順 *gojū-on jun* in order of the kana — 7, 12, 347 「syllabary
		順調 *junchō* favorable, smooth, without a hitch — 342

	770 3q4.4 口 广 亠 一 18 14 1 序	**JO** – beginning; preface; order; precedence
序		順序 *junjo* order, method, procedure — 769
		序説 *josetsu* introduction, preface — 400
		序論 *joron* introduction, preface — 293
		序文 *jobun* preface, foreword, introduction — 111
		序曲 *jokyoku* overture, prelude — 366

	771	***KUN*** – Japanese reading of a kanji; teaching, precept	
訓	7a3.6 ⊞	訓 育 *kun'iku* education, discipline	246
	言 儿 丨	教 訓 *kyōkun* teaching, precept, moral	245
	67 16 2	訓 練 *kunren* training	743
	訓	訓 辞 *kunji* an admonitory speech, instructions	688
		音 訓 *on-kun* Chinese and Japanese readings	347

	772	***JUN, tate*** – shield	
盾	5c4.8 ◻	後 ろ 盾 *ushirodate* support, backing; supporter, backer	48
	目 厂 十		
	55 18 12		
	盾		

	773	***MU, hoko*** – halberd	
矛	0a5.6 ⊟	矛 盾 *mujun* contradiction	772
	乛 一 丨	矛 先 *hokosaki* point of a spear; aim of an attack	50
	14 1 2		
	矛		

	774	***JŪ, NYŪ, yawa(rakai), yawa(raka)*** – soft	
柔	4a5.34 ⊟	柔 道 *jūdō* judo	149
	木 乛 一	柔 術 *jūjutsu* jujitsu	187
	41 14 1	柔 弱 *nyūjaku* weakness, enervation	218
	柔	柔 和 *nyūwa* gentle, mild(-mannered)	124
		物 柔 ら か *mono-yawaraka* mild(-mannered), quiet, gentle	79

	775	***HEN, ata(ri), -be*** – vicinity	
辺	2q2.1 ◻	近 辺 *kinpen* neighborhood, vicinity	445
	辶 力	周 辺 *shūhen* periphery, environs	91
	19 8	辺 地 *henchi* remote place, out-of-the-way place	118
	辺 邊	海 辺 *umibe* beach, seashore	117
		上 辺 *uwabe* exterior, surface; outward appearance	32

	776	***ko(mu)*** – be crowded, congested ***ko(meru)*** – include, count in; load (a gun); concentrate	
込	2q2.3 ◻	巻 き 込 む *makikomu* entangle, involve, implicate	507
	辶 亻	払 い 込 む *haraikomu* pay in	582
	19 3	申 し 込 み *mōshikomi* proposal, offer, application	309
	込 込	見 込 み *mikomi* prospects, outlook	63

	777	***JUN, megu(ru)*** – go around	
巡	2q3.3 ◻	巡 回 *junkai* tour, patrol, one's rounds	90
	辶 巛	巡 視 *junshi* tour of inspection, round of visits	606
	19 2	巡 査 *junsa* policeman, cop	624
	巡	巡 礼 *junrei* pilgrimage, pilgrim	620
		巡 業 *jungyō* tour (of a troupe/team)	279

	778	**JUN** – semi-, quasi-; level; correspond (to)	
準	2k11.1 🔲	水準 *suijun* water level; level, standard	21
	十 隹 氵	基準 *kijun* standard, criterion	450
	12 74 21	規準 *kijun* criterion, standard, norm	607
		準備 *junbi* preparation	768
	準	準決勝 *junkesshō* semifinal game/round	356, 509

	779	**SEN, so(maru)** – dye, color **so(meru)** – be dyed, imbued	
染	4a5.35 🔲	**shi(miru)** – soak into; be infected; smart, hurt **shi(mi)** – stain, blot, smudge	
	木 氵 十	(大気)汚染 *(taiki) osen* (air) pollution	26, 134, 693
	41 21 12	伝染病 *densenbyō* contagious disease	434, 380
	染	感染 *kansen* infection	262

	780	**KŌ, Ō, ki, [ko]** – yellow	
黄	3k8.16 🔲	黄葉 *kōyō* yellow (autumn) leaves	253
	卝 日 一	黄熱(病) *(k)ōnetsu(byō)* yellow fever	645, 380
	32 43 14	黄金 *ōgon, kogane* gold	23
		黄色 *kiiro* yellow	204
	黄 黄	黄身 *kimi* egg yolk	59

	781	**Ō, yoko** – side	
横	4a11.13🔲	専横 *sen'ō* arbitrariness, tyranny	600
	木 日 卝	横道 *yokomichi* side street; side issue, digression	149
	41 43 32	横切る *yokogiru* cross, traverse	39
		横顔 *yokogao* profile	277
	横 横	横目 *yokome* side glance; amorous glance	55

	782	**SAI, [SA], futata(bi)** – once more, again, twice	
再	0a6.26 ⬚	再会 *saikai* meeting again, reunion	158
	王 冂	再開 *saikai* reopening	396
	46 20	再編成 *saihensei* reorganization	682, 261
		再婚 *saikon* second marriage, remarriage	567
	再	再来週 *saraishū* week after next	69, 92

	783	**KŌ** – club; lecture; study	
講	7a10.3 🔲	講義 *kōgi* lecture	291
	言 王 卝	講演 *kōen* lecture, address	344
	67 46 32	講師 *kōshi* lecturer, instructor	409
		講堂 *kōdō* lecture hall	496
	講 講	講和 *kōwa* (make) peace	124

	784	**HEI, HYŌ** – soldier	
兵	2o5.6 🔲	兵器 *heiki* weapon	527
	⺍ 斤一	兵士 *heishi* soldier	572
	16 50 1	歩兵 *hohei* infantry; infantryman, foot soldier	431
		志願兵 *shiganhei* a volunteer (soldier)	573, 581
	兵	兵役 *heieki* military service, conscription	375

浜	**785** 3a7.7 田 氵斤几 21 50 16 浜 濱	**HIN, hama** – beach

海浜 *kaihin* seashore, beach　　　　　　　　117
京浜 *Kei-Hin* Tōkyō–Yokohama　　　　　　189
横浜 *Yokohama* (port city near Tōkyō)　　781
浜辺 *hamabe* beach, seashore　　　　　　　775
浜田 *Hamada* (surname)　　　　　　　　　35

座	**786** 3q7.2 □ 广 土 亻 18 22 3 座	**ZA** – seat; theater; constellation　*suwa(ru)* – sit down

座席 *zaseki* seat　　　　　　　　　　　　379
座談会 *zadankai* round-table discussion, symposium　593, 158
(通信) 講座 *(tsūshin) kōza* (correspondence)　　150, 157, 783
口座 *kōza* (savings) account　　┌course　54
銀座 *Ginza* (area of Tōkyō)　　　　　　　313

卒	**787** 2j6.2 目 亠 亻 卄 11 3 12 卒 卆	**SOTSU** – soldier, private; end

卒業 *sotsugyō* graduation　　┌examination　279
卒業試験 *sotsugyō shiken* graduation　279, 526, 532
卒業証書 *sotsugyō shōsho* diploma　279, 484, 131
卒中 *sotchū* cerebral stroke, apoplexy　　28
兵卒 *heisotsu* a private, common soldier　784

率	**788** 2j9.1 目 亠 冫 卄 11 5 12 率	**SOTSU, hiki(iru)** – lead, command　**RITSU** – rate, proportion

率直 *sotchoku* straightforward, frank　　423
軽率 *keisotsu* rash, hasty, heedless　　　547
能率 *nōritsu* efficiency　　　　　　　　386
倍率 *bairitsu* (degree of) magnification　　87
成長率 *seichōritsu* rate of growth　　261, 95

血	**789** 5h1.1 日 皿 丿 59 2 血	**KETSU, chi** – blood

血液 *ketsueki* blood　　　　　　　　　　472
血管 *kekkan* blood vessel　　　　　　　328
(内) 出血 *(nai)shukketsu* (internal) hemorrhage　84, 53
止血剤 *shiketsuzai* a hemostatic, styptic (agent)　477, 550
流血 *ryūketsu* bloodshed　　　　　　　247

傘	**790** 2a10.7 ⋯ 亻 卄 3 12 傘	**SAN, kasa** – umbrella

傘下 *sanka* affiliated　　　　　　　　　31
日傘 *higasa* parasol　　　　　　　　　　5
雨傘 *amagasa* umbrella　　　　　　　　30
傘立て *kasatate* umbrella stand　　　　121
こうもり傘 *kōmorigasa* umbrella, parasol

舎	**791** 2a6.23 日 亻 土 口 3 22 24 舎 舍	**SHA** – house, hut, quarters

校舎 *kōsha* schoolhouse, school building　115
兵舎 *heisha* barracks　　　　　　　　　784
国民宿舎 *kokumin shukusha* government-sponsored
　　　　　　　　　　　　hostels　40, 177, 179
田舎 *inaka* the country, rural areas　　　35

衆	792 5h7.1 ⊟ 血 礻 | 59 57 2 衆	**SHŪ, [SHU]** – multitude, populace

公衆 (電話) *kōshū (denwa)* public (telephone)　126, 108, 238
大衆文学 *taishū bungaku* popular literature　26, 111, 109
民衆 *minshū* the people, masses　177
衆議院 *Shūgiin* the House of Representa tives　292, 614
アメリカ合衆国 *Amerika Gasshūkoku* U.S.A.　159, 40

君	793 3d4.23 ⊡ 口 ⋽ | 24 39 2 君	**KUN** – (suffix for male personal names); ruler　*kimi* – you (in masculine speech); ruler

田中君 *Tanaka-kun* Tanaka (male sur name)　35, 28
和夫君 *Kazuo-kun* Kazuo (male given name)　124, 315
君主 *kunshu* monarch, sovereign 「constitutional monarchy 155
立憲君主政 (国) *rikken kunshusei (koku)*　121, 521, 155, 483, 40

群	794 3d10.14 ⊞ 口 王 ⋽ 24 46 39 群 羣	**GUN, mu(re), [mura]** – group, herd　*mu(reru)* – crowd, flock

群衆 *gunshū* crowd of people　792
群集 *gunshū* crowd of people　436
群像 *gunzō* group of people (in an artwork)　740
魚群 *gyogun* school of fish　290
群島 *guntō* group of islands, archipelago　286

隊	795 2d9.7 ⊞ 阝 犭 儿 7 27 16 隊 隊	**TAI** – party, squad, unit

軍隊 *guntai* troops, army, the military　438
部隊 *butai* military unit, squad　86
兵隊 *heitai* soldier; troops　784
探検隊 *tankentai* expedition, expeditionary group　535, 531
楽隊 *gakutai* (musical) band　358

豚	796 4b7.2 ⊡ 月 犭 ㇄ 42 27 10 豚	**TON, buta** – pig

養豚 *yōton* pig raising　402
豚カツ *tonkatsu* pork cutlet
豚肉 *butaniku* pork　223
豚小屋 *butagoya* pigsty, pigpen　27, 167

劇	797 2f13.2 ⊡ 刂 犭 厂 16 27 18 劇	**GEKI** – drama, play

劇場 *gekijō* theater, playhouse　154
演劇 *engeki* drama, theatrical performance　344
歌劇 *kageki* opera　392
劇的 *gekiteki* dramatic　210
劇薬 *gekiyaku* powerful medicine; virulent poison　359

比	798 2m3.5 ⊡ ⵏ 13 比	**HI** – compare; (short for) Philippines　*kura(beru)* – compare

比率 *hiritsu* ratio　788
比例 *hirei* proportion　612
対比 *taihi* contrast, contradistinction　365
比重 *hijū* specific gravity　227
見比べる *mikuraberu* compare　63

799	**KON, ma(zeru)** – mix **ma(zaru/jiru)** – be mixed	
3a8.14 ⊞	混乱 *konran* confusion, disorder, chaos	689
氵 日 ⼔	混雑 *konzatsu* confusion, congestion	575
21 43 13	混合 *kongō* mixture 「half-breed	159
混	混血の人 *konketsu no hito* person of mixed race,	789, 1
	混ぜ物 *mazemono* adulteration	79

800	**SEN, era(bu)** – choose, select	
2q12.3 ▣	当選 *tōsen* be elected	77
辶 弓 艹	改選 *kaisen* reelection	514
19 28 32	精選 *seisen* careful selection	659
選	予選 *yosen* preliminary match; primary election	393
	選手 *senshu* (sports) player	57

801	**KYO** – all, whole; arrest, capture; name, give, cite **a(geru)** – name, give, enumerate; arrest, apprehend **a(garu)** – be apprehended; be found, recovered	
3n7.1 目		
⺍ 扌 儿	選挙 *senkyo* election	800
35 23 16	挙党 *kyotō* the whole party	495
挙 擧	列挙 *rekkyo* enumerate, list	611

802	**YO, homa(re)** – glory, honor	
3n10.1 目	栄誉 *eiyo* honor, glory	723
⺍ 言 儿	名誉 *meiyo* honor	82
35 67 16	名誉職 *meiyoshoku* honorary post	82, 385
誉 譽	名誉教授 *meiyo kyōju* professor emeritus	82, 245, 602
	名誉市民 *meiyo shimin* honorary citizen	82, 181, 177

803	**HŌ, ho(meru)** – praise	
2j13.1 目	褒賞 *hōshō* prize	500
亠 衤 木	褒美 *hōbi* reward	401
11 57 41	過褒 *kahō* excessive/undeserved praise	413
褒 襃	褒め上げる *homeageru* praise very highly, extol	32
	褒め立てる *hometateru* admire, praise highly	121

804	**HŌ, tsutsu(mu)** – wrap up	
0a5.9 ⬚	包容力 *hōyōryoku* capacity; tolerance, catholicity	654, 100
勹 ㇕	包丁 *hōchō* kitchen knife	184
28 15	小包み *kozutsumi* parcel	27
包 包	紙包み *kamizutsumi* parcel wrapped in paper	180
	包み紙 *tsutsumigami* wrapping paper, wrapper	180

805	**KIN** – equal, even	
3b4.8 ▥	平均 *heikin* average	202
土 ㇕ ⼂	均一 *kin'itsu* uniform	2
22 15 5	均等 *kintō* equality, uniformity, parity	569
均	均質 *kinshitsu* homogeneous	176
	均分 *kinbun* divide equally	38

	806	**MITSU** – close, dense, crowded; minute, fine; secret	
密	3m8.5 目	機密 *kimitsu* a secret	528
	宀 心 山	密輸 *mitsuyu* smuggling	546
	33 51 36	(人口)密度 *(jinkō) mitsudo* (population) density	1, 54, 377
	密	密接 *missetsu* close, intimate	486
		精密 *seimitsu* minute, accurate, precision	659

	807	**HI, hi(meru)** – keep secret	
秘	5d5.6 ⊞	秘密 *himitsu* a secret	806
	禾 心 丨	極秘 *gokuhi* strict secrecy, top secret	336
	56 51 2	秘書 *hisho* secretary	131
	秘 祕	神秘 *shinpi* mystery	310
		便秘 *benpi* constipation	330

	808	**HŌ** – country; Japan ⌜America)	
邦	2d4.7 ⊞	(在米)邦人 *(zaibei) hōjin* Japanese (living in	268, 224, 1
	⻏ 十 二	邦字新聞 *hōji shinbun* Japanese-language	110, 174, 64
	7 12 4	邦楽 *hōgaku* (traditional) Japanese music ⌞newspaper	358
	邦	連邦 *renpō* federation, federal	440
		連邦政府 *renpō seifu* federal government	440, 483, 504

	809	**RIN, tonari** – next door **tona(ru)** – be neighboring	
隣	2d13.1 ⊞	隣国 *ringoku* neighboring country/province	40
	⻖ 米 夕	隣席 *rinseki* next seat, seat next to one	379
	7 62 30	隣接 *rinsetsu* border on, be contiguous, adjoin	486
	隣 鄰	隣人 *rinjin* a neighbor	1
		隣り合う *tonariau* adjoin/be next door to each other	159

	810	**BU, ma(u)** – dance, flutter about **mai** – dance	
舞	0a15.1 ⊟	舞台 *butai* the stage	492
	艹 夕 ⼃	舞楽 *bugaku* old Japanese court-dance music	358
	32 30 15	歌舞き *kabuki* Kabuki	392
	舞	仕舞 *shimai* end, conclusion	333
		(お)見舞い *(o)mimai* visit, inquiry (after someone's health)	63

	811	**MU, yume** – dream	
夢	3k10.14目	夢想 *musō* dream, vision, fancy	147
	艹 目 夕	悪夢 *akumu* bad dream, nightmare	304
	32 55 30	夢中 *muchū* rapture; absorption, intentness; franctic	28
	夢 梦	夢を見る *yume o miru* (have a) dream	63
		夢にも *yume nimo* (not) even in a dream	

	812	**SŌ, hōmu(ru)** – bury, inter	
葬	3k9.15 目	葬儀, 葬式 *sōgi, sōshiki* funeral	727, 525
	艹 夕 ⼷	火葬 *kasō* cremation	20
	32 30 13	葬列 *sōretsu* funeral procession	611
	葬	副葬品 *fukusōhin* burial accessories	714, 230
		改葬 *kaisō* reburial, reinterment	514

813	**BI, hana** – nose	
5f9.3 目	鼻先 *hanasaki* tip of the nose	50
甲 刂 艹	鼻血 *hanaji* nosebleed, bloody nose	789
58 55 32	鼻薬 *hanagusuri* a bribe	359
	耳鼻いんこう専門医 *jibiinkō senmon'i* ear,	56, 600, 161, 220
鼻	鼻音 *bion* nasal sound ⌊nose, and throat specialist	347

814	**I, chiga(u)** – be different; be mistaken **chiga(eru)** – alter	
2q10.5 凵	相違 *sōi* difference, disparity	146
辶 刂 艹	違反 *ihan* violation	324
19 24 12	違法 *ihō* illegal	123
	違憲 *iken* unconstitutionality	521
違	間違い *machigai* mistake, error; accident, mishap	43

815	**EI** – defend, protect	
3i13.3 ⊞	防衛 *bōei* defense	513
彳 刂 艹	自衛隊 *Jieitai* (Japanese) Self-Defense Forces	62, 795
29 24 12	衛生 *eisei* hygiene, sanitation	44
	衛星 *eisei* satellite	730
衞 衞	前衛 *zen'ei* advance guard; avant-garde	47

816	**KŌ, ki(ku)** – be effective	
2g6.2 ⊟	効力 *kōryoku* effectiveness, effect, validity	100
力 亠 儿	効果 *kōka* effect, effectiveness	487
8 11 16	有効 *yūkō* validity, effectiveness	265
	無効 *mukō* invalidity, ineffectiveness	93
効 效	時効 *jikō* prescription (in statute of limitations)	42

817	**KŌ** – suburbs, rural areas	
2d6.8 ⊟	近郊 *kinkō* suburbs, outskirts	445
阝 亠 儿	郊外 *kōgai* suburbs, outskirts	83
7 11 16		
郊		

818	**KŌ, [KU]** – merits, success	
2g3.2 ⊡	成功 *seikō* success	261
力 工	功労 *kōrō* meritorious service	233
8 38	功業 *kōgyō* achievement, exploit	279
	功名 *kōmyō* great achievement, glorious deed	82
功	年功 *nenkō* long service/experience	45

819	**KŌ, se(meru)** – attack	
4i3.2 ⊡	攻勢 *kōsei* the offensive	646
攵 工	攻防 *kōbō* offense and defense	513
49 38	攻守 *kōshu* offense and defense	490
	攻城 *kōjō* siege	720
攻	専攻 *senkō* one's major (study)	600

	820 6a3.6 □ 糸 工 61 38 紅	**KŌ, [KU], kurenai** – deep red **beni** – rouge, lipstick	
紅		紅葉　*kōyō, momiji*　red (autumn) leaves; maple tree	253
		紅茶　*kōcha*　black tea	251
		紅白　*kōhaku*　red and white	205
		真紅　*shinku*　crimson, scarlet	422
		口紅　*kuchibeni*　lipstick	54

	821 3a3.8 □ 氵 工 21 38 江	**KŌ, e** – inlet, bay	
江		江湖　*kōko*　the public, world	467
		入り江　*irie*　inlet, small bay	52
		江ノ島　*Enoshima*　(island near Kamakura)	286
		江戸　*Edo*　(old name for Tōkyō)	152
		江戸っ子　*Edokko*　true Tōkyōite	152, 103

	822 3n14.1 🗒 ⺍ 耳 攵 35 65 49 嚴 嚴	**GEN, [GON], kibi(shii)** – severe, strict, rigorous, intense **ogoso(ka)** – solemn, grave, stately	
嚴		厳重　*genjū*　strict, stringent, rigid	227
		厳格　*genkaku*　strict, stern, severe	643
		厳禁　*genkin*　strict prohibition	482
		尊厳　*songen*　dignity	704

	823 6c4.2 □ 舟 亠 冂 63 11 20 航	**KŌ** – navigation, sailing	
航		航空便　*kōkūbin*　airmail	140, 330
		航空券　*kōkūken*　flight/airplane ticket	140, 506
		航路　*kōro*　sea route, course	151
		航海　*kōkai*　sea voyage/navigation	117
		巡航　*junkō*　a cruise	777

	824 3c4.15 🗄 扌 亠 冂 23 11 20 抗	**KŌ** – resist	
抗		対抗　*taikō*　opposition, confrontation	365
		抵抗　*teikō*　resistance	560
		反抗　*hankō*　resistance, opposition	324
		抗議　*kōgi*　protest	292
		抗争　*kōsō*　contention, dispute	302

	825 3q7.1 🗇 广 車 18 69 庫	**KO, [KU]** – storehouse	
庫		車庫　*shako*　garage	133
		金庫　*kinko*　a safe	23
		国庫　*Kokko*　the (National) Treasury	40
		文庫本　*bunkobon*　small cheap paperback	111, 25
		在庫品　*zaikohin*　goods in stock, inventory	268, 230

	826 3q4.1 🗇 广 木 18 41 床 牀	**SHŌ, toko** – bed; floor **yuka** – floor	
床		起床　*kishō*　rise, get up (from bed)	373
		病床　*byōshō*　sickbed	380
		温床　*onshō*　hotbed, breeding ground	634
		床屋　*tokoya*　barber, barbershop	167
		床の間　*tokonoma*　alcove in Japanese-style room	43

827	**Ō** – reply, respond; comply with; fulfill, satisfy	
3q4.2	反応 *hannō* reaction	324
广 忄	順応 *junnō* adaption, adjustment	769
18 51	相応 *sōō* correspond, be suitable	146
	応用 *ōyō* (practical) application	107
応 應	応接間 *ōsetsuma* reception room	486, 43

828	**JŪ** – fill **a(teru)** – allot, allocate, apply (to)	
2j4.5	充分 *jūbun* enough, sufficient (cf. No. 38)	38
亠 厶 儿	充満 *jūman* fullness, abundance	201
11 17 16	充足 *jūsoku* sufficiency	58
	充実 *jūjitsu* repletion, perfection	203
充	充血した目 *jūketsu shita me* bloodshot eyes	789, 55

829	**JŪ** – gun	
8a6.9	銃器 *jūki* firearm	527
金 亠 厶	小銃 *shōjū* rifle	27
72 11 17	短銃 *tanjū* pistol, revolver	215
	機関銃 *kikanjū* machine gun	528, 398
銃	銃殺 *jūsatsu* shoot dead	576

830	**TŌ, su(beru)** – govern, control	
6a6.10	統制 *tōsei* control, regulation	427
糸 亠 厶	統治 *tōchi, tōji* reign, rule	493
61 11 17	統一 *tōitsu* unity, unification	2
	統計 *tōkei* statistics	340
統	伝統 *dentō* tradition	434

831	**REI** – order, command	
2a3.9	命令 *meirei* an order	578
亻 一 丨	号令 *gōrei* an order, command	266
3 1 2	訓令 *kunrei* instructions, directive	771
	政令 *seirei* cabinet order, government ordinance	483
令	発令 *hatsurei* official announcement	96

832	**REI, tsume(tai)** – cold **hi(yasu), sa(masu)** – chill, cool
2b5.3	**hi(eru), sa(meru)** – become cold **hi(ya)** – cold water; cold sakè
冫 亻 一	**hi(yakasu)** – poke fun at, tease; browse
5 3 1	

	冷水 *reisui* cold water	21
	冷戦 *reisen* cold war	301
冷	冷静 *reisei* calm, cool, dispassionate	663

833	**REI** – age	
6b11.5	年齢 *nenrei* age	45
米 卜 冂	学齢 *gakurei* (of) school age	109
62 13 20	老齢 *rōrei* old age	543
	高齢 *kōrei* old/advanced age	190
齢 齡	月齢 *getsurei* phase of the moon; age in months	17

	834	**RYŌ** – govern, rule	
領	9a5.2 田	領 土, 領 地 *ryōdo, ryōchi* territory	24, 118
	頁 亻 一	大 統 領 *daitōryō* president (of a country)	26, 830
	77 3 1	領 事 *ryōji* consul	80
	領	領 収 書/証 *ryōshūsho/shō* receipt	757, 131, 484
		横 領 *ōryō* usurpation, embezzlement	781

	835	**SHIN, JIN** – retainer, subject	
臣	2t4.3 回	大 臣 *daijin* (government) minister	26
	匚 丨	総 理 大 臣 *sōri daijin* prime minister	697, 143, 26
	20 2	臣 民 *shinmin* subject	177
	臣	臣 下 *shinka* subject, retainer	31
		君 臣 *kunshin* sovereign and subject, ruler and ruled	793

	836	**RIN, nozo(mu)** – face, confront; attend, assist at	
臨	2t15.1 田	臨 時 *rinji* temporary, provisional, extraordinary	42
	匚 口 ㇗	臨 床 *rinshō* clinical	826
	20 24 15	臨 終 *rinjū* one's last moments/deathbed	458
	臨	臨 席 *rinseki* attendance, presence	379
		君 臨 *kunrin* reign, rule	793

	837	**KAKU** – tower; palace; the cabinet	
閣	8e6.3 回	内 閣 *naikaku* the cabinet	84
	門 夂口	閣 議 *kakugi* meeting of the cabinet	292
	76 49 24	組 閣 *sokaku* formation of a cabinet	418
	閣	閣 下 *kakka* Your/His Excellency	31
		金 閣 寺 *Kinkakuji* Temple of the Golden Pavilion	23, 41

	838	**GAKU** – amount; framed picture **hitai** – forehead	
額	9a9.6 田	金 額 *kingaku* amount of money	23
	頁 夂宀	額 面 *gakumen* face value, par	274
	77 49 33	総 額 *sōgaku* total amount, sum total	697
	額	差 額 *sagaku* the difference, balance	658
		半 額 *hangaku* half the amount/price	88

	839	**RAKU, o(chiru)** – fall **o(tosu)** – drop; lose	
落	3k9.13 田	転 落 *tenraku* a fall	433
	艹 夂氵	落 第 *rakudai* failure in an examination	404
	32 49 21	部 落 *buraku* village, settlement	86
	落	落 語 *rakugo* Japanese comic storytelling	67
		落 ち 着 い た *ochitsuita* calm, composed	657

	840	**RAKU, kara(mu), kara(maru)** – get entangled	
絡	6a6.6 ⊞	連 絡 *renraku* contact, liaison, communication	440
	糸 夂口	連 絡 駅 *renraku-eki* connecting station, junction	440, 284
	61 49 24	連 絡 線 *renraku-sen* connecting line	440, 299
	絡	絡 み 付 く *karamitsuku* coil around, cling to	192
		絡 み 合 う *karamiau* intertwine	159

略	**841** 5f6.4 □ 田 夂口 58 49 24 略 畧	***RYAKU*** – abbreviation, omission

省略 *shōryaku* omission, abridgment, abbreviation 145
略語 *ryakugo* abbreviation 67
略歴 *ryakureki* brief personal history 480
計略 *keiryaku* plan, strategem, scheme 340
戦略 *senryaku* strategy 301

司	**842** 3d2.14 □ 口 一 24 1 司	***SHI*** – administer, conduct

司法 *shihō* administration of justice, judicial 123
司令 *shirei* commandant, commanding officer 831
司会者 *shikaisha* master of ceremonies, chairman 158, 164
司書 *shisho* librarian 131
上司 *jōshi* one's superior (officer) 32

詞	**843** 7a5.15 □ 言 口 一 67 24 1 詞	***SHI*** – words

品詞 *hinshi* part of speech 230
名詞 *meishi* noun 82
(他)動詞 *(ta)dōshi* (transitive) verb 120, 231
歌詞 *kashi* lyrics, words to a song 392
賀詞 *gashi* congratulations, greetings 756

肖	**844** 3n4.1 日 ⺍月 35 42 肖	***SHŌ*** – resemble

肖像画 *shōzōga* portrait 740, 343
不肖 *fushō* unlike/unworthy of one's father; (humble) I 94

消	**845** 3a7.16 田 氵月 小 21 42 35 消 消	***SHŌ, ke(su)*** – extinguish ***ki(eru)*** – go out; disappear

消防(車) *shōbō(sha)* fire fighting (engine) 513, 133
消火器 *shōkaki* fire extinguisher 20, 527
消費者 *shōhisha* consumer 749, 164
消化 *shōka* digestion 254
消極的 *shōkyokuteki* negative, passive 336, 210

退	**846** 2q6.3 □ 辶 艮 19 73 退	***TAI, shirizo(ku)*** – retreat ***shirizo(keru)*** – drive away, repel

退職 *taishoku* retirement, resignation 385
退院 *taiin* leave/be discharged from the hospital 614
退学 *taigaku* leave/drop out of school 109
引退 *intai* retire (from public life) 216
進退 *shintai* advance of retreat, movement 437

限	**847** 2d6.1 □ 阝 艮 7 73 限	***GEN, kagi(ru)*** – limit

無限 *mugen* unlimited, infinite 93
制限 *seigen* restriction, limitation 427
限度 *gendo* a limit 377
期限 *kigen* term, time limit, deadline 449
権限 *kengen* authority, competence, jurisdiction 335

848 眼	**GAN, [GEN], manako** – eye
5c6.1 ⊞ 目 艮 55 73 眼	両眼 *ryōgan* both eyes 200 近眼 *kingan* nearsightedness, shortsightedness 445 眼科医 *gankai* eye doctor, ophtalmologist 320, 220 眼識 *ganshiki* discernment, insight 681 千里眼 *senrigan* clairvoyance, clairvoyant 15, 142
849 眠	**MIN, nemu(ru)** – sleep **nemu(i)** – tired, sleepy
5c5.2 ⊞ 目 尸 十 55 40 12 眠	不眠 *fumin* sleeplessness, insomnia 94 安眠 *anmin* a quiet/sound sleep 105 冬眠 *tōmin* hibernation 459 居眠り *inemuri* a doze, falling asleep in one's seat 171 眠り薬 *nemurigusuri* sleeping drug/pills 359
850 況	**KYŌ** – circumstances, situation
3a5.21 ⊞ 氵口 儿 21 24 16 況 況	状況, 情況 *jōkyō* conditions, situation 626, 209 現況 *genkyō* present situation 298 実況 *jikkyō* actual state of affairs 203 市況 *shikyō* market conditions, the market 181 不況 *fukyō* recession, economic slump 94
851 祝	**SHUKU, [SHŪ], iwa(u)** – celebrate, congratulate
4e5.5 ⊞ 礻口 儿 45 24 16 祝 祝	祝辞 *shukuji* (speech of) congratulations 688 祝電 *shukuden* telegram of congratulations 108 祝賀 *shukuga* celebration; congratulations 756 祝日 *shukujitsu* festival day, holiday 5 祝儀 *shūgi* (wedding) celebration; gift 727
852 競	**KYŌ, KEI, kiso(u)** – compete, vie for **se(ru)** – compete, vie; bid for
5b15.1 ⊞ 立 口 儿 54 24 16 競 競	競争 *kyōsō* competition 302 競走 *kyōsō* race 429 競売 *kyōbai* auction 239 競馬 *keiba* horse racing 283
853 景	**KEI** – view, scene
4c8.8 目 日 口 小 43 24 35 景	景色 *keshiki* scenery 204 風景 *fūkei* scenery 29 景勝 (地) *keishō(chi)* (place of) picturesque scenery 509, 118 景気 *keiki* business conditions 134 不景気 *fukeiki* hard times, recession 94, 134
854 影	**EI, kage** – light; shadow, silhouette; figure; trace
3j12.1 ⊞ 彡日 口 31 43 24 影	影像 *eizō* image, shadow 740 人影 *hitokage, jin'ei* silhouette, human figure 1 影法師 *kagebōshi* person's shadow 123, 409 影絵 *kagee* shadow picture, silhouette 345 面影 *omokage* face, traces, vestiges 274

	855	**KYŌ** – village, native place **GŌ** – rural area, country	
	2d8.14	故郷 *kokyō* one's hometown, native place	173
	阝 食 厶	郷里 *kyōri* one's hometown, native place	142
	7 73 17	郷土 *kyōdo* one's hometown	24
		望郷 の 念 *bōkyō no nen* homesickness, nostalgia	673, 579
	郷 郷	近郷 *kingō* neighboring districts	445

	856	**KYŌ, hibi(ku)** – sound, resound, be echoed; affect	
	4c15.3	影響 *eikyō* effect, influence	854
	日 食 立	反響 *hankyō* echo, response	324
	43 73 54	音響 *onkyō* sound	347
		交響曲/楽 *kōkyōkyoku/gaku* symphony	114, 366, 358
	響 響	響き渡る *hibikiwataru* resound, reverberate	378

	857	**SHŌ** – chapter; badge, mark	
	5b6.3	文章 *bunshō* composition, writing	111
	立 日 十	第三章 *dai-sanshō* Chapter 3	404, 4
	54 43 12	第三楽章 *dai-san gakushō* third movement	404, 4, 358
		憲章 *kenshō* charter, constitution	521
	章	記章 *kishō* medal, badge	371

	858	**SHŌ, sawa(ru)** – hinder, interfere with; harm, hurt	
	2d11.2	保障 *hoshō* guarantee, security	489
	阝 立 日	支障 *shishō* hindrance, impediment	318
	7 54 43	障害 *shōgai* obstacle, impediment	518
		故障 *koshō* trouble, breakdown, out of order	173
	障	障子 *shōji* Japanese sliding paper door	103

	859	**CHO, arawa(su)** – write, publish **ichijiru(shii)** – marked, striking, remarkable, conspicuous	
	3k8.4	著者 *chosha* author	164
	艹 日 土	著書 *chosho* a (literary) work	131
	32 43 22	名著 *meicho* a famous/great work	82
	著 著	著名 *chomei* prominent, well-known	82

	860	**SHO** – government office, station	
	5g8.1	税務署 *zeimusho* tax office	399, 235
	罒 日 土	消防署 *shōbōsho* fire station, firehouse	845, 513
	55 43 22	警察署 *keisatsusho* police station	706, 619
		部署 *busho* one's post/place of duty	86
	署 署	署名 *shomei* signature, autograph	82

	861	**SHO** – all, various	
	7a8.3	諸国 *shokoku* all/various countries	40
	言 日 土	諸島 *shotō* islands	286
	67 43 22	諸説 *shosetsu* various views/accounts	400
		諸事 *shoji* various matters/affairs	80
	諸 諸	諸君 *shokun* (Ladies and) Gentlemen!	793

	862 6a8.3 □ 糸 日 土 61 43 22 緒 緒	**SHO, [CHO]** – beginning **o** – cord, strap, thong	
		緒 戦 *shosen, chosen* beginning of war	301
		緒 論 *shoron, choron* introduction	293
		由 緒 *yuisho* history; pedigree, lineage	363
		情 緒 *jōcho, jōsho* emotion, feeling	209
		鼻 緒 *hanao* clog thong, *geta* strap	813

	863 8a11.6 □ 金 立 日 72 54 43 鏡	**KYŌ, kagami** – mirror	
		鏡 台 *kyōdai* dressing table	492
		三 面 鏡 *sanmenkyō* a dresser with 3 mirrors	4, 274
		望 遠 鏡 *bōenkyō* telescope	673, 446
		手 鏡 *tekagami* hand mirror	57
		眼 鏡 *megane, gankyō* eyeglasses	848

	864 3b11.1 □ 土 立 日 22 54 43 境	**KYŌ, [KEI], sakai** – boundary	
		国 境 *kokkyō* border	40
		境 界 *kyōkai* boundary, border	454
		苦 境 *kukyō* distress, difficulties	545
		境 内 *keidai* precincts, grounds	84
		境 目 *sakaime* borderline; crisis	55

	865 4f13.1 □ 王 日 衤 46 55 57 環 環	**KAN** – ring; surround	
		環 境 *kankyō* environment	864
		環 状 *kanjō* ring-shaped, annular	626
		光 環 *kōkan* corona	138
		一 環 *ikkan* a link, part	2

	866 2q13.4 □ 辶 日 衤 19 55 57 還	**KAN** – return	
		返 還 *henkan* return, restoration; repayment	442
		帰 還 *kikan* return home, repatriation	317
		送 還 *sōkan* sending home, repatriation	441
		還 元 *kangen* restoration; reduction	137

	867 2d8.7 □ 阝 亻 厶 7 3 17 陰	**IN** – negative, hidden; shadow, secret **kage** – shadow; back **kage(ru)** – get dark/clouded	
		陰 陽 *in'yō* yin and yang, positive and negative	630
		陰 性 *insei* negative; dormant, latent	98
		陰 気 *inki* gloomy, dismal, melancholy	134
		日/木 陰 *hi/kokage* shade from the sun/of a tree	5, 22

	868 2d11.3 □ 阝 心 彐 7 51 39 隠 隱	**IN, kaku(reru)** – (intr.) hide **kaku(su)** – (tr.) hide	
		隠 語 *ingo* secret language; argot, jargon	67
		隠 者 *inja* hermit	164
		隠 居 *inkyo* retirement from active life	171
		隠 し 芸 *kakushigei* parlor trick; hidden talent ⌈chest)	435
		隠 し 引き 出 し *kakushi hikidashi* secret compartment (in a	16, 53

	869	**ON, oda(yaka)** – calm, quiet, mild, peaceful, moderate	
穏	5d11.4 ⊞	穏和 *onwa* mild, gentle, genial	124
	禾 心 彐	平穏 *heion* calmness, quiet, serenity	202
	56 51 39	平穏無事 *heion-buji* peace and quiet	202, 93, 80
		穏当 *ontō* proper, appropriate; gentle	77
	穏 穩	穏便 *onbin* gentle, quiet, amicable	330

	870	**SHI, eda** – branch	
枝	4a4.18 ⊞	枝葉 *shiyō, edaha* branches and leaves; digression	253
	木 十 又	大枝 *ōeda* bough, limb	26
	41 12 9	小枝 *koeda* twig	27
		枝切り *edakiri* lopping off/pruning of branches	39
	枝	枝接ぎ *edatsugi* grafting	486

	871	**GI, waza** – technique; ability; feat	
技	3c4.16 ⊞	技術 *gijutsu* technique, technology	187
	扌 十 又	技師 *gishi* engineer	409
	23 12 9	技能 *ginō* technical skill, ability	386
		演技 *engi* acting, performance	344
	技	競技 *kyōgi* match, contest, competition	852

	872	**KI** – forked road	
岐	3o4.1 ⊞	分岐 *bunki* divergence, branching	38
	山 十 又	分岐点 *bunkiten* point of divergence, junction	38, 169
	36 12 9	岐路 *kiro* fork in the road, crossroads	151
	岐		

	873	**CHŪ, mushi** – bug, insect	
虫	6d0.1 ☐	益/害虫 *eki/gaichū* beneficial/harmful insect	716, 518
	虫	殺虫剤 *satchūzai* insecticide	576, 550
	64	毛虫 *kemushi* hairy caterpillar	287
		油虫 *aburamushi* cockroach; hanger-on, parasite	364
	虫 蟲	虫歯 *mushiba* decayed tooth, cavity	478

	874	**SHOKU, sawa(ru), fu(reru)** – touch	
触	6d7.10 ⊞	触覚 *shokkaku* sense of touch	605
	虫 月 ⺈	接触 *sesshoku* touch, contact	486
	64 42 15	感触 *kanshoku* the touch, feel	262
		触角 *shokkaku* feeler, antenna, tentacle	473
	触 觸	抵触 *teishoku* conflict	560

	875	**SŌ, sawa(gu)** – make noise	
騒	10a8.5 ⊞	騒音 *sōon* noise	347
	馬 虫 又	騒動 *sōdō* disturbance, riot	231
	78 64 9	騒然 *sōzen* noisy, tumultuous	651
		大騒ぎ *ōsawagi* clamor, uproar, hullabaloo	26
	騒 騷	騒ぎ立てる *sawagitateru* raise a great fuss/furor	121

876 4n3.1 戈 艹 52 32 戒	**KAI, imashi(meru)** – admonish, warn	
	警戒 *keikai* caution, precaution, warning	706
	訓戒 *kunkai* admonition, warning	771
	厳戒 *genkai* strict watch/guard	822
	戒律 *kairitsu* (Buddhist) precepts	667
	十戒 *jikkai* the Ten Commandments	12

877 4n8.4 戈 厶 亻 52 17 3 幾	**KI, iku** – how much/many; some	
	幾何学 *kikagaku* geometry	390, 109
	幾日 *ikunichi* how many days; what day of the month	5
	幾分 *ikubun* some, a portion, more or less	38
	幾つ *ikutsu* how much/many/old	
	幾ら *ikura* how much/long/expensive	

878 2a8.27 亻 口 一 3 24 14 倹 儉	**KEN** – thrifty, simple, modest	
	倹約 *ken'yaku* thriftiness, economy	211
	節倹 *sekken* frugality, economy	464
	勤倹 *kinken* diligence and thrift	559

879 2f8.5 刂 口 亻 16 24 3 剣 劍	**KEN, tsurugi** – sword	
	剣道 *kendō* Kendo, Japanese fencing	149
	刀剣 *tōken* swords	37
	短剣 *tanken* short sword, dagger	215
	剣劇 *kengeki* swordplay/samurai drama	797
	真剣 *shinken* serious, earnest	422

880 6f6.2 𥫗 木 冂 66 41 20 策	**SAKU** – plan, means, measure, policy	
	政策 *seisaku* policy	483
	対策 *taisaku* measure, countermeasure	365
	具体策 *gutaisaku* specific measure	420, 61
	策略 *sakuryaku* stratagem, scheme, tactic	841
	術策 *jussaku* artifice, stratagem, intrigue	187

881 2f6.2 刂 木 冂 16 41 20 刺	**SHI, sa(su)** – pierce **sa(saru)** – stick, get stuck	
	名刺 *meishi* name/business card	82
	風刺 *fūshi* satire	29
	刺し殺す *sashikorosu* stab to death	576
	刺し傷 *sashikizu* a stab; (insect) bite	633
	刺身 *sashimi* sashimi, sliced raw fish	59

882 3g2.1 犭 卩 27 7 犯	**HAN, oka(su)** – commit (a crime), violate, defy	
	犯人 *hannin* criminal, culprit	1
	犯行 *hankō* crime	68
	現行犯で *genkōhan de* in the act, red-handed	298, 68
	共犯 *kyōhan* complicity	196
	防犯 *bōhan* crime prevention/fighting	513

狂	**883** 3g4.2 □ 犭 王 27 46 狂	***KYŌ, kuru(u)*** – go crazy; run amuck; get out of order ***kuru(oshii)*** – be nearly mad (with worry/grief)	
		狂言 *kyōgen* play, drama; Noh farce	66
		発狂 *hakkyō* insanity, madness	96
		狂気 *kyōki* insanity, madness	134
		狂乱 *kyōran* frenzy, madness	689

獄	**884** 3g11.1 Ⅲ 犭 言 27 67 獄	***GOKU*** – prison	
		地獄 *jigoku* hell ⌐examinations	118
		受験地獄 *juken jigoku* the ordeal of	260, 532, 118
		獄舎 *gokusha* prison, jail (building)	791
		出獄 *shutsugoku* release from prison	53
		獄死 *gokushi* die in prison	85

罪	**885** 5g8.4 目 罒 二 儿 55 4 16 罪	***ZAI, tsumi*** – crime, sin, guilt	
		犯罪 *hanzai* crime	882
		罪人 *zainin* criminal	1
		tsumibito sinner	
		有罪 *yūzai* guilty	265
		罪業 *zaigō* sin	279

罰	**886** 5g9.1 目 罒 言 儿 55 67 16 罰 罰	***BATSU*** – punishment, penalty ***BACHI*** – (divine) punishment	
		罰金 *bakkin* a fine	23
		体罰 *taibatsu* corporal punishment	61
		厳罰 *genbatsu* severe punishment	822
		天罰 *tenbatsu* punishment from God/heaven	141
		罰当たり *bachiatari* damned, cursed	77

刑	**887** 2f4.2 目 刂 廾 一 16 32 1 刑	***KEI*** – penalty, punishment, sentence	
		刑事 *keiji* criminal case; (police) detective	80
		刑法 *keihō* criminal law, the Criminal Code	123
		刑罰 *keibatsu* punishment, penalty	886
		死刑 *shikei* capital punishment	85
		刑務所 *keimusho* prison	235, 153

型	**888** 3b6.11 目 土 廾 儿 22 32 16 型	***KEI, kata*** – model, form	
		類型的 *ruikeiteki* stereotyped; typical	226, 210
		原型 *genkei* prototype, model	136
		紙型 *kamigata, shikei* papier-mâché mold	180
		血液型 *ketsuekigata* blood type	789, 472
		大型トラック *ōgata torakku* large truck	26

補	**889** 5e7.1 □ 衤 月 十 57 42 12 補	***HO, ogina(u)*** – supply, make up for, compensate for	
		補給 *hokyū* supply, replenishment	346
		補正 *hosei* revision, compensation	275
		補助 *hojo* assistance, supplement, subsidy	623
		補充 *hojū* supplement, replacement	828
		補習教育 *hoshū kyōiku* continuing education	591, 245, 246

	890 3c7.3 □ 扌 月 十 23 42 12 捕	**HO, to(ru), to(raeru), tsuka(maeru)** – catch, grasp **to(rawareru), tsuka(maru)** – be caught; hold on to
		捕鯨 *hogei* whaling — 700
		捕鯨船 *hogeisen* whaling ship — 700, 376
		だ捕 *daho* capture, seize
		生け捕り *ikedori* capturing alive — 44

	891 2q8.2 ▣ 辶 氵 ヨ 19 21 39 逮	**TAI** – chase
		逮捕 *taiho* arrest — 890
		逮捕状 *taihojō* arrest warrant — 890, 626
		逮夜 *taiya* eve of the anniversary of a death — 471

	892 2q6.2 ▣ 辶 ヨ 十 19 39 12 建	**KEN, [KON], ta(teru)** – build **ta(tsu)** – be built
		建設 *kensetsu* construction — 577
		建立 *konryū* erection, building — 121
		建物 *tatemono* a building — 79
		二階建て *nikaidate* 2-story — 3, 588
		建て前 *tatemae* erection of the framework; principle — 47

	893 2a8.34 □ 亻 ヨ 辶 3 39 19 健	**KEN, suko(yaka)** – healthy
		保健 *hoken* preservation of health, hygiene — 489
		穏健 *onken* moderate, sound — 869
		強健 *kyōken* robust health, strong physique — 217
		健在 *kenzai* healthy, sound — 268
		健勝 *kenshō* healthy — 509

	894 3q8.1 ▣ 广 氵 ヨ 18 21 39 康	**KŌ** – peace, composure
		健康 *kenkō* health — 893
		不健康 *fukenkō* not healthy, unhealthful — 94, 893
		小康 *shōkō* lull, brief respite — 27

	895 3m4.5 ▤ 宀 儿 十 33 16 12 究	**KYŪ, kiwa(meru)** – investigate thoroughly/exhaustively
		究明 *kyūmei* study, investigation, inquiry — 18
		探究 *tankyū* research, investigation — 535
		学究 *gakkyū* scholar, student — 109
		究極 *kyūkyoku* final, ultimate — 336
		論究 *ronkyū* discuss thoroughly — 293

	896 5a4.1 ⊞ 石 艹 一 53 32 1 研 研	**KEN, to(gu)** – whet, hone, sharpen; polish, wash (rice)
		研究 *kenkyū* research — 895
		研究所 *kenkyūjo* research institute — 895, 153
		研学 *kengaku* study — 109

窮	897	**KYŪ, kiwa(maru)** – reach an extreme; come to an end
	3m12.4 ⊞	**kiwa(meru)** – carry to extremes; bring to an end
	宀 月 弓	窮 極 目 的 *kyūkyoku mokuteki* ultimate goal 336, 55, 210
	33 42 28	窮 地, 窮 境 *kyūchi, kyūkyō* predicament 118, 864
	窮	窮 乏 *kyūbō* poverty 754
		困 窮 *konkyū* poverty 558

突	898	**TOTSU, tsu(ku)** – thrust, poke, strike
	3m5.11 ☐	突 然 *totsuzen* suddenly 651
	宀 大 儿	突 破 *toppa* break through, overcome 665
	33 34 16	突 入 *totsunyū* rush in, storm 52
	突 突	羽 根 突 き *hanetsuki* Japanese badminton 590, 314
		突 き 当 た る *tsukiataru* run/bump into; reach the end 77

穴	899	**KETSU, ana** – hole; cave
	3m2.2 ☐	穴 居 人 *kekkyojin* caveman 171, 1
	宀 儿	落 と し 穴 *otoshiana* pitfall, trap 839
	33 16	穴 あ け 器 *ana akeki* punch, perforator 527
	穴 穴	送 り 穴 *okuriana* (film) perforations, sprocket holes 441
		穴 子 *anago* conger eel 103

射	900	**SHA, i(ru)** – shoot
	0a10.8 ⊞	発 射 *hassha* fire, launch 96
	月 寸 l	射 殺 *shasatsu* shoot dead 576
	42 37 2	注 射 *chūsha* injection, shot 357
	射	放 射 能 *hōshanō* radioactivity 512, 386
		反 射 *hansha* reflection; reflex 324

謝	901	**SHA** – gratitude; apology **ayama(ru)** – apologize
	7a10.1 Ⅲ	感 謝 *kansha* gratitude 262
	言 月 寸	謝 礼 *sharei* remuneration, honorarium 620
	67 42 37	月 謝 *gessha* monthly tuition 17
	謝	謝 罪 *shazai* apology 885
		代 謝 *taisha* metabolism (cf. No. 1405) 256

至	902	**SHI** – utmost **ita(ru)** – arrive, lead to
	3b3.6 ☐	必 至 *hisshi* inevitable 520
	土 ム 一	至 急 *shikyū* urgency, urgent 303
	22 17 1	夏 至 *geshi* summer solstice 461
	至	至 る 所 *itaru tokoro* everywhere 153
		至 東 京 *itaru Tōkyō* To Tōkyō (at the edge of a map) 71, 189

致	903	**CHI, ita(su)** – do (deferential, used like *suru*); bring about
	4i6.2 ⊞	一 致 *itchi* agreement, consistency 2
	攵 土 ム	合 致 *gatchi* agreement, consistency 159
	49 22 17	致 命 傷 *chimeishō* fatal wound 578, 633
	致	致 死 量 *chishiryō* lethal dose 85, 411
		風 致 地 区 *fūchi chiku* scenic area 29, 118, 183

904 到

TŌ – arrive, reach

2f6.4 田

刂土 厶
16 22 17

到

到着	tōchaku	arrival	657
到来	tōrai	arrival, advent	69
到達	tōtatsu	reach, attain	448
殺到	sattō	rush, stampede	576
周到	shūtō	meticulous	91

905 倒

TŌ, tao(reru) – fall over, collapse tao(su) – knock down, topple, defeat

2a8.5 Ⅲ

亻土 儿
3 22 16

倒

卒倒	sottō	faint	787
倒産	tōsan	bankruptcy	278
倒閣	tōkaku	overthrowing the cabinet	837
共倒れ	tomodaore	mutual destruction, common ruin	196

906 誤

GO, ayama(ru) – err, make a mistake

7a7.2 田

言 口 儿
67 24 16

誤 誤

誤解	gokai	misunderstanding	474
誤報	gohō	erroneous report/information	685
誤算	gosan	miscalculation	747
誤植	goshoku	a misprint	424
読み誤る	yomiayamaru	misread	244

907 互

GO, taga(i) – mutual, reciprocal, each other

0a4.15 日

一 一
14 1

互

相互	sōgo	mutual	146
交互	kōgo	mutual; alternating	114
互助	gojo	mutual aid	623
互選	gosen	mutual election	800
互い違いに	tagaichigai ni	alternately	814

908 系

KEI – system; lineage, group

6a1.1 ...

糸 丨
61 2

系

体系	taikei	system	61
系統	keitō	system; lineage, descent	830
日系	nikkei	of Japanese descent	5
直系	chokkei	direct descent	423
系図	keizu	genealogy, family tree	339

909 係

KEI, kaka(ru) – relate to, concern kakari – charge, duty; person in charge, clerk

2a7.8 Ⅲ

亻 糸 丨
3 61 2

係

関係	kankei	relation, relationship, connection	398
連係	renkei	connection, link, contact	440
係争	keisō	dispute, contention	302
係員	kakariin	clerk in charge, attendant	163

910 孫

SON, mago – grandchild

2c7.1 Ⅲ

子 糸 丨
6 61 2

孫

子孫	shison	descendant	103
皇孫	kōson	imperial grandchild/descendant	297
天孫	tenson	of divine descent	141
そう孫	sōson	great-grandchild	
ひ孫	himago	great-grandchild	

911

懸

4k16.2 ⊞

心 糸 目
51 61 55

懸

KEN, [KE], ka(karu) – hang　**ka(keru)** – offer, give

一生懸命	isshōkenmei	utmost effort, all one's	2, 44, 578
懸案	ken'an	unsettled problem ⌐might	106
懸賞	kenshō	offer of a prize	500
懸念	kenen	fear, apprehension	579
命懸け	inochigake	risking one's life	578

912

派

3a6.21 ⊡

氵厂乀
21 18 10

派

HA – group, faction, sect, school (of thought)

宗派	shūha	sect	616
党派	tōha	party, faction	495
左派, 右派	saha, uha	the left wing, the right wing	75, 76
派出所	hashutsujo	branch office; police box	53, 153
特派員	tokuhain	correspondent	282, 163

913

脈

4b6.8 ⊡

月 厂 乀
42 18 10

脈　脉

MYAKU – pulse, vein, blood vessel

動脈	dōmyaku	artery	231
静脈	jōmyaku	vein	663
山脈	sanmyaku	mountain range	34
文脈	bunmyaku	context	111
脈略	myakuraku	logical connection, coherence, context	841

914

貫

7b4.3 ⊟

貝 女 丨
68 25 2

貫

KAN, tsuranu(ku) – pierce; carry out

一貫	ikkan	consistency, coherence, integrated	2
貫通	kantsū	pass through, pierce	150
貫流	kanryū	flow through	247
突貫	tokkan	rush, storm	898
貫き通す	tsuranukitōsu	carry out (one's will)	150

915

慣

4k11.9 ⊞

心 貝 女
51 68 25

慣

KAN, na(reru) – get used (to)　**na(rasu)** – make used (to); tame

習慣	shūkan	custom, practice	591
慣習	kanshū	custom, practice	591
慣例	kanrei	custom, convention	612
見慣れる	minareru	get used to seeing	63

916

複

5e9.3 ⊞

衤 日 攵
57 43 49

複

FUKU – double, multiple, composite; again

複雑	fukuzatsu	complicated	575
複合	fukugō	composition, compound, complex	159
重複	chōfuku, jūfuku	duplication, overlapping	227
複製	fukusei	reproduction, duplicate, facsimile	428
複数	fukusū	plural	225

917

復

3i9.4 ⊞

彳 日 攵
29 43 49

復

FUKU – return; be restored

復習	fukushū	review	591
反復	hanpuku	repetition	324
復活	fukkatsu	revival	237
復興	fukkō	reconstruction, revival	368
回復	kaifuku	recovery, recuperation	90

	918	**Ō** – go	
往	3i5.6	往復 *ōfuku* round trip	917
	彳王丨	往来 *ōrai* comings and goings, traffic; street, way	69
	29 46 2	立ち往生 *tachiōjō* standstill, getting stalled	121, 44
	往 往	右往左往 *uō-saō* rush about in confusion	76, 75
		往年 *ōnen* the past, formerly	45

	919	**EN, kemuri** – smoke **kemu(ru)** – smoke, smolder	
煙	4d9.3	**kemu(i)** – smoky	
	火 口 土	禁煙 *kin'en* No Smoking	482
	44 24 22	煙突 *entotsu* chimney	898
		発煙 *hatsuen* emitting smoke, fuming	96
	煙 烟	黒煙 *kokuen* black smoke	206

	920	**SHŌ, ya(keru)** – (intr.) burn; be roasted, broiled, baked	
焼	4d8.4	**ya(ku)** – (tr.) burn, roast, broil, bake	
	火 艹 十	全焼 *zenshō* be totally destroyed by fire	89
	44 32 12	焼(き)鳥 *yakitori* grilled chicken	285
		日焼け *hiyake* sunburn, suntan	5
	焼 燒	夕焼け *yūyake* glow of sunset	81

	921	**SEN** – move, change; climb	
遷	2q12.1	変遷 *hensen* undergo changes	257
	辶 口 弓	左遷 *sasen* demotion	75
	19 24 28	遷都 *sento* transfer of the capital	188
	遷		

	922	**HYŌ** – slip of paper, ballot, vote	
票	4e6.2	一票 *ippyō* a vote	2
	礻 口 一	得票 *tokuhyō* votes obtained	374
	45 24 14	反対票 *hantaihyō* no vote, adverse vote	324, 365
		開票 *kaihyō* vote counting	396
	票	伝票 *denpyō* slip of paper	434

	923	**HYŌ** – sign, mark	
標	4a11.8	目標 *mokuhyō* goal, purpose	55
	木 礻 口	標語 *hyōgo* slogan, motto	67
	41 45 24	標準語 *hyōjungo* the standard language	778, 67
		標本 *hyōhon* specimen, sample	25
	標	商標 *shōhyō* trademark	412

	924	**HYŌ, tadayo(u)** – drift about, float	
漂	3a11.9	漂流 *hyōryū* drift, be adrift	247
	氵 礻 口	漂着 *hyōchaku* drift ashore	657
	21 45 24	漂白剤 *hyōhakuzai* bleach	205, 550
		漂然 *hyōzen* aimless; sudden, unexpected	651
	漂	漂々 *hyōhyō* light, buoyant	

	925	**MEI, na(ku)** – (animals) cry, sing, howl **na(ru)** – (intr.) sound, ring **na(rasu)** – (tr.) sound, ring	
鳴	3d11.1 口 口 鳥 24 80 鳴	共 鳴 *kyōmei* resonance; sympathy	196
		鳴 動 *meidō* rumble	231
		鳴 き 声 *nakigoe* cry, call, chirping (of animals)	746
		海 鳴 り *uminari* rumbling/noise of the sea	117

	926	**KEI, niwatori** – chicken, hen, rooster	
鶏	11b8.4 田 鳥 小 大 80 35 34 鶏 鷄	鶏 肉 *keiniku* chicken, fowl	223
		養 鶏 *yōkei* poultry raising	402
		鶏 舎 *keisha* chicken coop, henhouse	791
		鶏 鳴 *keimei* cockcrow, rooster's call	925
		鶏 頭 *keitō* cockscomb (flower)	276

	927	**sa(ku)** – bloom	
咲	3d6.12 田 口 大 儿 24 34 16 咲	咲 き 出 す *sakidasu* begin to bloom	53
		咲 き 乱 れ る *sakimidareru* bloom in profusion	689
		遅 咲 き *osozaki* blooming late	702
		狂 い 咲 き *kuruizaki* flowering out of season	883
		返 り 咲 き *kaerizaki* second bloom; comeback	442

	928	**Ō, sakura** – cherry tree	
桜	4a6.15 田 木 小 女 41 35 25 桜 櫻	桜 花 *ōka* cherry blossoms	255
		八 重 桜 *yaezakura* double-petal cherry blossoms	10, 227
		桜 ん ぼ *sakuranbo* cherry	
		桜 色 *sakurairo* pink, cerise	204
		桜 肉 *sakuraniku* horsemeat	223

	929	**SHI, sugata** – form, figure, shape, appearance, posture	
姿	3e6.10 田 女 夂 冫 25 49 5 姿	姿 勢 *shisei* posture, stance	646
		容 姿 *yōshi* face and figure, appearance	654
		姿 態 *shitai* figure, pose	387
		姿 見 *sugatami* full-length mirror	63
		後 ろ 姿 *ushiro-sugata* view (of someone) from behind	48

	930	**DA** – peace, contentment	
妥	3e4.9 日 女 小 丨 25 35 2 妥 安	妥 協 *dakyō* compromise	234
		妥 結 *daketsu* compromise, agreement	485
		妥 当 *datō* proper, appropriate, adequate	77
		妥 協 案 *dakyōan* compromise plan	234, 106

	931	**SAI, na** – vegetable; rape, mustard plant	
菜	3k8.25 目 艹 木 小 32 41 35 菜 菜	野 菜 *yasai* vegetable	236
		菜 園 *saien* vegetable garden	447
		菜 食 *saishoku* vegetarian/herbivorous diet	322
		山 菜 *sansai* edible wild plant	34
		菜 種 *natane* rapeseed, coleseed, colza	228

	932	**SAI, irodo(ru)** – color	
彩	3j8.1 田	色彩 *shikisai* color, coloration	204
	彡 木 小	彩色 *saishiki* coloring, coloration	204
	31 41 35	多彩 *tasai* colorful	229
	彩	光彩 *kōsai* luster, brilliancy	138
		水彩画 *suisaiga* a watercolor painting	21, 343

	933	**SAI, to(ru)** – take (on), accept, employ; collect	
採	3c8.14 田	採用 *saiyō* adopt; employ	107
	扌 木 小	採決 *saiketsu* voting	356
	23 41 35	採集 *saishū* collecting (plants/butterflies)	436
	採 採	採録 *sairoku* record (in a book)	538
		採算 *saisan* a profit	747

	934	**SHŪ, [JU], tsu(ku)** – take (a seat); engage (in an occupation) **tsu(keru)** – employ	
就	3d9.21 田		
	口 小 尤	就職 *shūshoku* find employment	385
	24 35 27	就任 *shūnin* assumption of office	334
	就	就業時間 *shūgyō jikan* working hours	279, 42, 43
		成就 *jōju* accomplish, attain	261

	935	**BOTSU** – sink, go down	
没	3a4.15 田	没落 *botsuraku* downfall, ruin	839
	氵 冂 又	没入 *botsunyū* become immersed (in)	52
	21 20 9	出没 *shutsubotsu* appear and disappear, frequent	53
	没 没	没収 *bosshū* confiscation, forfeiture	757
		没交渉 *bokkōshō* unrelated, independent	114, 432

	936	**CHIN, shizu(mu)** – (intr.) sink **shizu(meru)** – (tr.) sink	
沈	3a4.9 田	沈没 *chinbotsu* sinking	935
	氵 冂 丨	沈下 *chinka* sinking, subsidence, settling	31
	21 20 2	沈静 *chinsei* stillness, stagnation	663
	沈	沈着 *chinchaku* composed, calm	657
		沈思 *chinshi* meditation, contemplation	99

	937	**SEN** – dive, hide **mogu(ru)** – dive; crawl into **hiso(mu)** – lurk, lie hidden	
潜	3a12.6 田		
	氵 日 大	潜水 *sensui* dive, submerge	21
	21 43 34	潜水夫 *sensuifu* diver	21, 315
	潜 潜	潜在 *senzai* hidden, latent, potential	268
		潜入 *sennyū* infiltrate (into)	52

	938	**FU, u(kabu)** – float, rise to the surface **u(kaberu)** – set afloat; show **u(ku)** – float, rise to the surface **u(kareru)** – feel buoyant, be in high spirits	
浮	3a6.11 田		
	氵 小 子	思い浮ぶ *omoiukabu* come to mind, occur to	99
	21 35 6	浮かぬ顔 *ukanu kao* dejected look	277
	浮 浮	浮世絵 *ukiyoe* Japanese woodblock print	252, 345

	939	**NYŪ, chichi, chi** – mother's milk; breast
乳	3n4.4	牛乳 *gyūnyū* (cow's) milk — 281
		母乳 *bonyū* mother's milk — 112
	35 6 2	乳がん *nyūgan* breast cancer
	乳	乳首 *chikubi, chichikubi* nipple — 148
		乳母車 *ubaguruma* baby carriage — 112, 133

	940	**KŌ** – hole; Confucius
孔	2c1.1	気孔 *kikō* pore — 134
		通気孔,空気孔 *tsūkikō, kūkikō* air hole — 150, 134, 140
	6 2	鼻孔 *bikō* nostril — 813
		多孔 *takō* porous — 229
	孔	孔子 *Kōshi* Confucius — 103

	941	**RYŌ** – finish, complete; understand
了	2c0.3	終了 *shūryō* end, completion, expiration — 458
		完了 *kanryō* completion; perfect tense 「of office) — 613
	(6) 1 2	(任期)満了 *(ninki) manryō* expiration (of a term — 334, 449, 201
		校了 *kōryō* final proofreading — 115
	了	了解 *ryōkai* understanding; Roger! (on a radio) — 474

	942	**SHŌ, uketamawa(ru)** – hear, be told
承	0a7.7	承知 *shōchi* consent; be aware of — 214
		承認 *shōnin* approval — 738
	21 4 1	承服 *shōfuku* consent, acceptance — 683
		了承 *ryōshō* acknowledgment — 941
	承	伝承 *denshō* hand down (from generation to generation) — 434

	943	**JŌ, mu(su)** – steam; be sultry **mu(rasu)** – steam **mu(reru)** – be steamed; get hot and stuffy
蒸	3k9.19	(水)蒸気 *(sui)jōki* (water) vapor, steam — 21, 134
		蒸発 *jōhatsu* evaporate; disappear into thin air — 96
	32 44 21	蒸し暑い *mushiatsui* hot and humid, sultry — 638
	蒸	蒸し返す *mushikaesu* reheat; repeat, rehash — 442

	944	**KŌ** – season; weather **sōrō** – (classical verb suffix)
候	2a8.10	天候 *tenkō* weather — 141
		気候 *kikō* climate — 134
	3 34 15	測候所 *sokkōjo* meteorological station — 610, 153
		候補者 *kōhosha* candidate — 889, 164
	候	居候 *isōrō* hanger-on, parasite — 171

	945	**SHŪ, [SHU], osa(meru)** – study; master **osa(maru)** – govern oneself
修	2a8.11	修理 *shūri* repair — 143
		修業 *shūgyō, shugyō* pursuit/completion of one's studies — 279
	3 49 31	修正 *shūsei* revise, correct, retouch — 275
	修	修行 *shugyō* training, study — 68

946 隆

2d8.6

阝 夂 牛
7 49 47

隆 隆

RYŪ – prosperity; high

隆盛	*ryūsei* prosperity	719
興隆	*kōryū* rise, prosperity, flourishing	368
隆起	*ryūki* protuberance, rise, elevation	373
隆々	*ryūryū* prosperous, thriving; muscular	
法隆寺	*Hōryūji* (temple in Nara)	123, 41

947 降

2d7.7

阝 夂 十
7 49 12

降

KŌ, o(riru) – go down, descend, get off (a bus) **o(rosu)** – let off (a passenger), dismiss **fu(ru)** – fall (rain/snow)

降雨量	*kōuryō* (amount of) rainfall	30, 411
降下	*kōka* descent, fall, landing	31
以降	*ikō* since, from ... on	46
飛び降りる	*tobioriru* jump down (from)	530

948 霜

8d9.2

雨 目 木
75 55 41

霜

SŌ, shimo – frost

霜害	*sōgai* frost damage	518
霜柱	*shimobashira* ice/frost columns	598
霜解け	*shimodoke* thawing	474
霜焼け	*shimoyake* frostbite	920
霜降り	*shimofuri* marbled (meat), salt-and-pepper pattern	947

949 雪

8d3.2

雨 彐
75 39

雪 雪

SETSU, yuki – snow

雪害	*setsugai* damage from snow	518
新雪	*shinsetsu* new-fallen snow	174
初雪	*hatsuyuki* first snow of the year/winter	679
大雪	*ōyuki* heavy snowfall	26
雪合戦	*yukigassen* snowball fight	159, 301

950 霧

8d11.1

雨 夂 力
75 49 8

霧

MU, kiri – fog

五里霧中	*gori-muchū* in a fog, mystified	7, 142, 28
霧雨	*kirisame* misty rain, drizzle	30
朝霧	*asagiri* morning mist/fog	469
夕霧	*yūgiri* evening mist/fog	81
黒い霧	*kuroi kiri* dark machinations	206

951 露

8d13.1

雨 卩 夂
75 70 49

露

RO, [RŌ] – open, public **tsuyu** – dew

露天で	*roten de* outdoors, in the open air	141
露店	*roten* street stall, booth	168
露出	*roshutsu* (indecent/film) exposure	53
露見	*roken* discovery, detection, exposure	63
朝露	*asatsuyu* morning dew	469

952 雷

8d5.1

雨 田
75 58

雷

RAI, kaminari – thunder

雷鳴	*raimei* thunder	925
落雷	*rakurai* thunderbolt, bolt of lightning	839
雷雨	*raiu* thunderstorm	30
地雷	*jirai* (land) mine	118
魚雷	*gyorai* torpedo	290

953	
8d7.3 日	**SHIN, furu(eru), furu(u)** – tremble, shake
雨 衤 厂 75 57 18	地震 *jishin* earthquake 118 震動 *shindō* tremor, vibration 231 震度 5 *shindo go* magnitude 5 (on the Japanese scale of 7) 377 震央, 震源 *shin'ō, shingen* epicenter 351, 580 身震い *miburui* shivering, trembling 59
震	

954	
3c7.14 □	**SHIN, fu(ruu)** – swing, wield; flourish **fu(ru)** – wave, shake
扌 衤 厂 23 57 18	振興 *shinkō* advancement, promotion 368 振動 *shindō* swing, oscillation, vibration 231 不振 *fushin* inactivity, stagnation, slump 94 振り替え *furikae* transfer 744 振り返る *furikaeru* turn one's head, look back 442
振	

955	
3e4.3 □	**NIN** – conception; pregnancy
女 王 25 46	妊婦 *ninpu* pregnant woman 316 妊婦服 *ninpufuku* maternity dress 316, 683 不妊 *funin* sterile, infertile 94 妊産婦 *ninsanpu* expectant and nursing mothers 278, 316
妊 妊	

956	
3e7.10 □	**SHIN** – pregnancy
女 衤 厂 25 57 18	妊娠 *ninshin* pregnancy 955 妊娠中絶 *ninshin chūzetsu* abortion 955, 28, 742
娠	

957	
3a13.7 田	**NŌ, ko(i)** – dark, thick, heavy, strong (coffee)
氵 衤 日 21 57 43	濃度 *nōdo* (degree of) concentration 377 濃厚 *nōkō* thickness, richness, strength 639 濃霧 *nōmu* dense fog 950
濃	

958	
3d4.22 目	**TŌ, [ZU], mame** – bean, pea; (prefix) miniature
口 儿 一 24 16 1	大豆 *daizu* soybean 26 小豆 *azuki* adzuki bean 27 枝豆 *edamame* green soybean 870 コーヒー豆 *kōhīmame* coffee bean 豆本 *mamehon* miniature book, pocket edition 25
豆	

959	
3d10.15目	**HŌ, yuta(ka)** – abundant, rich
口 日 儿 24 43 16	豊富 *hōfu* abundance, wealth 713 豊作 *hōsaku* good harvest 360 豊漁 *hōryō* good catch (of fish) 699 豊年 *hōnen* fruitful year 45 豊満 *hōman* plump, voluptuous, buxom 201
豊 豐	

登	**960** 3d9.26 目 口 火 儿 24 44 16 登	**TŌ, TO, nobo(ru)** – climb

登 山 *tozan* mountain climbing — 34
登 場 *tōjō* stage entrance; appearance — 154
登 記 *tōki* registration — 371
登 録 *tōroku* registration — 538
登 用 *tōyō* appointment; promotion — 107

廃	**961** 3q9.3 广 广 火 艹 18 44 32 廃 廢	**HAI, suta(reru), suta(ru)** – become outmoded, go out of fashion, be on the wane

廃 止 *haishi* abolition, abrogation — 477
廃 業 *haigyō* going out of business — 279
退 廃 *taihai* degeneracy, decadence — 846
廃 人 *haijin* cripple, invalid — 1

棄	**962** 2j11.5 目 亠 木 艹 11 41 32 棄 弃	**KI** – abandon, throw out, give up

廃 棄 物 *haikibutsu* waste (matter) — 961, 79
放 棄 *hōki* give up, renounce, waive — 512
棄 権 *kiken* abstention, nonvoting; renunciation — 335
自 棄 *jiki* self-abandonment — 62
破 棄 *haki* destruction; annulment, revocation — 665

帯	**963** 3f7.1 目 巾 艹 冂 26 32 20 帯 帶	**TAI** – belt, zone **obi** – belt, sash **o(biru)** – wear; be entrusted (with)

包 帯 *hōtai* bandage — 804
地 帯 *chitai* zone, area, region, belt — 118
熱 帯 *nettai* the tropics — 645
所 帯 *shotai* household — 153

滞	**964** 3a10.14 目 氵 艹 巾 21 32 26 滞 滯	**TAI** – stay, stopping over **todokō(ru)** – be left undone; fall into arrears, be overdue, be left unpaid

滞 在 *taizai* stay, sojourn — 268
遅 滞 *chitai* delay, procrastination — 702
滞 納 *tainō* delinquency (in payment) — 758
沈 滞 *chintai* stagnation, inactivity — 936

純	**965** 6a4.3 口 糸 十 冂 61 12 20 純	**JUN** – pure

純 毛 *junmō* pure/100 percent wool — 287
純 益 *jun'eki* net profit — 716
純 文 学 *junbungaku* pure literature, belles lettres — 111, 109
純 日 本 風 *jun Nihon-fū* classical Japanese style — 5, 25, 29
単 純 *tanjun* simple — 300

鈍	**966** 8a4.2 口 金 十 冂 72 12 20 鈍	**DON, nibu(i)** – dull, thick, slow-witted, sluggish, blunt, dim **nibu(ru)** – become dull/blunt, weaken

鈍 感 *donkan* obtuse, thick, insensitive — 262
鈍 重 *donjū* dull-witted, phlegmatic, stolid — 227
鈍 角 *donkaku* obtuse angle — 473
鈍 器 *donki* blunt object (used as a weapon) — 527

	967 2q6.1 □ 辶 米 19 62 迷	**MEI, mayo(u)** – be perplexed, vacillate; get lost; go astray
		迷宮, 迷路 *meikyū, meiro* maze, labyrinth　721, 151
		迷信 *meishin* superstition　157
		迷彩 *meisai* camouflage　932
		低迷 *teimei* be low, in a slump (market prices)　561
		迷子 *maigo* lost child　103

	968 2q5.3 辶 朮 丨 19 41 2 述	**JUTSU, no(beru)** – state, mention, refer to, explain
		供述 *kyōjutsu* testimony, deposition　197
		記述 *kijutsu* description　371
		上述 *jōjutsu* above-mentioned　32
		口述 *kōjutsu* oral statement; dictation　54
		著述家 *chojutsuka* writer, author　859, 165

	969 4k8.16 心 戈 口 51 52 24 惑	**WAKU, mado(u)** – go astray, be misguided, be tempted
		迷惑 *meiwaku* trouble, inconvenience　967
		当惑 *tōwaku* puzzlement, confusion　77
		思惑 *omowaku* opinion, intention, expectation　99
		惑星 *wakusei* planet　730
		戸惑い *tomadoi* become disoriented/flurried　152

	970 3b8.3 土 戈 口 22 52 24 域	**IKI** – region, area
		地域 *chiiki* region, area, zone　118
		区域 *kuiki* boundary, zone, district　183
		領域 *ryōiki* territory, domain　834
		流域 *ryūiki* (river) basin, valley　247
		聖域 *seiiki* sacred ground　674

	971 2a15.4 亻 貝 小 3 68 35 償	**SHŌ, tsuguna(u)** – make up for, compensate, indemnify, atone for
		補償 *hoshō* compensation, indemnification　889
		弁償 *benshō* compensation, reimbursement　711
		報償 *hōshō* compensation, remuneration　685
		無償 *mushō* free of charge, gratis　93

	972 3s5.2 回 口 十 24 12 固	**KO, kata(i)** – hard **kata(maru/meru)** – (intr./tr.) harden
		固体 *kotai* a solid　61
		固有 *koyū* own, peculiar, characteristic　265
		固定 *kotei* fixed　355
		固執 *koshitsu* hold fast to, persist in, insist on　686
		強固 *kyōko* firm, solid, strong　217

	973 2a8.36 亻 口 十 3 24 12 個 个	**KO** – individual; (counter for various objects)
		個人 *kojin* an individual　1
		個体 *kotai* an individual　61
		個性 *kosei* individuality　98
		個別的 *kobetsuteki* individual, separate　267, 210
		一個 *ikko* 1 piece　2

枯	**974** 4a5.26 ⊞ 木 口 十 41 24 12 枯	**KO, ka(reru)** – wither **ka(rasu)** – blight, let wither

枯死 *koshi* wither away, die — 85
栄枯 *eiko* ups and downs, vicissitudes — 723
枯れ木 *kareki* dead/withered tree — 22
枯れ葉 *kareha* dead/withered leaf — 253
木枯らし *kogarashi* cold winter wind — 22

975 2h3.1 ▯ 又 厂 9 18 皮
HI, kawa – skin, hide, leather, pelt, bark, rind
皮肉 *hiniku* irony — 223
皮相 *hisō* superficiality, shallowness — 146
毛皮 *kegawa* fur — 287
皮細工 *kawazaiku* leatherwork — 695, 139
皮切り *kawakiri* beginning, start — 39

976 5e5.3 ▱ 衤 厂 又 57 18 9 被
HI, kōmu(ru) – incur, suffer, receive
被害者 *higaisha* victim — 518, 164
被告 (人) *hikoku(nin)* defendant — 690, 1
被選挙資格 *hisenkyo shikaku* eligibility for election — 800, 801, 750, 643
被服 *hifuku* covering, coating — 683

977 3i5.2 ▱ 彳 厂 又 29 18 9 彼
HI – he; that *kare* – he *[kano]* – that
彼岸 *higan* equinoctial week; goal — 586
彼ら *karera* they
彼氏 *kareshi* he; boyfriend, lover — 566
彼女 *kanojo* she; girlfriend, lover — 102

978 5d5.8 ▱ 禾 小 𠂉 56 35 15 称 稱
SHŌ – name, title
名称 *meishō* name, designation — 82
愛称 *aishō* term of endearment, pet name — 259
尊称 *sonshō* honorific title — 704
称号 *shōgō* title, degree — 266
相称, 対称 *sōshō, taishō* symmetry — 146, 365

979 8b5.3 ▱ 食 巾 𠂉 73 26 15 飾 餝
SHOKU, kaza(ru) – decorate, adorn
修飾 *shūshoku* embellishment; modify (in grammar) — 945
飾り付け *kazaritsuke* decoration — 192
飾り気 *kazarike* affectation, love of display — 134
首飾り *kubikazari* necklace, choker — 148
着飾る *kikazaru* dress up — 657

980 2d6.5 ▱ 阝 食 7 73 郎 郞
RŌ – man, husband; (suffix for male given names)
新郎新婦 *shinrō-shinpu* bride and groom — 174, 316
郎等, 郎党 *rōtō, rōdō* vassals, retainers — 569, 495
野郎 *yarō* guy — 236
太郎 *Tarō* (male given name) — 629
二郎, 次郎 *Jirō* (male given name) — 3, 384

981 廊

RŌ – corridor, hall

3q8.4

广 食 阝
18 73 7

廊 廊

廊 下	*rōka*	corridor, hall	31
回 廊	*kairō*	corridor, gallery	90
画 廊	*garō*	picture gallery	343

982 甲

KŌ – A, No. 1 (in a series); shell, tortoise shell **KAN** – high (voice)

0a5.34

日 丨
43 2

甲

甲 鉄	*kōtetsu*	armor, armor plating	312
甲 状 せ ん	*kōjōsen*	thyroid gland	626
甲 種	*kōshu*	Grade A, first class	228
甲 高 い	*kandakai*	high-pitched, shrill	190

983 乙

OTSU – B, No. 2 (in a series); the latter; duplicate; bass (voice); strange; stylish; fine

0a1.5

一
1

乙

甲 乙	*kō-otsu*	A and B; discrimination, gradation	982
乙 女	*otome*	virgin, maiden	102
乙 な 味	*otsu na aji*	delicate flavor	307

984 丙

HEI – C, No. 3 (in a series)

0a5.21

一 冂 丨
14 20 2

丙

| 甲 乙 丙 | *kō-otsu-hei* | A, B, C; Nos. 1, 2, 3 | 982, 983 |
| 丙 午 | *hinoeuma* | (year in the Chinese 60-year cycle; it is said a woman born in such a year [1906, 1966 ...] will be domineering and will lead her husband to an early grave) | 49 |

985 柄

HEI, gara – pattern, design; build; character **e** – handle

4a5.9

木 一 冂
41 14 20

柄

横 柄	*ōhei*	arrogance	781
身 柄	*migara*	one's person	59
人 柄	*hitogara*	character, personality	1
事 柄	*kotogara*	matters, affairs	80
間 柄	*aidagara*	relation, relationship	43

986 押

Ō, o(su) – push **o(saeru)** – restrain, hold in check, suppress

3c5.5

扌 日 丨
23 43 2

押

押 収	*ōshū*	confiscation	757
押 韻	*ōin*	rhyme	349
押 し 入 れ	*oshiire*	closet, wall-cupboard	52
後 押 し	*atooshi*	push, support, back	48
押 し 付 け る	*oshitsukeru*	press against; force (upon)	192

987 抽

CHŪ – pull, extract

3c5.7

扌 日 丨
23 43 2

抽

抽 出	*chūshutsu*	extraction, sampling	53
抽 象	*chūshō*	abstraction	739
抽 象 的	*chūshōteki*	abstract	739, 210
抽 せ ん	*chūsen*	drawing, lottery	
抽 せ ん 券	*chūsenken*	lottery/raffle ticket	506

軸	**988**	***JIKU*** – axis, axle, shaft; (picture) scroll
	7c5.1	車軸 *shajiku* axle　　　　　　　　　　　　　　　133
	車 日 ∣	地軸 *chijiku* earth's axis　　　　　　　　　　　118
	69 43 2	自転軸 *jitenjiku* axis of rotation　　　　　62, 433
	軸	

搜	**989**	***SŌ, saga(su)*** – look/search for
	3c7.5	捜査 *sōsa* investigation　　　　　　　┌premises　624
	扌 日 又	家宅捜査 *kataku sōsa* search of the house/　165, 178, 624
	23 43 9	捜査本部 *sōsa honbu* investigation headquarters　624, 25, 86
	捜 捜	捜し回る *sagashimawaru* search around for　　　90
		捜し当てる *sagashiateru* find out, discover, locate　77

宇	**990**	***U*** – heaven
	3m3.3	宇内 *udai* the whole world　　　　　　　　　84
	宀 ｢ 一	気宇広大 *kiu-kōdai* magnanimous　　　134, 694, 26
	33 14 1	宇都宮 *Utsunomiya* (capital of Tochigi Prefecture)　188, 721
	宇	

宙	**991**	***CHŪ*** – midair; space, heaven
	3m5.5	宇宙 *uchū* space, the universe　　　　　　　990
	宀 日 ∣	宇宙旅行 *uchū ryokō* space flight　　　990, 222, 68
	33 43 2	宇宙飛行士 *uchū hikōshi* astronaut　990, 530, 68, 572
	宙	大宇宙 *daiuchū* macrocosm, the universe　26, 990
		宙返り *chūgaeri* somersault　　　　　　　442

届	**992**	***todo(ku)*** – reach, arrive　***todo(keru)*** – report, notify; send, deliver
	3r5.1	欠席届け *kessekitodoke* report of nonattendance　383, 379
	尸 日 ∣	欠勤届け *kekkintodoke* report of absence　　383, 559
	40 43 2	無届け *mutodoke* (absence) without notice　　　93
	届 届	届け先 *todokesaki* where to report; receiver's address　50

択	**993**	***TAKU*** – selection, choice
	3c4.21	選択 *sentaku* selection, choice　　　　　　　800
	扌 尸 ∣	選択科目 *sentaku kamoku* an elective (subject)　800, 320, 55
	23 40 2	採択 *saitaku* adoption, selection　　　　　　933
	択 擇	二者択一 *nisha-takuitsu* either-or alternative　3, 164, 2

沢	**994**	***TAKU, sawa*** – swamp, marsh
	3a4.18	光沢 *kōtaku* luster, gloss　　　　　　　　　138
	氵 尸 ∣	ぜい沢 *zeitaku* luxury, extravagance
	21 40 2	毛沢東 *Mō Takutō* Mao Zedong, Mao Tse-tung　287, 71
	沢 澤	金沢 *Kanazawa* (capital of Ishikawa Prefecture)　23

	995	**SHŌ, me(su)** – (honorific) summon; wear; take (a bath/bus)
召	2f3.3 ⊟	召集 *shōshū* convene (the Diet) 436
	刂 口 力	応召 *ōshō* be drafted, called up ⌐Shakespeare) 827
	(16) 24 8	お気に召すまま *O-ki ni Mesu Mama* (As You Like It – 134
	召	召し上がる *meshiagaru* eat, drink, have 32
		お召し物 *omeshimono* food, drink, clothing (polite) 79

	996	**SHŌ, numa** – swamp, marsh
沼	3a5.24 ⊞	沼沢 *shōtaku* marsh, swamp, bog 994
	氵 口 力	湖沼 *koshō* lakes and marshes 467
	21 24 8	沼地 *numachi* marshland, swampland 118
	沼	沼田 *numata* marshy rice field 35

	997	**SHŌ** – bright, clear
昭	4c5.4 ⊞	昭和 *Shōwa* (Japanese era, 1926–1989) 124
	日 口 力	昭和 6 3 年 *Shōwa rokujūsan-nen* 1988 124, 45
	43 24 8	昭和年間 *Shōwa nenkan* the Shōwa era 124, 45, 43
	昭	昭和元年 *Shōwa gannen* first year of the Shōwa
		era (1926) 124, 137, 45

	998	**SHŌ, te(ru)** – shine *te(rasu)* – shine on
照	4d9.12 ⊞	*te(reru)* – feel embarrassed
	火 日 口	照明 *shōmei* illumination, lighting 18
	44 43 24	対照 *taishō* contrast 365
	照	参照 *sanshō* reference 710
		東照宮 *Tōshōgū* (shrine in Nikkō) 71, 721

	999	**SHŌ** – fire; impatience; yearning *ko(gasu)* – scorch, singe; pine
焦	8c4.3 ⊟	for *ko(geru)* – get scorched *ko(gareru)* – yearn for *ase(ru)* – be
	隹 火	in a hurry, hasty, impatient
	74 44	焦点 *shōten* focal point, focus 169
	焦	焦熱地獄 *shōnetsu jigoku* an inferno 645, 118, 884
		黒焦げ *kurokoge* charred, burned 206

	1000	**CHŌ, ko(su), ko(eru)** – cross, go over, exceed
超	3b9.18 ⊡	超過 *chōka* excess 413
	土 口 力	超音速 *chōonsoku* supersonic speed 347, 502
	22 24 8	超大国 *chōtaikoku* a superpower 26, 40
	超	超満員 *chōman'in* crowded beyond capacity 201, 163
		超人 *chōjin* a superman 1

	1001	**ETSU, ko(su), ko(eru)** – cross, go over, exceed
越	4n8.2 ⊡	超越 *chōetsu* transcendence 1000
	戈 土 卜	越権 *ekken* overstepping one's authority 335
	52 22 13	越境 *ekkyō* jumping the border 864
	越	引っ越す *hikkosu* move, change residences 216
		勝ち越し *kachikoshi* a net win, being ahead 509

	1002	**SHU, omomuki** – purport, gist; taste, elegance; appearance	
趣	6e9.1 ⋯	趣味 *shumi* interest, liking, taste; hobby	307
	耳 土 又	趣向 *shukō* plan, idea	199
	65 22 9	趣意 *shui* purport, meaning; aim, object	132
		情趣 *jōshu* mood; artistic effect	209
	趣	野趣 *yashu* rural life and beauty, rusticity	236

	1003	**YŪ, [YU], aso(bu)** – play, enjoy oneself, be idle	
遊	2q8.3 ⊡	遊歩道 *yūhodō* promenade, mall, boardwalk	431, 149
	辶 方 ⌐	周遊(券) *shūyū(ken)* excursion (ticket)	91, 506
	19 48 15	遊説 *yūzei* speaking tour, political campaigning	400
		遊休 *yūkyū* idle, unused	60
	遊	遊び相手 *asobiaite* playmate	146, 57

	1004	**SHI, SE, hodoko(su)** – give, bestow; carry out, perform, conduct	
施	4h5.1 ⊞	施設 *shisetsu* facilities, institution	577
	方 ⌐ 十	施行 *shikō* enforce; put in operation	68
	48 15 12	施政 *shisei* administration, governing	483
	施	実施 *jisshi* carry into effect, enforce, implement	203

	1005	**SEN** – go around, revolve, rotate	
旋	4h7.2 ⊞	旋回 *senkai* turning, revolving, circling	90
	方 ⌐ ⌐	周旋 *shūsen* good offices, mediation	91
	48 15 14	旋律 *senritsu* melody	667
		旋風 *senpū* whirlwind, cyclone, tornado	29
	旋	あっ旋 *assen* good offices, mediation	

	1006	**KI, hata** – flag, banner	
旗	4h10.1 ⊞	国旗 *kokki* flag (of a country)	40
	方 艹 ⌐	校旗 *kōki* school banner/flag	115
	48 32 15	半旗 *hanki* flag at half-mast	88
		星条旗 *seijōki* the Stars and Stripes (U.S. flag)	730, 564
	旗	旗色 *hatairo* the tide of war; things, the situation	204

	1007	**RI** – an official	
吏	0a6.22 ⋯	官吏 *kanri* an official	326
	口 十 |	吏員 *riin* an official	163
	24 12 2	能吏 *nōri* capable official	386
	吏 吏	吏党 *ritō* party of officials	495

	1008	**KŌ, sara** – anew, again, furthermore **fu(kasu)** – stay up till late (at night) **fu(keru)** – grow late	
更	0a7.12 ⋯	変更 *henkō* alteration, change, modification	257
	日 ⌐ |	更衣室 *kōishitsu* clothes-changing room	677, 166
	43 14 2	更年期 *kōnenki* menopause	45, 449
	更 更	更生 *kōsei* rebirth, rehabilitation	44

1009 硬 5a7.1 □ 石 日 一 53 43 14 硬	**KŌ, kata(i)** – hard, firm
	硬質 *kōshitsu* hard, rigid — 176
	硬度 *kōdo* (degree of) hardness — 377
	硬化 *kōka* hardening — 254
	硬貨 *kōka* coin; hard currency — 752
	強硬 *kyōkō* firm, unyielding — 217
1010 構 4a10.10 □ 木 艹 王 41 32 46 構 構	**KŌ, kama(eru)** – build, set up; assume a posture/position **kama(u)** – mind, care about; meddle in; look after
	機構 *kikō* mechanism, structure, organization — 528
	構成 *kōsei* composition, makeup — 261
	構想 *kōsō* conception, plan — 147
	心構え *kokorogamae* mental attitude, readiness — 97
1011 購 7b10.3 □ 貝 艹 王 68 32 46 購	**KŌ** – buy, purchase
	購入 *kōnyū* purchase — 52
	購入者 *kōnyūsha* purchaser, buyer — 52, 164
	購買 *kōbai* purchase — 241
	購読 *kōdoku* subscription — 244
	購読料 *kōdokuryō* subscription price/fee — 244, 319
1012 溝 3a10.9 □ 氵 艹 王 21 32 46 溝	**KŌ, mizo** – ditch, gutter, groove
	下水溝 *gesuikō* drainage ditch, sewage pipe — 31, 21
	海溝 *kaikō* an ocean deep, sea trench — 117
	日本海溝 *Nihon/Nippon Kaikō* Japan Deep/Trench — 5, 25, 117
1013 譲 7a13.1 □ 言 礻 艹 67 57 32 譲 譲	**JŌ, yuzu(ru)** – transfer, assign; yield, concede
	譲歩 *jōho* concession, compromise — 431
	割譲 *katsujō* cede (territory) — 519
	互譲 *gojō* mutual concession — 907
	譲り渡す *yuzuriwatasu* turn over, transfer — 378
	親譲り *oyayuzuri* inheritance from a parent — 175
1014 暴 4c11.2 目 日 艹 氵 43 32 21 暴	**BŌ, aba(reru)** – act violently, rage, rampage, run amuck **[BAKU], aba(ku)** – disclose, expose, bring to light
	暴力団 *bōryokudan* gangster syndicate — 100, 491
	暴風 *bōfū* high winds, windstorm — 29
	乱暴 *ranbō* violence, roughness — 689
	暴露 *bakuro* expose, bring to light — 951
1015 爆 4d15.2 □ 火 日 艹 44 43 32 爆	**BAKU** – explode
	爆発 *bakuhatsu* explosion — 96
	爆発的 *bakuhatsuteki* explosive — 96, 210
	原爆 *genbaku* atomic bomb — 136
	被爆者 *hibakusha* bombing victim — 976, 164
	爆薬 *bakuyaku* explosives — 359

	1016	**GEKI, u(tsu)** – attack; fire, shoot	
撃	3c11.7	攻撃 *kōgeki* attack	819
	扌 車 冂	反撃 *hangeki* counterattack	324
	23 69 20	爆撃 *bakugeki* bombing raid	1015
	撃 撃	撃沈 *gekichin* (attack and) sink	936
		目撃者 *mokugekisha* eyewitness	55, 164

	1017	**GEKI, hage(shii)** – violent, fierce, strong, intense	
激	3a13.1	過激派 *kagekiha* radicals, extremist faction	413, 912
	氵 日 方	感激 *kangeki* deep emotion/gratitude	262
	21 43 48	激情 *gekijō* violent emotion, passion	209
	激	激動 *gekidō* violent shaking; excitement, stir	231
		激流 *gekiryū* swift current	247

	1018	**TŌ, u(tsu)** – attack	
討	7a3.3	検討 *kentō* examination, investigation, study	531
	言 寸	討論 *tōron* debate, discussion	293
	67 37	討議 *tōgi* discussion, deliberation, debate	292
	討	討ち死に *uchijini* fall in battle	85
		討ち取る *uchitoru* capture; kill	65

	1019	**TEI** – correcting	
訂	7a2.3	訂正 *teisei* correction, revision	275
	言 一	校訂 *kōtei* revision	115
	67 14	改訂 *kaitei* revision	514
	訂	増訂 *zōtei* revised and enlarged (edition)	712

	1020	**DA, u(tsu)** – hit, strike	
打	3c2.3	打開 *dakai* a break, development, new turn	396
	扌 一	打算的 *dasanteki* calculating, selfish, mercenary	747, 210
	23 14	打楽器 *dagakki* percussion instrument	358, 527
	打	打ち合わせ *uchiawase* previous arrangement	159
		打ち消し *uchikeshi* denial; negation	845

	1021	**TŌ, na(geru)** – throw	
投	3c4.18	投票 *tōhyō* vote	922
	扌 冂 又	投書 *tōsho* letter to the editor, contribution	131
	23 20 9	投資 *tōshi* investment	750
	投	投機 *tōki* speculation	528
		投影 *tōei* projection	854

	1022	**Ō** – Europe	
欧	4j4.2	欧州 *Ōshū* Europe	195
	欠 冂 十	西欧 *Seiō* Western Europe	72
	49 20 12	欧米 *Ō-Bei* Europe and America/the U.S.	224
	欧 歐	欧州同盟 *Ōshū Dōmei* the European Union	195, 198, 717
		北欧諸国 *hokuō shokoku* Scandinavian countries	73, 861, 40

	1023	**SŪ** – pivot	
枢	4a4.22	枢軸 *sūjiku* pivot, axis, center	988
	木 冂 艹	中枢 *chūsū* center	28
	41 20 12	枢要 *sūyō* important	419
	枢 樞	枢密 *sūmitsu* state secret	806

	1024	**DAN** – decision, judgement **kotowa(ru)** – decline, refuse; give	
断	6b5.6	notice/warning; prohibit **ta(tsu)** – cut off	
	米 斤 l	決断 *ketsudan* (prompt) decision, resolution	356
	62 50 2	油断 *yudan* inattention, negligence	364
	断 斷	横断 *ōdan* crossing	781
		断念 *dannen* abandonment, giving up	579

	1025	**KEI, tsu(gu)** – follow; succeed to, inherit	
継	6a7.8	後継 *kōkei* succession	48
	糸 米 l	継承 *keishō* succession, inheritance	942
	61 62 2	継続 *keizoku* continuance	243
	継 繼	中継 *chūkei* (radio/TV) relay, hookup	28
		受け継ぐ *uketsugu* inherit, succeed to	260

	1026	**HAN** – stamp, seal **BAN** – (paper) size	
判	2f5.2	判断 (力) *handan(ryoku)* judgment	1024, 100
	リ 小 二	判決 *hanketsu* a decision, ruling	356
	16 35 4	判事 *hanji* a judge	80
	判	公判 *kōhan* (public) trial	126
		判明 *hanmei* become clear, be ascertained	18

	1027	**HAN, BAN, tomona(u)** – go with, accompany; entail,	
伴	2a5.4	be accompanied by, be associated with	
	亻 小 二	同伴 *dōhan* keep (someone) company	198
	3 35 4	伴りょ *hanryo* companion, comrade, partner	
	伴	相伴う *aitomonau* accompany	146

	1028	**HYŌ** – criticism, comment	
評	7a5.3	評論 *hyōron* criticism, critique, commentary	293
	言 小 二	論評 *ronpyō* criticism, comment, review	293
	67 35 4	評価 *hyōka* appraisal	421
	評	評判 *hyōban* fame, popularity; rumor, gossip	1026
		書評 *shohyō* book review	131

	1029	**HI** – critique	
批	3c4.13	批判 *hihan* critique	1026
	扌 卜	批判的 *hihanteki* critical	1026, 210
	23 13	批評 *hihyō* critique, criticism, review	1028
	批	批評眼 *hihyōgan* critical eye	1028, 848
		文芸批評 *bungei hihyō* literary criticism	111, 435, 1028

	1030	**NI** – two (in documents)
弐	4n3.3 […]	弐万円 *niman'en* 20,000 yen 16, 13
	戈 二 丨 52 4 2	
	弐 貳	

	1031	**BU, MU** – military
武	4n5.3 […]	武器 *buki* weapon, arms 527
	戈 ﾄ 一 52 13 1	武力 *buryoku* military force 100
	武	武道 *budō* military arts 149
		武士 *bushi* samurai, warrior 572
		武者 *musha* warrior 164

	1032	**YŪ, ure(eru)** – grieve, be distressed, be anxious **ure(i/e)** – grief, distress, anxiety **u(i)** – unhappy, gloomy
憂	4i12.1 目	憂国 *yūkoku* patriotism 40
	夊 月 心 49 42 51	物憂い *monoui* languid, weary, listless 79
	憂	憂き目 *ukime* grief, misery, hardship 55
		憂い顔 *ureigao* sorrowful face, troubled look 277

	1033	**YŪ, sugu(reru)** – excel **yasa(shii)** – gentle, tender, kindhearted
優	2a15.1 ⊞	優勢 *yūsei* predominance, superiority 646
	亻 月 心 3 42 51	優勝 *yūshō* victory, championship 509
	優	優先 *yūsen* priority 50
		優柔不断 *yūjū-fudan* indecision, vacillation 774, 94, 1024
		女優 *joyū* actress 102

	1034	**HI, kana(shii)** – sad **kana(shimu)** – be sad, lament, regret
悲	4k8.18 目	悲劇 *higeki* tragedy 797
	心 一 儿 51 4 16	悲恋 *hiren* disappointed love 258
	悲	悲鳴 *himei* shriek, scream 925
		悲観 *hikan* pessimism 604

	1035	**HAI** – actor
俳	2a8.8 ⊞	俳優 *haiyū* actor 1033
	亻 二 儿 3 4 16	俳句 *haiku* haiku, 17-syllable Japanese poem in 5-7-5 form 337
	俳	俳人 *haijin* haiku poet 1

	1036	**HAI** – exclude; reject, expel
排	3c8.8 ⊞	排気ガス *haikigasu* exhaust gas/fumes 134
	扌 二 儿 23 4 16	排液 *haieki* drainage (in surgery) 472
	排	排撃 *haigeki* reject, denounce 1016
		排日 *hai-Nichi* anti-Japanese 5
		排他的 *haitateki* exclusive, cliquish 120, 210

1037	**HAI** – fellow, colleague, companion	
7c8.7	先輩 *senpai* one's senior (at school/work)	50
車 二 儿	後輩 *kōhai* one's junior, younger people	48
69 4 16	年輩 *nenpai* age, elderliness ⌜same age	45
輩	同年輩の人 *dōnenpai no hito* someone of the	198, 45, 1
	輩出 *haishutsu* appear one after another	53

1038	**TOKU** – virtue	
3i11.3	道徳 *dōtoku* marality, morals	149
彳目 心	公徳 *kōtoku* public morality	126
29 55 51	人徳 *jintoku, nintoku* one's natural virtue	1
徳 悳	不徳 *futoku* lack of virtue, vice, immorality	94
	徳川 *Tokugawa* (historical surname)	33

1039	**CHŌ, ki(ku)** – hear, listen	
6e11.3	聴取 *chōshu* listening	65
耳目 心	聴衆 *chōshū* audience	792
65 55 51	聴講 *chōkō* attendance at a lecture	783
聴 聴	公聴会 *kōchōkai* public hearing	126, 158
	聴覚 *chōkaku* sense of hearing	605

1040	**SHI, mune** – purport, content, gist; instructions	
4c2.2	趣旨 *shushi* purport, content, gist	1002
日 ト	要旨 *yōshi* gist, essential points	419
43 13	本旨 *honshi* main purpose, true aim	25
旨	論旨 *ronshi* point/drift of an argument	293

1041	**SHI, yubi** – finger **sa(su)** – point to	
3c6.15	指導 *shidō* guidance, leadership	703
扌目 ト	指令 *shirei* order, instruction	831
23 43 13	指名 *shimei* nomination, designation	82
指	指定席 *shiteiseki* reserved seat	355, 379
	人さし指 *hitosashiyubi* index finger, forefinger	1

1042	**SHI, abura** – (animal) fat	
4b6.7	油脂 *yushi* oils and fats	364
月目 ト	脂身 *aburami* fat (of meat)	59
42 43 13	脂っ濃い *aburakkoi* greasy, rich (foods)	957
脂		

1043	**IN** – seal, stamp **shirushi** – sign, mark	
2e4.1	印象 *inshō* impression	739
卩 厂 二	調印 *chōin* signing, signature	342
7 18 4	印税 *inzei* a royalty (on a book)	399
印	印紙 *inshi* revenue stamp	180
	矢印 *yajirushi* (direction) arrow	213

刷	**1044** 2f6.9 □ 刂尸巾 16 40 26 刷	**SATSU, su(ru)** – print 印刷 *insatsu* printing　　1043 印刷物 *insatsubutsu* printed matter　　1043, 79 増刷 *zōsatsu* additional printing, reprinting　　712 刷新 *sasshin* reform　　174 刷り直す *surinaosu* reprint to correct mistakes　　423
片	**1045** 2j2.5 ⸛ ⺌⼃ 11 15 片	**HEN** – part　**kata-** – one (of two) 破片 *hahen* broken piece, fragment, splinter　　665 断片 *danpen* fragment, piece, snippet　　1024 木片 *mokuhen* block/chip of wood, wood shavings　　22 片目 *katame* one eye　　55 片道 *katamichi* one way, each way　　149
版	**1046** 2j6.8 □ ⺌⼃厂 11 15 18 版	**HAN** – printing block/plate; printing; edition 出版社 *shuppansha* publishing house　　53, 308 版権 *hanken* copyright　　335 初版 *shohan* first edition　　679 改訂版 *kaiteiban* revised edition　　514, 1019 版画 *hanga* print, woodblock print　　343
板	**1047** 4a4.21 □ 木厂又 41 18 9 板	**HAN, BAN, ita** – a board 甲板 *kanpan, kōhan* deck (of a ship)　　982 合板 *gōban, gōhan* plywood　　159 黒板 *kokuban* blackboard　　206 床板 *yukaita* floorboard　　826 表示板 *hyōjiban* indicator-board　　272, 615
販	**1048** 7b4.2 □ 貝厂又 68 18 9 販	**HAN** – sell 販売 *hanbai* sales, selling　　239 販売値段 *hanbai nedan* selling price　　239, 425, 362 自動販売機 *jidō hanbaiki* vending machine　62, 231, 239, 528 市販 *shihan* marketing　　181 販路 *hanro* market (for goods), outlet　　151
仮	**1049** 2a4.15 □ 亻厂又 3 18 9 仮假	**KA, [KE], kari** – temporary, provisional, tentative, supposing 仮説 *kasetsu* hypothesis, supposition　　400 仮定 *katei* supposition, assumption, hypothesis　　355 仮面 *kamen* a mask　　274 仮名 *kamei* fictitious name　　82 仮病 *kebyō* pretended illness, malingering　　380
寛	**1050** 3m10.3 □ 宀貝卝 33 68 32 寛寛	**KAN** – leniency, generosity 寛大 *kandai* magnanimity, tolerance, leniency　　26 寛容 *kan'yō* magnanimity, generosity, forbearance　　654 寛厚 *kankō* generous, large-hearted　　639 寛厳 *kangen* severity and leniency　　822

1051

KAN, susu(meru) – recommend, offer, advise, encourage

2g11.1

力 隹 宀
8 74 15

勧 勸

勧告	kankoku	recommendation, advice	690
勧業	kangyō	encouragement of industry	279
勧進	kanjin	soliciting religious contributions	437

1052

KAN – joy, pleasure

4j11.1

欠 隹 宀
49 74 15

歓 歡

歓待	kantai	hospitality	452
歓談	kandan	pleasant chat	593
歓声	kansei	shout of joy, cheer	746
歓楽街	kanrakugai	amusement center	358, 186
歓心を買う	kanshin o kau	curry favor	97, 241

1053

I, era(i) – great, eminent, extraordinary, excellent

2a10.5

亻 口 十
3 24 12

偉

偉大	idai	great, mighty, grand	26
偉人	ijin	great man	1
偉才	isai	man of extraordinary talent	551
偉業	igyō	great achievement	279
偉観	ikan	a spectacular sight	604

1054

I – woof (horizontal thread in weaving); latitude

6a10.7

糸 口 十
61 24 12

緯

緯度	ido	latitude	377
緯線	isen	a parallel (of latitude)	299
北緯	hokui	north latitude	73
南緯	nan'i	south latitude	74
経緯	keii	longitude and latitude; the details	548

1055

GEI, muka(eru) – go to meet, receive; invite, send for

2q4.4

辶 厂 阝
19 18 7

迎

歓迎	kangei	welcome	1052
迎合	geigō	flattery	159
送迎	sōgei	welcome and sendoff	441
出迎え	demukae	meeting (someone) on arrival, reception	53
迎え撃つ	mukaeutsu	fight to repulse (an attack)	1016

1056

GYŌ, [KŌ], ao(gu) – look up at; look up to, respect; ask for, rely (on) **ō(se)** – what you say, (your/his) wish

2a4.10

亻 厂 阝
3 18 7

仰

仰視	gyōshi	look up (at)	606
仰天	gyōten	be astonished, frightened	141
信仰	shinkō	faith, religious conviction	157
仰向け	aomuke	facing upward, on one's back, supine	199

1057

YOKU, osa(eru) – hold down/in check, suppress, control

3c4.12

扌 厂 阝
23 18 7

抑

抑制	yokusei	control, restrain, suppress	427
抑留	yokuryū	dentention, internment	761
抑止	yokushi	deter, stave off	477
抑揚	yokuyō	rising and falling of tones, intonation	631

		1058	**RAN, tamago** – egg (cf. No. 295)	
卵	2e5.2 ⊞ 卩厂丨 7 18 2 卵		鶏 卵 *keiran* (hen's) egg 産 卵 *sanran* egg-laying, spawning 卵 黄 *ran'ō* yolk 卵 管 *rankan* Fallopian tube, oviduct 卵 形 *tamagogata, rankei* egg-shaped, oval	926 278 780 328 395

		1059	**SAKU** – rope, cord; search for	
索	2k8.2 ⊟ 十 糸 冂 12 61 20 索		索 引 *sakuin* an index 捜 索 *sōsaku* search ⌈premises 家 宅 捜 索 *kataku sōsaku* search of the house/ 165, 178, 探 索 *tansaku* search, inquiry, investigation 思 索 *shisaku* thinking, speculation, contemplation	216 989 989 535 99

		1060	**RUI** – involvement, trouble; accumulation; continually	
累	5f6.5 ⊟ 田 糸 58 61 累		累 加/増 *ruika/zō* acceleration, successive increase 709, 712 累 積 *ruiseki* accumulation, cumulative 累 計 *ruikei* (sum) total 係 累 *keirui* family encumbrances, dependents 累 進 *ruishin* successive/progressive promotions	 656 340 909 437

		1061	**I, koto** – be different	
異	5f6.7 ⊟ 田 艹 儿 58 32 16 異		異 常 *ijō* unusual, abnormal 異 質 *ishitsu* heterogeneity 異 国 *ikoku* foreign country 異 議 *igi* objection 異 教 *ikyō* heathenism, paganism, heresy	497 176 40 292 245

		1062	**YOKU, tsubasa** – wing	
翼	2o15.2 ⊟ 丷 田 ヨ 16 58 39 翼 翼		左 翼 *sayoku* the left wing, leftist 右 翼 *uyoku* the right wing, rightist 両 翼 *ryōyoku* both wings 比 翼 の 鳥 *hiyoku no tori* happily married couple 798, 285	75 76 200

		1063	**YO, ama(ru)** – be left over, in excess **ama(su)** – leave over	
余	2a5.24 ⊟ 亻 木 一 3 41 1 余 餘		二 十 余 年 *nijūyonen* more than 20 years 3, 12, 45 余 命 *yomei* the rest of one's life 余 計 *yokei* too much, unwanted, uncalled-for 余 地 *yochi* room, margin 余 波 *yoha* aftereffect	 578 340 118 666

		1064	**KA, hima** – free time, leisure	
暇	4c9.1 ⊞ 日 尸 二 43 40 4 暇		休 暇 *kyūka* holiday, vacation, time off 余 暇 *yoka* leisure, spare time 暇 つぶし *himatsubushi* a waste of time, killing time 暇 取 る *himadoru* take a long time, be delayed 暇 な 時 *hima na toki* leisure time, when one is free	60 1063 65 42

除	**1065** 2d7.10 □ 阝 木 イ 7 41 3 除	**JO, [JI], nozo(ku)** – get rid of, exclude

解 除 *kaijo* cancellation	474
除 名 *jomei* remove (someone's) name, expel	82
除 外 *jogai* except, exclude	83
免 除 *menjo* exemption	733
取 り 除 く *torinozoku* remove, rid	65

徐	**1066** 3i7.2 □ 彳 木 イ 29 41 3 徐	**JO** – slowly

徐 々 に *jojo ni* slowly, gradually	
徐 行 *jokō* go/drive slowly	68
徐 歩 *joho* walk slowly, saunter, mosey	431

叙	**1067** 2h7.1 □ 又 木 イ 9 41 3 叙 敍	**JO** – narrate, describe

叙 述 *jojutsu* description, narration	968
叙 景 *jokei* description of scenery	853
叙 情 詩 *jojōshi* lyric poem/poetry	209, 570
叙 事 詩 *jojishi* epic poem/poetry	80, 570
自 叙 伝 *jijoden* autobiography	62, 434

剰	**1068** 2f9.1 □ 刂 木 艹 16 41 32 剰 剩	**JŌ** – surplus

剰 余 (金) *jōyo(kin)* a surplus 「births)	1063, 23
(出 生) 過 剰 *(shussei) kajō* surplus, excess (of	53, 44, 413
余 剰 *yojō* surplus	1063
剰 員 *jōin* superfluous personnel, overstaffing	163

斜	**1069** 2a9.21 □ イ 木 艹 3 41 12 斜	**SHA, nana(me)** – slanting, diagonal, oblique

斜 面 *shamen* a slope, slant, incline	274
斜 線 *shasen* slanting line, slash [/]	299
斜 辺 *shahen* oblique side, hypotenuse	775
斜 陽 *shayō* setting sun	630
斜 視 *shashi* squint	606

垂	**1070** 0a8.12 … 王 艹 一 46 32 1 垂	**SUI, ta(reru/rasu)** – (intr./tr.) hang down, dangle, drip

垂 直 *suichoku* perpendicular, vertical	423
垂 線 *suisen* a perpendicular (line)	299
懸 垂 *kensui* suspension, dangling; doing chin-ups	911
虫 垂 *chūsui* the appendix	873
雨 垂 れ *amadare* raindrops	30

睡	**1071** 5c8.2 □ 目 王 艹 55 46 32 睡	**SUI** – sleep

睡 眠 *suimin* sleep	849
睡 眠 不 足 *suimin-busoku* lack of sleep	849, 94, 58
午 睡 *gosui* nap, siesta	49
熟 睡 *jukusui* sound/deep sleep	687
こ ん 睡 (状 態) *konsui (jōtai)* coma	626, 387

1072

途

2q7.16

辶 木 亻
19 41 3

途 途

TO – way, road

途 中	*tochū* on the way, midway	28
前 途	*zento* one's future, prospects	47
途 絶 え る	*todaeru* come to a stop	742
帰 途	*kito* one's way home ⌐country	317
(開 発) 途 上 国	*(kaihatsu) tojōkoku* developing	396, 96, 32, 40

1073

塗

3b10.10

土 木 氵
22 41 21

塗

TO, nu(ru) – paint

塗 料	*toryō* paints, paint and varnish	319
塗 布	*tofu* apply (salve)	675
塗 り 物	*nurimono* lacquerware	79
塗 り 立 て	*nuritate* freshly painted	121
塗 り 替 え る	*nurikaeru* repaint, put on a new coating	744

1074

華

3k7.1

艹 王
32 46

華

KA, [KE], hana – flower, florid, showy, brilliant

華 道	*kadō* (Japanese) flower arranging	149
華 美	*kabi* splendor, pomp, gorgeousness	401
中 華 料 理	*chūka ryōri* Chinese food/cooking	28, 319, 143
中 華 人 民 共 和 国	*Chūka Jinmin Kyōwakoku*	
	People's Republic of China	28, 1, 177, 196, 124, 40

1075

革

3k6.2

艹 口 一
32 24 14

革

KAKU – reform   **kawa** – leather

革 命	*kakumei* revolution	578
革 新	*kakushin* reform	174
改 革	*kaikaku* reform, reorganization	514
変 革	*henkaku* reform, innovation, revolutionize	257
皮 革	*hikaku* leather	975

1076

靴

3k10.34

艹 口 亻
32 24 3

靴

KA, kutsu – shoe

製 靴	*seika* shoemaking	428
革 靴	*kawagutsu* leather shoes	1075
靴 下	*kutsushita* socks, stockings	31
靴 屋	*kutsuya* shoe store	167
靴 一 足	*kutsu issoku* 1 pair of shoes	2, 58

1077

侵

2a7.15

亻 彐 冂
3 39 20

侵

SHIN, oka(su) – invade; violate, infringe on; damage

侵 略	*shinryaku* aggression, invasion	841
侵 入	*shinnyū* invasion, raid, trespass	52
侵 害	*shingai* infringement ⌐pact	518
不 可 侵 条 約	*fukashin jōyaku* nonaggression	94, 388, 564, 211
侵 食	*shinshoku* erosion, weathering	322

1078

浸

3a7.17

氵 彐 冂
21 39 20

浸

SHIN, hita(ru) – be soaked, steeped   **hita(su)** – dip, immerse

浸 水	*shinsui* inundation, submersion	21
浸 出	*shinshutsu* exuding, oozing out, percolation	53
浸 食	*shinshoku* erosion, corrosion	322
水 浸 し	*mizubitashi* submersion, inundation	21

	1079	**SHIN, ne(ru)** – go to bed, sleep **ne(kasu)** – put to bed
寝	3m10.1	寝室 *shinshitsu* bedroom
	宀 ⼹ ⼃	寝台 *shindai* bed
	33 39 5	寝具 (類) *shingu(rui)* bedclothes, bedding
	寝 寝	昼寝 *hirune* (daytime) nap, siesta
		寝苦しい *negurushii* unable to sleep well

	166
	492
	420, 226
	470
	545

	1080	**SŌ, ha(ku)** – sweep
掃	3c8.22	(大)掃除 *(ō)sōji* (general) housecleaning
	扌 ⼹ 帚	清掃夫 *seisōfu* street sweeper, cleaning man
	23 39 26	掃除婦 *sōjifu* cleaning lady
	掃 掃	掃討 *sōtō* sweeping, clearing, mopping up
		一掃 *issō* sweep away, eradicate, stamp out

	26, 1065
	660, 315
	1065, 316
	1018
	2

	1081	**KEN, ka(neru)** – combine, double as **-ka(neru)** – cannot
兼	2o8.1	兼業 *kengyō* a side business
	⼍ ⼹ 一	兼任 *kennin* hold 2 posts (simultaneously)
	16 39 14	待ち兼ねる *machikaneru* cannot wait, wait impatiently
	兼	首相兼外相 *shushō ken gaishō* prime minister who is also foreign minister

	279
	「for 334
	452
	148, 146, 83

	1082	**JIN, tazu(neru)** – search for; ask, inquire
尋	3d9.29	尋問 *jinmon* questioning, interrogation
	口 ⼹ ⼯	尋常 *jinjō* normal, ordinary
	24 39 38	尋ね人 *tazunebito* person being sought, missing person
	尋 尋	

	162
	497
	1

	1083	**SO** – crop tax, tribute
租	5d5.7	租税 *sozei* taxes
	禾 月 一	地租 *chiso* (obsolete) land tax
	56 42 1	租借 *soshaku* lease (land)
	租	租界 *sokai* (foreign) settlement, concession
		租借地 *soshakuchi* leased territory

	399
	118
	766
	454
	766, 118

	1084	**SO, ara(i)** – coarse, rough
粗	6b5.2	粗末 *somatsu* coarse, plain, crude, rough, rude
	米 月 一	粗暴 *sobō* wild, rough, rude, violent
	62 42 1	粗野 *soya* rustic, loutish, vulgar, ill-bred
	粗	粗悪 *soaku* coarse, crude, base, inferior
		粗食 *soshoku* coarse food, plain diet

	305
	1014
	236
	304
	322

	1085	**SO, haba(mu)** – hamper
阻	2d5.1	阻止 *soshi* obstruct, impede
	阝 月 一	阻害 *sogai* check, impediment, hindrance
	7 42 1	険阻 *kenso* steep, precipitous, rugged
	阻	

	477
	518
	533

宜	**1086** 3m5.7 目 宀 月 一 33 42 1 宜	**GI** – good, all right	
		便宜 *bengi* convenience, expediency	330
		便宜上 *bengijō* for convenience/expediency	330, 32
		時宜 *jigi* right time/opportunity	42
		適宜 *tekigi* suitable, appropriate, fitting	415

畳	**1087** 5f7.3 目 田 月 冂 58 42 20 畳 疊	**JŌ, tatami** – tatami, straw floor-mat ***tata(mu)*** – fold up	
		四畳半 *yojōhan* 4 1/2-mat room	6, 88
		畳表 *tatami-omote* woven covering of a tatami	272
		畳替え *tatamigae* replacing *tatami-omote*/tatami	744
		畳屋 *tatamiya* tatami maker/store	167

援	**1088** 3c9.7 田 扌 小 又 23 35 9 援 援	**EN** – help, assistance	
		援助 *enjo* assistance, aid	623
		応援 *ōen* aid, support, backing, cheering	827
		後援 *kōen* support, backing	48
		声援 *seien* shout of encouragement, cheers, rooting	746
		援軍 *engun* reinforcements	438

緩	**1089** 6a9.8 田 糸 小 又 61 35 9 緩	**KAN, yuru(mu)** – become loose, abate, slacken ***yuru(meru)*** – loosen, relieve, relax, slacken ***yuru(i)*** – loose; generous; lax; gentle (slope); slow ***yuru(yaka)*** – loose, slack; magnanimous; gentle, easy, slow	
		緩和 *kanwa* relieve, ease, lighten	124
		緩急 *kankyū* fast and slow speed; emergency	303

筋	**1090** 6f6.4 田 ⺮ 月 力 66 42 8 筋	**KIN, suji** – muscle, tendon; blood vessel; line; reason, logic; plot (of a story); coherence; source (of information)	
		筋肉 *kinniku* muscle	223
		筋道 *sujimichi* reason, logic, coherence	149
		筋違い *sujichigai, sujikai* a cramp; illogical; wrong	814
		筋書き *sujigaki* synopsis, outline, plan	131

箱	**1091** 6f9.4 田 ⺮ 目 木 66 55 41 箱	**hako** – box	
		本箱 *honbako* bookcase	25
		貯金箱 *chokinbako* savings box, (piggy) bank	762, 23
		重箱 *jūbako* nested boxes	227
		豚箱 *butabako* police lockup, jail, hoosegow	796
		箱根 *Hakone* (resort area near Mt. Fuji)	314

範	**1092** 6f9.3 田 ⺮ 車 阝 66 69 7 範	**HAN** – example, model, pattern; limit	
		範例 *hanrei* example	612
		師範 *shihan* teacher, master	409
		規範 *kihan* norm, criterion	607
		広範 *kōhan* extensive, wide, far-reaching	694

1093 丹	0a4.34 冂 一 丨 20 1 2 丹 丹	**TAN** – red	
		丹念 *tannen* application, diligence	579
		丹誠 *tansei* sincerity; efforts, diligence	718
		丹精 *tansei* exertion, diligence, painstaking care	659
		丹前 *tanzen* man's padded kimono	47

1094 舟	6c0.1 舟 63 舟 舟	**SHŪ, fune, [funa]** – boat	
		小舟 *kobune* boat, skiff	27
		舟遊び *funaasobi* boating	1003
		舟歌 *funauta* sailor's song, chantey	392

1095 舶	6c5.2 舟 日 丨 63 43 2 舶	**HAKU** – ship	
		船舶 *senpaku* ship, vessel; shipping	376
		舶来 *hakurai* imported	69
		舶来品 *hakuraihin* imported article/goods	69, 230

1096 般	6c4.3 舟 冂 又 63 20 9 般	**HAN** – carry; all, general	
		一般的 *ippanteki* general	2, 210
		一般化 *ippanka* generalization, popularization	2, 254
		全般 *zenpan* the whole	89
		全般的 *zenpanteki* general, overall	89, 210
		先般 *senpan* recently, some time ago	50

1097 皿	5h0.1 皿 59 皿	**sara** – plate, dish, saucer	
		皿洗い *saraarai* washing dishes	692
		サラダ一皿 *sarada hitosara* 1 plate of salad	2
		大皿 *ōzara* large dish, platter	26
		小皿 *kozara* small plate	27
		受け皿 *ukezara* saucer	260

1098 盤	5h10.2 皿 舟 冂 59 63 20 盤	**BAN** – (chess/go) board, tray, platter, basin	
		基盤 *kiban* basis, foundation	450
		円盤 *enban* disk; discus	13
		空飛ぶ円盤 *soratobu enban* flying saucer	140, 530, 13
		水盤 *suiban* basin	21
		終盤戦 *shūbansen* end game	458, 301

1099 盆	2o7.6 皿 儿 力 59 16 8 盆 盆	**BON** – Buddhist Festival of the Dead; tray	
		盆地 *bonchi* basin, valley	118
		盆景 *bonkei* miniature landscape on a tray	853
		(お)盆 *(O)Bon* the Bon Festival	
		(o)bon tray	

	1100	**TŌ, nusu(mu)** – steal
盗	5h6.2 ⊞	強盗 *gōtō* burglar, robber — 217
	皿 攵 冫	盗難 (保険) *tōnan (hoken)* theft (insurance) — 557, 489, 533
	59 49 5	盗用 *tōyō* embezzlement; surreptitious use, plagiarism — 107
	盗 盗	盗作 *tōsaku* plagiarism — 360
		盗品 *tōhin* stolen goods, loot — 230

	1101	**EN, shio** – salt
塩	3b10.4 ⊞	食塩 *shokuen* table salt — 322
	土 皿 口	塩分 *enbun* salt content, salinity — 38
	22 59 24	塩酸 *ensan* hydrichloric acid — 516
	塩 鹽	塩水 *shiomizu, ensui* salt water, brine — 21
		塩入れ *shioire* saltshaker — 52

	1102	**BON, [HAN]** – common, ordinary
凡	2s1.1 ▢	凡人 *bonjin* ordinary person, man of mediocre ability — 1
	几 丨	平凡 *heibon* commonplace, miediocre — 202
	20 2	凡才 *bonsai* common ability, mediocre talent — 551
	凡	凡例 *hanrei* introductory remarks — 612

	1103	**HAN, ho** – sail
帆	3f3.1 ⊞	出帆 *shuppan* sailing, departure — 53
	巾 冂 丨	帆走 *hansō* sailing — 429
	26 20 2	帆船 *hansen, hobune* sailing ship, sailboat — 376
	帆	帆柱 *hobashira* mast — 598

	1104	**BŌ, oka(su)** – risk, brave, defy, dare; desecrate
冒	4c5.6 ⊟	冒険 *bōken* adventure — 533
	日 目	冒険小説 *bōken shōsetsu* adventure novel — 533, 27, 400
	43 55	冒頭 *bōtō* beginning, opening, lead — 276
	冒 冒	感冒 *kanbō* a cold — 262
		冒とく *bōtoku* blasphemy, sacrilege, defilement

	1105	**BŌ** – cap, hat, headgear
帽	3f9.1 ⊞	帽子 *bōshi* hat, cap — 103
	巾 日 目	宇宙帽 *uchūbō* space helmet — 990, 991
	26 55 43	赤帽 *akabō* redcap, luggage porter — 207
	帽	無帽 *mubō* hatless, bareheaded — 93
		帽章 *bōshō* badge on a cap — 857

	1106	**CHŌ, ha(ru)** – stretch, spread
張	3h8.1 ⊞	主張 *shuchō* insistence, assertion, contention — 155
	弓 礻 二	出張 *shutchō* business trip — 53
	28 57 4	出張所 *shutchōjo* branch office, agency — 53, 153
	張	引っ張る *hipparu* pull, tug at — 216
		見張る *miharu* keep watch, be on the lookout — 63

1107

帳

3f8.2 ⊞

巾 衤 二
26 57 4

帳

CHŌ – notebook; register; curtain

手帳 *techō* (picket) notebook　　　　　　　　　　　　57
電話帳 *denwachō* telephone book/directory　　108, 238
(貯金)通帳 *(chokin) tsūchō* bankbook, passbook　762, 23, 150
帳面 *chōmen* notebook, account book　　　　　　274
帳消し *chōkeshi* cancellation, writing off (debts)　　845

1108

伸

2a5.3 ⊞

イ 日 丨
3 43 2

伸

SHIN, no(biru) – stretch, lengthen, grow　**no(basu)** – stretch out, lenghten, extend

伸張 *shinchō* extend, expand　　　　　　　　　1106
二伸 *nishin* postscript, P.S.　　　　　　　　　　3
伸び伸び *nobinobi* at ease, relieved, refreshed

1109

紳

6a5.2 ⊞

糸 日 丨
61 43 2

紳

SHIN – gentleman

紳士 *shinshi* gentleman　　　　　　　　　　　572
紳士用 *shinshiyō* men's, for men　　　　　572, 107
紳士服 *shinshifuku* men's clothing　　　　572, 683
紳士協定 *shinshi kyōtei* gentleman's agreement
　　　　　　　　　　　　　　　　　　572, 234, 355

1110

縮

6a11.9 ⊞

糸 日 宀
61 43 33

縮

SHUKU, chiji(maru/mu) – shrink, contract　**chiji(meru)** – shorten, condense　**chiji(reru)** – become curly　**chiji(rasu)** – make curly

伸縮 *shinshuku* expansion and contraction, flexibility　1108
短縮 *tanshuku* shortening, reduction　　　　　　215
縮図 *shukuzu* reduced/scaled-down drawing　　　339
軍縮 *gunshuku* arms reduction　　　　　　　　438

1111

廷

2q4.2 ⊞

辶 王
19 46

廷

TEI – imperial court; government office

宮廷 *kyūtei* imperial court　　　　　　　　　721
法廷 *hōtei* (law) court　　　　　　　　　　　123
開廷 *kaitei* holding (law) court　　　　　　　396
出廷 *shuttei* appearance in court　　　　　　53
廷臣 *teishin* court official, courtier　　　　　835

1112

庭

3q6.3 ⊡

广 王 辶
18 46 19

庭

TEI, niwa – garden

家庭 *katei* home, family　　　　　　　　　　165
校庭 *kōtei* schoolyard, school grounds　　　　115
庭球 *teikyū* tennis　　　　　　　　　　　　726
庭園 *teien* garden　　　　　　　　　　　　447
前庭 *maeniwa, zentei* front garden　　　　　47

1113

拡

3c5.25 ⊡

扌 厂 ム
23 18 17

拡 擴

KAKU – extend, expand

拡大 *kakudai* magnification, expansion　　　　26
拡張 *kakuchō* extension, expansion　　　　　1106
拡充 *kakujū* expansion, amplification　　　　828
拡散 *kakusan* diffusion　　　　　　　　　　767
拡声機, 拡声器 *kakuseiki* loudspeaker　746, 528, 527

	1114	**SEI** – conquer	
征	3i5.3	征 服 *seifuku* conquer, subjugate	683
	彳 工 一	征 服 者 *seifukusha* conqueror	683, 164
	29 38 1	出 征 *shussei* going to the front, taking the field	53
	征	遠 征 *ensei* (military) expedition; playing tour	446
		長 征 *chōsei* the Long March (in China)	95

	1115	**EN, no(basu/beru)** – lengthen, prolong, postpone	
延	2q5.4	**no(biru)** – be postponed, delayed, prolonged	
	辶 ㇒ 一	延 長 *enchō* extension	95
	19 13 11	延 期 *enki* postponement, extension	449
	延	遅 延 *chien* delay, being behind time	702
		引 き 延 ばす *hikinobasu* draw out, prolong, enlarge	216

	1116	**TAN** – birth	
誕	7a7.15	誕 生 *tanjō* birth	44
	言 辶 ㇒	誕 生 日 *tanjōbi* birthday	44, 5
	67 19 13	誕 生 祝 い *tanjōiwai* birthday celebration	44, 851
	誕	生 誕 (百 年) *seitan (hyakunen)* (centenary of someone's)	
		birth	44, 14, 45

	1117	**SEKI** – achievements; spinning	
績	6a11.8	成 績 *seiseki* performance, results	261
	糸 貝 土	成 績 表 *seisekihyō* list of grades, report card	261, 272
	61 68 22	業 績 *gyōseki* work, achievements; business performance	279
	績	功 績 *kōseki* meritorious service	818
		実 績 *jisseki* record of performance, actual results	203

	1118	**SAI** – debt, loan	
債	2a11.11	負 債 *fusai* debt, liabilities	510
	亻 貝 土	国 債 *kokusai* national debt, public loan	40
	3 68 22	債 券 *saiken* bond, debenture	506
	債	債 権 (者) *saiken(sha)* credit(or)	335, 164
		債 務 (者) *saimu(sha)* debt(or)	235, 164

	1119	**KŌ** – empress	
后	3d3.11	皇 后 *kōgō* empress	297
	口 厂 一	皇 后 陛 下 *kōgō-heika* Her Majesty the Empress	297, 589, 31
	24 18 1	皇 太 后 *kōtaigō, kōtaikō* the empress dowager	297, 629
	后		

	1120	**KŌ** – manuscript, draft	
稿	5d10.5	原 稿 (用 紙) *genkō (yōshi)* manuscript (paper)	136, 107, 180
	禾 口 亠	草 稿 *sōkō* rough draft, notes	249
	56 24 11	投 稿 *tōkō* contribution (to a periodical)	1021
	稿 槀	稿 料 *kōryō* fee for a manuscript/article/artwork	319

	1121 5d6.1 ⊞ 禾 夕 56 30 移	**I, utsu(ru)** – move (one's residence), change; be catching **utsu(su)** – move (one's residence/office); transfer; infect
		移動 *idō* moving, migration — 231 移転 *iten* move, change of address — 433 移(住)民 *i(jū)min* emigrant, immigrant — 156, 177 移植 *ishoku* transplant — 424

	1122 3o8.7 ⊞ 凵 月 36 42 崩 崩	**HŌ, kuzu(reru)** – fall to pieces, collapse **kuzu(su)** – demolish; change, break (a large bill); write (cursive simplified kanji)
		崩御 *hōgyo* death of the emperor — 708 山崩れ *yamakuzure* landslide — 34 荷崩れ *nikuzure* a load falling off (a truck) — 391 切り崩す *kirikuzusu* cut through, level (a mountain) — 39

	1123 5e6.9 ⁝ 礻 戈 十 57 52 12 裁	**SAI, saba(ku)** – pass judgment **ta(tsu)** – cut out (cloth/leather)
		裁判 *saiban* trial, hearing — 1026 裁決 *saiketsu* decision, ruling — 356 独裁 *dokusai* dictatorship — 219 総裁 *sōsai* president, general director — 697 洋裁 *yōsai* (Western-style) dressmaking — 289

	1124 7c6.5 ⁝ 車 戈 十 69 52 12 載	**SAI, no(ru)** – be recorded, appear (in print) **no(seru)** – place on top of; load (luggage); publish, run (an ad)
		積載 *sekisai* loading, carrying — 656 満載 *mansai* fully loaded — 201 記載 *kisai* statement, mention — 371 連載 *rensai* a serial — 440

	1125 4n6.1 ⁝ 戈 木 十 52 41 12 栽	**SAI** – planting
		盆栽 *bonsai* a bonsai, potted dwarf tree — 1099

	1126 2a7.17 ⊡ 亻 火 口 3 44 24 俗	**ZOKU** – customs, manners; the world, laity; vulgar
		俗語 *zokugo* colloquial language — 67 俗名 *zokumyō* secular name — 82 民俗 *minzoku* folk — 177 風俗 *fūzoku* manners, customs; public morals — 29 通俗文学 *tsūzoku bungaku* popular literature — 150, 111, 109

	1127 4j7.1 ⊡ 欠 火 口 49 44 24 欲 慾	**YOKU** – covetousness, desire **hos(suru)** – desire, want **ho(shii)** – want
		食欲 *shokuyoku* appetite — 322 性欲 *seiyoku* sexual desire, sex drive — 98 欲望 *yokubō* desire, appetite, craving — 673 無欲 *muyoku* free from avarice, unselfish — 93

	1128	**YOKU, a(biru)** – be bathed in **a(biseru)** – pour over, shower
浴	3a7.18 □	入浴 *nyūyoku* bathing, (hot) bath　　　　　　52
	氵火口	浴室 *yokushitsu* bathroom　　　　　　　166
	21 44 24	海水浴場 *kaisuiyokujō* (swimming) beach　117, 21, 154
		日光浴 *nikkōyoku* sunbathing　　　　　　5, 138
	浴	浴衣 *yukata* cotton kimono for summer　　　677

	1129	**TEN** – expand
展	3r7.2 □	展示(会) *tenji(kai)* show, exhibition　　615, 158
	尸衤艹	展望台 *tenbōdai* observation platform　　673, 492
	40 57 32	親展 *shinten* confidential　　　　　　　175
		進展 *shinten* development, evolution　┌country　437
	展	発展途上国 *hatten tojōkoku* developing　96, 1072, 32, 40

	1130	**DEN, TEN** – hall, palace; mister **tono** – lord **-dono** – Mr.
殿	3r10.1 田	宮殿 *kyūden* palace　　　　　　　　　721
	尸艹几	御殿 *goten* palace　　　　　　　　　708
	40 32 16	殿下 *denka* His/Your Highness　　　　　31
		湯殿 *yudono* bathroom　　　　　　　　632
	殿	

	1131	**EN** – relation, connection; marriage; fate; veranda **fuchi** – edge, brink, rim, border
縁	6a9.10 田	絶縁 *zetsuen* (electrical) insulation; break off relations　742
	糸ヨ豸	因縁 *innen* causality, connection, fate　　554
	61 39 27	縁側 *engawa* veranda, porch, balcony　　609
	縁 縁	額縁 *gakubuchi* (picture) frame　　　　838

	1132	**TSUI** – fall
墜	3b11.7 □	墜落 *tsuiraku* fall, (airplane) crash　　　839
	土豸阝	墜死 *tsuishi* fatal fall, fall to one's death　85
	22 27 7	撃墜 *gekitsui* shoot down (a plane)　　1016
		失墜 *shittsui* loss, fall　　　　　　　311
	墜	

	1133	**SUI, to(geru)** – accomplish, attain, carry through
遂	2q9.13 □	遂行 *suikō* accomplish, execute, perform　　68
	辶豸儿	完遂 *kansui* successful execution, completion　613
	19 27 16	(殺人)未遂 *(satsujin) misui* attempted (murder)　576, 1, 306
		(自殺)未遂 *(jisatsu) misui* attempted (suicide)　62, 576, 306
	遂	やり遂げる *yaritogeru* go through with, carry out

	1134	**CHIKU** – drive away, pursue, follow
逐	2q7.6 □	放逐 *hōchiku* expulsion, banishment　　　512
	辶豸七	逐語訳 *chikugoyaku* word-for-word/literal translation　67, 594
	19 27 10	逐次 *chikuji* one after another, one by one　384
		逐一 *chikuichi* one by one, in detail　　　2
	逐	逐電 *chikuden, chikuten* abscond, make a getaway　108

1135

4k13.12 田
心 食 犭
51 73 27
懇

KON, nengo(ro) – intimacy, friendship

懇 談	*kondan*	familiar talk, friendly chat	593
懇 意	*kon'i*	intimacy, friendship	132
懇 切	*konsetsu*	cordial; exhaustive, detailed	39
懇 願	*kongan*	entreaty, earnest appeal	581
懇 親 会	*konshinkai*	social gathering	175, 158

1136

3b13.6 田
土 食 犭
22 73 27
墾

KON – opening up farmland, cultivation

開 墾	*kaikon*	clearing, reclamation (of land)	396
開 墾 地	*kaikonchi*	developed/cultivated land	396, 118

1137

4i2.2 凵
夂 冂
49 20
処 處

SHO – deal with, treat; sentence, condemn; behave, act

処 分	*shobun*	disposal, disposition; punishment	38
処 置	*shochi*	disposition, measures, steps	426
処 理	*shori*	treat, manage, deal with	143
対 処	*taisho*	cope with, tackle	365
処 女	*shojo*	virgin	102

1138

3c5.26 凵
扌 夂 冂
23 49 20
拠 據

KYO, KO – be due to, based on

根 拠	*konkyo*	basis, grounds	314
拠 点	*kyoten*	(military) position, base	169
準 拠	*junkyo*	be based on, conform to	778
論 拠	*ronkyo*	grounds/basis of an argument	293
証 拠	*shōko*	evidence	484

1139

2o10.2 目
ﾛ 王 口
16 46 24
善 譱

ZEN, yo(i) – good

善 悪	*zen'aku*	good and evil; quality (whether good or bad)	304
善 良	*zenryō*	good, honest, virtuous	321
善 意	*zen'i*	good intentions; favorable sense	132
親 善	*shinzen*	friendship	175
改 善	*kaizen*	improvement, betterment	514

1140

6a12.2 田
糸 王 口
61 46 24
繕

ZEN, tsukuro(u) – repair, mend

修 繕	*shūzen*	repair	945
営 繕	*eizen*	building and repairs	722

1141

3p3.1 日
士 口
22 24
吉

KICHI, KITSU – good luck

吉 報	*kippō*	good news, glad tidings	685
吉 日	*kichinichi*	lucky day	5
不 吉	*fukitsu*	ill omen, portentous	94
石 部 金 吉	*Ishibe Kinkichi*	man of strict morals	78, 86, 23
吉 田	*Yoshida*	(surname)	35

	1142	**KITSU, tsu(mu)** – be pressed into, closely packed
詰	7a6.7 ⊞	**tsu(meru)** – cram, stuff; shorten **tsu(maru)** – be stopped up, jammed; shrink; be cornered
	言 土 口	詰 問 *kitsumon* cross-examination, tough questioning 162
	67 22 24	詰 め 込 む *tsumekomu* cram, stuff 776
詰		気 詰 ま り *kizumari* embarrassment, awkwardness 134

	1143	**KI, yoroko(bu)** – be glad
喜	3p9.1 🔲	喜 劇 *kigeki* a comedy 797
	吉 口 儿	歓 喜 *kanki* joy, delight 1052
	22 24 16	狂 喜 *kyōki* wild joy, exultation 883
喜 㐂		一 喜 一 憂 *ikki-ichiyū* alternation of joy and sorrow 2, 1032
		大 喜 び *ōyorokobi* great joy 26

	1144	**JU** – tree, bush
樹	4a12.3 ▥	樹 木 *jumoku* tree 22
	木 土 口	果 樹 *kaju* fruit tree 487
	41 22 24	樹 皮 *juhi* bark (of a tree) 975
樹		樹 脂 *jushi* resin 1042
		樹 立 *juritsu* establish, found 121

	1145	**BŌ, fuku(reru), fuku(ramu)** – swell, bulge, rise (dough),
膨	4b12.1 ▥	expand; sulk, pout
	月 土 口	膨 大 *bōdai* swelling; large, enormous 26
	42 22 24	青 膨 れ *aobukure* dropsical swelling 208
膨		膨 れ っ 面 *fukurettsura* sullen/sulky look 274
		下 膨 れ *shimobukure* full-cheeked, round-faced 31

	1146	**SHI** – limbs
肢	4b4.7 ⊞	肢 体 *shitai* limbs; body and limbs 61
	月 十 又	下 肢 *kashi* lower limbs, legs 31
	42 12 9	上 肢 *jōshi* upper limbs, arms 32
肢		四 肢 *shishi* the limbs, members 6

	1147	**KO, tsuzumi** – hand drum
鼓	3p10.2 ⊞	太 鼓 *taiko* drum 629
	吉 口 儿	鼓 手 *koshu* drummer 57
	22 24 16	鼓 動 *kodō* (heart) beat 231
鼓 皷		鼓 舞 *kobu* encouragement, inspiration 810

	1148	**HATSU, kami** – hair (on the head)
髪	3j11.3 ⊞	散 髪 *sanpatsu* haircut, hairdressing 767
	彡 十 又	洗 髪 *senpatsu* hair washing, a shampoo 692
	31 12 9	間 一 髪 *kan-ippatsu* by a hairsbreadth 43, 2
髪 髮		金 髪 *kinpatsu* blond 23
		白 髪 *hakuhatsu, shiraga* white/gray hair 205

	1149	**CHŌ, ho(ru)** – carve, engrave, chisel, sculpt	
彫	3j8.2 ⬚	彫像 *chōzō* carved statue	740
	彡月 口	彫金 *chōkin* chasing, metal carving	23
	31 42 24	木彫 *mokuchō* wood carving	22
		木彫り *kibori* wood carving	22
	彫	浮き彫り *ukibori* relief	938

	1150	**RETSU, oto(ru)** – be inferior	
劣	3n3.4 ⬚	劣等 *rettō* inferiority	569
	⺌ 力 丨	劣等感 *rettōkan* inferiority complex	569, 262
	35 8 2	劣性 *ressei* inferior; recessive (gene)	98
		劣勢 *ressei* numerical inferiority	646
	劣	優劣 *yūretsu* superiority or inferiority, relative merit	1033

	1151	**SA, SHA, suna** – sand	
砂	5a4.3 ⬚	砂利 *jari* gravel	329
	石 小 丨	土砂降り *doshaburi* pouring rain, downpour	24, 947
	53 35 2	土砂崩れ *doshakuzure* washout, landslide	24, 1122
		砂浜 *sunahama* sandy beach	785
	砂	砂時計 *sunadokei* hourglass	42, 340

	1152	**BYŌ** – second (of time/arc)	
秒	5d4.2 ⬚	秒針 *byōshin* second hand (of a clock)	341
	禾 小 丨	数秒 *sūbyō* several seconds	225
	56 35 2	1分20秒 *ippun nijūbyō* 1 minute 20 seconds	38
		秒読み *byōyomi* countdown ⌐second	244
	秒	秒速5メートル *byōsoku gomētoru* 5 meters per	502

	1153	**SHŌ** – selection, summary, excerpt	
抄	3c4.11 ⬚	抄録 *shōroku* excerpt, abstract, summary	538
	扌 小 丨	抄本 *shōhon* extract, abridged transcript	25
	23 35 2	抄訳 *shōyaku* abridged translation	594
	抄	詩抄 *shishō* a selection of poems	570

	1154	**MYŌ** – strange, odd; a mystery; adroitness, knack	
妙	3e4.5 ⬚	奥妙 *ōmyō* secret, mystery	476
	女 小 丨	妙案 *myōan* good idea, ingenious plan	106
	25 35 2	妙技 *myōgi* extraordinary skill	871
		妙手 *myōshu* expert, master, virtuoso	57
	妙	絶妙 *zetsumyō* miraculous, superb, exquisite	742

	1155	**HAI, sakazuki** – wine cup (for sakè)	
杯	4a4.11 ⬚	一杯 *ippai* a glass (of); a drink; full	2
	木 一 丨	二杯 *nihai* 2 glasses (of)	3
	41 14 2	祝杯 *shukuhai* a toast	851
		銀杯 *ginpai* silver cup	313
	杯 盃	デ杯 (戦) *Dehai(sen)* Davis Cup (tournament)	301

1156	**MAI** – (counter for thin, flat objects)	
4a4.4 □	紙一枚 *kami ichimai* 1 sheet of paper	180, 2
木 攵	何枚 *nanmai* how many (sheets/plates/stamps)	390
41 49	枚挙 *maikyo* enumerate, count, list	801
枚	枚数 *maisū* number of sheets	225
	大枚 *taimai* a big sum (of money)	26

1157	**SATSU** – paper money, slip of paper *fuda* – chit, card, label	
4a1.1 □	千円札 *sen-ensatsu* 1,000-yen bill/note	15, 13
木 丨	札束 *satsutaba* bundle/roll of bills	501
41 2	改札口 *kaisatsuguchi* wicket, ticket gate	514, 54
札	標札, 表札 *hyōsatsu* nameplate	923, 272
	入札 *nyūsatsu* a bid, tender	52

1158	**SATSU** – (counter for books) **SAKU** – book	
0a5.42 [..]	十二冊 *jūnisatsu* 12 books/volumes	12, 3
卄 冂	別冊 *bessatsu* separate volume	267
32 20	分冊 *bunsatsu* individual/separate volumes	38
冊 冊	冊子 *sasshi* booklet, brochure, pamphlet	103
	短冊 *tanzaku* strip of fancy paper (for a poem)	215

1159	**HEN, katayo(ru)** – lean, incline; be one sided, partial	
2a9.16 □	不偏 (不党) *fuhen (futō)* nonpartisan	94, 495
亻 尸 卄	偏向 *henkō* propensity, leaning, deviation	199
3 40 32	偏見 *henken* biased view, prejudice	63
偏 偏	偏食 *henshoku* unbalanced diet	322
	偏差 *hensa* deviation, deflection, declination	658

1160	**HEN** – far, widespread, general	
2q9.16 □	遍歴 *henreki* travel, pilgrimage	480
辶 尸 卄	遍路 *henro* pilgrim	151
19 40 32	一遍 *ippen* once, one time	2
遍 遍		

1161	**BIN** – bottle	
2o9.6 ⊞	花瓶 *kabin* vase	255
ソ 卄 一	瓶詰 *binzume* bottled, in a glass jar	1142
16 32 14	ビール瓶 *bīrubin* beer bottle	
瓶 瓶	鉄瓶 *tetsubin* iron kettle	312
	空き瓶 *akibin* empty bottle	140

1162	**HEI, awa(seru)** – put together, unite, combine	
2a6.17 ⊞	合併 *gappei* merger	159
亻 卄 儿	併合 *heigō* annexation, amalgamation, merger	159
3 32 16	併用 *heiyō* use jointly/in combination	107
併 併	併発 *heihatsu* (medical) complications	96
	併記 *heiki* write side by side/on the same page	371

倫	1163	**RIN** – principle, code	
	2a8.28 ⊞	倫理 *rinri* ethics, morals	143
	亻 艹 冂	倫理学 *rinrigaku* ethics, moral philosophy	143, 109
	3 32 20	人倫 *jinrin* humanity, morality	1
	倫	不倫 *furin* immoral, illicit	94
		絶倫 *zetsurin* peerless, unsurpassed	742

輪	1164	**RIN, wa** – wheel, ring, circle; (counter for flowers)	
	7c8.4 ⊞	車輪 *sharin* wheel	133
	車 艹 亻	輪番 *rinban* taking turns, in rotation	185
	69 32 3	五輪 (大会) *gorin (taikai)* the Olympic Games	7, 26, 158
	輪	競輪 *keirin* bicycle race	852
		指輪 *yubiwa* (finger) ring	1041

並	1165	**HEI, nara(bu)** – be lined up **nara(beru)** – arrange, put side by	
	2o6.1 ⊟	side **nara(bi ni)** – and **nami** – ordinary, average	
	丷 工 l	並行 *heikō* parallel	68
	16 38 2	並列 *heiretsu* stand in a row; parataxis	611
	並 竝	並木 *namiki* row of trees, roadside trees	22
		平年並み *heinennami* as in an average/normal year	202, 45

普	1166	**FU** – general, universal	
	2o10.5 ⊟	普通 *futsū* usual, ordinary	150
	丷 日 工	普(通)選(挙) *fu(tsū) sen(kyo)* general elections	150, 800, 801
	16 43 38	普遍的 *fuhenteki* universal, ubiquitous	1160, 210
	普	普請 *fushin* building, construction	661
		普段 *fudan* usual, ordinary, everyday	362

譜	1167	**FU** – (sheet) music, notes, staff, score; a genealogy; record	
	7a12.2 ⊞	楽譜 *gakufu* (written) notes, the score	358
	言 日 工	譜面 *fumen* sheet music, score	274
	67 43 38	暗譜 *anpu* learning the notes by heart	348
	譜 譜	年譜 *nenpu* chronological record	45
		系譜 *keifu* genealogical chart, family tree	908

霊	1168	**REI, RYŌ, tama** – soul, spirit	
	8d7.2 ⊟	霊肉 *reiniku* body and soul/spirit	223
	雨 工 儿	亡霊 *bōrei* soul/spirit of a dead person	672
	75 38 16	聖霊 *seirei* the Holy Spirit	674
	霊 靈	霊園 *reien* cemetery park	447
		万物の霊長 *banbutsu no reichō* crown of ⌐creation, man	16, 79, 95

湿	1169	**SHITSU, shime(ru)** – become damp **shime(su)** – moisten	
	3a9.22 ⊞	湿気 *shikke, shikki* moisture, humidity	134
	氵 日 儿	湿度 *shitsudo* humidity	377
	21 43 16	湿地 *shitchi* damp ground, bog	118
	湿 濕	湿布 *shippu* wet compress, poultice	675

顕	**1170** 9a9.5 ⊞ 頁 日 儿 77 43 16 顕 顯	**KEN** – clear, plain obvious
		露顕 *roken* dicovery, disclosure, exposure 951
		顕著 *kencho* notable, striking, marked 859
		顕花植物 *kenka shokubutsu* flowering plant 255, 424, 79

貴	**1171** 7b5.7 ☐ 貝 口 亠 68 24 11 貴	**KI, tatto(i), tōto(i)** – valuable, noble **tatto(bu), tōto(bu)** – value, esteem, respect
		貴重 *kichō* valuable, precious 227
		貴重品 *kichōhin* valuables 227, 230
		貴族 *kizoku* nobleman, the nobility 221
		富貴 *fūki* riches and honors, wealth and rank 713

遺	**1172** 2q12.4 ☐ 辶 貝 口 19 68 24 遺	**I, [YUI]** – leave behind, bequeath
		遺伝 *iden* heredity 434
		遺体 *itai* corpse, the remains 61
		遺産 *isan* an inheritance, estate 278
		遺族 *izoku* family of the deceased, survivors 221
		遺言 *yuigon* will, last wishes 66

遣	**1173** 2q10.2 ☐ 辶 口 尸 19 24 40 遣	**KEN, tsuka(wasu)** – send; give **tsuka(u)** – use
		派遣 *haken* dispatch, send (a person) 912
		小遣い(銭) *kozukai(sen)* pocket money 27, 648
		気遣い *kizukai* worry, apprehension 134
		心遣い *kokorozukai* solicitude, consideration 97

追	**1174** 2q6.4 ☐ 辶 尸 冂 19 40 20 追	**TSUI, o(u)** – drive away; pursue
		追放 *tsuihō* banishment, purge 512
		追求 *tsuikyū* pursue, follow up 724
		追加 *tsuika* addition, supplement 709
		追い風 *oikaze* favorable/tail wind 29
		追い越す *oikosu* overtake, pass 1001

迫	**1175** 2q5.5 ☐ 辶 日 丨 19 43 2 迫	**HAKU, sema(ru)** – press (someone) for, urge; approach, draw near
		切迫 *seppaku* draw near, press, be imminent 39
		迫力 *hakuryoku* force, power, impressiveness 100
		迫害 *hakugai* persecution 518
		窮迫 *kyūhaku* straitened circumstances, poverty 897

伯	**1176** 2a5.7 ⊞ 亻 日 丨 3 43 2 伯	**HAKU** – eldest brother (cf. No.1667); count, earl
		画伯 *gahaku* great artist, master painter 343
		伯母 *oba* aunt (elder sister of parent) 112
		伯父 *oji* uncle (elder brother of parent) 113

	1177	***HAKU, to(maru/meru)*** – (intr./tr.) put up (for the night), lodge	
泊	3a5.15 ⊞	宿 泊　*shukuhaku*　lodging	179
	氵日 丨	一 泊　*ippaku*　overnight stay	2
	21 43 2	漂 泊　*hyōhaku*　wander, drift	924
	泊	泊 り 賃　*tomarichin*　hotel charges	751
		泊 り 客　*tomarikyaku*　house guest; (hotel) guest	641

	1178	***HAKU, HYŌ*** – beat (in music)	
拍	3c5.14 ⊞	拍 手　*hakushu*　handclapping, applause	57
	扌日 丨	拍 車　*hakusha*　a spur	133
	23 43 2	拍 子　*hyōshi*　time, tempo; chance, the moment	103
	拍 拍	拍 子 木　*hyōshigi*　wooden clappers	103, 22
		脈 拍　*myakuhaku*　pulse	913

	1179	***TEI*** – emperor	
帝	2j7.1 ⊟	帝 国　*teikoku*　empire	40
	亠巾 儿	帝 国 主 義　*teikoku shugi*　imperialism	40, 155, 291
	11 26 16	帝 政　*teisei*　imperial rule	483
	帝 帝	皇 帝　*kōtei*　emperor	297
		カ ー ル 大 帝　*Kāru Taitei*　Charlemagne	26

	1180	***TEI, shi(meru)*** – tie, tighten　***shi(maru)*** – be shut; tighten	
締	6a9.11 ⊞	条 約 の 締 結　*jōyaku no teiketsu*　conclusion of　564, 211, 485	
	糹巾 亠	取 り 締 ま り　*torishimari*　control, supervision └a treaty	65
	61 26 11	締 め 切 り　*shimekiri*　closing (date), deadline	39
	締	締 め 出 す　*shimedasu*　shut/lock out	53
		引 き 締 め る　*hikishimeru*　ighten, stiffen	216

	1181	***HŌ, tazu(neru), otozu(reru)*** – visit	
訪	7a4.1 ⊡	訪 問　*hōmon*　visit	162
	言 方	来 訪　*raihō*　visit	69
	67 48	訪 日　*hōnichi*　visit to Japan	5
	訪	訪 客　*hōkyaku*　visitor, guest	641
		探 訪　*tanbō*　making inquiries, inquiring into	535

	1182	***BŌ, samata(geru)*** – prevent, obstruct, hamper	
妨	3e4.1 ⊡	妨 害　*bōgai*　obstruction, disturbance, interference	518
	女 方		
	25 48		
	妨		

	1183	***BŌ, katawa(ra)*** – side	
傍	2a10.6 ⊞	傍 観　*bōkan*　look on, remain a spectator	604
	亻方 亠	傍 聴　*bōchō*　hearing, attendance	1039
	3 48 11	傍 系　*bōkei*　collateral (descendant)	908
	傍	傍 証　*bōshō*　supporting evidence, corroboration	484
		傍 受　*bōju*　intercept, monitor (a radio message)	260

亭 **1184** 2j7.5 目 ⼀ ⼝ ⼐ 11 24 20 亭	**TEI** – restaurant, pavilion, arbor 亭主 *teishu* host; innkeeper; husband　　　　155 料亭 *ryōtei* (Japanese) restaurant　　　　319
停 **1185** 2a9.14 田 亻⼝ ⼀ 3 24 11 停	**TEI** – stop 停止 *teishi* suspension, stopping　　　　477 停滞 *teitai* stagnation, accumulation　　　　964 調停 *chōtei* mediation, arbitration　　　　342 停留所 *teiryūjo* (bus/streetcar) stop　　　　761, 153 各駅停車 *kakueki teisha* a local (train)　　642, 284, 133
轄 **1186** 7c10.1 田 車 ⼧ ⼟ 69 33 22 轄	**KATSU** – a wedge; control, administration 管轄 *kankatsu* jurisdiction, competence　　　　328 管轄官庁 *kankatsu kanchō* the proper　　328, 326, 763 所轄 *shokatsu* jurisdiction 　┌authorities　　153 統轄 *tōkatsu* supervision, general control　　　830 直轄 *chokkatsu* direct control/jurisdiction　　　423
軒 **1187** 7c3.1 □ 車 ⼀ ⼀ 69 14 1 軒	**KEN** – (counter for buildings) **noki** – eaves 一軒 *ikken* 1 house　　　　2 軒数 *kensū* number of houses　　　　225 軒並 *nokinami* row of houses　　　　1165 軒先 *nokisaki* edge of the eaves; front of the house　　50
汗 **1188** 3a3.6 □ 氵⼀ ⼀ 21 14 1 汗	**KAN, ase** – sweat 発汗 *hakkan* perspire, sweat　　　　96 冷汗 *reikan, hiyaase* a cold sweat　　　　832 汗顔 *kangan* sweating from shame　　　　277
幹 **1189** 4c9.8 田 ⽇ ⼗ 亻 43 12 3 幹	**KAN** – main part **miki** – (tree) trunk 幹部 *kanbu* key officers, executives, management　　86 幹事長 *kanjichō* executive secretary, secretary-general　80, 95 根幹 *konkan* basis, root, nucleus　　　　314 語幹 *gokan* stem of a word　　　　67 新幹線 *Shinkansen* New Trunk Line, bullet train　174, 299
乾 **1190** 4c7.14 田 ⽇ ⼗ ⼄ 43 12 15 乾	**KAN, kawa(ku/kasu)** – (intr./tr.) dry, dry out 乾季 *kanki* the dry season　　　　465 乾電池 *kandenchi* dry cell, battery　　　108, 119 乾物 *kanbutsu* dry provisions, groceries　　　79 乾杯 *kanpai* a toast; Cheers!　　　　1155

綿	**1191** 6a8.8 ⊞ 糸 日 巾 61 43 26 綿 縣	**MEN, wata** – cotton

木綿　*momen*　cotton　22
綿布　*menpu*　cotton (cloth)　675
綿織物　*men'orimono*　cotton fabrics, cotton goods　680, 79
海綿　*kaimen*　a sponge　117
綿密　*menmitsu*　minute, close, meticulous　806

| 泉 | **1192**
3a5.33 目
氵日 |
21 43 2
泉 㵎 | **SEN, izumi** – spring, fountainhead, fountain |

温泉　*onsen*　hot spring, spa　634
冷泉　*reisen*　cold mineral spring　832
泉水　*sensui*　garden pond, fountain　21
源泉　*gensen*　fountainhead, source　580
平泉　*Hiraizumi*　(town in Tōhoku)　202

| 井 | **1193**
0a4.46 ⊡
卅 一
32 1
井 | **SEI, [SHŌ], i** – a well |

井泉　*seisen*　a well　1192
油井　*yusei*　oil well　364
天井　*tenjō*　ceiling　141
井戸　*ido*　a well　⌐Tōkyō) 152
軽井沢　*Karuizawa*　(summer resort town NW of　547, 994

| 囲 | **1194**
3s4.2 回
口 卅 一
24 32 1
囲 圍 | **I, kako(mu/u)** – surround, enclose; lay siege to |

範囲　*han'i*　extent, scope, range　1092
周囲　*shūi*　circumference, surroundings　91
包囲　*hōi*　encirclement, siege　804
取り囲む　*torikakomu*　surround, enclose; besiege　65

| 囚 | **1195**
3s2.1 回
口 亻
24 3
囚 | **SHŪ** – arrest, imprison, prisoner |

囚人　*shūjin*　prisoner, convict　1
未決囚　*miketsushū*　unconvicted prisoner　306, 356
死刑囚　*shikeishū*　criminal sentenced to death　85, 887
女囚　*joshū*　female prisoner　102
免囚　*menshū*　released prisoner, ex-convict　733

| 耕 | **1196**
0a10.13 ⊞
木 卅 一
41 32 4
耕 畊 | **KŌ, tagaya(su)** – till, plow, cultivate |

耕地　*kōchi*　arable land, cultivated land　118
耕作　*kōsaku*　cultivation, farming　360
農耕　*nōkō*　agriculture, farming　369

| 耗 | **1197**
0a10.12 ⊞
木 一 卅
41 4 12
耗 耗 | **MŌ, [KŌ]** – decrease |

消耗　*shōmō*　consumption, wear and tear　845
損耗　*sonmō*　wear, wastage, loss　350
心神耗弱　*shinshin kō/mōjaku*　feebleminded　97, 310, 218
心神耗弱者　*shinshin kō/mōjakusha*　feebleminded person
　97, 310, 218, 164

籍	**1198** 6f14.1 ⽵ 木 日 66 41 43 籍	**SEKI** – (family) register

戸 籍 *koseki* census registration 152
本 籍 *honseki* one's domicile, legal residence 25
除 籍 *joseki* removal from the register 1065
国 籍 *kokuseki* nationality 40
書 籍 *shoseki* books 131

| 錯 | **1199** 8a8.10 釒 日 ⺿ 72 43 32 錯 | **SAKU** – mix, be in disorder |

錯 覚 *sakkaku* illusion 605
錯 誤 *sakugo* error 906
錯 乱 *sakuran* distraction, derangement 689
交 錯 *kōsaku* mixture; intricacy 114
倒 錯 *tōsaku* perversion 905

| 措 | **1200** 3c8.20 扌 日 ⺿ 23 43 32 措 | **SO** – give up, discontinue, set aside |

措 置 *sochi* measures, steps 426
報 復 措 置 *hōfuku sochi* retaliatory measures 685, 917, 426

| 拝 | **1201** 3c5.3 扌 王 一 23 46 1 拝 拜 | **HAI, oga(mu)** – pray, venerate |

参 拝 *sanpai* visit (a shrine/grave) 710
礼 拝 *reihai* worship, (church) services 620
拝 見 *haiken* see, have a look at 63
拝 借 *haishaku* borrow 766
拝 み 倒 す *ogamitaosu* entreat (someone) into consent 905

| 欄 | **1202** 4a16.4 木 門日 41 76 43 欄 欄 | **RAN** – (newspaper) column; railing |

家 庭 欄 *kateiran* home-life section 165, 1112
投 書 欄 *tōshoran* letters-to-the-editor column 1021, 131
欄 外 *rangai* margin (of a page) 83
空 欄 *kūran* blank column/space 140
欄 干 *rankan* railing, banister 584

| 潤 | **1203** 3a12.20 氵 門王 21 76 46 潤 | **JUN, uruo(su)** – moisten, wet, water; profit, enrich **uruo(u)** – become wet; profit, become rich **uru(mu)** – become wet/blurred/turbid/clouded |

浸 潤 *shinjun* permeation, infiltration 1078
利 潤 *rijun* profits 329
潤 飾, 潤 色 *junshoku* embellishment 979, 204

| 涼 | **1204** 3a8.31 氵 日 小 21 24 35 涼 涼 | **RYŌ, suzu(shii)** – cool, refreshing **suzu(mu)** – cool off, enjoy the evening cool |

清 涼 飲 料 *seiryō inryō* carbonated beverage 660, 323, 319
涼 味 *ryōmi* the cool, coolness 307
涼 風 *ryōfū, suzukaze* cool breeze 29
夕 涼 み *yūsuzumi* the evening cool 81

1205 凍

2b8.2 ⼌
氵 木 日
5 41 43

凍

TŌ, kō(ru) – freeze (up) **kogo(eru)** – become frozen/numb

冷凍器	*reitōki* refrigerator, freezer	832, 527
凍結	*tōketsu* freeze (assets)	485
凍傷	*tōshō* frostbite	633
凍死	*tōshi* freeze to death	85
凍え死に	*kogoejini* freeze to death	85

1206 氷

3a1.2 […]
氵 丨
21 2

氷 冰

HYŌ, kōri, hi – ice **kō(ru)** – freeze (up)

氷山	*hyōzan* iceberg	34
氷河	*hyōga* glacier	389
流氷	*ryūhyō* floating ice, ice floe	247
氷点(下)	*hyōten(ka)* (below) the freezing point	169, 31
氷結	*hyōketsu* freeze (over)	485

1207 永

3a1.1 日
氵 丨
21 2

永

EI, naga(i) – long (time)

永住	*eijū* permanent residence	156
永遠	*eien* eternity	446
永眠	*eimin* eternal sleep, death	849
永続	*eizoku* permanence, perpetuity	243
永田町	*Nagatachō* (area of Tōkyō)	35, 182

1208 泳

3a5.14 田
氵 丨
21 2

泳

EI, oyo(gu) – swim

水泳	*suiei* swimming	21
競泳	*kyōei* swimming race	852
泳法	*eihō* swimming style/stroke	123
遠泳	*en'ei* long-distance swim	446
平泳ぎ	*hiraoyogi* the breaststroke	202

1209 詠

7a5.14 田
言 氵 丨
67 21 2

詠 咏

EI, yo(mu) – compose, write (a poem)

詠歌	*eika* composition of a poem; (Buddhist) chant	392
詠草	*eisō* draft of a poem	249

1210 久

0a3.7 […]
⼃ 丨
15 2

久

KYŪ, [KU], hisa(shii) – long (time)

永久	*eikyū* permanence, perpetuity, eternity	1207
長久	*chōkyū* long continuance, eternity	95
持久	*jikyū* endurance, persistence	451
久遠	*kuon* eternity	446
久し振り	*hisashiburi* (after) a long time	954

1211 刻

2f6.7 田
刂 宀 厶
16 11 17

刻

KOKU, kiza(mu) – cut fine, chop up; carve, engrave

彫刻	*chōkoku* sculpture	1149
深刻	*shinkoku* grave, serious	536
時刻	*jikoku* time	42
一刻	*ikkoku* moment; stubborn	2
夕刻	*yūkoku* evening	81

1212

核

核 核

4a6.22 田

木 宀 厶
41 11 17

KAKU – core, nucleus

核心	*kakushin* core, kernel	97
原子核	*genshikaku* (atomic) nucleus	136, 103
核燃料	*kakunenryō* nuclear fuel	652, 319
核兵器	*kakuheiki* nuclear weapons	784, 527
結核	*kekkaku* tuberculosis	485

1213

該

該

7a6.10 田

言 宀 厶
67 11 17

GAI – (prefix) the said

当該官庁	*tōgai kanchō* relevant authorities	77, 326, 763
当該人物	*tōgai jinbutsu* the said person	77, 1, 79
該当	*gaitō* pertain (to), come/fall under	77
該博な知識	*gaihaku na chishiki* profound/vast learning	601, 214, 681

1214

診

診

7a5.9 田

言 彡 亻
67 31 3

SHIN, mi(ru) – diagnose, examine

診察	*shinsatsu* medical examination	619
検診	*kenshin* medical examination	531
診断	*shindan* diagnosis	1024
打診	*dashin* percussion, tapping; sound out	1020
往診	*ōshin* doctor's visit to a patient, house call	918

1215

珍

珍 珎

4f5.6 田

王 彡 亻
46 31 3

CHIN, mezura(shii) – rare, unusual

珍品	*chinpin* a rarity, curiosity	230
珍談	*chindan* amusing story, anecdote	593
珍味	*chinmi* a delicacy	307
珍重	*chinchō* value highly, prize	227
珍客	*chinkyaku* least-expected/welcome visitor	641

1216

旧

旧 舊

4c1.1 田

日 丨
43 2

KYŪ – old, former

旧式	*kyūshiki* old-type, old-fashioned	525
復旧	*fukkyū* recovery, restoration	917
新旧	*shinkyū* old and new	174
旧悪	*kyūaku* one's past misdeed	304
旧約(聖書)	*Kyūyaku (Seisho)* Old Testament	211, 674, 131

1217

児

児 兒

4c3.3 田

日 儿 丨
43 16 2

JI, [NI] – small child, infant

児童	*jidō* child, juvenile	410
育児園	*ikujien* daycare nursery	246, 447
産児制限	*sanji seigen* birth control	278, 427, 847
乳児	*nyūji* (nursing) baby, infant	939
小児科医	*shōnikai* pediatrician	27, 320, 220

1218

陥

陥 陷

2d7.11 田

阝 日 宀
7 43 15

KAN, ochii(ru) – fall, get, run (into); fall, be reduced
otoshii(reru) – ensnare, entice; capture

欠陥	*kekkan* defect, shortcoming	383
陥落	*kanraku* fall, capitulation	839
陥没	*kanbotsu* depression, subsidence, cave-in	935
陥せい	*kansei* pitfall, trap, plot	

	1219	**KEI, E, megu(mu)** – bestow a favor; bless	
恵	4k6.16 心 日 十 51 43 12 恵 惠	天 恵 *tenkei* gift of nature, natural natural advantage 恩 恵 *onkei* benefit, favor 互 恵 *gokei* mutual benefit, reciprocity 知 恵 *chie* wisdom, sense, brains, intelligence 知 恵 者 *chiesha* wise/resourceful man	141 555 907 214 214, 164
稲	1220 5d9.2 禾 日 小 56 43 35 稲 稻	**TŌ, ine, [ina-]** – rice plant 水 稲 *suitō* paddy rice 稲 作 *inasaku* rice crop 稲 荷 *Inari* god of harvests, fox deity 早 稲 *wase* (early-ripening variety of rice) 早 稲 田 *Waseda* (area of Tōkyō)	21 360 391 248 248, 35
穂	1221 5d10.2 禾 日 心 56 43 51 穂 穗	**SUI, ho** – ear, head (of grain) 稲 穂 *inaho* ear of rice 穂 先 *hosaki* tip of an ear/spear/knife/brush 穂 波 *honami* waves of grain	1220 50 666
菌	1222 3k8.32 艹 禾 刂 32 56 24 菌	**KIN** – fungus, germ, bacteria 細 菌 *saikin* bacteria 保 菌 者 *hokinsha* (germ) carrier 殺 菌 *sakkin* sterilization 無 菌 *mukin* germ-free, sterilized 抗 菌 性 *kōkinsei* antibacterial	695 489, 164 576 93 824, 98
畜	1223 2j8.7 亠 田 厶 11 58 17 畜	**CHIKU** – animal raising; domestic animals 家 畜 *kachiku* domestic animal, livestock 畜 産 *chikusan* stock raising 牧 畜 業 *bokuchikugyō* stock farming, cattle 畜 舍 *chikusha* cattle shed, barn 畜 生 *chikushō* beast, brute; Dammit!	165 278 731, 279 791 44
蓄	1224 3k10.16 艹 田 亠 32 58 11 蓄	**CHIKU, takuwa(eru)** – store, save, put aside 貯 蓄 *chochiku* savings, saving 備 蓄 *bichiku* saving for emergencies, storing 蓄 積 *chikuseki* accumulation 蓄 電 池 *chikudenchi* storage battery	762 768 656 108, 119
玄	1225 2j3.2 亠 厶 丨 11 17 2 玄	**GEN** – dark, mystery 玄 関 *genkan* entranceway 玄 関 番 *genkanban* doorkeeper, doorman, porter 玄 米 *genmai* unpolished/brown rice 玄 人 *kurōto* expert, professional, specialist	398 398, 185 224 1

	1226	**GEN, tsuru** – string; bowstring	
弦	3h5.1 ⊞	弦楽器 *gengakki* string instrument, the strings	358, 527
	弓 宀 ム	管弦楽 (団) *kangengaku(dan)* orchestra	328, 358, 491
	28 11 17	正弦曲線 *seigen kyokusen* sine curve	275, 366, 299
	弦	上弦 *jōgen* first quarter (of the moon)	32
		下弦 *kagen* last quarter (of the moon)	31

	1227	**GEN, maboroshi** – illusion, phantom, vision	
幻	0a4.6 ⊞	幻覚 *genkaku* hallucination	605
	ム 一 丨	幻影 *gen'ei* vision, phantom, illusion	854
	17 1 2	幻想 *gensō* fantasy, illusion	147
	幻	夢幻 *mugen* dreams and phantasms	811

	1228	**YŪ** – quiet, deep	
幽	3o6.6 ⊡	幽玄 *yūgen* the profound, occult	1225
	山 ム 丨	幽霊 *yūrei* ghost	1168
	36 17 2	幽閉 *yūhei* confinement, imprisonment	397
	幽	幽谷 *yūkoku* deep ravine, narrow valley	653
		幽門 *yūmon* pylorus	161

	1229	**YŌ, osana(i)** – very young; infantile, childish	
幼	2g3.3 ⊞	幼児 *yōji* baby, small child, tot	1217
	力 ム 丨	幼少 *yōshō* infancy, childhood	144
	8 17 2	幼虫 *yōchū* larva	873
	幼	幼子 *osanago* little child	103
		幼心 *osanagokoro* child's mind/heart	97

	1230	**CHI** – child	
稚	5d8.1 ⊞	幼稚園 *yōchien* kindergarten	1229, 447
	禾 隹	稚気 *chiki* childlike state of mind	134
	56 74	稚児 *chigo* child; child in a Buddhist procession	1217
	稚 稺		

	1231	**I** – tie, rope	
維	6a8.1 ⊞	維持 *iji* maintenance, support	451
	糸 隹	維持費 *ijihi* upkeep expenses	451, 749
	61 74	明治維新 *Meiji Ishin* Meiji Restoration	18, 493, 174
	維		

	1232	**JUN** – apply correspondingly, imitate, pattern after	
准	2b8.1 ⊞	批准 *hijun* ratify	1029
	冫 隹		
	5 74		
	准		

	1233	**SUI, o(su)** – infer, deduce; recommend, propose	
推	3c8.1	推 定 *suitei* presumption, inference	355
	扌 隹	推 論 *suiron* reasoning, inference	293
	23 74	推 理 *suiri* reasoning, inference	143
		類 推 *ruisui* (inference by) analogy	226
	推	推 進 *suishin* propulsion, drive	437

	1234	**YUI, [I]** – solely, only, merely	
唯	3d8.1	唯 物 論 *yuibutsuron* materialism	79, 293
	口 隹	唯 心 論 *yuishinron* spiritualism, idealism	97, 293
	24 74	唯 理 論 *yuiriron* rationalism	143, 293
		唯 美 主 義 *yuibi shugi* estheticism	401, 155, 291
	唯	唯 一 *yuiitsu* the only, sole	2

	1235	**SHŌ, wara(u)** – laugh, smile *e(mu)* – smile	
笑	6f4.1	苦 笑 *kushō* wry smile, forced laugh	545
	竹 大 丨	冷 笑 *reishō* scornful laugh, sneer	832
	66 34 2	談 笑 *danshō* friendly talk, chat	593
		大 笑 い *ōwarai* loud laughter, hearty laugh	26
	笑	笑 顔 *egao* smiling face	277

	1236	**KYŪ, na(ku)** – cry	
泣	3a5.1	感 泣 *kankyū* be moved to tears	262
	氵 立	号 泣 *gōkyū* wailing, lamentation	266
	21 54	泣 き 声 *nakigoe* tearful voice, sob, whimper	746
		泣 き 虫 *nakimushi* crybaby ⌐tears	873
	泣	泣 き 落 と す *nakiotosu* obtain (someone's) consent by	839

	1237	**BŌ,** – a room; tassel *fusa* – tassel, tuft, cluster	
房	4m4.2	暖 房 *danbō* heating	635
	戸 方	独 房 *dokubō* solitary (prison) cell	219
	40 48	官 房 長 (官) *kanbōchō(kan)* chief secretary	326, 95
		文 房 具 *bunbōgu* stationery	111, 420
	房 房	女 房 *nyōbō* (one's own) wife	102

	1238	**REI, modo(ru)** – go/come back, return *modo(su)* – give/send	
戻	4m3.1	back, return, restore; throw up, vomit	
	戸 大	取 り 戻 す *torimodosu* regain	65
	40 34	払 い 戻 す *haraimodosu* pay back, refund	582
		差 し 戻 す *sashimodosu* send back (to a lower court)	658
	戻 戻	逆 戻 り *gyakumodori* going backward, retrogression	444

	1239	**RUI, namida** – teardrop	
涙	3a7.21	感 涙 *kanrui* tears of strong emotion	262
	氵 戸 大	血 涙 *ketsurui* tears of blood, bitter tears	789
	21 40 34	空 涙 *soranamida* false/crocodile tears	140
		涙 声 *namidagoe* tearful voice	746
	涙 泪	涙 ぐ ま し い *namidagumashii* touching, moving	

1240 喫	喫 3d9.7 ⼝ ⼝ ⼟ 大 24 22 34 喫	**KITSU** – eat, drink, smoke

喫茶店 *kissaten* teahouse, café — 251, 168
喫煙 *kitsuen* smoking — 919
満喫 *mankitsu* eat/drink one's fill, enjoy fully — 201
喫する *kissuru* eat, drink, smoke

1241 潔

3a12.10 ⽥ 氵 糸 士 21 61 22 潔 潔

KETSU – pure *isagiyo(i)* – brave, manly, righteous, pure

清潔 *seiketsu* clean, neat — 660
純潔 *junketsu* pure, chaste — 965
潔白 *keppaku* pure, upright, of integrity — 205
高潔 *kōketsu* noble, lofty, high-minded — 190
不潔 *fuketsu* impure, unclean, filthy — 94

1242 息

4k6.17 ⽬ 心 日 丨 51 55 2 息

SOKU – son; breath *iki* – breath

休息 *kyūsoku* a rest, breather — 60
消息 *shōsoku* news, information — 845
利息 *risoku* interest (on a loan) — 329
息切れ *ikigire* shortness of breath — 39
息子 *musuko* son — 103

1243 憩

4k12.10 ⽥ 心 日 ⼝ 51 55 24 憩 憩

KEI, iko(i) – rest *iko(u)* – rest

休憩 *kyūkei* rest, recess — 60
休憩所 *kyūkeijo* resting place, lobby — 60, 153
休憩時間 *kyūkei jikan* rest period, recess — 60, 42, 43
小憩, 少憩 *shōkei* brief recess, a break — 27, 144

1244 臭

5c4.3 ⽬ 日 大 丨 55 34 2 臭 臭

SHŪ, kusa(i) – foul-smelling, smelling of

臭気 *shūki* offensive odor, stink — 134
悪臭 *akushū* bad odor, stench — 304
俗臭 *zokushū* low taste, vulgarity — 1126
古臭い *furukusai* old, outdated; trite, hackneyed — 172
かび臭い *kabikusai* musty, moldy

1245 腐

3q11.3 ⼌ 广 寸 亻 18 37 3 腐

FU, kusa(ru), kusa(reru) – rot, go bad, spoil, turn sour
kusa(rasu) – spoil, rot, putrefy, corrode

豆腐 *tōfu* tofu, bean curd — 958
腐食 *fushoku* corrosion — 322
腐敗 *fuhai* decomposition, decay; corruption — 511
腐心 *fushin* take pains, be intent on — 97

1246 嘆

3d10.8 ⽥ ⼝ 艹 大 24 32 34 嘆 嘆

TAN, nage(ku) – grieve, lament, bemoan; deplore, regret
nage(kawashii) – deplorable, regrettable

感嘆 *kantan* admiration, exclamation — 262
嘆願 *tangan* entreaty, petition — 581
嘆息 *tansoku* sigh; lament — 1242
悲嘆 *hitan* grief, sorrow, lamentation — 1034

謹	1247	**KIN, tsutsushi(mu)** – be respectful	
	7a10.6	謹 聴 *kinchō* listen attentively	1039
	言 艹 口	謹 賀 新 年 *kinga shinnen* Happy New Year.	756, 174, 45
	67 32 24	謹 言 *kingen* Sincerely/Respectfully yours	66
	謹 謹	謹 ん で *tsutsushinde* respectfully, humbly	

否	1248	**HI, ina** – no	
	3d4.20	否 定 *hitei* denial, negation	355
	口 一 丨	否 認 *hinin* denial, repudiation, disavow	738
	24 14 2	否 決 *hiketsu* rejection, voting down	356
	否	賛 否 *sanpi* approval or disapproval, yes or no	745
		安 否 *anpi* how (someone) is getting on	105

含	1249	**GAN, fuku(mu)** – hold in one's mouth; bear in mind; contain, include **fuku(meru)** – include; give instructions	
	2a5.25	含 蓄 *ganchiku* significance, implication	1224
	亻 口 一	包 含 *hōgan* include, cover, imply	804
	3 24 1	含 有 *gan'yū* contain	265
	含		

吟	1250	**GIN** – sing, chant, recite	
	3d4.8	独 吟 *dokugin* (vocal) solo	219
	口 亻 一	詩 吟 *shigin* recitation of Chinese poems	570
	24 3 1	吟 詠 *gin'ei* sing, recite; compose a poem	1209
	吟	吟 味 *ginmi* close inquiry, scrutiny	307

琴	1251	**KIN, koto** – koto, Japanese zither	
	4f8.11	心 の 琴 線 *kokoro no kinsen* heartstrings	97, 299
	王 亻 一	木 琴 *mokkin* xylophone	22
	46 3 1	風 琴 *fūkin* organ, harmonium	29
	琴	手 風 琴 *tefūkin* accordion, concertina	57, 29
		た て 琴 *tategoto* harp, lyre	

叫	1252	**KYŌ, sake(bu)** – shout, cry out	
	3d3.4	絶 叫 *zekkyō* scream, exclamation	742
	口 十 丨	叫 び 声 *sakebigoe* a shout, cry, scream	746
	24 12 2		
	叫 叫		

吐	1253	**TO, ha(ku)** – spew, vomit, throw up; express, give vent to	
	3d3.1	吐 血 *toketsu* vomit blood	789
	口 土	吐 息 *toiki* a sigh	1242
	24 22	吐 露 *toro* express, voice, speak out	951
	吐	吐 き 気 *hakike* nausea	134
		吐 き 出 す *hakidasu* vomit, disgorge, spew out	53

1254

KO, yo(bu) – call, send for, invite, name

3d5.4

口 小 一
24 35 1

呼

点 呼	*tenko* roll call	169
呼 応	*koō* act in concert	827
呼 び 声	*yobigoe* a call, cry, shout ⌐a loudspeaker)	746
呼 び 出 す	*yobidasu* page, call (on the telephone/	53
呼 び 戻 す	*yobimodosu* call back, recall	1238

1255

SUI, fu(ku) – blow

3d4.3

口 欠
24 49

吹

鼓 吹	*kosui* inspire, instill	1147
吹 雪	*fubuki* snowstorm	949
吹 き 込 む	*fukikomu* blow in; record (a song); inspire	776
吹 き 飛 ぶ	*fukitobu* be blown away	530
吹 き 出 物	*fukidemono* skin rash, spots, pimple	53, 79

1256

KYŪ, su(u) – suck in, inhale; smoke

3d3.5

口 力 |
24 8 2

吸

呼 吸	*kokyū* breathing	1254
吸 入	*kyūnyū* inhale	52
吸 引	*kyūin* absorb (by suction)	216
吸 収	*kyūshū* absorb	757
吸 い 取 り 紙	*suitorigami* blotting paper	65, 180

1257

KYŪ, oyo(bu) – reach, amount to, extend to, match, equal
oyo(bosu) – exert **oyo(bi)** – and, as well as

0a3.24

力 |
8 2

及

普 及	*fukyū* spread, come into wide use	1166
及 第 点	*kyūdaiten* passing mark/grade	404, 169
言 及	*genkyū* refer to, mention	66
言 い 及 ぶ	*iioyobu* refer to, touch upon	66

1258

atsuka(u) – handle

3c3.5

扌 力 |
23 8 2

扱 扱

取 り 扱 う	*toriatsukau* treat, deal with, handle	65
取 り 扱 い 方	*toriatsukaikata* how to handle	65, 70
取 (り) 扱 (い) 注 意	*toriatsukai chūi* Handle with Care	
		65, 357, 132
客 扱 い	*kyakuatsukai* hospitality, service to customers	641

1259

ZETSU, shita – tongue

3d3.9

口 十 |
24 12 2

舌

舌 戦	*zessen* verbal warfare, war of words	301
弁 舌	*benzetsu* eloquence, tongue, speech	711
毒 舌	*dokuzetsu* venomous tongue, malicious remarks	522
二 枚 舌	*nimaijita* forked tongue, duplicity	3, 1156
舌 打 ち	*shitauchi* clicking one's tongue, tsk, tch	1020

1260

KATSU – tie together, fasten

3c6.12

扌 口 十
23 24 12

括

一 括	*ikkatsu* lump together, summarize	2
総 括	*sōkatsu* generalization, summarization	697
包 括 的	*hōkatsuteki* comprehensive, general, sweeping	
		804, 210

絹	**1261** 6a7.3 糸月口 61 42 24 絹	**KEN, kinu** – silk	
		人絹 *jinken* artificial silk, rayon	1
		絹布 *kenpu* silk fabric, silk	675
		絹糸 *kenshi, kinuito* silk thread	242
		絹織物 *kinuorimono* silk fabrics	680, 79
		絹針 *kinubari* needle for silk	341
肯	**1262** 4b4.11 月 卜 亠 42 13 11 肯	**KŌ** – agree to, consent	
		肯定 *kōtei* affirmation, affirmative	355
		首肯 *shukō* assent, consent	148
脅	**1263** 2g8.2 力月 8 42 脅	**KYŌ, obiya(kasu), odo(kasu), odo(su)** – threaten	
		脅迫 *kyōhaku* threat, intimidation	1175
		脅迫状 *kyōhakujō* threatening letter	1175, 626
		脅し文句 *odoshimonku* threatening words	111, 337
肩	**1264** 4m4.1 戸月 40 42 肩 肩	**KEN, kata** – shoulder	
		肩章 *kenshō* epaulet, shoulder pips	857
		比肩 *hiken* rank (with), be comparable (to)	798
		肩書き *katagaki* one's title, degree	131
		肩身が広い *katami ga hiroi* feel proud	59, 694
		肩代わり *katagawari* take-over, transfer (of business)	256
背	**1265** 4b5.15 月 卜 一 42 13 1 背	**HAI, se** – back; height **sei** – height, stature **somu(ku)** – act contrary (to) **somu(keru)** – avert, turn away	
		背景 *haikei* background	853
		背信 *haishin* breach of faith, betrayal, infidelity	157
		背中 *senaka* the back	28
		背広 *sebiro* business suit	694
骨	**1266** 4b6.14 月冂一 42 20 1 骨	**KOTSU, hone** – bone	
		骨格 *kokkaku* skeleton, framework	643
		頭骨 *tōkotsu* skull	276
		骨子 *kosshi* essential part, main points	103
		鉄骨 *tekkotsu* steel frame	312
		骨惜しみ *honeoshimi* avoid effort, spare oneself	765
滑	**1267** 3a10.6 氵月冂 21 42 20 滑	**KATSU, sube(ru)** – slide, glide; slip **name(raka)** – smooth	
		滑走路 *kassōro* runway	429, 151
		潤滑油 *junkatsuyu* lubricating oil	1203, 364
		円滑 *enkatsu* smooth, harmonious, amicable	13
		滑り台 *suberidai* (playground) slide	492

	1268	**I** – stomach
胃	5f4.3	胃病 *ibyō* stomach disorder/trouble 380
	甲 月	胃酸 *isan* stomach acid 516
	58 42	胃がん *igan* stomach cancer
	胃	胃下垂 *ikasui* gastric ptosis 31, 1070
		胃弱 *ijaku* weak digestion, indigestion, dyspepsia 218

	1269	**FU** – the skin
膚	2m13.1	皮膚 *hifu* the skin 975
	广 甲 月	皮膚病 *hifubyō* skin disease 975, 380
	13 58 42	皮膚移植 *hifu ishoku* skin graft/transplant 975, 1121, 424
	膚	完膚なきまで *kanpu-naki made* thoroughly, completely 613

	1270	**CHŌ** – intestines, entrails
腸	4b9.8	胃腸 *ichō* stomach and intestines 1268
	月 日 彡	大腸 *daichō* large intestine, colon 26
	42 43 27	腸閉そく *chōheisoku* intestinal obstruction, ileus 397
		腸ねん転 *chōnenten* twist in the intestines, volvulus 433
	腸 腸	断腸の思い *danchō no omoi* heartrending grief 1024, 99

	1271	**FUKU, hara** – belly; heart, mind
腹	4b9.4	切腹 *seppuku* hara-kiri 39
	月 日 夂	立腹 *rippuku* anger, offense 121
	42 43 49	空腹 *kūfuku* empty belly, hunger 140
		腹巻き *haramaki* belly/stomach band 507
	腹	太っ腹 *futoppara* magnanimous; bold, daring 629

	1272	**KAN, kimo** – liver; heart, spirit
肝	4b3.2	肝硬変 *kankōhen* cirrhosis of the liver 1009, 257
	月 一 一	肝油 *kan'yu* cod-liver oil 364
	42 14 1	肝要 *kan'yō* important, vital 419
		肝心 *kanjin* main, vital, essential 97
	肝	肝っ玉 *kimottama* pluck, courage, grit 295

	1273	**TAN** – gallbladder; courage
胆	4b5.6	胆石 *tanseki* gallstone 78
	月 日 一	大胆 *daitan* bold, daring 26
	42 43 1	胆力 *tanryoku* courage, mettle 100
		落胆 *rakutan* discouragement, disappointment 839
	胆 膽	

	1274	**TAN, katsu(gu)** – carry on the shoulder; choose (someone); trick (someone) **nina(u)** – carry on the shoulder; bear, take on
担	3c5.20	担当 *tantō* being in charge, overseeing 77
	扌 日 一	担任 *tannin* charge, responsibility 334
	23 43 1	負担 *futan* burden, load, liability 510
	担 擔	担保 *tanpo* a security, guarantee 489

	1275	**KŌ** – always	
恒	4k6.5	恒久 *kōkyū* permanence, perpetuity	1210
	心 日 二	恒星 *kōsei* fixed star, sidereal	730
	51 43 4	恒心 *kōshin* constancy, steadfastness	97
		恒例 *kōrei* established practice, custom	612
	恒 恆	恒常 *kōjō* constancy	497

	1276	**kaki** – fence, hedge	
垣	3b6.5	石垣 *ishigaki* stone wall	78
	土 日 二	竹垣 *takegaki* bamboo fence	129
	22 43 4	生け垣 *ikegaki* hedge	44
		垣根 *kakine* fence, hedge	314
	垣	垣間見る *kaimamiru* peek in, get a glimpse	43, 63

	1277	**HAI** – lung	
肺	4b5.9	肺病 *haibyō* lung/pulmonary disease	380
	月 巾 一	肺結核 *haikekkaku* pulmonary tuberculosis	485, 1212
	42 26 11	肺がん *haigan* lung cancer	
		肺活量 *haikatsuryō* lung capacity	237, 411
	肺	肺肝 *haikan* lungs and liver; one's innermost heart	1272

	1278	**NŌ** – brain	
脳	4b7.7	頭脳 *zunō* brains, intelligence	276
	月 小 冂	脳下垂体 *nōkasuitai* pituitary gland	31, 1070, 61
	42 35 20	脳卒中 *nōsotchū* cerebral hemorrhage	787, 28
		洗脳 *sennō* brainwashing	692
	脳 腦	首脳会談 *shunō kaidan* summit conference	148, 158, 593

	1279	**NŌ, naya(mu)** – be troubled, be distressed, suffer **naya(masu)** – afflict, beset, worry	
悩	4k7.11	苦悩 *kunō* affliction, distress, agony	545
	心 小 冂	悩殺 *nōsatsu* enchant, captivate	576
	51 35 20	伸び悩む *nobinayamu* continue stagnant, level off	1108
	悩 惱	恋の悩み *koi no nayami* the torments of love	258

	1280	**KYŌ** – evil, misfortune	
凶	0a4.19	凶作 *kyōsaku* bad harvest	360
	冂 十	凶行 *kyōkō* violence, crime, murder	68
	20 12	凶悪 *kyōaku* heinous, brutal	304
		凶器 *kyōki* murder/lethal weapon	527
	凶	吉凶 *kikkyō* good or ill luck, fortune	1141

	1281	**RI, hana(reru)** – separate, leave **hana(su)** – separate, keep apart	
離	8c10.3	分離 *bunri* separation, secession, segregation	38
	隹 亠 冂	離婚 *rikon* divorce	567
	74 11 20	離反 *rihan* estrangement, alienation, breakaway	324
		離陸 *ririku* (airplane) takeoff	647
	離	切り離す *kirihanasu* cut off, sever	39

	1282	**ka(ru)** – cut (hair), clip, mow	
刈	2f2.1 ⊡	刈り入れ *kariire* harvest, reaping	52
	リ 十	稲刈り *inekari* rice reaping/harvesting	1220
	16 12	刈り取る *karitoru* mow, cut down	65
		刈り込む *karikomu* cut, trim, prune	776
	刈	芝刈り機 *shibakariki* lawn mower	250, 528

	1283	**KYŌ, mune, [muna]** – breast, chest	
胸	4b6.9 ⊡	胸像 *kyōzō* (sculptured) bust	740
	月 勹 凵	胸部 *kyōbu* the chest	86
	42 15 20	胸囲 *kyōi* girth/circumference of the chest	1194
		胸中 *kyōchū* one's bosom, heart, feelings	28
	胸	度胸 *dokyō* courage, daring, nerve	377

	1284	**HŌ** – sac, sheath; placenta	
胞	4b5.5 ⊡	細胞 *saibō, saihō* cell	695
	月 弓 勹	単細胞 *tansaibō* 1 cell, single cell	300, 695
	42 28 15	脳細胞 *nōsaibō* brain cell	1278, 695
		胞子 *hōshi* spore	103
	胞 胞	同胞 *dōhō* brethren, countrymen	198

	1285	**HŌ, da(ku)** – hug, hold in one's arms **ida(ku)** – embrace; harbor (feelings) **kaka(eru)** – carry in one's arms; have (dependents); employ, hire	
抱	3c5.15 ⊡		
	扌 弓 勹	抱負 *hōfu* aspiration, ambition	510
	23 28 15	介抱 *kaihō* nursing, care	453
	抱 抱	抱き合う *dakiau* embrace each other	159

	1286	**ZŌ, kura** – storehouse, warehouse, repository	
蔵	3k12.17 ⊟	冷蔵庫 *reizōko* refrigerator	832, 825
	艹 戈 凵	蔵書 *zōsho* collection of books, one's library	131
	32 52 20	貯蔵 *chozō* storage	762
		蔵相 *zōshō* minister of finance	146
	蔵 藏	大蔵省 *Ōkurashō* Ministry of Finance	26, 145

	1287	**ZŌ** – internal organs	
臓	4b15.2 ⊞	内臓 *naizō* internal organs, viscera	84
	月 戈 艹	臓器 *zōki* internal organs, viscera	527
	42 52 32	心臓 *shinzō* the heart	97
		肺臓 *haizō* the lungs	1277
	臓 臟	肝臓 *kanzō* the liver	1272

	1288	**KEN, kashiko(i)** – wise, intelligent	
賢	7b9.2 ⊟	賢明 *kenmei* wise, intelligent	18
	貝 臣 又	先賢 *senken* wise men of old, ancient sages	50
	68 20 9	賢人 *kenjin* wise man, sage, the wise	1
		賢母 *kenbo* wise mother	112
	賢	悪賢い *warugashikoi* sly, wily, cunning	304

	1289	**KEN, kata(i)** – firm, hard, solid	
堅	3b9.13	堅実 *kenjitsu* solid, sound, reliable	203
	土 冂 又	堅固 *kengo* strong, solid, steadfast	972
	22 20 9	中堅 *chūken* mainstay, backbone, nucleus	28
		堅持 *kenji* hold fast to, adhere to	451
	堅	手堅い *tegatai* firm, solid, dependable	57

	1290	**KIN** – hard, tight	
緊	6a9.17	緊張 *kinchō* tension	1106
	糸 冂 又	緊迫 *kinpaku* tension	1175
	61 20 9	緊急 *kinkyū* emergency	303
		緊縮 *kinshuku* contraction; austerity	1110
	緊	緊密 *kinmitsu* close, tight	806

	1291	**RAN** – see, look at	
覧	5c12.7	展/博覧会 *ten/hakurankai* an exhibition	1129, 601, 158
	目 貝 冂	遊覧船 *yūransen* excursion ship, pleasure boat	1003, 376
	55 68 20	観覧 *kanran* viewing, inspection	604
		一覧表 *ichiranhyō* table, list	2, 272
	覧 覽	回覧 *kairan* read-and-pass-on circulation	90

	1292	**HAN** – fullness, luxury; frequency	
繁	6a10.13	繁栄 *han'ei* prosperity	723
	糸 攵 女	繁盛 *hanjō* prosperity; success	719
	61 49 25	繁華街 *hankagai* thriving shopping area	1074, 186
	繁 繁		

	1293	**KYO** – large, gigantic	
巨	2t2.2	巨大 *kyodai* huge, gigantic, enormous	26
	⊏	巨人 *kyojin* giant	1
	20	巨漢 *kyokan* very large man, big fellow	556
		巨星 *kyosei* giant star; great/prominent man	730
	巨	巨万 *kyoman* millions, immense amount	16

	1294	**KYO** – distance	
距	7d5.8	距離 *kyori* distance	1281
	𧾷 冂	短/近距離 *tan/kinkyori* short distance	215, 445, 1281
	70 20	長/遠距離 *chō/enkyori* long distance	95, 446, 1281
		中距離競走 *chūkyori kyōsō* medium-distance race	
	距		28, 1281, 852, 429

	1295	**KYO, koba(mu)** – refuse, decline	
拒	3c5.29	拒否 *kyohi* denial, refusal; rejection, veto	1248
	扌 冂	拒否権 *kyohiken* right of veto	1248, 335
	23 20	拒絶 *kyozetsu* refusal, rejection, repudiation	742
	拒		

	1296	**TAI** – womb, uterus	
胎	4b5.10 ⊞ 月 口 厶 42 24 17 胎	胎盤 *taiban* placenta, afterbirth 母胎 *botai* mother's womb/uterus 受胎 *jutai* conception 胎児 *taiji* embryo, fetus 胎動 *taidō* fetal movement, quickening	1098 112 260 1217 231
怠	1297 4k5.21 ☰ 心 口 厶 51 24 17 怠	**TAI, nama(keru)** – be idle, be lazy, neglect **okota(ru)** – neglect, be remiss in, default on 怠業 *taigyō* work stoppage, slowdown strike けん怠 *kentai* fatigue, weariness 怠け者 *namakemono* idler, lazybones	 279 164
腰	1298 4b9.3 ⊞ 月 口 女 42 24 25 腰	**YŌ, koshi** – pelvic region, loins, hips, small of back 腰部 *yōbu* pelvic region, waist, hips, loins 腰布 *koshinuno* loincloth 弱腰 *yowagoshi* without backbone, faint-hearted 物腰 *monogoshi* one's manner, demeanor 本腰 *hongoshi* serious, in earnest	 86 675 218 79 25
腕	1299 4b8.6 ⊞ 月 宀 夕 42 33 30 腕	**WAN, ude** – arm; ability, talent, skill 手腕 *shuwan* ability, capability, skill 腕力 *wanryoku* physical strength 腕前 *udemae* ability, skill 腕輪 *udewa* bracelet 腕時計 *udedokei* wristwatch	 57 100 47 1164 42, 340
胴	1300 4b6.10 ⊡ 月 口 冂 42 24 20 胴	**DŌ** – torso, trunk 胴体 *dōtai* the body, torso; fuselage 胴回り *dōmawari* one's girth 胴上げ,胴揚げ *dōage* hoist (someone) shoulder-high	 61 90 32, 631
洞	1301 3a6.25 ⊡ 氵 口 冂 21 24 20 洞	**DŌ, hora** – cave 洞察 *dōsatsu* discernment, insight 空洞 *kūdō* cave, cavity 洞穴 *dōketsu, horaana* cave 洞くつ *dōkutsu* cave, grotto 洞門 *dōmon* cave entrance	 619 140 899 161
我	1302 0a7.10 … 戈 十 丨 52 12 2 我	**GA, ware, wa** – I, self; my, our 自我 *jiga* self, ego 我利 *gari* one's own interests, self-interest 無我 *muga* self-effacement, selflessness 我勝ち *waregachi* each striving to be first 我が国 *wagakuni* our country	 62 329 93 509 40

	1303	**GA** – starve	
餓	8b7.1 □ 食 戈 十 73 52 12 餓	餓死 *gashi* starve to death	85

	1304	**KI, u(eru)** – starve	
飢	8b2.1 □ 食 几 73 20 飢	飢餓 *kiga* hunger, starvation 飢きん *kikin* famine 飢死に *uejini* starve to death	1303 85

	1305	**KI, tsukue** – desk	
机	4a2.4 木 几 41 20 机	机上 *kijō* desk-top, academic, theoretical 机上の空論 *kijō no kūron* mere academic theorizing 事務机 *jimuzukue* office desk 書き物机 *kakimono-zukue* writing desk	32 32, 140, 293 80, 235 131, 79

	1306	**hada** – the skin; disposition, character, temperament	
肌	4b2.2 □ 月 几 42 20 肌	肌色 *hadairo* flesh-colored 地肌 *jihada* one's skin; surface of the ground 肌着 *hadagi* underwear 肌触り *hadazawari* the touch, feel 肌寒い *hadasamui, hadazamui* chilly	204 118 657 874 457

	1307	**SŌ, kura** – storehouse, warehouse, depository	
倉	2a8.37 □ 亻食 口 (3) 73 24 倉	倉庫 *sōko* warehouse 倉荷 *kurani* warehouse goods	825 391

	1308	**SŌ** – creation	
創	2f10.3 □ 刂食 口 16 73 24 創	創造 *sōzō* creation 創作 *sōsaku* (literary) creation 創立 *sōritsu* establishment, founding 独創 *dokusō* originality, creativity 創価学会 *Sōka Gakkai* (Buddhist sect)	691 360 121 219 421, 109, 158

	1309	**FUN, furu(u)** – be enlivened, rouse up	
奮	5f11.2 日 田 隹 大 58 74 34 奮	興奮 *kōfun* excitement 奮発 *funpatsu* exertion, strenuous effort; splurge 奮起 *funki* rouse oneself (to action), be inspired 奮って *furutte* energetically, willingly	368 96 373

	1310	**DATSU, uba(u)** – snatch away, take by force; captivate	
奪	8c6.4 ⊟	争奪 (戦) *sōdatsu(sen)* a competition, struggle	302, 301
	隹大寸 74 34 37	略奪 *ryakudatsu* plunder, pillage, despoliation	841
		強奪 *gōdatsu* seizure, robbery	217
	奪	奪回, 奪還 *dakkai, dakkan* recapture, retaking	90, 866
		奪い合う *ubaiau* scramble, struggle (for)	159

	1311	**SEKI** – (counter for ships); one (of a pair)	
隻	8c2.1 ⊟	三隻 *sanseki* 3 ships	4
	隹又 74 9	数隻 (の船) *sūseki (no fune)* several (ships)	225, 376
		隻眼 *sekigan* one-eyed	848
	隻	一隻眼 *issekigan* discerning eye	2, 848
		隻手 *sekishu* one-armed	57

	1312	**GO** – defend, protect	
護	7a13.3 ⊞	弁護士 *bengoshi* lawyer, attorney	711, 572
	言隹艹 67 74 32	保護 *hogo* protection, preservation	489
		援護 *engo* support, backing, protection	1088
	護	護衛 *goei* guard, escort	815
		護符 *gofu* amulet, talisman	505

	1313	**KAKU, e(ru)** – obtain, acquire, gain	
獲	3g13.1 ⊞	獲得 *kakutoku* acquire, gain, win	374
	犭隹艹 27 74 32	捕獲 *hokaku* catch; capture, seizure	890
		漁獲 *gyokaku* fishing, a catch of fish	699
	獲	乱獲 *rankaku* excessive fishing/hunting	689
		獲物 *emono* game, a catch, trophy	79

	1314	**KAKU** – harvest	
穫	5d13.4 ⊞	収穫 *shūkaku* harvest, harvesting	757
	禾隹艹 56 74 32	収穫高 *shūkakudaka* the yield, crop	757, 190
	穫	収穫期 *shūkakuki* harvest time	757, 449

	1315	**KAN, wazura(u)** – be ill, suffer (from)	
患	4k7.18 ⊟	患者 *kanja* a patient	164
	心口丨 51 24 2	急患 *kyūkan* person suddenly taken ill	303
		患部 *kanbu* affected/diseased part	86
	患	長患い *nagawazurai* long illness	95

	1316	**KAN** – see	
看	5c4.4 ⊡	看護婦 *kangofu* nurse	1312, 316
	目扌 55 23	看病 *kanbyō* tending the sick, nursing	380
		看守 *kanshu* (prison) guard	490
	看	看破 *kanpa* see through, detect	665
		看板 *kanban* sign, signboard	1047

催 _{1 3 5 / 2 6 7 8 / 11 13 12}	**1317** 2a11.12 ⊞ 亻 催 山 3 74 36 催	**SAI, moyō(su)** – hold, sponsor; feel

開催　*kaisai*　hold (a meeting)　396
主催　*shusai*　sponsorship, promotion　155
催眠　*saimin*　hypnosis　849
催涙ガス　*sairuigasu*　tear gas　1239
催し物　*moyōshimono*　(program of) entertainments　79

症 _{1 / 4 2 / 5 9 7 8 / 10}	**1318** 5i5.4 ⊡ 疒 一 60 38 1 症	**SHŌ** – illness, symptoms

病症　*byōshō*　nature of a disease　380
症状, 症候　*shōjō, shōkō*　symptom　626, 944
不眠症　*fuminshō*　insomnia　94, 849
自閉症　*jiheishō*　autism　62, 397
露出症　*roshutsushō*　exhibitionism　951, 53

疫 _{1 2 / 4 3 / 5 8 / 6 9}	**1319** 5i4.2 ⊡ 疒 冂 又 60 20 9 疫	**EKI, [YAKU]** – epidemic

疫病　*ekibyō*　epidemic, plague　380
悪疫　*akueki*　plague, pestilence, epidemic　304
防疫　*bōeki*　prevention of epidemics　513
検疫　*ken'eki*　quarantine　531
免疫　*men'eki*　immunity　733

痛 _{1 2 / 4 6 7 / 5 8 10 / 11}	**1320** 5i7.7 ⊡ 疒 月 一 60 42 1 痛	**TSŪ, ita(mu)** – feel painful, hurt; be damaged　**ita(meru)** – hurt, damage; cause pain　**ita(i)** – painful

苦痛　*kutsū*　pain　545
頭痛　*zutsū*　headache　276
痛飲　*tsūin*　drink heavily, carouse　323
痛手　*itade*　severe wound; hard blow　57

疲 _{1 2 / 4 3 7 8 / 5 6 9 / 10}	**1321** 5i5.2 ⊡ 疒 厂 又 60 18 9 疲	**HI, tsuka(reru)** – get tired　**tsuka(rasu)** – (tr.) fatigue, tire

疲労　*hirō*　fatigue, weariness　233
気疲れ　*kizukare*　mental fatigue/exhaustion　134
疲れ果てる　*tsukarehateru*　be completely exhausted　487
(お)疲れ様　*(o)tsukaresama*　Thank you (for your tiring work)　403

療 _{1 2 3 / 4 6 7 8 10 / 5 9 / 11 12 17 / 16 15 13 14}	**1322** 5i12.3 ⊡ 疒 火 日 60 44 43 療	**RYŌ** – heal, cure; treat medically

治療　*chiryō*　medical treatment, therapy　493
医療　*iryō*　medical treatment　220
診療　*shinryō*　diagnosis and treatment　1214
施療　*seryō*　free medical treatment　1004
療養所　*ryōyōsho, ryōyōjo*　sanatorium, nursing home　402, 153

寮 _{2 1 3 / 4 5 6 / 7 8 10 / 9 11 15 / 14 13 12}	**1323** 3m12.2 ⊟ 宀 火 日 33 44 43 寮	**RYŌ** – hostel, dormitory

学生寮　*gakuseiryō*　dormitory　109, 44
社員寮　*shain'ryō*　company dormitory　308, 163
独身寮　*dokushin'ryō*　dormitory for bachelors　219, 59
寮長　*ryōchō*　dormitory director　95
寮生　*ryōsei*　student living in a dormitory　44

1324	**RYŌ** – an official; companion	
2a12.4	官 僚 *kanryō* bureaucrat ⌐bureaucracy	326
亻火日	官 僚 主 義 *kanryō shugi* bureaucratism,	326, 155, 291
3 44 43	閣 僚 *kakuryō* cabinet member/minister	837
	同 僚 *dōryō* colleague, coworker	198
僚	僚 友 *ryōyū* fellow worker, colleague	264

1325	**JŌ** – (unit of length, about 3m) *take* – one's height	
0a3.26	丈 夫 *jōbu* strong and healthy; strong, durable	315
十 丨	偉 丈 夫 *ijōfu* great man	1053, 315
12 2	気 丈 *kijō* stout-hearted, courageous	134
	八 丈 島 *Hachijō-jima* (island south of Tōkyō)	10, 286
丈 丈	背 丈 *setake* one's height	1265

1326	**SŌ** – manly, strong	
2b4.2	壮 大 *sōdai* magnificent, grand, imposing	26
冫 士 丨	強 壮 *kyōsō* strong, robust, husky	217
5 22 2	壮 健 *sōken* healthy, hale and hearty	893
	悲 壮 *hisō* tragic, touching, pathetic	1034
壮 壯	壮 年 *sōnen* prime of manhood/life	45

1327	**SŌ** – villa, inn; solemn	
3k6.12	別 荘 *bessō* country house, cottage, villa	267
艹 士 冫	山 荘 *sansō* mountain villa	34
32 22 5	荘 重 *sōchō* solemn, sublime, impressive	227
	荘 厳 *sōgon* sublime, grand, majestic	822
荘 莊		

1328	**SŌ, SHŌ, yosō(u)** – wear; feign, pretend, disguise oneself as	
5e6.8	服 装 *fukusō* style of dress, attire	683
衤 士 冫	変 装 *hensō* disguise	257
57 22 5	装 置 *sōchi* device, apparatus, equipment	426
	装 飾 *sōshoku* ornament, decoration	979
装 裝	武 装 *busō* arms, armament	1031

1329	**TAI, fukuro** – sack, bag	
5e5.11	手 袋 *tebukuro* glove	57
衤 戈 亻	足 袋 *tabi* Japanese socks (worn with kimono)	58
57 52 3	紙 袋 *kamibukuro* paper sack/bag	180
	袋 小 路 *fukurokōji* blind alley, cul-de-sac	27, 151
袋	胃 袋 *ibukuro* stomach	1268

1330	**RETSU, sa(keru/ku)** – (intr./tr.) split, tear, rip	
5e6.7	分 裂 *bunretsu* breakup, dissolution, division	38
衤 夕 儿	核 分 裂 *kakubunretsu* nuclear fission	1212
57 30 16	破 裂 *haretsu* burst, rupture, explode	665
	決 裂 *ketsuretsu* (negotiations) break down	356
裂	裂 け 目 *sakeme* a rip, split, crack, fissure	55

1331	**RETSU** – violent, intense

烈震　*resshin*　violent earthquake　953
熱烈　*netsuretsu*　ardent, fervent, vehement　645
壮烈　*sōretsu*　heroic, brave　1326
強烈　*kyōretsu*　intense, severe　217
痛烈　*tsūretsu*　severe, fierce, bitter　1320

4d6.3
火 夕 儿　44 30 16
烈

1332	**SHŌ** – urge, encourage

奨学金　*shōgakukin*　a scholarship　109, 23
奨学生　*shōgakusei*　student on a scholarship　109, 44
勧奨　*kanshō*　encouragement, promotion　1051
推奨　*suishō*　recommendation, commendation　1233

3n10.4
⺍ 大 寸　35 37 34
奨 奨

1333	**TŌ, hi** – a light, lamp

電灯　*dentō*　electric light/lamp　108
灯火　*tōka*　a light, lamplight　20
街灯　*gaitō*　streetlight　186
船灯　*sentō*　ship light　376
灯台　*tōdai*　lighthouse　492

4d2.1
火 一　44 14
灯 燈

1334	**CHŌ, su(mu)** – become clear　**su(masu)** – make clear, perk (one's ears); look prim/unconcerned/nonchalant

清澄　*seichō*　clear, limpid, lucid, serene　660
澄み切る　*sumikiru*　become perfectly clear　39
澄み渡る　*sumiwataru*　be crystal clear　378
澄まし顔　*sumashigao*　unconcerned look　277

3a12.11
氵 火 口　21 44 24
澄 澂

1335	**SAI, wazawa(i)** – misfortune, disaster

災難　*sainan*　mishap, accident, calamity　557
災害　*saigai*　disaster, accident　518
火災　*kasai*　fire, blaze, conflagration　20
天災　*tensai*　natural disaster/calamity　141
震災　*shinsai*　earthquake disaster　953

4d3.3
火 〳　44 2
災

1336	**EN, honō** – flame

火炎瓶　*kaenbin*　firebomb, Molotov cocktail　20, 1161
炎症　*enshō*　inflammation　1318
肺炎　*haien*　pneumonia　1277
脳炎　*nōen*　brain inflammation, encephalitis　1278
中耳炎　*chūjien*　inflammation of the middle ear　28, 56

4d4.4
火　44
炎

1337	**TAN, awa(i)** – light, faint, pale; transitory

濃淡　*nōtan*　light and shade, shading　957
淡彩　*tansai*　light coloring　932
冷淡　*reitan*　indifferent, apathetic　832
淡水　*tansui*　fresh water　21
淡雪　*awayuki*　light snow　949

3a8.15
氵 火　21 44
淡

	1338	**METSU, horo(biru)** – fall to ruin, perish, die out
滅	3a10.26 ☐	**horo(bosu)** – ruin, destroy, overthrow, annihilate
	氵 戈 火	破 滅 hametsu ruin, downfall, collapse 665
	21 52 44	滅 亡 metsubō downfall, destruction 672
		消 滅 shōmetsu extinction, disappearance 845
	滅	幻 滅 genmetsu disillusionment 1227

	1339	**I** – authority, dignity, majesty; threat
威	4n5.2	権 威 ken'i authority 335
	戈 女 一	威 勢 isei power, influence; high spirits 646
	52 25 1	威 厳 igen dignity, stateliness 822
		威 信 ishin prestige, dignity 157
	威	脅 威 kyōi menace, threat, danger 1263

	1340	**REI** – encouragement; diligence **hage(mu)** – be diligent
励	2g5.4 ☐	**hage(masu)** – encourage, urge on
	力 厂 一	奨 励 shōrei encouragement, promotion 1332
	8 18 14	激 励 gekirei urging, encouragement 1017
		精 励 seirei diligence, industriousness 659
	励 勵	励 行 reikō strict enforcement 68

	1341	**YAKU** – misfortune, disaster
厄	2p2.3 ☐	厄 介 yakkai troublesome, burdensome; help, care 453
	厂 卩	厄 介 者 yakkaimono a dependent; burden 453, 164
	18 7	厄 日 yakubi unlucky day; critical day 5
		厄 年 yakudoshi unlucky year; critical age 45
	厄	厄 払 い yakubarai, yakuharai exorcism 582

	1342	**ATSU** – pressure
圧	2p3.1 ☐	圧 力 atsuryoku pressure 100
	厂 土	圧 迫 appaku pressure, oppression 1175
	18 22	気 圧 kiatsu atmospheric pressure 134
		抑 圧 yokuatsu restraint, suppression 1057
	圧 壓	圧 倒 的 attōteki overwhelming 905, 210

	1343	**KAI, hai** – ash
灰	2p4.1 ☐	灰 じ ん kaijin ashes
	厂 火	石 灰 sekkai (chemical) lime 78
	18 44	灰 皿 haizara ashtray 1097
		火 山 灰 kazanbai volcanic ash 20, 34
	灰	灰 色 haiiro gray 204

	1344	**TAN, sumi** – charcoal
炭	3o6.5 ☐	石 炭 sekitan coal 78
	山 火 厂	木 炭 mokutan charcoal 22
	36 44 18	採 炭 saitan coal mining 933
		炭 素 tanso carbon 271
	炭 炭	炭 酸 tansan carbonic acid 516

1345 岩	**GAN, iwa** – rock	
3o5.10 ☷	岩石 *ganseki* rock	78
屮 石	火成岩 *kaseigan* igneous rock	20, 261
36 53	岩塩 *gan'en* rock salt	1101
岩	岩屋 *iwaya* cave, cavern	167
	岩登り *iwanobori* rock climbing	960

1346 沖	**CHŪ, oki** – open sea	
3a4.5 ☐	沖合 *okiai* open sea, offshore	159
氵口丨	沖積世 *chūsekisei* the alluvial epoch	656, 252
21 24 2	沖積期 *chūsekiki* the alluvial epoch	656, 449
沖 沖		

1347 仲	**CHŪ, naka** – personal relations	
2a4.7 ☐	仲裁 *chūsai* arbitration	1123
亻口丨	仲介 *chūkai* mediation	453
3 24 2	伯仲 *hakuchū* be nearly equal, evenly matched	1176
仲	仲良く *nakayoku* on good terms, like good friends	321
	仲人 *nakōdo* go-between, matchmaker	1

1348 忠	**CHŪ** – loyality, faithfulness	
4k4.6 ☷	忠実 *chūjitsu* faithful, devoted, loyal	203
心口丨	忠義 *chūgi* loyalty	291
51 24 2	忠誠 *chūsei* loyalty, allegiance	718
忠	忠告 *chūkoku* advice, admonition	690
	忠臣蔵 *Chūshingura* (the 47 *Rōnin* story)	835, 1286

1349 縫	**HŌ, nu(u)** – sew	
6a9.15 ☐	裁縫 *saihō* sewing	1123
糸夂辶	縫合 *hōgō* a suture, stitch	159
61 49 19	天衣無縫 *ten'i-muhō* of flawless beauty, perfect	141, 677, 93
縫 縫	縫い目 *nuime* seam, stitch	55
	仮縫い *karinui* temporary sewing, basting, fitting	1049

1350 峰	**HŌ, mine** – peak, summit	
3o7.6 ☐	連峰 *renpō* mountain range	440
屮夂十	高峰 *kōhō* lofty peak	190
36 49 12	霊峰 *reihō* sacred mountain	1168
峰 峯		

1351 峠	**tōge** – mountain pass	
3o6.3 ☐	峠道 *tōgemichi* road through a mountain pass	149
屮卜一	峠を越す *tōge o kosu* cross a pass	1001
36 13 14	十国峠 *Jikkoku Tōge* (pass in Hakone)	12, 40
峠		

1352 3o6.1 ▯ 山 火 二 36 44 4 峡 峽	**KYŌ** – gorge, ravine 山峡 *sankyō* (mountain) gorge 34 峡谷 *kyōkoku* gorge, ravine, canyon 653 海峡 *kaikyō* strait, channel, narrows 117 峡湾 *kyōwan* fjord 670
1353 3g6.2 ▯ 犭 火 二 27 44 4 狭 狹	**KYŌ, sema(i)** – narrow, small (in area) **seba(maru/meru)** – (intr./ tr.) narrow, contract 狭量 *kyōryō* narrow-minded 411 偏狭 *henkyō* narrow-minded, parochial ⌐pectoris 1159 狭心症 *kyōshinshō* stricture of the heart, angina 97, 1318 狭苦しい *semakurushii* cramped 545
1354 3c6.1 ▯ 扌 火 二 23 44 4 挟 挾	**KYŌ, hasa(mu)** – put between, interpose **hasa(maru)** – get between, get caught/hemmed/sandwiched between 挟撃 *kyōgeki* pincer attack 1016 挟み撃ち *hasamiuchi* pincer attack 1016 挟み込む *hasamikomu* put between, insert 776 挟み上げる *hasamiageru* pick up (with chopsticks) 32
1355 3g9.6 ▤ 犭 月 十 27 42 12 献 獻	**KEN, [KON]** – present, offer 献金 *kenkin* gift of money, contribution 23 献血 *kenketsu* blood donation 789 献上 *kenjō* presentation 32 文献 *bunken* the literature, documentary records 111 献立 *kondate* menu; arrangements, plan, program 121
1356 2a4.1 ▯ 亻 犭 3 27 伏	**FUKU, fu(su)** – bend down, lie down/prostrate **fu(seru)** – cast down (one's eyes); turn over; cover, put over; conceal 降伏 *kōfuku* surrender, capitulation 947 伏兵 *fukuhei* an ambush 784 潜伏 *senpuku* hide; be dormant, latent 937 伏線 *fukusen* foreshadowing 299
1357 0a5.12 ▤ 斤 一 50 1 丘	**KYŪ, oka** – hill 砂丘 *sakyū* sand dune 1151
1358 3o5.12 ▤ 山 斤 一 36 50 1 岳 嶽	**GAKU, take** – mountain, peak 山岳 *sangaku* mountains 34 山岳部 *sangakubu* mountaineering club 34, 86 岳父 *gakufu* father of one's wife 113 谷川岳 *Tanigawa-dake* (mountain about 150 km north of Tōkyō) 653, 33

	1359	**SHŌ** – workman, artisan	
匠	2t4.2 ⊟	巨 匠 *kyoshō* (great) master	1293
	⎡ 斤	名 匠 *meishō* master craftsman	82
	20 50	師 匠 *shishō* master, teacher	409
		宗 匠 *sōshō* master, teacher	616
	匠	意 匠 *ishō* a design	132

	1360	**KI** – strange, curious	
奇	3d5.17 ⊟	好 奇 心 *kōkishin* curiosity	104, 97
	口 大 一	奇 妙 *kimyō* strange, curious, odd	1154
	24 34 14	奇 術 *kijutsu* conjuring, sleight of hand	187
		奇 病 *kibyō* strange disease	380
	奇 畜	奇 数 *kisū* odd number	225

	1361	**KI, yo(ru)** – approach, draw near; meet; drop in **yo(seru)** – bring near; push aside; gather together; send	
寄	3m8.8 ⊟	寄 付 *kifu* contribution, donation	192
	宀 大 口	寄 宿 舎 *kishukusha* dormitory	179, 791
	33 34 24	寄 生 *kisei* parasitism	44
	寄	立 ち 寄 る *tachiyoru* drop in, stop (at)	121

	1362	**saki** – cape, promontory, headland, point (of land)	
崎	3o8.3 ⊞	長 崎 *Nagasaki* (city on western coast of Kyūshū)	95
	山 大 口	宮 崎 *Miyazaki* (city on southern coast of Kyūshū)	721
	36 34 24		
	崎 嵜		

	1363	**misaki** – promontory, headland, point (of land)	
岬	3o5.4 ⊡	宗 谷 岬 *Sōya-misaki* (northern tip of Hokkaidō)	616, 653
	山 日 丨	知 床 岬 *Shiretoko-misaki* (eastern tip of Hokkaidō)	214, 826
	36 43 2	潮 岬 *Shio-no-misaki* (southern tip of Kii Peninsula)	468
	岬	足 ず り 岬 *Ashizuri-misaki* (southern tip of Shikoku)	58

	1364	**ZŌ, [SŌ], oku(ru)** – give, present, bestow	
贈	7b11.2 ⊞	贈 与 (証 書) *zōyo (shōsho)* gift (certificate)	539, 484, 131
	貝 田日	寄 贈 *kizō, kisō* presentation, donation, contribution	1361
	68 58 43	贈 答 *zōtō* exchange of gifts	160
		贈 り 物 *okurimono* gift, present	79
	贈 贈	贈 り 主 *okurinushi* sender (of a gift)	155

	1365	**ZŌ, niku(mu)** – hate **niku(i), niku(rashii)** – hateful, horrible, repulsive **niku(shimi)** – hatred, animosity	
憎	4k11.7 ⊞	愛 憎 *aizō* love and hate; partiality	259
	心 田日	憎 悪 *zōo* hatred	304
	51 58 43	憎 ま れ っ 子 *nikumarekko* bad/naughty boy	103
	憎 憎	憎 ま れ 口 *nikumareguchi* offensive/malicious remarks	54

1366	SŌ – Buddhist priest/monk	
2a11.7	僧 院　sōin　temple; monastery	614
亻 田 日	僧 正　sōjō　Buddhist high priest, bishop	275
3 58 43	高 僧　kōsō　high/exemplary priest	190
	僧 服　sōfuku　priestly robe, monk's habit	683
僧 僧	小 僧　kozō　young priest; apprentice; boy	27

1367	SŌ – layer, level	
3r11.2	上 層　jōsō　upper layer/classes/floors	32
尸 田 日	多 層　tasō　multilayer	229
40 58 43	層 雲　sōun　stratus (cloud)	636
	読 者 層　dokushasō　class/level of readers	244, 164
層 層	階 層　kaisō　social stratum, class	588

1368	ETSU – joy	
4k7.15	喜 悦　kietsu　joy, delight	1143
心 口 儿	悦 楽　etsuraku　joy, pleasure, gaiety	358
51 24 16	法 悦　hōetsu　religious exultation; ecstasy	123
	満 悦　man'etsu　delighted, very satisfied	201
悦 悦	悦 に 入 る　etsu ni iru　be pleased (with)	52

1369	ETSU – inspection, review	
8e7.2	閲 覧　etsuran　perusal, inspection, reading	1291
門 口 儿	閲 覧 室　etsuranshitsu　reading room	1291, 166
76 24 16	校 閲　kōetsu　revision (of a manuscript)	115
	検 閲　ken'etsu　censorship	531
閲	閲 歴　etsureki　one's career/personal history	480

1370	DATSU – omit; escape　nu(gu) – take off (clothes)	
	nu(geru) – come off, slip off (footwear/clothing)	
4b7.8	脱 衣 所　datsuisho, datsuijo　changing/dressing room	677, 153
月 口 儿	脱 線　dassen　derailment; digression	299
42 24 16	離 脱　ridatsu　secession, breakaway	1281
脱 脱	脱 税　datsuzei　tax evasion	399

1371	EI, surudo(i) – sharp	
8a7.12	鋭 利　eiri　sharp	329
釒 口 儿	鋭 気　eiki　spirit, mettle, energy	134
72 24 16	精 鋭　seiei　elite, choice	659
	新 鋭　shin'ei　fresh, new	174
鋭 鋭	鋭 角　eikaku　acute angle	473

1372	KOKU – conquer	
2k5.1	克 服　kokufuku　conquest, subjugation	683
十 口 儿	克 己　kokki　self-denial, self-control	370
12 24 16	克 明　kokumei　faithful, conscientious	18
克		

	1373	**BŌ, isoga(shii)** – busy
忙	4k3.2 田	多忙 *tabō* busy, hectic 229
	心 亠 丨	繁忙 *hanbō* (very) busy 1292
	51 11 2	忙殺される *bōsatsu sareru* be busily occupied 576
	忙	

	1374	**BŌ, wasu(reru)** – forget
忘	2j5.4 目	健忘(症) *kenbō(shō)* forgetfulness 893, 1318
	亠 心 丨	忘恩 *bōon* ingratitude 555
	11 51 2	忘年会 *bōnenkai* year-end party 45, 158
	忘 忘	忘れ物 *wasuremono* article left behind 79
		度/胴忘れ *do/dōwasure* forget for the moment 377, 1300

	1375	**MŌ** – blindness; ignorance
盲	2j6.6 目	盲人 *mōjin* blind person, the blind 1
	亠 目 丨	盲目 *mōmoku* blindness 55
	11 55 2	色盲 *shikimō* color blindness 204
	盲 盲	文盲 *monmō* illiteracy 111
		盲腸 *mōchō* caecum, appendix 1270

	1376	**MŌ, BŌ** – without reason/authority
妄	2j4.6 目	迷妄 *meimō* illusion, fallacy 967
	亠 女 丨	妄想 *mōsō* wild fancy, foolish fantasy, delusion 147
	11 25 2	妄信 *mōshin, bōshin* blind belief, overcredulity 157
	妄	被害妄想 *higai mōsō* delusions of persecution, paranoia 976, 518, 147

	1377	**KŌ, ara(i)** – rough, wild, violent **a(reru)** – get rough/stormy, run
荒	3k6.18 目	wild, go to ruin **a(rasu)** – devastate, lay waste
	艹 亠 儿	荒廃 *kōhai* desolation, devastation 961
	32 11 16	荒野 *kōya, areno* wilderness, wasteland 236
	荒	荒れ狂う *arekuruu* rage, run amuck 883
		荒仕事 *arashigoto* heavy work, hard labor 333, 80

	1378	**KŌ, awa(teru)** – get flustered, be in a flurry, panic
慌	4k9.10 田	**awa(tadashii)** – bustling, flurried, confused
	心 艹 亠	大慌て *ōawate* great haste 26
	51 32 11	慌て者 *awatemono* absentminded person, scatterbrain 164
	慌	

	1379	**FUKU** – fortune, blessing; wealth, welfare
福	4e9.1 田	幸福 *kōfuku* happiness 684
	礻 甲 口	祝福 *shukufuku* blessing 851
	45 58 24	福音 *fukuin* the Gospel; good news 347
	福 福	福引き *fukubiki* lottery, raffle 216
		七福神 *Shichifukujin* the Seven Gods of Good Fortune 9, 310

	1380	**FUKU, haba** – width, breadth, range; influence	
幅	3f9.2 田	振 幅 *shinpuku* amplitude	954
	巾 田 卩	大 幅 *ōhaba* broad; large, wholesale, substantial	26
	26 58 24	幅 の 広 い *haba no hiroi* wide, broad	694
		横 幅 *yokohaba* breadth, width	781
	幅	幅 が 利 く *haba ga kiku* be influential	329

	1381	**HAN** – squad, group	
班	4f6.3 Ⅲ	首 班 *shuhan* head, chief	148
	王 儿	班 長 *hanchō* squad/group leader	95
	46 16	救 護 班 *kyūgohan* relief squad	725, 1312
	班	班 点 *hanten* spot, speckle, dot	169

	1382	**HAN** – feudal clan/lord	
藩	3k15.4 田	藩 主 *hanshu* lord of a feudal clan	155
	艹 米 田	藩 学 *hangaku* samurai school for clan children	109
	32 62 58	廃 藩 置 県 *haihan-chiken* abolition of clans and estab-	
	藩	lishment of prefectures 961, 426, 194	

	1383	**SHIN** – hearing, investigation, trial	
審	3m12.1 …	審 査 *shinsa* examination, investigation	624
	宀 米 田	審 議 *shingi* deliberation, consideration	292
	33 62 58	審 問 *shinmon* trial, hearing, inquiry	162
		不 審 *fushin* doubt, suspicion	94
	審	審 判 *shinpan* decision, judgment, refereeing	1026

	1384	**RYO** – thought, consideration	
慮	2m13.2 冂	考 慮 *kōryo* consideration, reflection	541
	卜 田 心	遠 慮 *enryo* reserve, restraint, hesitation	446
	(13) 58 51	配 慮 *hairyo* consideration, solicitude	515
		憂 慮 *yūryo* apprehension, concern	1032
	慮	焦 慮 *shōryo* impatience; worry	999

	1385	**RYO** – captive	
虜	2m11.2 冂	捕 虜 *horyo* prisoner of war	890
	卜 田 厂	捕 虜 収 容 所 *horyo shūyōjo* POW camp 890, 757, 654, 153	
	(13) 58 18		
	虜 虜		

	1386	**YŪ, isa(mu)** – be spirited, lively, encouraged	
勇	2g7.3 目	勇 気 *yūki* courage	134
	力 田 一	武 勇 *buyū* bravery, valor	1031
	8 58 1	勇 士 *yūshi* brave warrior, hero	572
		勇 退 *yūtai* retire voluntarily	846
	勇	勇 み 足 *isamiashi* overeagerness, rashness	58

	1387	**YŪ** – male; brave; great **osu, o** – male	
雄	8c4.1	英 雄 *eiyū* hero	353
	隹 十 ム	雄 弁 *yūben* eloquence	711
	74 12 17	雄 大 *yūdai* grand, magnificent	26
	雄	雄 鳥 *ondori* rooster, male bird	285
		両 雄 *ryōyū* 2 great men (rivals)	200

	1388	**SHI, mesu, me** – female	
雌	8c6.1	雌 伏 *shifuku* remain in obscurity, lie low	1356
	隹 匕 丨	雌 雄 *shiyū* male and female; victory or defeat	1387
	74 13 2	雌 犬 *mesuinu* a bitch	280
	雌	雌 牛 *meushi* (female) cow	281
		雌 花 *mebana* female flower	255

	1389	**SHI, murasaki** – purple	
紫	6a6.15	紫 外 線 *shigaisen* ultraviolet rays	83, 299
	糸 匕 丨	紫 煙 *shien* tobacco smoke, blue cigarette smoke	919
	61 13 2	紫 雲 *shiun* auspicious purple clouds	636
	紫	山 紫 水 明 *sanshi-suimei* beautiful scenery	34, 21, 18
		紫 色 *murasakiiro* purple	204

	1390	**SHI** – happiness	
祉	4e4.1	福 祉 *fukushi* welfare, well-being	1379
	木 止	福 祉 国 家 *fukushi kokka* welfare state	1379, 40, 165
	45 13 11	社 会 福 祉 *shakai fukushi* social/public welfare	
	祉 祉		308, 158, 1379

	1391	**YŪ** – surplus	
裕	5e7.3	余 裕 *yoyū* room, margin, leeway; composure	1063
	木 火 口	富 裕 *fuyū* wealth, affluence	713
	57 44 24	裕 福 *yūfuku* wealth, affluence	1379
	裕	余 裕 し ゃ く し ゃ く *yoyū-shakushaku* calm and	
			composed 1063

	1392	**YŌ, to(keru)** – (intr.) melt, dissolve **to(kasu), to(ku)** – (tr.) melt, dissolve	
溶	3a10.15	溶 解 *yōkai* (intr.) melt, dissolve	474
	氵 火 宀	溶 岩 *yōgan* lava	1345
	21 44 33	溶 液 *yōeki* solution	472
	溶	水 溶 性 *suiyōsei* water-soluble	21, 98

	1393	**SEKI** – divide, take apart, analyze	
析	4a4.12	分 析 *bunseki* analysis	38
	木 斤	分 析 化 学 *bunseki kagaku* analytical chemistry	38, 254, 109
	41 50	市 場 分 析 *shijō bunseki* market analysis	181, 154, 38
	析	解 析 *kaiseki* analysis	474

	1394	**SETSU, o(reru)** – (intr.) break; be folded; yield, compromise
折	3c4.7 □	**o(ru)** – (tr.) break; fold, bend **ori** – occasion, opportunity
	扌 斤	右折禁止 *usetsu kinshi* No Right Turn 76, 482, 477
	23 50	折半 *seppan* divide into halves 88
	折	曲折 *kyokusetsu* twists and turns, complications 366
		折り紙 *origami* paper folding; paper for origami 180

	1395	**SEI, chika(u)** – swear, pledge, vow
誓	7a7.17 ⊞	誓約 *seiyaku* oath, vow, pledge 211
	言 斤 扌	宣誓 *sensei* oath 625
	67 50 23	折誓 *kisei* oath, vow 621
	誓	誓文 *seimon* written oath 111

	1396	**SEI, yu(ku)** – die
逝	2q7.8 ⬚	逝去 *seikyo* death 414
	辶 斤 扌	急逝 *kyūsei* sudden/untimely death 303
	19 50 23	
	逝 逝	

	1397	**TETSU** – wisdom
哲	3d7.13 ⊞	哲学 *tetsugaku* philosophy 109
	口 斤 扌	哲学者 *tetsugakusha* philosopher 109, 164
	24 50 23	賢哲 *kentetsu* wise man, sage 1288
	哲	先哲 *sentetsu* wise man of the past, sage of old 50
		哲人 *tetsujin* wise man, philosopher 1

	1398	**KEI** – open; say
啓	3d8.17 ⊞	啓発 *keihatsu* enlightenment, edification 96
	口 攵 尸	啓示 *keiji* revelation 615
	24 49 40	天啓 *tenkei* divine revelation 141
	啓	拝啓 *haikei* Dear Sir: 1201
		啓もう *keimō* enlightenment, instruction

	1399	**ZAN** – (for) a while
暫	4c11.3 ⊞	暫時 *zanji* (for) a short time 42
	日 車 斤	暫定 *zantei* tentative, provisional 355
	43 69 50	
	暫	

	1400	**ZEN** – gradually
漸	3a11.2 ⊞	漸次 *zenji* gradually, step by step 384
	氵 車 斤	漸進 *zenshin* gradual progress 437
	21 69 50	漸増 *zenzō* increase gradually 712
	漸	漸減 *zengen* decrease gradually, taper off 715

斥	**1401** 0a5.18 □ 斤丨 50 2 斥	**SEKI** – retreat, recede; repel, reject 排斥 *haiseki* rejection, exclusion, boycott 1036 排斥運動 *haiseki undō* agitation for expulsion/exclusion 1036, 439, 231
訴	**1402** 7a5.2 □ 言 斤丨 67 50 2 訴	**SO, utta(eru)** – sue; complain of; appeal (to) 起訴 *kiso* prosecution, indictment 373 提訴 *teiso* bring before (the court), file (suit) 628 告訴 *kokuso* complaint, accusation, charges 690 敗訴 *haiso* losing a suit/case 511 勝訴 *shōso* winning a suit/case 509
訟	**1403** 7a4.6 □ 言 儿 厶 67 16 17 訟	**SHŌ** – accuse 訴訟 *soshō* lawsuit, litigation 1402 刑事訴訟 *keiji soshō* criminal suit 887, 80, 1402 民事訴訟 *minji soshō* civil suit 177, 80, 1402 離婚訴訟 *rikon soshō* suit for divorce 1281, 567, 1402 訴訟費用 *soshō hiyō* costs of litigation 1402, 749, 107
陣	**1404** 2d7.1 □ 阝 車 7 69 陣	**JIN** – battle position, camp 陣営 *jin'ei* camp, encampment 722 陣地 *jinchi* (military) position 118 陣容 *jin'yō* battle array, lineup 654 退陣 *taijin* decampment, withdrawal 846 陣痛 *jintsū* labor (pains) 1320
陳	**1405** 2d8.2 □ 阝 木 日 7 41 43 陳	**CHIN** – state, explain; show; old 陳列 *chinretsu* display, exhibit 611 陳情 *chinjō* petition, appeal 209 陳述 *chinjutsu* statement, declaration 968 陳謝 *chinsha* apology 「regeneration 901 新陳代謝 *shinchin taisha* metabolism; 174, 256, 901
棟	**1406** 4a8.3 □ 木 日 41 43 棟	**TŌ, mune, [muna]** – ridge of a roof 上棟式 *jōtōshiki* roof-laying ceremony 32, 525 病棟 *byōtō* (hospital) ward 380 別棟 *betsumune* separate building 267 棟上げ式 *muneageshiki* roof-laying ceremony 32, 525 棟木 *munagi* ridgepole, ridge beam 22
壊	**1407** 3b13.3 □ 土 衤 日 22 57 55 壊 壊	**KAI, kowa(reru)** – get broken, break **kowa(su)** – break, tear down, destroy, damage 壊滅 *kaimetsu* destruction, annihilation 1338 破壊 *hakai* destruction, wrecking 665 崩壊 *hōkai* collapse, breakdown, cave-in 1122 壊血病 *kaiketsubyō* scurvy 789, 380

懷	**1408** 4k13.9 ⊞ 心 目 礻 51 55 57 懷 懷	***KAI*** – pocket; nostalgia ***natsu(kashii)*** – dear, fond, longed-for ***natsu(kashimu)*** – yearn for ***natsu(ku)*** – take kindly (to) ***natsu(keru)*** – win over; tame ***futokoro*** – breast (pocket) 懷中電灯 *kaichū dentō* flashlight 28, 108, 1333 述懷 *jukkai* (relating) one's thoughts and reminiscences 968 懷柔 *kaijū* conciliation 774

快	**1409** 4k4.2 ⊡ 心 六 一 51 34 1 快	***KAI, kokoroyo(i)*** – pleasant, delightful 快適 *kaiteki* comfortable, pleasant, agreeable 415 快活 *kaikatsu* cheerful, lighthearted 237 全快 *zenkai* complete recovery (from illness) 89 快晴 *kaisei* fine weather, clear skies 662 快速電車 *kaisoku densha* express train 502, 108, 133

慢	**1410** 4k11.8 ⊞ 心 目 日 51 55 43 慢	***MAN*** – be lazy, neglect 我慢 *gaman* exercise patience, tolerate 1302 自慢 *jiman* pride, boasting, vanity 62 怠慢 *taiman* negligence, dereliction 1297 緩慢 *kanman* slow, sluggish 1089 慢性 *mansei* chronic 98

漫	**1411** 3a11.11 ⊞ 氵目 日 21 55 43 漫	***MAN*** – aimless, random; involuntarily 漫画 *manga* cartoon, comic book/strip 343 漫談 *mandan* chat, idle talk 593 散漫 *sanman* vague, loose, desultory 767 漫然 *manzen* random, rambling, discursive 651 漫才 *manzai* comic (stage) dialogue 551

寧	**1412** 3m11.8 ⊟ 宀 目 心 33 55 51 寧 寧	***NEI*** – peaceful, quiet; rather, preferably 丁寧 *teinei* polite; careful, meticulous 184 安寧 *annei* public peace/order 105

刃	**1413** 0a3.22 ⊡ カ 丨 8 2 刃 双	***JIN, ha*** – blade 白刃 *hakujin* naked blade, drawn sword 205 刃先 *hasaki* edge (of a blade) 50 刃物 *hamono* edged tool, cutlery 79 もろ刃の剣 *moroha no tsurugi* double-edged sword 879

忍	**1414** 4k3.3 心 カ 丨 51 8 2 忍 忍	***NIN, shino(bu)*** – bear, endure; hide, lie hidden; avoid (being seen) ***shino(baseru)*** – hide, conceal 忍苦 *ninku* endurance, stoicism 545 残忍 *zannin* brutal, ruthless 650 忍者 *ninja* (feudal) professional spy/assassin 164 忍び足 *shinobiashi* stealthy steps 58

	1415	**TAI, ta(eru)** – endure, bear, withstand; be fit, competent
耐	2r7.1 ⊞ 冂 寸 一 20 37 14 耐	忍耐 *nintai* perseverance, patience 1414 耐熱 *tainetsu* heatproof, heat-resistant 645 耐火 *taika* fireproof, fire-resistant 20 耐久 *taikyū* endurance; durability 1210 耐乏生活 *taibō seikatsu* austerity 754, 44, 237

	1416	**JU** – request, need, demand
需	8d6.1 ☰ 雨 一 冂 75 14 20 需	需要 (供給) *juyō (kyōkyū)* demand (and supply) 419, 197, 346 需給 *jukyū* supply and demand 346 特需 *tokuju* special procurement (in wartime) 282 軍需品 *gunjuhin* military supplies, matériel 438, 230 必需品 *hitsujuhin* necessary articles, necessities 520, 230

	1417	**JU** – Confucianism
儒	2a14.1 ⊞ 亻 雨 一 3 75 14 儒	儒教 *jukyō* Confucianism 245 儒学 *jugaku* Confucianism 109 儒学者 *jugakusha* Confucian scholar 109, 164 儒家 *juka* Confucian scholar, Confucianist 165

	1418	**TAN** – correct; end, tip **hashi** – end, edge **hata** – side, edge, nearby **ha** – edge
端	5b9.2 ⊞ 立 山 一 54 36 14 端	極端 *kyokutan* extreme, ultra- 336 異端 *itan* heresy, heathenism 1061 道端 *michibata* roadside, wayside 149 端折る *hashoru* tuck up; cut short, abridge 1394

	1419	**BI** – minute, slight
微	3i10.1 ⊞ 彳 攵 山 29 49 36 微 微	微妙 *bimyō* delicate, subtle 1154 微笑 *bishō* smile 1235 微熱 *binetsu* a slight fever 645 微生物 *biseibutsu* microorganism, microbe 44, 79 顕微鏡 *kenbikyō* microscope 1170, 863

	1420	**CHŌ** – collect; demand; sign, symptom
徴	3i11.2 ⊞ 彳 王 攵 29 46 49 徴 徴	徴候 *chōkō* sign, indication, symptom 944 象徴 *shōchō* symbol 739 特徴 *tokuchō* distinctive feature 282 徴税 *chōzei* tax collection 399 徴兵 *chōhei* conscription, military service; draftee 784

	1421	**CHŌ, ko(rasu), ko(rashimeru)** – chastise, punish, discipline **ko(riru)** – learn by experience, be taught a lesson, be sick of
懲	4k14.3 ☷ 心 王 攵 51 46 49 懲 懲	懲罰 *chōbatsu* disciplinary measure, punishment 886 懲役 *chōeki* penal servitude, imprisonment 375 勧善懲悪 *kanzen-chōaku* good over evil, poetic justice 1051, 1139, 304

1422

徹

3i12.2 �

彳 月 攵
29 42 49

徹

TETSU – pierce, go through

徹底的	*tetteiteki*	thorough	562, 210
貫徹	*kantetsu*	carry through, accomplish	914
徹夜	*tetsuya*	stay up all night	471
冷徹	*reitetsu*	coolheaded, levelheaded	832

1423

撤

3c12.3 ▦

扌 月 攵
23 42 49

撤

TETSU – withdraw, remove

撤回	*tekkai*	withdraw, retract, rescind	90
撤去	*tekkyo*	withdraw, evacuate, remove	414
撤退	*tettai*	withdraw, pull out, retreat	846
撤兵	*teppei*	withdraw troops, disengage	784
撤廃	*teppai*	abolish, do away with, repeal	961

1424

崇

3o8.9 ⊟

山 礻 宀
36 45 33

崇

SŪ – respect, revere; lofty, sublime

崇拝	*sūhai*	worship, adoration	1201
祖先崇拝	*sosen sūhai*	ancestor worship	622, 50, 1201
崇敬	*sūkei*	veneration, reverence	705
崇高	*sūkō*	lofty, sublime, noble	190

1425

模

4a10.16 ⊞

木 日 艹
41 43 32

模 模

MO, BO – copy, imitate; model

模様	*moyō*	pattern, design; appearance; situation	403
模範	*mohan*	model, exemplar	1092
模型	*mokei*	(scale) model; a mold	888
模造	*mozō*	imitation	691
規模	*kibo*	scale, scope	607

1426

膜

4b10.6 ⊞

月 日 艹
42 43 32

膜

MAKU – membrane

角膜	*kakumaku*	cornea	473
鼓膜	*komaku*	eardrum	1147
処女膜	*shojomaku*	hymen	1137, 102
腹膜炎	*fukumakuen*	peritonitis	1271, 1336
結膜炎	*ketsumakuen*	conjunctivitis, pinkeye	485, 1336

1427

漠

3a10.18 ⊞

氵 日 艹
21 43 32

漠

BAKU – vague, obscure; desert; wide

砂漠	*sabaku*	desert	1151
広漠	*kōbaku*	vast, boundless	694
漠然	*bakuzen*	vague, hazy, nebulous	651

1428

暮

3k11.14 ⊟

艹 日 大
32 43 34

暮

BO, ku(reru) – grow dark, come to an end **ku(rasu)** – live

歳暮	*seibo*	end of the year; year-end gift	479
野暮	*yabo*	uncouth, rustic, boorish	236
夕暮れ	*yūgure*	evening, twilight	81
一人暮らし	*hitorigurashi*	living alone	2, 1

墓	**1429** 3k10.18目 艹 日 土 32 43 22 墓	**BO, haka** – a grave	
		墓地　bochi　cemetery	118
		墓標　bohyō　grave marker/post	923
		墓石　boseki　gravestone	78
		墓穴　boketsu　grave (pit)	899
		墓参り　hakamairi　visit to a grave	710
募	**1430** 3k9.23目 艹 日 大 32 43 34 募	**BO, tsuno(ru)** – appeal for, invite, raise; grow intense	
		募集　boshū　recruiting, solicitation	436
		応募　ōbo　apply for, enlist, enroll	827
		応募者　ōbosha　applicant, entrant	827, 164
		募金　bokin　fund raising	23
		公募　kōbo　offer for public subscription	126
慕	**1431** 3k11.12目 艹 日 心 32 43 51 慕	**BO, shita(u)** – yearn for, love dearly; idolize	
		慕情　bojō　longing, love, affection	209
		思慕　shibo　longing (for), deep attachment (to)	99
		敬慕　keibo　love and respect	705
		恋慕　renbo　love, affection	258
		追慕　tsuibo　cherish (someone's) memory, sigh for	1174
幕	**1432** 3k10.19目 艹 日 巾 32 43 26 幕	**MAKU** – (stage) curtain; act (of a play)　**BAKU** – shogunate	
		開幕　kaimaku　commencement of a performance	396
		序幕　jomaku　opening act, prelude	770
		除幕　jomaku　unveiling	1065
		内幕　uchimaku, naimaku　behind-the-scenes story	84
		幕府　Bakufu　Japan's feudal government, shogunate	504
添	**1433** 3a8.22 田 氵 心 大 21 51 34 添	**TEN, so(eru)** – add (to), append　**so(u)** – accompany	
		添加　tenka　annex, append, affix	709
		添付　tenpu　attach, append	192
		添乗員　tenjōin　tour conductor	523, 163
		力添え　chikarazoe　help, assistance	100
		付き添い　tsukisoi　attending (someone), escorting	192
恭	**1434** 3k7.16目 艹 心 几 32 51 16 恭	**KYŌ, uyauya(shii)** – respectful, reverent, deferential	
		恭順　kyōjun　fealty, allegiance	769
		恭敬　kyōkei　reverence, respect	705
		恭賀新年　kyōga shinnen　Best wishes for a happy New Year.	756, 174, 45
洪	**1435** 3a6.14 田 氵 艹 几 21 32 16 洪	**KŌ** – flood, inundation; vast	
		洪水　kōzui　flood, inundation, deluge	21
		洪積層　kōsekisō　diluvium, diluvial formation	656, 1367

呉 呉呉	**1436** 2o5.7 目 ソ 口 一 16 24 1	***GO*** – Wu (dynasty of ancient China) 呉服 *gofuku* drapery, dry goods　683 呉服屋 *gofukuya* draper's shop, dry-goods dealer　683, 167 呉越 *Go-Etsu* Wu and Yue/Yüeh (rival states of China)　1001
娯 娯娯	**1437** 3e7.3 田 女 口 儿 25 24 16	***GO*** – pleasure, enjoyment 娯楽 *goraku* amusement, enterainment　358 娯楽番組 *goraku bangumi* entertainment program 358, 185, 418
悟 悟	**1438** 4k7.5 田 心 口 一 51 24 14	***GO, sato(ru)*** – perceive, understand, realize, be enlightened 覚悟 *kakugo* readiness, preparedness, resoluteness　605 悟り *satori* comprehension, understanding; satori, spiritual awakening
項 項	**1439** 9a3.1 口 頁 工 77 38	***KŌ*** – item, clause, paragraph 事項 *jikō* matters, facts; items, particulars　80 事項索引 *jikō sakuin* subject index　80, 1059, 216 要項 *yōkō* essential points, gist　419 条項 *jōkō* provision, clause　564 項目 *kōmoku* heading, item　55
頂 頂	**1440** 9a2.1 口 頁 一 77 14	***CHŌ, itadaki*** – summit, top ***itada(ku)*** – be capped with; receive 頂上 *chōjō* summit, peak, top; climax　32 山頂 *sanchō* summit, mountain top　34 頂点 *chōten* zenith, peak, climax　169 絶頂 *zetchō* peak, height, climax　742
傾 傾	**1441** 2a11.3 田 亻 頁 ⻖ 3 77 13	***KEI, katamu(ku/keru)*** – (intr./tr.) lean, incline, tilt 傾向 *keikō* tendency, trend; inclination　199 傾斜 *keisha* inclination, slant, slope　1069 左傾 *sakei* leftward leanings, radicalization　75 傾聴 *keichō* listen　1039 傾倒 *keitō* devote oneself (to), be absorbed (in)　905
浦 浦	**1442** 3a7.2 口 氵 月 十 21 42 12	***HO, ura*** – bay, inlet; seashore 浦波 *uranami* wave breaking on the beach, breaker　666 津々浦々 *tsutsu-uraura* throughout the land, the entire country　668 浦島太郎 *Urashima Tarō* (character in a folk tale) 286, 629, 980

278

	1443	**HO** – shop, store; pavement	
舗	3b12.4	店舗 *tenpo* shop, store	168
	土 月 口	老舗 *shinise, rōho* long-established store	543
	22 42 24	舗装 *hosō* pave	1328
舖 舗		舗(装)道(路) *ho(sō) dō(ro)* paved road/street	1328, 149, 151

	1444	**SHA, su(teru)** – throw away; abandon, forsake	
捨	3c8.26	取捨 *shusha* adoption or rejection, selection	65
	扌 土 口	喜捨 *kisha* charity, almsgiving, donation	1143
	23 22 24	捨て子 *sutego* abandoned child, foundling	103
捨 捨		見捨てる *misuteru* abandon, desert, forsake	63
		切り捨てる *kirisuteru* cut down; discard, omit	39

	1445	**SHŪ, hiro(u)** – pick up, find **JŪ** – ten (in documents)	
拾	3c6.14	拾得物 *shūtokubutsu* an acquisition	374, 79
	扌 口 亻	収拾 *shūshū* get under control, deal with	757
	23 24 3	拾い物 *hiroimono* something found lying on the ground, a find	79
拾		(金)拾万円 *(kin) jūman en* (amount of) 100,000 yen	23, 16, 13

	1446	**TEKI, shizuku** – a drop **shitata(ru)** – drip, trickle	
滴	3a11.14	水滴 *suiteki* drop of water	21
	氵口 亠	雨滴 *uteki* raindrop	30
	21 24 11	滴下 *tekika* drip, trickle down	31
滴		点滴 *tenteki* falling drop of water/rain; (intravenous) drip	169

	1447	**TEKI, tsu(mu)** – pick, pluck, nip	
摘	3c11.5	摘発 *tekihatsu* exposure, disclosure	96
	扌 口 亠	摘出 *tekishutsu* pluck out, extract; expose	53
	23 24 11	指摘 *shiteki* point out	1041
摘		摘要 *tekiyō* summary, synopsis	419
		茶摘み *chatsumi* tea picking	251

	1448	**BAKU, shiba(ru)** – tie up, bind	
縛	6a10.3	束縛 *sokubaku* restraint, constraint, shackles	501
	糸 日 寸	捕縛 *hobaku* capture, apprehension, arrest	890
	61 43 37	金縛り *kanashibari* be bound; be tied down with money	23
縛 縛		縛り首 *shibarikubi* (execution by) hanging	148

	1449	**HAKU, usu(i)** – thin (paper), weak (tea), light (color) **usu(maru/ragu/reru)** – thin out, fade **usu(meru)** – dilute	
薄	3k13.11	浅薄 *senpaku* shallow, superficial	649
	艹 日 氵	薄情 *hakujō* unfeeling, heartless, coldhearted	209
	32 43 21	薄弱 *hakujaku* feebleness	218
薄		薄明 *hakumei* twilight	18

簿	**1450** 6f13.4 ⺮ 日 氵 66 43 21 簿 筟	**BO** – record book, ledger, register 簿記　*boki*　bookkeeping　　371 帳簿　*chōbo*　account book, ledger　　1107 家計簿　*kakeibo*　housekeeping account book　　165, 340 名簿　*meibo*　list of names, roster　　82 会員名簿　*kaiin meibo*　list of members　　158, 163, 82
敷	**1451** 4i11.1 女 田 方 49 43 48 敷	**FU, shi(ku)** – spread, lay, put down 敷設　*fusetsu*　laying, construction　　577 屋敷　*yashiki*　mansion; residential lot　　167 座敷　*zashiki*　a room, reception room　　786 敷金　*shikikin*　a deposit, security　　23 敷布　*shikifu*　(bed) sheet　　675
絞	**1452** 6a6.9 糸 亠 儿 61 11 16 絞	**KŌ, shi(meru)** – strangle, wring　**shi(maru)** – be wrung out, pressed together　**shibo(ru)** – wring, squeeze, press, milk 絞殺　*kōsatsu*　strangle to death; hang　　576 絞首刑　*kōshukei*　(execution by) hanging　　148, 887 お絞り　*oshibori*　wet towel (provided in restaurants)
較	**1453** 7c6.3 車 亠 儿 69 11 16 較	**KAKU** – compare 比較　*hikaku*　comparison　　798 比較的　*hikakuteki*　comparatively, relatively　　798, 210 比較級　*hikakukyū*　the comparative (of an adjective)　　798, 568 比較文学　*hikaku bungaku*　comparative literature 　　798, 111, 109
紋	**1454** 6a4.9 糸 亠 十 61 11 12 紋	**MON** – (family) crest; (textile) pattern 紋章　*monshō*　crest, coat of arms　　⌐crest　857 菊の御紋　*kiku no gomon*　imperial chrysanthemum　　475, 708 紋切り形/型　*monkirigata*　conventional pattern　39, 395, 888 指紋　*shimon*　a fingerprint　　1041 波紋　*hamon*　a ripple　　666
芽	**1455** 3k5.9 艹 一 十 32 14 11 芽 芽	**GA, me** – a sprout, bud 発芽　*hatsuga*　germinate, sprout, bud　　96 麦芽　*bakuga*　malt　　270 新芽　*shinme*　new bud, sprout, shoot　　174 芽生え　*mebae*　bud, sprout, seedling　　44 木の芽　*ki no me*　leaf bud; Japanese pepper bud　　22
雅	**1456** 8c5.1 隹 一 一 74 14 11 雅 雅	**GA** – elegance, gracefulness 優雅　*yūga*　elegance, grace, refinement　　1033 風雅　*fūga*　elegance, refinement, (good) taste　　29 雅趣　*gashu*　elegance, tastefulness, artistry　　1002 雅楽　*gagaku*　ancient Japanese court music　　358

	1457	JA – evil, wrong	
邪	2d5.8	邪推 *jasui* groundless suspicion, mistrust	1233
	阝 一 亠	邪道 *jadō* evil course, vice; heresy	149
	7 14 11	邪教 *jakyō* heretical religion, heathenism	245
	邪 邪	邪宗 *jashū* heretical sect, heathenism	616
		風邪 *kaze* a cold	29

	1458	KI, sude (ni) – already	
既	0a10.5	既成 (の) 事実 *kisei (no) jijitsu* accomplished fact	261, 80, 203
	艮 一 亠	既製服 *kiseifuku* ready-made clothes	428, 683
	73 14 11	既婚 *kikon* married	567
	既 既	既報 *kihō* previous report	685
		既往症 *kiōshō* previous illness; medical history	918, 1318

	1459	GAI – general, approximate	
概	4a10.2	概算 *gaisan* rough estimate	747
	木 艮 一	概略 *gairyaku* outline, summary	841
	41 73 14	概括 *gaikatsu* summary, generalization	1260
	概 概	概況 *gaikyō* general situation, outlook	850
		概念 *gainen* concept	579

	1460	GAI – regret, lament, deplore	
慨	4k10.3	慨嘆 *gaitan* regret, lament, deplore	1246
	心 艮 一	感慨 *kangai* deep emotion	262
	51 73 14	感慨無量 *kangai-muryō* filled with deep emotion	262, 93, 411
	慨 慨		

	1461	GAI – shore; end, limit	
涯	3a8.33	生涯 *shōgai* a life, one's lifetime	44
	氵 土 厂	生涯教育 *shōgai kyōiku* continuing education	44, 245, 246
	21 22 18	一生涯 *isshōgai* one's (whole) life (long)	2, 44
	涯	天涯 *tengai* horizon; a distant land	141

	1462	KA – good, beautiful	
佳	2a6.10	佳人 *kajin* beautiful woman, a beauty	1
	亻 土	佳作 *kasaku* a fine piece of work	360
	3 22	風光絶佳 *fūkō-zekka* scenic beauty	29, 138, 742
	佳	佳境 *kakyō* interesting part, climax (of a story)	864

	1463	FŪ – seal HŌ – fief	
封	3b6.13	同封 *dōfū* enclose (with a letter)	198
	土 寸	封入 *fūnyū* enclose (with a letter)	52
	22 37	封書 *fūsho* sealed letter/document	131
	封	開封 *kaifū* open (a letter)	396
		封建制度 *hōken seido* the feudal system	892, 427, 377

掛	**1464** 3c8.6 ⊞ 扌 土 ㇏ 23 22 13 掛	**ka(karu)** – hang; cost, take **ka(keru)** – hang up; put on top of; spend; multiply **kakari** – expenses; tax; relation, connection 腰掛け *koshikake* seat, bench; stepping-stone 1298 掛け布団 *kakebuton* quilt, bedspread 675, 491 掛け軸 *kakejiku* hanging scroll 988 心掛け *kokorogake* intention; attitude; attention 97
赴	**1465** 3b6.14 ⟁ 土 ㇏ 亻 22 13 3 赴	**FU, omomu(ku)** – go, proceed; become 赴任 *funin* proceed to one's new post ⌐appointment 334 赴任地 *funinchi* one's post, one's place of 334, 118 赴任先 *funinsaki* one's post, one's place of appointment 334, 50
朴	**1466** 4a2.3 ⊞ 木 ㇏ 41 13 朴	**BOKU** – simple, plain 素朴 *soboku* simple, unsophisticated 271 質朴 *shitsuboku* simplehearted, unsophisticated 176 朴直 *bokuchoku* simple and honest, ingenuous 423 朴とつ *bokutotsu* ruggedly honest, rudely simple
茂	**1467** 3k5.7 目 艹 戈 丨 32 52 2 茂 梻	**MO, shige(ru)** – grow thick/rank 繁茂 *hanmo* luxuriant growth 1292 生い茂る *oishigeru* grow luxuriantly 44
苗	**1468** 3k5.2 目 艹 田 32 58 苗	**BYŌ, nae, [nawa]** – seedling, sapling 苗木 *naegi* sapling, seedling, young tree 22 苗床 *naedoko* nursery, seedbed 826 苗代 *nawashiro* bed for rice seedlings 256 苗字 *myōji* family name, surname 110
描	**1469** 3c8.21 ⊞ 扌 田 艹 23 58 32 描	**BYŌ, ega(ku)** – draw, paint, sketch, depict, portray 描写 *byōsha* depiction, portrayal, description 540 心理描写 *shinri byōsha* psychological 97, 143, 540 素描 *sobyō* rough sketch ⌐description 271 絵描き *ekaki* painter, artist 345
猫	**1470** 3g8.5 ⊞ 犭 田 艹 27 58 32 猫	**BYŌ, neko** – cat 山猫 *yamaneko* wildcat, lynx 34 山猫争議 *yamaneko sōgi* wildcat strike 34, 302, 292 猫なで声 *nekonadegoe* coaxing voice 746 招き猫 *manekineko* porcelain cat beckoning customers 455 愛猫 *aibyō* pet/favorite cat ⌐in stores 259

笛	1471	**TEKI, fue** – flute, whistle
	6f5.6 ⊟	警笛 *keiteki* alarm whistle; (automobile) horn 706
	⺮ ⽇ ｜	汽笛 *kiteki* steam whistle 135
	66 43 2	霧笛 *muteki* foghorn 950
		口笛 *kuchibue* a whistle 54
	笛	角笛 *tsunobue* bugle; huntsman's horn 473

筒	1472	**TŌ, tsutsu** – pipe, tube
	6f6.15 ⊟	封筒 *fūtō* envelope 1463
	⺮ ⼝ ⼌	水筒 *suitō* canteen, flask 21
	66 24 20	発煙筒 *hatsuentō* smoke candle 96, 919
		円筒 (形) *entō(kei)* cylinder 13, 395
	筒	竹筒 *takezutsu* bamboo tube 129

箇	1473	**KA** – (single) object; (counter for inanimate objects)
	6f8.15 ⊟	箇所 *kasho* place, part, passage (in a book) 153
	⺮ ⼝ ⼗	箇条 *kajō* article, provision, item 564
	66 24 12	箇条書き *kajōgaki* an itemization 564, 131
	箇 ケ	一箇年 *ikkanen* 1 year 2, 45

茎	1474	**KEI, kuki** – stalk, stem
	3k5.23 ⊟	地下茎 *chikakei* underground stem, rhizome 118, 31
	⺾ ⼟ ⼜	球茎 *kyūkei* (tulip) bulb 726
	32 22 9	陰茎 *inkei* penis 867
	茎 莖	歯茎 *haguki* gums 478

径	1475	**KEI** – path; diameter
	3i5.5 ⊞	直径 *chokkei* diameter 423
	⼻ ⼟ ⼜	半径 *hankei* radius 88
	29 22 9	口径 *kōkei* caliber 54
		径路 *keiro* course, route, process 151
	径 徑	直情径行 *chokujō keikō* straightforwardness 423, 209, 68

怪	1476	**KAI, aya(shii)** – dubious; suspicious-looking; strange, mysterious; poor, clumsy **aya(shimu)** – doubt, be sceptical; marvel at, be surprised
	4k5.11 ⊞	
	⼼ ⼟ ⼜	怪物 *kaibutsu* monster, apparition; mystery man 79
	51 22 9	奇怪 *kikai* strange, mysterious; outrageous 1360
	怪 恠	

斉	1477	**SEI** – equal
	2j6.5 ⊟	一斉に *issei ni* all at one, all together 2
	⼇ ⼗ ⼉	均斉 *kinsei* symmetry, good balance 805
	11 12 16	
	斉 齊	

斎 2j9.6 ☐ 亠 小 十 11 35 12 斎 齋	**1478**	*SAI* – religious purification; a room
		書斎 *shosai* a study, library 131 斎戒 *saikai* purification 876 斎戒もく浴 *saikai mokuyoku* ablution, purification 876, 1128
循 3i9.6 ☐ 彳 日 厂 29 55 18 循	**1479**	*JUN* – follow; circulate
		循環 *junkan* circulation 865 血液循環 *ketsueki junkan* blood circulation 789, 472, 865 悪循環 *akujunkan* vicious circle 304, 865
孤 2c6.2 ☐ 子 厂 厶 6 18 17 孤	**1480**	*KO* – lone, alone
		孤独 *kodoku* solitary, lonely 219 孤立 *koritsu* isolation 121 孤島 *kotō* solitary/desert island 286 孤客 *kokaku* solitary traveler 641 孤児(院) *koji(in)* orphan(age) 1217, 614
弧 3h6.2 ☐ 弓 厂 厶 28 18 17 弧	**1481**	*KO* – arc
		弧状 *kojō* arc-shaped 626 円弧 *enko* circular arc 13 括弧 *kakko* parentheses ( ) 1260
従 3i7.3 ☐ 彳 儿 一 29 16 14 従 從	**1482**	*JŪ, [JU], [SHŌ], shitaga(u)* – obey, comply with, follow *shitaga(eru)* – be attended by; conquer
		服従 *fukujū* obedience, submission 683 盲従 *mōjū* blind obedience 1375 従来 *jūrai* up to now, usual, conventional 69 従業員 *jūgyōin* employee 279, 163
縦 6a10.2 ☐ 糸 彳 儿 61 29 16 縦 縱	**1483**	*JŪ, tate* – height, length; vertical
		縦線 *jūsen* vertical line 299 放縦 *hōjū* self-indulgent, dissolute, licentious 512 縦横 *jūō, tateyoko* length and breadth 781 縦断 *jūdan* vertical section; traverse, travel across 1024
為 4d5.8 ☐ 灬 十 一 44 12 1 為 爲	**1484**	*I* – do
		為政者 *iseisha* statesman, administrator 483, 164 人為的 *jin'iteki* artificial 1, 210 行為 *kōi* act, deed; behaviour, conduct 68 無為 *mui* idleness, inaction 93 為替 *kawase* money order; (foreign) exchange 744

1485 2a9.2	***GI, itsuwa(ru)*** – lie, misrepresent, feign, deceive ***nise*** – fake, sham, bogus, counterfeit	
偽	偽造 *gizō* forgery	691
	偽証 *gishō* perjury	484
	真偽 *shingi* true or false, truth	422
	偽物 *nisemono* fake, imitation, counterfeit	79

1486 2a5.11	***JI, ni(ru)*** – be similar (to), be like, resemble	
似	類似 *ruiji* resemblance, similarity	226
	相似 *sōji* resemblance, similarity	146
	似顔 *nigao* likeness, portrait	277
	空似 *sorani* accidental resemblance	140
	似合う *niau* be becoming, suit, go well (with)	159

1487 5b2.2	***SHIN, kara(i)*** – hot, spicy, salty; hard, trying	
辛	辛苦 *shinku* hardships, labor, trouble	545
	辛酸 *shinsan* hardships, privations	516
	辛勝 *shinshō* win after a hard fight	509
	辛抱 *shinbō* patience, perseverance	1285
	辛味 *karami* pungent taste, spiciness	307

1488 3m7.2	***SAI*** – manage, rule	
宰	主宰 *shusai* superintendence, presiding over	155
	主宰者 *shusaisha* president, chairman, leader	155, 164
	宰相 *saishō* prime minister, premier	146

1489 3b13.7	***HEKI, kabe*** – wall	
壁	障壁 *shōheki* fence, wall, barrier, obstacle	858
	防壁 *bōheki* protective wall, bulwark	513
	岩壁 *ganpeki* rock wall/face	1345
	壁画 *hekiga* fresco, mural	343
	壁紙 *kabegami* wallpaper	180

1490 5i13.2	***HEKI, kuse*** – personal habit, quirk, propensity	
癖	性癖 *seiheki* disposition, proclivity	98
	悪癖 *akuheki* bad habit	304
	潔癖 *keppeki* love of cleanliness, fastidiousness	1241
	盗癖 *tōheki* kleptomania	1100
	口癖 *kuchiguse* habit of saying, favorite phrase	54

1491 2q13.3	***HI, sa(keru)*** – avoid	
避	回避 *kaihi* evasion, avoidance	90
	不可避 *fukahi* unavoidable	94, 388
	避難 *hinan* refuge, evacuation	557
	避妊 *hinin* contraception	955
	避雷針 *hiraishin* lightning rod	952, 341

甘	**1492** 0a5.32 ⸛ 艹 一 32 4 甘	**KAN, ama(i)** – sweet; insufficiently salted; indulgent; over-optimistic **ama(eru)** – coax, wheedle, act spoiled, presume upon (another's) love **ama(yakasu)** – be indulgent 甘味料 *kanmiryō* sweetener　307, 319 甘美 *kanbi* sweet, dulcet　401 甘言 *kangen* honeyed words, flattery　66
紺	**1493** 6a5.5 ⬚ 糸 艹 一 61 32 4 紺	**KON** – dark/navy blue 紺色 *kon'iro* dark/navy blue　204 濃紺 *nōkon* deep/dark/navy blue　957 紺屋 *kon'ya, kōya* dyer, dyer's shop　167
某	**1494** 4a5.33 日 木 艹 一 41 32 4 某	**BŌ** – a certain 某所 *bōsho* a certain place　153 某氏 *bōshi* a certain person　566 某国 *bōkoku* a certain country　40 某日 *bōjitsu* a certain day, one day　5 何某 *nanibō* a certain person　390
謀	**1495** 7a9.8 ⬚ 言 木 艹 67 41 32 謀	**BŌ, [MU], haka(ru)** – plan, devise; deceive 陰謀 *inbō* plot, intrigue, conspiracy　867 共謀 *kyōbō* conspiracy, collusion　196 主謀者 *shubōsha* ringleader, mastermind　155, 164 謀略 *bōryaku* strategem, scheme　841 参謀 *sanbō* (general) staff　710
媒	**1496** 3e9.2 ⬚ 女 木 艹 25 41 32 媒	**BAI** – go-between 触媒 *shokubai* catalyst　874 触媒作用 *shokubai sayō* catalytic action　874, 360, 107 媒介 *baikai* mediation; matchmaking　453 媒介物 *baikaibutsu* a medium; carrier (of a disease)　453, 79 霊媒 *reibai* (spiritualistic) medium　1168
搾	**1497** 3c10.9 ⬚ 扌 宀 儿 23 33 16 搾	**SAKU, shibo(ru)** – squeeze, press, extract, milk 圧搾 *assaku* pressure, compression　1342 圧搾器 *assakuki* press, compressor　1342, 527 搾乳 *sakunyū* milk (a cow)　939 搾取 *sakushu* exploitation　65 搾り取る *shiboritoru* press out, extract　65
詐	**1498** 7a5.6 ⬚ 言 𠂉 卜 67 15 13 詐	**SA** – lie, deceive 詐称 *sashō* misrepresent oneself　978 詐取 *sashu* fraud, swindle　65

	1499	**GI, azamu(ku)** – deceive, dupe
欺	4j8.1 田 欠 艹 二 49 32 4 欺	詐欺 *sagi* fraud　1498 詐欺師 *sagishi* swindler　1498, 409

	1500	**HITSU** – compare; alone　*hiki* – (counter for animals)
匹	2t2.3 回 匚 儿 20 16 匹	匹敵 *hitteki* be a match (for), comparable (to)　416 匹夫 *hippu* man; man of humble position　315 犬一匹 *inu ippiki* 1 dog　280, 2

	1501	**JIN, hanaha(da/dashii)** – very much, extreme, great, enormous, intense
甚	0a9.10 日 艹 二 一 32 4 14 甚	甚大 *jindai* very great, immense, serious, heavy　26 激甚 *gekijin* intense, violent, severe　1017 幸甚 *kōjin* very glad, much obliged　684 甚六 *jinroku* simpleton, blockhead　8

	1502	**KAN** – perception, intuition, sixth sense
勘	2g9.3 田 力 艹 二 8 32 4 勘	勘定 *kanjō* counting, accounts, bill　355 割り勘 *warikan* splitting the bill equally, Dutch treat　519 勘弁 *kanben* pardon, forgive, overlook　711 勘違い *kanchigai* misunderstanding, mistaken idea　814 勘当 *kandō* disown, disinherit　77

	1503	**SHU** – scarlet
朱	0a6.13 … 牛 儿 47 16 朱	朱色 *shuiro* scarlet, cinnabar, vermilion　204 朱印 *shuin* red seal　1043 朱肉 *shuniku* red ink pad　223 朱筆を加える *shuhitsu o kuwaeru* correct, retouch　130, 709

	1504	**SHU** – pearl
珠	4f6.2 田 王 牛 儿 46 47 16 珠	真珠 *shinju* pearl　422 珠玉 *shugyoku* jewel, gem　295 珠算 *shuzan* calculation on the abacus　747 数珠 *juzu* rosary　225 真珠湾 *Shinju-wan* Pearl Harbor　422, 670

	1505	**SHU, koto (ni)** – especially, in particular
殊	0a10.7 田 牛 夕 儿 47 30 16 殊	特殊 *tokushu* special, unique　282 特殊性 *tokushusei* special characteristics, peculiarity　282, 98 殊勝 *shushō* admirable, praiseworthy　509 殊の外 *koto no hoka* exceedingly, exceptionally　83

殖	**1506** 5c7.4 田 日 夕 十 55 30 12 殖	**SHOKU, fu(eru)** – grow in number, increase **fu(yasu)** – increase 増 殖　*zōshoku*　increase, multiply, proliferate　712 生 殖　*seishoku*　reproduction, procreation　44 繁 殖　*hanshoku*　breeding, reproduction　1292 養 殖　*yōshoku*　raising, culture, cultivation　402
迭	**1507** 2q5.2 凵 辶 大 宀 19 34 15 迭	**TETSU** – alternation 更 迭　*kōtetsu*　change (in personnel), reshuffle　1008
秩	**1508** 5d5.2 田 禾 大 宀 56 34 15 秩	**CHITSU** – order, sequence 秩 序　*chitsujo*　order, system, regularity　770 安 寧秩 序　*annei-chitsujo*　peace and order　105, 1412, 770 無 秩序　*muchitsujo*　disorder, chaos, confusion　93, 770 秩 父　*Chichibu*　(resort area NW of Tōkyō)　113
伐	**1509** 2a4.5 凵 亻 戈 3　52 伐	**BATSU** – attack; cut down 征 伐　*seibatsu*　conquest, subjugation　1114 討 伐　*tōbatsu*　subjugation, suppression　1018 殺 伐　*satsubatsu*　bloody, savage, warlike, fierce　576 伐 採　*bassai*　timber felling, lumbering　933 乱 伐　*ranbatsu*　reckless deforestation, overcutting　689
閥	**1510** 8e6.2 囗 門 戈 亻 76 52 3 閥	**BATSU** – clique, clan, faction 派 閥　*habatsu*　clique, faction　912 財 閥　*zaibatsu*　financial combine　553 軍 閥　*gunbatsu*　military clique, the militarists　438 藩 閥　*hanbatsu*　clan, clique, faction　1382 門 閥　*monbatsu*　lineage; distinguished family　161
闘	**1511** 8e10.2 囗 門 口 寸 76 24 37 闘 鬪	**TŌ, tataka(u)** – fight, struggle 闘 争　*tōsō*　struggle, conflict; strike　302 戦 闘　*sentō*　battle, combat　301 奮 闘　*funtō*　hard fighting, strenuous efforts　1309 春 闘　*shuntō*　spring (labor) offensive　460 格 闘　*kakutō*　hand-to-hand fighting, scuffle　643
頼	**1512** 9a7.1 囗 頁 木 口 77 41 24 頼 賴	**RAI, tano(mu)** – ask for, request; entrust (to) **tano(moshii)** – reliable, dependable; promising **tayo(ru)** – rely, depend (on) 依 頼　*irai*　request; entrust (to); reliance　678 信 頼　*shinrai*　reliance, trust, confidence　157 頼 信 紙　*raishinshi*　telegram form　157, 180

	1513	*se* – shallows; rapids	
瀬	3a16.3 ⊞	浅瀬 *asase* shoal, shallows, sandbank; ford	649
	氵 頁木	早瀬 *hayase* swift current, rapids ⌐war)	248
	21 77 41	瀬戸際 *setogiwa* crucial moment, crisis, brink (of	152, 618
	瀬 瀬	瀬戸物 *setomono* porcelain, china, earthenware	152, 79
		瀬戸内海 *Seto Naikai* Seto Inland Sea	152, 84, 117

	1514	*SO, uto(mu)* – shun, neglect, treat coldly	
疎	0a11.4 ⊞	*uto(i)* – distant, estranged; know little (of)	
	木 ㅁ ㅏ	疎遠 *soen* estrangement, alienation	446
	41 24 13	疎開 *sokai* evacuation, removal	396
	疎 疎	空疎 *kūso* empty, unsubstantial ⌐understanding	140
		(意志 の) 疎通 *(ishi no) sotsū* mutual	132, 573, 150

	1515	*SO, ishizue* – cornerstone, foundation (stone)	
礎	5a13.2 ⊞	基礎 *kiso* foundation, basis ⌐groundwork	450
	石 木 一	基礎工事 *kiso kōji* foundation work,	450, 139, 80
	53 41 14	基礎知識 *kiso chishiki* elementary knowledge	450, 214, 681
	礎	礎石 *soseki* foundation (stone)	78
		定礎式 *teisoshiki* laying of the cornerstone	355, 525

	1516	*GI, utaga(u)* – be doubtful of, be suspicious of, distrust	
疑	2m12.1 ⊞	疑問 *gimon* question, doubt, problem	162
	ㅏ 大 ㅏ	疑惑 *giwaku* suspicion, distrust, misgivings	969
	13 34 15	疑獄 *gigoku* scandal	884
	疑	容疑者 *yōgisha* a suspect ⌐(session)	654, 164
		質疑応答 *shitsugi-ōtō* question and answer	176, 827, 160

	1517	*GI* – imitate	
擬	3c14.2 ⊞	擬人 *gijin* personification	1
	扌 大 ㅏ	擬音 *gion* an imitated sound; sound effects	347
	23 34 13	模擬 *mogi* imitation, simulated	1425
	擬	模擬試験 *mogi shiken* mock/trial examination	
			1425, 526, 532

	1518	*GYŌ, ko(ru)* – grow stiff; be engrossed (in); be fastidious,	
凝	2b14.1 ⊞	elaborate (about) *ko(rasu)* – concentrate, strain	
	氵 大 ㅏ	凝固 *gyōko* solidification, coagulation, freezing	972
	5 34 13	凝結 *gyōketsu* coagulation, curdling, condensation	485
	凝	凝視 *gyōshi* stare at, watch intently	606
		凝り性 *korishō* fastidiousness, perfectionism	98

	1519	*SATSU, su(reru)* – rub, chafe; become worn; lose one's simplicity	
擦	3c14.5 ⊞	*su(ru)* – rub, file	
	扌 木 宀	擦過傷 *sakkashō* an abrasion, scratch	413, 633
	23 45 33	靴擦れ *kutsuzure* shoe sore	1076
	擦	擦れ違う *surechigau* pass by each other	814
		擦り傷 *surikizu* an abrasion, scratch	633

	1520	**SATSU** – pick, pinch; summarize **to(ru)** – take (a picture)	
撮	3c12.13	撮影 *satsuei* photography, filming	854
	扌 耳 日	撮影所 *satsueijo* movie studio	854, 153
	23 65 43	夜間撮影 *yakan satsuei* night photography	471, 43, 854
	撮	戸/野外撮影 *ko/yagai satsuei* outdoor photography, outdoor shooting	152, 236, 83, 854

	1521	**HI, iya(shimeru/shimu)** – despise, look down on	
卑	5f4.8	**iya(shii)** – humble, lowly; base, ignoble, vulgar	
	田 十 丨	卑俗 *hizoku* vulgar, coarse	1126
	58 12 2	卑劣漢 *hiretsukan* mean bastard, low-down skunk	1150, 556
	卑 卑	卑語 *higo* vulgar word/expression ⌈over women	67
		男尊女卑 *danson-johi* predominance of men	101, 704, 102

	1522	**HI** – tombstone, monument	
碑	5a9.2	記念碑 *kinenhi* monument, memorial	371, 579
	石 田 十	墓碑 *bohi* tombstone, gravestone	1429
	53 58 12	石碑 *sekihi* tombstone, (stone) monument	78
	碑 碑	碑文 *hibun* epitaph, inscription	111

	1523	**KI, oni** – ogre, demon, devil; soul of a dead person	
鬼	5f5.6	鬼神 *kijin, kishin, onigami* fierce god; departed soul	310
	田 儿 厶	餓鬼 *gaki* hungry ghost; little brat	1303
	58 16 17	鬼才 *kisai* genius, man of remarkable talent	551
	鬼	鬼ごっこ *onigokko* tag; blindman's buff	

	1524	**KAI, katamari** – lump, clod, clump	
塊	3b10.2	土塊 *dokai* clod of dirt	24
	土 田 儿	金塊 *kinkai* gold nugget/bar	23
	22 58 16	肉塊 *nikkai* piece of meat	223
	塊	塊根 *kaikon* tuberous root	314
		塊状 *kaijō* massive	626

	1525	**KON, tamashii** – soul, spirit	
魂	5f9.2	霊魂 *reikon* the soul	1168
	田 二 厶	商魂 *shōkon* commercial spirit, salesmanship	412
	58 4 17	魂胆 *kontan* soul; ulterior motive	1273
	魂	負けじ魂 *makeji-damashii* unyielding spirit	510
		大和魂 *Yamato-damashii* the Japanese spirit	26, 124

	1526	**MI** – charm, enchant, fascinate	
魅	5f10.1	魅力 *miryoku* charm, appeal, fascination	100
	田 木 儿	魅力的 *miryokuteki* fascinating, captivating	100, 210
	58 41 16	魅了 *miryō* charm, captivate, hold spellbound	941
	魅	魅惑 *miwaku* fascination, charm, lure	969

醜	**1527** 7e10.1 ⊞ 酉 甶 儿 71 58 16 醜	***SHŪ, miniku(i)*** – ugly

醜聞 *shūbun* scandal — 64
醜悪 *shūaku* ugly, abominable, scandalous — 304
醜態 *shūtai* unseemly sight; disgraceful behavior — 387
醜女 *shūjo, shikome* ugly woman — 102
美醜 *bishū* beauty or ugliness, appearance — 401

魔	**1528** 3q18.2 ⊡ 广 甶 木 18 58 41 魔	***MA*** – demon, devil, evil spirit

悪魔 *akuma* devil — 304
魔術 *majutsu* black magic, sorcery, witchcraft — 187
魔法 *mahō* magic — 123
魔法瓶 *mahōbin* thermos bottle — 123, 1161
邪魔 *jama* encumbrance, interruption, disturbance — 1457

麻	**1529** 3q8.3 广 木 18 41 麻	***MA, asa*** – flax, hemp

大麻 *taima, ōasa* hemp, marijuana — 26
麻薬 *mayaku* narcotics, drugs — 359
麻ひ *mahi* paralysis
小児麻ひ *shōni mahi* infantile paralysis, polio — 27, 1217
麻糸 *asaito* hempen yarn, linen thread — 242

摩	**1530** 3q12.6 ⊡ 广 木 扌 18 41 23 摩	***MA*** – rub, rub off, scrape

摩擦 *masatsu* friction — 1519
冷水摩擦 *reisui masatsu* rubdown with a wet towel — 832, 21, 1519
あん摩 *anma* massage; masseur, masseuse

磨	**1531** 3q13.3 ⊡ 广 石 木 18 53 41 磨	***MA, miga(ku)*** – polish, brush

研磨 *kenma* grind, polish; study hard — 896
磨滅 *mametsu* wear, abrasion — 1338
達磨 *daruma* Bodhidharma; quadruple amputee; prostitute — 448
歯磨き *hamigaki* toothpaste — 478
磨き上げる *migakiageru* polish up — 32

閑	**1532** 8e4.2 ⊡ 門 木 76 41 閑	***KAN*** – leisure

閑静 *kansei* quiet, peaceful — 663
森閑 *shinkan* stillness, quiet — 128
安閑 *ankan* idleness — 105
閑散 *kansan* leisure; (market) inactivity — 767
農閑期 *nōkanki* the slack season for farming — 369, 449

簡	**1533** 6f12.5 ⊟ 竹 門 日 66 76 43 簡	***KAN*** – simple, brief

簡単 *kantan* simple, brief — 300
簡略 *kanryaku* simple, concise — 841
簡潔 *kanketsu* concise — 1241
簡素 *kanso* plain and simple — 271
書簡 *shokan* letter, correspondence — 131

1534	**REKI, koyomi** – calendar
2p12.3	西暦 *seireki* the Western calendar, A.D. 72
厂木日	旧暦 *kyūreki* the old (lunar) calendar 1216
18 41 43	太陽暦 *taiyōreki* the solar calendar 629, 630
	還暦 *kanreki* one's 60th birthday 866
暦暦	花暦 *hanagoyomi* floral calendar 255

1535	**KA** – cake; fruit
3k8.2	(お)菓子 *(o)kashi* candy, confections, pastry 103
艹日木	菓子屋 *kashiya* candy store, confectionery shop 103, 167
32 43 41	和菓子 *wagashi* Japanese-style confection 124, 103
	茶菓 *chaka, saka* tea and cake, refreshments 251
菓	水菓子 *mizugashi* fruit 21, 103

1536	**RA, hadaka** – naked
5e8.1	裸婦 *rafu* nude woman 316
衤日木	裸体画 *rataiga* nude picture 61, 343
57 43 41	赤裸々 *sekirara* naked; frank, outspoken 207
	裸馬 *hadakauma* unsaddled horse ⌐body 283
裸	裸一貫 *hadaka-ikkan* with no property but one's own 2, 914

1537	**KIN, eri** – neck; collar, lapel
5e13.2	胸襟 *kyōkin* bosom, heart 1283
衤木衤	開襟シャツ *kaikin shatsu* open-necked shirt 396
57 41 45	襟巻き *erimaki* muffler, scarf 507
	襟首 *erikubi* nape, back/scruff of the neck 148
襟	襟元 *erimoto* the neck 137

1538	**SŌ, su** – nest
3n8.1	卵巣 *ransō* ovary ⌐inflammation 1058
艹日木	炎症病巣 *enshō byōsō* focus of an 1336, 1318, 380
35 43 41	古巣 *furusu* old nest, one's old haunt 172
	空き巣(ねらい) *akisu(nerai)* sneak thief 140
巣巣	巣立ち *sudachi* leave the nest, become independent 121

1539	**DAN, tama** – bullet **hazu(mu)** – bounce; be stimulated; fork out, splurge on **hi(ku)** – play (piano/guitar)
3h9.3	
弓日小	爆弾 *bakudan* a bomb 1015
28 43 35	弾薬 *dan'yaku* ammunition 359
	弾丸 *dangan* projectile, bullet, shell 644
弾彈	弾力 *danryoku* elasticity 100

1540	**ZEN** – Zen Buddhism
4e9.2	禅宗 *Zenshū* the Zen sect 616
衤日小	座禅 *zazen* religious meditation (done while sitting) 786
45 43 35	禅僧 *zensō* Zen priest 1366
	禅寺 *zendera* Zen temple ⌐dialogue 41
禅禪	禅問答 *zen mondō* Zen dialogue; incomprehensible 162, 160

奉	**1541** 0a8.13 […] 大 一 十 34 4 12 奉	**HŌ, [BU], tatematsu(ru)** – offer, present; revere 奉 納 *hōnō* dedication, offering　758 奉 献 *hōken* dedication, consecration　1355 信 奉 *shinpō* belief, faith　157 奉 仕 *hōshi* attendance; service　333 奉 公 *hōkō* public duty; domestic service　126
俸	**1542** 2a8.18 ☐ 亻 大 一 3 34 4 俸	**HŌ** – salary 俸 給 *hōkyū* salary, pay　346 年 俸 *nenpō* annual salary　45 号 俸 *gōhō* pay level, salary class　266 減 俸 *genpō* salary reduction, pay cut ⌐allowance　715 年 功 加 俸 *nenkō kahō* long-service pension/　45, 818, 709
棒	**1543** 4a8.20 ☐ 木 大 一 41 34 4 棒	**BŌ** – stick, pole 鉄 棒 *tetsubō* iron bar; the horizontal bar (in gymnastics)　312 心 棒 *shinbō* axle, shaft　97 棒 立 ち *bōdachi* standing bolt upright　121 相 棒 *aibō* pal; accomplice　146 棒 暗 記 *bōanki* indiscriminate/rote memorization　348, 371
奏	**1544** 0a9.17 […] 大 一 一 34 4 1 奏	**SŌ, kana(deru)** – play (a musical instrument) 演 奏 会 *ensōkai* concert, recital　344, 158 前 奏 *zensō* prelude　47 独 奏 *dokusō* a solo (performance)　219 二 重 奏 *nijūsō* duet　3, 227 伴 奏 *bansō* accompaniment　1027
泰	**1545** 3a5.34 […] 氵 大 一 21 34 4 泰	**TAI** – calm, peace 泰 然 自 若 *taizen jijaku* imperturbability　651, 62, 544 安 泰 *antai* tranquility; security　105 泰 平 *taihei* peace, tranquility　202 泰 西 *taisei* Occident, the West　72 泰 西 名 画 *taisei meiga* famous Western painting　72, 82, 343
漆	**1546** 3a11.10 ☐ 氵 木 亻 21 41 3 漆	**SHITSU, urushi** – lacquer 漆 器 *shikki* lacquerware　527 漆 黒 *shikkoku* jet-black, pitch-black ⌐Buddha)　206 乾 漆 像 *kanshitsuzō* dry-lacquered image (of　1190, 740 漆 く い *shikkui* mortar, plaster 漆 塗 り *urushinuri* lacquered, japanned　1073
慈	**1547** 2o11.1 ☐ 丷 心 厶 16 51 17 慈 慈	**JI, itsuku(shimu)** – love, treat with affection 慈 善 *jizen* charity, philanthropy　1139 慈 悲 *jihi* mercy, benevolence, pity　1034 慈 恵 *jikei* charity　1219 慈 愛 *jiai* affection, kindness, love　259 慈 雨 *jiu* beneficial/welcome rain　30

磁	1548 5a9.6 ⊞ 石 儿 ム 53 16 17 磁	JI – magnetism; porcelain
		磁気 *jiki* magnetism, magnetic 134
		磁石 *jishaku* magnet 78
		電磁石 *denjishaku* electromagnet 108, 78
		磁場 *jiba, jijō* magnetic field 154
		磁器 *jiki* porcelain 527

滋	1549 3a9.27 ⊞ 氵 儿 ム 21 16 17 滋	JI – more and more, luxuriant
		滋養 *jiyō* nourishment, nutrition 402
		滋養分 *jiyōbun* nutritious element, nutriment 402, 38
		滋賀県 *Shiga-ken* Shiga Prefecture 756, 194

寿	1550 0a7.15 … 寸 十 一 37 12 4 寿 壽	JU, kotobuki – congratulations; longevity
		寿命 *jumyō* lifespan, life 578
		天寿 *tenju* one's natural span of life 141
		長寿 *chōju* longevity 95
		喜寿 *kiju* one's 77th birthday 1143
		寿司 *sushi* raw fish and other delicacies with vinegared ⌐rice 842

鋳	1551 8a7.2 ⊡ 金 寸 十 72 37 12 鋳 鑄	CHŪ, i(ru) – cast (metal)
		鋳造 *chūzō* casting; minting, coinage 691
		鋳鉄 *chūtetsu* cast iron 312
		改鋳 *kaichū* recoinage; recasting 514
		鋳型 *igata* a mold, cast 888
		鋳物 *imono* an article of cast metal, a casting 79

銘	1552 8a6.4 ⊡ 金 夕 口 72 30 24 銘	MEI – inscription, signature, name; precept, motto
		銘記 *meiki* bear in mind 371
		感銘 *kanmei* deep impression 262
		銘柄 *meigara* a brand (name) 985
		座右銘 *zayūmei* motto 786, 76
		碑銘 *himei* inscription; epitaph 1522

雇	1553 4m8.1 ⊡ 戸 隹 40 74 雇 雇	KO, yato(u) – employ; charter
		終身雇用制 *shūshin koyōsei* lifetime employment system 458, 59, 107, 427
		解雇 *kaiko* dismiss, fire 474
		雇い人 *yatoinin* employee; servant 1
		雇い主 *yatoinushi* employer 155

顧	1554 9a12.2 ⊡ 頁 隹 尸 77 74 40 顧 顧	KO, kaeri(miru) – look back; take into consideration
		回顧 *kaiko* recollection, retrospect 90
		回顧録 *kaikoroku* reminiscences, memoirs 90, 538
		顧慮 *koryo* regard, consideration 1384
		顧問 *komon* adviser 162
		顧客 *kokaku, kokyaku* customer 641

	1555	**SEN, ōgi** – fan, folding fan	
	4m6.1	扇子　*sensu*　folding fan	103
	戸 ヨ	扇風機　*senpūki*　electric fan	29, 528
	40　39	扇形　*senkei, ōgigata*　fan shape, sector, segment	395
	扇	扇動　*sendō*　incitement, instigation, agitation	231
		舞扇　*maiōgi*　dancer's fan	810

	1556	**HI, tobira** – door; title page	
	4m8.2	開扉　*kaihi*　opening of the door	396
	戸 儿 二	門扉　*monpi*　the doors of a gate	161
	40　16　4		
	扉 扉		

	1557	**SOKU, unaga(su)** – urge, prompt, spur on	
	2a7.3	促進　*sokushin*　promotion, acceleration	437
	亻 𠯢	催促　*saisoku*　press, urge, demand	1317
	3　70	促成　*sokusei*　artificially accelerate, force (growth)	261
	促		

	1558	**YŌ, odo(ru)** – dance　**odo(ri)** – a dance, dancing	
	7d7.2	舞踊　*buyō*　a dance, dancing	810
	𧾷 月 一	盆踊り　*Bon odori*　Bon Festival dance	1099
	70　42　1	踊り子　*odoriko*　dancer, dancing girl	103
	踊 踴	踊り狂う　*odorikuruu*　dance ecstatically	883
		踊り場　*odoriba*　dance hall/floor; (stairway) landing	154

	1559	**TŌ, fu(mu)** – step on　**fu(maeru)** – stand on, be based on	
	7d8.3	舞踏会　*butōkai*　ball, dance party	810, 158
	𧾷 日 氵	雑踏　*zattō*　hustle and bustle, (traffic) congestion	575
	70　43　21	踏査　*tōsa*　survey, field investigation	624
	踏 蹈	踏切　*fumikiri*　railroad crossing	39
		足踏み　*ashibumi*　step, stamp, mark time	58

	1560	**YAKU, odo(ru)** – jump, leap, hop	
	7d14.2	飛躍　*hiyaku*　a leap; activity; rapid progress	530
	𧾷 隹 ヨ	活躍　*katsuyaku*　active, action	237
	70　74　39	暗躍　*an'yaku*　behind-the-scenes maneuvering	348
	躍	躍進　*yakushin*　advance by leaps and bounds	437
		躍動　*yakudō*　lively motion	231

	1561	**TAKU** – wash, rinse	
	3a14.5	洗濯　*sentaku*　washing, the wash, laundry	692
	氵 隹 ヨ	洗濯機　*sentakuki*　washing machine, washer	692, 528
	21　74　39	洗濯物　*sentakumono*　the wash, laundry	692, 79
	濯 濯		

	1562	**CHŌ** – sign, indication; trillion **kiza(shi)** – sign, symptoms
	2b4.4	**kiza(su)** – show signs; sprout, germinate
	亻儿乀 5 16 10	兆候 *chōkō* sign, indication 944
		前兆 *zenchō* omen, portent, foreshadowing 47
	兆兆	吉兆 *kitchō* good omen/sign 1141
		億兆 *okuchō* the multitude, the people 382

	1563	**CHŌ, to(bu), ha(neru)** – leap, spring up, jump, bounce
	7d6.3	跳躍 *chōyaku* spring, jump, leap 1560
	𧾷亻儿 70 5 16	跳び上がる *tobiagaru* jump up 32
		跳ね上がる *haneagaru* jump up ⌐jump 32
	跳	走り高跳び *hashiri-takatobi* the (running) high 429, 190
		飛び跳ねる *tobihaneru* jump up and down 530

	1564	**CHŌ, ido(mu)** – challenge
	3c6.5	挑戦 *chōsen* challenge 301
	扌亻儿 23 5 16	挑戦者 *chōsensha* challenger 301, 164
		挑発 *chōhatsu* arouse, excite, provoke 96
	挑	挑発的 *chōhatsuteki* provocative, suggestive 96, 210

	1565	**CHŌ, naga(meru)** – look at, watch, gaze at
	5c6.2	眺望 *chōbō* a view (from a window) 673
	目亻儿 55 5 16	
	眺	

	1566	**TŌ, ni(geru)** – run away, escape, flee **noga(reru)** – escape
	2q6.5	**ni(gasu), noga(su)** – let go, set free; let escape
	辶亻儿 19 5 16	逃走 *tōsō* escape, flight, desertion 429
		逃亡 *tōbō* escape, flight, desertion 672
	逃逃	逃げ出す *nigedasu* break into a run, run off/away 53
		見逃す *minogasu* overlook 63

	1567	**TŌ, momo** – peach
	4a6.10	桃色 *momoiro* pink 204
	木亻儿 41 5 16	桃の節句 *Momo no Sekku* Doll Festival (March 3) 464, 337
		桃山時代 *Momoyama jidai* Momoyama period
	桃	(1583–1602) 34, 42, 256
		桃源郷/境 *Tōgenkyō* Shangri-la, paradise on earth 580, 855, 864

	1568	**SEN** – step, step up; realize, put into practice
	7d6.1	実践 *jissen* practice 203
	𧾷戈丨 70 52 2	実践的 *jissenteki* practical 203, 210
		実践理性批判 *Jissen Risei Hihan* (Critique of Practical
	践踐	Reason – Kant) 203, 143, 98, 1029, 1026

	1569	**SEKI, ato** – mark, traces, vestiges, remains, ruins	
跡	7d6.7 ⊞	遺 跡 *iseki* remains, ruins, relics	1172
	𧾷 一 儿	史 跡 *shiseki* historic site/relics	332
	70 11 16	足 跡 *ashiato, sokuseki* footprint	58
		傷 跡 *kizuato* a scar	633
	跡	跡 継 ぎ *atotsugi* successor, heir	1025

	1570	**SHA** – forgive	
赦	4i7.3 ⊞	大 赦 *taisha* (general) amnesty	26
	攵 土 儿	恩 赦 *onsha* an amnesty, general pardon	555
	49 22 16	赦 免 *shamen* pardon, clemency	733
		特 赦 *tokusha* an amnesty	282
	赦	容 赦 *yōsha* pardon, forgiveness, mercy	654

	1571	**SEN** – fine, slender	
繊	6a11.1 ⊡	繊 維 *sen'i* fiber, textiles	1231
	糸 戈 十	繊 維 工 業 *sen'i kōgyō* textile industry	1231, 139, 279
	61 52 12	合 成 繊 維 *gōsei sen'i* synthetic fiber	159, 261, 1231
		化 繊 *kasen* synthetic fiber	254
	繊 纖	繊 細 *sensai* delicate, fine, subtle	695

	1572	**KYO, [KO]** – empty	
虚	2m9.1 ⊡	虚 無 主 義 *kyomu shugi* nihilism	93, 155, 291
	⼧ ⼚ 十	虚 栄 (心) *kyoei(shin)* vanity	723, 97
	(13) 18 12	虚 弱 *kyojaku* weak, feeble, frail	218
		虚 偽 *kyogi* false, untrue	1485
	虚 虛	虚 空 *kokū* empty space, the air	140

	1573	**GI, tawamu(reru)** – play, sport; jest, flirt	
戯	4n11.1 ⊡	遊 戯 *yūgi* amusement	1003
	戈 ⼚ 十	戯 曲 *gikyoku* drama, play	366
	52 18 12	前 戯 *zengi* (sexual) foreplay	47
		戯 画 *giga* a caricature	343
	戯 戲	悪 戯 *akugi, itazura* mischief, prank; lewdness	304

	1574	**GYAKU, shiita(geru)** – oppress, tyrannize	
虐	2m7.3 ⊡	虐 待 *gyakutai* treat cruelly, mistreat	452
	⼧ ⼚ 十	暴 虐 *bōgyaku* tyrannical, cruel	1014
	(13) 18 12	虐 殺 *gyakusatsu* massacre, slaughter, butchery	576
		残 虐 *zangyaku* cruel, brutal, inhuman	650
	虐 虐	自 虐 的 *jigyakuteki* self-torturing	62, 210

	1575	**SHŪ, oso(u)** – attack, assail; succeed to, inherit	
襲	5e16.2 ⊟	来 襲 *raishū* attack, assault, invasion	69
	⻂ 立 月	空 襲 *kūshū* air raid	140
	57 54 42	夜 襲 *yashū* night attack	471
		世 襲 *seshū* hereditary	252
	襲	因 襲 *inshū* long-established custom, convention	554

祥	**1576** 4e6.1 ⊞ 木 王 儿 45 46 16 祥 祥	**SHŌ** – happiness; good omen 不祥事 *fushōji* scandal 　　　　　　　　　94, 80 発祥 *hasshō* origin 　　　　　　　　　　　96 発祥地 *hasshōchi* birthplace, cradle 　　96, 118 吉祥 *kisshō* good omen 　　　　　　　　1141 吉祥天 *Kichijōten, Kisshōten* (Buddhist goddess) 1141, 141
詳	**1577** 7a6.12 ⊞ 言 王 儿 67 46 16 詳	**SHŌ, kuwa(shii)** – detailed, full; familiar with (something) 詳細 *shōsai* details, particulars 　　　　695 不詳 *fushō* unknown, unidentified 　　　94 未詳 *mishō* unknown, unidentified 　　306 詳報 *shōhō* full/detailed report 　　　685 詳述 *shōjutsu* detailed explanation, full account 968
黙	**1578** 4d11.5 ⊟ 火 日 土 44 43 22 黙 默	**MOKU, dama(ru)** – become silent, say nothing 沈黙 *chinmoku* silence 　　　　　　　936 黙認 *mokunin* tacit approval 　　　　738 黙殺 *mokusatsu* take no notice of, ignore 576 黙秘権 *mokuhiken* right against self-incrimination 807, 335
猛	**1579** 3g7.4 ⊞ 犭 皿 子 27 59 6 猛	**MŌ** – strong, fierce 猛烈 *mōretsu* fierce, violent, strong 　1331 猛打 *mōda* hard hit, heavy blow 　　1020 猛暑 *mōsho* fierce heat 　　　　　　638 猛犬 *mōken* vicious dog 　　　　　　280 猛者 *mosa* man of courage, stalwart veteran 164
猟	**1580** 3g8.6 ⊞ 犭 小 冂 27 35 20 猟 獵	**RYŌ** – hunting 猟師 *ryōshi* hunter 　　　　　　　　409 密猟者 *mitsuryōsha* poacher 　　　806, 164 猟犬 *ryōken* hunting dog 　　　　　280 猟銃 *ryōjū* hunting gun, shotgun 　　829 禁猟 *kinryō* prohibition on hunting 　482
狩	**1581** 3g6.5 ⊞ 犭 宀 寸 27 33 37 狩	**SHU, ka(ri)** – hunting　**ka(ru)** – hunt 狩猟(期) *shuryō(ki)* hunting (season) 1580, 449 狩り小屋 *karigoya* hunting cabin 　27, 167 狩人 *karyūdo* hunter 　　　　　　　　1 潮干狩り *shiohigari* shell gathering (at low tide) 468, 584 みかん狩り *mikangari* picking mandarin oranges
獣	**1582** 3g12.3 ⊟ 犭 田 小 27 58 35 獣 獸	**JŪ, kemono** – animal, beast 野獣 *yajū* wild animal 　　　　　　　236 猛獣 *mōjū* vicious animal, ferocious beast 1579 怪獣 *kaijū* monster 　　　　　　　1476 鳥獣保護区域 *chōjū hogo kuiki* 285, 489, 1312, 183, 970 獣医 *jūi* veterinarian 　⌞wildlife sanctuary　220

猶	**1583** 3g9.5 犭 酉 儿 27 71 16 猶	**YŪ** – delay; still, still more

猶予 *yūyo* postponement, deferment　393
猶予なく *yūyonaku* without delay, promptly　393
執行猶予 *shikkō yūyo* suspended sentence, probation
　　　　　686, 68, 393

猿	**1584** 3g10.3 犭 衤 土 27 57 22 猿	**EN, saru** – monkey

野猿 *yaen* wild monkey　236
類人猿 *rujin'en* anthropoid ape　226, 1
猿知恵 *sarujie* shallow cleverness　214, 1219
犬猿の仲 *ken'en no naka* hating each other, like cats
　　　　　and dogs　280, 1347

衡	**1585** 3i13.1 彳 田 大 29 58 34 衡	**KŌ** – scales, weigh

均衡 *kinkō* balance, equilibrium　805
平衡 *heikō* balance, equilibrium　202
平衡感覚 *heikō kankaku* sense of equilibrium　202, 262, 605
度量衡 *doryōkō* weights and measures　377, 411

換	**1586** 3c9.15 扌 大 宀 23 34 15 換 換	**KAN, ka(eru)** – substitute **ka(waru)** – be replaced

交換 *kōkan* exchange, substitution　114
転換 *tenkan* conversion, switchover; diversion　433
変換 *henkan* change, conversion　257
換算(率) *kansan(ritsu)* conversion, exchange (rate)　747, 788
乗り換える *norikaeru* transfer, change (trains)　523

喚	**1587** 3d9.19 口 大 宀 24 34 15 喚	**KAN** – call

召喚 *shōkan* summons, subpoena　「witness)　995
(証人)喚問 *(shōnin) kanmon* summons (of a　484, 1, 162
喚起 *kanki* evoke, awaken, call forth　373
叫喚 *kyōkan* shout, outcry, scream　1252
あ鼻叫喚 *abikyōkan* (2 Buddhist hells); bedlam　813, 1252

融	**1588** 6d10.5 虫 口 冂 64 24 20 融	**YŪ** – dissolve, melt

融合 *yūgō* fusion　159
融通 *yūzū* accomodation, loan; versatility　150
金融 *kin'yū* money, finance　23
金融機関 *kin'yū kikan* financial institution　23, 528, 398
融資 *yūshi* financing, loan　750

隔	**1589** 2d10.2 阝 口 冂 7 24 20 隔 隔	**KAKU, heda(teru)** – separate, interpose; estrange **heda(taru)** – be distant, apart; become estranged

間隔 *kankaku* space, spacing, interval　43
隔離 *kakuri* isolation, quarantine　1281
遠隔 *enkaku* distant, remote, outlying　446
横隔膜 *ōkakumaku* the diaphragm　781, 1426

1590	**TEI** – offer, present, exhibit	
3d4.14 ☐	進呈 *shintei* give, present	437
口 王	贈呈 *zōtei* present, donate	1364
24 46	献呈本 *kenteibon* presentation copy	1355, 25
	謹呈 *kintei* With the compliments of the author	1247
呈	露呈 *rotei* exposure, disclosure	951

1591	**ZE** – right, correct, just	
4c5.9 ☐	是非 *zehi* right and wrong; by all means	498
日 一 亻	是正 *zesei* correct, rectify	275
43 14 3	是認 *zenin* approval, sanction	738
是	是々非々 *zeze-hihi* being fair and unbiased	498

1592	**TEI, *tsutsumi*** – bank, embankment, dike	
3b9.7 ⊞	堤防 *teibō* embankment, dike, levee	513
土 日 一	防波堤 *bōhatei* breakwater	513, 666
22 43 14		
堤		

1593	***mata*** – again; also, moreover	
2h0.1 ☐	又聞き *matagiki* hearsay, secondhand information	64
又	又貸し *matagashi* sublease	748
9	又々 *matamata* once again	
又 又	又は *matawa* or, either … or …	

1594	**SŌ, *futa*** – pair, both	
2h2.1 ⊞	双方 *sōhō* both parties/sides	70
又	双生児 *sōseiji* twins	44, 1217
9	双眼鏡 *sōgankyō* binoculars	848, 863
	双肩 *sōken* one's shoulders	1264
双 雙	双子 *futago* twins	103

1595	**DO, *tsuto(meru)*** – exert oneself, make efforts, strive	
2g5.6 ⊞	努力 *doryoku* effort, endeavor	100
力 女 又	努力家 *doryokuka* hard worker	100, 165
8 25 9		
努		

1596	**DO, *oko(ru)*, *ika(ru)*** – get angry	
4k5.19 ⊞	怒気 *doki* (fit of) anger	134
心 女 又	激怒 *gekido* wild rage, wrath, fury ⌈be infuriated	1017
51 25 9	怒髪天を突く *dohatsu ten o tsuku*	1148, 141, 898
	怒号 *dogō* angry roar	266
怒	喜怒 *kido* joy and anger, emotion	1143

	1597	**YŪ** – distant; leisure	
悠	4k7.20 曰	悠然 *yūzen* calm, perfect composure	651
	心 夂 亻	悠長 *yūchō* leisurely, slow, easygoing	95
	51 49 3	悠々 *yūyū* calm, composed, leisurely	
		悠揚 *yūyō* composed, calm, serene	631
	悠	悠久 *yūkyū* eternity, perpetuity	1210

	1598	**YU** – joy, pleasure	
愉	4k9.13 曰	愉快 *yukai* pleasant, merry, cheerful	1409
	心 月 亻	不愉快 *fuyukai* unpleasant, disagreeable	94, 1409
	51 42 3	愉楽 *yuraku* pleasure, joy	358
	愉 愉		

	1599	**YU, sato(su)** – admonish, remonstrate, warn, counsel	
諭	7a9.13 曰	教諭 *kyōyu* teacher, instructor	245
	言 月 亻	説諭 *setsuyu* admonition, reproof, caution	400
	67 42 3	諭旨 *yushi* official suggestion (to a subordinate)	1040
	諭 諭		

	1600	**YU** – heal, cure	
癒	5i13.3 回	癒着 *yuchaku* heal up, adhere, knit together	657
	疒 月 心	治癒 *chiyu* healing, cure, recovery	493
	60 42 51	平癒 *heiyu* recovery	202
	癒 癒		

	1601	**SHŪ, ure(i)** – grief, sorrow, distress; anxiety, cares	
愁	4k9.16 曰	**ure(eru)** – grieve, be distressed; fear, be apprehensive	
	心 禾 火	郷愁 *kyōshū* homesickness, nostalgia	855
	51 56 44	旅愁 *ryoshū* loneliness on a journey	222
		憂愁 *yūshū* melancholy, grief, gloom	1032
	愁	ご愁傷様 *goshūshō-sama* My heartfelt sympathy.	633, 403

	1602	**KYŌ, oso(reru)** – fear, be afraid of	
恐	4k6.19 曰	**oso(roshii)** – terrible, frightful, awful	
	心 工 冂	恐縮 *kyōshuku* be very grateful; be sorry	1110
	51 38 20	恐慌 *kyōkō* panic	1378
		恐妻家 *kyōsaika* henpecked husband	671, 165
	恐 恐	空恐ろしい *soraosoroshii* have a vague fear	140

	1603	**CHIKU, kizu(ku)** – build, erect	
築	6f10.5 目	建築 *kenchiku* architecture, construction	892
	竹 木 工	建築家 *kenchikuka* architect	892, 165
	66 41 38	新築 *shinchiku* new construction	174
		改築 *kaichiku* rebuilding, reconstruction	514
	築	築山 *tsukiyama* mound, artificial hill	34

	1604	*KŌ* – ore
鉱	8a5.15	鉱石 *kōseki* ore, mineral, crystal ... 78
	金 厂 ム	鉱物 *kōbutsu* mineral ... 79
	72 18 17	鉄鉱 *tekkō* iron ore ... 312
		鉱山 *kōzan* a mine ... 34
	鉱 鑛	鉱業 *kōgyō* mining ... 279

	1605	*DŌ* – copper
銅	8a6.12	銅山 *dōzan* copper mine ... 34
	金 口 冂	銅版画 *dōhanga* copper print ... 1046, 343
	72 24 20	銅像 *dōzō* bronze statue ... 740
		青銅 *seidō* bronze ... 208
	銅	銅メダル *dōmedaru* bronze medal

	1606	*EN, namari* – lead
鉛	8a5.14	鉛筆 *enpitsu* pencil ... 130
	金 口 儿	黒鉛 *kokuen* graphite ... 206
	72 24 16	鉛版 *enban* stereotype, printing plate ... 1046
		鉛毒 *endoku* lead poisoning ... 522
	鉛	鉛色 *namariiro* lead color/gray ... 204

	1607	*EN, so(u)* – stand along (a street), run parallel (to)
沿	3a5.23	沿岸 *engan* coast, shore ... 586
	氵 口 儿	沿海 *enkai* coastal waters, coast ... 117
	21 24 16	沿線 *ensen* along the (train) line ... 299
		沿革 *enkaku* history, development ... 1075
	沿	川沿い *kawazoi* along the river ... 33

	1608	*KŌ, hagane* – steel
鋼	8a8.20	鋼鉄 *kōtetsu* steel ... 312
	金 ㎕ 冂	特殊鋼 *tokushukō* special steel ... 282, 1505
	72 36 20	鋼板 *kōhan, kōban* steel plate ... 1047
		製鋼所 *seikōjo* steel plant ... 428, 153
	鋼	製鋼業 *seikōgyō* steel industry ... 428, 279

	1609	*KŌ, tsuna* – rope, cord
綱	6a8.23	綱領 *kōryō* plan, program, platform ... 834
	糸 ㎕ 冂	綱紀 *kōki* official discipline, public order ... 372
	61 36 20	手綱 *tazuna* bridle, reins ... 57
		綱渡り *tsunawatari* tightrope walking ... 378
	綱	横綱 *yokozuna* sumo grand champion ... 781

	1610	*GŌ* – strength; hardness
剛	2f8.7	外柔内剛 *gaijū-naigō* gentle-looking but sturdy ... 83, 774, 84
	刂 ㎕ 冂	剛健 *gōken* strong and sturdy, virile ... 893
	16 36 20	剛勇 *gōyū* valor, bravery ... 1386
	剛	金剛石 *kongōseki* diamond ... 23, 78

1611 削

SAKU, kezu(ru) – whittle down, sharpen (a pencil); delete; curtail

2f7.4 刂月 小 16 42 35

削 削

削除	sakujo	deletion, elimination	1065
削減	sakugen	reduction, cutback	715
添削	tensaku	correction (of a composition)	1433
鉛筆削り	enpitsu-kezuri	pencil sharpener	1606, 130

1612 網

MŌ, ami – net

6a8.25 糸月儿 61 42 16

網

漁網	gyomō	fishing net	699
交通網	kōtsūmō	traffic network	114, 150
支店網	shitenmō	network of branch offices	318, 168
金網	kanaami	wire mesh/netting	23
網袋	amibukuro	net (shopping) bag	1329

1613 坑

KŌ – pit, hole

3b4.6 土 亠 门 22 11 20

坑

炭坑	tankō	coalpit, coal mine	1344
坑夫	kōfu	coal miner	315
坑道	kōdō	(mine) shaft, level, gallery	149
坑内事故	kōnai jiko	mine accident	84, 80, 173
廃坑	haikō	abandoned mine	961

1614 冗

JŌ – redundant, superfluous

2i2.1 宀 20

冗 冗

冗談	jōdan	a joke	593
冗語	jōgo	redundancy	67
冗員	jōin	superfluous member/personnel, overstaffing	163
冗長	jōchō	redundant, verbose	95
冗漫	jōman	wordy, verbose, rambling	1411

1615 冠

KAN, kanmuri – crown

2i7.2 宀 寸 二 20 37 4

冠

王冠	ōkan	(royal) crown; bottle cap	294
金冠	kinkan	gold crown	23
栄冠	eikan	crown (of victory), laurels	723
弱冠	jakkan	20 years of age; youth	218
草冠	kusa-kanmuri	Grapheme No. 3k [艹]	249

1616 亜

A – rank next, come after, sub-; Asia

0a7.14 亠 口 丨 38 24 2

亜 亞

亜熱帯	anettai	subtropical zones, subtropics	645, 963
亜鉛	aen	zinc	1606
亜麻	ama	flax	1529
亜流	aryū	follower, epigone	247
東亜	Tōa	East Asia	71

1617 尉

I – officer

4e6.4 礻 尸 寸 45 40 37

尉

尉官	ikan	officer below the rank of major	326
大尉	taii	captain	26
中尉	chūi	lieutenant	28
少尉	shōi	second lieutenant	144
准尉	jun'i	warrant officer	1232

慰	**1618** 4k11.13 心 ネ 尸 51 45 40 慰	*I, nagusa(meru)* – comfort, console, cheer up; amuse, divert *nagusa(mu)* – be diverted; banter; make a plaything of

慰問　*imon*　consolation, sympathy　　　　　　162
慰安　*ian*　comfort, recreation, amusement　　　105
慰霊祭　*ireisai*　a memorial service　　　1168, 617
慰謝料　*isharyō*　consolation money, solatium　901, 319

仁	**1619** 2a2.8 亻 二 3　4 仁	*JIN, [NI]* – virtue, benevolence, humanity, charity

仁義　*jingi*　humanity and justice　　　　　　291
仁愛　*jin'ai*　benevolence, charity, philanthropy　259
仁術　*jinjutsu*　benevolent act; the healing art　187
仁徳　*jintoku*　benevolence, goodness　　　　1038
仁王 (門)　*Niō(mon)*　Deva (gate)　　　　294, 161

尼	**1620** 3r2.2 尸 ㇒ 40　13 尼	*NI, ama* – nun

尼僧　*nisō*　nun　　　　　　　　　　　　1366
尼寺　*amadera*　convent　　　　　　　　　41

泥	**1621** 3a5.29 氵 尸 ㇒ 21　40　13 泥	*DEI, doro* – mud

泥炭　*deitan*　peat　　　　　　　　　　　1344
雲泥の差　*undei no sa*　enormous difference　636, 658
泥沼　*doronuma*　bog, quagmire　　　　　　996
泥棒　*dorobō*　thief, robber, burglar, burglary　1543

渇	**1622** 3a8.13 氵 日 ㇀ 21　43　15 渇 渇	*KATSU, kawa(ku)* – be thirsty

飢渇　*kikatsu*　hunger and thirst　　　　　1304
渇望　*katsubō*　craving, longing, thirst　　　673
枯渇　*kokatsu*　run dry, become depleted　　974
渇水　*kassui*　water shortage　　　　　　　21
渇きを覚える　*kawaki o oboeru*　feel thirsty　605

褐	**1623** 5e8.7 衤 日 ㇀ 57　43　15 褐 褐	*KATSU* – woolen/quilted clothing

褐色　*kasshoku*　brown　　　　　　　　　　204
茶褐色　*chakasshoku*　brown, chestnut brown　251, 204
赤褐色　*sekkasshoku*　reddish brown　　　207, 204
黒褐色　*kokkasshoku*　dark/blackish brown　206, 204

掲	**1624** 3c8.13 扌 日 ㇀ 23　43　15 掲 掲	*KEI, kaka(geru)* – put up (a sign), hoist (a flag); publish, print

掲揚　*keiyō*　hoist, raise, fly (a flag)　　　　631
掲示　*keiji*　notice, bulletin　　　　　　　615
掲示板　*keijiban*　bulletin board　　　　615, 1047
掲載　*keisai*　publish, print, carry, mention　1124
前掲　*zenkei*　shown above, aforementioned　　47

1625

濁

3a13.8

氵 虫 日
21 64 55

濁

DAKU, nigo(ru) – become muddy/turbid **nigo(su)** – make turbid

混濁	*kondaku* turbidity, muddiness	799
清濁	*seidaku* purity and impurity, good and evil	660
濁流	*dakuryū* muddy river, turbid waters	247
濁音	*dakuon* voiced sound; cardiac dullness	347

1626

潟

3a12.9

氵 火 ヨ
21 44 39

潟

kata – beach, lagoon, inlet

干潟	*higata* dry beach, beach at ebb tide	584
新潟県	*Niigata-ken* Niigata Prefecture	174, 194

1627

巧

0a5.7

工 一
38 14

巧

KŌ, taku(mi) – skill, dexterity, ingenuity

技巧	*gikō* art, craftsmanship, technical skill	871
巧妙	*kōmyō* skilled, clever, ingenious	1154
巧者	*kōsha* skilled, adroit, clever	164
精巧	*seikō* elaborate, exquisite, sophisticated	659
老巧	*rōkō* experienced, seasoned, veteran	543

1628

朽

4a2.6

木 一
41 14

朽

KYŪ, ku(chiru) – rot, decay

不朽	*fukyū* immortal, undying ⌈masterpiece	94
不朽の名作	*fukyū no meisaku* immortal	94, 82, 360
腐朽	*fukyū* deteriorate, rot away, molder	1245
老朽	*rōkyū* senescence, advanced age	543
朽ち葉	*kuchiba* decayed/dead leaves	253

1629

誇

7a6.9

言 大 二
67 34 4

誇

KO, hoko(ru) – boast of, be proud of

誇張	*kochō* exaggeration, overstatement	1106
誇大	*kodai* exaggeration, overstatement	26
誇大妄想 (狂)	*kodai mōsō(kyō)* delusions	26, 1376, 147, 883
誇示	*koji* display, flaunt ⌊of grandeur, megalomania	615
勝ち誇る	*kachihokoru* exult in one's triumph	509

1630

麗

3q16.5

广 門 ト
18 20 13

麗

REI, uruwa(shii) – beautiful, pretty

美麗	*birei* beautiful, pretty	401
華麗	*karei* glory, splendor, magnificence	1074
麗人	*reijin* beautiful woman	1
端麗	*tanrei* grace, elegance, beauty ⌈flourishes	1418
美辞麗句	*biji-reiku* speech full of rhetorical	401, 688, 337

1631

薦

3k13.25

艹 火 厂
32 44 18

薦

SEN, susu(meru) – recommend; advise; offer, present

推薦	*suisen* recommendation	1233
推薦状	*suisenjō* letter of recommendation	1233, 626
他薦	*tasen* recommendation (by another)	120
自薦	*jisen* self-recommendation	62

慶	**1632** 3q12.8 ⊟ 广 心 夂 18 51 49 慶	**_KEI_** – rejoice, be happy over; congratulate 慶賀 _keiga_ congratulation 756 慶祝 _keishuku_ congratulation; celebration 851 慶事 _keiji_ happy event, matter for congratulation 80 慶応 _Keiō_ (Japanese era, 1865–68) ⌐China 827 国慶節 _Kokkeisetsu_ Anniversary of Founding of P.R. 40, 464
覇	**1633** 4b15.4 ⊟ 月 口 艹 42 24 32 覇	**_HA_** – supremacy, domination, hegemony 覇権 _haken_ hegemony 355 覇者 _hasha_ supreme ruler; champion, titleholder 164 制覇 _seiha_ conquest, domination; championship 427 覇気 _haki_ ambition, aspirations 134 連覇 _renpa_ successive championships 440
覆	**1634** 4c14.6 ⊟ 日 夂口 43 49 24 覆 覆	**_FUKU, ō(u)_** – cover; conceal **_kutsugae(ru)_** – be overturned **_kutsugae(su)_** – overturn, overthrow 覆面 _fukumen_ mask 274 転覆 _tenpuku_ overturn, topple 433 覆水盆に返らず _fukusui bon ni kaerazu_ What's done is done. 21, 1099, 442
履	**1635** 3r12.1 ▢ 尸 日 夂 40 43 49 履	**_RI, ha(ku)_** – put on, wear (shoes/pants) 履歴書 _rirekisho_ curriculum vitae 480, 131 履行 _rikō_ perform, fulfill, implement 68 草履 _zōri_ (toe-strap) sandals 249 履き物 _hakimono_ footwear 79 履き古し _hakifurushi_ worn-out shoes/socks 172
託	**1636** 7a3.1 ▢ 言 十 丨 67 12 2 託	**_TAKU_** – entrust (to), leave in the care (of) 委託 _itaku_ trust, charge, commission 466 信託 _shintaku_ trust 157 託児所 _takujisho_ day nursery 1217, 153 託宣 _takusen_ oracle, revelation from God 625 結託 _kettaku_ conspiracy, collusion 485
属	**1637** 3r9.1 ▢ 尸 虫 冂 40 64 20 属 屬	**_ZOKU_** – belong (to) 所属 _shozoku_ belong, be assigned (to) 153 付属 _fuzoku_ attached, affiliated, incidental 192 金属 _kinzoku_ metal 23 専属 _senzoku_ belong exclusively (to) 600 従属 _jūzoku_ subordination, dependence 1482
嘱	**1638** 3d12.11▢ 口 虫 尸 24 64 40 嘱 囑	**_SHOKU_** – request, entrust, commission 嘱託 _shokutaku_ part-time worker 1636 委嘱 _ishoku_ commission, charge, request 466 嘱望 _shokubō_ expect much of 673

偶	**1639** 2a9.1 □ イ 日 ム 3 43 17 偶	**GŪ** – (married) couple; even number; doll; chance, accidental

偶然　*gūzen*　chance, accident　　　　　　　　651
偶発　*gūhatsu*　chance occurrence　　　　　　96
偶像　*gūzō*　image, statue, idol　　　　　　　740
配偶者　*haigūsha*　spouse　　　　　　　515, 164
偶数　*gūsū*　even number　　　　　　　　　225

隅	**1640** 2d9.1 □ 阝 日 ム 7 43 17 隅	**GŪ, sumi** – corner, nook

一隅　*ichigū*　corner, nook　　　　　　　　　2
片隅　*katasumi*　corner, nook　　　　　　　1045
四隅　*yosumi*　the 4 corners　　　　　　　　6
隅々　*sumizumi*　every nook and cranny, all over
隅田川　*Sumida-gawa*　Sumida River　　　35, 33

遇	**1641** 2q9.1 □ 辶 日 ム 19 43 17 遇	**GŪ** – treat, deal with; entertain; receive; meet

待遇　*taigū*　treatment; service; pay　　　　452
優遇　*yūgū*　cordial reception, hospitality　　1033
冷遇　*reigū*　cold reception, inhospitality　　832
境遇　*kyōgū*　one's circumstances　　　　　864
奇遇　*kigū*　chance meeting　　　　　　　1360

愚	**1642** 4k9.15 □ 心 日 ム 51 43 17 愚	**GU, oro(ka)** – foolish, stupid

愚劣　*guretsu*　stupidity, foolishness, nonsense　1150
愚鈍　*gudon*　stupid, dim-witted　　　　　966
愚問　*gumon*　stupid question　　　　　　162
愚連隊　*gurentai*　gang of hoodlums　　440, 795

遭	**1643** 2q11.2 □ 辶 日 艹 19 43 32 遭	**SŌ, a(u)** – meet, see, come across, encounter

遭難　*sōnan*　disaster, accident, mishap　　　557
遭難者　*sōnansha*　victim　　　　　　　557, 164
遭難信号　*sōnan shingō*　distress signal, SOS　557, 157, 266
遭遇　*sōgū*　encounter　　　　　　　　　1641
災難に遭う　*sainan ni au*　meet with disaster　1335, 557

槽	**1644** 4a11.7 □ 木 日 艹 41 43 32 槽	**SŌ** – tub, tank, vat

水槽　*suisō*　water tank, cistern　　　　　　21
浴槽　*yokusō*　bathtub　　　　　　　　　1128

晶	**1645** 4c8.6 □ 日 43 晶	**SHŌ** – clear; crystal

結晶　*kesshō*　crystal, crystallization　　　　485
愛の結晶　*ai no kesshō*　fruit of love, child　259, 485
晶化　*shōka*　crystallization　　　　　　　254
水晶　*suishō*　(rock) crystal, quartz　　　　21
紫水晶　*murasaki suishō*　amethyst　　1389, 21

1646

3d8.9 田

口 日

24 43

唱

SHŌ, tona(eru) – chant; cry; advocate, espouse

合唱 (団)	gasshō(dan) chorus	159, 491
独唱	dokushō vocal solo	219
唱歌	shōka singing	392
主唱, 首唱	shushō advocacy, promotion	155, 148
提唱	teishō advocate	628

1647

7a9.9 田

言 小 山

67 35 36

謡 謡

YŌ – song; Noh chanting **uta(u)** – sing

民謡	min'yō folk song	177
童謡	dōyō children's song	410
歌謡	kayō song	392
歌謡曲	kayōkyoku popular song	392, 366
謡曲	yōkyoku Noh song	366

1648

3c9.8 田

扌 小 山

23 35 36

揺 搖

YŌ, yu(reru), yu(ragu) yu(rugu) – shake, sway, vibrate, roll, pitch, joggle **yu(ru), yu(suru), yu(suburu), yu(saburu)** – shake, rock, joggle

動揺	dōyō shaking; unrest, tumult	231
揺(す)り起こす	yu(su)riokosu awaken by shaking	373
揺り返し	yurikaeshi aftershock	442

1649

2k4.6 ⊡

十 山 ⌐

(12) 36 15

缶 罐

KAN – can

缶詰	kanzume canned goods	1142
製缶工場	seikan kōjō cannery, canning factory	428, 139, 154
缶切り	kankiri can opener	39
空き缶	akikan empty can	140

1650

2d8.11 ⊡

阝 山 ⌐

7 36 15

陶

TŌ – porcelain, pottery

陶器	tōki china, ceramics, pottery	527
陶磁器	tōjiki ceramics, china and porcelain	1548, 527
陶芸	tōgei ceramic art	435
陶工	tōkō potter	139

1651

3c7.2 ⊡

扌 日 十

23 43 12

挿 插

SŌ, sa(su) – insert

挿入	sōnyū insertion	52
挿話	sōwa episode, little story	238
挿し木	sashiki a cutting	22
挿し絵	sashie an illustration	345

1652

3c9.14 ⊡

扌 車 冂

23 69 20

揮

KI – shake, brandish; direct, command; scatter

指揮	shiki command, direct, conduct	1041
指揮者	shikisha (orchestra) conductor	1041, 164
指揮官	shikikan commander	1041, 326
発揮	hakki exhibit, display, manifest	96
揮発	kihatsu volatilization	96

	1653	**KI, kagaya(ku)** – shine, gleam, sparkle, be brilliant	
輝	7c8.8 田	光輝 *kōki* brilliance, brightness; glory	138
	車 小 宀	輝度 *kido* (degree of) brightness	377
	69 35 14	光り輝く *hikarikagayaku* shine, beam, glisten	138
	輝	輝かしい *kagayakashii* bright, brilliant	

	1654	**ku(ru)** – reel, wind; spin (thread); turn (pages); consult (a reference book), look up; count	
繰	6a13.3 田		
	糸 木 口	繰り返す *kurikaesu* repeat	442
	61 41 24	繰り言 *kurigoto* same old story, complaint	66
		繰り延べ *kurinobe* postponement, deferment	1115
	繰	繰り上げる *kuriageru* advance, move up (a date)	32

	1655	**SŌ, ayatsu(ru)** – manipulate, operate **misao** – chastity; constancy, fidelity, honor	
操	3c13.3 田		
	扌 木 口	操縦 *sōjū* control, operate, manipulate	1483
	23 41 24	(遠隔)操作 *(enkaku) sōsa* (remote) control	446, 1589, 360
		体操 *taisō* gymnastics, exercises	61
	操	節操 *sessō* fidelity, integrity; chastity	464

	1656	**SŌ** – dry	
燥	4d13.6 田	乾燥 *kansō* dry (up/out)	1190
	火 木 口	乾燥機 *kansōki* (clothes) dryer	1190, 528
	44 41 24	無味乾燥 *mumi-kansō* dry, uninteresting	93, 307, 1190
	燥	焦燥 *shōsō* impatience, nervous restlessness	999

	1657	**SŌ, mo** – water plant	
藻	3k16.8 田	藻類 *sōrui* water plants	226
	艹 木 氵	海藻 *kaisō* saltwater plant, seaweed	117
	32 41 21	藻草 *mogusa* water plant	249
	藻		

	1658	**GYŌ, akatsuki** – dawn, daybreak	
暁	4c8.1 田	暁天 *gyōten* dawn, daybreak	141
	日 土 十	暁星 *gyōsei* morning stars; Venus	730
	43 22 12	今暁 *kongyō* early this morning	51
		通暁 *tsūgyō* thorough knowledge, mastery	150
	暁 曉	暁には *akatsuki niwa* in the event, in case (of)	

	1659	**HON** – run	
奔	2k6.5 …	奔走 *honsō* running about, efforts	429
	十 大 土	奔放 *honpō* wild, extravagant, uninhibited	512
	(12) 34 22	狂奔 *kyōhon* rush madly about	883
		奔馬 *honba* galloping/runaway horse	283
	奔	出奔 *shuppon* abscond; elope	53

1660

噴

3d12.8

口 貝 土
24 68 22

噴

FUN, fu(ku) – emit, spout, spew forth

噴火	*funka* (volcanic) eruption	20
噴水	*funsui* jet of water; fountain	21
噴出	*funshutsu* eruption, gushing, spouting	53
噴射	*funsha* jet, spray, injection	900
噴霧器	*funmuki* sprayer, vaporizer	950, 527

1661

憤

4k12.6

心 貝 土
51 68 22

憤

FUN, ikidō(ru) – resent, be enraged, be indignant

憤慨	*fungai* indignation, resentment	1460
公憤	*kōfun* public/righteous indignation	126
義憤	*gifun* righteous indignation	291
憤然と	*funzen to* indignantly	651
発憤	*happun* be stimulated, roused	96

1662

墳

3b12.1

土 貝 土
22 68 22

墳

FUN – burial mound, tomb

墳墓	*funbo* grave, tomb	1429
古墳	*kofun* ancient burial mound, old tomb	172
前方後円墳	*zenpō-kōen fun* ancient burial mound (square at the head and rounded at the foot)	47, 70, 48, 13

1663

監

5h10.1

血 冂 𠂉
59 20 15

監

KAN – keep watch over

監視	*kanshi* keeping watch, supervision, surveillance	606
監査	*kansa* inspection; auditing	624
総監	*sōkan* inspector/superintendent general	697
監禁	*kankin* imprison, confine	482
監獄	*kangoku* prison	884

1664

鑑

8a15.2

金 血 冂
72 59 20

鑑

KAN – model, pattern, example; mirror

鑑定	*kantei* appraisal, expert opinion	355
鑑賞	*kanshō* admiration, enjoyment	500
鑑別	*kanbetsu* discrimination, differentiation	267
年鑑	*nenkan* yearbook, almanac	45
印鑑	*inkan* one's seal, seal impression	1043

1665

艦

6c15.2

舟 血 冂
63 59 20

艦

KAN – warship

軍艦	*gunkan* warship	438
戦艦	*senkan* battleship	301
航空母艦	*kōkū bokan* aircraft carrier	823, 140, 112
潜水艦	*sensuikan* submarine	937, 21
艦隊	*kantai* fleet, squadron	795

1666

艇

6c6.2

舟 王 辶
63 46 19

艇

TEI – small boat

艦艇	*kantei* naval vessels	1665
舟艇	*shūtei* boat, craft	1094
巡視艇	*junshitei* patrol boat	777, 606
艇庫	*teiko* boathouse	825
艇身	*teishin* a boat length	59

1667		**SHUKU** – younger sibling of a parent (cf. No. 1176)	
2h6.1	田	叔母 *oba, shukubo* aunt	112
又 小 卜		叔父 *oji, shukufu* uncle	113
9 35 13			

叔

1668		**SHUKU** – graceful; polite; pure	
3a8.5	Ⅲ	淑女 *shukujo* lady, gentlewoman	102
氵 小 又		淑徳 *shukutoku* feminine virtues	1038
21 35 9		私淑 *shishuku* look up to as one's model	125

淑

1669		**JAKU, [SEKI], sabi(shii)** – lonely **sabi(reru)** – decline in prosperity **sabi** – elegant simplicity	
3m8.2	田	静寂 *seijaku* stillness, silence	663
宀 小 又		閑寂 *kanjaku* quietness, tranquility	1532
33 35 9		寂然 *sekizen, jakunen* lonesome, desolate	651
		寂りょう *sekiryō* loneliness, desolation	

寂

1670		**TOKU** – lead, command; superintend, supervise	
5c8.9	田	監督 *kantoku* supervision, direction; (movie) director	1663
目 小 又		督励 *tokurei* encourage, urge	1340
55 35 9		督促 *tokusoku* urge, press, dun	1557
		総督 *sōtoku* governor-general ⌐heirship	697
		家督相続 *katoku sōzoku* succession to a house,	165, 146, 243

督

1671		**GŌ** – strength, power; splendor, magnificence	
2j12.3	目	豪華 *gōka* splendor, gorgeousness, pomp	1074
亠 口 豸		豪壮 *gōsō* magnificent, grand	1326
11 24 27		富豪 *fugō* man of great wealth, multimillionaire	713
		豪族 *gōzoku* powerful/influential family	221
		豪雨 *gōu* heavy rainfall, torrential downpour	30

豪

1672		**KYŌ** – enjoy; receive	
2j5.1	目	享楽 *kyōraku* enjoyment ⌐hedonism	358
亠 口 子		享楽主義 *kyōraku shugi* epicureanism,	358, 155, 291
11 24 6		享受 *kyōju* enjoy, have, be given	260
		享有 *kyōyū* enjoyment, possession ⌐of 75	265
		享年７５歳 *kyōnen nanajūgo-sai* dead at the age	45, 479

享

1673		**KAKU** – enclosure, quarters; red-light district	
2d7.14	田	輪郭 *rinkaku* contours, outline	1164
阝 口 亠		外郭 *gaikaku* outer wall (of a castle); perimeter	83
7 24 11		外郭団体 *gaikaku dantai* auxiliary organization	83, 491, 61
		城郭 *jōkaku* castle, fortress; castle walls	720
		郭公 *kakkō* (Japanese) cuckoo	126

郭

	1674	**JUKU** – private school
	3b10.7 ⊞	私塾 *shijuku* private class at a teacher's home	125
	土 口 宀	学習塾 *gakushūjuku* (private) cram school	109, 591
	22 24 11	塾生 *jukusei* student of a *juku*	44

	1675	**AI, awa(re)** – sorrowful, piteous **awa(remu)** – pity, sympathize
	2j7.4 ⊟	哀愁 *aishū* sadness, sorrow, grief	1601
	宀 衤 口	悲哀 *hiai* sorrow, grief, misery	1034
	11 57 24	哀話 *aiwa* sad story, pathetic tale	238
		哀歌 *aika* doleful song, elegy, lament ⌐emotions	392
		喜怒哀楽 *kido-airaku* joy and pathos,	1143, 1596, 358

	1676	**SUI, otoro(eru)** – grow weak, decline, wane
	2j8.1 ⊟	老衰 *rōsui* feebleness of old age, senility	543
	宀 衤 口	衰弱 *suijaku* weakening, debility	218
	11 57 24	衰微 *suibi* decline, wane	1419
		衰亡 *suibō* decline and fall, ruin, downfall	672
		盛衰 *seisui* rise and fall, vicissitudes	719

	1677	**CHŪ** – heart, mind, inside
	0a9.9	衷心 *chūshin* one's inmost heart/feelings	97
	衤 口 十	衷情 *chūjō* one's inmost feelings	209
	57 24 12	苦衷 *kuchū* anguish, predicament	545
		和洋折衷 *Wa-yō setchū* blending of Japanese and
		Western styles 124, 289, 1394

	1678	**SŌ, mo** – mourning
	3b9.20 ⊟	喪失 *sōshitsu* loss	311
	土 衤 口	喪服 *mofuku* mourning clothes	683
	22 57 24	喪章 *moshō* mourning badge/band	857
		喪主 *moshu* chief mourner	155
		喪中 *mochū* period of mourning	28

	1679	**TAKU** – table, desk; high
	2m6.2 ⊟	食卓 *shokutaku* dining table	322
	⊦ 日 十	卓球 *takkyū* table tennis, ping-pong	726
	13 43 12	電卓 *dentaku* (desk-top) calculator	108
		卓上 *takujō* table-top, desk-top	32
		卓越 *takuetsu* be superior, excel, surpass	1001

	1680	**TŌ, ita(mu)** – grieve over, mourn, lament
	4k8.13 ⊞	追悼 *tsuitō* mourning	1174
	忄 日 ⊦	追悼会 *tsuitōkai* memorial services	1174, 158
	51 43 13	追悼式 *tsuitōshiki* memorial services	1174, 525
		哀悼 *aitō* condolence, mourning, grief	1675
		悼辞 *tōji* message of condolence, funeral address	688

1681
貞 **TEI** – chastity, constancy, righteousness

2m7.1

貞淑 *teishuku* chastity, feminine modesty 1668
貞節 *teisetsu* fidelity, chastity 464
貞操 *teisō* chastity, female honor, virginity 1655
貞潔 *teiketsu* chaste and pure 1241
不貞 *futei* unchastity, infidelity 94

1682
香 **KŌ, [KYŌ], kao(ri), ka** – fragrance, aroma **kao(ru)** – smell sweet

5d4.5

香気 *kōki* fragrance, aroma, sweet smell 134
香料 *kōryō* spices; perfume 319
線香 *senkō* stick of incense 299
色香 *iroka* color and scent; (feminine) beauty 204

1683
秀 **SHŪ, hii(deru)** – excel, surpass

5d2.4

優秀 *yūshū* excellent, superior 1033
秀逸 *shūitsu* superb, masterly 734
秀麗 *shūrei* graceful, beautiful, handsome 1630
秀才 *shūsai* talented man, bright boy/girl ⌐painter 551
けい秀画家 *keishū gaka* accomplished woman 343, 165

1684
誘 **YŪ, saso(u)** – invite; induce; lure, entice

7a7.4

誘惑 *yūwaku* temptation, seduction 969
勧誘 *kan'yū* invitation, canvassing, solicitation 1051
誘因 *yūin* enticement, inducement 554
誘発 *yūhatsu* induce, give rise to 96
誘い水 *sasoimizu* pump priming 21

1685
透 **TŌ, su(ku)** – be transparent; leave a gap **su(kasu)** – look through; leave a space **su(keru)** – shine through

2q7.10

透明 *tōmei* transparent 18
透視 *tōshi* seeing through; fluoroscopy; clairvoyance 606
浸透 *shintō* permeation, osmosis, infiltration 1078
透き通る *sukitōru* be transparent 150

1686
携 **KEI, tazusa(eru)** – carry (in one's hand); have with one **tazusa(waru)** – participate (in)

3c10.4

携帯 *keitai* carrying, bring with; portable 963
必携 *hikkei* handbook, manual; indispensable 520
提携 *teikei* cooperation, tie-up 628
連携 *renkei* cooperation, league, concert 440

1687
謙 **KEN** – modesty, humility

7a10.10

謙虚 *kenkyo* modest, humble 1572
謙譲 *kenjō* modest, humble ⌐modesty 1013
謙譲の美徳 *kenjō no bitoku* the virtue of 1013, 401, 1038
恭謙 *kyōken* modesty, humility, deference 1434
謙そん *kenson* modesty, humility

	1688	**KEN, [GEN], kira(u)** – dislike, hate	
3e10.7 ⊞	嫌悪	*ken'o* hatred, dislike, loathing	304
女 ヨ 儿	嫌疑	*kengi* suspicion	1516
25 39 16	機嫌	*kigen* mood, humor	528
	大嫌い	*daikirai* hate, strong aversion	26
嫌 嫌	毛嫌い	*kegirai* antipathy, prejudice	287

	1689	**REN** – pure; honest; low price	
3q10.1 ⊡	清廉	*seiren* integrity, uprightness	660
广 ヨ 儿	清廉潔白	*seiren-keppaku* spotless integrity	660, 1241, 205
18 39 16	廉売	*renbai* bargain sale	239
	廉価	*renka* low price	421
廉			

	1690	**CHI, haji** – shame, disgrace **ha(jiru)** – feel shame	
6e4.2 ⊡		**ha(jirau)** – be shy **ha(zukashii)** – shy, ashamed	
耳 心	無恥	*muchi* shameless, brazen	93
65 51	破廉恥	*harenchi* shameless, disgraceful	665, 1689
	恥毛	*chimō* pubic hair	287
恥 恥	恥知らず	*hajishirazu* shameless person	214

	1691	**KAN** – daring, bold	
4i8.5 ⊞	勇敢	*yūkan* brave, daring, courageous	1386
攵耳 一	果敢	*kakan* resolute, determined, bold, daring	487
49 65 14	敢然	*kanzen* bold, fearless	651
	敢闘	*kantō* fight courageously	1511
敢	敢行	*kankō* take decisive action, dare; carry out	68

	1692	**SETSU** – act in place of; take	
3c10.6 ⊞	摂取	*sesshu* take in, ingest	65
扌耳 冫	摂生	*sessei* taking care of one's health	44
23 65 5	摂政	*sesshō* regency; regent	483
	摂理	*setsuri* providence	143
摂 攝	摂氏２０度	*sesshi nijūdo* 20 degrees centigrade	566, 377

	1693	**JŪ, shibu(i)** – astringent, puckery; glum; quiet and tasteful	
3a8.19 ⊞		**shibu** – astringent juice (of unripe persimmons)	
氵 止 亠		**shibu(ru)** – hesitate, be reluctant	
21 13 11	渋滞	*jūtai* delay, retardation	964
	渋面	*jūmen, shibutsura, shibuzura* sour face, scowl	274
渋 澁	渋味	*shibumi* puckery taste; severe elegance	307

	1694	**RUI** – parapet, rampart; base (in baseball)	
5f7.2 ▤	堅塁	*kenrui* fortress, stronghold	1289
甲 土 冫	敵塁	*tekirui* enemy's fortress/position	416
58 22 5	塁審	*ruishin* base umpire	1383
	本塁打	*honruida* home run	25, 1020
塁 壘	満塁	*manrui* bases loaded	201

	1695	**SHUKU** – quietly, softly, solemnly	
肅	0a11.8	静粛 *seishuku* stillness, quiet, hush	663
	米 ⋿ 几	厳粛 *genshuku* solemnity, austerity, gravity	822
	62 39 16	自粛 *jishuku* self-discipline, self-control	62
		粛清 *shukusei* (political) purge	660
	粛 粛	粛党 *shukutō* purge disloyal elements from a party	495

	1696	**YŌ** – mediocre, ordinary	
庸	3q8.2	中庸 *chūyō* middle path, golden mean	28
	广月 ⋿	凡庸 *bon'yō* mediocre, run-of-the-mill	1102
	18 42 39	登庸 *tōyō* appointment, promotion	960
	庸		

	1697	**TŌ** – Tang, T'ang (Chinese dynasty) **Kara** – China, Cathay	
唐	3q7.3	唐突 *tōtotsu* abrupt	898
	广 ⋿ 口	毛唐 (人) *ketō(jin)* hairy barbarian, foreigner	287, 1
	18 39 24	遣唐使 *kentōshi* Japanese envoy to Tang China	1173, 331
	唐	唐様 *karayō* Chinese style	403

	1698	**TŌ** – sugar	
糖	6b10.3	砂糖 *satō* sugar	1151
	米 ⋿ 口	製糖 *seitō* sugar manufacturing	428
	62 39 24	糖分 *tōbun* sugar content	38
		糖質 *tōshitsu* sugariness, saccharinity	176
	糖	血糖 *kettō* blood sugar	789

	1699	**SHŌ** – adorn (one's person)	
粧	6b6.1	化粧 *keshō* makeup	254
	米 土 厂	化粧品 *keshōhin* cosmetics	254, 230
	62 22 18	化粧室 *keshōshitsu* dressing room; lavatory	254, 166
		化粧箱 *keshōbako* a vanity, dressing case	254, 1091
	粧	薄化粧 *usugeshō* light makeup	1449, 254

	1700	**RYŪ, tsubu** – a grain	
粒	6b5.1	粒状 *ryūjō* granular, granulated	626
	米 立	粒子 *ryūshi* (atomic) particle; grain (in film)	103
	62 54	素粒子 *soryūshi* elementary/subatomic particle	271, 103
		米粒 *kometsubu* grain of rice	224
	粒	雨粒 *amatsubu* raindrop	30

	1701	**FUN, kona, ko** – flour; powder	
粉	6b4.6	粉末 *funmatsu* powder	305
	米 几 力	製粉所 *seifunjo* flour mill	428, 153
	62 16 8	粉飾 *funshoku* makeup; embellishment	979
		粉ミルク *konamiruku* powdered milk	
	粉	メリケン粉 *merikenko* wheat flour	

	1702	**FUN, magi(reru)** – be mistaken (for), be hardly distinguishable; get mixed; disappear (among); be diverted **magi(rasu),** **magi(rawasu)** – divert, distract; conceal; evade **magi(rawashii)** – ambiguous, liable to be confused	
紛	6a4.8 ⊞ 糸 儿 力 61 16 8 紛	紛争 *funsō* dispute, strife 紛失 *funshitsu* loss, be missing	302 311

	1703	**KYŪ** – twist (rope); ask, inquire into	
糾	6a3.4 ⊡ 糸 十 丨 61 12 2 糾 糺	糾弾 *kyūdan* impeach, censure 糾明 *kyūmei* study, inquiry, investigation 糾問 *kyūmon* close examination, grilling 紛糾 *funkyū* complication, entanglement 糾合 *kyūgō* rally, muster	1539 18 162 1702 159

	1704	**RYŌ, [RŌ], kate** – food, provisions	
糧	6b12.1 ⊞ 米 日 土 62 43 22 糧 粮	食糧 *shokuryō* food, foodstuffs 糧食 *ryōshoku* provisions, food supplies 兵糧 *hyōrō* (military) provisions 日々の糧 *hibi no kate* one's daily bread 心の糧 *kokoro no kate* food for thought	322 322 784 5 97

	1705	**BOKU, sumi** – India ink, ink stick	
墨	3b11.4 ⊡ 土 日 火 22 43 44 墨 墨	水墨画 *suibokuga* India-ink painting 白墨 *hakuboku* chalk 墨守 *bokushu* adherence (to tradition) 墨絵 *sumie* India-ink drawing 入れ墨 *irezumi* tattooing; a tattoo	21, 343 205 490 345 52

	1706	**SEN, shi(meru)** – occupy, hold **urana(u)** – tell fortunes	
占	2m3.2 ⊟ 卜 口 13 24 占	占有 *sen'yū* occupancy, possession 占領 *senryō* occupation, capture 独占 *dokusen* monopoly 買い占め *kaishime* cornering (the market) 星占い *hoshiuranai* astrology; horoscope	265 834 219 241 730

	1707	**NEN, neba(ru)** – be sticky; stick to it, persevere	
粘	6b5.4 ⊞ 米 口 卜 62 24 13 粘 黏	粘着(力) *nenchaku(ryoku)* adhesion, viscosity 粘土 *nendo* clay 粘液 *nen'eki* mucus 粘膜 *nenmaku* mucous membrane 粘り強い *nebarizuyoi* tenacious, persistent	657, 100 24 472 1426 217

	1708	**SUI** – purity, essence; elite, choice; elegant, fashionable, chic; considerateness	
粋	6b4.5 ⊞ 米 十 62 12 粋 粹	純粋 *junsui* pure, genuine 粋人 *suijin* man of refined tastes, man about town 粋狂 *suikyō* whimsical, capricious 精粋 *seisui* pure, selfless	965 1 883 659

酔	**1709**	**SUI, yo(u)** – get drunk; be intoxicated; feel sick
	7e4.3	麻酔 *masui* anesthesia; narcosis 1529
	酉 十	泥酔 *deisui* get dead drunk 1621
	71 12	心酔 *shinsui* be fascinated (with), ardently admire 97
	酔 醉	酔っ払い *yopparai* a drunk 582
		船酔い *funayoi* seasickness 376

砕	**1710**	**SAI, kuda(keru)** – break, be smashed; condescend, get familiar
	5a4.6	**kuda(ku)** – break, smash, pulverize
	石 十	粉砕 *funsai* pulverize, shatter, crush 1701
	53 12	砕石 *saiseki* rubble, broken stone ⌐efforts 78
	砕 碎	粉骨砕身 *funkotsu-saishin* make one's utmost 1701, 1266, 59
		玉砕 *gyokusai* death for honor 295

酷	**1711**	**KOKU** – severe, harsh, cruel
	7e7.1	残酷 *zankoku* cruel 650
	酉 土 口	冷酷 *reikoku* heartless, cruel 832
	71 22 24	酷評 *kokuhyō* sharp/harsh criticism 1028
	酷	酷使 *kokushi* work (someone) hard 331
		酷暑 *kokusho* intense heat, swelter 638

披	**1712**	**HI** – open
	3c5.13	披露 *hirō* announcement 951
	扌 厂 又	結婚披露宴 *kekkon hirōen* wedding reception
	23 18 9	485, 567, 951, 640
	披	披歴 *hireki* express (one's opinion) 480
		披見 *hiken* open and read (a letter) 63

抜	**1713**	**BATSU, nu(ku)** – pull out; remove; leave out; outdistance, surpass
	3c4.10	**nu(keru)** – come/fall out; be omitted; be gone; escape
	扌 十 又	**nu(karu)** – make a blunder **nu(kasu)** – omit, skip over
	23 12 9	抜群 *batsugun* preeminent, outstanding 794
	抜 拔	選抜 *senbatsu* selection, picking out 800
		骨抜き *honenuki* unboned; emasculated, toothless 1266

握	**1714**	**AKU, nigi(ru)** – grasp, grip, take hold of
	3c9.17	握手 *akushu* shake hands 57
	扌 尸 土	掌握 *shōaku* hold, seize, grasp 499
	23 40 22	一握り *hitonigiri* handful 2
	握	握り飯 *nigirimeshi* rice ball 325
		握り締める *nigirishimeru* grasp tightly, clench 1180

擁	**1715**	**YŌ** – embrace
	3c13.5	抱擁 *hōyō* embrace 1285
	扌 隹 宀	擁護 *yōgo* protect, defend 1312
	23 74 11	擁立 *yōritsu* support, back 121
	擁	

窒	**1716** 3m8.9 目 宀 土 儿 33 22 16 窒	**CHITSU** – plug up, obstruct; nitrogen 窒息 *chissoku* suffocation, asphyxiation ... 1242 窒息死 *chissokushi* death from suffocation ... 1242, 85 窒素 *chisso* nitrogen ... 271
窃	**1717** 3m6.5 目 宀 十 儿 33 16 12 窃 竊	**SETSU** – steal 窃盗 *settō* theft, thief ... 1100 窃盗罪 *settōzai* theft, larceny ... 1100, 885 窃盗犯 *settōhan* thief ... 1100, 882 窃取 *sesshu* steal ... 65 ひょう窃 *hyōsetsu* plagiarism
控	**1718** 3c8.11 目 扌 宀 工 23 33 38 控	**KŌ, hika(eru)** – hold back, refrain from; note down; wait 控除 *kōjo* deduct, subtract ... 1065 控訴 *kōso* (intermediate) appeal (to a higher court) ... 1402 手控え *tebikae* note, memo; holding off/back ... 57 控え室 *hikaeshitsu* anteroom, lobby ... 166 控え目 *hikaeme* moderate, reserved ... 55
貢	**1719** 7b3.3 目 貝 工 68 38 貢	**KŌ, [KU], mitsu(gu)** – pay tribute; support (financially) 貢献 *kōken* contribution, services ... 1355 年貢 *nengu* annual tribute ... 45 貢ぎ (物) *mitsugi(mono)* tribute ... 79
拷	**1720** 3c6.2 目 扌 耂 一 23 22 1 拷	**GŌ** – beat, torture 拷問 *gōmon* torture ... 162 拷問具 *gōmongu* instrument of torture ... 162, 420
扶	**1721** 3c4.4 目 扌 大 一 23 34 1 扶	**FU** – help 扶養 *fuyō* support (a family) 「(someone) ... 402 扶養義務 *fuyō gimu* duty of supporting ... 402, 291, 235 扶養料 *fuyōryō* sustenance allowance, alimony ... 402, 319 扶助 *fujo* aid, support, relief ... 623 扶持 *fuchi* rice ration allotted to a samurai ... 451
搬	**1722** 3c10.2 目 扌 舟 几 23 63 20 搬	**HAN** – carry, transport 運搬 *unpan* transport, conveyance, delivery ... 439 搬送 *hansō* convey, carry ... 441 搬入 *hannyū* carry/send in ... 52 搬出 *hanshutsu* carry/take out ... 53

	1723	**HI, koe, ko(yashi)** – manure, dung, night soil **ko(yasu)** – fertilize
肥	4b4.5 ▢	**ko(eru)** – grow fat; grow fertile; have fastidious taste
	月 尸 ｜ 42 40 2	肥 料 *hiryō* manure, fertilizer 319
		肥 満 *himan* corpulence, fatness, obesity 201
	肥	肥 大 *hidai* fleshiness, corpulence 26

	1724	**HA** – take, grasp; bundle
把	3c4.5 ▢	把 握 *haaku* grasp, comprehend 1714
	扌 尸 ｜ 23 40 2	把 持 *haji* hold on to, grasp 451
		一 把 *ichiwa* 1 bundle 2
	把	三 把 *sanba* 3 bundles 4
		十 把 *jippa* 10 bundles 12

	1725	**SAN, ZAN, miji(me)** – piteous, wretched, miserable
惨	4k8.5 ▦	悲 惨 *hisan* misery, distress, tragedy 1034
	心 大 彡 51 34 31	惨 事 *sanji* disaster, tragic accident 80
		惨 状 *sanjō* miserable state, disastrous scene 626
	惨 惨	惨 敗 *sanpai, zanpai* crushing defeat 511
		惨 死 *zanshi* tragic/violent death 85

	1726	**JIN, tsu(kusu)** – exhaust, use up; render (service), make efforts
尽	3r3.1 ▣	**tsu(kiru)** – be exhausted, be used up, run out, end
	尸 ｜ 40 2	**tsu(kasu)** – exhaust, use up, run out of
		尽 力 *jinryoku* efforts, exertions; assistance 100
	尽 盡	無 尽 蔵 *mujinzō* inexhaustible supply 93, 1286
		論 じ 尽 く す *ronjitsukusu* discuss fully/exhaustively 293

	1727	**KAN** – article, section; goodwill, friendship
款	4j8.2 ▦	借 款 *shakkan* (international) loan 766
	欠 礻 土 49 45 22	長 期 借 款 *chōki shakkan* long-term loan 95, 449, 766
		定 款 *teikan* articles of association/incorporation 355
	款	約 款 *yakkan* agreement, provision, clause 211
		落 款 *rakkan* signature (and seal) 839

	1728	**KAKU, kara** – husk, hull, shell
殻	3p8.1 ▦	地 殻 *chikaku* the earth's crust 118
	壴 冂 又 22 20 9	地 殻 変 動 *chikaku hendō* movement of the earth's crust
		118, 257, 231
	殻 殻	貝 殻 *kaigara* seashell 240
		卵 の 殻 *tamago no kara* eggshell 1058

	1729	**KOKU** – grain, cereals
穀	5d9.4 ▦	穀 物 *kokumotsu* grain 79
	禾 土 冂 56 22 20	穀 類 *kokurui* grains ⌐beans) 226
		五 穀 *gokoku* the 5 grains (rice, wheat and barley, 2 millets, 7
	穀 穀	穀 倉 *kokusō* granary, grain elevator 1307
		脱 穀 機 *dakkokuki* threshing machine, thresher 1370, 528

	1730	***ICHI*** – one (in documents)	
壱	3p4.2 ⊟ 士 冂 ⺊ 22 20 13 壱 壹	金壱万円　*kin ichiman en*　10,000 yen	23, 16, 13

	1731	***KETSU*** – excel	
傑	2a11.6 ⊞ 亻 木 夕 3 41 30 傑 杰	傑出　*kesshutsu*　excel, be eminent 傑作　*kessaku*　masterpiece 傑物　*ketsubutsu*　great man, outstanding figure 豪傑　*gōketsu*　hero, great man 豪傑笑い　*gōketsu warai*　broad/hearty laugh	53 360 79 1671 1671, 1235

	1732	***SHUN, matata(ku)*** – wink, blink, twinkle	
瞬	5c13.1 ⊞ 目 小 夕 55 35 30 瞬 瞬	瞬間　*shunkan*　instant, moment 瞬時　*shunji*　moment, instant 一瞬　*isshun*　instant; for an instant 瞬刻　*shunkoku*　instant, moment	43 42 2 1211

	1733	***KAI, ku(iru)*** – regret, rue　***ku(yamu)*** – regret, rue; lament, mourn over; offer condolences　***kuya(shii)*** – vexatious, vexing	
悔	4k6.12 ⊞ 心 毎 宀 51 25 15 悔 悔	後悔　*kōkai*　regret 悔悟　*kaigo*　repentance, remorse 悔やみ (状)　*kuyami(jō)*　(letter of) condolence	48 1438 626

	1734	***BAI, ume*** – ume, Japanese plum/apricot (tree)	
梅	4a6.27 ⊞ 木 毎 宀 41 25 15 梅 楳	梅雨　*baiu, tsuyu*　the rainy season 紅梅　*kōbai*　ume with red/pink blossoms 梅見　*umemi*　ume-blossom viewing 梅酒　*umeshu*　ume brandy 梅干し　*umeboshi*　pickled ume	30 820 63 517 584

	1735	***BIN*** – agile, alert	
敏	4i6.3 ⊞ 攵 毎 宀 49 25 15 敏 敏	敏速　*binsoku*　promptness, alacrity 敏感　*binkan*　sensitive 鋭敏　*eibin*　sharp, keen, acute 機敏　*kibin*　smart, astute, alert 敏腕　*binwan*　able, capable	502 262 1371 528 1299

	1736	***BU, anado(ru)*** – despise	
侮	2a6.20 ⊞ 亻 毎 宀 3 25 15 侮 侮	軽侮　*keibu*　scorn, contempt 侮言　*bugen*　an insult 侮べつ　*bubetsu*　scorn, contempt	547 66

	1737	**SHIN, kuchibiru** – lip	
唇	3d7.12 ⊟	口 唇 *kōshin* lips	54
	口 衤 厂	紅 唇 *kōshin* red lips	820
	24 57 18	唇 音 *shin'on* a labial (sound)	347
	唇 脣	上 唇 *uwa-kuchibiru, jōshin* upper lip	32
		下 唇 *shita-kuchibiru, kashin* lower lip	31

	1738	**JOKU, hazukashi(meru)** – humiliate, disgrace	
辱	2p8.2 ⊟	侮 辱 *bujoku* insult	1736
	厂 衤 寸	恥 辱 *chijoku* disgrace, dishonor	1690
	18 57 37	汚 辱 *ojoku* disgrace, dishonor	693
	辱	雪 辱 *setsujoku* vindication; revenge	949

	1739	**WAI, makana(u)** – provide board; supply, furnish; pay, finance	
賄	7b6.1 ▥	贈 賄 *zōwai* giving a bribe, bribery	1364
	貝 月 十	収 賄 *shūwai* accepting a bribe, bribery	757
	68 42 12	賄 ろ *wairo* a bribe	
	賄	賄 い 付 き *makanaitsuki* with meals	192

	1740	**ZUI** – marrow	
髄	4b14.3 ⊞	骨 髄 *kotsuzui* bone marrow	1266
	月 冂 十	せ き 髄 *sekizui* spinal cord	
	42 20 12	脳 髄 *nōzui* brain	1278
	髄 髓	真 /神/心 髄 *shinzui* essence, quintessence, soul 422, 310, 97	
		精 髄 *seizui* essence, quintessence, soul	659

	1741	**ZUI** – follow	
随	2d8.10 ▥	追 随 *tsuizui* follow (someone)	1174
	阝 月 十	随 意 *zuii* voluntary, optional	132
	7 42 12	随 筆 *zuihitsu* essay, miscellaneous writings	130
	随 隨	付 随 現 象 *fuzui genshō* concomitant 192, 298, 739	
		随 一 *zuiichi* most, greatest, first ⌐phenomenon	2

	1742	**DA** – fall	
堕	3b8.14 ⊟	堕 落 *daraku* depravity, corruption	839
	土 月 阝	堕 胎 *datai* abortion	1296
	22 42 7		
	堕 墮		

	1743	**DA** – lazy, inactive	
惰	4k9.6 ⊞	怠 惰 *taida* laziness, idleness, sloth	1297
	心 月 亠	惰 性 *dasei* inertia; force of habit	98
	51 42 38	惰 気 *daki* inactivity, dullness	134
	惰	惰 眠 *damin* idle slumber, lethargy	849

1744

佐

2a5.9 ⊟

亻 工 十
3 38 12

佐

SA – help

補佐	*hosa*	aid; assistant, adviser	889
少佐	*shōsa*	major; lieutenant commander (in the navy)	144
大佐	*taisa*	colonel; captain (in the navy)	26
佐官	*sakan*	field officer	326
土佐	*Tosa*	(city and region in Shikoku)	24

1745

婿

3e9.3 ⊞

女 月 一
25 42 14

婿 壻

SEI, muko – son-in-law; bridegroom

花婿	*hanamuko*	bridegroom	255
婿養子	*mukoyōshi*	son-in-law taken into the family	402, 103
婿選び	*mukoerabi*	looking for a husband for one's daughter	800

1746

姓

3e5.3 ⊞

女 牛 一
25 47 1

姓

SEI, SHŌ – surname, family name

姓名	*seimei*	(one's full) name	82
同姓	*dōsei*	same surname; namesakes	198
改姓	*kaisei*	change one's surname	514
旧姓	*kyūsei*	one's former/maiden name	1216
百姓	*hyakushō*	farmer	14

1747

如

3e3.1 ⊡

女 口
25 24

如

JO, NYO – equal, like, as, as if

突如	*totsujo*	suddenly, unexpectedly	898
躍如	*yakujo*	vivid, lifelike	1560
欠如	*ketsujo*	lack, deficiency	383
如実	*nyojitsu*	true to life, realistic	203
如何	*ikaga*	how	390

1748

姻

3e6.8 ⊡

女 口 大
25 24 34

姻

IN – marriage

婚姻	*kon'in*	marriage, matrimony	567
婚姻法	*kon'inhō*	the Marriage Law	567, 123
姻族	*inzoku*	relatives by marriage	221

1749

嫁

3e10.6 ⊞

女 宀 犭
25 33 27

嫁

KA – marry (a man); blame   ***totsu(gu)*** – get married
yome – bride, young wife; daughter-in-law

転嫁	*tenka*	remarriage; impute (blame)	433
花嫁	*hanayome*	bride	255
嫁入り	*yomeiri*	marriage, wedding (of a woman)	52

1750

稼

5d10.3 ⊞

禾 宀 犭
56 33 27

稼

KA, kase(gu) – work, earn (a living)

稼働	*kadō*	operation, work	232
稼業	*kagyō*	one's trade/occupation	279
出稼ぎ	*dekasegi*	work away from home	53
時間稼ぎ	*jikankasegi*	playing/stalling for time	42, 43
稼ぎ手	*kasegite*	breadwinner; hard worker	57

1751

塚

3b9.10 ⊞
土 犭 冂
22 27 20

塚 塚

tsuka – mound, hillock

貝 塚	*kaizuka* heap of shells	240
あ り 塚	*arizuka* anthill	
一 里 塚	*ichirizuka* milepost, milestone	2, 142

1752

娘

3e7.2 □
女 食
25 73

娘

musume – daughter; girl

孫 娘	*magomusume* granddaughter	910
娘 婿	*musumemuko* son-in-law	1745
娘 盛 り	*musumezakari* (a girl in) the prime of youth	719
娘 心	*musumegokoro* girlish mind/innocence	97
田 舎 娘	*inaka-musume* country girl	35, 791

1753

浪

3a7.5 □
氵 食
21 73

浪

RŌ – waves; wander

波 浪	*harō* waves, high seas	666
浮 浪	*furō* vagrancy, vagabondage	938
流 浪	*rurō* vagrancy, wandering	247
浪 人	*rōnin* lordless samurai; unaffiliated person	1
浪 費	*rōhi* waste, squander	749

1754

朗

4b6.11 □
月 食
42 73

朗 脱

RŌ, hoga(raka) – clear, bright, cheerful

明 朗	*meirō* bright, clear, cheerful	18
朗 々	*rōrō* clear, sonorous	
朗 詠	*rōei* recite (a Japanese/Chinese poem)	1209
朗 読	*rōdoku* read aloud, recite	244
朗 報	*rōhō* good news, glad tidings	685

1755

恨

4k6.2 □
心 食
51 73

恨

KON, ura(mu) – bear ill will/a grudge against, feel resentment/reproachful **ura(meshii)** – reproachful, rueful, have a grudge, feel bitter (against)

遺 恨	*ikon* grudge, rancor, malice, enmity	1172
悔 恨	*kaikon* remorse, contrition	1733
痛 恨	*tsūkon* great sorrow, bitter regret	1320

1756

妃

3e3.2 □
女 弓
25 28

妃

HI – (married) princess

王 妃	*ōhi* queen, empress	294
皇 太 子 妃	*kōtaishihi* the crown princess	297, 629, 103
妃 殿 下	*hidenka* Her Imperial Highness	1130, 31

1757

姫

3e7.11 □
女 冂 丨
25 20 2

姫

hime – princess

姫 君	*himegimi* princess	793
舞 姫	*maihime* dancing girl, dancer	810
歌 姫	*utahime* songstress	392
姫 路	*Himeji* (city with a famous castle, 100 km west of Ōsaka)	151

竜	1758	**RYŪ, tatsu** – dragon	
	5b5.3 ⊟	飛竜 *hiryū* flying dragon	530
	立 日 ｜	竜宮 *ryūgū* Palace of the Dragon King	721
	54 43 2	恐竜 *kyōryū* dinosaur	1602
		竜骨 *ryūkotsu* keel	1266
	竜 龍	竜巻 *tatsumaki* tornado	507

滝	1759	**taki** – waterfall	
	3a10.8 ⊞	滝口 *takiguchi* top/crest of a waterfall	54
	氵立 日	滝つぼ *takitsubo* bottom/basin of a waterfall	
	21 54 43	滝登り *takinobori* (salmon) climbing a waterfall	960
		華厳の滝 *Kegon no Taki* (waterfall near Nikkō)	1074, 822
	滝 瀧		

縄	1760	**JŌ, nawa** – rope	
	6a9.1 ⊞	縄文 *jōmon* (ancient Japanese) straw-rope pattern	111
	糸 日 ｜	縄張 *nawabari* rope off; one's domain	1106
	61 43 2	縄跳び *nawatobi* skipping/jumping rope	1563
		自縄自縛に陥る *jijō-jibaku ni ochiiru* fall in one's	
	縄 繩	own trap	62, 1448, 1218

伺	1761	**SHI, ukaga(u)** – visit, call at; ask, inquire	
	2a5.23 ⊞	伺候 *shikō* wait upon, attend; make a courtesy call	944
	亻口 一	奉伺 *hōshi* attend, serve	1541
	3 24 1	暑中伺い *shochū ukagai* hot-season greeting	638, 28
		進退伺い *shintai ukagai* informal resignation	437, 846
	伺		

飼	1762	**SHI, ka(u)** – raise, keep (animals)	
	8b5.4 ⊞	飼育 *shiiku* raising, breeding	246
	食 口 一	飼料 *shiryō* feed, fodder	319
	73 24 1	飼い主 *kainushi* (pet) owner, master	155
		羊飼い *hitsujikai* shepherd	288
	飼	飼い犬 *kaiinu* pet dog	280

飽	1763	**HŌ, a(kiru)** – get (sick and) tired of **a(kasu)** – cloy, satiate, surfeit; tire, bore, make (someone) fed up	
	8b5.1 ⊞	飽食 *hōshoku* gluttony, engorgement	322
	食 弓 一	飽和 *hōwa* saturation	124
	73 28 15	見飽きる *miakiru* get tired of seeing	63
	飽	…に飽かして *…ni akashite* regardless of …	

砲	1764	**HŌ** – gun, cannon	
	5a5.3 ⊞	大砲 *taihō* cannon	26
	石 弓 一	鉄砲 *teppō* gun	312
	53 28 15	砲撃 *hōgeki* shelling, bombardment	1016
		砲兵 *hōhei* artillery; artilleryman, gunner	784
	砲 砲	(十字)砲火 *(jūji) hōka* (cross) fire	12, 110, 20

1765	**HŌ, awa** – bubble, foam, froth, suds	
3a5.18 ▢	気 泡 *kihō* (air) bubble	134
氵弓 宀	水 泡 *suihō* foam, bubble	21
21 28 15	発 泡 *happō* foaming	96
泡 泡	泡 立 つ *awadatsu* bubble, foam, lather up	121
	泡 を 食 う *awa o kuu* be flurried, lose one's head	322

1766	**SHO** – all; illegitimate child	
3q8.7 ▢	庶 務 *shomu* general affairs	235
广 火 艹	庶 務 課 *shomuka* general affairs section	235, 488
18 44 32	庶 民 *shomin* the (common) people	177
庶	庶 民 的 *shominteki* popular, common, democratic	177, 210
	庶 子 *shoshi* illegitimate child	103

1767	**SHA, saegi(ru)** – interrupt, obstruct, block	
2q11.4 ▢	遮 断 *shadan* interception, isolation, cutoff	1024
辶 火 艹	遮 断 機 *shadanki* railroad-crossing gate	1024, 528
19 44 32	遮 断 器 *shadanki* circuit breaker	1024, 527
遮 遮		

1768	**SHŌ** – sunken rock	
5a12.2 ▢	暗 礁 *anshō* sunken rock, unseen reef, snag	348
石 隹 火	岩 礁 *ganshō* (shore) reef	1345
53 74 44	環 礁 *kanshō* atoll	865
礁	さ ん ご 礁 *sangoshō* coral reef	
	離 礁 *rishō* get (a ship) off the rocks, refloat	1281

1769	**SHI, haka(ru)** – consult, confer, solicit advice	
7a9.4 ▢	諮 問 *shimon* question, inquiry	162
言 夂口	諮 問 機 関 *shimon kikan* advisory body	162, 528, 398
67 49 24		
諮		

1770	**DAKU** – consent, agree to	
7a8.10 ▢	承 諾 *shōdaku* consent, agreement	942
言 艹口	許 諾 *kyodaku* consent, approval, permission	737
67 32 24	受 諾 *judaku* acceptance (of an offer)	260
諾	内 諾 *naidaku* informal consent	84
	諾 否 *dakuhi* acceptance or refusal, definite reply	1248

1771	**TOKU** – shelter, hide	
2t8.2 ▢	匿 名 *tokumei* anonymity; pseudonym	82
匚 艹口	隠 匿 *intoku* conceal, stash away, cover up	868
20 32 24	隠 匿 者 *intokusha* hoarder, concealer	868, 164
匿	隠 匿 物 資 *intoku busshi* secret cache of goods	868, 79, 750

	1772	**SHŌ** – collision
衝	3i12.1 ⫿ 彳 車 二 29 69 4 衝	衝撃 *shōgeki* shock ⌐collision 1016 (正面) 衝突 *(shōmen) shōtotsu* (head-on) 275, 274, 898 緩衝地帯 *kanshō chitai* buffer zone 1089, 118, 963 折衝 *sesshō* negotiations 1394 衝動 (行為) *shōdō (kōi)* (acting on) impulse 231, 68, 1484

	1773	**KUN** – merit
勲	4d11.3 ⊟ 火 車 力 44 69 8 勲 勳	勲功 *kunkō* distinguished service, merits 818 勲章 *kunshō* order, decoration, medal 857 勲一等 *kun ittō* First Order of Merit 2, 569 殊勲 *shukun* distinguished service, meritorious deeds 1505 偉勲 *ikun* brilliant exploit, great achievement 1053

	1774	**KUN, kao(ru)** – be fragrant, smell good
薫	3k13.17⊟ 艹 車 火 32 69 44 薫	薫香 *kunkō* incense; fragrance 1682 薫風 *kunpū* balmy breeze 29 薫陶 *kuntō* discipline, training; education 1650 風薫る五月 *kaze kaoru gogatsu* the balmy month of May 29, 7, 17

	1775	**HŌ** – fragrance; (honoric prefix) **kanba(shii)** – sweetsmelling; favorable, fair
芳	3k4.1 ⊟ 艹 方 32 48 芳	芳香 *hōkō* fragrance, perfume, aroma 1682 芳名 *hōmei* good name/reputation; your name 82 (来客) 芳名録 *(raikyaku) hōmeiroku* visitor's 69, 641, 82, 538 芳紀 *hōki* age (of a young lady) ⌐book 372

	1776	**HŌ, nara(u)** – imitate, follow
倣	2a8.7 ⫿ 彳 方 攵 3 48 49 倣	模倣 *mohō* imitation 1425 先例に倣う *senrei ni narau* follow precedent 50, 612

	1777	**SHŌ, nobo(ru)** – rise, be promoted
昇	4c4.5 ⊟ 日 艹 | 43 32 2 昇	上昇 *jōshō* rise, ascent; upward trend 32 昇進 *shōshin* promotion, advancement 437 昇格 *shōkaku* promotion to a higher status, upgrading 643 昇給 *shōkyū* pay raise 346 昇級 *shōkyū* promotion to a higher grade 568

	1778	**KYŌ, odoro(ku)** – be surprised, astonished; be frightened **odoro(kasu)** – surprise, astonish; frighten
驚	10a12.4⊟ 馬 攵 艹 78 49 32 驚	驚嘆 *kyōtan* admiration, wonder 1246 驚異 *kyōi* wonder, miracle, marvel 1061 驚がく *kyōgaku* astonishment; alarm, consternation

326

謄	**1779** 4b13.1 □ 月 言 火 42 67 44 謄 謄	**TŌ** – copy 謄写 *tōsha* copy, duplication — 540 謄写器 *tōshaki* mimeograph machine — 540, 527 謄写版 *tōshaban* mimeograph — 540, 1046 謄本 *tōhon* transcript, copy — 25
騰	**1780** 4b16.3 □ 月 馬 火 42 78 44 騰 騰	**TŌ** – rise (in prices) (物価) 騰貴 *(bukka) tōki* rise (in prices) — 79, 421, 1171 暴騰 *bōtō* sudden/sharp rise — 1014 高騰 *kōtō* sudden rise, jump (in prices) — 190
幣	**1781** 3f12.4 □ 巾 攵 小 26 49 35 幣 幣	**HEI** – Shinto zigzag paper offerings; money 紙幣 *shihei* paper money — 180 貨幣 *kahei* money; coin, coinage ⌈currency — 752 貨幣価値 *kahei kachi* the value of money/ — 752, 421, 425 造幣局 *Zōheikyoku* Mint Bureau — 691, 170 幣制 *heisei* monetary system — 427
弊	**1782** 4i11.3 □ 攵 小 卄 49 35 32 弊 弊	**HEI** – evil; abuse, vice; (humble prefix) our 弊害 *heigai* an evil, ill effect — 518 疲弊 *hihei* impoverishment, exhaustion — 1321 旧弊 *kyūhei* an old evil; old-fashioned — 1216 弊社 *heisha* our company, we — 308
却	**1783** 2e5.3 □ 冂 土 厶 7 22 17 却 卻	**KYAKU** – pull back, withdraw 却下 *kyakka* reject, dismiss — 31 返却 *henkyaku* return, repay — 442 退却 *taikyaku* retreat — 846 売却 *baikyaku* sale, disposal by sale — 239 忘却 *bōkyaku* forget, lose sight of — 1374
脚	**1784** 4b7.3 □ 月 土 阝 42 22 7 脚	**KYAKU, [KYA], ashi** – leg 橋脚 *kyōkyaku* bridge pier — 597 失脚 *shikkyaku* lose one's position/standing — 311 脚注 *kyakuchū* footnote — 357 脚本 *kyakuhon* play, script — 25 脚色 *kyakushoku* dramatization, stage/film adaption — 204
慎	**1785** 4k10.4 □ 心 目 十 51 55 12 慎 愼	**SHIN, tsutsushi(mu)** – be discreet, careful; restrain oneself, refrain from 謹慎 *kinshin* good behavior; house arrest — 1247 慎重 *shinchō* cautious — 227 慎み深い *tsutsushimibukai* discreet, cautious — 536

1786

CHIN, shizu(meru) – calm, quell **shizu(maru)** – calm down

8a10.6 ⊞

72 55 12

鎮 鎮

鎮静剤	*chinseizai* a sedative	663, 550
鎮痛剤	*chintsūzai* pain-killer	1320, 550
鎮圧	*chin'atsu* suppression, quelling	1342
鎮魂曲/歌	*chinkonkyoku/ka* requiem	1525, 366, 392
鎮守	*chinju* local/tutelary deity	490

1787

KI – wheel track, rut, railway, orbit

7c2.1 ⊡

69 12

軌

軌道	*kidō* railroad track; orbit	149
狭軌鉄道	*kyōki tetsudō* narrow-gauge railway	1353, 312, 149
常軌	*jōki* normal course of action	497
軌範	*kihan* model, example	1092
軌跡	*kiseki* (geometrical) locus	1569

1788

NAN, yawa(rakai/raka) – soft

7c4.1 ⊡

69 49

軟

柔軟	*jūnan* soft, pliable	774
軟化	*nanka* become soft; relent	254
軟弱	*nanjaku* weak, weak-kneed	218
軟骨	*nankotsu* cartilage	1266
軟着陸	*nanchakuriku* soft landing	657, 647

1789

YŌ, kama – kiln

3m12.5 ⊟

33 46 44

窯 窰

窯業	*yōgyō* ceramic industry, ceramics	279
窯元	*kamamoto* place where pottery is made	137

1790

RO – furnace, hearth

4d4.2 ⊡

44 40

炉 爐

暖炉	*danro* fireplace	635
溶鉱炉	*yōkōro* smelting/blast furnace	1392, 1604
原子炉	*genshiro* atomic reactor	136, 103
核反応炉	*kaku hannōro* nuclear reactor	1212, 324, 827
増殖炉	*zōshokuro* breeder reactor	712, 1506

1791

SUI, ta(ku) – burn; light a fire; boil, cook

4d4.1 ⊡

44 49

炊

炊事	*suiji* cooking	80
自炊	*jisui* do one's own cooking	62
炊飯器	*suihanki* rice cooker	325, 527
雑炊	*zōsui* porridge of rice and vegetables	575
炊き出し	*takidashi* emergency group cooking	53

1792

FUTSU, wa(ku) – boil, seethe **wa(kasu)** – (bring to a) boil

3a5.3 ⊡

21 28 16

沸

沸騰	*futtō* boiling; excitement, agitation	1780
沸(騰)点	*fut(tō)ten* boiling point	1780, 169
沸き立つ	*wakitatsu* boil up, seethe	121
湯沸かし(器)	*yuwakashi(ki)* hot-water heater	632, 527

	1793	***tsu(keru)*** – soak, immerse; pickle, preserve ***tsu(karu)*** – soak, steep, be submersed; be well seasoned	
漬	3a11.12 田		
	氵貝土 21 68 22	漬物 *tsukemono* pickled vegetables	79
		漬物石 *tsukemono-ishi* weight stone (used in making pickles)	79, 78
	漬	塩漬 *shiozuke* food preserved with salt	1101

	1794	***JŪ, shiru*** – juice, sap; soup, broth, gravy	
汁	3a2.1 口		
	氵十 21 12	(天然) 果汁 *(tennen) kajū* (natural) fruit juice	141, 651, 487
		肉汁 *nikujū* meat juices, gravy	223
		墨汁 *bokujū* India ink	1705
	汁	汁粉 *shiruko* adzuki-bean soup with rice cake	1701
		みそ汁 *misoshiru* miso soup	

	1795	***SHA, ni(eru/ru)*** – (intr./tr.) boil, cook ***ni(yasu)*** – boil, cook	
煮	4d8.9 日		
	火 日 土 44 43 22	煮沸 *shafutsu* boiling	1792
		雑煮 *zōni* rice-cake soup with vegetables	575
		生煮え *namanie* half-cooked, underdone	44
	煮 煮	煮返す *nikaesu* reboil, cook over again	442
		業を煮やす *gō o niyasu* become exasperated	279

	1796	***CHŌ, tomura(u)*** – mourn, condole	
弔	0a4.41 ⋯		
	弓 丨 28 2	弔意 *chōi* condolence, sympathy	132
		弔辞 *chōji* words/message of condolence	688
		弔電 *chōden* telegram of condolence	108
	弔	弔問 *chōmon* visit of condolence	162
		慶弔 *keichō* congratulations and condolences	1632

	1797	***KI, i(mu)*** – hate, loathe; avoid, shun ***i(mawashii)*** – abominable, disgusting, scandalous; ominous	
忌	4k3.4 日		
	心 弓 51 28	忌中 *kichū* in mourning	28
		忌避 *kihi* evasion, shirking; (legal) challenge	1491
	忌	忌み言葉 *imikotoba* word taboo by superstition	66, 253

	1798	***JIN*** – fast	
迅	2q3.5 口		
	⻌ 十 一 19 12 1	迅速 *jinsoku* quick, rapid, speedy	502
		迅雷 *jinrai* thunderclap	952
	迅	奮迅 *funjin* roused to powerful action	1309

	1799	***JUN*** – follow into death, lay down one's life	
殉	4c6.9 田		
	日 夕 ⼔ 43 30 15	殉教者 *junkyōsha* martyr	245, 164
		殉難 *junnan* martyrdom	557
		殉職 *junshoku* die in the line of duty	385
	殉	殉国 *junkoku* dying for one's country	40
		殉死 *junshi* kill oneself on the death of one's lord	85

	1800	*KŌ* – seize, arrest; adhere to	
拘	3c5.28 □	拘束 *kōsoku* restriction, restraint	501
	扌 口 宀	拘留 *kōryū* detention, custody	761
	23 24 15	拘置 *kōchi* keep in detention, confine, hold	426
		拘置所 *kōchisho* house of detention, prison	426, 153
拘		拘泥 *kōdei* adhere (to), be a stickler (for)	1621

	1801	*SETSU* – unskillful, clumsy	
拙	3c5.11 □	拙劣 *setsuretsu* clumsy, bungling, unskillful	1150
	扌 屮 冂	稚拙 *chisetsu* artless, crude, naive	1230
	23 36 20	拙策 *sessaku* poor policy, imprudent measure	880
		拙速 *sessoku* not elaborate but fast, rough-and-ready	502
拙		巧拙 *kōsetsu* skill, dexterity	1627

	1802	*KUTSU* – bend; yield	
屈	3r5.2 □	屈曲 *kukkyoku* crookedness; refraction; curvature	366
	尸 屮 冂	不屈 *fukutsu* indomitability, dauntlessness	94
	40 36 20	屈辱 *kutsujoku* humiliation, indignity	1738
		卑屈 *hikutsu* lack of moral courage, servility	1521
屈		退屈 *taikutsu* tedious, monotonous, boring	846

	1803	*KUTSU, ho(ru)* – dig	
掘	3c8.32 □	採掘 *saikutsu* mining, digging	933
	扌 尸 屮	発掘 *hakkutsu* excavation; exhumation	96
	23 40 36	掘り抜く *horinuku* dig through, bore	1713
		掘り返す *horikaesu* dig up	⌐bargain 442
掘		掘り出し物 *horidashimono* treasure trove; lucky find;	53, 79

	1804	*hori* – moat; canal, ditch	
堀	3b8.11 □	堀割 *horiwari* canal, waterway	519
	土 尸 屮	堀江 *horie* canal	821
	22 40 36	堀川 *horikawa* canal	33
		内堀 *uchibori* inner moat	84
堀		外堀 *sotobori* outer moat	83

	1805	*HEI* – wall, fence	
塀	3b9.11 □	板塀 *itabei* board fence	1047
	土 尸 艹	石塀 *ishibei* stone fence	78
	22 40 32	土塀 *dobei* mud/earthen wall	24
塀 塀			

	1806	*RŌ, mo(ru/reru)* – leak, slip from *mo(rasu)* – let leak, divulge	
漏	3a11.19 □	漏電 *rōden* electric leakage, short circuit	108
	氵 雨 尸	脱漏 *datsurō* be omitted, left out	1370
	21 75 40	遺漏なく *irōnaku* without omission, exhaustively	1172
		雨漏り *amamori* leak in the roof	30
漏		聞き漏らす *kikimorasu* fail to hear, miss (a word)	64

	1807	**ZOKU** – rebel, robber	
賊	7b6.3 □	盗 賊 *tōzoku* thief, burglar, robber	1100
	貝 戈 十	海 賊 *kaizoku* pirate	117
	68 52 12	山 賊 *sanzoku* mountain robber, bandit	34
		賊 軍 *zokugun* rebel army, rebels	438
	賊	国 賊 *kokuzoku* traitor	40

	1808	**FU** – tribute; payment, installment; prose poem	
賦	7b8.4 □	月 賦 *geppu* monthly installment	17
	貝 戈 ト	賦 税 *fuzei* taxation	399
	68 52 13	賦 課 *fuka* levy, assessment	488
		賦 役 *fueki* compulsory labor, corvée	375
	賦	天 賦 *tenpu* inherent nature; inborn, natural	141

	1809	**KA** – calamity, misfortune	
禍	4e9.4 ⊞	禍 根 *kakon* root of evil, source of calamity	314
	礻 口 冂	災 禍 *saika* accident, disaster	1335
	45 24 20	戦 禍 *senka* the ravages of war, war damage	301
		禍 福 *kafuku* fortune and misfortune	1379
	禍 禍	舌 禍 *zekka* unfortunate slip of the tongue	1259

	1810	**KA, uzu** – swirl, vortex, whirlpool, eddy	
渦	3a9.36 ⊞	渦 流 *karyū* eddy, whirlpool	247
	氵 口 冂	渦 中 *kachū* maelstrom, vortex	28
	21 24 20	戦 渦 *senka* the confusion of war	301
	渦	渦 巻 き *uzumaki* eddy, vortex, whirlpool; spiral	507

	1811	**RI** – diarrhea	
痢	5i7.2 ▯	下 痢 *geri* diarrhea	31
	疒 禾 几	赤 痢 *sekiri* dysentery	207
	60 56 16	疫 痢 *ekiri* children's dysentery, infant diarrhea	1319
	痢		

	1812	**SHITSU** – illness, disease; fast	
疾	5i5.12 ▯	疾 患 *shikkan* disease, ailment	1315
	疒 大 ᅳ	悪 疾 *akushitsu* malignant disease	304
	60 34 15	廃 疾 *haishitsu* disablement, disabiltiy	961
		疾 走 *shissō* run at full speed	429
	疾	疾 風 *shippū* strong wind, gale	29

	1813	**CHI** – foolish	
痴	5i8.1 ▯	白 痴 *hakuchi* idiocy; idiot	205
	疒 大 口	痴 漢 *chikan* molester of women, masher	556
	60 34 24	痴 情 *chijō* foolish passion, blind love; jealousy	209
		音 痴 *onchi* tone-deaf	347
	痴 癡	愚 痴 *guchi* idle complaint, grumbling	1642

怖	**1814** 4k5.6 □ 心 巾 十 51 26 12 怖	**FU, kowa(i)** – frightening, scary, dreadful; eerie, weird 恐 怖 *kyōfu* fear, terror 1602 恐 怖 政 治 *kyōfu seiji* reign of terror 1602, 483, 493 恐 怖 症 *kyōfushō* phobia, morbid dread 1602, 1318 高 所 恐 怖 症 *kōsho kyōfushō* acrophobia 190, 153, 1602, 1318
憾	**1815** 4k13.3 ⊞ 心 戈 口 51 52 24 憾	**KAN** – regret 遺 憾 *ikan* regrettable 1172
錬	**1816** 8a8.3 □ 釒 木 日 72 41 43 錬 錬	**REN** – forge, temper (iron); polish, refine; train, drill 精 錬 所 *seirensho* refinery 659, 153 錬 金 術 *renkinjutsu* alchemy 23, 187 錬 成 *rensei* training 261 修 錬 *shūren* training, discipline 945
鍛	**1817** 8a9.5 Ⅲ 釒 厂 冂 72 18 20 鍛	**TAN, kita(eru)** – forge, temper; train, drill, discipline 鍛 工 *tankō* metalworker, smith 139 鍛 錬 *tanren* temper, anneal; train, harden 1816 鍛 え 上 げ る *kitaeageru* become highly trained 32
錠	**1818** 8a8.12 ⊞ 釒 宀 二 72 33 14 錠	**JŌ** – lock, padlock; pill, tablet 錠 前 *jōmae* a lock 47 組 み 合 わ せ 錠 *kumiawasejō* combination lock 418, 159 手 錠 *tejō* handcuffs 57 錠 剤 *jōzai* tablet, pill 550 一 錠 *ichijō* 1 tablet/pill 2
鎖	**1819** 8a10.2 ⊞ 釒 貝 小 72 68 35 鎖	**SA** – close, shut **kusari** – chain 封 鎖 *fūsa* blockade 1463 閉 鎖 *heisa* closing, shutdown, lockout 397 鎖 国 *sakoku* national isolation 40 連 鎖 反 応 *rensa hannō* chain reaction 440, 324, 827 金 鎖 *kingusari* gold chain 23
鉢	**1820** 8a5.4 □ 釒 木 一 72 41 1 鉢	**HACHI, [HATSU]** – bowl, pot; brainpan; crown 火 鉢 *hibachi* hibachi, charcoal brazier 20 植 木 鉢 *uekibachi* flowerpot 424, 22 衣 鉢 *ihatsu* the mantle, secrets (of one's master) 677 す り 鉢 *suribachi* (conical) earthenware mortar 鉢 巻 き *hachimaki* cloth tied around one's head 507

	1821	**SHŌ, kane** – bell	
鐘	8a12.6 ⊞ 金 立 日 72 54 43 鐘	晩鐘 *banshō* evening bell 警鐘 *keishō* alarm bell 半鐘 *hanshō* fire bell 鐘乳洞 *shōnyūdō* stalactite cave	736 706 88 939, 1301
鈴	1822 8a5.11 ⊞ 金 亻 一 72 3 1 鈴	**REI, RIN, suzu** – bell 電鈴 *denrei* electric bell 呼び鈴 *yobirin* doorbell, (hotel) service bell 風鈴 *fūrin* wind-bell 鈴虫 *suzumushi* "bell-ring" insect 鈴木 *Suzuki* (surname)	108 1254 29 873 22
零	1823 8d5.4 日 雨 亻 一 75 3 1 零	**REI** – zero 零点 *reiten* (a score of) zero 零時 *reiji* 12 o'clock 零度 *reido* zero (degrees), the freezing point 零下 *reika* below zero, subzero 零細 *reisai* small, trifling	169 42 377 31 695
霧	1824 8d4.2 日 雨 儿 力 75 16 8 霧	**FUN** – fog 雰囲気 *fun'iki* atmosphere, ambience	1194, 134
棺	1825 4a8.25 ⊞ 木 宀 尸 41 33 40 棺	**KAN** – coffin 棺おけ *kan'oke* coffin 石棺 *sekkan* stone coffin, sarcophagus 納棺 *nōkan* place (a body) in the coffin 出棺 *shukkan* start of a funeral procession	78 758 53
埋	1826 3b7.2 ⊞ 土 日 22 43 埋	**MAI, u(maru)** – be buried (under); filled up **u(meru)** – bury; fill up **u(moreru)** – be buried; sink into obscurity 埋葬 *maisō* burial, interment 埋没 *maibotsu* be buried; fall into oblivion 埋蔵 *maizō* buried stores, underground reserves 埋め立て *umetate* land reclamation	812 935 1286 121
彰	1827 3j11.1 ⊞ 彡 立 日 31 54 43 彰	**SHŌ** – clear 顕彰 *kenshō* manifest, exhibit, exalt 表彰 *hyōshō* official commendation 表彰状 *hyōshōjō* certificate of commendation, citation	1170 272 272, 626

培	**1828** 3b8.6　田 土 立 口 22　54　24 培	**BAI, tsuchika(u)** – cultivate, foster 栽 培　*saibai*　cultivation, culture, growing　　　　　1125 培 養　*baiyō*　cultivation, culture　　　　　　　　402 培 養 液　*baiyōeki*　culture fluid/solution　　　402, 472 純 粋 培 養　*junsui baiyō*　pure culture　965, 1708, 402
賠	**1829** 7b8.1　田 貝 立 口 68　54　24 賠	**BAI** – indemnify 賠 償　*baishō*　reparation, indemnification　　　　971 損 害 賠 償　*songai baishō*　compensation for damages 　　　　　　　　　　　　　　　　　　350, 518, 971 賠 償 金　*baishōkin*　indemnities, reparations, damages　971, 23
剖	**1830** 2f8.1　田 刂 立 口 16　54　24 剖 剖	**BŌ** – divide 解 剖　*kaibō*　dissection, autopsy, analysis　　　　474 解 剖 学　*kaibōgaku*　anatomy　　　　　　　474, 109 生 体 解 剖　*seitai kaibō*　vivisection　　　44, 61, 474
賜	**1831** 7b8.2　田 貝 日 勿 68　43　27 賜	**SHI, tamawa(ru)** – grant, bestow, confer 下 賜　*kashi*　imperial grant, donation　　　　　　31 恩 賜　*onshi*　imperial gift　　　　　　　　　　555 賜 暇　*shika*　leave of absence, furlough　　　　1064
据	**1832** 3c8.33　田 扌 尸 口 23　40　24 据	**su(eru)** – set, place, put into position　**su(waru)** – sit, be set 据 え 付 け る　*suetsukeru*　set into position, install　192 据 え 置 く　*sueoku*　leave as is, let stand　　　　426 腹 を 据 え る　*hara o sueru*　decide, make up one's mind　1271
拓	**1833** 3c5.1　田 扌 石 23　53 拓	**TAKU** – open, clear, break up (land) 開 拓　*kaitaku*　reclamation, clearing　　　　　　396 開 拓 者　*kaitakusha*　settler, pioneer　　　　396, 164 拓 殖　*takushoku*　colonization, settlement　　　1506 干 拓　*kantaku*　land reclamation by drainage　　584 拓 本　*takuhon*　a rubbing (of an inscription)　　　25
碁	**1834** 5a8.9　田 石 廾 一 二 53　32　4 碁	**GO** – (the board game) go 囲 碁　*igo*　(the game of) go　　　　　　　　　1194 碁 石　*goishi*　go stone　　　　　　　　　　　　78 碁 会 所　*gokaisho, gokaijo*　go club　　　　158, 153 碁 盤　*goban*　go board　　　　　　　　┌layout 1098 碁 盤 の 目　*goban no me*　go-board grid, checker-board 1098, 55

	1835	**KI** – go, shōgi, Japanese chess	
棋	4a8.14 ⊞ 木 艹 儿 41 32 16 棋 棊	将 棋 *shōgi* shōgi, Japanese chess 将 棋 盤 *shōgiban* shōgi board 棋 譜 *kifu* record of a game of go/shōgi 棋 士 *kishi* (professional) go/shōgi player 将 棋 倒 し *shōgidaoshi* fall down (like dominoes)	627 627, 1098 1167 572 627, 905

	1836	**JŌ** – daughter; young lady	
嬢	3e13.1 ⊞ 女 衤 艹 25 57 32 嬢 孃	お 嬢 さ ん *ojōsan* (your) daughter; young lady (御) 令 嬢 *(go)reijō* (your) daughter; young lady 愛 嬢 *aijō* one's dear/favorite daughter	 708, 831 259

	1837	**JŌ, kamo(su)** – brew; bring about, give rise to	
醸	7e13.1 ⊞ 酉 衤 艹 71 57 32 醸 釀	醸 造 所 *jōzōsho* brewery, distillery 醸 成 *jōsei* brew; cause, bring about	691, 153 261

	1838	**SO** – modeling, molding	
塑	3b10.8 ⊞ 土 月 儿 22 42 16 塑	塑 像 *sozō* modeling, molding 可 塑 性 *kasosei* plasticity 彫 塑 *chōso* carving and (clay) modeling, plastic arts	740 388, 98 1149

	1839	**DAN, [TAN]** – rostrum, dais, podium	
壇	3b13.5 ⊞ 土 日 回 22 43 24 壇	演 壇 *endan* (speaker's) platform, rostrum 祭 壇 *saidan* altar 文 壇 *bundan* the literary world 花 壇 *kadan* flower bed ⌐execution 土 壇 場 *dotanba* last/critical moment; place of	344 617 111 255 24, 154

	1840	**TŌ** – tower	
塔	3b9.9 ⊞ 土 艹 口 22 32 24 塔	監 視 塔 *kanshitō* watchtower 管 制 塔 *kanseitō* control tower 広 告 塔 *kōkokutō* poster column, advertising pillar 象 げ の 塔 *zōge no tō* ivory tower 五 重 の 塔 *gojū no tō* 5-story pagoda	1663, 606 328, 427 694, 690 739 7, 227

	1841	**RŌ** – tower, turret, lookout	
楼	4a9.10 ⊞ 木 米 女 41 62 25 楼 樓	鐘 楼 *shōrō* bell tower, belfry 楼 閣 *rōkaku* many-storied building, castle 楼 門 *rōmon* 2-story gate 摩 天 楼 *matenrō* skyscraper	1821 837 161 1530, 141

	1842	**SEN** – stopper, cork, plug, spigot	
栓	4a6.26 田 木 王 亻 41 46 3 栓	消火栓 *shōkasen* fire hydrant 給水栓 *kyūsuisen* water tap, hydrant 水道栓 *suidōsen* hydrant, tap ガス栓 *gasusen* gas tap 栓抜き *sennuki* bottle opener	845, 20 346, 21 21, 149 1713

	1843	**FU** – attach; accompany (cf. No. 192)	
附	2d5.4 ⊞ 阝 寸 亻 7 37 3 附	附属 *fuzoku* belonging to, accessory 寄附 *kifu* contribution, donation 附近 *fukin* neighborhood, vicinity 附録 *furoku* supplement, appendix 附随 *fuzui* accompany, be entailed by	1637 1361 445 538 1741

	1844	**RYŌ, misasagi** – imperial tomb, mausoleum	
陵	2d8.5 ⊞ 阝 夂 土 7 49 22 陵	丘陵 *kyūryō* hill 丘陵地帯 *kyūryō chitai* hilly area 御陵 *goryō* tomb of the emperor/empress	1357 1357, 118, 963 708

	1845	**SHUN** – excellence, genius	
俊	2a7:10 ⊞ 亻 夂 厶 3 49 17 俊	俊秀 *shunshū* person of outstanding talent 俊英 *shun'ei* talent, gifted person 俊才 *shunsai* genius, outstanding talent 俊傑 *shunketsu* great man 俊敏 *shunbin* keen, quick-witted	1683 353 551 1731 1735

	1846	**SA, sosonoka(su)** – tempt, entice; incite, abet	
唆	3d7.8 ⊞ 口 夂 厶 24 49 17 唆	示唆 *shisa* suggestion 教唆 *kyōsa* instigation, incitement	615 245

	1847	**HIN** – occur repeatedly	
頻	9a8.2 ⊞ 頁 小 ト 77 35 13 頻 頻	頻度 *hindo* frequency, rate of occurrence 頻発 *hinpatsu* frequency, frequent occurrence 頻繁 *hinpan* frequency, rapid succession 頻々と *hinpin to* frequent, in rapid succession	377 96 1292

	1848	**GAN** – stubborn, obstinate	
頑	9a4.6 ⊞ 頁 二 儿 77 4 16 頑	頑固 *ganko* stubborn, obstinate 頑迷 *ganmei* bigoted, obstinate 頑強 *gankyō* stubborn, obstinate, unyielding 頑健 *ganken* strong and robust, in excellent health 頑張る *ganbaru* persist in, stick to it, hang in there	972 967 217 893 1106

	1849	**HAN, [BON]**, *wazura(u)* – worry about; be ill, suffer from
煩	4d9.1 ☐	*wazura(wasu)* – trouble, bother, annoy

火 頁		
44 77		

| 煩 | | |

煩雑	*hanzatsu*	complicated, troublesome	575
煩忙	*hanbō*	busy, pressed with business	1373
煩悩	*bonnō*	evil passions, carnal desires	1279
煩わしい	*wazurawashii*	troublesome, tangled	

	1850	**HAN** – divide, distribute
頒	9a4.3 ⊞	

頁 儿 力		
77 16 8		

| 頒 | | |

頒布	*hanpu*	distribute, circulate	675

	1851	**KA** – alone, widowed; few, small
寡	3m11.2 ☐	

宀 月 一		
33 42 14		

| 寡 | | |

多寡	*taka*	quantity, number, amount	229
寡婦	*kafu*	widow	316
寡聞	*kabun*	little knowledge, ill-informed	64
寡黙	*kamoku*	taciturn, reticent	1578
寡占	*kasen*	oligopoly	1706

	1852	**HIN** – guest
賓	3m12.3 ☐	

宀 貝 小		
33 68 35		

| 賓 賓 | | |

賓客	*hinkaku, hinkyaku*	honored guest, visitor	641
貴賓	*kihin*	distinguished guest, guest of honor	1171
主賓	*shuhin*	guest of honor	155
来賓	*raihin*	guest, visitor	69
迎賓館	*geihinkan*	reception hall; guest mansion	1055, 327

	1853	**SHŌ** – further; value, respect
尚	3n5.2 ☐	

⺌ ⼝ 冂		
35 24 20		

| 尚 尚 | | |

高尚	*kōshō*	lofty, noble, refined	190
尚武	*shōbu*	militaristic, martial	1031
尚早	*shōsō*	premature, too early	248
時機尚早	*jiki-shōsō*	too soon, time is not ripe	42, 528, 248
和尚	*oshō*	Buddhist priest	124

	1854	**SHŌ, yoi** – early evening
宵	3m7.7 ☐	

宀 月 小		
33 42 35		

| 宵 宵 | | |

春宵	*shunshō*	spring evening	460
徹宵	*tesshō*	all night long	1422
宵の口	*yoi no kuchi*	early evening	54
宵っ張り	*yoippari*	staying up till late; night owl	1106
宵越し	*yoigoshi*	(left over) from the previous evening	1001

	1855	**SHŌ** – saltpeter
硝	5a7.6 ⊞	

石 月 小		
53 42 35		

| 硝 | | |

硝酸	*shōsan*	nitric acid	516
硝石	*shōseki*	saltpeter	78
硝煙	*shōen*	gunpowder smoke	919

硫	**1856** 5a7.3 石 宀 ム 53 11 17 硫	**RYŪ** – sulfur 硫酸 *ryūsan* sulfuric acid 516 硫化水素 *ryūka suiso* hydrogen sulfide 254, 21, 271 硫黄 *iō* sulfur 780
肪	**1857** 4b4.2 月 方 42 48 肪	**BŌ** – (animal) fat 脂肪 *shibō* fat 1042 皮下脂肪 *hika shibō* subcutaneous fat 975, 31, 1042 脂肪ぶとり *shibōbutori* fat, obese 1042 脂肪層 *shibōsō* layer of fat ⌈fat 1042, 1367 植物性脂肪 *shokubutsusei shibō* vegetable 424, 79, 98, 1042
坊	**1858** 3b4.1 土 方 22 48 坊	**BŌ, [BO']** – priest's residence; Buddhist priest; boy 坊主 *bōzu* Buddhist priest, bonze 155 朝寝坊 *asanebō* a late riser 469, 1079 けちん坊 *kechinbō* stingy person, tightwad 赤ん坊 *akanbō* baby 207 坊ちゃん *botchan* (your) son, young master, boy
紡	**1859** 6a4.1 糸 方 61 48 紡	**BŌ, tsumu(gu)** – spin, make yarn 紡績 *bōseki* spinning 1117 紡績工場 *bōseki kōjō* spinning mill 1117, 139, 154 紡織 *bōshoku* spinning and weaving 680 混紡 *konbō* mixed/blended spinning 799
羅	**1860** 5g14.1 罒 隹 糸 55 74 61 羅	**RA** – silk gauze, thin silk 羅列 *raretsu* enumerate, cite 611 羅針 *rashin* compass needle 341 羅針盤 *rashinban* compass 341, 1098 網羅 *mōra* be all-inclusive, comprehensive 1612 一張羅 *itchōra* one's best/only clothes 2, 1106
罷	**1861** 5g10.2 罒 月 ム 55 42 17 罷	**HI** – end, discontinue, stop; leave, withdraw 罷免 *himen* dismissal (from one's post) 733 罷業 *higyō* strike, walkout 279
釣	**1862** 8a3.5 金 勹 丨 72 15 2 釣	**CHŌ, tsu(ru)** – fish, angle; decoy, allure, take in 釣り道具 *tsuridōgu* fishing tackle 149, 420 釣り針 *tsuribari* fishhook 341 釣り堀 *tsuribori* fishing pond 1804 釣り銭 *tsurisen* (make) change 648 釣り合い *tsuriai* balance, equilibrium, proportion 159

酌	**1863** 7e3.3 ▢ 酉 宀 丨 71 15 2 酌	**SHAKU** – pour (wine), serve at table 媒酌 *baishaku* matchmaking ... 1496 媒酌人 *baishakunin* matchmaker, go-between ... 1496, 1 晩酌 *banshaku* evening drink ... 736 独酌 *dokushaku* drinking alone ... 219 しん酌 *shinshaku* take into consideration
酬	**1864** 7e6.2 ▢ 酉 儿 71 16 酬	**SHŪ** – reward, compensation 報酬 *hōshū* remuneration ... 685 無報酬 *muhōshū* without remuneration, free of charge ... 93, 685 応酬 *ōshū* reply, response, retort ... 827
酪	**1865** 7e6.4 ▢ 酉 夂口 71 49 24 酪	**RAKU** – whey 酪農(場) *rakunō(jō)* dairy, dairy farm ... 369, 154 酪製品 *rakuseihin* dairy products ... 428, 230 酪農家 *rakunōka* dairy farmer, dairyman ... 369, 165
酵	**1866** 7e6.1 ▢ 酉 土 子 71 22 6 酵	**KŌ** – fermentation; yeast 酵母 *kōbo* yeast ... 112 酵母菌 *kōbokin* yeast fungus ... 112, 1222 酵素 *kōso* enzyme ... 271 発酵 *hakkō* fermentation ... 96
酢	**1867** 7e5.3 ▢ 酉 宀 ト 71 15 13 酢 醋	**SAKU, su** – vinegar 酢酸 *sakusan* acetic acid ... 516 酢漬け *suzuke* pickling in vinegar ... 1793 酢の物 *su no mono* vinegared dish ... 79 甘酢 *amazu* sweet vinegar ... 1492
尾	**1868** 3r4.2 ▢ 尸 龷 一 40 12 1 尾	**BI, o** – tail 末尾 *matsubi* the end ... 305 首尾 *shubi* beginning and end; result, outcome ... 148 尾行 *bikō* shadow, tail (someone) ... 68 尾灯 *bitō* taillight ... 1333 徹頭徹尾 *tettō-tetsubi* thoroughly ... 1422, 276
尿	**1869** 3r4.1 ▢ 尸 氵 40 21 尿	**NYŌ** – urine 尿素 *nyōso* urea ... 271 尿酸 *nyōsan* uric acid ... 516 排尿 *hainyō* urination ... 1036 夜尿症 *yanyōshō* nocturnal enuresis, bedwetting ... 471, 1318 糖尿病 *tōnyōbyō* diabetes ... 1698, 380

	1870	**HITSU, HI** – flow, secrete
泌	3a5.10 ⊞	分泌 *bunpitsu, bunpi* secretion 38
	氵 必 丨	内分泌 *naibunpi, naibunpitsu* internal secretion 84, 38
	21 51 2	分泌物 *bunpibutsu, bunpitsubutsu* a secretion 38, 79
	泌	泌尿器 *hinyōki* urinary organs 1869, 527
		泌尿器科 *hinyōkika* urology 1869, 527, 320

	1871	**RYŪ, yanagi** – willow tree
柳	4a5.17 ⊞	川柳 *senryū* humorous 17-syllable Japanese poem 33
	木 厂阝	花柳界 *karyūkai* demimonde, red-light district 255, 454
	41 18 7	柳び *ryūbi* beautiful eyebrows
	柳	枝垂れ柳 *shidare yanagi* weeping willow 870, 1070
		柳腰 *yanagi-goshi* slender graceful hips 1298

	1872	**sugi** – Japanese cedar
杉	4a3.2 ⊞	杉並木 *suginamiki* avenue of sugi trees 1165, 22
	木 彡	杉並区 *Suginami-ku* Suginami Ward (Tōkyō) 1165, 183
	41 31	
	杉	

	1873	**SŌ, kuwa** – mulberry tree
桑	2h8.1 ⊟	桑門 *sōmon* Buddhist priest/monk 161
	又 木	桑園 *sōen* mulberry farm/orchard 447
	9 41	桑田 *sōden* mulberry orchard 35
	桑	桑畑 *kuwabatake* mulberry field ⌜God! 36
		桑原桑原 *kuwabara-kuwabara* Heaven forbid! Thank 136

	1874	**KON** – elder brother; later; insect
昆	4c4.10 ⊟	昆虫 *konchū* insect 873
	日 ⊢	昆虫学 *konchūgaku* entomology 873, 109
	43 13	昆虫採集 *konchū saishū* insect collecting 873, 933, 436
	昆	昆布 *konbu, kobu* sea tangle, tang, kelp 675
		昆布茶 *kobucha* tang tea 675, 251

	1875	**JA, DA, hebi** – snake
蛇	6d5.7 ⊞	蛇の目 *janome* bull's-eye design (on oilpaper umbrella) 55
	虫 宀 ⊢	蛇腹 *jabara* accordion-like folds, bellows; cornice 1271
	64 33 13	蛇行 *dakō* meander, zigzag, fishtail 68
	蛇	蛇足 *dasoku* superfluous (like legs on a snake) 58
		長蛇の列 *chōda no retsu* long queue/line of people 95, 611

	1876	**ka** – mosquito
蚊	6d4.5 ⊞	蚊帳, 蚊屋 *kaya* mosquito net 1107, 167
	虫 亠 十	蚊取り線香 *katori senkō* mosquito-repellent incense
	64 11 12	65, 299, 1682
	蚊	蚊柱 *kabashira* column of swarming mosquitoes 598

	1877	**SAN, kaiko** – silkworm	
蚕	6d4.8 ⊟	養蚕 *yōsan* sericulture, silkworm raising	402
	虫 大 一	蚕糸 *sanshi* silk thread/yarn	242
	64 34 1	蚕食 *sanshoku* encroachment, inroads	322
	蚕 蠶		

	1878	**KEI, hotaru** – firefly, glowworm	
蛍	3n8.2 ⊟	蛍光灯 *keikōtō* fluorescent lamp	138, 1333
	⺌ 虫 冂	蛍光塗料 *keikō-toryō* fluorescent paint	138, 1073, 319
	35 64 20	蛍雪の功 *keisetsu no kō* the fruits of diligent study	949, 818
	蛍 螢	蛍狩り *hotarugari* firefly catching	1581

	1879	**BAN** – barbarian	
蛮	2j10.1 ⊟	(野)蛮人 *(ya)banjin* barbarian, savage	236, 1
	一 虫 儿	南蛮 *nanban* southern barbarian, European (hist.)	74
	11 64 16	蛮風 *banpū* barbarous ways/customs	29
	蛮 蠻	蛮行 *bankō* act of barbarity, brutality	68
		蛮勇 *ban'yū* recklessness; brute force	1386

	1880	**DA** – pack horse; footwear; of poor quality	
駄	10a4.1 ☐	駄賃 *dachin* reward, recompense, tip	751
	馬 大 丨	駄菓子 *dagashi* cheap candy	1535, 103
	78 34 2	駄作 *dasaku* poor work, worthless stuff	360
	駄	無駄 *muda* futile, useless, in vain	93
		下駄 *geta* geta, Japanese wooden clogs	31

	1881	**KI** – horse riding; (counter for horsemen)	
騎	10a8.3 ⊞	騎手 *kishu* rider, jockey	57
	馬 大 口	騎士 *kishi* rider, horseman	572
	78 34 24	騎兵 *kihei* cavalry soldier	784
	騎	騎馬 *kiba* on horseback, mounted	283
		一騎打ち *ikkiuchi* single combat, man-to-man fight	2, 1020

	1882	**KU, ka(keru)** – gallop; run, rush **ka(ru)** – drive, spur on	
駆	10a4.5 ☐	先駆 *senku* forerunner, pioneer	50
	馬 冂 十	駆逐 *kuchiku* drive away, expel, get rid of	1134
	78 20 12	駆除 *kujo* exterminate	1065
	駆 驅	駆け回る *kakemawaru* run around	90
		駆け足 *kakeashi* running, galloping	58

	1883	**TOKU** – serious; cordial	
篤	6f10.1 ⊟	危篤 *kitoku* critically ill	534
	⺮ 馬	篤行 *tokkō* good deed, act of charity	68
	66 78	篤志家 *tokushika* benefactor, volunteer	573, 165
	篤	篤農家 *tokunōka* exemplary farmer	369, 165
		篤学 *tokugaku* love of learning, diligence in studies	109

	1884	**KEI** – valley	
渓	3a8.16 ⊞	渓谷 *keikoku* ravine, gorge, valley	653
	氵 小 大	渓流 *keiryū* mountain stream, torrent	247
	21 35 34	雪渓 *sekkei* snowy valley/ravine	949
	渓 渓	渓間 *keikan* ravine; in the valley	43

	1885	**SHŌ, mikotonori** – imperial edict	
詔	7a5.10 ⊞	大詔 *taishō* imperial rescript	26
	言 口 力	詔書 *shōsho* imperial edict/rescript	131
	67 24 8		
	詔		

	1886	**CHOKU** – imperial decree	
勅	2g7.1 ⊞	勅語 *chokugo* imperial message, speech from the throne	67
	力 木 口	勅命 *chokumei* imperial order/commission	578
	8 41 24	詔勅 *shōchoku* imperial proclamation	1885
	勅 敕	勅使 *chokushi* imperial messenger/envoy	331

	1887	**JI** – imperial seal	
璽	4f14.2 ⊟	国璽 *kokuji* great seal, seal of state	40
	王 罒 儿	御璽 *gyoji* imperial/privy seal	708
	46 75 16	玉璽 *gyokuji* imperial seal	295
	璽	璽書 *jisho* document with the imperial seal	131

	1888	**BOKU** – I (in masculine speech); manservant	
僕	2a12.1 ⊞	従僕 *jūboku* servant, attendant	1482
	亻 王 儿	家僕 *kaboku* manservant	165
	3 46 16	僕ら *bokura* we (in masculine speech)	
	僕		

	1889	**BOKU** – hit, strike	
撲	3c12.1 ⊞	打撲傷 *dabokushō* bruise, contusion	1020, 633
	扌 王 儿	撲滅 *bokumetsu* eradication, extermination	1338
	23 46 16	相撲 *sumō* sumo wrestling	146
	撲	相撲取り *sumōtori* sumo wrestler	146, 65
		大相撲 *ōzumō* grand sumo tournament; exciting bout	26, 146

	1890	**HYŌ, tawara** – straw bag/sack	
俵	2a8.21 ⊞	土俵 *dohyō* sandbag; sumo ring	24
	亻 耒 二	米俵 *komedawara* straw rice-sack; bag of/for rice	224
	3 57 4	炭俵 *sumidawara* sack for charcoal	1344
	俵	一俵 *ippyō* 1 bag/sack	2

1891

仙

2a3.1

亻 凵

3　36

仙

SEN – hermit; wizard

仙人	*sennin* mountain wizard; hermit, settler	1
仙女	*sennyo* fairy, nymph	102
酒仙	*shusen* heavy drinker	517
水仙	*suisen* narcissus	21
仙台	*Sendai* (city in Tōhoku)	492

1892

凸

0a5.13

一 丨

1　2

凸

TOTSU – protruding, convex

凸レンズ	*totsurenzu* convex lens	
凸面	*totsumen* convex (surface)	274
両凸	*ryōtotsu* biconvex	200
凸版(印刷)	*toppan (insatsu)* letter(press), relief (printing)	1046, 1043, 1044

1893

凹

0a5.14

一 丨

1　2

凹

Ō – indentation, hollowed out, sunken in, concave

凹凸	*ōtotsu* uneven, jagged, rough	1892
凹面鏡	*ōmenkyō* concave mirror	274, 863
凹レンズ	*ōrenzu* concave lens	

1894

寸

0a3.17

寸

37

寸

SUN – (unit of length, about 3 cm)

寸法	*sunpō* measurements; plan	123
寸評	*sunpyō* brief comment	1028
寸暇	*sunka* a moment's leisure, spare moments	1064
寸前	*sunzen* immediately/right before	47
寸断	*sundan* cut/tear to pieces	1024

1895

尺

3r1.1

尸 丨

40　2

尺

SHAKU – (unit of length, about 30 cm); measure, length

尺貫法	*shakkanhō* old Japanese system of weights and measures	914, 123
巻き尺	*makijaku* tape measure, surveying tape	507
縮尺	*shukushaku* reduced scale (map)	1110
尺八	*shakuhachi* Japanese end-blown bamboo flute	10

1896

坪

3b5.4

土 一 儿

22　14　16

坪 坪

tsubo – (unit of area, about 3.3 m²)

坪数	*tsubosū* number of *tsubo*, area	225
延べ坪(数)	*nobetsubo(sū)* total area (of all floors)	1115, 225
建坪	*tatetsubo* floor space/area	892
坪二万円	*tsubo niman en* 20,000 yen per *tsubo*	3, 16, 13
坪当たり	*tsuboatari* per *tsubo*	77

1897

斤

0a4.3

斤

50

斤

KIN – (unit of weight, about 600 g)

一斤	*ikkin* 1 *kin*	2
斤量	*kinryō* weight	411

升	**1898** 0a4.32 ⋯ 艹 丨 32 2 升	***SHŌ, masu*** – (unit of volume, 1.8 liters) 一 升 *isshō* 1 *shō* 2 一 升 瓶 *isshōbin* 1.8-liter bottle 2, 1161
斗	**1899** 0a4.17 ⋯ 艹 丨 12 2 斗	***TO*** – (unit of volume, 18 liters) 一 斗 *itto* 1 *to* 2 斗 酒 *toshu* kegs of sakè 517 北 斗 (七) 星 *hokuto(shichi)sei* the Big Dipper 73, 9, 730
厘	**1900** 2p7.1 冂 厂 日 土 18 43 22 厘	***RIN*** – (old unit of currency, 1/1,000 yen); (unit of length, about 0.3 mm) 二 銭 五 厘 *nisen gorin* 2 *sen* 5 *rin*, 2.5 *sen* 3, 648, 7 一 分 一 厘 *ichibu ichirin* 1 *bu* 1 *rin*, 1.1 *bu*; some, little, slight 2, 38 厘 毛 *rinmō* a trifle; unimportant, insignificant 287
畝	**1901** 5f5.5 田 田 亠 厶 58 11 15 畝 畝	***se*** – (unit of area, about 1 are) ***une*** – ridge (between furrows); rib (in fabric) 畝 間 *unema* space between ridges, furrow 43 畝 織 *uneori* rep, ribbed fabric 680
匁	**1902** 0a4.38 ⋯ ク 十 15 12 匁	***monme*** – (unit of weigth, about 3.75 g)
勺	**1903** 0a3.5 冂 ク 丨 15 2 勺	***SHAKU*** – (unit of volume, about 18 ml)
錘	**1904** 8a8.2 田 金 土 艹 72 22 32 錘	***SUI, tsumu*** – spindle 紡 錘 *bōsui* spindle 1859 錘 状 *suijō* spindle-shaped 626

銑	**1905** 8a6.6 ⊞ 釒 土 儿 72 22 16 銑	*SEN* – pig iron 銑鉄　*sentetsu*　pig iron	312
桟	**1906** 4a6.1 ⼞ 木 戈 二 41 52 4 桟 棧	*SAN* – crosspiece, frame, bolt (of a door) 桟橋　*sanbashi*　wharf, jetty 　　　*sankyō*　wharf; bridge 桟道　*sandō*　plank bridge	597 149
枠	**1907** 4a4.19 ⊞ 木 十 41 12 枠	*waku* – frame, framework; limit, confines 窓枠　*madowaku*　window frame 枠内　*wakunai*　within the limits 枠組　*wakugumi*　frame, framework; framing	698 84 418
棚	**1908** 4a8.10 ⫿⫿⫿ 木 月 41 42 棚	*tana* – shelf 本棚　*hondana*　bookshelf 戸棚　*todana*　cupboard 棚上げ　*tanaage*　put on the shelf, shelve 大陸棚　*tairikudana*　continental shelf 棚卸　*tanaoroshi*　inventory, stock taking	25 152 32 26, 647 707
芋	**1909** 3k3.1 ⊟ 艹 丆 一 32 14 1 芋	*imo* – potato じゃが芋　*jagaimo*　(white) potato 焼き芋　*yakiimo*　baked sweet potato 里芋　*satoimo*　taro 芋掘り　*imohori*　digging sweet potatoes	 920 142 1803
薪	**1910** 3k13.3 ⊞ 艹 立 木 32 54 41 薪	*SHIN, takigi* – firewood 薪水　*shinsui*　firewood and water 薪炭　*shintan*　firewood and charcoal, fuel	21 1344
繭	**1911** 3k15.7 ⊞ 艹 糸 虫 32 61 64 繭	*KEN, mayu* – cocoon 繭糸　*kenshi*　cocoon and (silk) thread; silk thread 繭玉　*mayudama*　(type of New Year's decoration)	242 295

壤	**1912** 3b13.4 ⊞ 土 木 艹 22 57 32 壤｜壤	***JŌ*** – soil 土壌　*dojō*　soil　　24
堪	**1913** 3b9.1 ⊞ 土 艹 二 22 32 4 堪	***KAN, ta(eru)*** – endure 堪忍　*kannin*　patience, forbearance; forgiveness　1414 堪弁　*kanben*　pardon, forgive　711 堪え忍ぶ　*taeshinobu*　bear patiently　1414 堪えかねる　*taekaneru*　cannot bear
抹	**1914** 3c5.9 ⊡ 扌 木 一 23 41 1 抹	***MATSU*** – erase, expunge 抹殺　*massatsu*　expunge; deny; ignore　576 抹消　*masshō*　erase, cross out　845 一抹　*ichimatsu*　a tinge of　2 抹茶　*matcha*　powdered tea　251 抹香　*makkō*　incense powder, incense　1682
搭	**1915** 3c9.10 ⊞ 扌 艹 口 23 32 24 搭	***TŌ*** – ride 搭乗　*tōjō*　board, get on　523 搭乗券　*tōjōken*　boarding pass　523, 506 搭載　*tōsai*　load, embark　1124
拐	**1916** 3c5.21 ⊞ 扌 口 力 23 24 8 拐｜拐	***KAI*** – kidnap 誘拐　*yūkai*　kidnap　1684 拐帯　*kaitai*　abscond with money　963
嗣	**1917** 3d10.13⊟ 口 艹 冂 24 32 20 嗣	***SHI*** – heir 嗣子　*shishi*　heir　103 後嗣　*kōshi*　heir　48
嚇	**1918** 3d14.1 ⊞ 口 土 儿 24 22 16 嚇	***KAKU*** – threat 威嚇　*ikaku*　threat, menace　1339

喝	**1919** 3d8.8 ⊞ 口 日 乚 24 43 15 喝 喝	**KATSU** – scold 恐喝 *kyōkatsu* threaten, blackmail 1602 喝破 *kappa* declare, proclaim 665
謁	**1920** 7a8.6 ⊞ 言 日 乚 67 43 15 謁 謁	**ETSU** – audience (with someone) 謁見 *ekken* have an audience (with) 63 拝謁 *haietsu* have an audience (with) 1201 謁する *essuru* have an audience (with)
朕	**1921** 4b6.6 ⊞ 月 大 儿 42 34 16 朕 朕	**CHIN** – (imperial) we 朕思うに *Chin omou ni* We, the emperor, think: 99
脹	**1922** 4b8.1 ⊞ 月 衤 卜 42 57 13 脹	**CHŌ** – swell 膨脹 *bōchō* expansion 1145
爵	**1923** 5g12.1 目 罒 食 小 (55) 73 35 爵	**SHAKU** – peerage, court rank 男爵 *danshaku* baron 101 公爵 *kōshaku* prince, duke 126 伯爵 *hakushaku* count, earl 1176 爵位 *shakui* peerage, court rank 122 授爵 *jushaku* elevate to the peerage, create a peer 602
侯	**1924** 2a7.21 ⊞ 亻 大 乚 3 34 15 侯	**KŌ** – marquis 王侯 *ōkō* royalty 294 諸侯 *shokō* feudal lords 861 侯爵 *kōshaku* marquis 1923
矯	**1925** 3d14.5 ⊞ 口 大 乚 24 34 15 矯	**KYŌ, ta(meru)** – straighten; correct 矯正 *kyōsei* correct, reform 275 矯激 *kyōgeki* radical, extreme 1017 奇矯 *kikyō* eccentric conduct 1360 矯め直す *tamenaosu* set up again, correct, reform, cure 423

且	**1926** 0a5.15 日 月 一 42 1 且	**ka(tsu)** – and 且つ又 *katsumata* and　　　　　　　　　　　　　　1593
但	**1927** 2a5.14 田 亻 日 一 3 43 1 但	**tada(shi)** – but, however, provided 但し書き *tadashigaki* proviso　　　　　　　　　　　131
偵	**1928** 2a9.15 田 亻 貝 ﾄ 3 68 13 偵	**TEI** – spy 探偵 *tantei* detective　　　　　　　┌whodunit　535 探偵小説 *tantei shōsetsu* detective story,　535, 27, 400 偵察 *teisatsu* reconnaissance　　　　　　　　619 内偵 *naitei* scouting; private inquiry　　　　　84
曹	**1929** 4c7.10 日 日 艹 43 32 曹	**SŌ** – friend 法曹 *hōsō* the legal profession; lawyer　　　　123 法曹界 *hōsōkai* legal circles, the bench and bar　123, 454
翁	**1930** 2o8.6 田 ﾞ 彐 厶 16 39 17 翁 翁	**Ō** – old man 老翁 *rōō* old man　　　　　　　　　　　　　543
婆	**1931** 3e8.9 田 女 氵 厂 25 21 18 婆	**BA** – old woman 老婆 *rōba* old woman　　　　　　　　　　　543 産婆 *sanba* midwife　　　　　　　　　　　278 お転婆 *otenba* tomboy　　　　　　　　　　433 塔婆 *tōba* wooden grave tablet　　　　　　1840
嫡	**1932** 3e11.5 田 女 口 亠 25 24 11 嫡 嫡	**CHAKU** – legitimate 嫡(出)子 *chaku(shutsu)shi* legitimate child　53, 103 嫡嗣 *chakushi* legitimate heir　　　　　　　1917 嫡流 *chakuryū* lineage of the eldest son　　　247 嫡男 *chakunan* eldest son, heir, legitimate son　101 嫡孫 *chakuson* eldest son of one's son and heir　910

奴	**1933** 3e2.2 ▯ 女 又 25 9 奴	**DO** – servant, slave; fellow 守銭奴 *shusendo* miser　　　　　　490, 648 農奴 *nōdo* serf　　　　　　　　　　369 売国奴 *baikokudo* traitor　　　　239, 40
隷	**1934** 4e11.1 ▦ ネ 土 彐 45 22 39 隷 隷	**REI** – servant 奴隷 *dorei* slave　　　　　　　　　1933 隷従 *reijū* slavery　　　　　　　　1482 隷属 *reizoku* be subordinate (to)　　1637 隷書 *reisho* (ancient squared style of kanji)　131
帥	**1935** 3f6.1 ▯ 巾 尸 冂 26 40 20 帥	**SUI** – leading troops 元帥 *gensui* field marshal, admiral　　137 総帥 *sōsui* commander in chief　　　697 統帥 *tōsui* supreme/high command　　830
屯	**1936** 0a4.35 ▦ 冂 十 20 12 屯	**TON** – barracks 駐屯 *chūton* be stationed　　　　　599 駐屯地 *chūtonchi* military post　　599, 118
逓	**1937** 2q7.5 ▯ 辶 巾 厂 19 26 18 逓 遞	**TEI** – in turn; send 逓信 *teishin* communications　　　157 逓送 *teisō* convey, send by mail, forward　441 逓減 *teigen* successive diminution　715 逓増 *teizō* gradual increase　　　　712
遵	**1938** 2q12.8 ▯ 辶 酋 寸 19 71 37 遵	**JUN** – follow, obey 遵守 *junshu* obey, comply with　　490 遵奉 *junpō* observe, adhere to, abide by　1541 遵法 *junpō* law abiding; work-to-rule (tactics)　123
劾	**1939** 2g6.1 ▦ 力 亠 厶 8 11 17 劾	**GAI** – criminal investigation 弾劾 *dangai* impeachment　　　　1539

毆 殴 毆	**1940** 2t6.1 ⊞ 匚 十 又 20 12 9	**Ō, nagu(ru)** – beat, hit, strike 毆 打 *ōda* assault (and battery) 1020 毆 り 殺 す *nagurikorosu* beat to death, strike dead 576 毆 り 付 け る *naguritsukeru* strike, beat, thrash 192 毆 り 込 み *nagurikomi* an attack, raid 776 ぶ ん 毆 る *bunnaguru* give a good whaling/thrashing
虞 虞 虞	**1941** 2m11.1 ⊏ ﾄ 口 厂 (13) 24 18	**osore** – fear, danger, risk
痘 痘	**1942** 5i7.8 ⊏ 疒 口 儿 60 24 16	**TŌ** – smallpox 種 痘 *shutō* vaccination 228 痘 苗 *tōbyō* vaccine 1468 天 然 痘 *tennentō* smallpox 141, 651 水 痘 *suitō* chickenpox 21
陪 陪	**1943** 2d8.3 ⊞ 阝 立 口 7 54 24	**BAI** – follow, accompany, attend on 陪 審 *baishin* jury 1383 陪 席 *baiseki* sitting as an associate (judge) 379 陪 食 *baishoku* dining with a superior 322
濫 濫	**1944** 3a15.3 ⊞ 氵 皿 囗 21 59 20	**RAN** – overflow 濫 用 *ran'yō* abuse, misuse, misappropriation 107 濫 費 *ranpi* waste, extravagance 749 濫 作 *ransaku* overproduction 360 濫 伐 *ranbatsu* reckless deforestation 1509 濫 獲 *rankaku* overfishing, overhunting 1313
畔 畔 畔	**1945** 5f5.1 ⊟ 田 小 儿 58 35 4	**HAN** – rice-paddy ridge, levee 湖 畔 *kohan* lakeshore 467 河 畔 *kahan* riverside 389

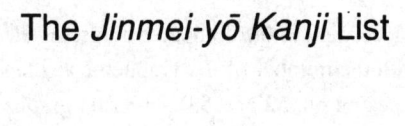

The *Jinmei-yō Kanji* List

Explanation of the *Jinmei-yō Kanji* List

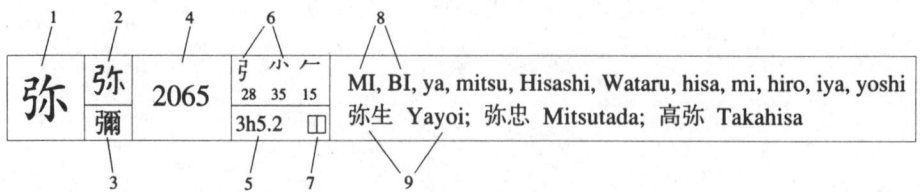

1. The kanji printed large

2. The kanji in pen form (*pen-ji*)

3. Variant of the kanji (usually an obsolete form)

4. Number of the kanji in this book (in this case, 2065)

5. Name of the radical (3h) of the kanji and descriptor (3h5.2) giving the kanji's location in Spahn & Hadamitzky's *Kanji Dictionary* and *The Learner's Kanji Dictionary*

6. Up to three graphemes, according to the computer programs *SUNRISE Kanji Dictionary* and *SUNRISE Script*, with the number of the grapheme written beneath each grapheme (see the table of graphemes on pp. 52 and 53). The first grapheme is always the kanji's radical. When the kanji's radical is only a part of a grapheme in the kanji (as 目 is a part of 見 in 観), the first grapheme appears in parentheses (see K&K number 604).

7. Structure of the kanji according to the computer programs *SUNRISE Kanji Dictionary* and *SUNRISE Script* (for a list of the structures, see p. 45)

8. Most important readings of the kanji, arranged by frequency within *on* and *kun* readings, with *on* readings in uppercase and *kun* readings in lowercase. A reading that occurs by itself as an independent given name is indicated by an underlined first letter (among the *on* readings) or by a capitalized first letter (among the *kun* readings).

9. Multiple-kanji given names in which the kanji occurs, with transliteration; names of famous persons (family name followed by given name) in whose given name (and sometimes also the family name) the kanji occurs, with transliteration and a short description; words in which the kanji occurs, with transliteration and translation or explanatory note.

丑	丑	2001	十 一 12 1 0a4.39 ⊟	CHŪ, ushi, hiro 丑松 Ushimatsu; 丑治, 丑二 Ushiji; 丑徳 Hironori
丞	丞	2002	了 氵 一 (6) 21 1 2c4.3 ⊟	JŌ, SHŌ, suke, Susumu, Tasuku, tsugu, Akira 鹿之丞 Shikanojō; 丞子 Jōko; 守丞 Morisuke
乃	乃	2003	力 8 0a2.10 ▢	NAI, DAI, no, Osamu, Imashi, yuki 乃武 Naibu, Nobu; 信乃 Shino; 乃木 Nogi (surname)
之	之	2004	一 丨 1 2 0a2.9 ⊟	SHI, no, yuki, kore, Itaru, yoshi, nobu, yori, hide, hisa, kuni 之乃布 Shinobu; 信之, 宣之, 誠之 Nobuyuki
也	也	2005	十 丨 12 2 0a3.29 ⋯	YA, nari, ari, mata, tada, kore 也寸志 Yasushi; 道也 Michinari; 匡也 Masatada
亘	亘 亙	2006	日 二 43 4 4c2.4 ⋯	KŌ, SEN, KAN, Wataru, Tōru, nobu, Hiroshi, Watari, hiro 亘康 Nobuyasu; 亘志 Kōji; 亘国 Hirokuni
亦	亦	2007	亠 儿 11 16 2j4.4 ⊟	EKI, YAKU, mata 亦介, 亦助 Matasuke; 亦次郎 Matajirō; 亦無 Yakumu
亥	亥	2008	亠 厶 亻 11 17 3 2j4.1 ⊟	GAI, KAI, i, ri 亥治郎 Gaijirō; 亥代子 Iyoko; 亥一 Iichi; 茂亥 Shigeri
亨	亨	2009	亠 口 一 11 24 1 2j4.2 ⊟	KYŌ, KŌ, HŌ, Tōru, michi, yuki, Akira, naga, Susumu, aki 亨子 Michiko; 盛亨 Moriyuki; 亨一 Kyōichi, Kōichi
亮	亮	2010	亠 口 冂 11 24 20 2j7.6 ⊟	RYŌ, Akira, Makoto, suke, Tōru, aki, yori, yoshi, katsu 亮太 Ryōta; 亮道 Akimichi; 誠亮 Seisuke; 亮夫 Yorio
伊	伊	2011	亻 彐 丨 3 39 2 2a4.6 ▢	I, kore, yoshi, tada, Osamu, isa 伊知郎 Ichirō; 伊尹 Koretada; 伊子 Yoshiko
伎	伎	2012	亻 十 又 3 12 9 2a4.13 ▢	GI, KI, SHI 伎茶夫 Gisao; 歌舞伎 Kabuki Kabuki
伍	伍	2013	亻 䒑 一 3 14 1 2a4.8 ▢	GO, Hitoshi, Atsumu, itsu, kumi, tomo 伍一 Goichi; 蓬伍 Hōitsu; 伍子 Kumiko
伽	伽	2014	亻 口 力 3 24 8 2a5.12 ▥	KA, GA, KYA 伽藍 garan temple, cathedral; 伽羅 kyara aloeswood
佑	佑	2015	亻 口 ナ 3 24 12 2a5.8 ▢	YŪ, U, suke, Tasuku　⌈(1947 –) (female) writer 佑吉 Yūkichi; 誠佑 Kanesuke; 津島佑子 Tsushima Yūko

353

伶	伶	2016	イ 一 丨 3 1 2 2a5.17 田	REI 伶俐(な) reiri(na) *clever, sharp-witted*
侃	侃	2017	イ 口 儿 3 24 16 2a6.12 田	<u>K</u>AN, Tsuyoshi, Tadashi, Akira, Sunao, nao, tada, yasu 侃二, 侃士 Kanji; 侃左 Naosuke; 侃一 Kan'ichi, Naokazu
侑	侑	2018	イ 月 十 3 42 12 2a6.5 □	YŪ, Susumu, Tasuku, yuki, Atsumu 侑広, 侑晃 Yūkō; 侑宏 Yukihiro; 侑男 Yukio
倭	倭	2019	イ 禾 女 3 56 25 2a8.16 田	WA, I, shizu, masa, Yamato, yasu, kazu 倭夫 Shizuo, Kazuo; 倭子 Masako, Shizuko; 倭蔵 Yasuzō
倖	倖	2020	イ 立 十 3 54 12 2a8.23 田	KŌ, GYŌ, sachi
偲	偲	2021	イ 田 心 3 58 51 2a9.7 田	SHI, SAI, Shinobu　　　　　　　　　　⌐temple, Kyōto 友山士偲 Yūzan Shishi *(1301–1370) abbot of Tōfuku*
允	允	2022	ム 儿 17 16 0a4.13 目	IN, EN, Makoto, masa, nobu, yoshi, mitsu, chika, suke, tada 成允 Narimasa, Shigemitsu; 允昭 Nobuaki
冴	冴	2023	冫 一 亠 5 14 11 2b5.2 □	GO, KO, sae 冴子 Saeko
冶	冶	2024	冫 口 厶 5 24 17 2b5.4 田	YA 冶生子 Yaeko; 亨冶 Tōru; 冶金 yakin *metallurgy*
凌	凌	2025	冫 夂 土 5 49 22 2b8.5 田	<u>R</u>YŌ, Shinogu, Noboru, Wataru 凌雲 Ryōun; 凌雪 Ryōsetsu
凛	凛	2026	冫 禾 口 5 56 24 2b13.1 田	RIN 凛子 Rinko; 凛気 rinki *cold air*
凪	凪	2027	几 ㅏ 亠 20 13 11 2s4.3 □	nagi, nagu 凪子 Nagiko; 夕凪 yūnagi *evening calm*
凱	凱	2028	几 山 口 20 36 24 2s10.1 田	GAI, KAI, yoshi, toki, Tanoshi, Katsumi, katsu 凱一 Tokiichi, Yoshikazu; 凱子 Katsuko, Tokiko
勁	勁	2029	力 工 一 8 38 1 2g7.2 田	<u>K</u>EI, Tsuyoshi 勁吉 Keikichi
匡	匡	2030	匸 王 20 46 2t4.1 目	KYŌ, masa, Tadasu, tada, Tadashi, Tasuku, Masashi 匡徳 Masanori, Tadanori; 匡介, 匡輔 Kyōsuke

卯	卯	2031	`卩 厂 丨` 7　18　2 2e3.1　□	U, BŌ, shige, Shigeru, Akira 卯吉 Ukichi; 卯外 Shigekado; 卯木 Uboku, Haruki
叡	叡	2032	`又 目 火` 9　55　44 2h14.1　田	EI, Satoshi, Akira, Tōru, toshi, yoshi, masa, tada, sato 乙叡 Takatoshi; 叡麓 Eiroku; 比叡山 Hieizan (mountain)
叶	叶	2033	`口 十` 24　12 3d2.1　□	KYŌ, Kanō, Kanai, yasu　　　　　　　┌(surname) 叶 Kanō, 叶井 Kanai, 叶内 Kanauchi, Kanouchi
只	只	2034	`口 儿` 24　16 3d2.8　日	SHI, tada, kore 只一 Tadaichi, Tadakazu; 只誠 Shisei
吾	吾	2035	`口 一 一` 24　14　1 3d4.17　日	GO, a, michi, waga, Gorō, ware, nori 正吾, 省吾, 尚吾, 章吾 Shōgo; 吾樹 Aki; 鎮吾 Masamichi
呂	呂	2036	`口 丨` 24　2　02 3d4.16　目	RO, RYO, naga, tomo, oto, fue 比呂司 Hiroshi; 吉呂 Yoshinaga; 呂久 Tomohisa
哉	哉	2037	`戈 口 十` 52　24　12 4n5.4　□	SAI, ya, chika, ka, kana, Hajime, ki, toshi, suke, ei 英哉 Eisai; 喜哉, 祥哉 Yoshichika; 清哉 Kiyoka
啄	啄	2038	`口 豸 ヽ` 24　27　10 3d8.4　□	TAKU, TOKU 石川啄木 Ishikawa Takuboku (1886–1912) poet
唄	唄	2039	`口 貝` 24　68 3d7.1　□	BAI, HAI, uta 唄子 Utako; 美唄 Miuta; Bibai (city in Hokkaidō)
喬	喬	2040	`口 大 冂` 24　34　20 3d9.25　日	KYŌ, taka, Takashi, nobu, tada, Tadashi, suke, moto, yasu 喬太郎 Kyōtarō; 喬樹 Takaki; 喬言 Nobukoto
嘉	嘉	2041	`吉 口 儿` 22　24　16 3p11.1　目	KA, Yoshi, Yoshimi, Yomishi, hiro, taka, Konomu 忠嘉 Tadahiro; 嘉村 Kamura, Yoshimura (surname)
圭	圭	2042	`土` 22 3b3.2　日	KEI, KE, tama, yoshi, kiyo, Kiyoshi, kado, ka, taka, aki 圭介 Keisuke; 圭雄 Tamao; 信圭 Nobukado
尭	尭 堯	2043	`土 儿 一` 22　16　14 3b9.3　日	GYŌ, taka, Takashi, aki, nori, Yutaka, tomi 尭三 Gyōzō; 尭爾 Takaji; 尭一 Akikazu; 尭治 Noriharu
奈	奈	2044	`礻 大` 45　34 4e3.3　□	NA, DAI, nani 奈々子 Nanako; 奈良 Nara (city); (surname)
奎	奎	2045	`土 大` 22　34 3b6.12　日	KEI, KE, KI, fumi 奎吾 Keigo; 奎彦 Fumihiko

		2046	大 十 34 12 / 0a11.7 [...]	S̱Ō, Akira, saya, sa, Sawa, Sayako, aki 爽司 Sōji; 爽子 Sayako, Sawako; 爽生子 Saoko
媛	媛	2047	女 小 一 25 35 14 / 3e9.4 ⊞	EN, Hime 愛媛 Ehime (prefecture)
嬉	嬉	2048	女 土 口 25 22 24 / 3e12.3 ⊞	KI, yoshi 嬉子 Kishi, Yoshiko
孟	孟	2049	子 皿 6 59 / 2c5.1 ⊟	M̱Ō, take, Takeshi, Tsutomu, Hajime, moto, tomo, osa, naga 孟夫 Takeo; 孟郎 Osao, Takeshirō
宏	宏	2050	宀 十 厶 33 12 17 / 3m4.3 ⊟	ḴŌ, hiro, Hiroshi, atsu, Fukashi 宏一 Kōichi, Hiroichi, Hirokazu; 宏彦 Atsuyoshi
宥	宥	2051	宀 月 十 33 42 12 / 3m6.1 ⊟	YŪ, Hiroshi, hiro, Yutaka, suke 宥全 Yūzen; 氏宥 Ujihiro; 宥子 Hiroko
寅	寅	2052	宀 日 一 33 43 14 / 3m8.4 ⊟	IN, I, Tora, nobu, taka, tomo, tsura, fusa 寅次郎 Torajirō Tora-san (movie hero); 吉寅 Yoshinobu
峻	峻	2053	山 夊 厶 36 49 17 / 3o7.4 ⊞	SHUN, taka, Takashi, toshi, mine, chika, michi 峻峰 Shunpō; 峻雄 Takao; 峻次 Toshitsugu
崚	崚	2054	山 夊 土 36 49 22 / 3o8.1 ⊞	RYŌ
嵐	嵐	2055	山 虫 冂 36 64 20 / 3o9.4 ⊟	RAN, Arashi ⌐嵐山 Arashiyama (mountain in Kyōto) 藤沢嵐子 Fujisawa Ranko (1925 –) (female) tango singer;
嵯	嵯	2056	山 王 工 36 46 38 / 3o10.2 [...]	SA, SHI 嵯峨 Saga (district of Kyōto); (surname)
嵩	嵩	2057	山 口 宀 36 24 11 / 3o10.4 ⊟	SŪ, SHŪ, taka, Takashi, take, Takabu 嵩渓 Sūkei; 嵩年 Takatoshi; 庸嵩 Tsunetaka
嶺	嶺	2058	山 頁 亻 36 77 3 / 3o14.2 ⊞	REI, RYŌ, mine, ne 嶺南 Reinan; 嶺男, 嶺雄 Mineo; 孝嶺 Takane
巌	巌 巖	2059	山 耳 夊 36 65 49 / 3o17.2 ⊟	G̱AN, GEN, Iwao, iwa, yoshi, o, mine, michi, toshi, itsu 巌松 Ganshō; 巌根 Iwane; 季巌 Sueyoshi; 松巌 Matsuo
巳	巳	2060	尸 40 / 0a3.16 ☐	SHI, mi ⌐(1905–69) movie director 巳熊 Mikuma; 己巳子 Kishiko; 成瀬巳喜男 Naruse Mikio

巴	巴	2061	尸 丨 40 2 0a4.16 ⊡	HA, tomo, Tomoe ⌐(1883–1957) wood-block artist 巴絵 Tomoe; 宗巴 Sōha; 川瀬巴水 Kawase Hasui
巽	巽	2062	ⸯ 弓 廾 16 28 32 2o10.7 ⊟	SON, Tatsumi, yoshi, yuku, Hajime ⌐(1905–73) poet 巽斎 Sonsai; 巽子 Yoshiko; 巽聖歌 Tatsumi Seika
庄	庄	2063	广 土 18 22 3q3.1 ⊡	SHŌ, SŌ, masa, Taira ⌐Shōgo 庄司 Shōji (surname or given name); 庄五 Masakazu,
弘	弘	2064	弓 厶 28 17 3h2.1 ⊞	KŌ, hiro, Hiroshi, Hiromu, mitsu, o 義弘 Yoshihiro; 宗弘 Munemitsu; 弘子 Mitsuko, Hiroko
弥	弥 彌	2065	弓 小 宀 28 35 15 3h5.2 ⊞	MI, BI, ya, mitsu, Hisashi, Wataru, hisa, mi, hiro, iya, yoshi 弥生 Yayoi; 弥忠 Mitsutada; 高弥 Takahisa
彗	彗	2066	ヨ 十 二 39 12 4 0a11.9 ⊞	SUI, EI 彗星 Suisei comet
彦	彦 ⸌	2067	立 彡 丨 54 31 2 5b4.4 ⊟	GEN, Hiko, yoshi, yasu, o, sato, hiro, tsune 彦斎 Gensai; 安彦 Yasuhiko, Yasuo; 彦正 Yoshimasa
彪	彪	2068	彡 厂 十 31 18 12 3j8.3 ⊡	HYŌ, HYŪ, Akira, Takeshi, take, aya, tora, Tsuyoshi, Kaoru 光彪 Kōhyō; 彪夫 Ayao, Takeo; 正彪 Masatora
彬	彬	2069	木 彡 41 31 4a7.3 ⊞	HIN, Akira, Aki, Yoshi, mori, Shigeshi, aya, hide, Hitoshi 彬光 Akimitsu; 彬江 Yoshie; 彬男 Ayao; 季彬 Suehide
怜	怜	2070	心 亻 一 51 3 1 4k5.10 ⊞	REI, RYŌ, REN, Satoshi, sato, Satoru, toki 怜子 Reiko, Satoko; 迪怜 Michisato
恕	恕	2071	心 女 口 51 25 24 4k6.18 ⊞	JO, SHO, hiro, Hiroshi, Yuki, yoshi, michi, nori, Hakaru 恕軒 Joken; 恕子 Hiroko, Michiko; 周恕 Chikayuki
悌	悌	2072	心 弓 儿 51 28 16 4k7.14 ⊞	TEI, Yasushi, yasu, Yoshi, tomo, Sunao 悌三 Teizō; 悌成 Yasunari; 光悌 Mitsuyoshi
惟	惟	2073	心 隹 51 74 4k8.1 ⊞	I, YUI, kore, tada, nobu, yoshi, ari, Tamotsu 惟謙 Iken; 惟親 Korechika; 惟俊 Tadatoshi
惣	惣	2074	心 牛 犭 51 47 27 4k8.17 ⊞	SŌ, SU, Osamu, nobu, fusa, michi 惣兵衛 Sōbei
惇	惇	2075	心 口 亠 51 24 11 4k7.12 ⊞	JUN, TON, Atsushi, Makoto, Tsutomu, atsu, toshi, Sunao 惇一 Jun'ichi; 惇信 Atsunobu; 惇郎 Toshirō, Junrō

慧	慧	2076	心 ヨ 十 51 39 12 4k11.16 ⊟	KEI, E, Satoshi, Satoru, Akira, Toshi, sato ⌜*Buddhist scholar* 大慧 Hirosato; 河口慧海 Kawaguchi Ekai *(1866–1945)*	
憧	憧	2077	心 立 日 51 54 43 4k12.5 ⊞	SHŌ, DŌ, TŌ 憧憬 dōkei *yearn for, aspire to*	
拳	拳	2078	扌 火 二 23 44 4 3c6.18 ⌷	KEN, GEN, Tsutomu, Katashi 緒形拳 Ogata Ken *(1937–) actor*; 拳闘 kentō *boxing*	
捷	捷	2079	扌 ヨ 十 23 39 12 3c8.4 ⊟	SHŌ, Katsu, toshi, haya, Satoshi, Masaru, Suguru, kachi 捷世 Katsuyo; 征捷 Yukitoshi; 捷郎 Hayao; 捷男 Kachio	
捺	捺	2080	扌 礻 大 23 45 34 3c8.17 ⊟	NATSU, toshi 捺印 natsuin *seal, stamp*	
敦	敦	2081	攵 口 亠 49 24 11 4i7.4 ⊟	TON, TAI, atsu, Atsushi, toshi, tsuru, Tsutomu, Osamu, yoi 敦介 Taisuke; 敦史 Atsushi; 敦子 Atsuko, Toshiko	
斐	斐	2082	亠 儿 二 11 16 04 2j10.4 ⊟	HI, Aya, Akira, yoshi, i, naka, naga, Ayaru ⌜斐之 Yoshiyuki 有斐閣 Yūhikaku *(a publishing company)*; 斐子 Ayako;	
魁	魁	2083	鬼 儿 厶 58 16 17 5f9.1 ⌷	KAI, Isao, Isamu, Tsutomu, Hajime, Yasushi, sakigake, o 魁蕾 Kairai; 東山魁夷 Higashiyama Kaii *(1908–) painter*	
於	於	2084	方 亻 丨 48 3 2 4h4.2 ⊞	O ⌜*Nobel-prize-winning physicist* 於菟吉 Otokichi; 江崎玲於奈 Esaki Reona *(1925–)*	
旦	旦	2085	日 一 43 1 4c1.2 ⊟	TAN, Akira, aki, Tadashi, Asa, ake, masa 安旦 Yasuaki; 旦夫 Asao; 元旦 gantan *New Year's Day*	
旭	旭	2086	日 十 43 12 4c2.6 ⊡	KYOKU, Akira, Asahi, teru, aki, asa 旭信 Terunobu; 正旭 Masaaki, Masaakira; 旭彦 Asahiko	
旺	旺	2087	日 王 43 46 4c4.2 ⊟	Ō, Akira, mori ⌜*company)* 旺輔 Ōsuke; 旺夫 Morio; 旺文社 Ōbunsha *(a publishing*	
昂	昂 昂	2088	日 厂 阝 43 18 7 4c5.11 ⊟	KŌ, taka, Takashi, Noboru, Akira, aki 昂一 Kōichi; 昂式 Takatsune; 彦昂 Hikoaki	
昌	昌	2089	日 43 4c4.4 ⊟	SHŌ, Masa, Aki, yoshi, Akira, Masashi, Sakae, suke, Masaru 昌治 Shōji; 昌植 Masatane; 昌女 Akime; 昌裕 Yoshihiro	
昴	昴	2090	日 厂 阝 43 18 7 4c5.12 ⊞	BŌ, Subaru	

晏	晏	2091	日 宀 女 43 33 25 / 4c6.4 目	AN, Yasushi, yasu, haru, sada, oso 晏代 Yasuyo; 晏正 Yasumasa; 清晏 Kiyoharu
晃	晃	2092	日 小 一 43 35 14 / 4c6.5 目	KŌ, aki, teru, Akira, mitsu, Hikaru, Noboru, kira 晃葉 Kōyō; 正晃 Masaaki, Masaakira; 晃央 Teruo
晋	晋	2093	日 エ 儿 43 38 16 / 4c6.8 目	SHIN, Susumu, kuni, yuki, aki, nobu 景晋 Kagekuni; 晋匡 Yukimasa; 健晋 Katsuaki
晟	晟	2094	日 戈 宀 43 52 15 / 4c7.5 目	SEI, Akira, masa, teru, Noboru, Shigeru 晟千代 Masachiyo; 晟子 Teruko
晨	晨	2095	日 扌 厂 43 57 18 / 4c7.7 目	SHIN, Toki, aki, asa, Akira, masa, teru, toyo 晨江 Tokie; 常晨 Tsuneaki; 晨生 Asao; 守晨 Moritoki
暉	暉	2096	日 車 冂 43 69 20 / 4c9.6 田	KI, Teru, aki, Akira, Terasu, Hikaru 暉衛 Terue; 暉昌 Akimasa
暢	暢	2097	日 豸 丨 43 27 2 / 4c10.4 田	CHŌ, Nobu, Tōru, masa, Mitsuru, mitsu, Noboru, naga, Itaru 暢夫 Nobuo; 暢美 Masayoshi; 貴暢 Takamitsu
曙	曙	2098	日 目 土 43 55 22 / 4c14.2 田	SHO, ake, Akira, Akebono 曙山 Shozan; 曙覧, 曙生, 曙海, 曙美 Akemi
智	智	2099	日 矢 口 43 34 24 / 4c8.11 田	CHI, Tomo, toshi, Satoshi, Satoru, nori, sato, Masaru, Akira 智恵子 Chieko; 智子 Tomoko, Satoko; 義智 Yoshitoshi
朋	朋	2100	月 42 / 4b4.1 田	HŌ, tomo, toshi 名朋子 Nahoko; 朋子 Tomoko; 朋夫 Toshio
朔	朔	2101	月 儿 一 42 16 14 / 4b6.12 田	SAKU, Hajime, kita, moto 朔郎 Sakuo, Sakurō, Kitarō; 猶朔 Naomoto
杏	杏	2102	木 口 41 24 / 4a3.13 目	KYŌ, AN, KŌ, Anzu　　「杏林大学 Kyōrin daigaku 杏子 Kyōko, Kyōshi, Momoko, Yōko; 杏奴 Annu;
杜	杜	2103	木 土 41 22 / 4a3.1 田	TO, ZU, mori, akanashi 杜人 Morito, Tojin; 北杜夫 Kita Morio *(1927–) writer*
李	李	2104	木 子 41 6 / 4a2.7 目	RI, momo 李子 Momoko; 李白 Rihaku *Li Bai (701–62) Chinese poet*
柊	柊	2105	木 夂 丨 41 49 2 / 4a5.24 田	SHŪ, hiiragi 柊郎 Shūrō; 宮柊二 Miya Shūji *(1912–) poet*

柚	柚	2106	木 日 | 41 43 2 4a5.5 ⬚	YŪ, YU, yuzu 柚岡 Yūkō; 柚木 Yunoki *(surname)*
柾	柾	2107	木 ㅗ 一 41 38 1 4a5.15 ⬚	Masa, Masaki, Masashi 柾子 Masako; 柾木 Masaki *(surname or given name)*
栞	栞	2108	木 ㄧ 一 41 14 1 4a6.34 ⬚	KAN, KEN, Shiori, ki 栞城 Kijō
桂	桂	2109	木 土 41 22 4a6.13 ⬚	KEI, Katsura, yoshi, katsu 桂花, 桂華 Keika; 桂木 Katsuragi *(surname)*
桐	桐	2110	木 口 冂 41 24 20 4a6.30 ⬚	TŌ, DŌ, kiri, hisa ⌐Kirimaro 桐谷 Tōkoku; 桐郎 Kirio, Kirirō; 桐美 Hisami; 桐麿
栗	栗	2111	木 口 一 41 24 14 4a6.32 ⬚	RITSU, Kuri 栗園 Ritsuen; 栗田 Kurita, 小栗 Oguri *(surnames)*
梧	梧	2112	木 口 一 41 24 14 4a7.9 ⬚	GO 梧郎, 梧楼 Gorō; 梧堂 Godō
梓	梓	2113	木 立 十 41 54 12 4a7.5 ⬚	SHI, Azusa 梓みちよ Azusa Michiyo *(1943 –) pop (female) singer*
梢	梢	2114	木 月 小 41 42 35 4a7.13 ⬚	SHŌ, Kozue, taka, sue 兼梢 Kanetaka
梨	梨	2115	木 禾 儿 41 56 16 4a7.24 ⬚	RI, nashi 梨子 Nashiko; 梨園 rien *the world of the theater*
椎	椎	2116	木 隹 41 74 4a8.1 ⬚	TSUI, SUI, shii, Tsuchi ⌐chinquapin 椎名 Shiina *(surname)*; 椎の実 shiinomi *sweet acorn,*
椋	椋	2117	木 口 小 41 24 35 4a8.31 ⬚	RYŌ, kura, Muku ⌐of children's books 椋園 Ryōen; 椋鳩十 Muku Hatojū *(1905 – 1987) author*
椿	椿	2118	木 日 大 41 43 34 4a9.16 ⬚	CHIN, Tsubaki 椿椿山 Tsubaki Chinzan *(1801 – 1854) painter*
楠	楠	2119	木 月 十 41 42 12 4a9.25 ⬚	NAN, DAN, Kusu, na, Kusunoki, toshi 虎楠 Konan; 楠緒子 Naoko; 楠雄 Kusuo, Toshio
楓	楓	2120	木 虫 冂 41 64 20 4a9.28 ⬚	FŪ, Kaede ⌐(1840 – 1925) painter 楓麻呂 Kaedemaro; 松本楓湖 Matsumoto Fūko

梛	梛	2121	木 耳 阝 41 65 7 / 4a8.6 ⊞	YA, yashi 梛子 Yashiko
楊	楊	2122	木 日 犭 41 43 27 / 4a9.17 ⊞	YŌ, yasu 楊一郎 Yōichirō; 楊枝 yōji *toothpick*
樺	樺	2123	木 王 艹 41 46 32 / 4a10.15 ⊞	KA, kaba, Kanba 樺 Kanba *(surname)*
榛	榛	2124	木 禾 大 41 56 34 / 4a10.11 ⊞	SHIN, haru, hari 榛名 Haruna *(surname or given name)*; 真榛 Mahari
槙	槙	2125	木 目 十 41 55 12 / 4a10.27 ⊞	SHIN, maki, Kozue, Shigeru 槙太郎 Makitarō; 槙村 Makimura *(surname)*
槻	槻	2126	木 貝 大 41 68 34 / 4a11.4 ⊞	KI, tsuki 槻子 Tsukiko; 大槻 Ōtsuki *(surname)*
橘	橘	2127	木 口 宀 41 24 14 / 4a12.11 ⊞	KITSU, Tachibana 橘三郎 Kitsusaburō; 橘之助 Kitsunosuke, Kichinosuke
檀	檀	2128	木 日 口 41 43 24 / 4a13.11 ⊞	DAN, SEN, Mayumi ⌐parishioner 檀 Dan *(surname)*; 檀家 danka *Buddhist temple*
欣	欣	2129	欠 斤 49 50 / 4j4.1 ⊞	KIN, GON, yoshi, Yasushi, Motomu 欣秀 Yoshihide; 欣子 Yoshiko; 欣喜 Kinki
欽	欽	2130	釒 欠 72 49 / 8a4.1 ⊞	KIN, yoshi, Hitoshi, Makoto, tada, koku, uya, Shitau 欽一 Yoshikazu; 萩本欽一 Hagimoto Kin'ichi *comedian*
毅	毅	2131	立 犭 乚 54 27 10 / 5b10.1 ⊞	KI, GI, take, Takeshi, Tsuyoshi, Kowashi, Tsuyoki, Hatasu 毅作 Kisaku; 正毅 Masaki, Masatoshi; 毅彦 Takehiko
毬	毬	2132	丿 氵 十 (5) 21 12 / 2b9.1 ⊡	KYŪ, mari 毬子 Mariko
汀	汀	2133	氵 丁 21 14 / 3a2.2 ⊞	TEI, Nagisa, Migiwa ⌐poet 汀川 Teisen; 中村汀女 Nakamura Teijo *(1900–88) haiku*
汐	汐	2134	氵 夕 21 30 / 3a3.9 ⊞	SEKI, shio, kiyo, 汐明 Shioaki; 汐美 Shiomi
沙	沙	2135	氵 小 丨 21 35 2 / 3a4.13 ⊞	SA, SHA, suna, isa, su, isago 美沙子 Misako; 沙雄 Sunao; 沙萌 Shabō

汰	汰	2136	氵 大 丨 21 34 2 3a4.8 □	**TA, TAI** 沙汰 sata *tidings, information; affair*
洸	洸	2137	氵 小 宀 21 35 14 3a6.15 田	**KŌ**, Takeshi, Hiroshi, hiro, Akira, Takashi, Fukashi 「*writer* 洸江 Hiroe; 藤浦洸 Fujiura Takashi *(1898–1979) copy-*
洲	洲	2138	氵 儿 21 16 3a6.10 Ⅲ	**SHŪ, SU**, kuni, shima 「*Sharaku wood-block master* 洲子 Kuniko; 洲人 Shimahito; 東洲斎写楽 Tōshūsai
洵	洵	2139	氵 日 勹 21 43 15 3a6.23 □	**JUN, SHUN**, Makoto, nobu, Hitoshi 洵一郎 Jun'ichirō; 洵治 Junji; 洵盛 Nobumori
浩	浩	2140	氵 土 口 21 22 24 3a7.9 田	**KŌ**, hiro, Hiroshi, Yutaka, Kiyoshi, Isamu, haru, Ōi, yō 浩通 Hiromitsu; 直浩 Naoharu; 浩二 Kōji, Hiroji
淳	淳	2141	氵 口 亠 21 24 11 3a7.19 田	**JUN**, atsu, Atsushi, Kiyoshi, Sunao, Makoto, kiyo, Tadashi 淳教 Atsunori; 淳浩 Kiyohiro; 淳高 Toshitaka
渚	渚 渚	2142	氵 日 土 21 43 22 3a9.1 □	**SHO**, Nagisa 「*(1932–) movie director and critic* 渚石 Shoseki; 渚男 Nagisao; 大島渚 Ōshima Nagisa
渥	渥	2143	氵 尸 土 21 40 22 3a9.33 □	**AKU**, atsu, Atsushi, hiku 渥子 Atsuko; 渥美 Atsumi *(surname)*
湧	湧	2144	氵 田 力 21 58 8 3a9.31 田	**YŌ, YŪ**, waku, waki, waka 湧子 Wakuko, Yūko
滉	滉	2145	氵 日 小 21 43 35 3a10.12 田	**KŌ**, Hiroshi, hiro, Akira 滉一 Kōichi
漱	漱	2146	氵 木 攵 21 41 49 3a11.4 Ⅲ	**SŌ**, Susugu 「*novelist* 漱平 Sōhei; 夏目漱石 Natsume Sōseki *(1867–1916)*
澪	澪	2147	氵 雨 亻 21 75 3 3a13.6 田	**REI, RYŌ**, Mio 澪子 Mioko; 澪人 Reijin
熙	熙	2148	火 口 尸 44 24 40 4d9.11 田	**KI, I**, hiro, Hiroshi, Hiromu, teru, sato, oki, yoshi, nori 熙庵 Kian; 熙子 Teruko; 光熙 Terusato; 頼熙 Yorioki
熊	熊	2149	火 月 厶 44 42 17 4d10.6 田	**YŪ**, kuma, kage 「*(city or prefecture); (surname)* 熊山 Yūzan; 熊吉 Kumakichi; 熊本 Kumamoto
燎	燎	2150	火 日 小 44 43 35 4d12.4 田	**RYŌ** 野田燎 Noda Ryō *(1948–) saxophone player*

燦	燦	2151	火 半 夕 44 62 30 / 4d13.3	SAN
燿	燿	2152	火 隹 日 44 74 39 / 4d14.3	YŌ, teru 燿胤 Terutane; 増燿 Masuteru
采	采	2153	朮 小 ⎸ 41 35 2 / 4a4.24	SAI, une, aya, koto ⌐Ayako 采真 Saishin; 采女 Uneme, uneme *lady-in-waiting*; 采子
爾	爾	2154	雨 儿 ⎸ 75 16 2 / 0a14.3	JI, NI, chika, Chikashi, shika, Mitsuru, Akira, mi 爾也 Chikaya; 辰爾 Tokishika; 久爾子 Kuniko
猪	猪 猪	2155	犭 日 土 27 43 22 / 3g8.1	CHO, i, shishi ⌐*political commentator* 正猪 Masai; 戸川猪佐武 Togawa Isamu *(1923–)*
玖	玖	2156	王 宀 ⎸ 46 15 2 / 4f3.1	KU, KYŪ, ki, hisa, tama 玖十郎 Kyūjūrō; 玖満子 Kumako; 玖次 Hisaji
玲	玲	2157	王 亻 一 46 3 1 / 4f5.7	REI, RE, RYŌ, RŌ, Akira, tama, aki ⌐Reisen 玲子 Reiko; 玲奈 Reina; 玲枝 Tamae; 玲雄 Akio; 玲川
琢	琢 琢	2158	王 犭 乀 46 27 10 / 4f8.1	TAKU, taka, aya, Migaku, Migaki, shige ⌐*entrepreneur* 琢禅 Takayoshi; 高琢 Takaaya; 団琢磨 Dan Takuma
瑛	瑛	2159	王 艹 大 46 32 34 / 4f8.6	EI, YŌ, Akira, teru, aki, yō 瑛泉 Eisen; 瑛代 Teruyo; 瑛子 Akiko, Eiko, Teruko, Yōko
琳	琳	2160	王 木 46 41 / 4f8.2	RIN 琳庵 Rin'an; 尾形光琳 Ogata Kōrin *(1658–1716) painter*
瑚	瑚	2161	王 月 口 46 42 24 / 4f9.3	KO, GO 珊瑚 sango *coral*
瑞	瑞	2162	王 山 一 46 36 14 / 4f9.6	ZUI, SUI, mizu, Tama, Makoto, Yutaka, mitsu 瑞雲 Zuiun; 瑞穂 Mizuho; 瑞樹 Tamaki; 瑞雄 Mitsuo
瑤	瑤 瑤	2163	王 小 山 46 35 36 / 4f9.5	YŌ, tama ⌐*(1940–93) (female) writer* 瑤泉 Yōsen; 真瑤 Matama; 森瑤子 Mori Yōko
瑳	瑳	2164	王 工 儿 46 38 16 / 4f10.6	SA 瑳五郎 Sagorō; 瑳助 Sasuke; 瑳磨介 Samanosuke
瑠	瑠	2165	王 留 厂 46 58 18 / 4f10.3	RU, RYŪ 瑠璃子 Ruriko; 瑠璃 ruri *lapis lazuli*

璃	璃	2166	王 一 冂 46 11 20 4f10.5 田	RI, aki 璃子 Akiko; 浄瑠璃 Jōruri (type of ballad-drama)
甫	甫	2167	月 十 丨 42 12 2 0a7.11	HO, FU, Hajime, toshi, suke, yoshi, nami, moto, nori, masa 甫子 Toshiko; 泰甫 Taisuke; 甫信 Yoshinobu; 甫安 Hoan
皋	皋	2168	月 十 二 43 12 4 4c7.12 目	KŌ, Susumu, taka, Takashi, sawa 皋雨郎 Kōurō; 勝皋 Katsutaka; 皋月 Satsuki, Kōgetsu
皓	皓	2169	日 土 口 43 22 24 4c8.13 田	KŌ, Akira, teru, Hiroshi, tsugu, hiro, aki, Hikaru 皓子 Teruko, Hiroko; 皓年 Tsugutoshi; 順皓 Yasuaki
眉	眉	2170	目 尸 丨 55 40 2 5c4.9 囗	BI, MI, mayu ⌐eyebrows 眉山 Bizan; 眉子 Mayuko; 眉間 miken between the
眸	眸	2171	目 牛 厶 55 47 17 5c6.3 田	BŌ, Hitomi 明眸 meibō bright/beautiful eyes
睦	睦	2172	目 土 儿 55 22 16 5c8.6 田	BOKU, mutsu, Mutsumi, chika, Atsushi, Chikashi, nobu 睦子 Mutsuko, Chikako; 睦夫 Mutsuo, Nobuo
瞳	瞳	2173	目 立 曰 55 54 43 5c12.2 田	DŌ, TŌ, Hitomi, Akira 安達瞳子 Adachi Tōko (1936–) (female) ikebana artist
瞭	瞭	2174	目 火 曰 55 44 43 5c12.4 田	RYŌ, Akira, aki ⌐忠瞭 Tadaakira 上野瞭 Ueno Ryō (1928–) author of children's books;
矩	矩	2175	匚 夫 尸 20 34 15 2t7.1 囗	KU, nori, tsune, kado, Tadashi, Tadasu, Kane 規矩雄 Kikuo; 高矩 Takanori; 規矩 Noritsune
碧	碧	2176	石 王 曰 53 46 43 5a9.7 田	HEKI, Midori, Kiyoshi, ao, tama ⌐Hekihō 碧子 Midoriko, Hekishi; 碧海 Hekikai, Aomi; 碧峰
磯	磯	2177	石 戈 厶 53 52 17 5a12.1 囗	KI, Iso, shi 小磯 Koiso; 磯次 Isoji; 磯村 Isomura (surname)
祐	祐 祐	2178	礻 口 十 45 24 12 4e5.3 囗	YŪ, YU, suke, hiro, Tasuku, sachi, masa, yoshi, masu 祐輔 Yūsuke; 祐之 Sukeyuki; 祐典 Hironori, Yūten
禄	禄 祿	2179	礻 ヨ 氵 45 39 21 4e8.2 田	ROKU, yoshi, toshi, sachi, tomi 禄郎 Rokurō; 禄夫 Yoshio; 光禄 Mitsutoshi
禎	禎 禎	2180	礻 貝 卜 45 68 13 4e9.3 田	TEI, sada, yoshi, tada, Tadashi, sachi, Sadamu, tsugu, tomo 禎子 Teiko, Sadako, Sachiko; 禎栄 Yoshie; 正禎 Masatada

秦	秦	2181	禾 大 一 56 34 4 5d5.10 [...]	SHIN, hata, kuni 「(surname) 秦山 Shinzan; 秦男 Kunio; 秦誦 Hatazumi; 秦野 Hatano
稀	稀	2182	禾 巾 艹 56 26 12 5d7.5 ⊞	KI, KE, mare 稀雄 Mareo; 稀薄な kihaku na *thin, diluted, rarefied*
稔	稔	2183	禾 心 亻 56 51 3 5d8.5 ⊞	NEN, JIN, Minoru, toshi, naru, nari, Yutaka, nori, mine 稔男 Toshio; 稔彦 Naruhiko; 稔斎 Nensai
稜	稜	2184	禾 夂 土 56 49 22 5d8.4 ⊞	RYŌ, taka, taru, izu, kado, sumi 稜厳 Ryōgon; 稜人 Takato; 稜彦 Taruhiko, Izuhiko
穣	穣 穰	2185	禾 衤 艹 56 57 32 5d13.2 ⊞	JŌ, Minoru, Yutaka, Yuzura, Minori, Osamu, shige 穣治 Jōji; 康穣 Yasushige
竣	竣	2186	立 夂 厶 54 49 17 5b7.2 ⊞	SHUN 竣介 Shunsuke
靖	靖	2187	立 月 土 54 42 22 5b8.1 ⊞	SEI, JŌ, yasu, Yasushi, Kiyoshi, Osamu, nobu, shizu, haru 靖子 Yasuko, Seiko, Shizuko; 靖久 Yasuhisa, Nobuhisa
笙	笙	2188	竹 生 一 66 47 1 6f5.4 ⊟	SHŌ, SEI 笙一郎 Shōichirō
笹	笹	2189	竹 艹 一 66 32 1 6f5.3 ⊟	sasa 笹丸 Sasamaru; 笹川 Sasagawa *(surname)*
紘	紘	2190	糸 厶 61 12 17 6a4.11 ⊞	KŌ, hiro, Hiroshi, Hiromu, Osamu, aya, tsuna 紘一 Kōichi, Hirokazu, Hiroichi; 紘子 Hiroko, Ayako
紗	紗	2191	糸 小 丨 61 35 2 6a4.6 ⊞	SA, SHA, tae, Suzu 「[from the Dutch saraça] 紗子 Taeko; 更紗 sarasa *printed cotton, chintz, calico*
絃	絃	2192	糸 一 厶 61 11 17 6a5.12 ⊞	GEN, KEN, tsuru, ito, o, fusa 絃阿弥 Gen'ami; 絃喜 Genki; 絃司 Genji; 絃夫 Tsuruo
紬	紬	2193	糸 日 丨 61 43 2 6a5.3 ⊞	CHŪ, SHŪ, tsumugi 「silk from Ōshima) 紬子 Tsumugiko; 大島紬 ōshima-tsumugi *(hand-woven*
絢	絢	2194	糸 日 勹 61 43 15 6a6.14 ⊞	JUN, KEN, Aya 「Jun'ya 絢子 Ayako; 絢彦 Ayahiko, Junko; 絢海 Kenkai; 絢也
綺	綺	2195	糸 大 口 61 34 24 6a8.16 ⊞	KI, aya 「(1872–1939) dramatist 綺語堂 Kigodō; 綺子 Ayako; 岡本綺堂 Okamoto Kidō

365

綜	綜	2196	糸 木 宀 61 45 33 6a8.12 ⊞	SŌ, osa 綜子 Osako
緋	緋	2197	糸 二 儿 61 4 16 6a8.4 ⊞	HI, aka 緋佐子 Hisako; 緋陶志 Hitoshi
綾	綾	2198	糸 夂 土 61 49 22 6a8.10 ⊞	RYŌ, aya 綾山 Ryōzan; 綾彦 Ayahiko; 綾郁, 綾香 Ayaka
綸	綸	2199	糸 艹 亻 61 32 3 6a8.18 ⊞	RIN, o, kumi 綸二 Rinji; 経綸 Tsuneo; 綸子 Kumiko; rinzu *silk*
翔	翔	2200	⺌ 王 ヨ 16 46 39 2o10.8 ⊞	SHŌ, sane 柴田翔 Shibata Shō *(1935 –) writer*
翠	翠	2201	十 ヨ 亠 12 39 11 2k12.2 ⊟	SUI, Midori, Akira 翠軒 Suiken; 翠子 Suiko, Midoriko; 翡翠 hisui *jade*
耀	耀	2202	隹 ⺌ ヨ 74 35 39 8c12.1 ⊞	YŌ, Akira, aki, teru 耀蔵 Yōzō; 栄耀 Hideaki; 耀男 Teruo
聡	聡	2203	耳 心 儿 65 51 16 6e8.2 ⊞	SŌ, Satoshi, sato, Akira, Toshi, fusa, Satoru, aki, tomi, toki 聡明 Toshiaki, Sōmei, Satoshi; 聡子 Satoko, Toshiko
肇	肇	2204	戸 夂 ヨ 40 49 39 4m10.1 ⊟	CHŌ, TŌ, Hajime, Hajimu, hatsu, tada, Tadashi, toshi, koto 肇一 Chōichi; 肇子 Hatsuko; 肇生 Tadao; 肇男 Toshio
胤	胤	2205	月 儿 厶 42 16 17 4b5.16 ⸛	IN, Tane, tsugu, tsugi, kazu, Tsuzuki, mi 胤子 Inshi; 胤貞 Tanesada; 義胤, 栄胤 Yoshitsugu
胡	胡	2206	月 口 十 42 24 12 4b5.12 ⊞	KO, GO, hisa 胡夷 Koi; 胡保 Hisayasu; 胡江 Hisae
脩	脩	2207	亻 夂 月 3 49 42 2a9.6 ⊞	SHŪ, Osamu, naga, nobu, osa, haru, suke, nao, moro, sane 脩造 Shūzō; 正脩 Masanaga; 脩夫 Nobuo; 公脩 Kin'osa
舜	舜	2208	⺥ 夕 冂 35 30 20 3n10.2 ⊞	SHUN, kiyo, toshi, yoshi, mitsu, Hitoshi, Akira 舜一 Shun'ichi; 泰舜 Yasukiyo; 舜世 Toshiyo
艶	艶	2209	口 日 尸 24 43 40 3d16.3 ⊞	EN, Tsuya, yoshi, moro, ō　　　「(1912–)(female) critic 艶二 Enji; 艶太 Tsuyata, 三宅艶子 Miyake Tsuyako
芹	芹	2210	艹 斤 32 50 3k4.5 ⊟	KIN, KI, seri 芹坡 Kinpa; 芹沢 Serizawa, 芹田 Serita *(surnames)*

芙	芙	2211	艹 夫 一 32 34 1 3k4.4 ⽥	FU, hasu ⌐(female) writer 芙代 Hasuyo; 林芙美子 Hayashi Fumiko (1903–1951)	
苑	苑	2212	艹 夕 阝 32 30 7 3k5.17 ⽥	EN, ON, sono, Shigeru 千苑 Chisono; 苑子 Sonoko; 紫苑 Shion	
茄	茄	2213	艹 口 力 32 24 8 3k5.19 ⽥	KA 茄子 nasu eggplant	
茅	茅	2214	艹 亅 一 32 14 1 3k5.26 ⽬	BŌ, chi, kaya 茅子 Kayako; 茅野 Kayano, Chino (surname)	
茉	茉	2215	艹 木 一 32 41 1 3k5.6 ⽥	MA, MATSU 森茉莉 Mori Mari (1903–1987) (female) writer	
茜	茜	2216	艹 口 ⼀ 32 24 14 3k6.3 ⽥	SEN, Akane 茜山 Senzan	
莞	莞	2217	艹 宀 二 32 33 4 3k7.14 ⽬	KAN 莞爾 Kanji	
莉	莉	2218	艹 禾 儿 32 56 16 3k7.5 ⽥	RI, REI 岡田茉莉子 Okada Mariko (1933–) actress	
菫	菫	2219	艹 王 口 32 46 24 3k8.1 ⽥	KIN, Sumire, tada 菫哉 Kinsai; 泣菫 Kyūkin	
菖	菖	2220	艹 日 32 43 3k8.22 ⽬	SHŌ, Ayame 菖渓 Shōkei; 菖蒲 shōbu iris, flag	
萌	萌	2221	艹 日 月 32 43 42 3k8.11 ⽥	HŌ, BŌ, moe, Kizashi, me, Megumi, memi, moyu 萌二 Hōji; 俵萌子 Tawara Moeko (1930–)(female) critic	
葵	葵	2222	艹 癶 大 32 44 34 3k9.17 ⽥	KI, GI, Mamoru, Aoi ⌐(1887–1957) politician 葵村 Kison; 葵山 Kizan; 重光葵 Shūgemitsu Mamoru	
萩	萩	2223	艹 禾 火 32 56 44 3k9.5 ⽥	SHŪ, Hagi 萩径 Shukei; 萩雄 Hagio; 萩麿 Hagimaro	
蒔	蒔	2224	艹 日 土 32 43 22 3k10.7 ⽥	SHI, JI, maki 蒔子 Makiko; 蒔田 Makita, 蒔村 Makimura (surnames)	
蒼	蒼	2225	艹 倉 口 32 73 24 3k10.22⽥	SŌ, Shigeru, tami ⌐company) 蒼梧 Sōgo; 蒼子 Tamiko; 蒼樹社 Sōjusha (a publishing	

蓉	蓉	2226	艹 火 宀 32 44 33 3k10.20	YŌ, hasu 蓉子 Yōko; 蓉身 Hasumi; 芙蓉 fuyō *lotus; cotton rose*
蓮	蓮	2227	艹 車 辶 32 69 19 3k10.31	REN, hasu 蓮蔵 Renzō; 蓮光 Hasumitsu; 蓮実 Hasumi *(surname)*
蔦	蔦	2228	艹 鳥 32 80 3k11.1	CHŌ, Tsuta ⌐*(a publishing company)* 蔦斎 Chōsai; 蔦夫, 蔦生 Tsutao; 蔦屋 Tsutaya
蕉	蕉	2229	艹 隹 火 32 74 44 3k12.6	SHŌ ⌐*poet* 蕉園 Shōen; 松尾芭蕉 Matsuo Bashō *(1644–94) haiku*
蕗	蕗	2230	艹 𧾷 夂 32 70 49 3k13.4	RO, Fuki 蕗子 Fukiko
藤	藤	2231	艹 月 火 32 42 44 3k15.3	TŌ, DŌ, Fuji, Katsura, tsu, hisa ⌐*Confucian scholar* 藤美 Fujimi; 松藤次 Matsuji; 中江藤樹 Nakae Tōju
藍	藍	2232	艹 血 皿 32 59 20 3k15.5	RAN, ai 藍洲 Ranshū; 藍子 Aiko
蘭	蘭	2233	艹 門 木 32 76 41 3k16.9	RAN, ka 蘭台 Randai; 蘭子 Ranko; 和蘭 Oranda *Holland*
虎	虎	2234	卜 厂 十 (13) 18 12 2m6.3	KO, Tora, take 龍虎 Ryūko, Tatsutora; 小虎 Kotora; 行虎 Michitake
虹	虹	2235	虫 工 64 38 6d3.1	KŌ, niji 虹児 Kōji; 虹子 Nijiko
蝶	蝶	2236	虫 朮 艹 64 41 32 6d9.7	CHŌ ⌐*(1897–1972) actress* 蝶介 Chōsuke; 蝶二 Chōji; 飯田蝶子 Iida Chōko
衿	衿	2237	礻 亻 一 57 3 1 5e4.5	KIN, eri 岸田衿子 Kishida Eriko *(1929–) poetess*
袈	袈	2238	礻 口 力 57 24 8 5e5.10	KE, KA, kesa 袈裟太郎 Kesatarō; 袈裟六 Kesaroku; 袈枝 Kesae
裟	裟	2239	礻 氵 小 57 21 35 5e7.6	SA, SHA 袈裟美 Kesami; 袈裟 kesa *surplice, monk's robe*
詢	詢	2240	訁 日 勹 67 43 15 7a6.17	JUN, SHUN, Makoto 交詢社 Kōjunsha *(a publishing company)*

誼	誼	2241	言 月 宀 67 42 33 7a8.11	GI, yoshi, Yoshimi, koto 誼夫 Giyoo; 誼衡 Yoshihiro; 正誼 Masayoshi
諄	諄	2242	言 口 宀 67 24 11 7a7.11	JUN, SHUN, Atsushi, atsu, Makoto, Itaru, shige, tomo, 諄子 Atsuko ⌐nobu, sane
諒	諒	2243	言 口 小 67 24 35 7a8.14	RYŌ, Makoto, Masa, Aki, asa 諒一 Masakazu; 諒兄 Akie
赳	赳	2244	土 ⌐ 亅 22 13 3 3b7.10	KYŪ, take, Takeshi, Isamu, isa ⌐prime minister (1977–78) 赳夫 Takeo, Isao; 赳城 Takeki; 福田赳夫 Fukuda Takeo
輔	輔	2245	車 月 十 69 42 12 7c7.1	HO, FU, BU, suke, Tasuku, Tasuke 輔之 Hoshi; 輔信 Sukenobu; 泰輔 Taisuke
辰	辰	2246	厂 衤 18 57 2p5.1	SHIN, tatsu, toki, Noburu, nobu, yoshi ⌐Nobuyoshi 辰斎 Shinsai; 辰夫 Tatsuo, Tokio, Yoshio; 辰由
迪	迪	2247	辶 日 亅 19 43 2 2q5.1	TEKI, Susumu, Michi, Tadasu, hira, tada, fumi, Tadashi 迪斎 Tekisai; 重迪 Shigemichi; 俊迪 Toshihira
遙	遙	2248	辶 小 山 19 35 36 2q10.3	YŌ, Haruka, michi, tō, haru, nobu, sumi, nori 遙子 Yōko; 遙秋 Michiaki
遼	遼	2249	辶 火 日 19 44 43 2q12.5	RYŌ, Haruka, tō, Toshi ⌐writer 遼一 Ryōichi; 司馬遼太郎 Shiba Ryōtarō (1923–)
邑	邑	2250	口 尸 亅 24 40 2 3d4.15	YŪ, mura, kuni, Satoshi, sato, sumi 良邑 Yoshimura; 吉邑 Yoshikuni
那	那	2251	阝 力 二 7 08 04 2d4.6	NA, DA, tomo, yasu, fuyu ⌐支那 Shina China 那津子 Natsuko; 那子 Tomoko, Fuyuko; 宗那 Muneyasu;
郁	郁	2252	阝 月 十 7 42 12 2d6.6	IKU, kuni, Kaoru, Takashi, ka, aya, fumi, Kaori 郁生, 郁雄 Ikuo, Kunio; 盛郁 Morika; 郁夫 Ayao, Ikuo
耶	耶	2253	耳 阝 65 7 6e2.1	YA, JA, SHA 耶馬台 Yamatai (ancient name for Japan)
酉	酉	2254	酉 71 7e0.1	YŪ, YU, Tori, Minoru, naga 酉吉 Yukichi; 酉平 Torihei; 酉雄 Nagao; 酉癸 Yuki
醇	醇	2255	酉 口 宀 71 24 11 7e7.5	JUN, SHUN, Atsushi, atsu 醇斎 Junsai; 政醇 Masaatsu

錦	錦	2256	金 日 巾 72 43 26 / 8a8.6 田	KIN, kane, nishiki 錦之介 Kinnosuke; 錦文 Kanefumi; 錦木 Nishikigi
鎌	鎌	2257	金 ヨ 儿 72 39 16 / 8a10.8 田	KEN, REN, kama, kane, kata 鎌吉 Kanakichi; 重鎌 Shigekane; 高鎌 Takakata
阿	阿	2258	阝 口 一 7 24 14 / 2d5.6 ⊡	A, kuma, o 阿佐緒 Asao; 照阿 Terukuma; 阿部 Abe (surname)
隼	隼	2259	隹 十 74 12 / 8c2.2 ⊟	SHUN, JUN, haya, taka, Hayashi, Hayato, Hayabusa, toshi 隼三 Junzō; 隼人 Hayato; 隼男 Hayao, Takao
雛	雛	2260	隹 ⺈ 冂 74 15 20 / 8c10.1	SŪ, SU, JU, hina　　　　　⌐(displayed in tiers) 雛子 Hinako; 雛助 Hinasuke; 雛人形 hinaningyō dolls
霞	霞	2261	雨 尸 二 75 40 4 / 8d9.1 田	KA, KO, Kasumi　　　⌐Kasumigaseki (district of Tōkyō) 朝霞 Asaka (district of Tōkyō); 霞庵 Koan; 霞ヶ関
鞠	鞠	2262	米 卄 勹 62 32 24 / 6b11.6 ⊡	KIKU, KYŪ, Mari, mitsu, tsugu 鞠塢 Kikuu; 鞠子 Mariko
須	須	2263	彡 頁 31 77 / 3j9.1 ⊡	SU, SHU, Motomu, mochi, matsu 須三男 Sumio; 須磨子 Sumako; 須猶 Mochinao
頌	頌	2264	頁 儿 厶 77 16 17 / 9a4.4 田	SHŌ, JU, nobu, tsugu, tada, uta, oto, yomu 頌一郎 Shōichirō; 容頌 Katanobu; 正頌 Masatsugu
碩	碩	2265	石 頁 53 77 / 5a9.1 ⊡	SEKI, hiro, Hiroshi, Mitsuru, michi, ō, Yutaka 碩哉 Hiroya, Sekiya; 碩彦 Michihiko; 碩人 Ōto
颯	颯	2266	立 虫 冂 54 64 20 / 5b9.4 ⊡	SATSU, SŌ, haya 颯々 Satsusatsu; 颯子 Satsuko; 颯夫 Hayao
馨	馨	2267	日 禾 土 43 56 22 / 4c16.2 田	KEI, KYŌ, Kaoru, ka, Kaori, kiyo, yoshi 馨六 Keiroku; 貞馨 Sadaka; 信馨 Nobukiyo
駒	駒	2268	馬 口 宀 78 24 15 / 10a5.5 ⊡	KU, koma 駒雄, 駒緒 Komao; 生駒 Ikoma; 駒村 Kuson
駿	駿	2269	馬 夂 厶 78 49 17 / 10a7.1 田	SHUN, Toshi, Hayashi, Hayao, Takashi, Susumu 駿介, 駿助 Shunsuke; 駿男, 駿雄 Toshio; 武駿 Taketoshi
鮎	鮎	2270	魚 口 卜 79 24 13 / 11a5.7 田	DEN, NEN, SEN, ayu 鮎子 Ayuko; 鮎之助 Ayunosuke

鯉	鯉	2271	魚 日 土 79 43 22 11a7.2	RI, koi 鯉吉 Rikichi; 鯉友 Riyū; 鯉之助 Koinosuke; 鯉洋 Riyō
鯛	鯛	2272	魚 月 口 79 42 24 11a8.11	CHŌ, tai 鯛子 Taiko; 鯛助 Taisuke; 鯛造 Taizō
鳩	鳩	2273	鳥 十 80 12 11b2.1	KYŪ, KU, hato, yasu 鳩翁 Kyūō; 鳩子 Hatoko; 鳩彦 Yasuhiko
鳳	鳳	2274	几 鳥 一 20 80 14 2s12.1	HŌ, FŪ, taka, Ōtori　　　　　　　　　　⌈actress 鳳山 Hōzan; 季鳳 Suetaka; 鳳蘭 Ōtori Ran (1946–)
鴻	鴻	2275	氵 鳥 エ 21 80 38 3a14.2	KŌ, Hiroshi, hiro, toki, Hitoshi, taka　　　⌈Yoshitoki 鴻秀 Kōshū; 鴻之 Takayuki; 重鴻 Shigehiro; 吉鴻
鵬	鵬	2276	月 鳥 42 80 4b15.1	HŌ, tomo, yuki 鵬磨 Hōma; 鵬一 Tomoichi; 忠鵬 Tadayuki
鶴	鶴	2277	鳥 隹 冂 80 74 20 11b10.1	KAKU, Tsuru, zu, tazu, tsu, kazu　　　　　⌈Mitsuo 鶴堂 Kakudō; 珠鶴, 省鶴 Suzu; 鶴美 Tazumi; 三鶴夫
鷹	鷹	2278	广 鳥 隹 18 80 74 3q21.1	YŌ, Ō, Taka 鷹山 Yōzan; 鷹衛 Takae; 三鷹 Mitaka (district of Tōkyō)
鹿	鹿	2279	广 儿 冂 18 16 20 3q8.5	ROKU, Shika, ka, shishi 鹿之助 Shikanosuke; 義鹿 Yoshika
麟	麟	2280	米 夕 厂 62 30 18 6b18.1	RIN　　　　　　　　　　　　　　　　⌈writer 麟太郎 Rintarō; 椎名麟三 Shiina Rinzō (1911–73)
麿	麿	2281	广 木 口 18 41 24 3q15.2	maro　　　　　⌈Utamaro (1753–1806) wood-block master 秀麿 Hidemaro; 麿枝 Maroe; 喜多川歌麿 Kitagawa
黎	黎	2282	氵 禾 ノ 21 56 15 3a10.29	REI, RI, tami, asa 黎吉 Reikichi; 黎子 Reiko, Tamiko
黛	黛	2283	火 戈 日 44 52 43 4d13.7	TAI, Mayuzumi　　　　　　　　　　　⌈composer 黛眉 Taibi; 黛敏郎 Mayuzumi Toshirō (1929–)
亀	亀	2284	勹 日 丨 15 43 2 2n9.1	KI, kame, hisa, Hisashi, Susumu, Nagashi, ama, aya 亀鶴 Kikaku; 亀一郎 Kiichirō, Kameichirō; 亀夫 Hisao

Index by Radicals

– 0a –		毛	287	毎	116	– 2a 亻–		含	1249	偏	1159	7	孫	910
1 一	2	丹	1093	再	782	0 人	1	6 依	678	斜	1069		– 2d 阝–	
乙	983	屯	1936	曲	366	2 仏	583	使	331	10 備	768	4	防	513
2 二	3	勾	1902	7 良	321	化	254	価	421	偉	1053		那	2251
入	52	丑	2001	身	59	仁	1619	侑	2018	傍	1183		邦	808
丁	184	中	28	来	69	介	453	例	612	傘	790	5	阻	1085
之	2004	弔	1796	承	942	今	51	佳	1462	11 働	232		附	1843
乃	2003	井	1193	束	501	3 仙	1891	侍	571	傾	1441		阿	2258
七	9	5 以	46	里	142	仕	333	侃	2017	傑	1731		邪	1457
九	11	北	73	我	1302	代	256	供	197	僧	1366		邸	563
3 三	4	矛	773	甫	2167	他	120	併	1162	傷	633	6	限	847
川	33	巧	1627	更	1008	付	192	侮	1736	債	1118		郎	980
勺	1903	包	804	亜	1616	令	831	舎	791	催	1317		郁	2252
工	139	丘	1357	寿	1550	4 伏	1356	念	579	12 僕	1888		郊	817
久	1210	凸	1892	8 非	498	休	60	命	578	僚	1324	7	陣	1404
万	16	凹	1893	長	95	件	732	7 信	157	像	740		陛	589
乏	754	且	1926	表	272	伐	1509	促	1557	13 儀	727		降	947
已	370	必	520	画	343	伊	2011	便	330	億	382		院	614
夕	81	斥	1401	果	487	仲	1347	係	909	14 儒	1417		除	1065
巳	2060	矢	213	東	71	伍	2013	俊	1845	15 優	1033		陥	1218
寸	1894	左	75	垂	1070	任	334	保	489	償	971		郡	193
大	26	丙	984	奉	1541	仰	1056	侵	1077					郭	1673
刃	1413	出	53	毒	522	伎	2012	俗	1126	– 2b 冫–		8	陳	1405
与	539	民	177	事	80	伝	434	侯	1924	4 次	384		陪	1943
及	1257	半	88	9 飛	530	仮	1049	8 倒	905	壮	1326		陸	647
丈	1325	本	25	発	96	全	89	倣	1776	兆	1562		陵	1844
才	551	末	305	衷	1677	企	481	俳	1035	羽	590		隆	946
丸	644	未	306	甚	1501	合	159	候	944	5 状	626		陰	867
也	2005	失	311	巻	507	会	158	修	945	冴	2023		険	533
4 不	94	生	44	専	600	肉	223	倍	87	冷	832		随	1741
斤	1897	弁	711	奏	1544	5 位	122	倭	2019	冶	2024		陶	1650
元	137	甘	1492	重	227	伸	1108	俸	1542	求	724		郵	524
幻	1227	央	351	乗	523	伴	1027	借	766	8 准	1232		都	188
予	393	甲	982	10 既	1458	体	61	倖	2020	凍	1205		郷	855
允	2022	由	363	殊	1505	伯	1176	倹	878	将	627		部	86
互	907	母	112	射	900	佑	2015	倫	1163	凌	2025	9	隅	1640
巴	2061	世	252	残	650	佐	1744	値	425	9 毬	2132		陽	630
斗	1899	史	332	耗	1197	作	360	健	893	13 凜	2026		階	588
太	629	申	309	耕	1196	似	1486	個	973	14 凝	1518		隊	795
凶	1280	冊	1158	11 疎	1514	伽	2014	倉	1307			10	隔	1589
天	141	6 多	229	野	236	但	1927	9 偶	1639	– 2c 子–		11	際	618
内	84	死	85	爽	2046	低	561	偽	1485	0 子	103		障	858
氏	566	気	134	粛	1695	伶	2016	側	609	了	941		隠	868
五	7	両	200	彗	2066	住	156	脩	2207	1 孔	940	13	隣	809
夫	315	朱	1503	13 業	279	何	390	偲	2021	3 存	269			
升	1898	年	45	14 爾	2154	伺	1761	停	1185	4 丞	2002		– 2e 冂–	
		西	72	15 舞	810	余	1063	偵	1928	5 孟	2049	3	卯	2031
		更	1007							6 孤	1480			

4 印 1043　　勇 1386　　版 1046　　占 1706　　瓶 1161　　7 連 440　　7 段 362
5 即 463　　8 脅 1263　　7 帝 1179　　正 275　　10 着 657　　速 502　　10 凱 2028
卵 1058　　9 動 231　　変 257　　比 798　　善 1139　　逓 1937　　12 鳳 2274
却 1783　　勘 1502　　哀 1675　　6 卓 1679　　尊 704　　逐 1134　　
7 卸 707　　10 勤 559　　亭 1184　　虎 2234　　普 1166　　逝 1396　　**– 2t 匚 –**
　　　　11 勧 1051　　亮 2010　　7 貞 1681　　巽 2062　　透 1685　　2 区 183
– 2f 刂 –　　勢 646　　8 衰 1676　　点 169　　翔 2200　　造 691　　巨 1293
0 刀 37　　　　　　恋 258　　虐 1574　　11 慈 1547　　途 1072　　匹 1500
2 刈 1282　　**– 2h 又 –**　　高 190　　9 虚 1572　　義 291　　通 150　　4 匡 2030
切 39　　0 又 1593　　畜 1223　　11 虞 1941　　13 養 402　　8 進 437　　匠 1359
3 刊 585　　2 双 1594　　9 率 788　　虜 1385　　14 興 368　　逮 891　　臣 835
召 995　　収 757　　斎 1478　　12 疑 1516　　15 翼 1062　　遊 1003　　5 医 220
4 州 195　　友 264　　商 412　　13 膚 1269　　　　逸 734　　6 殴 1940
刑 887　　3 皮 975　　10 蛮 1879　　慮 1384　　**– 2p 厂 –**　　週 92　　7 矩 2175
列 611　　6 叔 1667　　斐 2082　　　　2 反 324　　9 遇 1641　　8 匿 1771
5 判 1026　　受 260　　11 裏 273　　**– 2n ⼛ –**　　厄 1341　　達 448　　15 臨 836
別 267　　7 叙 1067　　棄 962　　4 色 204　　3 圧 1342　　運 439
6 制 427　　8 桑 1873　　12 豪 1671　　争 302　　4 灰 1343　　遂 1133　　**– 3a 氵 –**
刺 881　　14 叡 2032　　13 褒 803　　危 534　　5 辰 2246　　道 149　　0 水 21
到 904　　　　　　5 角 473　　6 厚 639　　遍 1160　　1 永 1207
刻 1211　　**– 2i 冖 –**　　**– 2k 十 –**　　6 免 733　　7 厘 1900　　遅 702　　氷 1206
刷 1044　　2 冗 1614　　0 十 12　　7 負 510　　8 原 136　　過 413　　2 汁 1794
券 506　　3 写 540　　1 干 584　　急 303　　辱 1738　　10 遺 1173　　汀 2133
7 削 1611　　7 軍 438　　千 15　　8 勉 735　　11 農 369　　遥 2248　　3 池 119
契 565　　冠 1615　　2 支 318　　9 亀 2284　　12 暦 1534　　遠 446　　汚 693
8 剖 1830　　　　午 49　　10 象 739　　歴 480　　違 814　　汗 1188
剣 879　　**– 2j 亠 –**　　3 古 172　　　　　　11 遭 1643　　江 821
剤 550　　1 亡 672　　平 202　　**– 2o ⼋ –**　　**– 2q 辶 –**　　適 415　　汐 2134
剛 1610　　2 六 8　　4 孝 542　　0 八 10　　2 辺 775　　遮 1767　　4 沖 1346
帰 317　　文 111　　考 541　　2 分 38　　込 776　　12 遷 921　　決 356
9 剰 1068　　片 1045　　老 543　　公 126　　巡 777　　選 800　　汰 2136
副 714　　3 市 181　　缶 1649　　父 113　　迅 1798　　遺 1172　　沈 936
10 割 519　　玄 1225　　5 克 1372　　羊 288　　4 廷 1111　　遼 2249　　沙 2135
創 1308　　4 亥 2008　　6 協 234　　5 弟 405　　近 445　　遵 1938　　没 935
13 劇 797　　亨 2009　　直 423　　谷 653　　迎 1055　　13 避 1491　　汽 135
　　交 114　　奔 1659　　兵 784　　返 442　　還 866　　沢 994
– 2g 力 –　　亦 2007　　7 南 74　　呉 1436　　5 迪 2247　　　　5 泣 1236
0 力 100　　充 828　　8 真 422　　6 並 1165　　迭 1507　　**– 2r 冂 –**　　沸 1792
3 加 709　　妄 1376　　索 1059　　典 367　　述 968　　2 円 13　　油 364
功 818　　5 享 1672　　10 博 601　　7 首 148　　延 1115　　3 用 107　　波 666
幼 1229　　忘 1374　　11 準 778　　前 47　　迫 1175　　4 同 198　　泌 1870
5 助 623　　対 365　　12 翠 2201　　美 401　　6 迷 967　　6 周 91　　泳 1208
励 1340　　6 夜 471　　　　盆 1099　　建 892　　7 耐 1415　　泊 1177
努 1595　　卒 787　　**– 2m ⼘ –**　　8 兼 1081　　退 846　　　　注 357
6 劾 1939　　京 189　　1 上 32　　差 658　　追 1174　　**– 2s 几 –**　　泡 1765
効 816　　育 246　　下 31　　益 716　　逃 1566　　1 凡 1102　　法 123
7 勒 1886　　斉 1477　　2 止 477　　翁 1930　　逆 444　　4 凪 2027　　況 850
勁 2029　　盲 1375　　3 外 83　　9 貧 753　　送 441　　7 風 29　　沿 1607

沼	996
治	493
泥	1621
河	389
泉	1192
泰	1545
6 浅	649
津	668
洲	2138
浮	938
洗	692
洪	1435
洸	2137
活	237
浄	664
洋	289
海	117
派	912
洵	2139
洞	1301
7 酒	517
浦	1442
浪	1753
浜	785
浩	2140
流	247
消	845
浸	1078
浴	1128
淳	2141
涙	1239
8 淑	1668
渇	1622
混	799
淡	1337
渓	1884
清	660
渋	1693
渉	432
深	536
添	1433
液	472
済	549
涼	1204
涯	1461
9 渚	2142
測	610
湖	467

港	669
湾	670
温	634
湿	1169
湯	632
満	201
滋	1549
湧	2144
渥	2143
渡	378
渦	1810
減	715
10 滑	1267
滝	1759
溝	1012
混	2145
滞	964
溶	1392
漢	556
漠	1427
源	580
滅	1338
黎	2282
11 漁	699
漸	1400
漱	2146
漂	924
漆	1546
漫	1411
漬	1793
演	344
滴	1446
漏	1806
12 潮	468
潜	937
潟	1626
潔	1241
澄	1334
潤	1203
13 激	1017
澪	2147
濃	957
濁	1625
14 鴻	2275
濯	1561
15 濫	1944
16 瀬	1513

– 3b 土 –

0 土	24
2 去	414
地	118
3 圭	2042
寺	41
至	902
先	50
在	268
4 坊	1858
坑	1613
坂	443
均	805
走	429
赤	207
5 坪	1896
幸	684
6 城	720
垣	1276
型	888
奎	2045
封	1463
赴	1465
7 埋	1826
趨	2244
起	373
8 域	970
培	1828
堀	1804
基	450
堕	1742
執	686
9 堪	1913
尭	2043
場	154
堤	1592
塔	1840
塚	1751
塀	1805
堅	1289
報	685
超	1000
喪	1678
10 塊	1524
塩	1101
塾	1674
塑	1838

塗	1073
11 境	864
増	712
墨	1705
墜	1132
12 墳	1662
舗	1443
13 壊	1407
壌	1912
壇	1839
墾	1136
壁	1489

– 3c 扌 –

0 手	57
2 払	582
打	1020
3 扱	1258
4 扶	1721
把	1724
折	1394
抜	1713
抄	1153
抑	1057
批	1029
抗	824
技	871
投	1021
択	993
5 拓	1833
拝	1201
押	986
抽	987
抹	1914
拙	1801
披	1712
拍	1178
抱	1285
抵	560
担	1274
拐	1916
招	455
拡	1113
拠	1138
拘	1800
拒	1295
6 挟	1354
拷	1720

挑	1564
持	451
括	1260
拾	1445
指	1041
拳	2078
7 挿	1651
捕	890
搜	989
振	954
捷	2079
掛	1464
排	1036
接	486
控	1718
掲	1624
採	933
授	602
探	535
捺	2080
8 推	1233
措	1200
描	1469
掃	1080
捨	1444
掘	1803
据	1832
9 提	628
揚	631
援	1088
揺	1648
搭	1915
揮	1652
換	1586
握	1714
10 搬	1722
携	1686
摂	1692
搾	1497
損	350
11 摘	1447
撃	1016
12 撲	1889
撤	1423
撮	1520
13 操	1655
擁	1715
14 擬	1517

擦	1519

– 3d 口 –

0 口	54
2 叶	2033
只	2034
兄	406
号	266
台	492
可	388
句	337
司	842
右	76
3 吐	1253
叫	1252
吸	1256
舌	1259
向	199
后	1119
名	82
4 吹	1255
吟	1250
呈	1590
邑	2250
呂	2036
吾	2035
告	690
否	1248
乱	689
豆	958
君	793
5 呼	1254
知	214
奇	1360
6 咲	927
品	230
7 唄	2039
唆	1846
員	163
唇	1737
哲	1397
8 唯	1234
啄	2038
喝	1919
唱	1646
啓	1398
9 喫	1240

喚	1587
就	934
喬	2040
登	960
短	215
尋	1082
10 嘆	1246
嗣	1917
群	794
豊	959
11 鳴	925
12 噴	1660
嘱	1638
器	527
14 嚇	1918
矯	1925
16 艶	2209

– 3e 女

0 女	102
2 好	104
奴	1933
3 如	1747
妃	1756
4 妨	1182
妊	955
妙	1154
妥	930
5 姓	1746
妹	408
姉	407
始	494
妻	671
6 姻	1748
姿	929
要	419
7 娘	1752
娯	1437
娠	956
姫	1757
8 婚	567
婦	316
婆	1931
9 媒	1496
婿	1745
媛	2047
10 嫁	1749
嫌	1688

11 嫡 1932
12 嬉 2048
13 嬢 1836

-3f 巾-
2 布 675
3 帆 1103
4 希 676
6 帥 1935
7 帯 963
師 409
8 帳 1107
9 帽 1105
幅 1380
12 幣 1781

-3g 犭-
0 犬 280
2 犯 882
4 狂 883
6 独 219
狭 1353
狩 1581
7 猛 1579
8 猪 2155
猫 1470
猟 1580
9 猶 1583
献 1355
10 猿 1584
11 獄 884
12 獣 1582
13 獲 1313

-3h 弓-
0 弓 212
1 引 216
2 弘 2064
5 弦 1226
弥 2065
6 弧 1481
7 弱 218
8 張 1106
強 217
9 弾 1539

-3i 彳-
3 行 68

4 役 375
5 彼 977
征 1114
径 1475
往 918
6 律 667
待 452
後 48
7 徒 430
徐 1066
従 1482
8 術 187
得 374
9 御 708
街 186
復 917
循 1479
10 微 1419
11 徴 1420
徳 1038
12 衝 1772
徹 1422
13 衡 1585
衛 815

-3j 彡-
4 形 395
5 参 710
8 彩 932
彫 1149
彪 2068
9 須 2263
11 彰 1827
髪 1148
12 影 854

-3k 艹-
2 芝 250
3 芋 1909
共 196
4 芳 1775
芙 2211
芹 2210
花 255
芸 435
5 苗 1468
英 353
茉 2215

茂 1467
芽 1455
若 544
苑 2212
茄 2213
茎 1474
苦 545
茅 2214
6 革 1075
茜 2216
荘 1327
草 249
荒 1377
茶 251
7 華 1074
莉 2218
荷 391
莞 2217
恭 1434
8 菫 2219
菓 1535
著 859
萌 2221
黄 780
菖 2220
菜 931
菊 475
菌 1222
9 萩 2223
落 839
葬 812
葵 2222
蒸 943
葉 253
慕 1430
10 蒔 2224
夢 811
蓄 1224
墓 1429
幕 1432
蓉 2226
蒼 2225
蓮 2227
靴 1076
11 蔦 2228
慕 1431
暮 1428

12 蕉 2229
蔵 1286
13 薪 1910
蕗 2230
薄 1449
薬 359
薫 1774
薦 1631
15 藤 2231
藩 1382
藍 2232
繭 1911
16 藻 1657
蘭 2233

-3m 宀-
2 字 110
穴 899
3 安 105
守 490
宇 990
宅 178
4 宏 2050
究 895
完 613
5 宗 616
宝 296
実 203
宙 991
官 326
宜 1086
定 355
突 898
空 140
6 宥 2051
宣 625
客 641
室 166
窃 1717
7 家 165
宰 1488
宴 640
害 518
宮 721
案 106
宵 1854
容 654
8 寂 1669

宿 179
寅 2052
密 806
窓 698
寄 1361
窒 1716
9 寒 457
富 713
10 寝 1079
寛 1050
11 寡 1851
察 619
寧 1412
12 審 1383
寮 1323
賓 1852
窮 897
窯 1789
13 憲 521

-3n 丷-
0 小 27
1 少 144
3 光 138
当 77
劣 1150
4 肖 844
学 109
労 233
乳 939
5 尚 1853
歩 431
6 栄 723
単 300
県 194
7 挙 801
党 495
8 巣 1538
蛍 1878
常 497
堂 496
9 営 722
覚 605
掌 499
10 誉 802
舜 2208
奨 1332
12 賞 500

14 厳 822

-3o 山-
0 山 34
4 岐 872
5 岬 1363
岩 1345
岸 586
岳 1358
6 峡 1352
峠 1351
炭 1344
幽 1228
7 峻 2053
峰 1350
島 286
8 崚 2054
崎 1362
崩 1122
崇 1424
9 嵐 2055
10 嵯 2056
嵩 2057
14 嶺 2058
17 巌 2059

-3p 士-
0 士 572
3 吉 1141
志 573
4 壱 1730
売 239
声 746
6 殻 1728
9 喜 1143
10 鼓 1147
11 嘉 2041

-3q 广-
2 広 694
庁 763
3 庄 2063
4 床 826
応 827
序 770
5 府 504
底 562
店 168

6 度 377
庭 1112
7 庫 825
座 786
唐 1697
席 379
8 康 894
庸 1696
麻 1529
廊 981
鹿 2279
9 廃 961
10 廉 1689
11 腐 1245
12 摩 1530
慶 1632
13 磨 1531
15 麿 2281
16 麗 1630
18 魔 1528
21 鷹 2278

-3r 尸-
1 尺 1895
2 尼 1620
3 尽 1726
4 尿 1869
尾 1868
局 170
5 届 992
屈 1802
居 171
6 屋 167
7 展 1129
9 属 1637
10 殿 1130
11 層 1367
12 履 1635

-3s 口-
2 囚 1195
四 6
3 回 90
因 554
団 491
4 困 558
囲 1194

377

図 339
5 国 40
固 972
6 面 274
9 圏 508
10 園 447

– 4a 木 –
0 木 22
1 札 1157
2 朴 1466
机 1305
朽 1628
李 2104
3 杜 2103
杉 1872
材 552
村 191
杏 2102
4 林 127
枚 1156
杯 1155
析 1393
松 696
枝 870
枠 1907
板 1047
枢 1023
采 2153
5 相 146
柚 2106
柄 985
柱 598
柾 2107
柳 1871
柊 2105
枯 974
査 624
某 1494
柔 774
染 779
架 755
6 桟 1906
株 741
根 314
桃 1567
桂 2109
桜 928

格 643
核 1212
校 115
栓 1842
梅 1734
桐 2110
栗 2111
栞 2108
殺 576
7 彬 2069
梓 2113
梧 2112
梢 2114
械 529
梨 2115
8 椎 2116
棟 1406
椰 2121
棚 1908
極 336
棋 1835
棒 1543
棺 1825
検 531
椋 2117
植 424
森 128
9 楼 1841
椿 2118
楊 2122
楠 2119
楓 2120
楽 358
10 概 1459
構 1010
榛 2124
樺 2123
模 1425
様 403
槙 2125
11 槻 2126
槽 1644
標 923
横 781
権 335
12 機 528
樹 1144
橋 597

橘 2127
13 檀 2128
16 欄 1202

– 4b 月 –
0 月 17
2 肌 1306
有 265
3 肝 1272
4 朋 2100
肪 1857
肥 1723
服 683
肢 1146
青 208
肯 1262
5 胞 1284
胆 1273
肺 1277
胎 1296
胡 2206
背 1265
胤 2205
6 朕 1921
脂 1042
脈 913
胸 1283
胴 1300
朗 1754
朔 2101
骨 1266
能 386
7 豚 796
脚 1784
脳 1278
脱 1370
8 脹 1922
勝 509
腕 1299
期 449
朝 469
9 腰 1298
腹 1271
腸 1270
10 膜 1426
静 663
12 膨 1145
13 膾 1779

14 髄 1740
15 鵬 2276
臓 1287
霸 1633
16 騰 1780

– 4c 日 –
0 日 5
1 旧 1216
旦 2085
白 205
2 早 248
旨 1040
百 14
亘 2006
旬 338
旭 2086
3 児 1217
4 明 18
旺 2087
昌 2089
昇 1777
易 759
昆 1874
的 210
者 164
5 映 352
昨 361
昭 997
冒 1104
星 730
是 1591
昂 2088
昴 2090
春 460
皆 587
昼 470
6 時 42
晏 2091
晃 2092
書 131
晋 2093
殉 1799
7 晟 2094
晨 2095
曹 1929
習 591
皐 2168

乾 1190
8 曉 1658
晴 662
晩 736
暑 638
晶 1645
景 853
量 411
最 263
智 2099
替 744
皓 2169
9 暇 1064
暗 348
暖 635
暉 2096
幹 1189
10 暢 2097
11 暫 1399
暴 1014
12 曡 637
14 曜 19
曙 2098
15 響 856
16 馨 2267

– 4d 火 –
0 火 20
2 灯 1333
3 災 1335
4 炊 1791
炉 1790
炎 1336
5 畑 36
為 1484
6 烈 1331
7 黒 206
8 焼 920
無 93
煮 1795
然 651
9 煩 1849
煙 919
熙 2148
照 998
10 熱 687
熊 2149

11 勲 1773
熱 645
黙 1578
12 燃 652
燎 2150
13 燦 2151
燥 1656
黛 2283
14 燿 2152
15 爆 1015

– 4e 示 –
0 示 615
1 礼 620
社 308
奈 2044
祉 1390
4 祈 621
5 神 310
祐 2178
祖 622
祝 851
6 祥 1576
票 922
祭 617
尉 1617
7 視 606
8 禄 2179
禁 482
9 福 1379
禅 1540
禎 2180
禍 1809
11 隷 1934

– 4f 王 –
0 王 294
玉 295
主 155
1 玖 2156
5 珍 1215
玲 2157
皇 297
6 珠 1504
班 1381
7 理 143
球 726
現 298

望 673
8 琢 2158
琳 2160
瑛 2159
琴 1251
9 瑚 2161
瑶 2163
瑞 2162
聖 674
10 瑠 2165
璃 2166
瑳 2164
13 環 865
14 璽 1887

– 4g 牛 –
0 牛 291
4 牧 731
物 79
5 牲 729
6 特 282
9 解 474
13 犠 728

– 4h 方 –
0 方 70
4 放 512
於 2084
5 施 1004
6 旅 222
7 旋 1005
族 221
10 旗 1006

– 4i 攵 –
2 冬 459
処 1137
3 改 514
攻 819
各 642
4 条 564
麦 270
5 政 483
故 173
6 教 245
致 903
敏 1735
7 救 725

赦 1570
敦 2081
夏 461
務 235
8 散 767
敬 705
敢 1691
9 数 225
10 愛 259
11 敷 1451
敵 416
弊 1782
12 憂 1032
整 503

– 4j 欠 –

0 欠 383
4 欣 2129
欧 1022
7 欲 1127
8 欺 1499
款 1727
10 歌 392
11 歓 1052

– 4k 心 –

0 心 97
3 忙 1373
忍 1414
忌 1797
4 快 1409
忠 1348
5 性 98
怖 1814
怜 2070
怪 1476
怒 1596
怠 1297
6 恨 1755
恒 1275
悔 1733
恵 1219
息 1242
恕 2071
恐 1602
恩 555
7 悟 1438
悩 1279
惇 2075
悌 2072
悦 1368
悪 304
患 1315
悠 1597
8 惟 2073
惨 1725
情 209
惜 765
悼 1680
惑 969
惣 2074
悲 1034
9 惰 1743
慌 1378
愉 1598
愚 1642
愁 1601
想 147
感 262
10 慨 1460
慎 1785
態 387
11 憎 1365
慢 1410
慣 915
慰 1618
慧 2076
12 憧 2077
憤 1661
憩 1243
13 憾 1815
憶 381
懐 1408
懇 1135
14 懲 1421
16 懸 911

– 4m 戸 –

0 戸 152
3 戻 1238
4 肩 1264
房 1237
所 153
6 扇 1555
8 雇 1553
扉 1556
10 肇 2204

– 4n 戈 –

2 成 261
3 戒 876
式 525
弐 1030
5 威 1339
武 1031
哉 2037
6 栽 1125
8 越 1001
幾 877
9 戦 301
歳 479
11 戯 1573

– 5a 石 –

0 石 78
4 研 896
砂 1151
砕 1710
5 破 665
砲 1764
7 硬 1009
硫 1856
硝 1855
8 碁 1834
9 碩 2265
碑 1522
磁 1548
碧 2176
10 確 603
12 磯 2177
礁 1768
13 礎 1515

– 5b 立 –

0 立 121
2 辛 1487
4 音 347
彦 2067
5 竜 1758
6 章 857
産 278
翌 592
7 竣 2186
童 410
8 靖 2187
意 132
新 174
辞 688
9 端 1418
颯 2266
10 毅 2131
11 親 175
15 競 852

– 5c 目 –

0 目 55
1 自 62
2 見 63
3 具 420
4 臭 1244
看 1316
省 145
盾 772
眉 2170
5 眠 849
6 眼 848
眺 1565
眸 2171
規 607
7 殖 1506
8 睡 1071
睦 2172
督 1670
9 導 703
12 瞳 2173
瞭 2174
覧 1291
13 瞬 1732
観 604

– 5d 禾 –

2 利 329
私 125
季 465
秀 1683
3 和 124
委 466
4 秋 462
秒 1152
科 320
香 1682
5 秩 1508
秘 807
租 1083
称 978
秦 2181
6 移 1121
7 程 417
税 399
稀 2182
8 稚 1230
稜 2184
稔 2183
9 種 228
稲 1220
穀 1729
10 穂 1221
稼 1750
稿 1120
11 穏 869
積 656
13 穣 2185
穫 1314

– 5e 衤 –

0 衣 677
2 初 679
4 衿 2237
5 被 976
袈 2238
袋 1329
6 裂 1330
装 1328
裁 1123
7 補 889
裕 1391
裟 2239
8 裸 1536
褐 1623
製 428
9 複 916
13 襟 1537
16 襲 1575

– 5f 田 –

0 田 35
2 町 182
男 101
4 胃 1268
思 99
界 454
卑 1521
5 畔 1945
留 761
畝 1901
鬼 1523
6 略 841
累 1060
異 1061
7 塁 1694
畳 1087
番 185
9 魁 2083
魂 1525
鼻 813
10 魅 1526
11 奮 1309

– 5g 罒 –

7 買 241
8 署 860
罪 885
置 426
9 罰 886
10 罷 1861
12 爵 1923
14 羅 1860

– 5h 皿 –

0 皿 1097
1 血 789
6 盛 719
盗 1100
7 衆 792
8 盟 717
10 監 1663
盤 1098

– 5i 疒 –

4 疫 1319
5 疲 1321
病 380
症 1318
疾 1812
7 痢 1811
痛 1320
痘 1942
8 痴 1813
12 療 1322
13 癖 1490
癒 1600

– 6a 糸 –

0 糸 242
1 系 908
3 級 568
糾 1703
紀 372
紅 820
約 211
4 紡 1859
純 965
紙 180
納 758
紗 2191
紛 1702
紋 1454
紘 2190
素 271
5 細 695
紳 1109
紬 2193
紺 1493
組 418
終 458
紹 456
経 548
絃 2192
6 結 485
絡 840
給 346
絵 345
絞 1452
統 830
絶 742
絢 2194
紫 1389
7 絹 1261
続 243
継 1025
8 維 1231
練 743
緒 862
緋 2197
綿 1191
綾 2198

6a 糸 (continued)

綜 2196 / 緑 537 / 綺 2195 / 綸 2199 / 総 697 / 綱 1609 / 網 1612
9 縄 1760 / 線 299 / 緩 1089 / 縁 1131 / 締 1180 / 編 682 / 縫 1349 / 緊 1290
10 縦 1483 / 縛 1448 / 緯 1054 / 繁 1292
11 繊 1571 / 績 1117 / 縮 1110
12 繕 1140 / 織 680
13 繰 1654

-6b 米-

0 米 224
4 料 319 / 粋 1708 / 粉 1701
5 粒 1700 / 粗 1084 / 粘 1707 / 釈 595 / 断 1024
6 粧 1699 / 奥 476 / 歯 478
8 精 659
10 糖 1698
11 齢 833 / 鞠 2262
12 糧 1704 / 翻 596
18 麟 2280

-6c 舟-

0 舟 1094
4 航 823 / 般 1096
5 舶 1095 / 船 376
6 艇 1666
15 艦 1665

-6d 虫-

0 虫 873
3 虹 2235
4 蚊 1876 / 蚕 1877
5 蛇 1875
7 触 874
9 蝶 2236
10 融 1588

-6e 耳-

0 耳 56
2 耶 2253 / 取 65
4 恥 1690
8 聡 2203
9 趣 1002
11 聴 1039
12 職 385

-6f ⺮-

0 竹 129
4 笑 1235
5 笹 2189 / 笙 2188 / 第 404 / 笛 1471 / 符 505
6 筆 130 / 策 880 / 筋 1090 / 等 569 / 答 160 / 筒 1472
7 節 464
8 算 747 / 管 328 / 箇 1473
9 範 1092 / 箱 1091
10 篤 1883 / 築 1603
12 簡 1533
13 簿 1450
14 籍 1198

-7a 言-

0 言 66
2 計 340 / 訂 1019
3 託 1636 / 討 1018 / 記 371 / 訓 771
4 訪 1181 / 許 737 / 訟 1403 / 設 577 / 訳 594
5 訴 1402 / 評 1028 / 証 484 / 詐 1498 / 診 1214 / 詔 1885 / 詠 1209 / 詞 843
6 誠 718 / 詩 570 / 詰 1142 / 話 238 / 誇 1629 / 該 1213 / 詳 1577 / 詢 2240 / 試 526
7 誤 906 / 誘 1684 / 語 67 / 誌 574 / 読 244 / 認 738 / 諄 2242 / 説 400 / 誕 1116 / 誓 1395
8 課 488 / 諸 861 / 謁 1920 / 談 593 / 請 661 / 諾 1770 / 誼 2241 / 論 293 / 諒 2243 / 調 342
9 諮 1769 / 謀 1495 / 謡 1647 / 諭 1599
10 謝 901 / 講 783 / 謹 1247 / 謙 1687
12 譜 1167 / 識 681 / 警 706
13 譲 1013 / 護 1312 / 議 292

-7b 貝-

0 貝 240
2 則 608
3 財 553 / 貢 1719
4 販 511 / 貫 1048 / 責 914 / 貨 752
5 貯 762 / 費 749 / 貴 1171 / 貿 760 / 貸 748 / 賀 756
6 賄 1739 / 賊 1807 / 賃 751 / 資 750
8 賠 1829 / 賜 1831
賦 1808 / 賛 745 / 質 176
9 賢 1288
10 購 1011
11 贈 1364
12 韻 349

-7c 車-

0 車 133
2 軌 1787
3 軒 1187
4 軟 1788 / 転 433
5 軸 988 / 軽 547
6 較 1453 / 載 1124
7 輔 2245
8 輪 1164 / 輩 1037 / 輝 1653
9 輸 546
10 轄 1186

-7d 足-

0 足 58
5 距 1294
6 践 1568 / 跳 1563 / 路 151 / 跡 1569
7 踊 1558
8 踏 1559
14 躍 1560

-7e 酉-

0 酉 2254
3 配 515 / 酌 1863
4 酔 1709
5 酢 1867
6 酵 1866 / 酬 1864 / 酪 1865
7 酷 1711 / 酸 516
醇 2255
10 醜 1527
13 醸 1837

-8a 金-

0 金 23
2 針 341
3 釣 1862
4 欽 2130 / 鈍 966
5 鉢 1820 / 鉄 312 / 鈴 1822 / 鉛 1606 / 鉱 1604
6 銭 648 / 銀 313 / 銘 1552 / 銑 1905 / 銃 829 / 銅 1605
7 鋳 1551 / 鋭 1371
8 錘 1904 / 錬 1816 / 錦 2256 / 錯 1199 / 錠 1818 / 録 538 / 鋼 1608
9 鍛 1817
10 鎖 1819 / 鎮 1786 / 鎌 2257
11 鏡 863
12 鐘 1821
15 鑑 1664

-8b 食-

0 食 322
2 飢 1304
4 飲 323 / 飯 325
5 飽 1763 / 飾 979 / 飼 1762
7 餓 1303
8 館 327

-8c 隹-

2 隻 1311 / 隼 2259
4 雄 1387 / 集 436 / 焦 999
5 雅 1456
6 雌 1388 / 雑 575 / 奪 1310
10 雛 2260 / 難 557 / 離 1281
12 耀 2202

-8d 雨-

0 雨 30
3 雪 949
4 雲 636 / 霧 1824 / 雷 952 / 電 108 / 零 1823
6 需 1416
7 霊 1168 / 震 953
9 霞 2261 / 霜 948
11 霧 950
13 露 951

-8e 門-

0 門 161
3 問 162 / 閉 397
4 閑 1532 / 間 43 / 開 396
6 閣 64 / 閥 1510 / 閤 837 / 関 398
7 閲 1369

380

10	闐	1511		頌	2264	9	類	226	**–10a 馬–**			駒	2268
				預	394		顏	277				7	駿	2269
–9a 頁–				頑	1848		顯	1170	0	馬	283	8	騎	1881
2	頂	1440	5	領	834		額	838	4	駄	1880		驗	532
3	項	1439	7	賴	1512		題	354		駅	284		騷	875
	順	769		頭	276	10	願	581		駆	1882			
4	頌	1850	8	頻	1847	12	顧	1554	5	駐	599	12	驚	1778

–11a 魚–			鯛	2272
0	魚	290	**–11b 鳥–**	
5	鮎	2270	0	鳥	285
6	鮮	701	2	鳩	2273
7	鯉	2271	8	鶏	926
8	鯨	700	10	鶴	2277

Index by Stroke Count

1 – 6 Strokes

– 1 –

一 2
乙 983

– 2 –

二 3
入 52
丁 184
之 2004
乃 2003
七 9
九 11
亻 人 1
子 子 103
了 941
刂 刀 37
力 力 100
又 又 1593
十 十 12
丷 八 10

– 3 –

三 4
川 33
勺 1903
工 139
久 1210
万 16
乏 754
己 370
夕 81
巳 2060
寸 1894
大 26
刃 1413
与 539
及 1257
丈 1325
才 551
丸 644
也 2005
子 孔 940
亠 亡 672
十 千 584
千 15
⺊ 上 32
下 31
八 凡 1102
土 土 24
口 口 54
女 女 102
弓 弓 212
⺌ 小 27
山 山 34
士 士 572

– 4 –

不 94
斤 1897
元 137
幻 1227
予 393
允 2022
互 907
巴 2061
斗 1899
太 629
凶 1280
天 141
内 84
氏 566
五 7
夫 315
升 1898
毛 287
丹 1093
屯 1936
匁 1902
丑 2001
中 28
弔 1796
井 1193
亻 仏 583
化 254
仁 1619
介 453
今 51
刂 刈 1282
切 39
又 双 1594
収 757
友 264
冖 冗 1614
亠 六 8
文 111
片 1045
十 支 318
午 49
⺊ 止 477
丷 分 38
公 126
父 113
厂 反 324
厄 1341
辶 辺 775
込 776
冂 円 13
匚 区 183
巨 1293
匹 1500
氵 水 21
永 1207
氷 1206
扌 手 57
犭 犬 280
弓 引 216
⺌ 少 144
尸 尺 1895
木 木 22
月 月 17
日 日 5
火 火 20
礻 示 615
王 王 294
玉 295
牛 牛 281
方 方 70
欠 欠 383
心 心 97
戸 戸 152

– 5 –

以 46
北 73
矛 773
巧 1627
包 804
丘 1357
凸 1892
凹 1893
且 1926
必 520
斥 1401
矢 213
左 75
丙 984
出 53
民 177
半 88
本 25
末 305
未 306
失 311
生 44
弁 711
甘 1492
央 351
甲 982
由 363
母 112
世 252
史 332
申 309
冊 1158
亻 仙 1891
仕 333
代 256
他 120
付 192
令 831
子 存 269
卩 卯 2031
刂 刊 585
召 995
力 加 709
功 818
幼 1229
又 皮 975
冖 写 540
亠 市 181
玄 1225
十 古 172
平 202
⺊ 外 83
占 1706
正 275
比 798
厂 圧 1342
辶 巡 777
迅 1798
冂 用 107
氵 汁 1794
汀 2133
土 去 414
扌 払 582
打 1020
口 叶 2033
只 2034
兄 406
号 266
台 492
可 388
句 337
司 842
右 76
女 好 104
奴 1933
巾 布 675
犭 犯 882
弓 弘 2064
艹 芝 250
宀 字 110
穴 899
广 広 694
庁 763
尸 尼 1620
囗 囚 1195
四 6
木 札 1157
日 旧 1216
旦 2085
白 205
礻 礼 620
王 主 155
石 石 78
立 立 121
目 目 55
衤 衣 677
田 田 35
皿 皿 1097

– 6 –

多 229
死 85
気 134
両 200
朱 1503
年 45
西 72
吏 1007
毎 116
再 782
曲 366
亻 伏 1356
休 60
件 732
伐 1509
伊 2011
仲 1347
伍 2013
任 334
仰 1056
伎 2012
伝 434
仮 1049
全 89
企 481
合 159
会 158
肉 223
冫 次 384
壮 1326
兆 1562
羽 590
子 丞 2002
阝 防 513
那 2251
邦 808
卩 印 1043
刂 州 195
刑 887
列 611
亠 亥 2008
亨 2009
交 114
亦 2007
充 828
妄 1376
十 孝 542
考 541
老 543
缶 1649
⺈ 色 204
争 302
危 534
丷 羊 288
厂 灰 1343
廴 廷 1111
近 445
迎 1055
返 442
冂 同 198
几 凪 2027
匚 匡 2030
匠 1359
臣 835
氵 池 119
汚 693
汗 1188
江 821
汐 2134
土 地 118
圭 2042
寺 41
至 902
先 50
在 268
扌 扱 1258
口 吐 1253
叫 1252
吸 1256
舌 1259
向 199
后 1119
名 82
女 如 1747
妃 1756
巾 帆 1103
彳 行 68
艹 芋 1909
共 196
宀 安 105
守 490
宇 990
宅 178
⺌ 光 138
当 77
劣 1150
士 吉 1141
广 庄 2063
尸 尽 1726
囗 回 90
因 554
団 491
木 朴 1466

机	1305	伶	2016
朽	1628	住	156
李	2104	何	390
月 肌	1306	伺	1761
有	265	余	1063
日 早	248	含	1249
旨	1040	冫 状	626
百	14	冴	2023
亘	2006	冷	832
旬	338	冶	2024
旭	2086	求	724
火 灯	1333	子 孟	2049
冬	459	阝 阻	1085
処	1137	附	1843
戈 成	261	阿	2258
自	62	邪	1457
血	789	邸	563
糸 糸	242	卩 即	463
米	224	卵	1058
舟	1094	却	1783
虫	873	刂 判	1026
耳	56	別	267
竹	129	力 助	623
		励	1340
– 7 –		努	1595
良	321	亠 享	1672
身	59	忘	1374
来	69	対	365
承	942	克	1372
束	501	宀 角	473
里	142	弟	405
我	1302	谷	653
甫	2167	兵	784
更	1008	呉	1436
亜	1616	厂 辰	2246
寿	1550	辷 迪	2247
亻 位	122	迭	1507
伸	1108	述	968
伴	1027	延	1115
体	61	迫	1175
伯	1176	匚 医	220
佑	2015	冲	1346
佐	1744	决	356
作	360	汰	2136
似	1486	沈	936
伽	2014	沙	2135
但	1927	没	935
低	561	汽	135

沢	994	乳	939
土 坊	1858	山 岐	872
坑	1613	士 志	573
坂	443	壱	1730
均	805	売	239
走	429	声	746
赤	207	广 床	826
扌 扶	1721	応	827
把	1724	序	770
折	1394	尸 尿	1869
抜	1713	尾	1868
抄	1153	局	170
抑	1057	口 困	558
批	1029	囲	1194
抗	824	図	339
技	871	木 杜	2103
投	1021	杉	1872
択	993	材	552
口 吹	1255	村	191
吟	1250	杏	2102
呈	1590	月 肝	1272
邑	2250	日 児	1217
呂	2036	火 災	1335
吾	2035	礻 社	308
告	690	奈	2044
否	1248	王 玖	2156
乱	689	攵 改	514
豆	958	攻	819
君	793	各	642
女 妨	1182	心 忙	1373
妊	955	忍	1414
妙	1154	忌	1797
妥	930	尸 戻	1238
巾 希	676	戈 戒	876
犭 狂	883	式	525
彳 役	375	弐	1030
彡 形	395	辛	1487
芳	1775	見	63
艹 芙	2211	利	329
芹	2210	私	125
花	255	季	465
芸	435	秀	1683
宀 宏	2050	耒 初	679
究	895	田 町	182
完	613	男	101
肖	844	糸 系	908
学	109	言 言	66
労	233	貝	240

車 車	133	斉	1477
足	58	盲	1375
酉 酉	2254	版	1046
		艹 協	234
– 8 –		直	423
非	498	奔	1659
長	95	卜 卓	1679
表	272	虎	2234
画	343	免	733
果	487	並	1165
東	71	典	367
垂	1070	厂 厚	639
奉	1541	辷 迷	967
毒	522	建	892
事	80	退	846
亻 依	678	追	1174
使	331	逃	1566
価	421	逆	444
侑	2018	送	441
例	612	門 周	91
佳	1462	匸 殴	1940
侍	571	泣	1236
侃	2017	沸	1792
供	197	油	364
侮	1736	波	666
舎	791	泌	1870
念	579	泳	1208
命	578	泊	1177
子 孤	1480	注	357
阝 限	847	泡	1765
郎	980	法	123
郁	2252	況	850
郊	817	沿	1607
刂 制	427	沼	996
刺	881	治	493
到	904	泥	1621
刻	1211	河	389
刷	1044	泉	1192
券	506	泰	1545
力 劾	1939	土 坪	1896
効	816	幸	684
又 叔	1667	扌 拓	1833
受	260	拝	1201
亠 夜	471	押	986
卒	787	抽	987
京	189	抹	1914
育	246	拙	1801
		披	1712

拍	1178
抱	1285
抵	560
担	1274
拐	1916
招	455
拡	1113
拠	1138
拘	1800
拒	1295
口 味	307
呼	1254
知	214
奇	1360
女 姓	1746
妹	408
姉	407
始	494
妻	671
弓 弦	1226
弥	2065
彳 彼	977
征	1114
径	1475
往	918
彡 参	710
艹 苗	1468
英	353
茉	2215
茂	1467
芽	1455
若	544
苑	2212
茄	2213
茎	1474
苦	545
茅	2214
昔	764
宀 宗	616
宝	296
実	203
宙	991
官	326
宜	1086
定	355
突	898
空	140
宀 尚	1853

歩 431	女 条 564	刂 削 1611	派 912	广 度 377	怖 1814	俳 1035
屮 岬 1363	麦 270	契 565	洶 2139	庭 1112	怜 2070	候 944
岩 1345	欠 欣 2129	力 勅 1886	洞 1301	尸 屋 167	怪 1476	修 945
岸 586	欧 1022	勁 2029	土 城 720	囗 面 274	怒 1596	倍 87
岳 1358	心 快 1409	勇 1386	垣 1276	扌 相 146	怠 1297	倭 2019
广 府 504	忠 1348	又 叙 1067	型 888	柚 2106	戈 威 1339	俸 1542
底 562	尸 肩 1264	冖 軍 438	奎 2045	柄 985	武 1031	俵 1890
店 168	房 1237	冠 1615	封 1463	柱 598	哉 2037	借 766
尸 届 992	所 153	亠 帝 1179	赴 1465	柾 2107	石 研 896	倖 2020
屈 1802	日 具 420	変 257	扌 挟 1354	柳 1871	砂 1151	倹 878
居 171	禾 和 124	哀 1675	拷 1720	柊 2105	砕 1710	倫 1163
囗 国 40	委 466	亭 1184	挑 1564	枯 974	音 347	値 425
固 972	耳 耶 2253	亮 2010	持 451	査 624	彦 2067	健 893
木 林 127	取 65	十 南 74	括 1260	某 1494	自 臭 1244	個 973
枚 1156	釒 金 23	卜 貞 1681	拾 1445	柔 774	看 1316	倉 1307
杯 1155	釒 食 322	点 169	指 1041	染 779	省 145	冫 准 1232
析 1393	雨 雨 30	虐 1574	拳 2078	架 755	盾 772	凍 1205
松 696	門 門 161	⺈ 負 510	口 咲 927	月 胞 1284	眉 2170	将 627
枝 870		急 303	品 230	胆 1273	禾 秋 462	凌 2025
枠 1907	**– 9 –**	⺌ 首 148	女 姻 1748	肺 1277	秒 1152	阝 陳 1405
板 1047	飛 530	前 47	姿 929	胎 1296	科 320	陪 1943
枢 1023	発 96	美 401	要 419	胡 2206	香 1682	陸 647
采 2153	衣 1677	皿 盆 1099	巾 帥 1935	背 1265	衤 衿 2237	陵 1844
月 朋 2100	甚 1501	厂 厘 1900	犭 独 219	胤 2205	罒 胃 1268	隆 946
肪 1857	卷 507	辶 連 440	狭 1353	日 映 352	思 99	陰 867
肥 1723	専 600	速 502	狩 1581	昨 361	界 454	険 533
服 683	奏 1544	通 1937	弓 弧 1481	昭 997	卑 1521	随 1741
肢 1146	重 227	逐 1134	彳 律 667	冒 1104	广 疫 1319	陶 1650
青 208	乗 523	逝 1396	待 452	星 730	糸 級 568	郵 524
肯 1262	亻 信 157	透 1685	後 48	是 1591	糾 1703	都 188
日 明 18	促 1557	造 691	艹 革 1075	昂 2090	紀 372	郷 855
旺 2087	便 330	途 1072	茜 2216	春 460	紅 820	部 86
昌 2089	係 909	通 150	荘 1327	皆 587	約 211	刂 剖 1830
昇 1777	俊 1845	門 耐 1415	草 249	昼 470	虫 虹 2235	剣 879
易 759	保 489	八 風 29	荒 1377	火 畑 36	言 計 340	剤 550
昆 1874	侵 1077	匸 段 362	茶 251	為 1484	訂 1019	剛 1731
的 210	俗 1126	矢 矩 2175	宀 宥 2051	礻 神 310	貝 則 608	帰 317
者 164	侯 1924	氵 津 668	宣 625	祐 2178	車 軌 1787	力 脅 1263
昂 2088	子 孫 910	浅 649	客 641	祖 622		又 桑 1873
火 炊 1791	阝 陣 1404	洲 2138	室 166	祝 851	**– 10 –**	一 衰 1676
炉 1790	陛 589	浮 938	窃 1717	王 珍 1215	既 1458	恋 258
炎 1336	降 947	洗 692	⺍ 栄 723	玲 2157	殊 1505	高 190
礻 祉 1390	院 614	洪 1435	単 300	皇 297	射 900	畜 1223
祈 621	除 1065	洸 2137	県 194	牛 牲 729	残 650	十 真 422
牛 牧 731	陥 1218	活 237	山 峡 1352	方 施 1004	耗 1197	索 1059
物 79	郡 193	浄 664	峠 1351	政 483	耕 1196	⺈ 勉 735
方 放 512	郭 1673	洋 289	炭 1344	故 173	亻 倒 905	兼 1081
於 2084	卩 卸 707	海 117	幽 1228	心 性 98	倣 1776	差 658

益	716
翁	1930
厂 原	136
辱	1738
辶 進	437
逮	891
遊	1003
逸	734
週	92
匚 匿	1771
氵 酒	517
浦	1442
浪	1753
浜	785
浩	2140
流	247
消	845
浸	1078
浴	1128
淳	2141
涙	1239
土 埋	1826
赳	2244
起	373
扌 挿	1651
捕	890
捜	989
振	954
口 唄	2039
唆	1846
員	163
唇	1737
哲	1397
女 娘	1752
娯	1437
娠	956
姫	1757
巾 帯	963
師	409
犭 猛	1579
弓 弱	218
彳 徒	430
徐	1066
従	1482
艹 華	1074
莉	2218
荷	391
莞	2217
恭	1434
宀 家	165
宰	1488
宴	640
害	518
宮	721
案	106
宵	1854
容	654
⺍ 挙	801
党	495
屵 峻	2053
峰	1350
島	286
广 庫	825
座	786
唐	1697
席	379
尸 展	1129
木 桟	1906
株	741
根	314
桃	1567
桂	2109
桜	928
格	643
核	1212
校	115
栓	1842
梅	1734
桐	2110
栗	2111
栞	2108
殺	576
月 朕	1921
脂	1042
脈	913
胸	1283
胴	1300
朗	1754
朔	2101
骨	1266
能	386
日 時	42
晏	2091
晃	2092
書	131
晋	2093
殉	1799
火 烈	1331
礻 祥	1576
票	922
祭	617
尉	1617
王 珠	1504
班	1381
牛 特	282
方 旅	222
攵 教	245
致	903
敏	1735
心 恨	1755
恒	1275
悔	1733
恵	1219
息	1242
恕	2071
恐	1602
恩	555
尸 扇	1555
戈 栽	1125
石 破	665
砲	1764
立 竜	1758
目 眠	849
禾 秩	1508
秘	807
租	1083
称	978
秦	2181
衤 被	976
裂	2238
袋	1329
田 畔	1945
留	761
歯	1901
鬼	1523
疒 疲	1321
病	380
症	1318
疾	1812
糸 紡	1859
純	965
紙	180
納	758
紗	2191
紛	1702
紋	1454
紘	2190
素	271
米 料	319
粋	1708
粉	1701
舟 航	823
般	1096
虫 蚊	1876
蚕	1877
耳 恥	1690
笑	1235
言 託	1636
討	1018
記	371
訓	771
貝 財	553
貢	1719
車 軒	1187
酉 配	515
酌	1863
金 針	341
飠 飢	1304
隹 隻	1311
隼	2259
馬 馬	283

- 11 -

疎	1514
野	236
爽	2046
粛	1695
彗	2066
亻 偶	1639
偽	1485
側	609
脩	2207
偲	2021
停	1185
偵	1928
偏	1159
斜	1069
氵 毬	2132
阝 隅	1640
陽	630
階	588
隊	795
刂 剰	1068
副	714
力 動	231
勘	1502
一 率	788
斎	1478
商	412
卜 虚	1572
⺈ 亀	2284
貝 貧	753
丷 瓶	1161
辶 遇	1641
達	448
運	439
遂	1133
道	149
遍	1160
遅	702
過	413
氵 淑	1668
渇	1622
混	799
淡	1337
渓	1884
清	660
渋	1693
渉	432
深	536
添	1433
液	472
済	549
涼	1204
涯	1461
土 域	970
培	1828
堀	1804
基	450
堕	1742
執	686
扌 推	1233
捷	2079
掛	1464
排	1036
接	486
控	1718
掲	1624
採	933
授	602
探	535
捺	2080
措	1200
描	1469
掃	1080
捨	1444
掘	1803
据	1832
口 唯	1234
啄	2038
喝	1919
唱	1646
啓	1398
女 婚	567
婦	316
婆	1931
巾 帳	1107
犭 猪	2155
猫	1470
猟	1580
弓 張	1106
強	217
彳 術	187
得	374
彡 彩	932
彫	1149
彪	2068
艹 菫	2219
菓	1535
著	859
萌	2221
菖	2220
菜	931
菊	475
菌	1222
宀 寂	1669
宿	179
寅	2052
密	806
窓	698
寄	1361
窒	1716
⺍ 巣	1538
蛍	1878
常	497
堂	496
屵 崚	2054
崎	1362
崩	1122
崇	1424
⺈ 殻	1728
广 康	894
庸	1696
麻	1529
廊	981
鹿	2279
庶	1766
木 彬	2069
梓	2113
梧	2112
梢	2114
械	529
梨	2115
月 豚	796
脚	1784
脳	1278
脱	1370
日 晟	2094
晨	2095
曹	1929
習	591
皐	2168
乾	1190
火 黒	206
礻 視	606
王 理	143
球	726
現	298
望	673
方 旋	1005
族	221
攵 救	725
赦	1570
敦	2081
夏	461
務	235
欠 欲	1127
心 悟	1438
悩	1279
惇	2075
悌	2072
悦	1368
悪	304
患	1315
悠	1597

立 章 857
産 278
羽 翌 592
目 眼 848
眺 1565
眸 2171
規 607
禾 移 1121
衣 裂 1330
装 1328
裁 1123
田 略 841
累 1060
異 1061
皿 盛 719
盗 1100
糸 細 695
紳 1109
紬 2193
紺 1493
組 418
終 458
紹 456
経 548
絃 2192
米 粒 1700
粗 1084
粘 1707
釈 595
断 1024
舟 舶 1095
船 376
虫 蛇 1875
竹 笹 2189
笙 2188
第 404
笛 1471
符 505
言 訪 1181
許 737
訟 1403
設 577
訳 594
貝 敗 511
販 1048
貫 914
責 655
貨 752

車 軟 1788
転 433
酉 酔 1709
金 釣 1862
雪 949
門 問 162
閉 397
頁 頂 1440
魚 魚 290
鳥 鳥 285

– 12 –

イ 備 768
偉 1053
傍 1183
傘 790
阝 隔 1589
刂 割 519
創 1308
力 勤 559
一 蛮 1879
斐 2082
十 博 601
ク 象 739
ソ 着 657
善 1139
尊 704
普 1166
巽 2062
翔 2200
辶 遣 1173
遥 2248
遠 446
違 814
几 凱 2028
氵 渚 2142
測 610
湖 467
港 669
湾 670
温 634
湿 1169
湯 632
満 201
滋 1549
湧 2144
渥 2143
渡 378

渦 1810
減 715
土 堪 1913
尭 2043
場 154
堤 1592
塔 1840
塚 1751
塀 1805
堅 1289
報 685
超 1000
喪 1678
扌 提 628
揚 631
援 1088
揺 1648
搭 1915
揮 1652
換 1586
握 1714
口 喫 1240
喚 1587
就 934
喬 2040
登 960
短 215
尋 1082
女 媒 1496
婿 1745
媛 2047
巾 帽 1105
幅 1380
犭 猶 1583
献 1355
弓 弾 1539
彳 御 708
街 186
復 917
循 1479
彡 須 2263
艹 萩 2223
落 839
葬 812
葵 2222
蒸 943
葉 253
募 1430

宀 寒 457
富 713
営 722
覚 605
掌 499
山 嵐 2055
喜 1143
广 廃 961
尸 属 1637
口 圏 508
木 椎 2116
棟 1406
椰 2121
棚 1908
極 336
棋 1835
棒 1543
棺 1825
検 531
椋 2117
植 424
森 128
月 腋 1922
勝 509
腕 1299
期 449
朝 469
日 暁 1658
晴 662
晩 736
暑 638
晶 1645
景 853
量 411
最 263
智 2099
替 744
皓 2169
火 焼 920
無 93
煮 1795
然 651
禾 禄 2179
禁 482
王 琢 2158
琳 2160
瑛 2159
琴 1251

攵 散 767
敬 705
敢 1691
欠 欺 1499
款 1727
心 惟 2073
惨 1725
情 209
惜 765
悼 1680
惑 969
惣 2074
悲 1034
尸 雇 1553
扉 1556
戈 越 1001
幾 877
石 硬 1009
硫 1856
硝 1855
竣 2186
童 410
日 殖 1506
禾 程 417
税 399
稀 2182
衤 補 889
裕 1391
娑 2239
罒 墾 1694
畳 1087
番 185
罒 買 241
皿 衆 792
广 痢 1811
痛 1320
痘 1942
糸 結 485
絡 840
給 346
絵 345
絞 1452
統 830
絶 742
絢 2194
紫 1389
米 粧 1699
奥 476

歯 478
艇 1666
釒 筆 130
策 880
筋 1090
等 569
答 160
筒 1472
言 訴 1402
評 1028
証 484
詐 1498
診 1214
詔 1885
詠 1209
詞 843
貝 貯 762
費 749
貴 1171
貿 760
貸 748
賀 756
車 軸 988
軽 547
⻊ 距 1294
酉 酢 1867
釒 欽 2130
鈍 966
飠 飲 323
飯 325
隹 雄 1387
集 436
焦 999
雲 636
雰 1824
門 閑 1532
間 43
開 396
頁 項 1439
順 769

– 13 –

業 279
イ 働 232
傾 1441
傑 1731
僧 1366
傷 633

債 1118
催 1317
阝 際 618
障 858
隠 868
力 勧 1051
勢 646
一 裏 273
棄 962
十 準 778
卜 虞 1941
虜 1385
丷 慈 1547
義 291
厂 農 369
辶 遭 1643
適 415
遮 1767
氵 滑 1267
滝 1759
溝 1012
滉 2145
滞 964
溶 1392
漢 556
漠 1427
源 580
滅 1338
黎 2282
土 塊 1524
塩 1101
塾 1674
塑 1838
塗 1073
扌 搬 1722
携 1686
摂 1692
搾 1497
損 350
口 嘆 1246
嗣 1917
群 794
豊 959
女 嫁 1749
嫌 1688
犭 猿 1584
彳 微 1419
艹 蒔 2224

388

夢 811
蓄 1224
墓 1429
幕 1432
蓉 2226
蒼 2225
蓮 2227
靴 1076
宀 寝 1079
寛 1050
⺍ 誉 802
舜 2208
奨 1332
山 嵯 2056
嵩 2057
士 鼓 1147
广 廉 1689
尸 殿 1130
囗 園 447
木 楼 1841
椿 2118
楊 2122
楠 2119
楓 2120
楽 358
月 腰 1298
腹 1271
腸 1270
日 暇 1064
暗 348
暖 635
暉 2096
幹 1189
火 煩 1849
煙 919
熙 2148
照 998
ネ 福 1379
禅 1540
禎 2180
禍 1809
王 瑚 2161
瑶 2163
瑞 2162
聖 674
牛 解 474
攵 数 225
心 惰 1743

慌 1378
愉 1598
愚 1642
愁 1601
想 147
感 262
戈 戦 301
歳 479
石 碁 1834
立 靖 2187
意 132
新 174
辞 688
目 睡 1071
睦 2172
督 1670
禾 稚 1230
稜 2184
稔 2183
衤 裸 1536
褐 1623
製 428
罒 署 860
罪 885
置 426
皿 盟 717
疒 痴 1813
糸 絹 1261
続 243
継 1025
虫 触 874
⺮ 節 464
言 誠 718
詩 570
詰 1142
話 238
誇 1629
該 1213
詳 1577
詢 2240
試 526
貝 賄 1739
賊 1807
賃 751
資 750
車 較 1453
載 1124
⻊ 践 1568

跳 1563
路 151
跡 1569
酉 酵 1866
酬 1864
酪 1865
金 鉢 1820
鉄 312
鈴 1822
鉛 1606
鉱 1604
食 飽 1763
飾 979
飼 1762
隹 雅 1456
雨 雷 952
電 108
零 1823
頁 頒 1850
頌 2264
預 394
頑 1848
鳥 鳩 2273

– 14 –

爾 2154
亻 僕 1888
僚 1324
像 740
亠 豪 1671
十 翠 2201
⺊ 疑 1516
厂 暦 1534
歴 480
⻌ 遷 921
選 800
遺 1172
遼 2249
遵 1938
几 鳳 2274
氵 漁 699
漸 1400
漱 2146
漂 924
漆 1546
漫 1411
漬 1793
演 344

滴 1446
漏 1806
土 境 864
増 712
墨 1705
墜 1132
扌 摘 1447
撃 1016
口 鳴 925
女 嫡 1932
犭 獄 884
彳 徴 1420
徳 1038
彡 彰 1827
髪 1148
艹 蔦 2228
慕 1431
暮 1428
宀 寡 1851
察 619
寧 1412
士 嘉 2041
广 腐 1245
尸 層 1367
木 概 1459
構 1010
榛 2124
樺 2123
模 1425
様 403
槙 2125
月 膜 1426
静 663
日 暢 2097
火 熟 687
熊 2149
王 瑠 2165
璃 2166
瑳 2164
方 旗 1006
攵 愛 259
欠 歌 392
心 慨 1460
慎 1785
態 387
戸 肇 2204
石 碩 2265
碑 1522

磁 1548
碧 2176
立 端 1418
颯 2266
目 導 703
禾 種 228
稲 1220
穀 1729
衤 複 916
罒 魁 2083
魂 1525
鼻 813
罒 罰 886
糸 維 1231
練 743
緒 862
緋 2197
綿 1191
綾 2198
綜 2196
緑 537
綺 2195
綸 2199
総 697
綱 1609
網 1612
米 精 659
耳 聡 2203
⺮ 算 747
管 328
箇 1473
言 誤 906
誘 1684
語 67
誌 574
読 244
認 738
諄 2242
説 400
誕 1116
誓 1395
車 輔 2245
⻊ 踊 1558
酉 酷 1711
丨 酸 516
醇 2255
金 銭 648
銀 313

銘 1552
銑 1905
銃 829
銅 1605
隹 雌 1388
雑 575
奪 1310
雨 需 1416
門 聞 64
閥 1510
閣 837
関 398
頁 領 834
馬 駄 1880
駅 284
駆 1882

– 15 –

舞 810
亻 儀 727
億 382
冫 凜 2026
阝 隣 809
刂 劇 797
亠 褒 803
⺊ 膚 1269
慮 1384
⺍ 養 402
⻌ 避 1491
還 866
氵 潮 468
潜 937
潟 1626
潔 1241
澄 1334
潤 1203
土 墳 1662
舗 1443
扌 撲 1889
撤 1423
撮 1520
口 噴 1660
嘱 1638
器 527
女 嬉 2048
巾 幣 1781
犭 獣 1582
彳 衝 1772

徹 1422
彡 影 854
艹 蕉 2229
蔵 1286
宀 審 1383
寮 1323
賓 1852
窮 897
窯 1789
⺍ 賞 500
广 摩 1530
慶 1632
尸 履 1635
木 槻 2126
槽 1644
標 923
横 781
権 335
日 暴 1014
暫 1399
火 勲 1773
熱 645
黙 1578
ネ 隷 1934
攵 敷 1451
敵 416
弊 1782
欠 歓 1052
心 憎 1365
慢 1410
慣 915
慰 1618
慧 2076
戈 戯 1573
石 確 603
立 毅 2131
禾 穂 1221
稼 1750
稿 1120
罒 魅 1526
罒 罷 1861
皿 監 1663
盤 1098
糸 縄 1760
線 299
緩 1089
縁 1131
締 1180

編 682
縫 1349
緊 1290
虫 蝶 2236
耳 趣 1002
⺮ 範 1092
箱 1091
言 課 488
諸 861
謁 1920
談 593
請 661
諾 1770
誼 2241
論 293
諒 2243
調 342
貝 賠 1829
賜 1831
賦 1808
賛 745
質 176
車 輪 1164
輩 1037
輝 1653
足 踏 1559
金 鋳 1551
鋭 1371
食 餓 1303
⻗ 霊 1168
震 953
門 閲 1369
馬 駐 599
駒 2268

– 16 –

亻 儒 1417

冫 凝 1518
又 叙 2032
⺍ 興 368
氵 激 1017
澪 2147
濃 957
濁 1625
土 壊 1407
壌 1912
壇 1839
墾 1136
壁 1489
扌 操 1655
擁 1715
女 嬢 1836
犭 獲 1313
亻 衡 1585
衛 815
艹 薪 1910
蕗 2230
薄 1449
薬 359
薫 1774
薦 1631
宀 憲 521
广 磨 1531
木 機 528
樹 1144
橋 597
橘 2127
月 膨 1145
日 曇 637
火 燃 652
燎 2150
女 憂 1032
整 503
心 憧 2077

憤 1661
憩 1243
立 親 175
手 穏 869
積 656
田 奮 1309
糸 縦 1483
縛 1448
緯 1054
繁 1292
米 糖 1698
虫 融 1588
⺮ 篤 1883
築 1603
言 諮 1769
謀 1495
謡 1647
諭 1599
貝 賢 1288
車 輸 546
金 錘 1904
錬 1816
錦 2256
錯 1199
錠 1818
録 538
鋼 1608
食 館 327
頁 頼 1512
頭 276
魚 鮎 2270

– 17 –

亻 優 1033
償 971
⺍ 翼 1062
匸 臨 836

氵 鴻 2275
濯 1561
扌 擬 1517
擦 1519
口 嚇 1918
矯 1925
⺍ 厳 822
⺾ 嶺 2058
木 檀 2128
月 膳 1779
火 燦 2151
燥 1656
黛 2283
王 環 865
牛 犠 728
心 憶 1815
憶 381
懐 1408
懇 1135
石 磯 2177
礁 1768
目 瞳 2173
瞭 2174
覧 1291
爵 1923
疒 療 1322
糸 繊 1571
績 1117
縮 1110
米 齢 833
鞠 2262
耳 聴 1039
言 謝 901
講 783
謹 1247
謙 1687
貝 購 1011

車 轄 1186
酉 醜 1527
金 鍛 1817
霞 2261
霜 948
頁 頻 1847
馬 駿 2269
鮮 701

– 18 –

氵 濫 1944
⺾ 藤 2231
藩 1382
藍 2232
璽 1911
广 麿 2281
月 髄 1740
日 曜 19
曙 2098
覆 1634
火 燿 2152
王 璽 1887
心 懲 1421
石 礎 1515
日 瞬 1732
観 604
禾 穣 2185
穫 1314
⻂ 襟 1537
疒 癖 1490
癒 1600
糸 繕 1140
織 680
米 糧 1704
翻 596
耳 職 385
⺾ 簡 1533

貝 贈 1364
金 鎖 1819
鎮 1786
鎌 2257
隹 雛 2260
難 557
離 1281
門 闘 1511
頁 類 226
顔 277
顎 1170
額 838
題 354
馬 騎 1881
験 532
騒 875
魚 鯉 2271

– 19 –

氵 瀬 1513
口 艶 2209
⺾ 藻 1657
蘭 2233
广 麗 1630
月 鵬 2276
臓 1287
覇 1633
日 響 856
火 爆 1015
⺫ 羅 1860
糸 繰 1654
⺾ 簿 1450
言 譜 1167
識 681
警 706
貝 韻 349
金 鏡 863

⻗ 霧 950
頁 願 581
魚 鯨 700
鯛 2272
鳥 鶏 926

– 20 –

⺍ 巌 2059
心 懸 911
木 欄 1202
月 騰 1780
香 馨 2267
立 競 852
⺾ 籍 1198
言 譲 1013
護 1312
議 292
酉 醸 1837
金 鐘 1821
隹 耀 2202

– 21 –

广 魔 1528
⻂ 襲 1575
舟 艦 1665
足 躍 1560
⻗ 露 951
頁 顧 1554
鳥 鶴 2277

– 22 –

馬 驚 1778

– 23 –

金 鑑 1664

– 24 –

广 鷹 2278
米 麟 2280

Index by Readings

– A –

Reading	Kanji	No.
A	亜	1616
	(悪)	AKU
	阿	2258
a	吾	2035
aba(ku)	暴	1014
aba(reru)	暴	1014
a(biru)	浴	1128
a(biseru)	浴	1128
abu(nai)	危	534
abura	油	364
	脂	1042
a(garu)	挙	801
	揚	631
	上	32
a(geru)	挙	801
	揚	631
	上	32
AI	哀	1675
	(衰)	SUI
	愛	259
ai	藍	2232
ai-	相	146
aida	間	43
aji	味	307
aji(wau)	味	307
aka	赤	207
	緋	2197
aka(i)	赤	207
akanashi	杜	2103
Akane	茜	2216
aka(rameru)	赤	207
aka(ramu)	赤	207
	明	18
a(kari)	明	18
aka(rui)	明	18
aka(rumu)	明	18
a(kasu)	明	18
	飽	1763
akatsuki	暁	1658
ake	旦	2085
	曙	2098
Akebono	曙	2098
a(keru)	空	140
	明	18
	開	396
Aki	昌	2089
	彬	2069
aki	諒	2243
	旦	2085
	旭	2086
	昂	2088
	晃	2092
	晋	2093
	晨	2095
	皓	2169
	暉	2096
	瞭	2174
	玲	2157
	瑛	2159
	璃	2166
	亨	2009
	圭	2042
	亮	2010
	秋	462
	爽	2046
	堯	2043
	聡	2203
	耀	2202
akina(u)	商	412
Akira	旦	2085
	旭	2086
	旺	2087
	昌	2089
	昂	2088
	晃	2092
	晟	2094
	晨	2095
	智	2099
	皓	2169
	滉	2145
	暉	2096
	瞭	2174
	曙	2098
	亨	2009
	亮	2010
	玲	2157
	瑛	2159
	爽	2046
	爾	2154
	彪	2068
	彬	2069
	叡	2032
	瞳	2173
	卯	2031
	丞	2002
	侃	2017
	洸	2137
	斐	2082
	舜	2208
	翠	2201
	聡	2203
	慧	2076
	耀	2202
aki(raka)	明	18
a(kiru)	飽	1763
AKU	渥	2143
	握	1714
	(屋)	OKU
	悪	304
	(亜)	A
a(ku)	空	140
	明	18
	開	396
a(kuru)	明	18
ama	天	141
	尼	1620
	雨	30
	亀	2284
ama(eru)	甘	1492
ama(i)	甘	1492
ama(ru)	余	1063
ama(su)	余	1063
ama(yakasu)	甘	1492
ame	天	141
	雨	30
ami	網	1612
	(綱)	tsuna
a(mu)	編	682
AN	安	105
	案	106
	晏	2091
	(宴)	EN
	暗	348
	(音)	ON
	行	68
	杏	2102
ana	穴	899
anado(ru)	侮	1736
ane	姉	407
ani	兄	406
Anzu	杏	2102
ao	青	208
	碧	2176
ao(gu)	仰	1056
Aoi	葵	2222
ao(i)	青	208
	荒	1377
	粗	1084
Arashi	嵐	2055
araso(u)	争	302
a(rasu)	荒	1377
ara(ta)	新	174
arata(maru)	改	514
arata(meru)	改	514
ara(u)	洗	692
arawa(reru)	表	272
	現	298
arawa(su)	表	272
	著	859
	現	298
a(reru)	荒	1377
ari	也	2005
	惟	2073
a(ru)	在	268
	有	265
aru(ku)	歩	431
Asa	旦	2085
asa	旭	2086
	晨	2095
	朝	469
	麻	1529
	黎	2282
	諒	2243
Asahi	旭	2086
asa(i)	浅	649
ase	汗	1188
ase(ru)	焦	999
ashi	足	58
	脚	1784
aso(bu)	遊	1003
ata(eru)	与	539
atai	価	421
	値	425
atama	頭	276
atara(shii)	新	174
ata(ri)	辺	775
a(taru)	当	77
atata(ka)	温	634
	暖	635
atata(kai)	温	634
	暖	635

Reading	Kanji	No.
atata(maru)	温	634
	暖	635
atata(meru)	温	634
	暖	635
a(teru)	充	828
	当	77
ato	後	48
	跡	1569
ATSU	圧	1342
	(庄)	SHŌ
atsu	淳	2141
	惇	2075
	敦	2081
	諄	2242
	醇	2255
	宏	2050
	渥	2143
atsu(i)	厚	639
	暑	638
	熱	645
atsuka(u)	扱	1258
atsu(maru)	集	436
atsu(meru)	集	436
Atsumu	伍	2013
	侑	2018
Atsushi	淳	2141
	惇	2075
	敦	2081
	諄	2242
	醇	2255
	渥	2143
	睦	2172
a(u)	合	159
	会	158
	遭	1643
awa	泡	1765
awa(i)	淡	1337
awa(re)	哀	1675
awa(remu)	哀	1675
awa(seru)	併	1162
a(waseru)	合	159
a(wasu)	合	159
awa(tadashii)		
	慌	1378
awa(teru)	慌	1378
Aya	斐	2082
	絢	2194
aya	紘	2190
	綾	2198
	綺	2195
	彪	2068
	彬	2069
	郁	2252
	采	2153
	亀	2284
	琢	2158
ayama(chi)	過	413
ayama(ru)	誤	906
	謝	901
ayama(tsu)	過	413
Ayame	菖	2220
Ayaru	斐	2082
aya(shii)	怪	1476
aya(shimu)	怪	1476
ayatsu(ru)	操	1655
aya(ui)	危	534
ayu	鮎	2270
ayu(mu)	歩	431
aza	字	110
azamu(ku)	欺	1499
aza(yaka)	鮮	701
azu(karu)	預	394
azu(keru)	預	394
Azusa	梓	2113

– B –

Reading	Kanji	No.
BA	婆	1931
	(波)	HA
	馬	283
ba	場	154
BACHI	罰	886
BAI	倍	87
	陪	1943
	培	1828
	賠	1829
	(部)	BU
	(剖)	BŌ
	唄	2039
	買	241
	(貝)	kai
	梅	1734
	(毎)	MAI
	(海)	KAI
	(敏)	BIN
	媒	1496
	(某)	BŌ
	(謀)	BŌ
	売	239
ba(kasu)	化	254
ba(keru)	化	254
BAKU	漠	1427
	幕	1432
	(漢)	KAN
	(募)	BO
	(墓)	BO
	(暮)	BO
	(模)	MO
	(膜)	MAKU
	博	601
	縛	1448
	(専)	SEN
	暴	1014
	爆	1015
	麦	270
BAN	伴	1027
	判	1026
	(半)	HAN
	番	185
	(審)	SHIN
	(藩)	HAN
	板	1047
	(反)	HAN
	蛮	1879
	(変)	HEN
	晩	736
	(免)	MEN
	盤	1098
	(般)	HAN
	万	16
BATSU	伐	1509
	閥	1510
	抜	1713
	(友)	YŪ
	(髪)	HATSU
	末	305
	罰	886
-be	辺	775
BEI	米	224
BEN	便	330
	(更)	KŌ
	弁	711
	勉	735
beni	紅	820
BETSU	別	267
BI	尾	1868
	(毛)	MŌ
	微	1419
	(徴)	CHŌ
	弥	2065
	美	401
	眉	2170
	備	768
	鼻	813
BIN	敏	1735
	(毎)	MAI
	(繁)	HAN
	便	330
	(更)	KŌ
	貧	753
	(分)	BUN
	瓶	1161
BO	募	1430
	墓	1429
	暮	1428
	慕	1431
	模	1425
	(漢)	BAKU
	簿	1450
	(専)	SEN
	(薄)	HAKU
	母	112
BO'	坊	1858
BŌ	防	513
	坊	1858
	妨	1182
	肪	1857
	房	1237
	紡	1859
	傍	1183
	(方)	HŌ
	亡	672
	妄	1376
	忘	1374
	忙	1373
	望	673
	卯	2031
	昂	2090
	(卵)	RAN
	(昂)	KŌ
	某	1494
	謀	1495
	冒	1104

393

Reading	Kanji	No.
	帽	1105
	剖	1830
	(倍)	BAI
	(部)	BU
	乏	754
	(之)	SHI
	棒	1543
	(奉)	BU
	茅	2214
	萌	2221
	眸	2171
	貿	760
	暴	1014
	膨	1145
BOKU	木	22
	朴	1466
	目	55
	睦	2172
	僕	1888
	撲	1889
	墨	1705
	(黒)	KOKU
	牧	731
BON	凡	1102
	(帆)	HAN
	盆	1099
	(分)	BUN
	煩	1849
BOTSU	没	935
BU	無	93
	舞	810
	奉	1541
	(俸)	HŌ
	(棒)	BŌ
	部	86
	(剖)	BŌ
	(倍)	BAI
	侮	1736
	(毎)	MAI
	不	94
	分	38
	歩	431
	武	1031
	輔	2245
BUN	文	111
	分	38
	聞	64
buta	豚	796
BUTSU	仏	583

Reading	Kanji	No.
	(払)	FUTSU
	物	79
BYAKU	白	205
BYŌ	苗	1468
	描	1469
	猫	1470
	秒	1152
	(少)	SHŌ
	(砂)	SA
	病	380
	(丙)	HEI
	平	202

– C –

Reading	Kanji	No.
CHA	茶	251
CHAKU	着	657
	(差)	SA
	嫡	1932
CHI	知	214
	智	2099
	痴	1813
	値	425
	置	426
	(直)	CHOKU
	池	119
	地	118
	治	493
	(台)	DAI
	(治)	YA
	(始)	SHI
	致	903
	(至)	SHI
	恥	1690
	遅	702
	稚	1230
	質	176
chi	血	789
	(皿)	sara
	千	15
	乳	939
	茅	2214
chichi	父	113
	乳	939
chiga(eru)	違	814
chiga(u)	違	814
chigi(ru)	契	565
chii(sai)	小	27
chiji(maru)	縮	1110

Reading	Kanji	No.
chiji(meru)	縮	1110
chiji(mu)	縮	1110
chiji(rasu)	縮	1110
chiji(reru)	縮	1110
chika	允	2022
	哉	2037
	峻	2053
	睦	2172
	爾	2154
chika(i)	近	445
chikara	力	100
Chikashi	睦	2172
	爾	2154
chika(u)	誓	1395
CHIKU	竹	129
	築	1603
	畜	1223
	蓄	1224
	逐	1134
CHIN	陳	1405
	(東)	TŌ
	(棟)	TŌ
	(陣)	JIN
	珍	1215
	(診)	SHIN
	朕	1921
	(朕)	saku
	椿	2118
	(春)	SHUN
	賃	751
	(任)	NIN
	鎮	1786
	(真)	SHIN
	沈	936
chi(rakaru)	散	767
chi(rakasu)	散	767
chi(rasu)	散	767
chi(ru)	散	767
CHITSU	秩	1508
	(失)	SHITSU
	窒	1716
	(室)	SHITSU
CHO	猪	2155
	著	859
	緒	862
	(者)	SHA
	(署)	SHO
	(諸)	SHO

Reading	Kanji	No.
	(都)	TO
	貯	762
	(丁)	CHŌ
CHŌ	丁	184
	庁	763
	町	182
	頂	1440
	(貯)	CHO
	(項)	KŌ
	(傾)	KEI
	兆	1562
	挑	1564
	眺	1565
	跳	1563
	(逃)	TŌ
	(桃)	TŌ
	長	95
	帳	1107
	張	1106
	脹	1922
	彫	1149
	調	342
	鯛	2272
	(周)	SHŪ
	腸	1270
	暢	2097
	(湯)	TŌ
	(場)	JŌ
	鳥	285
	蔦	2228
	(島)	TŌ
	徴	1420
	懲	1421
	(微)	BI
	朝	469
	潮	468
	澄	1334
	(豆)	TŌ
	(登)	TŌ
	弔	1796
	(弓)	KYŪ
	超	1000
	(召)	SHŌ
	蝶	2236
	(葉)	YŌ
	聴	1039
	(徳)	TOKU
	重	227

	釣	1862	(太)	TAI	DO	奴	1933		(衣)	I	
	肇	2204	台	492		努	1595		回	90	
CHOKU	直	423	(胎)	TAI		怒	1596		恵	1219	
	(値)	CHI	乃	2003		度	377	e	江	821	
	勅	1886	内	84		(席)	SEKI		柄	985	
	(束)	SOKU	奈	2044		(渡)	TO	-e	重	227	
CHŪ	中	28	題	354		土	24	eda	枝	870	
	仲	1347	DAKU	諾	1770	(吐)	TO	ega(ku)	描	1469	
	沖	1346	(若)	JAKU	DŌ	同	198	EI	永	1207	
	忠	1348	濁	1625		洞	1301		泳	1208	
	虫	873	(独)	DOKU		桐	2110		詠	1209	
	注	357	da(ku)	抱	1285	胴	1300		(水)	SUI	
	柱	598	dama(ru)	黙	1578	銅	1605		(氷)	HYŌ	
	駐	599	DAN	壇	1839	(筒)	TŌ		英	353	
	(主)	SHU	檀	2128		童	410		映	352	
	抽	987	暖	635		憧	2077		瑛	2159	
	宙	991	(援)	EN		瞳	2173		(央)	Ō	
	紬	2193	(緩)	KAN		動	231		栄	723	
	(由)	YŪ	男	101		働	232		営	722	
	衷	1677	(田)	DEN		(重)	CHŌ		(宮)	KYŪ	
	(哀)	AI	弾	1539		道	149		鋭	1371	
	昼	470	(単)	TAN		導	703		(悦)	ETSU	
	(旦)	TAN	楠	2119		(首)	SHU		(悦)	ETSU	
	鋳	1551	(南)	NAN		堂	496		(税)	ZEI	
	(寿)	JU	談	593		(党)	TŌ		(説)	SETSU	
	丑	2001	(炎)	EN		藤	2231		影	854	
			団	491	DOKU	読	244		(京)	KEI	
– D –			段	362		(売)	BAI		(景)	KEI	
DA	堕	1742	断	1024		(続)	ZOKU		彗	2066	
	惰	1743	da(su)	出	53	毒	522		(慧)	KEI	
	(随)	ZUI	DATSU	脱	1370	(母)	BO		衛	815	
	(髄)	ZUI	(悦)	ETSU		独	219		(偉)	I	
	打	1020	(説)	SETSU		(触)	SHOKU		叡	2032	
	(丁)	TEI	(閲)	ETSU	DON	鈍	966	ei	哉	2037	
	(灯)	TŌ	奪	1310		(屯)	TON	EKI	役	375	
	(訂)	TEI	(奮)	FUN		(純)	JUN		疫	1319	
	妥	930	DE	弟	405	畳	637		液	472	
	(桜)	Ō	(第)	DAI		(雲)	UN		(夜)	YA	
	駄	1880	DEI	泥	1621	-dono	殿	1130		亦	2007
	(太)	TAI	(尼)	NI	doro	泥	1621		易	759	
	那	2251	DEN	田	35					益	716
	蛇	1875	電	108	**– E –**				駅	284	
DAI	弟	405	殿	1130	E	会	158	e(mu)	笑	1235	
	第	404	(展)	TEN		絵	345	EN	遠	446	
	代	256	鮎	2270		慧	2076		猿	1584	
	(袋)	TAI	(占)	SEN		(急)	KYŪ		園	447	
	(貸)	TAI	伝	434		(彗)	EI		援	1088	
	大	26	de(ru)	出	53		依	678		媛	2047

Reading	Kanji	No.
	(暖)	DAN
	(緩)	KAN
	沿	1607
	鉛	1606
	(船)	SEN
	宴	640
	(安)	AN
	(案)	AN
	(晏)	AN
	延	1115
	(正)	SEI
	(延)	TEI
	炎	1336
	(火)	KA
	苑	2212
	(腕)	WAN
	縁	1131
	(緑)	RYOKU
	允	2022
	円	13
	塩	1101
	煙	919
	演	344
	艶	2209
era(bu)	選	800
era(i)	偉	1053
eri	衿	2237
	襟	1537
e(ru)	得	374
	獲	1313
ETSU	悦	1368
	閲	1369
	(脱)	DATSU
	(説)	SETSU
	謁	1920
	(渇)	KATSU
	(掲)	KEI
	(喝)	KATSU
	(褐)	KATSU
	越	1001

– F –

Reading	Kanji	No.
FU	付	192
	附	1843
	府	504
	符	505
fuchi	腐	1245
fuda	夫	315
fude		

Reading	Kanji	No.
	扶	1721
	芙	2211
	普	1166
	譜	1167
	(晋)	SHIN
	布	675
	怖	1814
	甫	2167
	輔	2245
	富	713
	(副)	FUKU
	(幅)	FUKU
	(福)	FUKU
	婦	316
	(帰)	KI
	(掃)	SŌ
	父	113
	(交)	KŌ
	浮	938
	(乳)	NYŪ
	膚	1269
	(胃)	I
	敷	1451
	(激)	GEKI
	賦	1808
	(武)	BU
	不	94
	歩	431
	負	510
	風	29
	赴	1465
FŪ	風	29
	楓	2120
	(虫)	CHŪ
	富	713
	(副)	FU
	(幅)	FU
	(福)	FU
	夫	315
	(扶)	FU
	(芙)	FU
	封	1463
	(付)	FU
	(圭)	KEI
	鳳	2274
fuchi	縁	1131
fuda	札	1157
fude	筆	130

Reading	Kanji	No.
fue	呂	2036
	笛	1471
fu(eru)	殖	1506
	増	712
Fuji	藤	2231
fuka(i)	深	536
fuka(maru)	深	536
fuka(meru)	深	536
Fukashi	宏	2050
	洸	2137
fu(kasu)	更	1008
fu(keru)	老	543
	更	1008
Fuki	蕗	2230
FUKU	復	917
	腹	1271
	複	916
	覆	1634
	(履)	RI
	副	714
	幅	1380
	福	1379
	(富)	FU
	伏	1356
	(犬)	KEN
	服	683
	(報)	HŌ
fu(ku)	吹	1255
	噴	1660
fuku(meru)	含	1249
fuku(mu)	含	1249
fuku(ramu)	膨	1145
fuku(reru)	膨	1145
fukuro	袋	1329
fu(maeru)	踏	1559
fumi	文	111
	迪	2247
	郁	2252
	奎	2045
fu(mu)	踏	1559
FUN	分	38
	紛	1702
	粉	1701
	雰	1824
	墳	1662
	噴	1660
	慎	1661
	奮	1309

Reading	Kanji	No.
	(奪)	DATSU
funa	舟	1094
	船	376
fune	舟	1094
	船	376
fu(reru)	触	874
fu(ru)	降	947
	振	954
furu(eru)	震	953
furu(i)	古	172
furu(su)	古	172
furu(u)	震	953
	奮	1309
fu(ruu)	振	954
fusa	房	1237
	寅	2052
	絃	2192
	惣	2074
	聡	2203
fuse(gu)	防	513
fu(seru)	伏	1356
fushi	節	464
fu(su)	伏	1356
futa	二	3
	双	1594
futata(bi)	再	782
futa(tsu)	二	3
futo(i)	太	629
futokoro	懐	1408
futo(ru)	太	629
FUTSU	払	582
	仏	583
	沸	1792
fu(yasu)	殖	1506
	増	712
fuyu	冬	459
	那	2251

– G –

Reading	Kanji	No.
GA	我	1302
	餓	1303
	(義)	GI
	伽	2014
	賀	756
	(加)	KA
	芽	1455
	雅	1456
	(邪)	JA

Reading	Kanji	No.
	画	343
GA'	合	159
GAI	亥	2008
	劾	1939
	該	1213
	(刻)	KOKU
	(核)	KAKU
	涯	1461
	街	186
	(術)	JUTSU
	概	1459
	慨	1460
	(既)	KI
	外	83
	(夕)	SEKI
	害	518
	(割)	KATSU
	凱	2028
GAKU	岳	1358
	(丘)	KYŪ
	(兵)	HEI
	額	838
	(各)	KAKU
	(客)	KAKU
	学	109
	(字)	JI
	楽	358
	(薬)	YAKU
GAN	元	137
	頑	1848
	願	581
	(完)	KAN
	(原)	GEN
	巌	2059
	(山)	SAN
	(敢)	KAN
	(厳)	GEN
	含	1249
	(今)	KON
	(吟)	GIN
	丸	644
	(九)	KYŪ
	岩	1345
	(石)	SEKI
	岸	586
	(干)	KAN
	眼	848
	(眠)	MIN
	顔	277
	(産)	SAN
gara	柄	985
GATSU	月	17
GE	下	31
	外	83
	華	1074
	夏	461
	解	474
GEI	迎	1055
	(仰)	GYŌ
	(抑)	YOKU
	(卯)	U
	(柳)	RYŪ
	芸	435
	(伝)	DEN
	(雲)	UN
	鯨	700
	(京)	KEI
GEKI	激	1017
	(敷)	FU
	撃	1016
	劇	797
GEN	幻	1227
	玄	1225
	弦	1226
	絃	2192
	(幼)	YŌ
	限	847
	眼	848
	(恨)	KON
	(根)	KON
	(銀)	GIN
	(眠)	MIN
	原	136
	源	580
	(願)	GAN
	厳	822
	巌	2059
	(敢)	KAN
	(惑)	WAKU
	(感)	KAN
	元	137
	(完)	KAN
	言	66
	(信)	SHIN
	現	298
	(見)	KEN
	嫌	1688
	(謙)	KEN
	彦	2067
GETSU	月	17
GI	義	291
	儀	727
	犠	728
	議	292
	(我)	GA
	伎	2012
	技	871
	(支)	SHI
	(岐)	KI
	宜	1086
	誼	2241
	(且)	ka(tsu)
	疑	1516
	擬	1517
	偽	1485
	(為)	I
	欺	1499
	(期)	KI
	戯	1573
	(虚)	KYO
	葵	2222
	毅	2131
	吟	1250
GIN	(今)	KIN
	(含)	GAN
	銀	313
	(金)	KIN
GO	五	7
	伍	2013
	吾	2035
	梧	2112
	悟	1438
	語	67
	呉	1436
	娯	1437
	誤	906
	午	49
	御	708
	(卸)	oroshi
	(許)	KYO
	胡	2206
	瑚	2161
	(古)	KO
	(湖)	KO
	期	449
	碁	1834
	(基)	KI
	護	1312
	(隻)	SEKI
	(獲)	KAKU
	(穫)	KAKU
	互	907
	後	48
	冴	2023
GŌ	合	159
	(拾)	JŪ
	(給)	KYŪ
	(答)	TŌ
	拷	1720
	(考)	KŌ
	号	266
	郷	855
	剛	1610
	強	217
	業	279
	豪	1671
GOKU	極	336
	獄	884
GON	厳	822
	(敢)	KAN
	(厳)	GEN
	欣	2129
	(斤)	KIN
	言	66
	勤	559
	権	335
	吾	2035
GU	愚	1642
	(偶)	GŪ
	(隅)	GŪ
	具	420
	(真)	SHIN
GŪ	偶	1639
	隅	1640
	験	532
	(倹)	KEN
	(険)	KEN
	(検)	KEN
	拳	2078
	(券)	KEN
	(巻)	KAN
	減	715

Reading	Kanji	Ref
	遇	1641
	(愚)	GU
	宮	721
	(営)	EI
GUN 郡		193
	群	794
	(君)	KUN
	軍	438
	(車)	SHA
	(運)	UN
	(揮)	KI
GYAKU 逆		444
	(朔)	SAKU
	(塑)	SO
	虐	1574
GYO 魚		290
	漁	699
	(鯨)	GEI
	御	708
	(卸)	oroshi
	(午)	GO
	(許)	KYO
GYŌ 尭		2043
	暁	1658
	(焼)	SHŌ
	仰	1056
	(卯)	U
	(迎)	GEI
	(抑)	YOKU
	(柳)	RYŪ
	倖	2020
	(幸)	KŌ
	凝	1518
	(疑)	GI
	行	68
	形	395
	業	279
GYOKU 玉		295
	(王)	Ō
GYŪ 牛		281

– H –

Reading	Kanji	Ref
HA	波	666
	破	665
	(皮)	HI
	(披)	HI
	(彼)	HI
	(被)	HI
hai	(疲)	HI
	(婆)	BA
	巴	2061
	把	1724
	(肥)	HI
	派	912
	(脈)	MYAKU
	覇	1633
HA'	法	123
ha	刃	1413
	羽	590
	葉	253
	歯	478
	端	1418
haba	幅	1380
haba(mu)	阻	1085
habu(ku)	省	145
HACHI	八	10
	鉢	1820
hada	肌	1306
hadaka	裸	1536
ha(e)	栄	723
ha(eru)	生	44
	栄	723
	映	352
hagane	鋼	1608
hage(masu)	励	1340
hage(mu)	励	1340
hage(shii)	激	1017
Hagi	萩	2223
haha	母	112
HAI	俳	1035
	排	1036
	輩	1037
	(非)	HI
	(悲)	HI
	唄	2039
	敗	511
	(貝)	kai
	背	1265
	(北)	HOKU
	廃	961
	(発)	HATSU
	拝	1201
	杯	1155
	肺	1277
	配	515
hai	灰	1343

Reading	Kanji	Ref
hai(ru)	入	52
haji	恥	1690
haji(maru)	始	494
Hajime	甫	2167
	孟	2049
	哉	2037
	朔	2101
	巽	2062
	肇	2204
	魁	2083
haji(me)	初	679
haji(meru)	始	494
haji(mete)	初	679
Hajimu	肇	2204
ha(jirau)	恥	1690
ha(jiru)	恥	1690
haka	墓	1429
haka(rau)	計	340
Hakaru	恕	2071
haka(ru)	図	339
	計	340
	測	610
	量	411
	諮	1769
	謀	1495
hako	箱	1091
hako(bu)	運	439
HAKU	白	205
	伯	1176
	迫	1175
	泊	1177
	拍	1178
	舶	1095
	博	601
	薄	1449
	(簿)	BO
	(縛)	BAKU
ha(ku)	吐	1253
	掃	1080
	履	1635
hama	浜	785
HAN	反	324
	坂	443
	版	1046
	板	1047
	販	1048
	飯	325
	(仮)	KA

Reading	Kanji	Ref
	(返)	HEN
	半	88
	伴	1027
	判	1026
	畔	1945
	般	1096
	搬	1722
	(盤)	BAN
	凡	1102
	帆	1103
	犯	882
	範	1092
	煩	1849
	頒	1850
	藩	1382
	(番)	BAN
	(審)	SHIN
	班	1381
	(王)	Ō
	繁	1292
	(敏)	BIN
hana	花	255
	華	1074
	鼻	813
hanaha(da)	甚	1501
hanaha(dashii)		
	甚	1501
hana(reru)	放	512
	離	1281
hanashi	話	238
hana(su)	放	512
	話	238
	離	1281
hana(tsu)	放	512
hane	羽	590
ha(neru)	跳	1563
hara	原	136
	腹	1271
ha(rasu)	晴	662
hara(u)	払	582
ha(reru)	晴	662
hari	針	341
	榛	2124
haru	春	460
	浩	2140
	晏	2091
	脩	2207
	遥	2248

Reading	Kanji	No.
	靖	2187
	榛	2124
ha(ru)	張	1106
Haruka	遥	2248
	遼	2249
hasa(maru)	挟	1354
hasa(mu)	挟	1354
hashi	端	1418
	橋	597
hashira	柱	598
hashi(ru)	走	429
hasu	芙	2211
	蓉	2226
	蓮	2227
hata	畑	36
	秦	2181
	旗	1006
	端	1418
	機	528
hatake	畑	36
hatara(ku)	働	232
Hatasu	毅	2131
ha(tasu)	果	487
ha(te)	果	487
ha(teru)	果	487
hato	鳩	2273
HATSU	発	96
(廃)	HAI	
	髪	1148
(友)	YŪ	
	鉢	1820
hatsu	肇	2204
hatsu-	初	679
haya	隼	2259
	捷	2079
	颯	2266
Hayabusa	隼	2259
haya(i)	早	248
	速	502
haya(maru)	早	248
haya(meru)	早	248
	速	502
Hayao	駿	2269
Hayashi	隼	2259
	駿	2269
hayashi	林	127
ha(yasu)	生	44
Hayato	隼	2259

Reading	Kanji	No.
ha(zukashii)	恥	1690
hazukashi(meru)		
	辱	1738
hazu(mu)	弾	1539
hazu(reru)	外	83
hazu(su)	外	83
hebi	蛇	1875
heda(taru)	隔	1589
heda(teru)	隔	1589
HEI	丙	984
	柄	985
	病	380
	併	1162
	塀	1805
	幣	1781
	弊	1782
	兵	784
(丘)	KYŪ	
	陛	589
(階)	KAI	
	閉	397
(才)	SAI	
	平	202
	並	1165
HEKI	壁	1489
	癖	1490
(避)	HI	
	碧	2176
HEN	偏	1159
	遍	1160
	編	682
	変	257
(恋)	REN	
(蛮)	BAN	
	片	1045
(版)	HAN	
	辺	775
(刀)	TŌ	
	返	442
(反)	HAN	
he(rasu)	減	715
he(ru)	経	548
	減	715
HI	皮	975
	披	1712
	彼	977
	被	976
	疲	1321

Reading	Kanji	No.
(破)	HA	
(婆)	BA	
	非	498
	斐	2082
	悲	1034
	扉	1556
	緋	2197
(輩)	HAI	
	泌	1870
	秘	807
(必)	HITSU	
	卑	1521
	碑	1522
(鬼)	KI	
	比	798
	批	1029
	避	1491
(壁)	HEKI	
(癖)	HEKI	
	妃	1756
(己)	KI	
	否	1248
(不)	FU	
	罷	1861
(能)	NŌ	
	肥	1723
	飛	530
	費	749
hi	火	20
	灯	1333
	氷	1206
	日	5
hibi(ku)	響	856
hidari	左	75
hide	之	2004
	彬	2069
hi(eru)	冷	832
higashi	東	71
hii(deru)	秀	1683
hiiragi	柊	2105
hika(eru)	控	1718
hikari	光	138
Hikaru	晃	2092
	皓	2169
	暉	2096
hika(ru)	光	138
hi(keru)	引	216
hiki	匹	1500

Reading	Kanji	No.
hiki(iru)	率	788
Hiko	彦	2067
hiku	渥	2143
	引	216
	弾	1539
hiku(i)	低	561
hiku(maru)	低	561
hiku(meru)	低	561
hima	暇	1064
Hime	媛	2047
hime	姫	1757
hi(meru)	秘	807
HIN	賓	1852
	頻	1847
(少)	SHŌ	
(歩)	HO	
	彬	2069
(林)	RIN	
(琳)	RIN	
	品	230
(口)	KŌ	
	浜	785
(兵)	HEI	
	貧	753
(分)	BUN	
hina	雛	2260
hira	平	202
	迪	2247
hira(keru)	開	396
hira(ku)	開	396
hiro	宏	2050
	祐	2178
	紘	2190
	宥	2051
	洸	2137
	渥	2145
	浩	2140
	皓	2169
	丑	2001
	弘	2064
	亘	2006
	弥	2065
	彦	2067
	恕	2071
	熙	2148
	嘉	2041
	碩	2265
	鴻	2275

Reading	Kanji	No.	Reading	Kanji	No.	Reading	Kanji	No.	Reading	Kanji	No.
hiro(garu)	広	694		欽	2130		(紡)	BŌ	honō	炎	1336
hiro(geru)	広	694		舜	2208		朋	2100	hora	洞	1301
hiro(i)	広	694		鴻	2275		崩	1122	hori	堀	1804
hiro(maru)	広	694	hito(shii)	等	569		鵬	2276	horo(biru)	滅	1338
hiro(meru)	広	694	hito(tsu)	一	2		鳳	2274	horo(bosu)	滅	1338
Hiromu	弘	2064	HITSU	必	520	(棚)	tana	ho(ru)	掘	1803
	紘	2190		泌	1870	(鳥)	CHŌ		彫	1149
	熙	2148	(秘)	HI		奉	1541	hoshi	星	730
Hiroshi	宏	2050		匹	1500		俸	1542	ho(shii)	欲	1127
	紘	2190	(四)	yo(tsu)	(奏)	SŌ	hoso(i)	細	695
	宥	2051		筆	130	(棒)	BŌ	hoso(ru)	細	695
	洸	2137	(書)	SHO		峰	1350	hos(suru)	欲	1127
	滉	2145	hitsuji	羊	288		縫	1349	ho(su)	干	584
	浩	2140	hi(ya)	冷	832		報	685	hotaru	蛍	1878
	皓	2169	hi(yakasu)	冷	832	(幸)	KŌ	hotoke	仏	583
	弘	2064	hi(yasu)	冷	832	(服)	FUKU	HOTSU	発	96
	亘	2006	HO	甫	2167		豊	959	HYAKU	百	14
	恕	2071		浦	1442	(曲)	KYOKU	(白)	HAKU
	熙	2148		捕	890	(豆)	TŌ	HYŌ	票	922
	碩	2265		補	889		亨	2009		漂	924
	鴻	2275		輔	2245	(享)	KYŌ		標	923
hiro(u)	拾	1445		舗	1443		法	123		表	272
hiru	昼	470	(甫)	FU	(去)	KYO		俵	1890
hi(ru)	干	584		歩	431		宝	296		兵	784
hiruga(eru)	翻	596	(止)	SHI	(玉)	GYOKU	(丘)	KYŪ
hirugae(su)	翻	596	(少)	SHŌ		封	1463	(岳)	GAKU
hisa	之	2004	(渉)	SHŌ	(佳)	KA		氷	1206
	玖	2156	(頻)	HIN		萌	2221	(永)	EI
	弥	2065		保	489	(明)	MEI		拍	1178
	胡	2206	HO'			法	123		褒	803	(白)	HAKU
	桐	2110	ho	火	20	(保)	HO		評	1028
	亀	2284		帆	1103		邦	808	(平)	HEI
	藤	2231		穂	1221	hodo	程	417		彪	2068
Hisashi	弥	2065	HŌ	包	804	hodoko(su)	施	1004	HYŪ	彪	2068
	亀	2284		泡	1765	hoga(raka)	朗	1754			
hisa(shii)	久	1210		抱	1285	hoka	外	83	– I –
hiso(mu)	潜	937		胞	1284	hoko	矛	773	I	偉	1053
hitai	額	838		砲	1764	hoko(ru)	誇	1629		違	814
hita(ru)	浸	1078		飽	1763	HOKU	北	73		緯	1054
hita(su)	浸	1078		方	70	homare	誉	802	(衛)	EI
hito	人	1		芳	1775	ho(meru)	褒	803		唯	1234
hito-	一	2		放	512	hōmu(ru)	葬	812		惟	2073
Hitomi	眸	2171		倣	1776	HON	翻	596		維	1231
	瞳	2173		訪	1181	(番)	BAN	(准)	JUN
hito(ri)	独	219	(防)	BŌ		反	324	(推)	SUI
Hitoshi	伍	2013	(坊)	BŌ		本	25	(稚)	CHI
	洵	2139	(妨)	BŌ		奔	1659		委	466
	彬	2069	(肪)	BŌ	hone	骨	1266		倭	2019

	(季) KI	i(kiru) 生 44	射 900	iya 弥 2065
	胃 1268	iko(i) 憩 1243	鋳 1551	iya(shii) 卑 1521
	異 1061	iko(u) 憩 1243	isa 伊 2011	iya(shimeru) 卑 1521
	(累) RUI	IKU 郁 2252	沙 2135	iya(shimu) 卑 1521
	衣 677	(有) YŪ	赳 2244	izu 稜 2184
	依 678	育 246	isagiyo(i) 潔 1241	izumi 泉 1192
	尉 1617	i(ku) 行 68	isago 沙 2135	
	慰 1618	iku- 幾 877	Isamu 浩 2140	**– J –**
	伊 2011	ikusa 戦 301	赳 2244	
	(君) KUN	ima 今 51	魁 2083	JA 邪 1457
	位 122	Imashi 乃 2003	isa(mu) 勇 1386	耶 2253
	(立) RITSU	imashi(meru)	Isao 魁 2083	蛇 1875
	医 220	戒 876	ishi 石 78	JAKU 若 544
	(矢) SHI	i(mawashii) 忌 1797	ishizue 礎 1515	(右) YŪ
	囲 1194	imo 芋 1909	Iso 磯 2177	弱 218
	(井) SEI	imōto 妹 408	isoga(shii) 忙 1373	(弓) KYŪ
	移 1121	i(mu) 忌 1797	iso(gu) 急 303	寂 1669
	(多) TA	IN 員 163	ita 板 1047	(叔) SHUKU
	意 132	韻 349	itadaki 頂 1440	着 657
	(音) IN	音 347	itada(ku) 頂 1440	(差) SA
	遺 1172	(損) SON	ita(i) 痛 1320	JI 寺 41
	(貴) KI	因 554	ita(meru) 痛 1320	侍 571
	以 46	姻 1748	傷 633	持 451
	易 759	(囚) SHŪ	ita(mu) 悼 1680	時 42
	威 1339	(困) KON	痛 1320	蒔 2224
	為 1484	院 614	傷 633	(待) TAI
	寅 2052	(完) KAN	Itaru 之 2004	(等) TŌ
	熙 2148	隠 868	暢 2097	(詩) SHI
i	井 1193	(穏) ON	譚 2242	滋 1549
	亥 2008	允 2022	ita(ru) 至 902	慈 1547
	猪 2155	引 216	ita(su) 致 903	磁 1548
	斐 2082	印 1043	ito 糸 242	爾 2154
ICHI	一 2	胤 2205	絃 2192	璽 1887
	壱 1730	陰 867	itona(mu) 営 722	治 493
ichi	市 181	寅 2052	ITSU 一 2	(台) DAI
ichijiru(shii)	著 859	飲 323	逸 734	(冶) YA
ida(ku)	抱 1285	ina 否 1248	itsu 五 7	(始) SHI
ido(mu)	挑 1564	ina- 稲 1220	伍 2013	次 384
ie	家 165	ine 稲 1220	巌 2059	(欠) KETSU
ika(ru)	怒 1596	inochi 命 578	itsuku(shimu)	(吹) SUI
i(kasu)	生 44	ino(ru) 祈 621	慈 1547	除 1065
ike	池 119	inu 犬 280	itsu(tsu) 五 7	(余) YO
i(keru)	生 44	i(reru) 入 52	itsuwa(ru) 偽 1485	(徐) JO
IKI	域 970	iro 色 204	i(u) 言 66	示 615
	(惑) WAKU	irodo(ru) 彩 932	iwa 岩 1345	(元) GEN
iki	息 1242	i(ru) 入 52	巌 2059	仕 333
ikidō(ru)	憤 1661	居 171	Iwao 巌 2059	(士) SHI
ikio(i)	勢 646	要 419	iwa(u) 祝 851	字 110
				(子) SHI

Reading	Kanji	No.
	地	118
	(池)	CHI
	自	62
	(目)	MOKU
	似	1486
	(以)	I
	児	1217
	(旧)	KYŪ
	辞	688
	(辛)	SHIN
	耳	56
	事	80
JI'	十	12
-ji	路	151
JIKI	直	423
	食	322
JIKU	軸	988
JIN	人	1
	仁	1619
	(入)	NYŪ
	陣	1404
	(車)	SHA
	(陳)	CHIN
	刃	1413
	(刀)	TŌ
	臣	835
	(巨)	KYO
	尽	1726
	(尺)	SHAKU
	神	310
	(申)	SHIN
	稔	2183
	(念)	NEN
	迅	1798
	甚	1501
	尋	1082
JITSU	日	5
	実	203
JO	除	1065
	叙	1067
	徐	1066
	(余)	YO
	女	102
	如	1747
	恕	2071
	序	770
	(予)	YO
	助	623
JŌ	壊	1912
	嬢	1836
	穣	2185
	譲	1013
	醸	1837
	浄	664
	静	663
	情	209
	靖	2187
	(青)	SEI
	(清)	SEI
	(精)	SEI
	(請)	SEI
	(争)	SŌ
	成	261
	城	720
	盛	719
	(誠)	SEI
	丞	2002
	蒸	943
	(承)	SHŌ
	乗	523
	剰	1068
	(垂)	SUI
	定	355
	錠	1818
	場	154
	(湯)	TŌ
	(腸)	CHŌ
	(暢)	CHŌ
	常	497
	(党)	TŌ
	(堂)	DŌ
	状	626
	(犬)	KEN
	畳	1087
	(且)	ka(tsu)
	縄	1760
	(亀)	KI
	丈	1325
	上	32
	冗	1614
	条	564
JOKU	辱	1738
	(唇)	SHIN
JU	受	260
	授	602
	需	1416
	儒	1417
	樹	1144
	(膨)	BŌ
	(鼓)	KO
	従	1482
	(縦)	JŪ
	就	934
	(京)	KYŌ
	寿	1550
	頌	2264
	雛	2260
JŪ	十	12
	汁	1794
	(計)	KEI
	(針)	SHIN
	充	828
	銃	829
	(統)	TŌ
	従	1482
	縦	1483
	住	156
	(主)	SHU
	(注)	CHŪ
	(駐)	CHŪ
	拾	1445
	(合)	GŌ
	柔	774
	(矛)	MU
	渋	1693
	(止)	SHI
	獣	1582
	(犬)	KEN
	重	227
JUKU	塾	1674
	熟	687
	(享)	KYŌ
	(熱)	NETSU
JUN	旬	338
	洵	2139
	殉	1799
	絢	2194
	詢	2240
	(句)	KU
	淳	2141
	惇	2075
	諄	2242
	醇	2255
	(享)	KYŌ
	(敦)	TON
	(亨)	KYŌ
	准	1232
	準	778
	(推)	SUI
	(唯)	YUI
	(集)	SHŪ
	稚	CHI
	(維)	I
	盾	772
	循	1479
	遵	1938
	(尊)	SON
	(導)	DŌ
	隼	2259
	(集)	SHŪ
	純	965
	(鈍)	DON
	順	769
	(訓)	KUN
	巡	777
	潤	1203
JUTSU	述	968
	術	187
	(街)	KAI

– K –

Reading	Kanji	No.
KA	加	709
	伽	2014
	茄	2213
	架	755
	袈	2238
	嘉	2041
	(賀)	GA
	可	388
	何	390
	河	389
	荷	391
	歌	392
	化	254
	花	255
	貨	752
	靴	1076
	(革)	KAKU
	果	487
	菓	1535
	課	488
	家	165

	嫁	1749
	稼	1750
	過	413
	渦	1810
	禍	1809
	華	1074
	樺	2123
	暇	1064
	霞	2261
	佳	1462
	(圭)	KEI
	(奎)	KEI
	(封)	FŪ
	科	320
	(斗)	TO
	(料)	RYŌ
	箇	1473
	(固)	KO
	(個)	KO
	仮	1049
	(反)	HAN
	下	31
	火	20
	価	421
	夏	461
	寡	1851
KA'	合	159
ka	香	1682
	馨	2267
	蚊	1876
	(虫)	mushi
	圭	2042
	郁	2252
	哉	2037
	鹿	2279
	蘭	2233
-ka	日	5
kaba	樺	2123
kabe	壁	1489
kabu	株	741
kachi	捷	2079
kado	圭	2042
	角	473
	門	161
	矩	2175
	稜	2184
Kaede	楓	2120
kaeri(miru)	省	145

	顧	1554
kae(ru)	返	442
	帰	317
ka(eru)	代	256
	変	257
	換	1586
	替	744
kae(su)	返	442
	帰	317
kagami	鏡	863
kagaya(ku)	輝	1653
kage	陰	867
	熊	2149
	影	854
kage(ru)	陰	867
kagi(ru)	限	847
KAI	海	117
	悔	1733
	(毎)	MAI
	(侮)	BU
	(梅)	BAI
	塊	1524
	魁	2083
	(鬼)	KI
	(魂)	KON
	(魅)	MI
	皆	587
	階	588
	(陛)	HEI
	介	453
	界	454
	会	158
	絵	345
	戒	876
	械	529
	壊	1407
	懐	1408
	亥	2008
	(刻)	KOKU
	(劾)	GAI
	(核)	KAKU
	(該)	GAI
	怪	1476
	(径)	KEI
	(茎)	KEI
	(経)	KEI
	(軽)	KEI
	灰	1343

	(火)	KA
	(炭)	TAN
	街	186
	(術)	JUTSU
	(圭)	KEI
	快	1409
	(決)	KETSU
	解	474
	(角)	KAKU
	回	90
	改	514
	拐	1916
	凱	2028
	開	396
kai	貝	240
kaiko	蚕	1877
kaka(eru)	抱	1285
kaka(geru)	掲	1624
kakari	係	909
	掛	1464
kaka(ru)	係	909
ka(karu)	架	755
	掛	1464
	懸	911
ka(keru)	欠	383
	架	755
	掛	1464
	駆	1882
	懸	911
kaki	垣	1276
kako(mu)	囲	1194
kako(u)	囲	1194
KAKU	各	642
	客	641
	格	643
	閣	837
	(略)	RYAKU
	(絡)	RAKU
	(額)	GAKU
	獲	1313
	穫	1314
	(隻)	SEKI
	(護)	GO
	確	603
	鶴	2277
	核	1212
	(亥)	GAI
	(刻)	KOKU

	(劾)	GAI
	(該)	GAI
	拡	1113
	(広)	KŌ
	郭	1673
	(享)	KYŌ
	殻	1728
	(穀)	KOKU
	隔	1589
	(融)	YŪ
	覚	605
	(見)	KEN
	較	1453
	(交)	KŌ
	嚇	1918
	(赤)	SEKI
	角	473
	画	343
	革	1075
ka(ku)	欠	383
	書	131
kaku(reru)	隠	868
kaku(su)	隠	868
kama	窯	1789
	鎌	2257
kama(eru)	構	1010
kama(u)	構	1010
kame	亀	2284
kami	上	32
	神	310
	紙	180
	髪	1148
kaminari	雷	952
kamo(su)	醸	1837
KAN	干	584
	刊	585
	汗	1188
	肝	1272
	栞	2108
	幹	1189
	乾	1190
	(岸)	GAN
	(軒)	KEN
	官	326
	棺	1825
	管	328
	館	327
	閑	1532

間 43		缶 1649	ka(riru)	借 766		(話) WA
関 398		亘 2006	karo(yaka)	軽 547		割 519
簡 1533		侃 2017	ka(ru)	刈 1282		轄 1186
完 613		陥 1218		狩 1581		(害) GAI
冠 1615		患 1315		駆 1882		滑 1267
荒 2217		寒 457	karu(i)	軽 547		(骨) KOTSU
(元) GAN		敢 1691	kasa	傘 790	Katsu	捷 2079
(宗) SHŪ	kan	神 310	kasa(naru)	重 227	katsu	亮 2010
監 1663	kana	金 23	kasa(neru)	重 227		桂 2109
艦 1665		哉 2037	kase(gu)	稼 1750		凱 2028
鑑 1664	kana(deru)	奏 1544	kashiko(i)	賢 1288	ka(tsu)	且 1926
(濫) RAN	Kanai	叶 2033	kashira	頭 276		勝 509
(覧) RAN	kanara(zu)	必 520	ka(su)	貸 748	katsu(gu)	担 1274
勧 1051	kana(shii)	悲 1034	Kasumi	霞 2261	Katsumi	凱 2028
歓 1052	kana(shimu)	悲 1034	kata	形 395	Katsura	桂 2109
観 604	Kanba	樺 2123		型 888		藤 2231
(権) KEN	kanba(shii)	芳 1775		方 70	ka(u)	交 114
感 262	Kane	矩 2175		肩 1264		買 241
憾 1815	kane	金 23		渇 1626		飼 1762
(減) GEN		錦 2256		鎌 2257	kawa	川 33
(惑) WAKU		鎌 2257	kata-	片 1045		皮 975
勘 1502		鐘 1821	katachi	形 395		河 389
堪 1913	ka(neru)	兼 1081	kata(i)	固 972		革 1075
(甚) JIN	kanga(eru)	考 541		堅 1289		側 609
貫 914	kanmuri	冠 1615		硬 1009	kawa(kasu)	乾 1190
慣 915	kano	彼 977		難 557	kawa(ku)	渇 1622
換 1586	Kanō	叶 2033	kataki	敵 416		乾 1190
喚 1587	kao	顔 277	katamari	塊 1524	ka(waru)	代 256
還 866	Kaori	郁 2252	kata(maru)	固 972		変 257
環 865		馨 2267	kata(meru)	固 972		換 1586
巻 507	kao(ri)	香 1682	katamu(keru)			替 744
(券) KEN	Kaoru	郁 2252		傾 1441	ka(wasu)	交 114
(圏) KEN		彪 2068	katamu(ku)	傾 1441	kaya	茅 2214
看 1316		馨 2267	katana	刀 37	kayo(u)	通 150
(手) SHU	kao(ru)	香 1682	kata(rau)	語 67	kaza-	風 29
(目) MOKU		薫 1774	kata(ru)	語 67	kaza(ru)	飾 979
漢 556	Kara	唐 1697	Katashi	拳 2078	kaze	風 29
(漠) BAKU	kara	空 140	katawa(ra)	傍 1183	kazo(eru)	数 225
(難) NAN		殻 1728	kataya(ru)	偏 1159	kazu	胤 2205
緩 1089	karada	体 61	kate	糧 1704		倭 2019
(援) EN	kara(i)	辛 1487	KATSU	渇 1622		数 225
(暖) DAN	kara(maru)	絡 840		喝 1919		鶴 2277
款 1727	kara(mu)	絡 840		褐 1623	KE	圭 2042
(隷) REI	kare	彼 977	(掲)	KEI		奎 2045
寛 1050	ka(reru)	枯 974	(謁)	ETSU		(佳) KA
(見) KEN	kari	仮 1049		活 237		(封) FŪ
甘 1492	ka(ri)	狩 1581		括 1260		袈 2238
甲 982			(舌)	ZETSU		(加) KA

Reading	Kanji	No.
	稀	2182
	(希)	KI
	化	254
	気	134
	仮	1049
	華	1074
	家	165
	懸	911
ke	毛	287
kega(rawashii)		
	汚	693
kega(reru)	汚	693
kega(su)	汚	693
KEI	径	1475
	茎	1474
	経	548
	軽	547
	(怪)	KAI
	圭	2042
	奎	2045
	桂	2109
	(佳)	KA
	(封)	FŪ
	刑	887
	形	395
	型	888
	系	908
	係	909
	(糸)	SHI
	京	189
	景	853
	(影)	EI
	敬	705
	警	706
	(驚)	KYŌ
	兄	406
	競	852
	鶏	926
	渓	1884
	掲	1624
	(渇)	KATSU
	(喝)	KATSU
	(褐)	KATSU
	(謁)	ETSU
	傾	1441
	(頂)	CHŌ
	(項)	KŌ
	契	565
	(喫)	KITSU
	境	864
	(鏡)	KYŌ
	継	1025
	(米)	BEI
	慧	2076
	(彗)	EI
	憩	1243
	(息)	SOKU
	勁	2029
	計	340
	恵	1219
	啓	1398
	蛍	1878
	携	1686
	慶	1632
	馨	2267
kemono	獣	1582
kemu(i)	煙	919
kemuri	煙	919
kemu(ru)	煙	919
KEN	倹	878
	険	533
	剣	879
	検	531
	験	532
	兼	1081
	嫌	1688
	謙	1687
	鎌	2257
	券	506
	圏	508
	拳	2078
	(巻)	KAN
	栞	2108
	軒	1187
	(干)	KAN
	堅	1289
	賢	1288
	(緊)	KIN
	犬	280
	献	1355
	建	892
	健	893
	県	194
	懸	911
	遣	1173
	(追)	TSUI
	(遺)	I
	権	335
	(歓)	KAN
	(観)	KAN
	件	732
	(牛)	GYŪ
	絃	2192
	(玄)	GEN
	絢	2194
	(旬)	JUN
	見	63
	肩	1264
	研	896
	間	43
	絹	1261
	憲	521
	繭	1911
	顕	1170
kesa	袈	2238
ke(su)	消	845
KETSU	結	485
	(吉)	KICHI
	(詰)	KITSU
	穴	899
	(八)	HACHI
	血	789
	(皿)	sara
	決	356
	(快)	KAI
	潔	1241
	(喫)	KITSU
	欠	383
	傑	1731
kewa(shii)	険	533
kezu(ru)	削	1611
KI	己	370
	忌	1797
	紀	372
	起	373
	記	371
	基	450
	棋	1835
	期	449
	旗	1006
	(欺)	GI
	奇	1360
	寄	1361
	綺	2195
	騎	1881
	揮	1652
	暉	2096
	輝	1653
	(軍)	GUN
	(運)	UN
	幾	877
	機	528
	磯	2177
	伎	2012
	岐	872
	(支)	SHI
	(技)	GI
	希	676
	稀	2182
	(布)	FU
	芹	2210
	祈	621
	(斤)	KIN
	気	134
	汽	135
	机	1305
	飢	1304
	規	607
	槻	2126
	喜	1143
	嬉	2048
	奎	2045
	(圭)	KEI
	(佳)	KA
	(封)	FŪ
	帰	317
	(掃)	SŌ
	(婦)	FU
	企	481
	(止)	SHI
	危	534
	(厄)	YAKU
	季	465
	(委)	I
	軌	1787
	(軟)	NAN
	亀	2284
	(縄)	JŌ
	既	1458
	鬼	1523
	葵	2222
	貴	1171

Reading	Kanji	No.
	棄	962
	熙	2148
	器	527
	毅	2131
ki	木	22
	栞	2108
	玖	2156
	哉	2037
	黄	780
ki-	生	44
kibi(shii)	厳	822
KICHI	吉	1141
ki(eru)	消	845
ki(koeru)	聞	64
KIKU	菊	475
	鞠	2262
ki(ku)	聞	64
	聴	1039
	利	329
	効	816
ki(maru)	決	356
ki(meru)	決	356
kimi	君	793
kimo	肝	1272
KIN	斤	1897
	近	445
	芹	2210
	欣	2129
	今	51
	袷	2237
	琴	1251
	(含)	GAN
	(吟)	GIN
	菫	2219
	勤	559
	謹	1247
	禁	482
	襟	1537
	(示)	SHI
	(林)	RIN
	金	23
	欽	2130
	緊	1290
	(堅)	KEN
	(賢)	KEN
	錦	2256
	(綿)	MEN
	均	805
kinu	絹	1261
kira	晃	2092
kira(u)	嫌	1688
ki(reru)	切	39
kiri	桐	2110
	霧	950
ki(ru)	切	39
	着	657
ki(seru)	着	657
kishi	岸	586
kiso(u)	競	852
kita	北	73
	朔	2101
kita(eru)	鍛	1817
kitana(i)	汚	693
kita(ru)	来	69
kita(su)	来	69
KITSU	吉	1141
	詰	1142
	(結)	KETSU
	喫	1240
	(契)	KEI
	(潔)	KETSU
	橘	2127
kiwa	際	618
kiwa(maru)	極	336
	窮	897
kiwa(meru)	究	895
	窮	897
	極	336
ko	極	336
kiyo	汐	2134
	淳	2141
	圭	2042
	舜	2208
	馨	2267
kiyo(i)	清	660
kiyo(maru)	清	660
kiyo(meru)	清	660
Kiyoshi	浩	2140
	淳	2141
	圭	2042
	靖	2187
	碧	2176
kiza(mu)	刻	1211
Kizashi	萌	2221
	筋	1090
	菌	1222
kiza(shi)	兆	1562
kiza(su)	兆	1562
kizu	傷	633
kizu(ku)	築	1603
KO	古	172
	固	972
	枯	974
	胡	2206
	故	173
	個	973
	湖	467
	瑚	2161
	(居)	KYO
	戸	152
	雇	1553
	顧	1554
	孤	1480
	弧	1481
	虎	2234
	虚	1572
	拠	1138
	(処)	SHO
	霞	2261
	(暇)	KA
	己	370
	去	414
	冴	2023
	呼	1254
	庫	825
	鼓	1147
	誇	1629
ko	子	103
	木	22
	粉	1701
	黄	780
ko-	小	27
KŌ	工	139
	巧	1627
	功	818
	江	821
	攻	819
	紅	820
	虹	2235
	貢	1719
	控	1718
	項	1439
	鴻	2275
	(空)	KŪ
	口	54
	向	199
	后	1119
	杏	2102
	拘	1800
	高	190
	格	643
	稿	1120
	興	368
	公	126
	弘	2064
	広	694
	宏	2050
	紘	2190
	鉱	1604
	(翁)	Ō
	交	114
	郊	817
	効	816
	校	115
	絞	1452
	(父)	FU
	(紋)	MON
	光	138
	洸	2137
	晃	2092
	滉	2145
	溝	1012
	構	1010
	講	783
	購	1011
	孔	940
	好	104
	厚	639
	孝	542
	考	541
	酵	1866
	行	68
	後	48
	衡	1585
	坑	1613
	抗	824
	航	823
	仰	1056
	昂	2088
	(抑)	YOKU
	(昂)	BŌ
	洪	1435

Reading	Kanji	No.
	港	669
	(共)	KYŌ
	(供)	KYŌ
	亘	2006
	恒	1275
	(宣)	SEN
	更	1008
	硬	1009
	(便)	BEN
	幸	684
	倖	2020
	(辛)	SHIN
	浩	2140
	皓	2169
	(告)	KOKU
	網	1609
	鋼	1608
	(剛)	GŌ
	侯	1924
	候	944
	荒	1377
	慌	1378
	皇	297
	皐	2168
	耗	1197
	耕	1196
	降	947
	(隆)	RYŪ
	康	894
	(逮)	TAI
	甲	982
	亨	2009
	肯	1262
	香	1682
	黄	780
kō	神	310
koba(mu)	拒	1295
koe	声	746
	肥	1723
ko(eru)	超	1000
	越	1001
	肥	1723
ko(gareru)	焦	999
ko(gasu)	焦	999
ko(geru)	焦	999
kogo(eru)	凍	1205
koi	恋	258
	鯉	2271
ko(i)	濃	957
koi(shii)	恋	258
kokono	九	11
kokono(tsu)	九	11
kokoro	心	97
kokoro(miru)	試	526
kokoroyo(i)	快	1409
kokorozashi	志	573
kokoroza(su)	志	573
KOKU	告	690
	酷	1711
	(造)	ZŌ
	刻	1211
	(亥)	GAI
	(劾)	GAI
	(核)	KAKU
	国	40
	(玉)	GYOKU
	黒	206
	(里)	RI
	穀	1729
	(殻)	KAKU
	石	78
	克	1372
	谷	653
koku	欽	2130
koma	駒	2268
koma(ka)	細	695
koma(kai)	細	695
koma(ru)	困	558
kome	米	224
ko(meru)	込	776
ko(mu)	込	776
kōmu(ru)	被	976
KON	根	314
	恨	1755
	(限)	GEN
	(眼)	GAN
	(銀)	GIN
	昆	1874
	混	799
	墾	1136
	懇	1135
	困	558
	(木)	BOKU
	(因)	IN
	魂	1525
	(鬼)	KI
	(塊)	KAI
	建	892
	(健)	KEN
	紺	1493
	(甘)	KAN
	献	1355
	(犬)	KEN
	今	51
	金	23
	婚	567
kona	粉	1701
Konomu	嘉	2041
kono(mu)	好	104
ko(rashimeru)	懲	1421
	凝	1518
ko(rasu)	懲	1421
kore	之	2004
	也	2005
	只	2034
	伊	2011
	惟	2073
kōri	氷	1206
ko(riru)	懲	1421
koro(bu)	転	433
koro(garu)	転	433
koro(gasu)	転	433
koro(geru)	転	433
koromo	衣	677
koro(su)	殺	576
ko(ru)	凝	1518
kō(ru)	氷	1206
	凍	1205
koshi	腰	1298
ko(su)	超	1000
	越	1001
	答	160
	答	160
koto	事	80
	采	2153
	殊	1505
	琴	1251
	肇	2204
	誼	2241
koto-	異	1061
-koto	言	66
kotobuki	寿	1550
kotowa(ru)	断	1024
KOTSU	骨	1266
ko(u)	恋	258
	請	661
kowa-	声	746
kowa(i)	怖	1814
kowa(reru)	壊	1407
Kowashi	毅	2131
kowa(su)	壊	1407
ko(yashi)	肥	1723
ko(yasu)	肥	1723
koyomi	暦	1534
Kozue	梢	2114
	槻	2125
KU	工	139
	功	818
	紅	820
	貢	1719
	(江)	KŌ
	(攻)	KŌ
	(空)	KŪ
	口	54
	句	337
	駒	2268
	(旬)	JUN
	九	11
	鳩	2273
	久	1210
	玖	2156
	区	183
	駆	1882
	供	197
	(共)	KYŌ
	苦	545
	(古)	KO
	宮	721
	(営)	EI
	庫	825
	(車)	SHA
KŪ	空	140
	(工)	KŌ
	矩	2175
kuba(ru)	配	515
kubi	首	148
kuchi	口	54
kuchibiru	唇	1737
ku(chiru)	朽	1628

407

kuda	管	328	kuru(shimeru)				(処)	SHO		興	368
kuda(keru)	砕	1710		苦	545		居	171	(同)		DŌ
kuda(ku)	砕	1710	kuru(shimu)	苦	545		(古)	KO		杏	2102
kuda(ru)	下	31	kuru(u)	狂	883		虚	1572		恐	1602
kuda(saru)	下	31	kusa	草	249		(戯)	GI		強	217
kuda(su)	下	31	kusa(i)	臭	1244		許	737	KYOKU	曲	366
ku(iru)	悔	1733	kusa(rasu)	腐	1245		(午)	GO		(典)	TEN
kujira	鯨	700	kusa(reru)	腐	1245	KYŌ	共	196		旭	2086
kuki	茎	1474	kusari	鎖	1819		供	197		局	170
kuma	阿	2258	kusa(ru)	腐	1245		恭	1434		極	336
	熊	2149	kuse	癖	1490		(洪)	KŌ	KYŪ	求	724
kumi	組	418	Kusu	楠	2119		挟	1354		毬	2132
	綸	2199	Kusunoki	楠	2119		狭	1353		球	726
	伍	2013	kusuri	薬	359		峡	1352		救	725
kumo	雲	636	KUTSU	屈	1802		(来)	RAI		及	1257
kumo(ru)	曇	637		掘	1803		兄	406		吸	1256
ku(mu)	組	418		(出)	SHUTSU		況	850		級	568
KUN	勲	1773	kutsu	靴	1076		競	852		(扱)	atsuka(u)
	薫	1774	kutsugae(ru)	覆	1634		亨	2009		九	11
	(重)	JŪ	kutsugae(su)	覆	1634		享	1672		究	895
	君	793	ku(u)	食	322		京	189		鳩	2273
	(伊)	I	kuwa	桑	1873		喬	2040		糾	1703
	訓	771	kuwada(teru)				橋	597		赳	2244
kuni	郁	2252		企	481		矯	1925		(叫)	KYŌ
	之	2004	kuwa(eru)	加	709		叶	2033		久	1210
	洲	2138	kuwa(shii)	詳	1577		叫	1252		玖	2156
	邑	2250	kuwa(waru)	加	709		(糾)	KYŪ		弓	212
	国	40	ku(yamu)	悔	1733		匡	2030		窮	897
	晋	2093	kuya(shii)	悔	1733		狂	883		旧	1216
	秦	2181	kuzu(reru)	崩	1122		(王)	Ō		(日)	NICHI
kura	倉	1307	kuzu(su)	崩	1122		凶	1280		休	60
	蔵	1286	KYA	伽	2014		胸	1283		(木)	BOKU
	椋	2117		(加)	KA		協	234		朽	1628
kura(beru)	比	798		脚	1784		脅	1263		(巧)	KŌ
kurai	位	122	KYAKU	却	1783		香	1682		泣	1236
kura(i)	暗	348		脚	1784		馨	2267		(立)	RITSU
ku(rasu)	暮	1428		(去)	KYO		郷	855		宮	721
ku(rau)	食	322		客	641		響	856		(営)	EI
kurenai	紅	820		(各)	KAKU		境	864		給	346
ku(reru)	暮	1428	KYO	巨	1293		鏡	863		(合)	GŌ
Kuri	栗	2111		拒	1295		経	548		丘	1357
kuro	黒	206		距	1294		(径)	KEI		急	303
kuro(i)	黒	206		挙	801		(怪)	KAI		鞠	2262
ku(ru)	来	69		(手)	SHU		驚	1778		– M –	
	繰	1654		(誉)	YO		(敬)	KEI			
kuruma	車	133		去	414		(警)	KEI	MA	麻	1529
kuru(oshii)	狂	883		(土)	DO		教	245		摩	1530
kuru(shii)	苦	545		拠	1138		(孝)	KŌ		磨	1531

Reading	Kanji	No.
	魔	1528
	(暦)	REKI
	(歴)	REKI
	茉	2215
	(末)	MATSU
ma	目	55
	真	422
	馬	283
	間	43
maboroshi	幻	1227
machi	町	182
	街	186
mado	窓	698
mado(u)	惑	969
mae	前	47
ma(garu)	曲	366
ma(geru)	曲	366
magi(rasu)	紛	1702
magi(rawashii)		
	紛	1702
magi(rawasu)		
	紛	1702
magi(reru)	紛	1702
mago	孫	910
MAI	毎	116
	(母)	BO
	(海)	KAI
	妹	408
	(未)	MI
	(味)	MI
	枚	1156
	(牧)	BOKU
	埋	1826
	(里)	RI
	米	224
mai	舞	810
mai(ru)	参	710
maji(eru)	交	114
ma(jiru)	交	114
	混	799
maji(waru)	交	114
makana(u)	賄	1739
maka(seru)	任	334
maka(su)	任	334
ma(kasu)	負	510
ma(keru)	負	510
maki	牧	731
	巻	507
	蒔	2224
	槙	2125
	淳	2141
	惇	2075
Makoto	諄	2242
	允	2022
	亮	2010
	洵	2139
	詢	2240
	欽	2130
	瑞	2162
	諒	2243
makoto	誠	718
MAKU	幕	1432
	膜	1426
	(漠)	BAKU
ma(ku)	巻	507
mame	豆	958
Mamoru	葵	2222
mamo(ru)	守	490
MAN	漫	1411
	慢	1410
	万	16
	満	201
mana(bu)	学	109
manako	眼	848
mane(ku)	招	455
manuka(reru)		
	免	733
mare	稀	2182
Mari	鞠	2262
mari	毬	2132
Maro	麿	2281
maru	丸	644
maru(i)	丸	644
	円	13
maru(meru)	丸	644
Masa	昌	2089
	柾	2107
	諒	2243
masa	旦	2085
	晟	2094
	晨	2095
	暢	2097
	允	2022
	匡	2030
	庄	2063
	甫	2167
	祐	2178
	倭	2019
	叡	2032
Masaki	柾	2107
masa (ni)	正	275
Masaru	昌	2089
	智	2099
	捷	2079
masa(ru)	勝	509
Masashi	匡	2030
	昌	2089
	柾	2107
masu	升	1898
	祐	2178
ma(su)	増	712
mata	又	1593
	也	2005
	亦	2007
matata(ku)	瞬	1732
mato	的	210
MATSU	末	305
	抹	1914
	茉	2215
	(未)	MI
matsu	松	696
	須	2263
ma(tsu)	待	452
matsu(ri)	祭	617
matsurigoto	政	483
matsu(ru)	祭	617
matta(ku)	全	89
ma(u)	舞	810
mawa(ri)	周	91
mawa(ru)	回	90
mawa(su)	回	90
mayo(u)	迷	967
mayu	眉	2170
	繭	1911
Mayumi	檀	2128
Mayuzumi	黛	2283
ma(zaru)	交	114
	混	799
ma(zeru)	交	114
	混	799
mazu(shii)	貧	753
me	女	102
	目	55
	芽	1455
	萌	2221
Megumi	萌	2221
me-	雌	1388
megu(mu)	恵	1219
megu(ru)	巡	777
MEI	名	82
	銘	1552
	明	18
	盟	717
	命	578
	(念)	NEN
	迷	967
	(米)	BEI
	鳴	925
	(鳥)	CHŌ
mekura	盲	1375
memi	萌	2221
MEN	綿	1191
	(線)	SEN
	(錦)	KIN
	免	733
	面	274
meshi	飯	325
mesu	雌	1388
me(su)	召	995
METSU	滅	1338
mezura(shii)	珍	1215
MI	未	306
	味	307
	魅	1526
	(妹)	MAI
	(末)	MATSU
	弥	2065
	眉	2170
mi	三	4
	巳	2060
	身	59
	弥	2065
	実	203
	胤	2205
	爾	2154
Michi	迪	2247
michi	峻	2053
	巌	2059
	恕	2071
	惣	2074
	道	149
	遥	2248

Reading	Kanji	No.	Reading	Kanji	No.	Reading	Kanji	No.	Reading	Kanji	No.
	亨	2009	mito(meru)	認	738	MOKU	木	22	MU	矛	773
	吾	2035	MITSU	密	806		目	55		務	235
	碩	2265	(必)		HITSU		黙	1578		霧	950
michibi(ku)	導	703	mitsu	弘	2064	momo	李	2104	(予)		YO
mi(chiru)	満	201		弥	2065		桃	1567		夢	811
mida(reru)	乱	689		晃	2092	MON	門	161	(夕)		YŪ
mida(su)	乱	689		暢	2097		問	162		謀	1495
Midori	翠	2201		允	2022		聞	64	(某)		BŌ
	碧	2176		舜	2208		文	111		武	1031
midori	緑	537		瑞	2162		紋	1454		無	93
mi(eru)	見	63		鞠	2262	(絞)		KŌ	mu	六	8
Migaki	琢	2158	mi(tsu)	三	4	monme	匁	1902	mugi	麦	270
Migaku	琢	2158	mitsu(gu)	貢	1719	mono	者	164	mui	六	8
miga(ku)	磨	1531	Mitsuru	爾	2154		物	79	muka(eru)	迎	1055
migi	右	76		暢	2097	moppa(ra)	専	600	mukashi	昔	764
Migiwa	汀	2133		碩	2265	mo(rasu)	漏	1806	mu(kau)	向	199
mijika(i)	短	215	mit(tsu)	三	4	mo(reru)	漏	1806	mu(keru)	向	199
miji(me)	惨	1725	miya	宮	721	mori	杜	2103	muko	婿	1745
miki	幹	1189	miyako	都	188		彬	2069	mu(kō)	向	199
mikotonori	詔	1885	mizo	溝	1012		森	128	Muku	椋	2117
mimi	耳	56	mizu	水	21		守	490	mu(ku)	向	199
MIN	民	177		瑞	2162		旺	2087	muku(iru)	報	685
	眠	849	mizuka(ra)	自	62	moro	脩	2207	muna	胸	1283
(眼)		GAN	mizuumi	湖	467		艶	2209		棟	1406
mina	皆	587	MO	模	1425	mo(ru)	盛	719	mune	旨	1040
minami	南	74	(膜)		MAKU		漏	1806		胸	1283
minamoto	源	580	(漠)		BAKU	mo(shikuwa)				棟	1406
minato	港	669		茂	1467		若	544	mura	邑	2250
mine	峻	2053	mo	喪	1678	mo(su)	燃	652		村	191
	峰	1350		藻	1657	mō(su)	申	309		群	794
	嶺	2058	MŌ	亡	672	moto	下	31	murasaki	紫	1389
	巌	2059		妄	1376		元	137	mu(rasu)	蒸	943
	稔	2183		盲	1375		本	25	mu(re)	群	794
miniku(i)	醜	1527		望	673		甫	2167	mu(reru)	蒸	943
Minori	穣	2185		毛	287		孟	2049		群	794
Minoru	稔	2183		耗	1197		朔	2101	muro	室	166
	穣	2185		孟	2049		基	450	mushi	虫	873
	酉	2254		猛	1579		喬	2040	mu(su)	蒸	943
mino(ru)	実	203		網	1612	motoi	基	450	musu(bu)	結	485
Mio	澪	2147	(綱)		KŌ	moto(meru)	求	724	musume	娘	1752
mi(ru)	見	63	mochi	須	2263	Motomu	欣	2129	mutsu	睦	2172
	診	1214	mochi(iru)	用	107		須	2263	mu(tsu)	六	8
misaki	岬	1363	modo(ru)	戻	1238	MOTSU	物	79	Mutsumi	睦	2172
misao	操	1655	modo(su)	戻	1238	mo(tsu)	持	451	mut(tsu)	六	8
misasagi	陵	1844	moe	萌	2221	motto(mo)	最	263	muzuka(shii)		
mise	店	168	mo(eru)	燃	652	mo(yasu)	燃	652		難	557
mi(seru)	見	63	mogu(ru)	潜	937	moyō(su)	催	1317	MYAKU	脈	913
mi(tasu)	満	201	mō(keru)	設	577	moyu	萌	2221	(派)		HA

Reading	Kanji	No.
MYŌ	妙	1154
(抄)	SHŌ	
(砂)	SA	
(秒)	BYŌ	
	命	578
(念)	NEN	
	名	82
	明	18
– N –		
NA	奈	2044
(捺)	NATSU	
	納	758
(内)	NAI	
	那	2251
	南	74
NA'	納	758
(内)	NAI	
na	名	82
	菜	931
	楠	2119
nae	苗	1468
naga	亨	2009
	孟	2049
	呂	2036
	酉	2254
	脩	2207
	斐	2082
	暢	2097
naga(i)	永	1207
	長	95
naga(meru)	眺	1565
naga(reru)	流	247
Nagashi	亀	2284
naga(su)	流	247
nage(kawashii)	嘆	1246
nage(ku)	嘆	1246
na(geru)	投	1021
nagi	凪	2027
Nagisa	汀	2133
	渚	2142
nago(mu)	和	124
nago(yaka)	和	124
nagu	凪	2027
nagu(ru)	殴	1940
nagusa(meru)	慰	1618
nagusa(mu)	慰	1618
NAI	乃	2003
	内	84
na(i)	亡	672
	無	93
naka	中	28
	仲	1347
	斐	2082
naka(ba)	半	88
na(ku)	泣	1236
	鳴	925
nama	生	44
nama(keru)	怠	1297
namari	鉛	1606
name(raka)	滑	1267
nami	甫	2167
	並	1165
	波	666
namida	涙	1239
NAN	南	74
	楠	2119
	納	758
(内)	NAI	
	軟	1788
(軌)	KI	
	難	557
(漢)	KAN	
	男	101
nan	何	390
nana	七	9
nana(me)	斜	1069
nana(tsu)	七	9
nani	何	390
	奈	2044
nano	七	9
nao	侃	2017
	脩	2207
nao(ru)	直	423
	治	493
nao(su)	直	423
	治	493
nara(beru)	並	1165
nara(bini)	並	1165
nara(bu)	並	1165
na(rasu)	鳴	925
	慣	915
nara(u)	倣	1776
	習	591
na(reru)	慣	915
nari	也	2005
	稔	2183
naru	稔	2183
na(ru)	成	261
	鳴	925
nasa(ke)	情	209
nashi	梨	2115
na(su)	成	261
NATSU	捺	2080
(奈)	NA	
natsu	夏	461
natsu(kashii)	懐	1408
natsu(kashimu)		
	懐	1408
natsu(keru)	懐	1408
natsu(ku)	懐	1408
nawa	苗	1468
	縄	1760
naya(masu)	悩	1279
naya(mu)	悩	1279
ne	音	347
	値	425
	根	314
	嶺	2058
neba(ru)	粘	1707
nega(u)	願	581
NEI	寧	1412
(丁)	TEI	
ne(kasu)	寝	1079
neko	猫	1470
nemu(i)	眠	849
nemu(ru)	眠	849
NEN	念	579
	稔	2183
(今)	KON	
(命)	MEI	
	粘	1707
	鮎	2270
(占)	SEN	
	然	651
	燃	652
	年	45
nengo(ro)	懇	1135
ne(ru)	寝	1079
	練	743
NETSU	熱	645
NI	二	3
	仁	1619
	弐	1030
	児	1217
(旧)	KYŪ	
	爾	2154
(璽)	JI	
	尼	1620
ni	荷	391
nibu(i)	鈍	966
nibu(ru)	鈍	966
NICHI	日	5
ni(eru)	煮	1795
niga(i)	苦	545
niga(ru)	苦	545
ni(gasu)	逃	1566
ni(geru)	逃	1566
nigi(ru)	握	1714
nigo(ru)	濁	1625
nigo(su)	濁	1625
nii-	新	174
niji	虹	2235
NIKU	肉	223
niku(i)	憎	1365
niku(mu)	憎	1365
niku(rashii)	憎	1365
niku(shimi)	憎	1365
NIN	任	334
	妊	955
(賃)	CHIN	
	忍	1414
	認	738
(刃)	JIN	
	人	1
	仁	1619
	担	1274
nina(u)		
ni(ru)	似	1486
	煮	1795
nise	偽	1485
nishi	西	72
nishiki	錦	2256
niwa	庭	1112
niwatori	鶏	926
no	之	2004
	乃	2003
	野	236
NŌ	悩	1279
	脳	1278
	農	369

Reading	Kanji	No.
	濃	957
	能	386
	(態)	TAI
	納	758
	(内)	NAI
no(basu)	伸	1108
	延	1115
no(beru)	述	968
	延	1115
no(biru)	伸	1108
	延	1115
Noboru	昂	2088
	晃	2092
	晟	2094
	凌	2025
nobo(ru)	上	32
	昇	1777
	登	960
nobo(seru)	上	32
nobo(su)	上	32
Nobu	暢	2097
nobu	亘	2006
	洵	2139
	晋	2093
	之	2004
	允	2022
	辰	2246
	脩	2207
	寅	2052
	遥	2248
	喬	2040
	惟	2073
	惣	2074
	靖	2187
	睦	2172
	頌	2264
	諄	2242
Noburu	辰	2246
	暢	2097
nochi	後	48
noga(reru)	逃	1566
noga(su)	逃	1566
noki	軒	1187
noko(ru)	残	650
noko(su)	残	650
no(mu)	飲	323
nori	甫	2167
	吾	2035

Reading	Kanji	No.
	矩	2175
	恕	2071
	遥	2248
	尭	2043
	智	2099
	熙	2148
	稔	2183
no(ru)	乗	523
	載	1124
no(seru)	乗	523
	載	1124
nozo(ku)	除	1065
nozo(mu)	望	673
	臨	836
nu(geru)	脱	1370
nu(gu)	脱	1370
nu(karu)	抜	1713
nu(kasu)	抜	1713
nu(keru)	抜	1713
nu(ku)	抜	1713
numa	沼	996
nuno	布	675
nu(ru)	塗	1073
nushi	主	155
nusu(mu)	盗	1100
nu(u)	縫	1349
NYAKU	若	544
NYO	女	102
	如	1747
NYŌ	尿	1869
	(水)	SUI
	女	102
NYŪ	入	52
	(人)	JIN
	乳	939
	(浮)	FU
	柔	774

– O –

Reading	Kanji	No.
O	悪	304
	(亜)	A
	汚	693
	於	2084
	和	124
o	絃	2192
	緒	862
	編	2199
	弘	2064

Reading	Kanji	No.
	阿	2258
	尾	1868
	彦	2067
	魁	2083
	巌	2059
o-	小	27
	雄	1387
Ō	王	294
	旺	2087
	皇	297
	殴	1940
	欧	1022
	(区)	KU
	黄	780
	横	781
	往	918
	(主)	SHU
	(注)	CHŪ
	(柱)	CHŪ
	応	827
	(心)	SHIN
	押	986
	(甲)	KŌ
	翁	1930
	(公)	KŌ
	鷹	2278
	(鳥)	CHŌ
	凹	1893
	央	351
	桜	928
	奥	476
ō	碩	2265
	艶	2209
ō-	大	26
obi	帯	963
o(biru)	帯	963
obiya(kasu)	脅	1263
obo(eru)	覚	605
ochii(ru)	陥	1218
o(chiru)	落	839
oda(yaka)	穏	869
odo(kasu)	脅	1263
odo(ri)	踊	1558
odoro(kasu)	驚	1778
odoro(ku)	驚	1778
odo(ru)	踊	1558
	躍	1560
odo(su)	脅	1263

Reading	Kanji	No.
o(eru)	終	458
oga(mu)	拝	1201
ōgi	扇	1555
ogina(u)	補	889
ogoso(ka)	厳	822
Ōi	浩	2140
ō(i)	多	229
ō(i ni)	大	26
o(iru)	老	543
oka	丘	1357
oka(su)	犯	882
	侵	1077
	冒	1104
oki	沖	1346
	熙	2148
ō(kii)	大	26
o(kiru)	起	373
okona(u)	行	68
oko(ru)	怒	1596
	興	368
o(koru)	起	373
oko(su)	興	368
o(kosu)	起	373
okota(ru)	怠	1297
OKU	億	382
	憶	381
	(意)	I
	屋	167
	(至)	SHI
	(室)	SHITSU
oku	奥	476
o(ku)	置	426
oku(rasu)	遅	702
oku(reru)	後	48
	遅	702
oku(ru)	送	441
	贈	1364
omo	主	155
	面	274
omo(i)	重	227
omomuki	趣	1002
omomu(ku)	赴	1465
omote	表	272
	面	274
omo(u)	思	99
ON	恩	555
	(因)	IN
	遠	446

Reading	Kanji	No.
(園)		EN
	温	634
(湯)		TŌ
	穏	869
(隠)		IN
	苑	2212
	音	347
on-	御	708
ona(ji)	同	198
oni	鬼	1523
onna	女	102
onoono	各	642
onore	己	370
o(reru)	折	1394
ori	折	1394
o(riru)	下	31
	降	947
oro(ka)	愚	1642
oroshi	卸	707
oro(su)	卸	707
o(rosu)	下	31
	降	947
o(ru)	折	1394
	織	680
osa	孟	2049
	脩	2207
	綜	2196
osa(eru)	抑	1057
o(saeru)	押	986
osa(maru)	収	757
	治	493
	修	945
	納	758
osa(meru)	収	757
	治	493
	修	945
	納	758
Osamu	乃	2003
	伊	2011
	紘	2190
	脩	2207
	敦	2081
	惣	2074
	靖	2187
	穣	2185
osana(i)	幼	1229
ō(se)	仰	1056
oshi(eru)	教	245

Reading	Kanji	No.
o(shii)	惜	765
o(shimu)	惜	765
oso	晏	2091
oso(i)	遅	702
osore	虞	1941
oso(reru)	恐	1602
oso(roshii)	恐	1602
oso(u)	襲	1575
oso(waru)	教	245
osu	雄	1387
o(su)	押	986
	推	1233
oto	呂	2036
	音	347
	頌	2264
otoko	男	101
Ōtori	鳳	2274
otoro(eru)	衰	1676
oto(ru)	劣	1150
otoshii(reru)	陥	1218
o(tosu)	落	839
otōto	弟	405
otozu(reru)	訪	1181
OTSU	乙	983
otto	夫	315
o(u)	生	44
	追	1174
	負	510
ō(u)	覆	1634
o(waru)	終	458
oya	親	175
ōyake	公	126
oyo(bi)	及	1257
oyo(bosu)	及	1257
oyo(bu)	及	1257
oyo(gu)	泳	1208

– R –

Reading	Kanji	No.
RA	裸	1536
(果)		KA
(課)		KA
	羅	1860
(維)		I
RAI	礼	620
	来	69
	雷	952
	頼	1512
RAKU	落	839
	絡	840
	酪	1865
(各)		KAKU
(略)		RYAKU
	楽	358
(薬)		YAKU
RAN	覧	1291
	濫	1944
	藍	2232
	卵	1058
(卵)		U
	乱	689
(舌)		ZETSU
	嵐	2055
(風)		FŪ
	蘭	2233
	欄	1202
RE	玲	2157
(令)		REI
	令	831
REI	伶	2016
	冷	832
	怜	2070
	玲	2157
	鈴	1822
	零	1823
	澪	2147
	嶺	2058
	齢	833
(領)		RYŌ
	隷	1934
(逮)		TAI
(康)		KŌ
(款)		KAN
	礼	620
(札)		SATSU
	戻	1238
(涙)		RUI
	例	612
(列)		RETSU
	莉	2218
(利)		RI
	励	1340
	黎	2282
	霊	1168
	麗	1630
REKI	暦	1534
	歴	480

Reading	Kanji	No.
REN	連	440
	蓮	2227
(車)		SHA
	廉	1689
	鎌	2257
(兼)		KEN
	練	743
	錬	1816
	怜	2070
(令)		REI
	恋	258
(変)		HEN
RETSU	列	611
	烈	1331
	裂	1330
(例)		REI
	劣	1150
RI	里	142
	理	143
	裏	273
	鯉	2271
(厘)		RIN
	利	329
	莉	2218
	梨	2115
	痢	1811
	璃	2166
	離	1281
	吏	1007
(史)		SHI
	李	2104
(季)		KI
	履	1635
(復)		FUKU
	黎	2282
	亥	2008
ri	律	667
RICHI		
RIKI	力	100
RIKU	陸	647
(凌)		RYŌ
(陵)		RYŌ
RIN	倫	1163
	綸	2199
	輪	1164
(論)		RON
	林	127
	琳	2160
(木)		BOKU

(彬)	HIN		録	538
隣	809		(縁)	EN
麟	2280		六	8
臨	836		鹿	2279
(臣)	SHIN	RON	論	293
(品)	HIN		(倫)	RIN
厘	1900		(輪)	RIN
(里)	RI	RU	留	761
鈴	1822		瑠	2165
凜	2026	RUI	流	247
RITSU 律	667		累	1060
(津)	SHIN		塁	1694	RYOKU
率	788		涙	1239
(卒)	SOTSU		(戻)	REI
立	121	RYAKU	類	226	RYŪ
栗	2111		略	841
RO 路	151		(各)	KAKU
蕗	2230	RYO	(絡)	RAKU
露	951		虜	1385	RYO
(各)	KAKU		慮	1384
(足)	SOKU		旅	222
炉	1790		(族)	ZOKU
(戸)	KO	RYŌ	呂	2036
呂	2036		僚	1324	RYŌ
RŌ 郎	980		遼	2249
浪	1753		寮	1323
朗	1754		燎	2150
廊	981		瞭	2174	SA
(良)	RYŌ		療	1322
(郷)	KYŌ		凌	2025
漏	1806		陵	1844
露	951		峻	2054
(雨)	U		稜	2184
(路)	RO		綾	2198
楼	1841		(陸)	RIKU
(桜)	Ō		怜	2070
(数)	SŪ		玲	2157
老	543		領	834
(考)	KŌ		澪	2147
労	233		嶺	2058
(力)	RYOKU		(令)	REI
玲	2157		涼	1204
(令)	REI		椋	2117
糧	1704		諒	2243
(量)	RYŌ		(京)	KYŌ
ROKU 禄	2179		量	411
緑	537		糧	1704
			料	319

(斗)	TO	sa	爽	2046
(科)	KA	SA'	早	248
漁	699	saba(ku)	裁	1123
(魚)	GYO	sabi	寂	1669
猟	1580	sabi(reru)	寂	1669
(犬)	KEN	sabi(shii)	寂	1669
了	941	sachi	祐	2178
両	200		禄	2179
良	321		禎	2180
亮	2010		幸	684
霊	1168		倖	2020
緑	537	RYOKU	sada	晏	2091
(録)	ROKU		禎	2180
力	100	sada(ka)	定	355
柳	1871	RYŪ	sada(maru)	定	355
留	761	sada(meru)	定	355
瑠	2165	Sadamu	禎	2180
(貿)	BŌ	sae	冴	2023
立	121	saegi(ru)	遮	1767
粒	1700	sa(garu)	下	31
竜	1758	saga(su)	捜	989
流	247		探	535
硫	1856	sa(geru)	下	31
隆	946		提	628
(降)	KŌ	sagu(ru)	探	535
		SAI	哉	2037

– S –

SA	左	75		栽	1125
佐	1744		裁	1123
差	658		歳	479
嵯	2056		載	1124
瑳	2164		采	2153
(着)	CHAKU		採	933
沙	2135		彩	932
砂	1151		菜	931
紗	2191		斎	1478
裟	2239		済	549
作	360		(斉)	SEI
詐	1498		(剤)	ZAI
(昨)	SAKU		才	551
(酢)	SAKU		財	553
唆	1846		(材)	ZAI
(俊)	SHUN		祭	617
(酸)	SAN		際	618
再	782		(察)	SATSU
茶	251		砕	1710
査	624		(枠)	waku
鎖	1819		(粋)	SUI
			(酔)	SUI

Reading	Character	No.
	債	1118
	(責)	SEKI
	(積)	SEKI
	(績)	SEKI
	切	39
	(刀)	TŌ
	宰	1488
	(辛)	SHIN
	偲	2021
	(思)	SHI
	最	263
	(取)	SHU
	西	72
	再	782
	災	1335
	妻	671
	殺	576
	細	695
	催	1317
saiwa(i)	幸	684
saka	坂	443
	逆	444
	酒	517
Sakae	昌	2089
saka(eru)	栄	723
sakai	境	864
saka(n)	盛	719
sakana	魚	290
saka(rau)	逆	444
saka(ru)	盛	719
sakazuki	杯	1155
sake	酒	517
sake(bu)	叫	1252
sa(keru)	裂	1330
	避	1491
saki	先	50
	崎	1362
sakigake	魁	2083
SAKU	作	360
	昨	361
	酢	1867
	搾	1497
	(詐)	SA
	錯	1199
	(昔)	SEKI
	(借)	SHAKU
	(措)	SO
	(惜)	SEKI
	朔	2101
	(塑)	SO
	(逆)	GYAKU
	削	1611
	(肖)	SHŌ
	索	1059
	(糸)	SHI
	策	880
	(刺)	SHI
	冊	1158
sa(ku)	咲	927
	裂	1330
	割	519
sakura	桜	928
sama	様	403
sa(masu)	冷	832
	覚	605
samata(geru)	妨	1182
sa(meru)	冷	832
	覚	605
samu(i)	寒	457
samurai	侍	571
SAN	参	710
	惨	1725
	桟	1906
	(浅)	SEN
	(残)	ZAN
	(銭)	SEN
	産	278
	(生)	SEI
	(彦)	GEN
	酸	516
	(俊)	SHUN
	(唆)	SA
	散	767
	(昔)	SEKI
	賛	745
	(替)	TAI
	三	4
	山	34
	蚕	1877
	傘	790
	算	747
	燦	2151
sane	脩	2207
	翔	2200
	諄	2242
sara	皿	1097
	更	1008
saru	猿	1584
sa(ru)	去	414
sasa	笹	2189
sasa(eru)	支	318
sa(saru)	刺	881
saso(u)	誘	1684
sa(su)	指	1041
	挿	1651
	刺	881
	差	658
sato	里	142
	邑	2250
	怜	2070
	彦	2067
	智	2099
	熙	2148
	聡	2203
	慧	2076
	叡	2032
Satoru	怜	2070
	智	2099
	聡	2203
	慧	2076
sato(ru)	悟	1438
	邑	2250
	怜	2070
Satoshi	捷	2079
	智	2099
	聡	2203
	慧	2076
	叡	2032
sato(su)	諭	1599
SATSU	察	619
	擦	1519
	(祭)	SAI
	(際)	SAI
	撮	1520
	(取)	SHU
	(最)	SAI
	札	1157
	(礼)	REI
	颯	2266
	(風)	FŪ
	冊	1158
	刷	1044
	殺	576
Sawa	爽	2046
sawa	沢	994
	皐	2168
sawa(gu)	騒	875
sawa(ru)	障	858
	触	874
saya	爽	2046
Sayako	爽	2046
sazu(karu)	授	602
sazu(keru)	授	602
SE	施	1004
	(旋)	SEN
	世	252
se	背	1265
	献	1901
	瀬	1513
seba(maru)	狭	1353
seba(meru)	狭	1353
SECHI	節	464
SEI	青	208
	清	660
	情	209
	晴	662
	靖	2187
	静	663
	精	659
	請	661
	生	44
	姓	1746
	性	98
	星	730
	牲	729
	笙	2188
	(産)	SAN
	正	275
	征	1114
	政	483
	整	503
	(延)	EN
	(症)	SHŌ
	(証)	SHŌ
	成	261
	晟	2094
	盛	719
	誠	718
	逝	1396
	誓	1395
	(折)	SETSU

制 427	銭 648	摂 1692	勺 1903
製 428	(残) ZAN	説 400	酌 1863
省 145	(桟) SAN	(悦) ETSU	(釣) tsu(ru)
(少) SHŌ	占 1706	(税) ZEI	石 78
勢 646	鮎 2270	(鋭) EI	赤 207
(熱) NETSU	鮮 701	折 1394	爵 1923
井 1193	先 50	(析) SEKI	**SHI** 止 477
世 252	洗 692	(誓) SEI	祉 1390
西 72	銑 1905	拙 1801	紫 1389
声 746	亘 2006	(出) SHUTSU	歯 478
斉 1477	宣 625	節 464	雌 1388
婿 1745	(恒) KŌ	(即) SOKU	司 842
聖 674	泉 1192	雪 949	伺 1761
歳 479	線 299	**SHA** 沙 2135	詞 843
sei 背 1265	船 376	砂 1151	嗣 1917
SEKI 昔 764	(沿) EN	紗 2191	飼 1762
惜 765	(鉛) EN	裟 2239	次 384
籍 1198	潜 937	(少) SHŌ	姿 929
(借) SHAKU	(替) TAI	舎 791	資 750
(措) SO	(賛) SAN	捨 1444	諮 1769
(錯) SAKU	仙 1891	者 164	(欠) KETSU
責 655	(山) SAN	煮 1795	士 572
積 656	茜 2216	射 900	仕 333
績 1117	(西) SEI	謝 901	志 573
(債) SAI	栓 1842	斜 1069	誌 574
赤 207	(全) ZEN	(斗) TO	支 318
跡 1569	旋 1005	(余) YO	伎 2012
(亦) YAKU	(施) SE	(科) KA	枝 870
石 78	選 800	(料) RYŌ	肢 1146
碩 2265	(巽) SON	写 540	市 181
夕 81	川 33	(与) YO	姉 407
汐 2134	千 15	赦 1570	師 409
斥 1401	専 600	(赤) SEKI	(帥) SUI
(斤) KIN	染 779	遮 1767	旨 1040
析 1393	扇 1555	(庶) SHO	指 1041
(折) SETSU	戦 301	社 308	脂 1042
席 379	遷 921	車 133	薜 2224
(度) DO	薦 1631	耶 2253	詩 570
寂 1669	檀 2128	**SHAKU** 尺 1895	(寺) JI
(淑) SHUKU	繊 1571	釈 595	(侍) JI
隻 1311	**seri** 芹 2210	(沢) TAKU	(持) JI
seki 関 398	**se(ru)** 競 852	(訳) YAKU	(時) JI
sema(i) 狭 1353	**SETSU** 切 39	(駅) EKI	史 332
sema(ru) 迫 1175	窃 1717	昔 764	使 331
se(meru) 攻 819	(刀) TŌ	借 766	(吏) RI
責 655	殺 576	(錯) SAKU	思 99
SEN 浅 649	設 577	(惜) SEKI	偲 2021
践 1568	接 486	(措) SO	(恩) ON

Reading	Kanji	No.
	氏	566
	紙	180
	示	615
	視	606
	私	125
	(仏)	BUTSU
	(払)	FUTSU
	始	494
	(台)	TAI
	(治)	JI
	之	2004
	(乏)	BŌ
	子	103
	(了)	RYŌ
	刺	881
	(策)	SAKU
	施	1004
	(旋)	SEN
	梓	2113
	(幸)	KŌ
	嵯	2056
	(差)	SA
	試	526
	(式)	SHIKI
	賜	1831
	(易)	EKI
	巳	2060
	失	213
	只	2034
	四	6
	死	85
	至	902
	自	62
	糸	242
shi	磯	2177
shiawa(se)	幸	684
shiba	芝	250
shiba(ru)	縛	1448
shibo(ru)	絞	1452
	搾	1497
shibu	渋	1693
shibu(i)	渋	1693
shibu(ru)	渋	1693
SHICHI	七	9
	質	176
shige	卯	2031
	琢	2158
	諄	2242

Reading	Kanji	No.
Shigeru	穣	2185
	苑	2212
	蒼	2225
	卯	2031
	晟	2094
	槙	2125
shige(ru)	茂	1467
Shigeshi	彬	2069
shii	椎	2116
shi(iru)	強	217
shiita(geru)	虐	1574
Shika	鹿	2279
shika	爾	2154
SHIKI	織	680
	識	681
	色	204
	式	525
shi(ku)	敷	1451
shima	洲	2138
	島	286
shi(maru)	絞	1452
	締	1180
	閉	397
shime(ru)	湿	1169
shi(meru)	絞	1452
	締	1180
	占	1706
	閉	397
shime(su)	示	615
	湿	1169
shi(mi)	染	779
shi(miru)	染	779
shimo	下	31
	霜	948
SHIN	辰	2246
	振	954
	唇	1737
	娠	956
	晨	2095
	震	953
	(辱)	JOKU
	辛	1487
	新	174
	薪	1910
	親	175
	(幸)	KŌ
	申	309
	伸	1108

Reading	Kanji	No.
	神	310
	紳	1109
	真	422
	槙	2125
	慎	1785
	(鎮)	CHIN
	侵	1077
	浸	1078
	寝	1079
	秦	2181
	榛	2124
	請	661
	(青)	SEI
	(清)	SEI
	(情)	SEI
	(晴)	SEI
	(静)	SEI
	(精)	SEI
	森	128
	(木)	BOKU
	(林)	RIN
	心	97
	(必)	HITSU
	臣	835
	(巨)	KYO
	津	668
	(律)	RITSU
	晋	2093
	(普)	FU
	針	341
	(計)	KEI
	深	536
	(探)	TAN
	診	1214
	(珍)	CHIN
	審	1383
	(番)	BAN
	身	59
	信	157
	進	437
shina	品	230
shino(baseru)	忍	1414
Shinobu	偲	2021
shino(bu)	忍	1414
Shinogu	凌	2025
shi(nu)	死	85
shio	汐	2134

Reading	Kanji	No.
	塩	1101
	潮	468
Shiori	栞	2108
shira	白	205
shira(beru)	調	342
shirizo(keru)	退	846
shirizo(ku)	退	846
shiro	代	256
	白	205
	城	720
shiro(i)	白	205
shiru	汁	1794
shi(ru)	知	214
shirushi	印	1043
shiru(su)	記	371
shishi	猪	2155
	鹿	2279
shita	下	31
	舌	1259
shitaga(eru)	従	1482
shitaga(u)	従	1482
shita(shii)	親	175
shita(shimu)	親	175
shitata(ru)	滴	1446
Shitau	欽	2130
shita(u)	慕	1431
SHITSU	室	166
	(至)	SHI
	(屋)	OKU
	疾	1812
	(矢)	SHI
	(医)	I
	執	686
	(幸)	KŌ
	(報)	HŌ
	失	311
	(夫)	FU
	湿	1169
	(顕)	KEN
	漆	1546
	質	176
shizu	靖	2187
	静	663
	倭	2019
shizu(ka)	静	663
shizuku	滴	1446
shizu(maru)	静	663
	鎮	1786

shizu(meru)	沈	936		生	44		(鮮)	SEN		節	979
	静	663		姓	1746		庄	2063		触	874
	鎮	1786		星	730		粧	1699		(独)	DOKU
shizu(mu)	沈	936		性	98		(圧)	ATSU		嘱	1638
SHO	渚	2142		笙	2188		憧	2077		(属)	ZOKU
	緒	862		尚	1853		鐘	1821		色	204
	諸	861		掌	499		(童)	DŌ	SHU	朱	1503
	暑	638		賞	500		升	1898		殊	1505
	署	860		償	971		昇	1777		珠	1504
	曙	2098		(常)	JŌ		丞	2002		(株)	kabu
	(者)	SHA		(堂)	DŌ		承	942		守	490
	(都)	TO		(党)	TŌ		傷	633		狩	1581
	(著)	CHO		正	275		(陽)	YŌ		取	65
	庶	1766		政	483		(湯)	TŌ		趣	1002
	(度)	DO		症	1318		(場)	JŌ		手	57
	(席)	SEKI		証	484		(揚)	YŌ		(毛)	MŌ
	(遮)	SHA		昌	2089		焼	920		主	155
	恕	2071		唱	1646		(尭)	GYŌ		(王)	Ō
	(如)	JO		菖	2220		(暁)	GYŌ		首	148
	処	1137		晶	1645		衝	1772		(目)	MOKU
	初	679		松	696		(行)	KŌ		修	945
	所	153		訟	1403		(重)	CHŌ		(候)	KŌ
	書	131		頌	2264		匠	1359		種	228
SHŌ	召	995		(公)	KŌ		(斤)	KIN		(重)	JŪ
	沼	996		(翁)	Ō		相	146		酒	517
	招	455		(窓)	SŌ		(想)	SŌ		須	2263
	昭	997		(総)	SŌ		従	1482	SHŪ	衆	792
	紹	456		青	208		(縦)	JŪ		州	195
	詔	1885		清	660		象	739		洲	2138
	照	998		精	659		(像)	ZŌ		酬	1864
	(超)	CHO		(情)	JŌ		勝	509		醜	1527
	小	27		(晴)	SEI		(券)	KEN		(鬼)	KI
	少	144		(請)	SEI		上	32		(塊)	KAI
	抄	1153		(静)	JŌ		井	1193		秋	462
	省	145		将	627		声	746		萩	2223
	称	978		装	1328		床	826		愁	1601
	渉	432		奨	1332		笑	1235		周	91
	(歩)	HO		(壮)	SŌ		商	412		週	92
	(妙)	MYŌ		章	857		捷	2079		(調)	CHŌ
	(砂)	SA		障	858		翔	2200		柊	2105
	(秒)	BYŌ		彰	1827	SHOKU	植	424		終	458
	(劣)	RETSU		焦	999		殖	1506		(冬)	TŌ
	肖	844		蕉	2229		(直)	CHOKU		修	945
	消	845		礁	1768		(値)	CHI		脩	2207
	宵	1854		祥	1576		織	680		(悠)	YŪ
	梢	2114		詳	1577		職	385		宗	616
	硝	1855		(羊)	YŌ		(識)	SHIKI		(示)	SHI
	(削)	SAKU		(洋)	YŌ		食	322		(完)	KAN

拾 1445
(合) GŌ
(捨) SHA
収 757
(又) mata
囚 1195
(人) JIN
臭 1244
(息) SOKU
執 686
(幸) KŌ
集 436
(隼) JUN
就 934
(京) KYŌ
衆 792
(血) KETSU
嵩 2057
(高) KŌ
舟 1094
秀 1683
祝 851
習 591
紬 2193
襲 1575
SHUKU 叔 1667
淑 1668
(寂) JAKU
(督) TOKU
宿 179
縮 1110
祝 851
(兄) KEI
(況) KYŌ
粛 1695
SHUN 俊 1845
峻 2053
竣 2186
駿 2269
(唆) SA
(酸) SAN
洵 2139
詢 2240
(旬) JUN
(殉) JUN
(絢) JUN
舜 2208
瞬 1732
諄 2242
醇 2255
隼 2259
(集) SHŪ
春 460
SHUTSU 出 53
SO 阻 1085
祖 622
租 1083
組 418
粗 1084
(且) ka(tsu)
(助) JO
素 271
(麦) BAKU
(表) HYŌ
措 1200
(昔) SEKI
(惜) SEKI
疎 1514
(束) SOKU
訴 1402
(斥) SEKI
想 147
(相) SŌ
塑 1838
礎 1515
SŌ 窓 698
総 697
聡 2203
(公) KŌ
僧 1366
層 1367
贈 1364
(増) ZŌ
壮 1326
荘 1327
装 1328
相 146
想 147
霜 948
倉 1307
創 1308
蒼 2225
曹 1929
遭 1643
槽 1644
操 1655
燥 1656
藻 1657
双 1594
桑 1873
(又) mata
宗 616
綜 2196
(示) SHI
(完) KAN
早 248
草 249
走 429
送 441
挿 1651
捜 989
巣 1538
(果) KA
(単) TAN
(菓) KA
掃 1080
(帰) KI
(婦) FU
庄 2063
(圧) ATSU
奏 1544
(奉) HŌ
葬 812
(死) SHI
颯 2266
(風) FŪ
争 302
爽 2046
喪 1678
惣 2074
漱 2146
騒 875
soda(teru) 育 246
soda(tsu) 育 246
so(eru) 添 1433
soko 底 562
soko(nau) 損 350
soko(neru) 損 350
SOKU 則 608
側 609
測 610
束 501
速 502
足 58
促 1557
息 1242
(臭) SHŪ
(憩) KEI
即 463
so(maru) 染 779
so(meru) 染 779
-so(meru) 初 679
somu(keru) 背 1265
somu(ku) 背 1265
SON 村 191
尊 704
(寸) SUN
孫 910
(系) KEI
(係) KEI
存 269
(在) ZAI
巽 2062
(選) SEN
損 350
(員) IN
sona(eru) 供 197
備 768
sona(waru) 備 768
sono 苑 2212
園 447
sora 空 140
so(rasu) 反 324
sōrō 候 944
so(ru) 反 324
soso(gu) 注 357
sosonoka(su)
唆 1846
soto 外 83
SOTSU 卒 787
率 788
so(u) 沿 1607
添 1433
SU 素 271
(麦) BAKU
(表) HYŌ
子 103
(了) RYŌ
主 155
(王) Ō
守 490
(寸) SUN

Reading	Kanji	No.
	惣	2074
	(物)	BUTSU
	数	225
	(楼)	RŌ
	洲	2138
	須	2263
	雛	2260
su	州	195
	(川)	SEN
	沙	2135
	巣	1538
	酢	1867
SŪ	枢	1023
	(区)	KU
	崇	1424
	(宗)	SHŪ
	数	225
	(楼)	RŌ
	嵩	2057
	雛	2260
Subaru	昂	2090
sube(ru)	滑	1267
su(beru)	統	830
sude (ni)	既	1458
sue	末	305
	梢	2114
su(eru)	据	1832
sugata	姿	929
sugi	杉	1872
su(giru)	過	413
su(gosu)	過	413
sugu(reru)	優	1033
Suguru	捷	2079
SUI	垂	1070
	睡	1071
	錘	1904
	(郵)	YŪ
	推	1233
	椎	2116
	(准)	JUN
	(唯)	YUI
	(維)	I
	吹	1255
	炊	1791
	(欠)	KETSU
	粋	1708
	酔	1709
	(砕)	SAI
	帥	1935
	(師)	SHI
	(追)	TSUI
	遂	1133
	(逐)	CHIKU
	(墜)	TSUI
	衰	1676
	(哀)	AI
	翠	2201
	(卒)	SOTSU
	穂	1221
	(恵)	KEI
	水	21
	出	53
	彗	2066
	瑞	2162
su(i)	酸	516
suji	筋	1090
su(kasu)	透	1685
suke	允	2022
	亮	2010
	甫	2167
	輔	2245
	佑	2015
	祐	2178
	丞	2002
	助	623
	昌	2089
	宥	2051
	哉	2037
	脩	2207
	喬	2040
su(keru)	透	1685
suko(shi)	少	144
suko(yaka)	健	893
su(ku)	好	104
	透	1685
suku(nai)	少	144
suku(u)	救	725
su(masu)	済	549
	澄	1334
su(mau)	住	156
sumi	邑	2250
	炭	1344
	隅	1640
	遥	2248
	稜	2184
	墨	1705
Sumire	菫	2219
sumi(yaka)	速	502
su(mu)	済	549
	澄	1334
	住	156
SUN	寸	1894
suna	沙	2135
	砂	1151
Sunao	淳	2141
	惇	2075
	侃	2017
	悌	2072
su(reru)	擦	1519
su(ru)	刷	1044
	擦	1519
surudo(i)	鋭	1371
Susugu	漱	2146
susu(meru)	進	437
	勧	1051
	薦	1631
Susumu	丞	2002
	亨	2009
	迪	2247
	侑	2018
	晋	2093
	亀	2284
	皐	2168
	駿	2269
susu(mu)	進	437
suta(reru)	廃	961
suta(ru)	廃	961
su(teru)	捨	1444
su(u)	吸	1256
suwa(ru)	座	786
su(waru)	据	1832
Suzu	紗	2191
	鈴	1822
suzu	涼	1204
suzu(mu)	涼	1204
suzu(shii)	涼	1204

– T –

Reading	Kanji	No.
TA	太	629
	汰	2136
	(大)	TAI
	他	120
	(也)	YA
	多	229
ta	手	57
	童	2219
	田	35
taba	束	501
ta(beru)	食	322
tabi	度	377
	旅	222
Tachibana	橘	2127
tada	也	2005
	允	2022
	只	2034
	伊	2011
	匡	2030
	迪	2247
	侃	2017
	董	2219
	喬	2040
	惟	2073
	欽	2130
	禎	2180
	頌	2264
	肇	2204
	叙	2032
tada(chi ni)	直	423
Tadashi	旦	2085
	匡	2030
	迪	2247
	侃	2017
	矩	2175
	淳	2141
	喬	2040
	禎	2180
	肇	2204
tada(shi)	但	1927
tada(shii)	正	275
Tadasu	匡	2030
	迪	2247
	矩	2175
	正	275
tada(su)	漂	924
tadayo(u)	漂	924
tae	紗	2191
ta(eru)	耐	1415
	堪	1913
	絶	742
taga(i)	互	907
tagaya(su)	耕	1196
TAI	代	256
	袋	1329
	貸	748
	黛	2283

Column 1	Column 2	Column 3	Column 4
台 492	梢 2114	濯 1561	(漢) KAN
胎 1296	皐 2168	(躍) YAKU	誕 1116
怠 1297	尭 2043	(曜) YŌ	(延) EN
(治) JI	琢 2158	卓 1679	鍛 1817
(始) SHI	稜 2184	拓 1833	(段) DAN
大 26	嘉 2041	ta(ku) 炊 1791	丹 1093
太 629	Takabu 嵩 2057	taku(mi) 巧 1627	反 324
汰 2136	taka(i) 高 190	takuwa(eru) 蓄 1224	短 215
退 846	taka(maru) 高 190	Tama 瑞 2162	端 1418
逮 891	taka(meru) 高 190	tama 玉 295	tana 棚 1908
(康) KŌ	takara 宝 296	玖 2156	Tane 胤 2205
対 365	Takashi 峻 2053	玲 2157	tane 種 228
耐 1415	駿 2269	球 726	tani 谷 653
帯 963	喬 2040	瑶 2163	tano(moshii) 頼 1512
滞 964	嵩 2057	圭 2042	tano(mu) 頼 1512
待 452	郁 2252	弾 1529	Tanoshi 凱 2028
(寺) JI	洸 2137	碧 2176	tano(shii) 楽 358
(侍) JI	昂 2088	霊 1168	tano(shimu) 楽 358
(持) JI	皐 2168	tamago 卵 1058	tao(reru) 倒 905
(時) JI	尭 2043	tamashii 魂 1525	tao(su) 倒 905
体 61	take 虎 2234	tamawa(ru) 賜 1831	ta(rasu) 垂 1070
(本) HON	彪 2068	tame(ru) 矯 1925	ta(reru) 垂 1070
(休) KYŪ	丈 1325	tame(su) 試 526	ta(riru) 足 58
隊 795	竹 129	tami 民 177	taru 稜 2184
(遂) SUI	孟 2049	黎 2282	ta(ru) 足 58
(墜) TSUI	岳 1358	蒼 2225	tashi(ka) 確 603
替 744	赳 2244	Tamotsu 惟 2073	tashi(kameru)
(潜) SEN	嵩 2057	tamo(tsu) 保 489	確 603
(贅) SAN	毅 2131	TAN 旦 2085	ta(su) 足 58
態 387	Takeshi 孟 2049	担 1274	tasu(karu) 助 623
(能) NŌ	洸 2137	胆 1273	Tasuke 輔 2245
(熊) YŪ	赳 2244	壇 1839	tasu(keru) 助 623
泰 1545	彪 2068	(但) tada(shi)	Tasuku 佑 2015
敦 2081	毅 2131	(昼) CHŪ	祐 2178
tai 鯛 2272	taki 滝 1759	単 300	丞 2002
Taira 庄 2063	takigi 薪 1910	(巣) SŌ	匡 2030
tai(ra) 平 202	TAKU 沢 994	(弾) DAN	侑 2018
Taka 鷹 2278	択 993	(禅) ZEN	輔 2245
taka 高 190	(尺) SHAKU	(戦) SEN	tataka(u) 戦 301
嵩 2057	(訳) YAKU	探 535	闘 1511
喬 2040	(駅) EKI	(深) SHIN	tatami 畳 1087
鳳 2274	宅 178	炭 1344	tata(mu) 畳 1087
鴻 2275	託 1636	(灰) KAI	tate 盾 772
圭 2042	啄 2038	(岩) GAN	縦 1483
昂 2088	琢 2158	淡 1337	tatematsu(ru)
峻 2053	度 377	(炎) EN	奉 1541
隼 2259	(席) SEKI	(談) DAN	ta(teru) 立 121
寅 2052	(庶) SHO	嘆 1246	建 892

Reading	Kanji	No.		Reading	Kanji	No.		Reading	Kanji	No.		Reading	Kanji	No.
tato(eru)	例	612			禎	2180		(微)	BI				逃	1566
TATSU	達	448			弟	405		(徴)	CHŌ				桃	1567
tatsu	辰	2246			悌	2072			迭	1507		(兆)	CHŌ	
	竜	1758		(第)	DAI				鉄	312		(挑)	CHŌ	
ta(tsu)	立	121			呈	1590		(失)	SHITSU			(眺)	CHŌ	
	建	892			程	417			哲	1397		(跳)	CHŌ	
	裁	1123			帝	1179		(折)	SETSU				到	904
	断	1024			締	1180		(逝)	SEI				倒	905
	絶	742			体	61		(誓)	SEI			(至)	SHI	
Tatsumi	巽	2062		(本)	HON	TO		土	24		(致)	CHI	
tatto(bu)	尊	704		(休)	KYŪ				吐	1253			桐	2110
	貴	1171			遞	1937			杜	2103			筒	1472
tatto(i)	尊	704	TEKI		適	415			度	377		(同)	DŌ	
	貴	1171			滴	1446			渡	378			憧	2077
tawamu(reru)					摘	1447		(席)	SEKI				瞳	2173
	戯	1573			敵	416		(庶)	SHO			(童)	DŌ	
tawara	俵	1890			迪	2247			登	960			唐	1697
ta(yasu)	絶	742			笛	1471			頭	276			糖	1698
tayo(ri)	便	330			的	210		(豆)	TŌ				膽	1779
tayo(ru)	頼	1512		(約)	YAKU			(豊)	HŌ				騰	1780
tazu	鶴	2277	TEN		店	168			途	1072			湯	632
tazu(neru)	訪	1181			点	169			塗	1073		(陽)	YŌ	
	尋	1082		(占)	SEN			(余)	YO			(揚)	YŌ	
tazusa(eru)	携	1686			天	141			斗	1899		(場)	JŌ	
tazusa(waru)	携	1686			添	1433			図	339			党	495
te	手	57			展	1129			都	188		(常)	JŌ	
TEI	丁	184			殿	1130		(者)	SHA			(堂)	DŌ	
	汀	2133			典	367		(走)	SŌ				統	830
	亭	1184		(曲)	KYOKU				十	12		(充)	JŪ	
	訂	1019			転	433	to		戸	152		(銃)	JŪ	
	停	1185		(伝)	DEN				豆	958			読	244
(灯)	TŌ		tera		寺	41	TŌ		登	960		(売)	BAI	
(打)	DA		Terasu		暉	2096			痘	1942		(続)	ZOKU	
	低	561	te(rasu)		照	998			頭	276			投	1021
	邸	563	te(reru)		照	998			闘	1511		(没)	BOTSU	
	抵	560	Teru		暉	2096		(豊)	HŌ				透	1685
	底	562	teru		旭	2086			東	71		(秀)	SHŪ	
(氐)	SHI				晃	2092			凍	1205			陶	1650
	廷	1111			晟	2094			棟	1406		(缶)	KAN	
	庭	1112			晨	2095		(陳)	CHIN				納	758
	艇	1666			燿	2152		(練)	REN			(内)	NAI	
(延)	EN				耀	2202		(錬)	REN				道	149
	定	355			皓	2169		(欄)	RAN			(首)	SHU	
	堤	1592			瑛	2159			塔	1840			悼	1680
	提	628			熙	2148			搭	1915		(卓)	TAKU	
(是)	ZE		te(ru)		照	998			答	160			等	569
	貞	1681	TETSU		撤	1423		(合)	GŌ			(寺)	JI	
	偵	1928			徹	1422							刀	37

Reading	Kanji	No.
tō	当	77
	冬	459
	灯	1333
	島	286
	討	1018
	盗	1100
	肇	2204
	稲	1220
	踏	1559
	藤	2231
	遥	2248
	遼	2249
	十	12
to(basu)	飛	530
tobira	扉	1556
tobo(shii)	乏	754
to(bu)	飛	530
	跳	1563
todo(keru)	届	992
todokō(ru)	滞	964
todo(ku)	届	992
tōge	峠	1351
to(geru)	遂	1133
to(gu)	研	896
to(i)	問	162
tō(i)	遠	446
to(jiru)	閉	397
to(kasu)	溶	1392
	解	474
to(keru)	溶	1392
	解	474
Toki	晨	2095
toki	辰	2246
	怜	2070
	時	42
	凱	2028
	聡	2203
	鴻	2275
toko	床	826
toko-	常	497
tokoro	所	153
TOKU	特	282
	(寺)	JI
	(持)	JI
	督	1670
	(目)	MOKU
	(叔)	SHUKU
	読	244
	(売)	BAI
	(続)	ZOKU
	匿	1771
	(若)	JAKU
	啄	2038
	(琢)	TAKU
	得	374
	(旦)	TAN
	徳	1038
	(聴)	CHŌ
	篤	1883
	(馬)	BA
to(ku)	溶	1392
	解	474
	説	400
to(maru)	止	477
	泊	1177
	留	761
to(meru)	止	477
	泊	1177
	留	761
tomi	堯	2043
	富	713
	禄	2179
	聡	2203
	智	2099
Tomo	共	196
tomo	供	197
	朋	2100
	鵬	2276
	巴	2061
	友	264
	伍	2013
	那	2251
	孟	2049
	呂	2036
	寅	2052
	悌	2072
	禎	2180
	諄	2242
Tomoe	巴	2061
tomona(u)	伴	1027
to(mu)	富	713
tomura(u)	弔	1796
TON	惇	2075
	敦	2081
	屯	1936
	団	491
	豚	796
ton	問	162
tona(eru)	唱	1646
tonari	隣	809
tona(ru)	隣	809
tono	殿	1130
Tora	虎	2234
	寅	2052
tora	彪	2068
to(raeru)	捕	890
to(rawareru)	捕	890
Tori	酉	2254
tori	鳥	285
to(ru)	取	65
	撮	1520
	捕	890
	採	933
	執	686
Tōru	亨	2009
	亮	2010
	亘	2006
	暢	2097
	叡	2032
tō(ru)	通	150
Toshi	遼	2249
	聡	2203
	慧	2076
	駿	2269
toshi	惇	2075
	敦	2081
	捷	2079
	捺	2080
	年	45
	甫	2167
	朋	2100
	哉	2037
	峻	2053
	隼	2259
	智	2099
	禄	2179
	舜	2208
	楠	2119
	稔	2183
	肇	2204
	叡	2032
	巌	2059
tō(su)	通	150
tōto(bu)	尊	704
	貴	1171
tōto(i)	尊	704
	貴	1171
totono(eru)	調	342
	整	503
totono(u)	調	342
	整	503
TOTSU	凸	1892
	突	898
totsu(gu)	嫁	1749
to(u)	問	162
toyo	晨	2095
to(zasu)	閉	397
TSU	通	150
	都	188
tsu	津	668
	藤	2231
	鶴	2277
TSŪ	通	150
	痛	1320
Tsubaki	椿	2118
tsubasa	翼	1062
tsubo	坪	1896
tsubu	粒	1700
Tsuchi	椎	2116
tsuchi	土	24
tsuchika(u)	培	1828
tsudo(u)	集	436
tsu(geru)	告	690
tsugi	次	384
	胤	2205
tsugu	丞	2002
	胤	2205
	皓	2169
	禎	2180
	頌	2264
	鞠	2262
tsu(gu)	次	384
	接	486
	継	1025
tsuguna(u)	償	971
TSUI	追	1174
	(帥)	SUI
	墜	1132
	(隊)	TAI
	対	365
	椎	2116
tsui(eru)	費	749

423

tsui(yasu)	費	749	tsuno(ru)	募	1430	**– U –**			une	采	2153
tsuka	塚	1751	tsura	面	274	U	右	76		畝	1901
tsuka(eru)	仕	333		寅	2052		佑	2015	uo	魚	290
tsuka(maeru)			tsura(naru)	連	440	(石)		SEKI	ura	浦	1442
	捕	890	tsura(neru)	連	440		卯	2031		裏	273
tsuka(maru)	捕	890	tsuranu(ku)	貫	914	(卵)		RAN	ura(meshii)	恨	1755
tsuka(rasu)	疲	1321	tsu(reru)	連	440		羽	590	ura(mu)	恨	1755
tsuka(reru)	疲	1321	Tsuru	鶴	2277		宇	990	urana(u)	占	1706
tsu(karu)	漬	1793	tsuru	弦	1226		有	265	ure(eru)	愁	1601
tsu(kasu)	尽	1726		絃	2192		雨	30		憂	1032
tsuka(u)	使	331		敦	2081	uba(u)	奪	1310	ure(i)	愁	1601
	遣	1173	tsu(ru)	釣	1862	ubu	産	278		憂	1032
tsuka(wasu)	遣	1173	tsurugi	剣	879	uchi	内	84	u(reru)	売	239
tsu(keru)	付	192	Tsuta	蔦	2228	ude	腕	1299		熟	687
	着	657	tsuta(eru)	伝	434	ue	上	32	u(ru)	売	239
	就	934	tsuta(u)	伝	434	u(eru)	飢	1304		得	374
	漬	1793	tsuta(waru)	伝	434		植	424	uru(mu)	潤	1203
tsuki	月	17	tsuto(maru)	勤	559	ugo(kasu)	動	231	uruo(su)	潤	1203
	槻	2126	tsuto(meru)	努	1595	ugo(ku)	動	231	uruo(u)	潤	1203
tsu(kiru)	尽	1726		務	235	u(i)	憂	1032	urushi	漆	1546
tsu(ku)	付	192		勤	559	ui-	初	679	uruwa(shii)	麗	1630
	突	898	Tsutomu	惇	2075	uji	氏	566	ushi	丑	2001
	着	657		敦	2081	u(kaberu)	浮	938		牛	281
	就	934		孟	2049	u(kabu)	浮	938	ushina(u)	失	311
tsukue	机	1305		拳	2078	ukaga(u)	伺	1761	ushi(ro)	後	48
tsukuro(u)	繕	1140		魁	2083	u(kareru)	浮	938	usu(i)	薄	1449
tsuku(ru)	作	360	tsutsu	筒	1472	u(karu)	受	260	usu(maru)	薄	1449
	造	691	tsutsumi	堤	1592	u(keru)	受	260	usu(meru)	薄	1449
tsu(kusu)	尽	1726	tsutsu(mu)	包	804		請	661	usu(ragu)	薄	1449
tsuma	妻	671	tsutsushi(mu)			uketamawa(ru)			usu(reru)	薄	1449
tsu(maru)	詰	1142		慎	1785		承	942	uta	唄	2039
tsu(meru)	詰	1142		謹	1247	u(ku)	浮	938		頌	2264
tsume(tai)	冷	832	Tsuya	艶	2209	uma	馬	283		歌	392
tsumi	罪	885	tsuyo(i)	強	217	u(mareru)	生	44	utaga(u)	疑	1516
tsu(moru)	積	656	Tsuyoki	毅	2131		産	278	utai	謡	1647
tsumu	錘	1904	tsuyo(maru)	強	217	u(maru)	埋	1826	uta(u)	歌	392
tsu(mu)	詰	1142	tsuyo(meru)	強	217	ume	梅	1734		謡	1647
	摘	1447	Tsuyoshi	侃	2017	u(meru)	埋	1826	uto(i)	疎	1514
	積	656		勁	2029	umi	海	117	uto(mu)	疎	1514
tsumugi	紬	2193		彪	2068	u(moreru)	埋	1826	u(tsu)	打	1020
tsumu(gu)	紡	1859		毅	2131	u(mu)	生	44		討	1018
tsuna	綱	1609	tsuyu	露	951		産	278		撃	1016
	(網)	ami	tsuzu(keru)	続	243	UN	運	439	utsuku(shii)	美	401
	紘	2190	Tsuzuki	胤	2205	(軍)		GUN	utsu(ru)	写	540
tsune	矩	2175	tsuzu(ku)	続	243		雲	636		映	352
	彦	2067	tsuzumi	鼓	1147	(曇)		DON		移	1121
	常	497				unaga(su)	促	1557	utsu(su)	写	540
tsuno	角	473								映	352

Reading	Kanji	No.
	移	1121
utsuwa	器	527
utta(eru)	訴	1402
uwa-	上	32
u(waru)	植	424
uya	欽	2130
uyama(u)	敬	705
uyauya(shii)	恭	1434
uzu	渦	1810

– W –

Reading	Kanji	No.
WA	話	238
	(舌)	ZETSU
	(活)	KATSU
	倭	2019
	(委)	I
	和	124
wa	我	1302
	輪	1164
waga	吾	2035
WAI	賄	1739
	(有)	YŪ
	(侑)	YŪ
waka	湧	2144
waka(i)	若	544
waka(reru)	別	267
wa(kareru)	分	38
wa(karu)	分	38
wa(kasu)	沸	1792
wa(katsu)	分	38
wake	訳	594
wa(keru)	分	38
waki	湧	2144
WAKU	惑	969
	(域)	IKI
waku	枠	1907
	湧	2144
wa(ku)	沸	1792
WAN	腕	1299
	(苑)	EN
	湾	670
warabe	童	410
wara(u)	笑	1235
ware	我	1302
	吾	2035
wa(reru)	割	519
wari	割	519
wa(ru)	割	519
waru(i)	悪	304
wasu(reru)	忘	1374
wata	綿	1191
watakushi	私	125
Watari	亘	2006
Wataru	亘	2006
	弥	2065
	凌	2025
wata(ru)	渡	378
wata(su)	渡	378
waza	技	871
	業	279
wazawa(i)	災	1335
wazura(u)	患	1315
	煩	1849
wazura(wasu)	煩	1849

– Y –

Reading	Kanji	No.
YA	也	2005
	(他)	TA
	耶	2253
	椰	2121
	冶	2024
	夜	471
	野	236
ya	八	10
	矢	213
	弥	2065
	屋	167
	哉	2037
	家	165
yabu(reru)	破	665
	敗	511
yabu(ru)	破	665
yado	宿	179
yado(ru)	宿	179
yado(su)	宿	179
ya(keru)	焼	920
YAKU	役	375
	疫	1319
	訳	594
	(尺)	SHAKU
	(沢)	TAKU
	(駅)	EKI
	躍	1560
	(濯)	TAKU
	(曜)	YŌ
	厄	1341
	(危)	KI
	亦	2007
	(赤)	SEKI
	約	211
	(勺)	SHAKU
	薬	359
	(楽)	GAKU
	益	716
ya(ku)	焼	920
yama	山	34
yamai	病	380
Yamato	倭	2019
ya(meru)	辞	688
ya(mu)	病	380
yanagi	柳	1871
yasa(shii)	易	759
	優	1033
yashi	椰	2121
yashina(u)	養	402
yashiro	社	308
yasu	叶	2033
	侃	2017
	喬	2040
	倭	2019
	晏	2091
yasu(i)	安	105
yasu(maru)	休	60
yasu(meru)	休	60
yasu(mu)	休	60
Yasushi	欣	2129
	晏	2091
	悌	2072
	靖	2187
	魁	2083
yato(u)	雇	1553
ya(tsu)	八	10
yat(tsu)	八	10
yawa(rageru)		
	和	124
yawa(ragu)	和	124
yawa(raka)	柔	774
	軟	1788
yawa(rakai)	柔	774
	軟	1788
YO	予	393
	預	394
	(矛)	MU
	(序)	JO
	誉	802
	(言)	GEN
	与	539
	余	1063
yo	世	252
	代	256
	四	6
	夜	471
YŌ	羊	288
	洋	289
	様	403
	養	402
	窯	1789
	遥	2248
	揺	1648
	瑶	2163
	謡	1647
	(缶)	KAN
	陽	630
	揚	631
	楊	2122
	(湯)	TŌ
	(場)	JŌ
	(傷)	SHŌ
	曜	19
	燿	2152
	耀	2202
	(濯)	TAKU
	(躍)	YAKU
	容	654
	溶	1392
	蓉	2226
	(谷)	KOKU
	用	107
	庸	1696
	要	419
	腰	1298
	葉	253
	(蝶)	CHŌ
	(世)	SEI
	(笹)	sasa

Reading	Kanji	No.		Reading	Kanji	No.
	幼	1229			酉	2254
	(幻)	GEN			(猶)	YŪ
	湧	2144			祐	2178
	(勇)	YŪ			(右)	YŪ
	瑛	2159			遊	1003
	(英)	EI		yu	湯	632
	踊	1558		YŪ	右	76
	擁	1715			佑	2015
	鷹	2278			祐	2178
yō	八	10			有	265
	浩	2140			侑	2018
	瑛	2159			宥	2051
yo(bu)	呼	1254			勇	1386
yogo(reru)	汚	693			湧	2144
yogo(su)	汚	693			(男)	DAN
yoi	宵	1854			由	363
	敦	2081			柚	2106
yo(i)	良	321			酉	2254
	善	1139			猶	1583
yoko	横	781			憂	1032
YOKU	浴	1128			優	1033
	欲	1127			郵	524
	(谷)	KOKU			(垂)	SUI
	(俗)	ZOKU			(睡)	SUI
	翌	592			(錘)	SUI
	翼	1062			裕	1391
	(羽)	U			(谷)	KOKU
	(習)	SHŪ			(俗)	ZOKU
	抑	1057			(浴)	YOKU
	(仰)	GYŌ			誘	1684
	(迎)	GEI			(秀)	SHŪ
	(卯)	U			(透)	TŌ
yome	嫁	1749			悠	1597
Yomishi	嘉	2041			(修)	SHŪ
yomu	頌	2264			熊	2149
yo(mu)	詠	1209			(態)	TAI
	読	244			融	1588
yon	四	6			(隔)	KAKU
yori	之	2004			友	264
	亮	2010			邑	2250
yoroko(bu)	喜	1143			幽	1228
yoru	夜	471			雄	1387
yo(ru)	因	554			遊	1003
	寄	1361		yū	夕	81
yo(seru)	寄	1361		yubi	指	1041
Yoshi	彬	2069		yue	故	173
	悌	2072		YUI	唯	1234
	嘉	2041			惟	2073

Reading	Kanji	No.		Reading	Kanji	No.
yoshi	祐	2178			遺	1172
	禄	2179			(貫)	KI
	禎	2180			(遣)	KEN
	允	2022			由	363
	亮	2010		yuka	床	826
	圭	2042		Yuki	恕	2071
	桂	2109		yuki	之	2004
	之	2004			乃	2003
	由	363			亨	2009
	伊	2011			侑	2018
	甫	2167			晋	2093
	辰	2246			雪	949
	弥	2065			鵬	2276
	昌	2089		yuku	巽	2062
	欣	2129		yu(ku)	行	68
	彦	2067			逝	1396
	恕	2071		yume	夢	811
	斐	2082		yumi	弓	212
	巽	2062		yu(ragu)	揺	1648
	凱	2028		yu(reru)	揺	1648
	惟	2073		yu(ru)	揺	1648
	欽	2130		yu(rugu)	揺	1648
	舜	2208		yuru(i)	緩	1089
	熙	2148		yuru(meru)	緩	1089
	嬉	2048		yuru(mu)	緩	1089
	誼	2241		yuru(su)	許	737
	叡	2032		yuru(yaka)	緩	1089
	艶	2209		yu(saburu)	揺	1648
	巌	2059		yu(suburu)	揺	1648
	馨	2267		yu(suru)	揺	1648
	誼	2241		Yutaka	稔	2183
	嘉	2041			穣	2185
Yoshimi					宥	2051
yosō(u)	装	1328			浩	2140
yo(tsu)	四	6			尭	2043
yot(tsu)	四	6			瑞	2162
yo(u)	酔	1709			碩	2265
yowa(i)	弱	218		yuta(ka)	豊	959
yowa(maru)	弱	218		yu(u)	結	485
yowa(meru)	弱	218		yu(waeru)	結	485
yowa(ru)	弱	218		yuzu	柚	2106
YU	愉	1598		Yuzura	穣	2185
	諭	1599		yuzu(ru)	譲	1013
	輸	546				
	癒	1600		**– Z –**		
yū	由	363		ZA	座	786
	油	364		ZAI	材	552
	柚	2106			財	553
	(抽)	CHŪ				

	(才)	SAI		説	400		(色)	SHOKU		(読)	DOKU
	剤	550		(脱)	DATSU		舌	1259		族	221
	(斉)	SEI	ZEN	善	1139	ZŌ	増	712		(旅)	RYO
	(済)	SAI		繕	1140		僧	1365		属	1637
	在	268		禅	1540		贈	1364		(嘱)	SHOKU
	(存)	SON		(単)	TAN		(僧)	SŌ		賊	1807
	罪	885		(弾)	DAN		象	739		(賦)	FU
	(非)	HI		(戦)	SEN		像	740	ZON	存	269
ZAN	残	650		(巣)	SŌ		蔵	1286		(在)	ZAI
	(浅)	SEN		然	651		臓	1287	ZU	豆	958
	(桟)	SAN		(黙)	MOKU		造	691		頭	276
	(銭)	SEN		(燃)	NEN		(告)	KOKU		図	339
	惨	1725		全	89		雑	575		杜	2103
	(参)	SAN		(王)	Ō	ZOKU	俗	1126		事	80
	暫	1399		漸	1400		(谷)	KOKU		鶴	2277
	(漸)	ZEN		(暫)	ZAN		(浴)	YOKU	zu	随	1741
ZATSU	雑	575		前	47		(裕)	YŪ	ZUI	髄	1740
ZE	是	1591	zeni	銭	648		続	243		瑞	2162
ZEI	税	399	ZETSU	絶	742		(売)	BAI			

427

Further instructional materials and reference works by the authors
concerning the Japanese writing system

W. Hadamitzky and M. Spahn
A Guide to Writing Kanji & Kana. Book 1.2
Rutland (Vermont) and Tokyo: Tuttle 1991
The two volumes accompanying Kanji & Kana *will help students master the writing of the two kana syllabaries and the 1,945 basic characters contained in volume 1 of* Kanji & Kana.

M. Spahn and W. Hadamitzy
The Kanji Dictionary.
Rutland (Vermont) and Tokyo: Tuttle 1996. 1748 p.
Revised and enlarged edition of the Japanese Character Dictionary *(1989). Contains 5,910 characters (7,062 counting variants) and over 48,000 multi-character compounds. Includes about 1,000 new entries not found in the 1989 edition. Uses a simple classic radical system (79 radicals). The only dictionary that allows the user to look up a compound via any of its constituent kanji. In addition, various tables, maps, and other supplements have been added for the user's edification and entertainment.*

M. Spahn and W. Hadamitzky
The Learners Kanji Dictionary.
Rutland (Vermont) and Tokyo: Tuttle 1997. approx. 900p.

SUNRISE Script 2000. Kanji learning program on CD-ROM
Berlin: JAPAN Media 1995
Release 3.1: 1 CD-ROM + 2 floppy disks + manual
Electronic version of Kanji & Kana, *with audio pronunciation for all kana and 2,000 kanji. Allows lookup of kanji by reading, meaning, or grapheme.*

SUNRISE Kanji Dictionary. Kanji dictionary with 7,000 kanji and 47,000 compounds on CD-ROM
Berlin: JAPAN Media 1995.
Release 1.3.1: 1 CD-ROM + 2 floppy disks + manual
Electronic version of Japanese Character Dictionary *(1989) by Spahn & Hadamitzky. Allows lookup of kanji and compounds by grapheme, reading, or meaning.*

Other Japanese Language Titles in the Tuttle Language Library

All-Romanized English Japanese Dictionary *by Hyojun Romaji Kai*

Basic Japanese Conversation Dictionary (English–Japanese/Japanese–English) *by Samuel E. Martin*

Character Dictionary Accompanying "Japanese: A Manual of Reading and Writing" *by Hamako Ito Chaplin & Samuel E. Martin*

Colloquial Japanese: With Important Construction and Grammar Notes *by Noboru Inamoto*

Complete Japanese Expression Guide *by Mizue Sasaki*

The Complete Japanese Verb Guide *compiled by the Hiroo Japanese Center*

Dictionary of Computer and Data Processing Terms (English–Japanese/Japanese–English) *by Gene Ferber*

Easy Japanese: A Direct Approach to Intermediate Conversation *by Samuel E. Martin*

English Loanwords in Japanese: A Selection *by Akira Miura*

Essential Japanese: An Introduction to the Standard Colloquial Language (3rd Revised Edition) *by Samuel E. Martin*

"Even Monkeys Fall from Trees" and Other Japanese Proverbs *by David Galef*

A Guide to Learning Hiragana & Katakana *by Kenneth G. Henshall with Tetsuo Takagaki*

A Guide to Reading & Writing Japanese: The 1,850 Basic Characters and the Kana Syllabaries (Revised Edition) *edited by Florence Sakade*

A Guide to Remembering Japanese Characters *by Kenneth G. Henshall*

Handbook of Japanese Grammer *by Masahiro Tanimori*

A Handbook of Japanese Usage *by Francis G. Drohan*

Hiragana Wall Chart

Hotel Japanese: Practical Japanese for the Hotel Industry *by Kazuo Nishiyama*

In Japan *by Philip Hinder*

Inoue's Japanese-English Dictionary *by Jukichi Inoue*

An Introduction to Written Japanese *by P. G. O'Neill and S. Yanada*

Introduction to Written Japanese: Hiragana *by Jim Gleeson*

Introduction to Written Japanese: Katakana *by Jim Gleeson*

Japanese: A Manual of Reading and Writing *by Hamako Ito Chaplin & Samuel E. Martin*

A Japanese and English Dictionary with an English and Japanese Index *by J. C. Hepburn*

Japanese Business Dictionary *by Boye De Mente*

Japanese for All Occasions: The Right Word at the Right Time *by Anne Kaneko*

Japanese for Fun: Make Your Stay in Japan More Enjoyable *by Taeko Kamiya*

The Japanese Language *by Haruhiko Kindaichi, translated by Umeyo Hirano*

Japanese Made Easy *by Tazuko Ajiro Monane*

Japanese Newspaper Compounds: The 1,000 Most Important in Order of Frequency *compiled by Tadashi Kikuoka*

A Japanese Reader: Graded Lessons for Mastering the Written Language *by Roy Andrew Miller*

Japanese Word-and-Phrase Book for Tourists *compiled by Eldora S. Thorlin*

Japanese Words and Their Uses *by Akira Miura*

Kana-a-Day Practice Pad *by Richard S. Keirstead*

Kanji-a-Day Practice Pad *by Richard S. Keirstead*

Kanji ABC *by Andreas Foerster & Naoko Tamura*

Kanji Power: A Workbook for Mastering Japanese Characters *by John Millen*

Kansai Japanese: The Language of Osaka, Kyoto, and Western Japan *by Peter Tse*

Katakana Wall Chart

Kinki Japanese: The Dialects & Culture of the Kansai Region *by D.C. Palter & Kaoru Horiuchi*

Let's Study Japanese *by Jun Maeda*

The Magical Power of Suru: Japanese Verbs Made Easy *by Nobuo Sato*

Martin's Concise Japanese Dictionary: Fully Romanized with Complete Kanji & Kana *by Samuel E. Martin*

Martin's Pocket Dictionary (English–Japanese/Japanese–English) *by Samuel E. Martin*

Nihongo Pera Pera: A User's Guide to Japanese Onomatopoeia *by Susan Millington*

Noodle Words: An Introduction to Chinese and Japanese Characters *by D. M. Murray and T. W. Wong*

The Original Modern Reader's Japanese-English Character Dictionary (2nd Revised Edition) *by Andrew N. Nelson*

A Programmed Course on Respect Language in Modern Japanese *by P. G. O'Neill*

Read Japanese Today *by Len Walsh*

A Reference Grammar of Japanese *by Samuel E. Martin*

Speak Japanese Today: A Self-Study Program for Learning Everyday Japanese *by Taeko Kamiya*

Tuttle Dictionary of Legal Terms: English–Japanese, Japanese–English (New Edition) *by Richard S. Keirstead*

Tuttle Kanji Cards *by Alexander Kask*

Tuttle New Loanwords in Japanese *by Taeko Kamiya*

Tuttle's Watch Pocket Dictionary: English-Japanese Dictionary

250 Essential Kanji for Everyday Use *by The Kanji Text Research Group, University of Tokyo*

Watashi No Nihon: Tuttle Activity Books for Young Learners of Japanese
    Book #1: My Homestay Family
    Book #2: My Day at School
    Book #3: My Day in Tokyo
by Kumi Kato, Donna Weeks & Judy Viney, Key Centre for Asian Languages & Studies

Wolfgang Hadamitzky is a librarian in the East Asia section of the Berlin State Library. He has worked in Oslo and Tokyo on the staff of the German Cultural Institute (Goethe-Institute).

Mark Spahn has a background in mathematics, engineering, and computer science. He has worked in Japan as a teacher, computer magazine writer, programmer, and translator. He presently resides in the United States, where he is active as a technical translator and consultant.

Table 15. The Syllabaries

Hiragana

ん	わ	ら	や	ま	は	な	た	さ	か	あ
	り			み	ひ	に	ち	し	き	い
	る		ゆ	む	ふ	ぬ	つ	す	く	う
	れ			め	へ	ね	て	せ	け	え
	を	ろ	よ	も	ほ	の	と	そ	こ	お

Katakana

ン	ワ	ラ	ヤ	マ	ハ	ナ	タ	サ	カ	ア
	リ			ミ	ヒ	ニ	チ	シ	キ	イ
	ル		ユ	ム	フ	ヌ	ツ	ス	ク	ウ
	レ			メ	ヘ	ネ	テ	セ	ケ	エ
	ヲ	ロ	ヨ	モ	ホ	ノ	ト	ソ	コ	オ